KB241849

나혼자 끝내는 토익 PART 1~4

신토익 실전12회

나혼자 끝내는 토익
PART 1~4 신토익 실전 12회

지은이 이주은
펴낸이 임상진
펴낸곳 (주)넥서스

초판 1쇄 발행 2015년 5월 10일
초판 2쇄 발행 2015년 5월 15일

2판 1쇄 발행 2016년 9월 5일
2판 2쇄 발행 2016년 9월 10일

3판 1쇄 발행 2017년 3월 15일
3판 2쇄 발행 2017년 3월 20일

출판신고 1992년 4월 3일 제311-2002-2호
10880 경기도 파주시 지목로 5
Tel (02)330-5500 Fax (02)330-5555

ISBN 979-11-5752-137-1 13740

가격은 뒤표지에 있습니다.
잘못 만들어진 책은 구입처에서 바꾸어 드립니다.

본 책은 〈TOEIC 파트별 실전 문제 PART 1~4〉의 개정판입니다.
www.nexusbook.com

나혼자 끝내는 토익 PART 1~4

신토익 실전12회

이주은 지음

넥서스

PREFACE

나의 30대를 딱 한마디로 표현한다면 주저 없이 '토익'이라는 단어가 떠오른다. 영어가 재미있고 토익이 좋아서 토익 강사를 시작한 지 벌써 10년이 다 되어 간다. 그동안 토익을 대표하는 어학원에서 또 온라인 강의를 통해서 수십만 명의 토익 수험생들을 만나고 함께 호흡하며 그들과 생생하게 소통해왔다. 또한 매달 토익 시험을 치르며 철저하게 유형과 난이도를 분석하고 차별화된 토익 솔루션을 연구했다. 수험생들이 더 빠르고 효율적으로 약점을 보완하고 목표 점수에 도달할 수 있도록 고민해 온 그간의 노력을 이 책에 고스란히 담을 수 있어 너무 기쁘고 뿌듯하다.

실전 모의고사라는 타이틀을 갖고 있지만 실제로는 정기 토익에 비해 지나치게 난이도가 높은 교재들, 토익 LC의 범위를 벗어나는 어휘와 표현들을 마구잡이로 포함시켜 수험생들의 시야를 가리는 교재들이 시중에 넘쳐날 때마다 느꼈던 안타까움과 아쉬움이 결국 저자의 오랜 미션이자 이 책을 완성하는 원동력이 되었다.

본 교재를 쓰기 위하여 지난 10년간 꾸준히 분석해 온 기출 문제 데이터를 다시 한 번 정리하여 토익에서 꾸준한 유형으로 큰 틀을 구성하였고, 지난 3년간의 최신 기출 트렌드만을 철저하게 반영하였다. 단 한 회를 풀더라도 수험생의 현재 실력과 약점이 정확하게 파악되도록 난이도를 계산하였고 빈출 질문의 비율을 고려하였다. 또한 수험생들의 시간 절약을 위해 토익 시험에 자주 등장하는 어휘와 표현, 배경 지식만으로 매회의 테스트를 채워 넣었으므로 이 교재를 풀고 철저히 복습하는 것만으로도 실전 대비가 될 것이라 자신한다.

내 수업에 사용하고 싶을 만큼 퀄리티 높은 교재를 쓰고 싶다는 욕심은 항상 있었지만 스케줄이 바쁘다는 이유로 혹은 건강이 허락하지 않는다는 핑계로 차일피일 미루고 있을 때 용기를 준 Catherine Lee님께 감사 인사를 전하고 싶다. 또한 첫 미팅부터 무한한 격려와 신뢰를 보내 주신 넥서스 편집부에도 진심으로 감사드린다. 그렇게 물꼬를 터 준 분들이 있었기에 결단을 내리고 집필 작업에 전념할 수 있었다.

언제나 나의 편에서 사랑과 응원을 보내 주시는 어머니 오채연 님과 그리운 아버지 故 이종권 님께 마음 깊이 감사한다. 마음의 안식처와 같은 소중한 친구 선재, 미경에게 감사하고, 이 교재의 완성도를 높이기 위해 어휘 하나를 놓고도 끝까지 함께 고민해 준 친구 John McKenna에게도 감사를 전한다.

내가 계속 앞으로 나아갈 수 있도록 해 주는 학생들이야말로 진정한 나의 에너지 원천임을 새삼 느끼게 된다. 그들이 있기에 더 좋은 강사가 되려고 오늘도 노력할 수 있어 행복하다.

토익이라는 매개체를 통하여 나와 인연을 맺었던 모든 분들과 미래의 독자들에게 이 책을 바친다.

마음을 담아

이주은

CONTENTS

FEATURES

1 **Part 1~4 신유형 완전 분석 & 반영**

더욱 어려워진 신토익 LC 경향을 파악하여 출제 원리와 어휘를 완전히 분석하고 반영하였다.

2 **Part 1~4 국내 최다 실전 문제 수록**

Part 1~4 총 12회분, 총 1,200문제의 국내 최다 문제를 수록하여 이 한 권만 풀어도 실전에 제대로 대비할 수 있다.

3 **문제+정답+번역+해설+어휘 한 권에 수록**

해설집을 따로 구매할 필요 없이 정답과 번역, 명쾌한 해설까지 딱 한 권으로 해결할 수 있다.

4 **빈출 어휘 리스트 및 테스트지 & 받아쓰기 테스트**

교재 전체에 등장한 모든 어휘를 언제든지 편리하게 활용하며 테스트지를 통해 최종 점검을 할 수 있다. 또한 청취력 향상을 위한 온라인 받아쓰기 테스트를 제공한다.
(QR 코드 또는 www.nexusbook.com 다운로드)

5 **저렴한 가격으로 제공하는 실전 모의고사**

LC 한 세트당 약 1,300원의 저렴한 가격으로 실제 시험과 동일한 구성의 토익 PART 1~4 실전 문제를 풀 수 있다.

6 **실전용·복습용·고사장 버전 MP3 무료 다운로드**

실전과 동일한 통파일 형태의 실전용, 개별 문항만 따로 들을 수 있는 복습용 MP3를 무료로 다운로드 할 수 있다. 추가로 고사장과 같은 환경의 음원을 들을 수 있도록 고사장 버전의 MP3를 제공한다.
(QR 코드 또는 www.nexusbook.com 다운로드)

2016년 5월 29일 정기시험부터 현재의 영어 사용 환경을 반영한 신(新)토익이 시행되었습니다. 전체 문항 수와 시험 시간은 동일하지만 각 파트별로 문항 수는 변화가 있으며 그동안 출제되지 않았던 그래프와 문자 메시지, 채팅, 삼중 지문 등 새로운 지문 유형과 문제가 출제됩니다.

신토익 시험의 구성

구성	Part	Part별 내용	문항수	시간	배점
Listening Comprehension	1	사진 묘사	6	45분	495점
	2	질의 응답	25		
	3	짧은 대화	39		
	4	설명문	30		
Reading Comprehension	5	단문 공란 채우기	30	75분	495점
	6	장문 공란 채우기	16		
	7	단일 지문	29		
		이중 지문	10		
		삼중 지문	15		
Total	7 Parts		200문제	120분	990점

신토익 이후 달라진 부분

❶ **Part 1** 문항 10개에서 6개로 감소
❷ **Part 2** 문항 30개에서 25개로 감소
❸ **Part 3** 문항 30개에서 39개로 증가, 〈3인 대화〉, 〈5턴 이상의 대화〉, 〈의도 파악, 시각 정보 연계 문제〉 추가
❹ **Part 4** 문항 30개로 기존과 동일, 〈의도 파악 문제〉, 〈시각 정보 연계 문제〉 추가
❺ **Part 5** 문항 40개에서 30개로 감소
❻ **Part 6** 문항 12개에서 16개로 증가, 〈알맞은 문장 고르기〉 추가
❼ **Part 7** 문항 48개에서 54개로 증가, 〈문자 메시지 · 온라인 채팅 지문〉, 〈의도 파악, 문장 삽입 문제〉, 〈삼중 지문〉 추가

신토익 핵심 정보

Part 3	화자의 의도 파악 문제	2~3문항	• 대화문에서 화자가 한 말의 의도를 묻는 유형
	시각 정보 연계 문제	2~3문항	• 대화문과 시각 정보(도표, 그래픽 등)간 연관 관계를 파악하는 유형
	3인 대화	대화 지문 1~2개	• 일부 대화문에서 세 명 이상의 화자가 등장함
	5턴 이상의 대화		• 주고 받는 대화가 5턴 이상으로 늘어난 대화 유형

Part 4	화자의 의도 파악 문제	2~3문항	• 담화문에서 화자가 한 말의 의도를 묻는 유형
	시각 정보 연계 문제	2~3문항	• 담화문과 시각 정보(도표, 그래픽 등)간 연관 관계를 파악하는 유형

Part 6	알맞은 문장 고르기	4문항 (지문당 1문항)	• 지문의 흐름상 빈칸에 들어갈 알맞은 문장 고르기 • 선택지가 모두 문장으로 제시되며 문맥 파악이 필수

Part 7	문장 삽입 문제	2문항 (지문당 1문항)	• 주어진 문장을 삽입할 수 있는 적절한 위치 고르기
	문자 메시지 · 온라인 채팅	각각 지문 1개	• 2명이 대화하는 문자 메시지, 다수가 참여하는 온라인 채팅
	의도 파악 문제	2문항 (지문당 1문항)	• 화자가 말한 말의 의도를 묻는 문제 • 문자 메시지, 온라인 채팅 지문에서 출제
	삼중 지문	지문 3개	• 세 개의 연계 지문에 대한 이해도를 묻는 문제

나혼토 실력 점검

테스트가 끝난 후 각 테스트별로 점검해 보세요. 테스트별로 맞은 개수를 확인하며 실력이 향상됨을 체크해 보세요.

	테스트 날짜	맞은 개수	체감 난이도
Actual Test 01			상 중 하
Actual Test 02			상 중 하
Actual Test 03			상 중 하
Actual Test 04			상 중 하
Actual Test 05			상 중 하
Actual Test 06			상 중 하
Actual Test 07			상 중 하
Actual Test 08			상 중 하
Actual Test 09			상 중 하
Actual Test 10			상 중 하
Actual Test 11			상 중 하
Actual Test 12			상 중 하

정답 및 해설 활용법

정답 및 해설집에는 스크립트뿐만 아니라 문제, 해석 및 해설이 자세하게 나와 있습니다. 틀린 문제는 정확하고 상세한 해설을 읽은 후, 스크립트에서 어떤 부분이 정답과 연관되어 있는지 밑줄을 긋고 문제 번호를 써 보세요. 그런 다음, 그 부분만 집중적으로 반복해서 들은 후, 다시 한 번 해당 지문 전체를 들어 보세요. 정답에 대한 실마리를 쉽게 찾을 수 있습니다.

온라인 받아쓰기 테스트 활용법

각 실전 테스트를 완료한 후, 청취력 향상 및 들으면서 반복 학습을 할 수 있는 온라인 받아쓰기 테스트를 제공합니다. 온라인 받아쓰기 테스트는 QR코드 또는 www.nexusbook.com을 통해 이용하실 수 있습니다.

Actual Test 1~12

LISTENING TEST

In the Listening test, you will be asked to demonstrate how well you understand spoken English. The entire Listening test will last approximately 45 minutes. There are four parts, and directions are given for each part. You must mark your answers on the separate answer sheet. Do not write your answers in your test book.

PART 1

Directions: For each question in this part, you will hear four statements about a picture in your test book. When you hear the statements, you must select the one statement that best describes what you see in the picture. Then find the number of the question on your answer sheet and mark your answer. The statements will not be printed in your test book and will be spoken only one time.

Example

Sample Answer

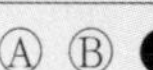  

Statement (C), "The man is working on a painting," is the best description of the picture, so you should select answer (C) and mark it on your answer sheet.

1

2

GO ON TO THE NEXT PAGE

3

4

5

6

GO ON TO THE NEXT PAGE

PART 2

Directions: You will hear a question or statement and three responses spoken in English. They will not be printed in your test book and will be spoken only one time. Select the best response to the question or statement and mark the letter (A), (B), or (C) on your answer sheet.

7 Mark your answer on your answer sheet.

8 Mark your answer on your answer sheet.

9 Mark your answer on your answer sheet.

10 Mark your answer on your answer sheet.

11 Mark your answer on your answer sheet.

12 Mark your answer on your answer sheet.

13 Mark your answer on your answer sheet.

14 Mark your answer on your answer sheet.

15 Mark your answer on your answer sheet.

16 Mark your answer on your answer sheet.

17 Mark your answer on your answer sheet.

18 Mark your answer on your answer sheet.

19 Mark your answer on your answer sheet.

20 Mark your answer on your answer sheet.

21 Mark your answer on your answer sheet.

22 Mark your answer on your answer sheet.

23 Mark your answer on your answer sheet.

24 Mark your answer on your answer sheet.

25 Mark your answer on your answer sheet.

26 Mark your answer on your answer sheet.

27 Mark your answer on your answer sheet.

28 Mark your answer on your answer sheet.

29 Mark your answer on your answer sheet.

30 Mark your answer on your answer sheet.

31 Mark your answer on your answer sheet.

PART 3

Directions: You will hear some conversations between two or more people. You will be asked to answer three questions about what the speakers say in each conversation. Select the best response to each question and mark the letter (A), (B), (C), or (D) on your answer sheet. The conversations will not be printed in your test book and will be spoken only one time.

32 Who is the man speaking to?

(A) A doctor
(B) A receptionist
(C) A sales person
(D) A patient

33 According to the woman, why is Dr. Howard unavailable now?

(A) He is out of town.
(B) He has been hospitalized.
(C) He is performing an operation.
(D) He is completing a research paper.

34 What does the woman suggest the man do?

(A) Complete a patient form
(B) Return the next day
(C) Find another doctor
(D) Buy some medication

---

35 What are the speakers mainly discussing?

(A) A new restaurant
(B) An outdoor market
(C) A foreign culture
(D) A travel destination

36 What is mentioned about the restaurant?

(A) The chef has won an award.
(B) It is located near the office.
(C) The ingredients are fresh.
(D) It serves authentic Thai food.

37 What time will the speakers probably meet tomorrow?

(A) At noon
(B) At 12:30 p.m.
(C) At 1:00 p.m.
(D) At 1:30 p.m.

38 What does the woman need to do?

(A) Attend a presentation
(B) Meet a deadline
(C) Make some copies
(D) Find a telephone number

39 What problem does the woman mention?

(A) A copier is out of ink.
(B) A delivery is late.
(C) Some equipment is broken.
(D) A coworker is not available.

40 What does the man suggest the woman do?

(A) Call a technician
(B) Pack some boxes
(C) Purchase some supplies
(D) Ask another colleague

---

41 What are the speakers mainly discussing?

(A) Building renovations
(B) Hiring temporary workers
(C) A work schedule
(D) An evening class

42 What problem does the woman mention?

(A) Lack of staff
(B) An equipment malfunction
(C) A missed deadline
(D) Insufficient work space

43 According to the woman, why will the production line be busier next month?

(A) A few employees have resigned.
(B) Large orders have been placed.
(C) A deadline has been moved up.
(D) Some workers are on vacation.

GO ON TO THE NEXT PAGE

44 What is happening in the meeting room?
(A) Some improvements are being made.
(B) Some furniture is on display.
(C) A fashion show is being held.
(D) A meeting is in progress.

45 What does the man say about his desk and chair?
(A) They are not comfortable.
(B) They are broken.
(C) They are fine.
(D) They are brand new.

46 What does the woman say about the new chairs?
(A) They are better than the old ones.
(B) They cost a lot of money.
(C) They are colorful.
(D) They are durable.

---

47 Who most likely is the man?
(A) A pharmacist
(B) A bus driver
(C) A store clerk
(D) A security guard

48 What problem does the man mention?
(A) The woman does not have a ticket.
(B) The street is being repaired.
(C) The traffic light is broken.
(D) The bus goes in the opposite direction.

49 What will the woman probably do next?
(A) Look at a map
(B) Get another ticket
(C) Cross the street
(D) Buy some medication

50 What did the woman forget to bring?
(A) A broken computer
(B) An original receipt
(C) An order form
(D) A user manual

51 What does the woman mean when she says, "Oh, that's convenient"?
(A) The store is located close to a subway station.
(B) She does not have to remember her order number.
(C) A free delivery service is provided.
(D) She can purchase an item online.

52 What will the man probably do next?
(A) Bring some merchandise
(B) Make a telephone call
(C) Go to the cashier
(D) Write down some information

---

53 Why is the woman calling?
(A) To inquire about a missing item
(B) To book a hotel room
(C) To cancel a flight
(D) To make travel arrangements

54 What does the woman say she will do in the afternoon?
(A) Go to a meeting
(B) Finalize an agreement
(C) Review a travel itinerary
(D) Stay in a hotel

55 What does the man agree to change?
(A) The location of an event
(B) A project deadline
(C) A holiday destination
(D) A delivery time

56 Why did the man want to talk to the woman?

(A) To announce his resignation
(B) To make some suggestions
(C) To request vacation days
(D) To discuss a new project

57 What type of company do the speakers probably work for?

(A) A theater company
(B) A newspaper
(C) A financial firm
(D) A police force

58 What does the man say about Boston?

(A) He was born there.
(B) It has many newspaper companies.
(C) It is popular with tourists.
(D) His family and friends live there.

---

59 What are the speakers mainly discussing?

(A) Mailing costs
(B) Preparations for an event
(C) Negative reviews
(D) Sales of a new book

60 What does the woman mean when she says, "You have a point there, Ron"?

(A) She organized the last opening.
(B) Ron has made a mistake.
(C) They need a larger space.
(D) The last event was overcrowded.

61 What does Ron suggest doing?

(A) Inviting local critics
(B) Advertising in the local newspaper
(C) Printing more brochures
(D) Sending out more invitations

Staff Lounge	OFFICE 2	
OFFICE 1	OFFICE 3	OFFICE 4

62 What does the woman ask the man to do?

(A) Lease office space
(B) Review the room assignments
(C) Submit a sales report
(D) Purchase some office furniture

63 Who will the woman meet with later today?

(A) Marketing experts
(B) The company president
(C) Sales staff
(D) An architect

64 Look at the graphic. Which office has been assigned to the man?

(A) Office 1
(B) Office 2
(C) Office 3
(D) Office 4

GO ON TO THE NEXT PAGE

Price list (Fax Machines)	
Item	Price
Paramount Fax Machine	$250
MP Fax Machine	$300
Neon Fax Machine	$350
Priority Fax Machine	$400

65 Why is the woman calling?

(A) To update contact information
(B) To inquire about a shipment
(C) To place an order
(D) To cancel an appointment

66 Look at the graphic. Which model did the woman order a week ago?

(A) Paramount Fax Machine
(B) MP Fax Machine
(C) Neon Fax Machine
(D) Priority Fax Machine

67 According to the man, when will the order arrive?

(A) Today
(B) Tomorrow
(C) In two days
(D) In a week

Employee Directory	
Name	Extension
Beth Hall	55
Jonathan Hastings	9
Sandra Larson	23
Melody Wong	15

68 What does the man say about the presentation?

(A) The woman did a good job on it.
(B) The company president attended it.
(C) It contained incorrect information.
(D) It took a lot of time.

69 Why is the woman concerned?

(A) She is not good at analyzing data.
(B) She has to finish another assignment.
(C) She is unavailable to attend a meeting.
(D) She will be on a business trip.

70 Look at the graphic. What extension will the man most likely call?

(A) 55
(B) 9
(C) 23
(D) 15

PART 4

Directions: You will hear some talks given by a single speaker. You will be asked to answer three questions about what the speaker says in each talk. Select the best response to each question and mark the letter (A), (B), (C), or (D) on your answer sheet. The talks will not be printed in your test book and will be spoken only one time.

71 What type of work is scheduled?
(A) Software testing
(B) Computer upgrades
(C) Telephone system replacement
(D) Plumbing maintenance

72 When will the work be completed?
(A) On Monday
(B) On Friday
(C) On Saturday
(D) On Sunday

73 What are listeners encouraged to do?
(A) Store water
(B) Speak to the manager
(C) Prepare for a presentation
(D) Return a phone call

---

74 What type of business is being advertised?
(A) A grocery store
(B) An electronics store
(C) A clothing store
(D) A photography studio

75 What will happen on Sunday?
(A) A new product will be released.
(B) A store will be relocated.
(C) A special offer will end.
(D) A business will be closed.

76 What is offered free of charge?
(A) Laptop cases
(B) Home delivery
(C) Computer software
(D) Refreshments

77 Who most likely is the speaker?
(A) The captain
(B) A mechanic
(C) A flight attendant
(D) An airport employee

78 Which city is the flight departing from?
(A) Seattle
(B) London
(C) Paris
(D) Singapore

79 What are passengers asked to do during take-off?
(A) Listen to a weather forecast
(B) Sit back and enjoy the view
(C) Speak to a flight attendant
(D) Turn off electronic devices

---

80 Who most likely are the listeners?
(A) Yoga teachers
(B) Center managers
(C) Prospective members
(D) Engineers

81 What special service does the fitness center offer?
(A) A cooking demonstration
(B) Some nutrition tips
(C) A charity concert
(D) A free shuttle bus

82 What will listeners probably do next?
(A) Sell tickets
(B) Complete a survey
(C) Reduce prices
(D) Go on a tour

GO ON TO THE NEXT PAGE

83 Who most likely are the listeners?

(A) Department heads
(B) New employees
(C) Raw material suppliers
(D) News reporters

84 What does the speaker mean when she says, "Be sure to read it carefully"?

(A) Employees should know how to report their work hours.
(B) Employees should not be late for work.
(C) Employees should set up an account.
(D) Employees should receive an orientation packet.

85 In what situation, should employees notify their manager?

(A) When they are injured
(B) When they forget a password
(C) When they work extra hours
(D) When their computers are broken

---

86 What is the speaker discussing?

(A) A revised company policy
(B) A staff restaurant
(C) A coupon book
(D) A healthy diet

87 According to the speaker, what are employees confused about?

(A) Difference in cost
(B) A facility's opening date
(C) Benefits of the membership
(D) Medical insurance

88 What does the speaker say employees can do?

(A) Request a breakfast menu
(B) Receive a discount on drinks
(C) Take time off after a meal
(D) Purchase meal coupons

89 What problem does the speaker mention about Modesta?

(A) Their focus on low price
(B) Their poor customer service
(C) Their staffing problems
(D) Their request to renew a contract

90 Why does the speaker say, "But here's the thing"?

(A) To hand out a document to listeners
(B) To change the subject
(C) To point out a problem to think about
(D) To recommend another supplier

91 What are the listeners encouraged to do?

(A) Design a new product
(B) Meet a deadline
(C) Deal with customer complaints
(D) Come up with ideas

---

92 What is the main topic of the announcement?

(A) An equipment installation
(B) A building inspection
(C) A corporate acquisition
(D) Orientation for new employees

93 What benefit does the new machine have?

(A) It consumes less power.
(B) It can be used for multiple purposes.
(C) It prints 20% more documents per hour.
(D) Free installation is offered.

94 What does the speaker ask some listeners to do?

(A) Consult a supervisor
(B) Go over a manual
(C) Install new machinery
(D) Work overtime

Spring 2016 **Event Schedule**	
Simple Diet Tips (Cindy)	1:00 ~ 1:50
Easy Recipes (Karen)	2:00 ~ 2:50
Coffee Break	3:00 ~ 3:30
Panel Discussion	4:30 ~ 5:50

95 What event does the community center plan?

(A) A health education event
(B) A cooking competition
(C) A seminar on home schooling
(D) A community festival

96 What does the speaker suggest?

(A) Bringing home-made desserts
(B) Adding a food tasting session
(C) Inviting some experts for a discussion
(D) Sharing ideas for recipes

97 Look at the graphic. What does the speaker want to remove from the schedule?

(A) Simple diet tips
(B) Easy recipes
(C) Coffee break
(D) Panel discussion

Price Estimate	
Type	**Package**
Weight	5kg
Length	20cm
Width	20cm
Height	6cm
Delivery option	Quick Delivery Co.
Total Estimate of Charges: $60.00	

98 What did Ms. O'Hara request?

(A) A change to a price estimate
(B) Her travel schedule
(C) A new telephone number
(D) Information on a cruise

99 Why does Ms. O'Hara want a package delivered by airmail?

(A) It is inexpensive.
(B) It is reliable.
(C) It is fast.
(D) It is popular.

100 Look at the graphic. According to the speaker, what information will be revised?

(A) Weight
(B) Height
(C) Delivery option
(D) Total charges

This is the end of the Listening test. Turn to Part 5 in your test book.

GO ON TO THE NEXT PAGE

LISTENING TEST

In the Listening test, you will be asked to demonstrate how well you understand spoken English. The entire Listening test will last approximately 45 minutes. There are four parts, and directions are given for each part. You must mark your answers on the separate answer sheet. Do not write your answers in your test book.

PART 1

Directions: For each question in this part, you will hear four statements about a picture in your test book. When you hear the statements, you must select the one statement that best describes what you see in the picture. Then find the number of the question on your answer sheet and mark your answer. The statements will not be printed in your test book and will be spoken only one time.

Example

Sample Answer

Statement (C), "The man is working on a painting," is the best description of the picture, so you should select answer (C) and mark it on your answer sheet.

1

2

GO ON TO THE NEXT PAGE

3

4

5

6

GO ON TO THE NEXT PAGE

PART 2

Directions: You will hear a question or statement and three responses spoken in English. They will not be printed in your test book and will be spoken only one time. Select the best response to the question or statement and mark the letter (A), (B), or (C) on your answer sheet.

7 Mark your answer on your answer sheet.

8 Mark your answer on your answer sheet.

9 Mark your answer on your answer sheet.

10 Mark your answer on your answer sheet.

11 Mark your answer on your answer sheet.

12 Mark your answer on your answer sheet.

13 Mark your answer on your answer sheet.

14 Mark your answer on your answer sheet.

15 Mark your answer on your answer sheet.

16 Mark your answer on your answer sheet.

17 Mark your answer on your answer sheet.

18 Mark your answer on your answer sheet.

19 Mark your answer on your answer sheet.

20 Mark your answer on your answer sheet.

21 Mark your answer on your answer sheet.

22 Mark your answer on your answer sheet.

23 Mark your answer on your answer sheet.

24 Mark your answer on your answer sheet.

25 Mark your answer on your answer sheet.

26 Mark your answer on your answer sheet.

27 Mark your answer on your answer sheet.

28 Mark your answer on your answer sheet.

29 Mark your answer on your answer sheet.

30 Mark your answer on your answer sheet.

31 Mark your answer on your answer sheet.

PART 3

Directions: You will hear some conversations between two or more people. You will be asked to answer three questions about what the speakers say in each conversation. Select the best response to each question and mark the letter (A), (B), (C), or (D) on your answer sheet. The conversations will not be printed in your test book and will be spoken only one time.

32 Where does the woman most likely work?
(A) At a hotel
(B) At a florist shop
(C) At a landscaping company
(D) At a construction company

33 What is the purpose of the man's call?
(A) To make a complaint
(B) To promote a special event
(C) To order some flowers
(D) To request some landscaping work

34 What does the man ask for as soon as possible?
(A) A list of companies
(B) A price estimate
(C) An appointment
(D) A corrected bill

---

35 What are the speakers talking about?
(A) An office complex
(B) Parking rules
(C) A new manager
(D) A community park

36 What does the man suggest the woman do?
(A) Purchase a new car
(B) Go for a walk
(C) Move a vehicle
(D) Check building regulations

37 What does the woman ask the man to do?
(A) Postpone a meeting
(B) Find a parking garage
(C) Recommend a mechanic
(D) Contact a moving company

38 Where is the conversation most likely taking place?
(A) In an office
(B) At a bus stop
(C) In a warehouse
(D) At a ticket office

39 How did the man learn about the delay?
(A) By speaking to a ticket agent
(B) By checking a schedule
(C) By hearing an announcement
(D) By reading a notice

40 Why is the woman pleased?
(A) She will arrive at work on time.
(B) There is no traffic jam.
(C) A bus fare has come down in price.
(D) She can purchase a ticket.

---

41 What are the speakers discussing?
(A) A food craving
(B) Travel arrangements
(C) International chefs
(D) A newly opened restaurant

42 What does the woman like about the chicken plate?
(A) The atmosphere
(B) The price
(C) The portion
(D) The location

43 When will the speakers meet?
(A) At 11:45 a.m.
(B) At 12:00 p.m.
(C) At 12:15 p.m.
(D) At 1:00 p.m.

GO ON TO THE NEXT PAGE

44 What is the woman having trouble with?

(A) A printer
(B) A delivery
(C) A security pass
(D) A password

45 How does the man say he will solve the problem?

(A) By changing a password
(B) By upgrading software
(C) By calling technical support
(D) By inspecting a building

46 What will the man do at 3 o'clock?

(A) Replace a computer
(B) Find a telephone
(C) Visit an office
(D) Review an instruction manual

---

47 Why was the man unable to hear the news report?

(A) He had a meeting with some clients.
(B) There was too much noise.
(C) He woke up late in the morning.
(D) His radio was out of order.

48 What is the subject of the news report?

(A) A sales meeting
(B) A company policy
(C) A traffic accident
(D) A council decision

49 What does the man imply when he says, "Wow, that's good news"?

(A) He will share a ride with the woman.
(B) He will experience less traffic congestion.
(C) A construction project will be cancelled.
(D) His work will be finished on time.

50 Where is the conversation most likely taking place?

(A) At an amusement park
(B) At a movie theater
(C) At a sports center
(D) At a museum

51 What does the woman ask about?

(A) Special events
(B) Discounts for children
(C) Directions to a gift shop
(D) Weather conditions

52 What additional information does the man give?

(A) A guided tour
(B) An event for children
(C) Business hours
(D) Benefits of a membership

---

53 What are the speakers mainly discussing?

(A) A new manager
(B) Employee benefits
(C) A project deadline
(D) Training classes

54 What does Stacey mean when she says, "I'm sorry but I'm not following"?

(A) She was not aware of the training classes.
(B) She wants to discuss another subject.
(C) She is an expert on marketing strategies.
(D) She is sorry about being late for work.

55 How can new employees register for the classes?

(A) By speaking to a manager
(B) By visiting a website
(C) By completing a form
(D) By upgrading software

56 What is the problem with the curtains?

(A) They are too dark.
(B) They look unattractive.
(C) They are the wrong size.
(D) They are out of stock.

57 What does the woman decide to do?

(A) Call for a brochure
(B) Request a refund
(C) Take measurements again
(D) Send a package by parcel

58 What does the man offer to check?

(A) Where to mail a shipment
(B) How to pay an additional fee
(C) Whether a product is available
(D) When a process will be completed

---

59 What type of business does the woman own?

(A) An advertising agency
(B) An online game company
(C) A florist shop
(D) A catering company

60 What does the woman say about her business?

(A) It has been unprofitable.
(B) It is adding a branch.
(C) It has hired a new advertising agent.
(D) It has a bad reputation.

61 What does the man offer to do?

(A) Bring his acquaintances
(B) Help prepare flower arrangements
(C) Review a contract
(D) Recommend the woman's business

62 What is mentioned about The XG-200?

(A) It is the newest model.
(B) It is slower than the previous model.
(C) It is the most expensive model.
(D) It comes in different colors.

63 What is the woman's concern?

(A) She prefers a faster printer.
(B) A product is unavailable right now.
(C) Her budget is limited.
(D) She has to go back to her office.

64 What advantage does Steven mention about last year's models?

(A) Free shipping is provided.
(B) They are lightweight.
(C) Self-installation is easy.
(D) They have come down in price.

GO ON TO THE NEXT PAGE

Library Check-out Policy

- 4 items at a time
- Books: 2 weeks
- Magazines and videos: 1-3 days
- Fines: 5 cents per day

65 What problem does the woman mention?

(A) She has an overdue item.
(B) Her library card has expired.
(C) She cannot find a book.
(D) The library is about to close.

66 Look at the graphic. How much will the woman have to pay for the overdue book tomorrow?

(A) 5 cents
(B) 15 cents
(C) 55 cents
(D) 2 dollars

67 What does the man offer to do?

(A) Revise a policy
(B) Find a magazine
(C) Reserve some books
(D) Arrange a meeting

Schedule	
Workshop	**Time**
Job Maintenance	10:00 a.m.
Dealing with Change	11:00 a.m.
Lunch	12:00 p.m.
Self Esteem	1:00 p.m.
Social Media	2:00 p.m.

68 What are the speakers mainly discussing?

(A) The upcoming workshops
(B) A company policy
(C) Online shopping
(D) Some Internet tools

69 What does the man suggest?

(A) Inviting the company CEO
(B) Viewing some photos online
(C) Using a larger space
(D) Changing the seating arrangement

70 Look at the graphic. According to the woman, which workshop will now be held last?

(A) Job Maintenance
(B) Dealing with Change
(C) Self Esteem
(D) Social Media

PART 4

Directions: You will hear some talks given by a single speaker. You will be asked to answer three questions about what the speaker says in each talk. Select the best response to each question and mark the letter (A), (B), (C), or (D) on your answer sheet. The talks will not be printed in your test book and will be spoken only one time.

71 Which department does the speaker most likely work in?
(A) Marketing
(B) Research and Development
(C) Human resources
(D) Customer service

72 What is the purpose of the message?
(A) To schedule an interview
(B) To request a document
(C) To introduce a new employee
(D) To invite a keynote speaker

73 What has already been prepared?
(A) A meeting room
(B) A user manual
(C) A list of questions
(D) A security badge

---

74 What is the purpose of the announcement?
(A) To announce the closing of a store
(B) To introduce a new line of products
(C) To explain a new refund policy
(D) To direct shoppers to the service desk

75 Where can shoppers find the sale items?
(A) Next to the checkout counters
(B) In the women's section
(C) In the children's section
(D) Near the event hall

76 What change will be implemented next weekend?
(A) A special sale will be held.
(B) A new manager will be hired.
(C) The store will have more stock.
(D) Business hours will be extended.

77 What is the topic of the talk show?
(A) Fashion
(B) Finance
(C) Health
(D) Politics

78 What are listeners invited to do?
(A) Join a discussion with experts
(B) Order a subscription
(C) Leave their contact information
(D) Take a tour of the radio station

79 What will listeners hear next?
(A) A traffic update
(B) A commercial
(C) The weather forecast
(D) A news report

---

80 What is the purpose of the message?
(A) To schedule a visit
(B) To discuss the licensing procedures
(C) To explain the results of an inspection
(D) To request a document

81 What does the speaker mean when he says, "Yes, it does"?
(A) The process takes a long time.
(B) An inspection is required to open a restaurant.
(C) Inspectors are available to visit the restaurant.
(D) There is a fee for the service.

82 What does the speaker say about renewing a license?
(A) A fee must be paid first.
(B) Staff training is required.
(C) The renewal form is available online.
(D) It must be done every year.

GO ON TO THE NEXT PAGE

83 What does the speaker mention about Blue Beverage Company?

(A) They have won an award.
(B) They will hire additional employees.
(C) They have developed a new product.
(D) Their sales have increased.

84 Who is Mike Anderson?

(A) A quality control expert
(B) A marketing expert
(C) A department head
(D) A sales representative

85 What will Mr. Anderson discuss?

(A) His recent book
(B) His marketing techniques
(C) His educational background
(D) His hard times

---

86 What is the purpose of the talk?

(A) To discuss a current social issue
(B) To report a local crime
(C) To present an award
(D) To introduce a speaker

87 Who is Gregory Bateman?

(A) A professor
(B) A news writer
(C) A policeman
(D) A politician

88 What will the audience most likely do after the talk?

(A) Enroll in a course
(B) Join an association
(C) Participate in a reception
(D) Register for a seminar

89 Who most likely are the listeners?

(A) Sales representatives
(B) Store customers
(C) Marketing staff
(D) Magazine reporters

90 What does the speaker mean when she says, "It is all because of everyone here"?

(A) Employees have developed a new product.
(B) Employees have organized tonight's event.
(C) Employees are able to multi-task.
(D) Employees have helped the company succeed.

91 What will the company do on September 1st?

(A) Open a branch overseas
(B) Launch a new product
(C) Conduct a marketing survey
(D) Celebrate an anniversary

---

92 What is the purpose of the meeting?

(A) To forecast the weather
(B) To discuss a problem
(C) To evaluate employees
(D) To assign a task

93 What does the speaker want to do?

(A) Reduce expenditures
(B) Boost profits
(C) Postpone a deadline
(D) Interview an applicant

94 What will happen on August 28th?

(A) A merger will be discussed.
(B) The CEO will be appointed.
(C) A meeting will take place.
(D) A product will be demonstrated.

List of Catering Companies	
Company	Price Quote
1. Daniel Catering	$3,000
2. Rose Catering	$4,500
3. The Lazy Gourmet	$7,000
4. Christine Catering	$3,500

95 What event will the company hold?

(A) A retirement party
(B) An awards banquet
(C) A press conference
(D) An annual convention

96 What does the speaker mention about Daniel Catering?

(A) The food was not good.
(B) The service was excellent.
(C) The price was expensive.
(D) The employees are well trained.

97 Look at the graphic. Which company does the speaker want to hire?

(A) Daniel Catering
(B) Rose Catering
(C) The Lazy Gourmet
(D) Christine Catering

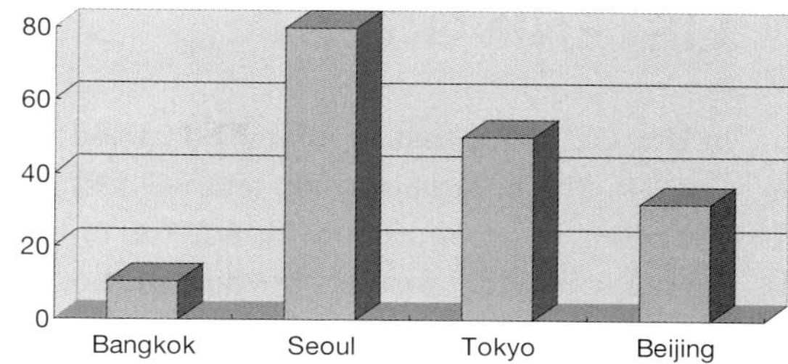

98 What is responsible for the increase in the company's profits?

(A) The company's new web site
(B) The decreased cost of operations
(C) Cheaper flight tickets
(D) Sales of city tours

99 According to the speaker, why do customers like Seoul?

(A) It is safe to travel around the city.
(B) They can enjoy the city day and night.
(C) There are many inexpensive hotels.
(D) It is easy to use public transportation.

100 Look at the graphic. What city will the listeners investigate?

(A) Bangkok
(B) Seoul
(C) Tokyo
(D) Beijing

This is the end of the Listening test. Turn to Part 5 in your test book.

GO ON TO THE NEXT PAGE

▶정답 및 해설 P46

LISTENING TEST

In the Listening test, you will be asked to demonstrate how well you understand spoken English. The entire Listening test will last approximately 45 minutes. There are four parts, and directions are given for each part. You must mark your answers on the separate answer sheet. Do not write your answers in your test book.

PART 1

Directions: For each question in this part, you will hear four statements about a picture in your test book. When you hear the statements, you must select the one statement that best describes what you see in the picture. Then find the number of the question on your answer sheet and mark your answer. The statements will not be printed in your test book and will be spoken only one time.

Example

Sample Answer

Statement (C), "The man is working on a painting," is the best description of the picture, so you should select answer (C) and mark it on your answer sheet.

1

2

GO ON TO THE NEXT PAGE

3

4

5

6

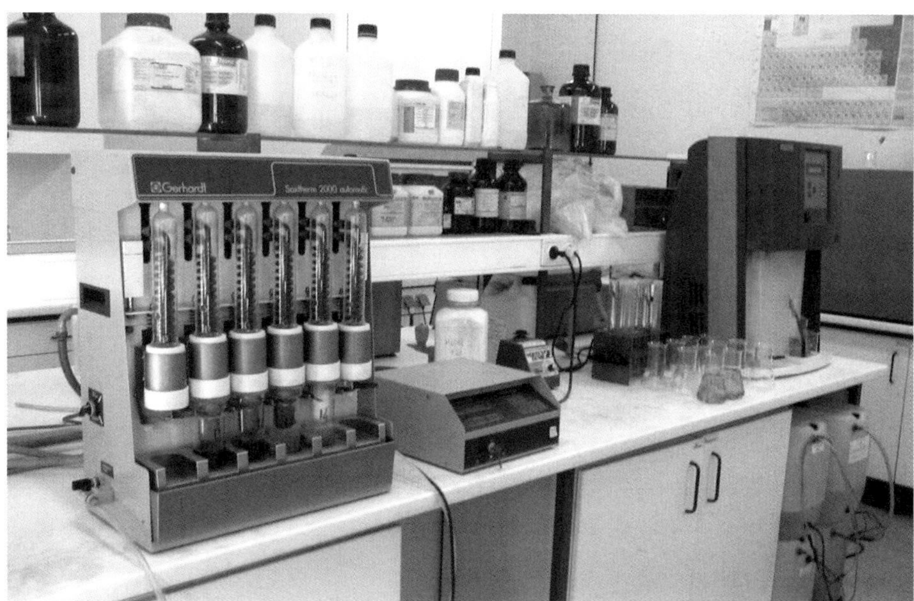

GO ON TO THE NEXT PAGE

PART 2

Directions: You will hear a question or statement and three responses spoken in English. They will not be printed in your test book and will be spoken only one time. Select the best response to the question or statement and mark the letter (A), (B), or (C) on your answer sheet.

7 Mark your answer on your answer sheet.

8 Mark your answer on your answer sheet.

9 Mark your answer on your answer sheet.

10 Mark your answer on your answer sheet.

11 Mark your answer on your answer sheet.

12 Mark your answer on your answer sheet.

13 Mark your answer on your answer sheet.

14 Mark your answer on your answer sheet.

15 Mark your answer on your answer sheet.

16 Mark your answer on your answer sheet.

17 Mark your answer on your answer sheet.

18 Mark your answer on your answer sheet.

19 Mark your answer on your answer sheet.

20 Mark your answer on your answer sheet.

21 Mark your answer on your answer sheet.

22 Mark your answer on your answer sheet.

23 Mark your answer on your answer sheet.

24 Mark your answer on your answer sheet.

25 Mark your answer on your answer sheet.

26 Mark your answer on your answer sheet.

27 Mark your answer on your answer sheet.

28 Mark your answer on your answer sheet.

29 Mark your answer on your answer sheet.

30 Mark your answer on your answer sheet.

31 Mark your answer on your answer sheet.

PART 3

Directions: You will hear some conversations between two or more people. You will be asked to answer three questions about what the speakers say in each conversation. Select the best response to each question and mark the letter (A), (B), (C), or (D) on your answer sheet. The conversations will not be printed in your test book and will be spoken only one time.

32 What are the speakers mainly discussing?
(A) A comic book
(B) A musical performance
(C) A comedy film
(D) A famous actor

33 Why was the man disappointed?
(A) Tickets were unavailable.
(B) The cinema was closed.
(C) Performers have changed.
(D) A colleague was busy.

34 What does the woman suggest the man do?
(A) Watch another movie
(B) Go to the cinema early
(C) Speak to a ticket agent
(D) Try getting tickets again

---

35 What is the woman's problem?
(A) She is unable to work overtime.
(B) She cannot make copies.
(C) She is not prepared for an interview.
(D) She has to go on a business trip.

36 What is the woman supposed to do at 3 o'clock?
(A) Go shopping
(B) Visit the headquarters
(C) Meet with a client
(D) Give a presentation

37 What will the woman probably do next?
(A) Go to a print shop
(B) Reschedule a meeting
(C) Request some help
(D) Contact another department

38 Where most likely are the speakers?
(A) At a post office
(B) At a coffee shop
(C) At a bank
(D) At a grocery store

39 What document does the man present?
(A) A passport
(B) A driver's license
(C) An application form
(D) A bank statement

40 What will the man probably do next?
(A) Make copies
(B) Take a photograph
(C) Complete a form
(D) Go to the lobby

---

41 What is the cause of the delay?
(A) Maintenance work
(B) Insufficient funds
(C) A labor shortage
(D) Weather conditions

42 Why is the man calling?
(A) To reserve a train ticket
(B) To ask for a timetable
(C) To change seats
(D) To postpone a meeting

43 When does the woman say she will be unavailable?
(A) On Tuesday
(B) On Wednesday
(C) On Thursday
(D) On Friday

GO ON TO THE NEXT PAGE

44 What does the man want to do?

(A) Select a vacation destination
(B) Take some time off work
(C) Submit an expense report
(D) Leave for the day

45 What is scheduled for next Wednesday?

(A) A company picnic
(B) A business trip
(C) A department meeting
(D) A safety inspection

46 What does the man agree to do?

(A) Cancel a flight ticket
(B) Contact an inspector
(C) Postpone his vacation
(D) Fill in for a coworker

---

47 What are the speakers discussing?

(A) Communicating by e-mail
(B) Addressing employee concerns
(C) Completing a course assignment
(D) Registering for a professional seminar

48 What does the woman imply when she says, "Well, I'm having the same problem"?

(A) She wants the man to help her with a project.
(B) She won't be able to finish her assignment on time.
(C) She has been out of town.
(D) She will report to a new director.

49 What will the man probably do next?

(A) Speak to a colleague
(B) Train some staff
(C) Confirm an appointment
(D) Request an extension

50 Where most likely are the speakers?

(A) At a public library
(B) At a school
(C) At a museum
(D) At a shopping mall

51 What is the man trying to locate?

(A) A robot exhibit
(B) A ticket office
(C) An exit
(D) An art show

52 What does the woman suggest the man do?

(A) Purchase a special gift
(B) Use an elevator
(C) Take a guided tour
(D) Find out the location of an event

---

53 Where most likely are the speakers?

(A) At a bus stop
(B) In an airport
(C) In a car
(D) At a taxi stand

54 What is the woman concerned about?

(A) Losing some luggage
(B) Locating a terminal
(C) Missing a connecting flight
(D) Changing seats

55 What does the man mean when he says, "But there is nothing I can do"?

(A) The flight for Dallas is fully booked.
(B) He cannot let the woman get on the flight.
(C) The woman has to leave the airport.
(D) He cannot help the woman find her gate.

56 Who most likely is the woman?

(A) A human resources manager
(B) A laboratory technician
(C) A factory worker
(D) A sales representative

57 What does the woman want to know about?

(A) The position that she will be working in
(B) The type of clients that she will be working with
(C) The kind of equipment that she will be using
(D) The instructions that she will follow

58 What does the man say the company did recently?

(A) Purchased some laboratory equipment
(B) Trained some new technicians
(C) Revised a company policy
(D) Relocated to a different building

---

59 Why does the man congratulate the woman?

(A) She has won an employee award.
(B) She has been promoted.
(C) She has been transferred overseas.
(D) She has started teaching at a university.

60 Where most likely do the speakers work?

(A) At an auto dealership
(B) At an advertising agency
(C) At an insurance firm
(D) At a university

61 What is the topic of the seminar series?

(A) Public speaking
(B) Event planning
(C) Sales techniques
(D) Product development

62 What will be discussed at an upcoming meeting?

(A) How to reduce costs
(B) Which office equipment supplier to hire
(C) Where to hold a company event
(D) How to meet sales goals

63 Which department do the speakers work in?

(A) Accounting
(B) Sales
(C) Payroll
(D) Shipping

64 What does Yuki suggest?

(A) Completing a budget report
(B) Turning off some office equipment
(C) Attending a board meeting
(D) Buying a new printer

GO ON TO THE NEXT PAGE

XDL DELIVERY SERVICE	
Delivery Type	Price
Standard Delivery	$50
Next Working Day	$70
XDL Premier	$120
Next Day Evening	$75

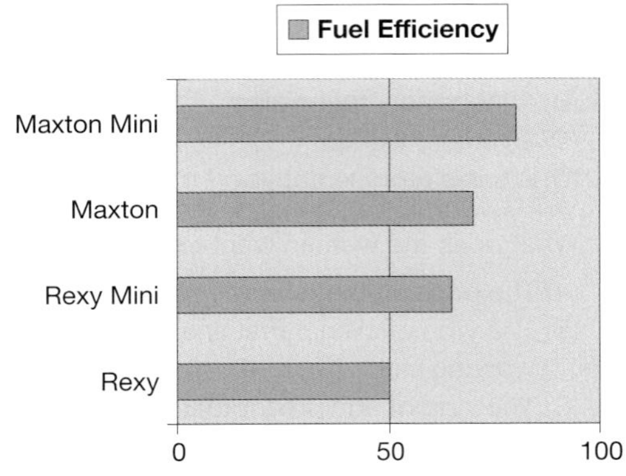

65 What is the purpose of Ms. Brown's call?

(A) To request a catalog
(B) To arrange a party
(C) To order some clothing
(D) To make a complaint

66 What is the cause of the delivery delay?

(A) An increased number of orders
(B) A missing document
(C) A system malfunction
(D) A shortage of delivery men

67 Look at the graphic. How much will the company pay for the delivery?

(A) $50
(B) $70
(C) $120
(D) $75

68 What is the man mainly looking for in a car?

(A) Safety features
(B) A powerful engine
(C) Fuel economy
(D) A discounted price

69 What does the man like about the Maxton?

(A) Its size
(B) Its design
(C) Its automatic transmission
(D) Its comfortable seating

70 Look at the graphic. Which car model will the man take for a test drive?

(A) The Maxton Mini
(B) The Maxton
(C) The Rexy Mini
(D) The Rexy

PART 4

Directions: You will hear some talks given by a single speaker. You will be asked to answer three questions about what the speaker says in each talk. Select the best response to each question and mark the letter (A), (B), (C), or (D) on your answer sheet. The talks will not be printed in your test book and will be spoken only one time.

71 What kind of class is the speaker interested in?

(A) Yoga
(B) Computer programming
(C) Swimming
(D) Public speaking

72 How did the speaker learn about the class?

(A) She saw a schedule online.
(B) She has taken the class before.
(C) It was advertised in a newspaper.
(D) It was recommended by a friend.

73 What information does the speaker request?

(A) The name of an instructor
(B) The starting date of a class
(C) The cost of a program
(D) The location of the center

---

74 What is being advertised?

(A) A vacation destination
(B) Local attractions
(C) Train service
(D) A bus tour

75 What is mentioned about the cost of traveling with Porter Railways?

(A) It is discounted for senior citizens.
(B) It has recently been reduced.
(C) It is more expensive during the peak season.
(D) It is cheaper than taking a plane.

76 Why should listeners visit the company's website?

(A) To view an updated timetable
(B) To book a ticket online
(C) To see a city map
(D) To sign up for a membership

77 Who most likely are the listeners?

(A) Restaurant employees
(B) Truck drivers
(C) Lunch customers
(D) Vegetable suppliers

78 What is the problem?

(A) A restaurant sign has been damaged.
(B) Some staff members called in sick.
(C) A popular dish is not available.
(D) A shipment was sent to the wrong address.

79 What will happen in a couple of hours?

(A) A delivery will arrive.
(B) A restaurant will be closed.
(C) Staff will start serving lunch.
(D) A new dish will be created.

---

80 Who most likely is the speaker?

(A) A taxi driver
(B) A magazine editor
(C) A radio reporter
(D) A police officer

81 How long has the weather been nice?

(A) For one day
(B) For three days
(C) For five days
(D) For seven days

82 What are listeners advised to do?

(A) Buy a new jacket
(B) Bring an umbrella
(C) Leave home early
(D) Use public transportation

GO ON TO THE NEXT PAGE

83 What is the purpose of the talk?

(A) To explain plans for a company merger
(B) To announce a new pay schedule
(C) To say farewell to a colleague
(D) To provide a conference schedule

84 When will the change take effect?

(A) This week
(B) Next week
(C) In two weeks
(D) In a month

85 What does the speaker mean when she says, "It should answer any questions you have"?

(A) Employees should go over the memo carefully.
(B) All questions should be directed to the manager.
(C) A questionnaire will be sent to employees.
(D) The article should be easy to understand.

---

86 What is the purpose of the meeting?

(A) To present an award
(B) To explain a new policy
(C) To discuss some candidates
(D) To introduce a new board member

87 What does Clifford Olson do?

(A) He cares for sick animals.
(B) He plans the annual budget.
(C) He advises local businesses on financial matters.
(D) He contributes articles to a medical journal.

88 What will listeners most likely do next?

(A) Interview the candidates
(B) Examine the credentials of an applicant
(C) Register for a training program
(D) Hear from the recipient of an award

89 What is the purpose of the telephone message?

(A) To apologize for a late shipment
(B) To schedule a meeting
(C) To ask about a new project
(D) To explain a report

90 What does the speaker mean when she says, "But the savings are worth it"?

(A) She needs to do additional research.
(B) Transporting by truck is a better option for the company.
(C) It is better to send packages by express mail.
(D) Meeting deadlines is the most important thing.

91 What does the speaker ask the listener to do?

(A) Review a report
(B) Change procedures
(C) Attend a presentation
(D) Develop a new product

---

92 Who is the intended audience of the talk?

(A) Department heads
(B) Marketing staff
(C) Office equipment suppliers
(D) International clients

93 What is the purpose of the talk?

(A) To welcome a company executive
(B) To explain a company policy
(C) To announce a special promotion
(D) To summarize some survey results

94 According to the speaker, what will Linda do?

(A) Prepare copies of a sales report
(B) Contact some suppliers
(C) Evaluate employees' performance
(D) Post some information

Lunch Order Form		
Item	Quantity	Cost
Burger	3	$3.50
French Fries	2	$1.50
Coke	3	$1.00
Frozen Yogurt	1	$1.50

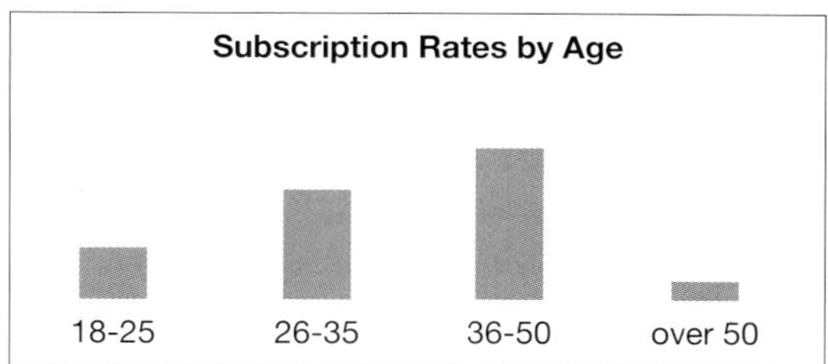

95 What is the purpose of the message?

(A) To inquire about costs
(B) To get directions to a restaurant
(C) To change an order
(D) To ask about business hours

96 Look at the graphic. Which item will not be delivered by noon?

(A) Burger
(B) French fries
(C) Coke
(D) Frozen yogurt

97 What is scheduled at 1 o'clock?

(A) A training session
(B) A meeting with clients
(C) An international event
(D) A video conference

98 Why does the company want to develop online applications?

(A) The company can save money on advertising.
(B) Online sales have decreased.
(C) They are inexpensive to develop.
(D) Customers prefer to read news online.

99 Look at the graphic. Which age group will the listeners look into?

(A) 18-25
(B) 26-35
(C) 36-50
(D) Over 59

100 What is scheduled for next Monday?

(A) A software upgrade
(B) A job interview
(C) A department meeting
(D) A political debate

This is the end of the Listening test. Turn to Part 5 in your test book.

GO ON TO THE NEXT PAGE

▶정답 및 해설 P66

LISTENING TEST

In the Listening test, you will be asked to demonstrate how well you understand spoken English. The entire Listening test will last approximately 45 minutes. There are four parts, and directions are given for each part. You must mark your answers on the separate answer sheet. Do not write your answers in your test book.

PART 1

Directions: For each question in this part, you will hear four statements about a picture in your test book. When you hear the statements, you must select the one statement that best describes what you see in the picture. Then find the number of the question on your answer sheet and mark your answer. The statements will not be printed in your test book and will be spoken only one time.

Example

Sample Answer

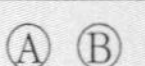  

Statement (C), "The man is working on a painting," is the best description of the picture, so you should select answer (C) and mark it on your answer sheet.

1

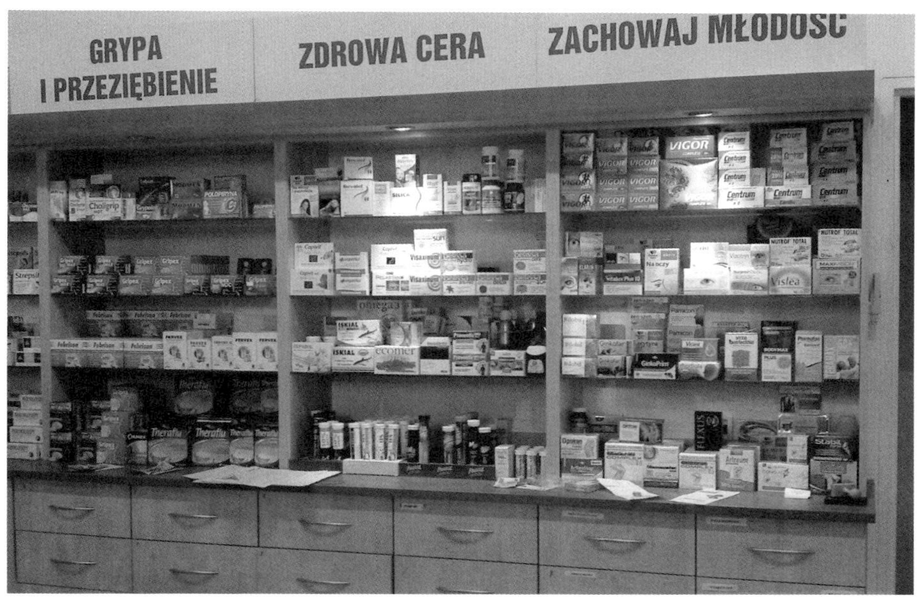

2

GO ON TO THE NEXT PAGE

3

4

5

6

GO ON TO THE NEXT PAGE

PART 2

Directions: You will hear a question or statement and three responses spoken in English. They will not be printed in your test book and will be spoken only one time. Select the best response to the question or statement and mark the letter (A), (B), or (C) on your answer sheet.

7 Mark your answer on your answer sheet.

8 Mark your answer on your answer sheet.

9 Mark your answer on your answer sheet.

10 Mark your answer on your answer sheet.

11 Mark your answer on your answer sheet.

12 Mark your answer on your answer sheet.

13 Mark your answer on your answer sheet.

14 Mark your answer on your answer sheet.

15 Mark your answer on your answer sheet.

16 Mark your answer on your answer sheet.

17 Mark your answer on your answer sheet.

18 Mark your answer on your answer sheet.

19 Mark your answer on your answer sheet.

20 Mark your answer on your answer sheet.

21 Mark your answer on your answer sheet.

22 Mark your answer on your answer sheet.

23 Mark your answer on your answer sheet.

24 Mark your answer on your answer sheet.

25 Mark your answer on your answer sheet.

26 Mark your answer on your answer sheet.

27 Mark your answer on your answer sheet.

28 Mark your answer on your answer sheet.

29 Mark your answer on your answer sheet.

30 Mark your answer on your answer sheet.

31 Mark your answer on your answer sheet.

PART 3

Directions: You will hear some conversations between two or more people. You will be asked to answer three questions about what the speakers say in each conversation. Select the best response to each question and mark the letter (A), (B), (C), or (D) on your answer sheet. The conversations will not be printed in your test book and will be spoken only one time.

32 Why did the man visit the community sports center?
(A) To report a lost item
(B) To participate in an event
(C) To volunteer for a carnival
(D) To ask for directions

33 What is the man instructed to do?
(A) Enroll in a college course
(B) Exercise on a regular basis
(C) Go to another place
(D) Distribute some flyers

34 What does the man ask for?
(A) A city map
(B) A registration form
(C) A list of participants
(D) Updated information

35 Where most likely do the speakers work?
(A) At a delivery company
(B) At a jewelry shop
(C) At a party planning firm
(D) At a florist shop

36 What problem does the woman mention?
(A) A client complained about the service.
(B) A party has been postponed.
(C) A delivery was late.
(D) Some work has not been completed.

37 Why will the man make a phone call?
(A) To request more supplies
(B) To cancel an order
(C) To apologize for a mistake
(D) To confirm the address

38 What problem does the man report?
(A) He's locked out of his room.
(B) The Internet connection is not working.
(C) A window is stuck.
(D) A safe is broken.

39 What does the woman say she will do?
(A) Replace a device
(B) Do some errands
(C) Send a maintenance person
(D) Arrange for transportation

40 Why does the man want the problem to be solved quickly?
(A) He cannot get into his room.
(B) He is storing some valuables.
(C) He is having some guests over.
(D) He has to catch a flight soon.

41 Where does the woman work?
(A) At a restaurant
(B) At an airport
(C) At a hotel
(D) At a coffee shop

42 Why is the man calling?
(A) To book a hotel room
(B) To confirm a flight booking
(C) To ask for directions
(D) To change a reservation

43 What alternative does the woman offer the man?
(A) Visiting on a different day
(B) Informing him if there is a cancellation
(C) Coming in at a later time
(D) Eating in an outdoor dining area

GO ON TO THE NEXT PAGE

44 What does the man want?

(A) A receipt for his purchase
(B) Directions to a drugstore
(C) A recommendation
(D) A reduced rate

45 What does the woman suggest the man do?

(A) Get a prescription
(B) Try a new remedy
(C) Fill out a form
(D) Consult another employee

46 What will the woman most likely do next?

(A) Make an announcement
(B) Issue a coupon
(C) Offer a map
(D) Page a colleague

---

47 Where most likely do the speakers work?

(A) At a software company
(B) At a computer repair shop
(C) At an architectural firm
(D) At a travel agency

48 What is the advantage of the new software?

(A) It is easy to use.
(B) It is reliable.
(C) It is inexpensive.
(D) It is fast.

49 What will happen on Thursday?

(A) A welcome reception will be held.
(B) A new employee will arrive.
(C) An expert will hold a seminar.
(D) A new task will be assigned.

50 What kind of business does the man own?

(A) A catering service
(B) An advertising firm
(C) A marketing company
(D) A web design company

51 What does the man say about his business?

(A) It will participate in a bid.
(B) It has hired an advertising agent.
(C) Its sales have been down.
(D) It is opening another branch.

52 What does the woman offer to do?

(A) Help organize an event
(B) Recommend the man's business
(C) Arrange a meeting
(D) Write a review

---

53 Where does the woman most likely work?

(A) At a moving company
(B) At a financial firm
(C) At an office supply store
(D) At a property development company

54 What does the man imply when he says, "Oh, I appreciate all your hard work, Ms. Lopez"?

(A) He has received a discount.
(B) He is satisfied with his office relocation.
(C) He wants the woman to try harder.
(D) A renovation project is ahead of schedule.

55 What does the woman ask the man about?

(A) How to get to a meeting room
(B) The cost of a special service
(C) Where to place a container
(D) The name of a company

56 Why is the woman at the Humax booth?

(A) To attend a meeting
(B) To introduce a product
(C) To get more information
(D) To register for a lecture

57 What has the woman recently done?

(A) Worked as a freelancer
(B) Obtained a diploma
(C) Demonstrated a product
(D) Relocated to a new city

58 What does the man want to know about?

(A) Relevant licenses
(B) The Interview process
(C) The location of the company
(D) Adequate work experience

---

59 What does the woman ask permission to do?

(A) Enter a restricted area
(B) Extend a project deadline
(C) Use some equipment for a presentation
(D) Change the time of a meeting

60 Why was the woman's presentation rescheduled?

(A) Some reports were incomplete.
(B) An event venue was unavailable.
(C) Some coworkers were in another meeting.
(D) There was a technical malfunction.

61 What does the man mean when he says, "Okay, that's no problem"?

(A) The woman should attend a meeting.
(B) The woman should make a reservation.
(C) The woman may leave work early.
(D) The woman may borrow his computer.

62 What problem is being discussed?

(A) Some ingredients are missing.
(B) A class has been cancelled.
(C) An employee is out sick.
(D) A customer has complained.

63 What does the woman mean when she says, "Oh, I'm afraid I can't, Mr. Gaines"?

(A) She cannot cover for her coworker.
(B) She has not made a reservation.
(C) She is unavailable to attend a meeting.
(D) She cannot reschedule an event.

64 What will Mark most likely do next?

(A) Prepare some food
(B) Contact a coworker
(C) Seat some customers
(D) Put on a uniform

GO ON TO THE NEXT PAGE

Material	Price
MDF	$250
metal	$380
Rubberwood	$420
Mahogany	$550

65 What does the man ask the woman to do?

(A) Contact her supervisor
(B) Repair some equipment
(C) Order some office furniture
(D) Find a new supplier

66 What problem does the woman mention?

(A) A product is out of stock.
(B) A vendor has increased its prices.
(C) A researcher has made a mistake.
(D) A budget proposal is incomplete.

67 Look at the graphic. How much will the speakers pay for a desk?

(A) $250
(B) $380
(C) $420
(D) $550

Company Directory	
Name	Extension
Andrew Graham	1
Elizabeth White	9
Nora Wong	11
Tyler Chang	15

68 Which department is looking to fill a vacancy?

(A) Sales
(B) Production
(C) Human resources
(D) Marketing

69 What does the woman say about production line workers?

(A) They have to wear protective gear.
(B) They are skilled workers.
(C) They are required to work overtime.
(D) They get paid well.

70 Look at the graphic. What number will the man most likely call?

(A) 1
(B) 9
(C) 11
(D) 15

PART 4

Directions: You will hear some talks given by a single speaker. You will be asked to answer three questions about what the speaker says in each talk. Select the best response to each question and mark the letter (A), (B), (C), or (D) on your answer sheet. The talks will not be printed in your test book and will be spoken only one time.

71 Where most likely does the speaker work?
(A) At a furniture store
(B) At a real estate agency
(C) At a moving company
(D) At an interior design firm

72 What does the speaker mention about the property?
(A) It has a parking lot.
(B) It is not available.
(C) It is in a good location.
(D) It has a nice view.

73 What has recently been renovated?
(A) A balcony
(B) A bathroom
(C) A kitchen
(D) A bedroom

---

74 Where is the event taking place?
(A) At a government office
(B) At a financial convention
(C) At a library
(D) At a job fair

75 What is the topic of the presentation?
(A) How to develop tax strategies
(B) How to travel on a small budget
(C) How to write a best-selling book
(D) How to plan for retirement

76 According to the speaker, what will be available online?
(A) A list of new publications
(B) A recording of the lecture
(C) Adrianne McCoy's columns
(D) Photographs of the event

77 What will take place tomorrow morning?
(A) Installation of equipment
(B) A factory renovation
(C) An annual road clean-up
(D) An emergency drill

78 According to the speaker, who will visit the factory?
(A) Electricians
(B) Inspectors
(C) Firefighters
(D) Union delegates

79 What are employees instructed to do?
(A) Complete a check list
(B) Distribute a manual
(C) Inspect some machines
(D) Read an evacuation plan

---

80 Where does the announcement most likely take place?
(A) In a museum
(B) In a bookstore
(C) In a theater
(D) In a radio studio

81 According to the speaker, who is Benjamin Han?
(A) A producer
(B) A conductor
(C) An actor
(D) A playwright

82 What are listeners told to do after the show?
(A) Reserve a seat
(B) Speak with the performers
(C) Attend a meeting
(D) Watch a movie

GO ON TO THE NEXT PAGE

83 What kind of event is taking place?

(A) An opening ceremony
(B) An annual conference
(C) An awards dinner
(D) A company outing

84 What is Dr. Evans famous for?

(A) Receiving a prestigious award
(B) Having written a series of books
(C) Developing a successful marketing strategy
(D) Expanding her own business overseas

85 What does the speaker mean when he says, "So please hold your questions until the end"?

(A) The audience should not interrupt the speaker.
(B) The audience should not leave their seats.
(C) The audience should applaud the speaker.
(D) The audience should answer some questions.

---

86 What have the listeners been learning?

(A) Writing techniques
(B) Advanced culinary skills
(C) Pencil drawing
(D) Martial arts for self defense

87 What are listeners asked to do?

(A) Complete a questionnaire
(B) Request a class schedule
(C) Exercise every day
(D) Apply for a membership

88 Why would listeners provide an e-mail address?

(A) To participate in a competition
(B) To receive some information
(C) To register for an exercise class
(D) To view some photos of an event

89 What did Mr. Hudson ask about?

(A) Online banking enrollment
(B) A high-interest savings account
(C) Directions to the nearest branch
(D) A lost credit card

90 What does the woman mean when she says, "Let me explain how it works"?

(A) She will assemble some equipment.
(B) She will send a repair person.
(C) She will offer detailed instructions.
(D) She will explain the hiring process.

91 What does the speaker say about a password?

(A) It must be updated every month.
(B) It is required to transfer funds.
(C) It can be used to check balances.
(D) It should be memorable.

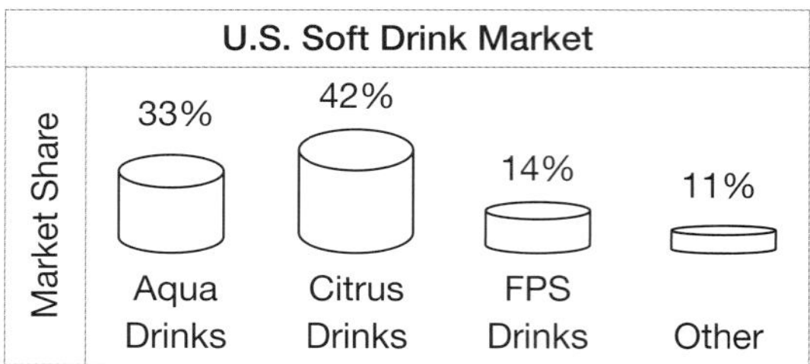

92 Which department does the speaker work in?

(A) Sales
(B) Advertising
(C) Personnel
(D) Product development

93 Look at the graphic. How much market share did the man's company have last quarter?

(A) 11%
(B) 14%
(C) 33%
(D) 42%

94 According to the speaker, what will happen on June 20th?

(A) A merger will take place.
(B) The division head will get a promotion.
(C) A new product will be introduced.
(D) Employees will submit proposals.

Program	
Lunch	12:00-1:00
Caitlin Stewart	1:00-1:30
Coffee break	1:30-3:00
Group discussion	3:00-3:30
Douglas Park	3:30-4:00

95 What are listeners asked to do at 1 o'clock?

(A) Provide feedback on a new product
(B) Break for lunch
(C) Analyze some data from customers
(D) Attend a presentation on time

96 What does the speaker mention about small group discussions?

(A) Solutions will be discussed.
(B) Testers will be selected.
(C) Interviews will be conducted.
(D) Errors will be corrected.

97 Look at the program. When will listeners actually have a coffee break?

(A) At 1:00
(B) At 1:30
(C) At 3:00
(D) At 3:30

Bare Root Prices		
Plant	Size	Price
Black Oak	6 in	$60
Chestnut Oak	6 in	$30
Bur Oak	8 in	$60
Red Oak	6 in	$30

98 What kind of business is the woman calling from?

(A) A delivery company
(B) An office supplies store
(C) A real estate agency
(D) A landscaping firm

99 Look at the graphic. Which oak tree has not gone down in price?

(A) Black
(B) Chestnut
(C) Bur
(D) Red

100 What should Mr. Sydney do if he is interested in mature oak trees?

(A) Send a price estimate
(B) Contact the company
(C) Plant some trees
(D) Apply for a membership

This is the end of the Listening test. Turn to Part 5 in your test book.

GO ON TO THE NEXT PAGE

▶정답 및 해설 P88

LISTENING TEST

In the Listening test, you will be asked to demonstrate how well you understand spoken English. The entire Listening test will last approximately 45 minutes. There are four parts, and directions are given for each part. You must mark your answers on the separate answer sheet. Do not write your answers in your test book.

PART 1

Directions: For each question in this part, you will hear four statements about a picture in your test book. When you hear the statements, you must select the one statement that best describes what you see in the picture. Then find the number of the question on your answer sheet and mark your answer. The statements will not be printed in your test book and will be spoken only one time.

Example

Sample Answer

Statement (C), "The man is working on a painting," is the best description of the picture, so you should select answer (C) and mark it on your answer sheet.

1

2

GO ON TO THE NEXT PAGE

3

4

5

6

GO ON TO THE NEXT PAGE

PART 2

Directions: You will hear a question or statement and three responses spoken in English. They will not be printed in your test book and will be spoken only one time. Select the best response to the question or statement and mark the letter (A), (B), or (C) on your answer sheet.

7 Mark your answer on your answer sheet.

8 Mark your answer on your answer sheet.

9 Mark your answer on your answer sheet.

10 Mark your answer on your answer sheet.

11 Mark your answer on your answer sheet.

12 Mark your answer on your answer sheet.

13 Mark your answer on your answer sheet.

14 Mark your answer on your answer sheet.

15 Mark your answer on your answer sheet.

16 Mark your answer on your answer sheet.

17 Mark your answer on your answer sheet.

18 Mark your answer on your answer sheet.

19 Mark your answer on your answer sheet.

20 Mark your answer on your answer sheet.

21 Mark your answer on your answer sheet.

22 Mark your answer on your answer sheet.

23 Mark your answer on your answer sheet.

24 Mark your answer on your answer sheet.

25 Mark your answer on your answer sheet.

26 Mark your answer on your answer sheet.

27 Mark your answer on your answer sheet.

28 Mark your answer on your answer sheet.

29 Mark your answer on your answer sheet.

30 Mark your answer on your answer sheet.

31 Mark your answer on your answer sheet.

PART 3

Directions: You will hear some conversations between two or more people. You will be asked to answer three questions about what the speakers say in each conversation. Select the best response to each question and mark the letter (A), (B), (C), or (D) on your answer sheet. The conversations will not be printed in your test book and will be spoken only one time.

32 What is the woman currently working on?
(A) Designing a book cover
(B) Writing an article
(C) Planning an event
(D) Preparing for a presentation

33 Why is the man unable to help the woman?
(A) He has been caught in traffic.
(B) He is late for a doctor's appointment.
(C) He is picking up his relatives.
(D) He is leaving for Singapore.

34 What does the woman say she will do?
(A) Speak to a coworker
(B) Read a manual
(C) Attend a conference
(D) Leave the office for the day

---

35 What are the speakers mainly discussing?
(A) Submitting a résumé
(B) Rescheduling a meeting
(C) Selecting a company
(D) Obtaining a document

36 What does the woman ask for?
(A) A certificate
(B) An address
(C) An order form
(D) A telephone number

37 What does the man say he will do?
(A) Receive the package
(B) Pay for a special service
(C) Choose a payment option
(D) Enroll in a training course

38 What idea does the man propose?
(A) Reading articles on beauty tips
(B) Changing the layout of the shop
(C) Getting new reading material
(D) Posting customer benefits online

39 What did the woman forget?
(A) The name of a magazine
(B) The date of a meeting
(C) A list of new books
(D) A company's name

40 What does the man suggest the woman do?
(A) Read some articles
(B) Visit a bookstore
(C) Send out some coupons
(D) Sign up for a subscription

---

41 Who most likely is the man?
(A) An editor
(B) A film director
(C) A conference organizer
(D) A software developer

42 What is the man preparing for?
(A) A demonstration
(B) A movie
(C) An assessment report
(D) A product proposal

43 What does the woman recommend the man do?
(A) Test the software
(B) Request some equipment
(C) Register for the event in advance
(D) Ask a colleague

GO ON TO THE NEXT PAGE

44 What problem does the woman mention?

(A) She does not know how to operate a machine.
(B) Her mobile phone is out of order.
(C) Her car has been damaged in an accident.
(D) She is late for an appointment.

45 What does the man suggest about Dominique's Mobile?

(A) Its employees are knowledgeable.
(B) Its after-sales service is excellent.
(C) It is conveniently located.
(D) It carries many kinds of cell phones.

46 What is the woman advised to do?

(A) Leave the office early
(B) Call a supplier
(C) Speak to an expert
(D) Bring a device with her

---

47 What are the speakers mainly discussing?

(A) A job opening
(B) A shipment of an order
(C) A conference call
(D) An e-mail address

48 What problem does the man mention?

(A) He does not know where to send an order.
(B) He cannot locate a missing document.
(C) Some items were sent to a wrong address.
(D) Some employees are out sick today.

49 What is the man asked to do now?

(A) Answer a customer's question
(B) Review some information
(C) Finish a project
(D) Contact another office

50 Who most likely are the speakers?

(A) Loan officers
(B) Factory workers
(C) Department heads
(D) Car dealers

51 What problem are the speakers discussing?

(A) Their company has been losing business.
(B) A competitor has won an award.
(C) Shipments have been delayed.
(D) Customers have complained about poor service

52 What does the man suggest to solve the problem?

(A) Renovating a facility
(B) Offering flexible payment plans
(C) Hiring skilled workers
(D) Soliciting customer feedback

---

53 Why is the man calling?

(A) To request a website address
(B) To find out about extended hours
(C) To apply for membership
(D) To reserve some tickets

54 What does the man imply when he says, "Oh, that sounds lovely"?

(A) The facilities stay open late.
(B) His children can have fun.
(C) Admission is free of charge.
(D) He enjoys outdoor activities.

55 What does the woman suggest?

(A) Taking public transportation
(B) Visiting outdoor markets
(C) Purchasing tickets online
(D) Arriving early

56 Where does the woman work?

(A) At a gym
(B) At a real estate agency
(C) At a newspaper
(D) At a printing company

57 What does the woman say about the special deal?

(A) It is only for house owners.
(B) It includes a discounted subscription.
(C) It is provided annually.
(D) It will not be valid tomorrow.

58 What does the man ask about the advertisement?

(A) The cost
(B) The period
(C) The word limit
(D) The seasonal change

---

59 Who most likely are the speakers?

(A) Building inspectors
(B) Home builders
(C) Personnel employees
(D) Professional gardeners

60 What does the man mean when he says, "That's not good"?

(A) A budget might not be approved.
(B) Some materials are out of stock.
(C) Heavy rains are forecast.
(D) A project might not be finished on time.

61 What do the speakers decide to do?

(A) Purchase from another supplier
(B) Cancel an order
(C) Hire more workers
(D) Contact a client

62 What does the man like about the restaurant?

(A) Food
(B) Wait staff
(C) Atmosphere
(D) Location

63 What does Lisa imply when she says, "Of course I can"?

(A) She enjoys spicy food.
(B) She can cook Indian food.
(C) She feels hungry.
(D) She does not need help.

64 What is served with the hot chicken curry?

(A) Steamed rice
(B) Bread and salad
(C) A beverage
(D) Grilled vegetables

GO ON TO THE NEXT PAGE

The 2016 Architecture Series @ Evans Museum		
Thursday, March 15	5:00-6:00 p.m.	Anthony McKean
Thursday, March 22	5:00-6:00 p.m.	Joan Rivers
Thursday, March 29	5:00-6:00 p.m.	Richard Brown
Thursday, April 6	5:00-6:00 p.m.	Sophia Witt

65 Who are the speakers?

(A) Museum employees
(B) News reporters
(C) Event planners
(D) Local artists

66 What problem does the woman mention?

(A) She cannot participate in a class discussion.
(B) She has misplaced her passport.
(C) She is unable to contact one of the speakers.
(D) She is unavailable to give a speech.

67 Look at the graphic. According to the speakers, whose lecture will now be held last?

(A) Anthony McKean
(B) Joan Rivers
(C) Richard Brown
(D) Sophia Witt

GRAND OPENING **Kitchen 105 Burger** New Location	
Where? 5301 Park Ave. Sacramento	When? Friday, November 28th
(916) 555-3890	

68 What are the speakers mainly discussing?

(A) A dinner reservation
(B) A meeting with clients
(C) A delivery of supplies
(D) Preparations for an event

69 Look at the graphic. According to the speakers, which information is incorrect?

(A) The name of a restaurant
(B) The opening date
(C) The address of a business
(D) The telephone number

70 What does the woman say she will do next?

(A) Contact the printers
(B) Review printed material
(C) Make an appointment
(D) Find an address

PART 4

Directions: You will hear some talks given by a single speaker. You will be asked to answer three questions about what the speaker says in each talk. Select the best response to each question and mark the letter (A), (B), (C), or (D) on your answer sheet. The talks will not be printed in your test book and will be spoken only one time.

71 What business is being advertised?

(A) An office supply store
(B) A delivery service
(C) A fitness center
(D) An electronics store

72 What service is now available?

(A) A reduced price
(B) An online registration system
(C) A renovated swimming pool
(D) Extended business hours

73 How can listeners get a discount?

(A) By becoming a member
(B) By presenting a coupon
(C) By calling the center
(D) By doing exercise at night

---

74 Who is the Cape Appledale Singing Contest intended for?

(A) Writers
(B) Vocalists
(C) Painters
(D) Photographers

75 What will the winners of the event receive?

(A) A convertible car
(B) A musical instrument
(C) A cash prize
(D) A chance to sing on stage

76 What should interested listeners do by February 28th?

(A) Submit an entry form online
(B) Read the rules for the competition
(C) Learn from a vocal trainer
(D) Tune in to a radio station

77 Where is the museum located?

(A) In the middle of the city
(B) A block from City Hall
(C) Next to a tea shop
(D) Across from the Chinese Embassy

78 What does the exhibition feature?

(A) Sculptures
(B) Silverware
(C) Tea ceremonies
(D) Antique furniture

79 Why would listeners stay on the line?

(A) To talk to a staff member
(B) To reserve a ticket
(C) To get directions
(D) To leave a message

---

80 Where does the caller work?

(A) At an event planning firm
(B) At a local restaurant
(C) At a catering company
(D) At a convention center

81 What problem does the caller mention?

(A) An incorrect price was charged.
(B) An event will be delayed.
(C) Requested items are unavailable.
(D) An order form is not complete.

82 According to the speaker, what should the listener do by 4 o'clock?

(A) Call the business
(B) Cancel an order
(C) Pay a bill online
(D) Speak to a supervisor

GO ON TO THE NEXT PAGE

83 Who is the speaker addressing?

(A) International clients
(B) Production workers
(C) Factory managers
(D) University students

84 According to the speaker, where will the listener go next?

(A) To a different building
(B) To the assembly floor
(C) To a manufacturing plant
(D) To a training room

85 What does the speaker mean when he says, "please get that ready"?

(A) Employees should read a document.
(B) Employees should unlock a door.
(C) Employees should have their identification handy.
(D) Employees should be prepared for a test.

---

86 What is the purpose of the talk?

(A) To suggest a cost-cutting measure
(B) To clarify the parking regulations
(C) To revise the hiring process
(D) To describe a company policy

87 What are employees encouraged to do in advance?

(A) Confirm the travel itinerary
(B) Request permission for travel
(C) Submit a progress report
(D) Meet a project deadline

88 What are employees asked to submit?

(A) Personal information
(B) A revised price list
(C) An original product proposal
(D) Expense receipts

89 What type of business is being advertised?

(A) A house repair shop
(B) A delivery company
(C) A furniture supplier
(D) An office supply store

90 What does the woman mean when she says, "And what's more"?

(A) She will add another important point.
(B) She wants to know more about the company.
(C) She has forgotten a word.
(D) She will introduce a new line of merchandise.

91 What can customers do online?

(A) Exchange items
(B) Customize a product
(C) Participate in an event
(D) Request a catalog

---

92 What is the purpose of the event?

(A) To introduce a local musician
(B) To celebrate the reopening of a concert hall
(C) To congratulate the purchaser of a building
(D) To recognize the contribution of an employee

93 Who will perform at the event?

(A) A famous vocalist
(B) A symphony orchestra
(C) A dance group
(D) A world-class artist

94 What is suggested about the brochure?

(A) It is only for members.
(B) It is available at the information desk.
(C) It lists the names of performers.
(D) It contains upcoming events.

PCA Clothing Order Form Customer: Eleanor Jackson Order Number: C00129		
Item	**Color**	**Quantity**
Zip-up hoodie	Yellow	20
T-shirt	White	10
Polo shirt	White	10
Swim shorts	Red	5

95 Why is the speaker calling?

(A) To book a venue
(B) To change an order
(C) To request some information
(D) To give directions to a store

96 Look at the graphic. Which item will be removed from the order?

(A) Zip-up hoodie
(B) T-shirt
(C) Polo shirt
(D) Swim shorts

97 What additional information does the speaker provide?

(A) What time a store closes
(B) How a payment should be made
(C) What date a sale begins on
(D) Where a business is located

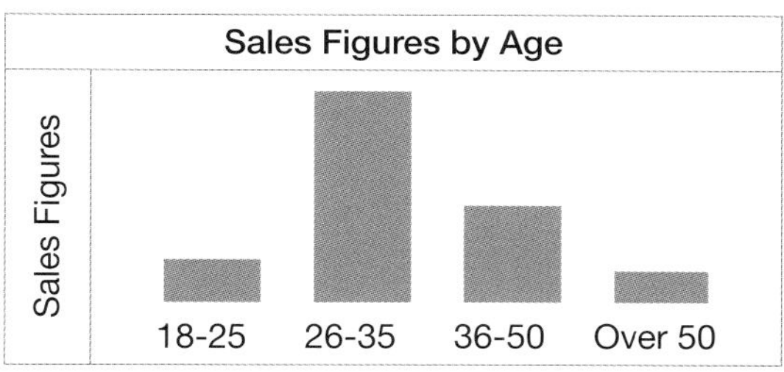

98 Who is the speaker addressing?

(A) Department heads
(B) Marketing staff
(C) Regular customers
(D) Environmentalists

99 According to the speaker, what did the company start?

(A) Expanding its business overseas
(B) Producing energy-efficient appliances
(C) Selling products on TV shopping channels
(D) Offering a free delivery service

100 Look at the graphic. Which age group is Damian asked to look into?

(A) 18-25
(B) 26-35
(C) 36-50
(D) Over 50

This is the end of the Listening test. Turn to Part 5 in your test book.

GO ON TO THE NEXT PAGE

▶정답 및 해설 P110

LISTENING TEST

In the Listening test, you will be asked to demonstrate how well you understand spoken English. The entire Listening test will last approximately 45 minutes. There are four parts, and directions are given for each part. You must mark your answers on the separate answer sheet. Do not write your answers in your test book.

PART 1

Directions: For each question in this part, you will hear four statements about a picture in your test book. When you hear the statements, you must select the one statement that best describes what you see in the picture. Then find the number of the question on your answer sheet and mark your answer. The statements will not be printed in your test book and will be spoken only one time.

Example

Sample Answer

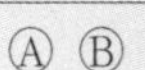  

Statement (C), "The man is working on a painting," is the best description of the picture, so you should select answer (C) and mark it on your answer sheet.

1

2

Test 06

GO ON TO THE NEXT PAGE

3

4

5

6

Test 06

GO ON TO THE NEXT PAGE

PART 2

Directions: You will hear a question or statement and three responses spoken in English. They will not be printed in your test book and will be spoken only one time. Select the best response to the question or statement and mark the letter (A), (B), or (C) on your answer sheet.

7 Mark your answer on your answer sheet.

8 Mark your answer on your answer sheet.

9 Mark your answer on your answer sheet.

10 Mark your answer on your answer sheet.

11 Mark your answer on your answer sheet.

12 Mark your answer on your answer sheet.

13 Mark your answer on your answer sheet.

14 Mark your answer on your answer sheet.

15 Mark your answer on your answer sheet.

16 Mark your answer on your answer sheet.

17 Mark your answer on your answer sheet.

18 Mark your answer on your answer sheet.

19 Mark your answer on your answer sheet.

20 Mark your answer on your answer sheet.

21 Mark your answer on your answer sheet.

22 Mark your answer on your answer sheet.

23 Mark your answer on your answer sheet.

24 Mark your answer on your answer sheet.

25 Mark your answer on your answer sheet.

26 Mark your answer on your answer sheet.

27 Mark your answer on your answer sheet.

28 Mark your answer on your answer sheet.

29 Mark your answer on your answer sheet.

30 Mark your answer on your answer sheet.

31 Mark your answer on your answer sheet.

PART 3

Directions: You will hear some conversations between two or more people. You will be asked to answer three questions about what the speakers say in each conversation. Select the best response to each question and mark the letter (A), (B), (C), or (D) on your answer sheet. The conversations will not be printed in your test book and will be spoken only one time.

32 Where is the conversation most likely taking place?
(A) In a store
(B) At a shipping company
(C) In a warehouse
(D) On the street

33 What does the man not like about the product?
(A) The size
(B) The fabric
(C) The color
(D) The price

34 What will the woman probably do next?
(A) Visit a shop
(B) Speak to a manager
(C) Contact a store
(D) Wrap a gift

---

35 What is the man calling about?
(A) A free trial
(B) A job interview
(C) A mistake on the bill
(D) A magazine subscription

36 What does the woman ask about?
(A) The location of an event
(B) The status of an order
(C) The name of a provider
(D) The cost of a service

37 Why does the woman ask the man to call her back?
(A) To revise an estimate
(B) To sign up for a service
(C) To complain about a poor service
(D) To complete a form

38 Who most likely is the man?
(A) A taxi driver
(B) A bank guard
(C) A realtor
(D) A parking attendant

39 What is the problem?
(A) The bank is closed.
(B) The woman doesn't have a parking ticket.
(C) The facility is full at the moment.
(D) The woman has lost her ticket.

40 What does the man suggest the woman do?
(A) Try a different location
(B) Buy a parking permit
(C) Return to the facility later
(D) Pay the fee by cash

---

41 Who most likely is the woman?
(A) A receptionist
(B) An insurance salesperson
(C) A pharmacist
(D) A doctor

42 What does the man want to do?
(A) Expedite a delivery
(B) Locate some documents
(C) Reschedule an appointment
(D) Speak to a doctor

43 What does the woman ask the man to do?
(A) Pay a bill in advance
(B) Fill out a set of questionnaires
(C) Bring his medical history form
(D) Provide his insurance information

GO ON TO THE NEXT PAGE

44 According to the woman, what change will the newspaper make?

(A) Another department will be added.
(B) A merger will take place.
(C) The headquarters will be moved.
(D) International coverage will increase.

45 What does the man say he needs to do?

(A) Rearrange the office
(B) Request detailed information
(C) Discuss with his spouse
(D) Contact his manager

46 What does the woman give the man?

(A) Flight tickets to Beijing
(B) Details of the work assignment
(C) A travel itinerary
(D) A deadline extension

---

47 Who did the man meet with last week?

(A) A product designer
(B) Sales representatives
(C) A company executive
(D) Product testers

48 What was the problem with one type of boots?

(A) Its material
(B) Its size
(C) Its price
(D) Its weight

49 What will the man do on Wednesday?

(A) Meet with some volunteers
(B) Present some product information
(C) Collect some data from questionnaires
(D) Sign an agreement

50 What are the speakers supposed to do tomorrow morning?

(A) Meet with some clients
(B) Give a demonstration
(C) Attend an international event
(D) Finish some product samples

51 Why is the woman asking the man a favor?

(A) She is leaving the company.
(B) She is not feeling well.
(C) She has planned a vacation.
(D) She has a scheduling conflict.

52 What does the woman imply when she says, "That's not a bad idea"?

(A) She agrees to a delay.
(B) She wants to schedule a meeting.
(C) She will review some documents.
(D) She will ask another colleague for help.

---

53 Where does the man most likely work?

(A) At a supermarket
(B) At a gift shop
(C) At a party planning firm
(D) At a restaurant

54 Why does the man need boxes?

(A) To store some items
(B) To pack up an order
(C) To categorize files
(D) To move to a new place

55 What will the man most likely do next?

(A) Buy groceries
(B) Call an acquaintance
(C) Talk to a store attendant
(D) Check the list

56 What problem are the speakers discussing?

(A) Some clients will be arriving late.
(B) A store is overcrowded with people.
(C) Some merchandise is out of stock.
(D) A business is currently closed.

57 What does the woman ask the man about?

(A) Payment options
(B) Directions to a shop
(C) The business hours
(D) His favorite food

58 What does the man mean when he says, "Lunch is on me"?

(A) He wants to stop by a bank.
(B) He will lend her some money.
(C) He will buy her lunch.
(D) He wants to eat somewhere else.

---

59 Why is the woman calling?

(A) To reserve a hotel room
(B) To recover a missing item
(C) To confirm a departure time
(D) To ask about a job opening

60 Where most likely does the man work?

(A) At an airport
(B) At a subway station
(C) At a delivery service
(D) At a hotel

61 What does the man offer to do?

(A) Mail a receipt
(B) Provide contact information
(C) Pay for shipping
(D) Arrange for a ride

62 What is scheduled to begin today?

(A) Some repair work
(B) A sporting event
(C) Building renovations
(D) A new theater production

63 According to Steve, what might delay the scheduled repairs?

(A) Special events
(B) Labor costs
(C) Changes in the weather
(D) Complaints from local residents

64 Why is traffic congestion expected at night?

(A) Some road crews are off sick.
(B) A bridge is not fully open to traffic.
(C) Many people are attending an event.
(D) Several cars are involved in an accident.

GO ON TO THE NEXT PAGE

Item	Price
MFC Laser Printer (Grey/Black)	$200
Concord Laser Printer (Grey/Black)	$220
SP Laser Printer (White/Black)	$300
Quantum Laser Printer (Black)	$500

65 What will take place next week?

(A) A sale
(B) A meeting
(C) A convention
(D) A product demonstration

66 What does the man suggest?

(A) Advertising the best-selling products
(B) Installing new software
(C) Ordering four different models of printers
(D) Requesting a price estimate

67 Look at the graphic. According to the speakers, which item will not be ordered?

(A) MFC Laser Printer
(B) Concord Laser Printer
(C) SP Laser Printer
(D) Quantum Laser Printer

GOMES directed by Audrey Woods		
Cast in order of appearance:		
Gomes	--------------	Roy Nichols
Lady Howe	--------------	Rachel Campbell
Emily	--------------	Sarah Braid
Dr. Colin Dennis	--------------	James Leith

68 Who is the man looking for?

(A) A stage director
(B) A costume designer
(C) A performer
(D) A repair person

69 Why is the stage director not available at the moment?

(A) She is working overseas.
(B) She is changing a flat tire.
(C) She is in a meeting.
(D) She is on vacation.

70 Look at the graphic. According to the speakers, which character in the story will Max Clifford be playing?

(A) Gomes
(B) Lady Howe
(C) Emily
(D) Dr. Colin Dennis

PART 4

Directions: You will hear some talks given by a single speaker. You will be asked to answer three questions about what the speaker says in each talk. Select the best response to each question and mark the letter (A), (B), (C), or (D) on your answer sheet. The talks will not be printed in your test book and will be spoken only one time.

71 What construction project does the speaker mention?
(A) A community college
(B) An airport terminal
(C) An international financial center
(D) A shopping mall complex

72 What is the cause of the delay?
(A) A shortage of funds
(B) Insufficient supplies
(C) Adverse weather conditions
(D) A series of strikes

73 According to the speaker, what will be available when the project is finished?
(A) Reduced air fares
(B) Wider restaurant selection
(C) Complimentary drinks
(D) More frequent service

---

74 Where does the speaker most likely work?
(A) At a stationary store
(B) At a laboratory
(C) At a factory
(D) At a retail store

75 What is the listener asked to do?
(A) Confirm the payment status of invoices
(B) Evaluate the accuracy of the statement
(C) Monitor the progress of renovation
(D) Check the availability of supplies

76 Why should the listener contact Jackson?
(A) To have a key copied
(B) To request an order form
(C) To have some items ordered
(D) To help him with the inventory

77 Why does the caller apologize?
(A) The online order system is not working.
(B) Some merchandise is out of stock.
(C) The sales price was incorrect.
(D) An item was shipped to the wrong place.

78 According to the speaker, when will the order be delivered to Ms. Harrison?
(A) On Tuesday
(B) On Wednesday
(C) On Thursday
(D) On Friday

79 What does the caller offer to do?
(A) Check the stockroom
(B) Recommend another product
(C) Ship an item by special delivery
(D) Provide a store credit

---

80 What are listeners encouraged to get from the farm store?
(A) A bottle of water
(B) A basket
(C) A cart
(D) A pair of gloves

81 According to the speaker, why are farm workers dressed in red?
(A) To be visible to the participants
(B) To feel a sense of belonging
(C) To harvest farm produce
(D) To give directions to the store

82 What will the speaker most likely do next?
(A) Serve refreshments
(B) Examine some products
(C) Distribute questionnaires
(D) Give a demonstration

GO ON TO THE NEXT PAGE

83 Where did the speaker meet Samuel Brown?

(A) At a trade fair
(B) At a business meeting
(C) At a seminar
(D) At a press conference

84 What is the purpose of the message?

(A) To exchange some devices
(B) To make a complaint
(C) To arrange for an event
(D) To apologize for being late

85 What does the speaker mean when she says, "So I really hope it is in your possession"?

(A) She would like to buy a new computer.
(B) She does not want to pay an extra fee.
(C) She hopes her computer hasn't gone missing.
(D) She wants to arrive at work on time.

---

86 What has been postponed?

(A) A maintenance project
(B) A monthly meeting
(C) A community event
(D) A charity concert

87 What does the speaker mention about the carnival?

(A) It attracted a record turnout.
(B) A large profit was made.
(C) Admission was free for children.
(D) It is an annual event.

88 What will listeners most likely do next?

(A) Attend an event
(B) Have a meal
(C) Receive a ballot
(D) Vote on a proposal

89 What does the company encourage employees to do?

(A) Participate in a walking project
(B) Recycle office supplies
(C) Share rides to work
(D) Attend a conference

90 What does the speaker mean when he says, "That's right"?

(A) He is interested in a new project.
(B) Expenses will be reimbursed.
(C) Employees should submit ideas.
(D) He emphasizes the benefit of reserved parking.

91 What information should interested employees provide?

(A) Their home address
(B) Their extension number
(C) Their medical history
(D) Their department code

---

92 Who most likely are the listeners?

(A) Factory managers
(B) Safety inspectors
(C) Company executives
(D) New assembly workers

93 Why is the program mandatory for the listeners?

(A) To receive a promotion
(B) To operate some machinery
(C) To pass a test
(D) To set safety standards

94 What will the listeners receive after finishing the sessions?

(A) A completion certificate
(B) A safety manual
(C) A team project
(D) A program schedule

INVOICE				
Platt Supply				
Bill to: Watson Manufacturing Company				
Due date: 2016. 06. 15			Date: 2016. 05. 29	
Date	Item	Quantity	Cost	Balance
2016. 05. 05	Copper Wire	60	$1.50 each	$90

95 What is the purpose of the message?

(A) To cancel an order
(B) To discuss a faulty product
(C) To expedite a delivery
(D) To report a billing problem

96 Look at the graphic. What information is incorrect?

(A) Date
(B) Item
(C) Quantity
(D) Cost

97 What does the speaker request?

(A) A corrected invoice
(B) A deadline extension
(C) An updated catalog
(D) A telephone number

Best Sellers in Thrillers (March)
1. *Double Trouble* by Josh Alexis
2. *December* by Neil Dawson
3. *Curse of the Sahara* by Howard Stone
4. *Nineteen Sixty Four* by George Bourne

98 Where most likely does the speaker work?

(A) At a bookstore
(B) At a television station
(C) At a publishing firm
(D) At an advertising agency

99 Look at the graphic. According to the speaker, which book will become the best seller in April?

(A) Double Trouble
(B) December
(C) Curse of the Sahara
(D) Nineteen Sixty Four

100 What are listeners asked to do?

(A) Help with some preparations
(B) Make travel arrangements
(C) Meet a project deadline
(D) Donate money to a charity

This is the end of the Listening test. Turn to Part 5 in your test book.

GO ON TO THE NEXT PAGE

▶정답 및 해설 P132

LISTENING TEST

In the Listening test, you will be asked to demonstrate how well you understand spoken English. The entire Listening test will last approximately 45 minutes. There are four parts, and directions are given for each part. You must mark your answers on the separate answer sheet. Do not write your answers in your test book.

PART 1

Directions: For each question in this part, you will hear four statements about a picture in your test book. When you hear the statements, you must select the one statement that best describes what you see in the picture. Then find the number of the question on your answer sheet and mark your answer. The statements will not be printed in your test book and will be spoken only one time.

Example

Sample Answer

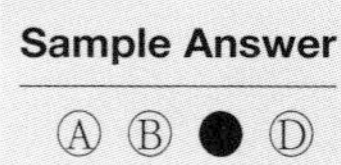

Statement (C), "The man is working on a painting," is the best description of the picture, so you should select answer (C) and mark it on your answer sheet.

1

2

Test 07

GO ON TO THE NEXT PAGE

3

4

5

6

Test 07

GO ON TO THE NEXT PAGE

PART 2

Directions: You will hear a question or statement and three responses spoken in English. They will not be printed in your test book and will be spoken only one time. Select the best response to the question or statement and mark the letter (A), (B), or (C) on your answer sheet.

7 Mark your answer on your answer sheet.

8 Mark your answer on your answer sheet.

9 Mark your answer on your answer sheet.

10 Mark your answer on your answer sheet.

11 Mark your answer on your answer sheet.

12 Mark your answer on your answer sheet.

13 Mark your answer on your answer sheet.

14 Mark your answer on your answer sheet.

15 Mark your answer on your answer sheet.

16 Mark your answer on your answer sheet.

17 Mark your answer on your answer sheet.

18 Mark your answer on your answer sheet.

19 Mark your answer on your answer sheet.

20 Mark your answer on your answer sheet.

21 Mark your answer on your answer sheet.

22 Mark your answer on your answer sheet.

23 Mark your answer on your answer sheet.

24 Mark your answer on your answer sheet.

25 Mark your answer on your answer sheet.

26 Mark your answer on your answer sheet.

27 Mark your answer on your answer sheet.

28 Mark your answer on your answer sheet.

29 Mark your answer on your answer sheet.

30 Mark your answer on your answer sheet.

31 Mark your answer on your answer sheet.

PART 3

Directions: You will hear some conversations between two or more people. You will be asked to answer three questions about what the speakers say in each conversation. Select the best response to each question and mark the letter (A), (B), (C), or (D) on your answer sheet. The conversations will not be printed in your test book and will be spoken only one time.

32 What does the woman want to do?
(A) Change her work schedule
(B) Carpool with her coworker
(C) Apply for a different position
(D) Volunteer at a school

33 What does the woman say she needs to do every morning?
(A) Pick up some materials
(B) Take a class
(C) Drive her child to school
(D) Exercise at a gym

34 What does the man tell the woman to do?
(A) Complete a time sheet every day
(B) Leave the office 30 minutes later
(C) Report to her supervisor
(D) Have another meeting with the man

---

35 Who most likely is the man?
(A) A repair person
(B) A waiter
(C) A client
(D) A shop manager

36 Where most likely is the conversation taking place?
(A) At a restaurant
(B) At an auto repair shop
(C) In a hotel lobby
(D) At an electronics store

37 For what does the woman thank the man?
(A) Delivering some ingredients
(B) Finishing the work quickly
(C) Recommending a restaurant
(D) Changing dinner reservations

38 What information does the woman request?
(A) A shipping cost
(B) A delivery time
(C) A street address
(D) An identification number

39 Who most likely are the speakers?
(A) Neighbors
(B) Coworkers
(C) Delivery people
(D) Gardeners

40 What does the man say he will do?
(A) Write a check list
(B) Purchase some tools
(C) Contact a company
(D) Change a delivery date

---

41 What does the woman ask the man to do?
(A) Read over some documents
(B) Submit a proposal
(C) Telephone a client
(D) Lead a training session

42 Why does the woman need to complete her work today?
(A) The office will be closed tomorrow.
(B) She has other tasks to take care of.
(C) She has to send it to a client.
(D) A director will visit in the morning.

43 What does the man suggest?
(A) Checking the documents herself
(B) Providing a list of references
(C) Negotiating the terms of a contract
(D) Asking another coworker

GO ON TO THE NEXT PAGE

44 Who most likely is the man?

(A) A sales representative
(B) A dentist
(C) A store clerk
(D) A research scientist

45 Why is the man calling?

(A) To report a defective product
(B) To sign up for a course
(C) To request some information
(D) To place an order

46 What does the woman offer to do?

(A) Contact another department
(B) Check the status of an order
(C) Send some brochures
(D) Arrange a meeting with a salesperson

---

47 What does the man say about his purchase?

(A) It comes with a tutorial.
(B) It is not user-friendly.
(C) It is hard to install.
(D) It is expensive.

48 What does the man ask about?

(A) A product exchange
(B) A training course
(C) A partial refund
(D) An extended warranty

49 What does the woman tell the man to do?

(A) Find a model code
(B) Visit a store
(C) Purchase a CD
(D) Request free service

50 What type of business is the man contacting?

(A) An electronics firm
(B) A moving company
(C) An advertising agency
(D) An office furniture store

51 What problem is the man discussing?

(A) A center was closed for business.
(B) A mover delivered his package to the wrong location.
(C) An unexpected fee was charged to him.
(D) An event was delayed.

52 What does the woman suggest about Mr. Dolan?

(A) He signed a contract.
(B) He organized an event.
(C) He will send a corrected bill.
(D) He will store some items.

---

53 What are the speakers discussing?

(A) A film screening
(B) A charity event
(C) An opening ceremony
(D) A sporting event

54 What does the man imply when he says "Well, it is quite possible though"?

(A) An outdoor event will be organized.
(B) Some equipment could be damaged.
(C) The concert is more likely to be cancelled.
(D) The weather will improve soon.

55 What does the man offer to do?

(A) Arrive half an hour early
(B) Call the park
(C) Go to the park
(D) Check for updates online

56 What is the man doing now?

(A) Collecting a fine
(B) Drafting a budget
(C) Preparing for a presentation
(D) Repairing a laptop computer

57 Why is the woman not able to assist the man?

(A) She has to meet another deadline.
(B) She has a gathering to attend.
(C) She has to go to a bank.
(D) She cannot access the information.

58 What will the man probably do next?

(A) Contact another coworker
(B) Check a book out of the library
(C) Calculate some figures
(D) Refer to a computer file

---

59 What are the speakers mainly discussing?

(A) Tax accounting
(B) A salary raise
(C) A job opening
(D) A reorganization of the company

60 What does the woman mean when she says "Actually I wasn't"?

(A) She thought the job she applied for was a full-time position.
(B) She thought she would work overseas.
(C) She thought the company pays well.
(D) She thought she was not qualified for the job.

61 What does the woman say she will consider?

(A) Offering benefits
(B) Applying for a different position
(C) Hiring more qualified workers
(D) Working as a part-timer

62 Who most likely is Isabelle Brooks?

(A) A receptionist
(B) A vice president
(C) A reporter
(D) A client

63 Why is the man unavailable for Ms. Brooks at the moment?

(A) She has arrived early for an appointment.
(B) He is in a meeting with an important client.
(C) A meeting room is being used by someone else.
(D) He has lost his mobile phone.

64 What will Ms. Brooks most likely do next?

(A) Return another day
(B) Make a copy
(C) Go to the lobby
(D) Read a newspaper

GO ON TO THE NEXT PAGE

Eyeglass Frames in Stock		
MODEL	COLOR	PRICE
Prism	Translucent	$50
Emory	Leopard	$50
Vernon	Red	$80
Bristol	Black	$40

65 What problem is being discussed?

(A) An item is out of stock.
(B) A manager is unavailable.
(C) A shipment has been delayed.
(D) Some lenses are damaged.

66 What does the woman mention about her new eyeglasses?

(A) She wants to try them on at the store.
(B) She wants to wear them on her trip.
(C) She has lost them on the subway.
(D) She purchased them at a reduced price.

67 Look at the graphic. Which model does the man recommend for the woman?

(A) Prism
(B) Emory
(C) Vernon
(D) Bristol

The Blue Line			
Roslyn	Joyce	Tenth Avenue	Meadow view

68 What is the main topic of the conversation?

(A) The location of a new station
(B) The hours of operation
(C) The cost of a monthly pass
(D) The addition of a new subway line

69 Look at the graphic. According to the speakers, what is the new station called?

(A) Roslyn
(B) Joyce
(C) Tenth Avenue
(D) Meadow view

70 Why is the man pleased?

(A) He has found helpful information online.
(B) He will move to another city.
(C) His commute will be more convenient.
(D) His coworker has been promoted.

PART 4

Directions: You will hear some talks given by a single speaker. You will be asked to answer three questions about what the speaker says in each talk. Select the best response to each question and mark the letter (A), (B), (C), or (D) on your answer sheet. The talks will not be printed in your test book and will be spoken only one time.

71 Who most likely are the listeners of the talk?
(A) Visiting professors
(B) Laboratory trainees
(C) Medical insurance employees
(D) Safety inspectors

72 What does the speaker say about the research center?
(A) It employs 32 technicians.
(B) It is up-to-date.
(C) It recently purchased a new device.
(D) It pays the researchers well.

73 What most likely will happen next?
(A) A group of people will go on a tour.
(B) Doctors will use the equipment.
(C) Technicians will begin a new project.
(D) Trainees will learn safety procedures.

---

74 What merchandise is being promoted?
(A) Office furniture
(B) Sporting goods
(C) Home decorative accessories
(D) Construction supplies

75 According to the speaker, how can shoppers find sale items?
(A) By going to a designated area
(B) By receiving a brochure
(C) By calling customer service
(D) By looking for special signs

76 Why should listeners visit the customer service desk?
(A) To return an item
(B) To report a defective product
(C) To sign up for a membership
(D) To pick up a discount coupon

77 What type of company is being advertised?
(A) A home repair company
(B) A landscaping business
(C) A local supermarket
(D) A flower store

78 What should customers do to receive a discount?
(A) Sign a one-year contract
(B) Recommend a new client
(C) Get a membership
(D) Change a garden design

79 Why does the speaker say, "Act fast"?
(A) To invite potential customers to the store
(B) To ask listeners to attend a special event
(C) To encourage listeners to purchase a service
(D) To offer additional discount to regular customers

---

80 Who most likely are the listeners?
(A) Airport lounge staff
(B) Restaurant employees
(C) Office workers
(D) Flight attendants

81 What is the talk mainly about?
(A) A customer satisfaction rating
(B) A promotional event
(C) Acceptable methods of payment
(D) A dress code at a workplace

82 Why are listeners advised to consult a manager?
(A) To update a work schedule
(B) To address a complaint
(C) To inquire about a policy
(D) To make a suggestion

GO ON TO THE NEXT PAGE

83 What is the topic of the training session?
(A) Online references
(B) Web design
(C) Computer software
(D) Home building

84 What does the speaker mean when he says, "So I'd really like you to take her place"?
(A) There was a computer malfunction.
(B) Some equipment needs to be installed.
(C) He wants the listener to lead a workshop.
(D) The listener needs to meet a deadline.

85 What will the caller probably do next?
(A) Send an agenda
(B) Visit a hospital
(C) Plan an event
(D) Call tech support

---

86 Where does the speaker work?
(A) At a hotel
(B) At a dance academy
(C) At a theater
(D) At a television station

87 What problem is mentioned by the speaker?
(A) They are understaffed.
(B) An auditorium is unavailable.
(C) Their rental fees have risen.
(D) Renovations are being carried out.

88 What does the speaker offer?
(A) A different location
(B) A dancing class
(C) A discounted rate
(D) A free stage effect

89 What will take place at the banquet?
(A) A demonstration will be given.
(B) Research results will be presented.
(C) Awards will be presented.
(D) A new president will be introduced.

90 What information can be found on the table?
(A) A list of participants
(B) Changes to some rules
(C) Information on nominations
(D) Tips to conserve natural resources

91 What is mentioned about Green Cross International?
(A) They are receiving an award.
(B) They are sponsoring the event.
(C) They donate used items every year.
(D) They are manufacturing electronic devices.

---

92 What is special about the desserts?
(A) They don't contain gluten.
(B) They are popular with children.
(C) They are created by an award-winning pastry chef.
(D) They can be custom-made.

93 What does the speaker mean when he says, "here's how you can do it"?
(A) He will explain the history of the company.
(B) He will give listeners easy baking recipes.
(C) He will provide information about the factory tours.
(D) He will announce the winners of a competition.

94 What is offered during the month of May?
(A) A catering service
(B) A complimentary breakfast
(C) A seasonal menu
(D) A store discount

Lectures and Events @ Winston History Museum April 2018	
Lecture/Event	**Time**
Museum Highlights Tour	Every Tuesday
Storytelling for Kids	Every Friday
History Lecture Series	Thursday, April 13th
Genealogy Workshops	Saturday, April 22nd

95 Why is the museum required to make changes?

(A) A budget has decreased.
(B) More events are being held.
(C) A building is being renovated.
(D) Some exhibits have been canceled.

96 Look at the graphic. Which event will not be held in May?

(A) Museum Highlights Tour
(B) Storytelling for Kids
(C) History Lecture Series
(D) Genealogy Workshops

97 What is Maria asked to do?

(A) Work overtime
(B) Complete a survey
(C) Train new employees
(D) Revise a work schedule

Linex 300 Printer	Linex 5X Photocopier
· Print in color	· Slow
· Two-sided copies	· Two-sided copies
· Assigned to each team	· Energy-saving
	· Located on each floor

98 Who is the speaker addressing?

(A) Marketing personnel
(B) Store attendants
(C) Factory workers
(D) Sales staff

99 Look at the graphic. According to the speaker, which information about Linex 5X Photocopier is not correct?

(A) It is slow.
(B) It makes two-sided copies.
(C) It has an energy-saving feature.
(D) It is located on each floor.

100 What can Michael help employees to do?

(A) Repair a new printer
(B) Connect pieces of equipment
(C) Order office supplies
(D) Upgrade computer software

This is the end of the Listening test. Turn to Part 5 in your test book.

GO ON TO THE NEXT PAGE

LISTENING TEST

In the Listening test, you will be asked to demonstrate how well you understand spoken English. The entire Listening test will last approximately 45 minutes. There are four parts, and directions are given for each part. You must mark your answers on the separate answer sheet. Do not write your answers in your test book.

PART 1

Directions: For each question in this part, you will hear four statements about a picture in your test book. When you hear the statements, you must select the one statement that best describes what you see in the picture. Then find the number of the question on your answer sheet and mark your answer. The statements will not be printed in your test book and will be spoken only one time.

Example

Sample Answer

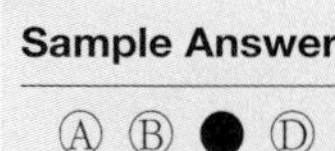

Statement (C), "The man is working on a painting," is the best description of the picture, so you should select answer (C) and mark it on your answer sheet.

1

2

Test 08

GO ON TO THE NEXT PAGE

3

4

5

6

Test 08

GO ON TO THE NEXT PAGE

PART 2

Directions: You will hear a question or statement and three responses spoken in English. They will not be printed in your test book and will be spoken only one time. Select the best response to the question or statement and mark the letter (A), (B), or (C) on your answer sheet.

7 Mark your answer on your answer sheet.

8 Mark your answer on your answer sheet.

9 Mark your answer on your answer sheet.

10 Mark your answer on your answer sheet.

11 Mark your answer on your answer sheet.

12 Mark your answer on your answer sheet.

13 Mark your answer on your answer sheet.

14 Mark your answer on your answer sheet.

15 Mark your answer on your answer sheet.

16 Mark your answer on your answer sheet.

17 Mark your answer on your answer sheet.

18 Mark your answer on your answer sheet.

19 Mark your answer on your answer sheet.

20 Mark your answer on your answer sheet.

21 Mark your answer on your answer sheet.

22 Mark your answer on your answer sheet.

23 Mark your answer on your answer sheet.

24 Mark your answer on your answer sheet.

25 Mark your answer on your answer sheet.

26 Mark your answer on your answer sheet.

27 Mark your answer on your answer sheet.

28 Mark your answer on your answer sheet.

29 Mark your answer on your answer sheet.

30 Mark your answer on your answer sheet.

31 Mark your answer on your answer sheet.

PART 3

Directions: You will hear some conversations between two or more people. You will be asked to answer three questions about what the speakers say in each conversation. Select the best response to each question and mark the letter (A), (B), (C), or (D) on your answer sheet. The conversations will not be printed in your test book and will be spoken only one time.

32 What problem are the speakers discussing?
(A) A bank is closed.
(B) The wait is long.
(C) An event is delayed.
(D) The food is pricey.

33 Where is the conversation most likely taking place?
(A) In a gym
(B) In a store
(C) In a restaurant
(D) In an office

34 What does the man say he will do?
(A) Reschedule an appointment
(B) Speak to a manager
(C) Return later
(D) Purchase an item

---

35 Who most likely are the speakers?
(A) Store attendants
(B) Bank clerks
(C) Repair people
(D) Office workers

36 What does the man say he will do?
(A) Repair some equipment
(B) Read a safety manual
(C) Check the gas valve
(D) Call a professional

37 What will the woman most likely do next?
(A) Make some tea
(B) Turn on a device
(C) Call a technician
(D) Go to a storage room

38 What are the speakers mainly discussing?
(A) A company outing
(B) A charity banquet
(C) An awards ceremony
(D) A community park

39 Why is the woman concerned?
(A) She cannot make it to a party.
(B) She does not have an umbrella.
(C) A performer is off sick.
(D) An event might be cancelled.

40 According to the woman, what will take place on Saturday afternoon?
(A) A barbecue dinner
(B) A used book sale
(C) A musical performance
(D) An office party

---

41 What problem are the speakers discussing?
(A) A worker is not available.
(B) A sign is damaged.
(C) A machine is out of order.
(D) A fee is incorrect.

42 What does the man say he will do next?
(A) Hang a sign
(B) Notify his supervisor
(C) Repair the machine
(D) Print out a document

43 Where most likely will the woman go next?
(A) To the elevator
(B) To the reception desk
(C) To the parking lot
(D) To the lounge

GO ON TO THE NEXT PAGE

44 Why is the man calling?

(A) To place an order
(B) To discuss an overdue book
(C) To renew a membership
(D) To inquire about a lost item

45 What does the woman ask about?

(A) Renting a facility
(B) Finding a new job
(C) Renewing a book
(D) Teaching a class

46 What is the woman planning to do today?

(A) Return an item
(B) Buy a present
(C) Visit a museum
(D) Take some time off

---

47 What did the man do on Tuesday?

(A) He mastered some techniques.
(B) He led a workshop.
(C) He moved to another city.
(D) He wrote a manual

48 What does the woman ask the man to do?

(A) Develop some software
(B) Make a change in travel plans
(C) Repeat a class
(D) Evaluate some workers

49 What does the man suggest?

(A) Reviewing some specifications
(B) Learning from another instructor
(C) Arranging an appointment for next week
(D) Removing outdated computers

50 Why is the man calling?

(A) To praise an employee
(B) To inquire about opening an account
(C) To offer a suggestion
(D) To request a statement

51 What does the woman ask about?

(A) The address of a customer
(B) The cost of a service
(C) The name of an associate
(D) The location of an event

52 What does the woman say she will do?

(A) Telephone a supplier
(B) Call a special meeting
(C) Check in a directory
(D) Speak to a colleague

---

53 What are the speakers mainly discussing?

(A) A company logo
(B) A foreign country
(C) A sales strategy
(D) A job opportunity

54 Who most likely is the woman?

(A) A department head
(B) A potential employee
(C) A language instructor
(D) A travel agent

55 What does the woman imply when she says, "Not at all"?

(A) She is willing to work abroad.
(B) She wants to attend a sales meeting.
(C) She does not speak a foreign language.
(D) She has not signed the contract.

56 What are the speakers mainly discussing?

(A) A business contract
(B) An art exhibit
(C) A new publication
(D) Company handbooks

57 What does the woman like about the book?

(A) The plot is interesting.
(B) It has been a best-seller.
(C) The characters are well developed.
(D) It has been written for children.

58 What does the woman say will happen next?

(A) A design will be created.
(B) A book signing will be held.
(C) A contract will be finalized.
(D) The story will be edited.

---

59 What is the woman interested in doing?

(A) Buying gardening equipment
(B) Moving into a new house
(C) Growing some flowers
(D) Hiring a landscaping company

60 What does the woman mean when she says, "Oh, that's exactly what I need"?

(A) She would like to learn from an expert.
(B) She would like to subscribe to a magazine.
(C) She would like to create a new website.
(D) She would like to go to another shop.

61 What does the man give the woman?

(A) A free trial membership
(B) A list of necessary supplies
(C) A reduced price
(D) A newsletter

62 What does the woman say she likes?

(A) Some pictures of the store
(B) The price of an item
(C) The appearance of some displays
(D) A newspaper article

63 What will happen tomorrow?

(A) A sale will be held.
(B) A reporter will visit the store.
(C) A television show will premiere.
(D) A new store will open.

64 What does Daniel ask about the advertisement?

(A) Where it should be placed
(B) How much he should spend on it
(C) How large it should be
(D) How many days it should appear

GO ON TO THE NEXT PAGE

Schedule	
Presenter	Time
Evelyn Whitney	10:00 ~ 10:50
Chris Hunter	11:00 ~ 11:50
Lunch	12:00 ~ 12:50
Jane Lopez	13:00 ~ 13:50
Chuck Tomlin	14:00 ~ 14:50

65 What is the man preparing to do?

(A) Conduct a job interview
(B) Lead a training session
(C) Write a company handbook
(D) Post some information online

66 Why does the man request a change to the schedule?

(A) His presentation notes are incomplete.
(B) His computer is out of order.
(C) He has a scheduling conflict.
(D) He is not feeling well.

67 Look at the graphic. What time will the man begin his presentation now?

(A) At 10 a.m.
(B) At 11 a.m.
(C) At 1 p.m.
(D) At 2 p.m.

ACE Car Rental	
Pick Up Location:	San Francisco Airport
Pick Up Date/Time:	Tue, 26 Jan 2017 12:00 P.M.
Drop Off Location:	San Francisco Airport
Drop Off Date/Time:	Fri, 29 Jan 2017 5:00 P.M.
Total Estimate of Charges: $600.00	

68 Where does the woman most likely work?

(A) At a hotel
(B) At a travel agency
(C) At an airline ticketing desk
(D) At a car rental agency

69 What does the man want to do?

(A) Return a vehicle to a different location
(B) Travel back home by car
(C) Rent a larger meeting space
(D) Take an early flight

70 Look at the graphic. How much will the man pay now?

(A) $80
(B) $600
(C) $680
(D) $1800

PART 4

Directions: You will hear some talks given by a single speaker. You will be asked to answer three questions about what the speaker says in each talk. Select the best response to each question and mark the letter (A), (B), (C), or (D) on your answer sheet. The talks will not be printed in your test book and will be spoken only one time.

71 What is the announcement about?
(A) An additional class
(B) Extended hours of operation
(C) A new facility
(D) Benefits for the members

72 Who is Heidi Grey?
(A) A receptionist
(B) A prospective member
(C) A center manager
(D) A yoga instructor

73 How can listeners learn more about the class?
(A) From a newsletter
(B) From an employee
(C) From a review
(D) From a magazine

---

74 What is the purpose of the talk?
(A) To announce the opening of an event
(B) To deliver a lecture
(C) To introduce a speaker
(D) To present an award

75 According to the speaker, what has Dr. Chan recently done?
(A) Wrote a book
(B) Started to teach at a school
(C) Planted various trees
(D) Resigned from a job

76 What will Dr. Chan discuss?
(A) Developing people skills
(B) Community volunteering
(C) Techniques for caring for trees
(D) A divisional budget

77 What kind of products does Troy's sell?
(A) Apparel
(B) Sporting goods
(C) Home decorations
(D) Household appliances

78 When does the special offer end?
(A) On Monday
(B) On Tuesday
(C) On Friday
(D) On Sunday

79 Why is the store having a half-off sale?
(A) It is undergoing renovation.
(B) It is making room for new arrivals.
(C) It is opening a new branch.
(D) It is celebrating its 10th anniversary.

---

80 What type of merchandise is being demonstrated?
(A) A kitchen appliance
(B) A vacuum cleaner
(C) A lawn mower
(D) A car repair tool

81 What is the most important aspect of the product?
(A) Its quality
(B) Its size
(C) Its durability
(D) Its color

82 What will happen at the end of the event?
(A) Some refreshments will be served.
(B) Some books will be handed out.
(C) Participants will receive a certificate.
(D) An expert will give a lecture.

GO ON TO THE NEXT PAGE

83 What is the destination of the flight?

(A) Paris
(B) Madrid
(C) Boston
(D) Mexico City

84 According to the speaker, what are passengers allowed to do?

(A) Use a mobile phone
(B) Move to a different seat
(C) Wear a life vest
(D) Order a drink

85 Why are passengers instructed to speak to a flight attendant?

(A) To receive a gift
(B) To purchase duty-free items
(C) To inquire about flight information
(D) To request a headset

---

86 What type of business is the speaker calling?

(A) A gardening company
(B) A roofing company
(C) An auto repair shop
(D) A home-improvement store

87 What does the speaker mean when he says, "And even more rain is forecast for the weekend"?

(A) A repair person will be late.
(B) He cannot keep windows open.
(C) A problem will get worse.
(D) He will have to change his schedule.

88 What does the speaker ask the listener to do?

(A) Visit his office
(B) Deliver some items to his home
(C) Call him back
(D) Give him a discount

89 What is the purpose of the call?

(A) To ask for directions to an office
(B) To provide some product information
(C) To place an order online
(D) To respond to a complaint

90 What needs to be repaired?

(A) An Internet device
(B) A photocopier
(C) An air conditioning system
(D) A light switch

91 According to the speaker, when will the technical problem be solved?

(A) This morning
(B) This evening
(C) Tomorrow evening
(D) This weekend

---

92 What is being advertised?

(A) A famous restaurant
(B) Boat rentals
(C) A city tour
(D) An online reservation

93 What does the speaker imply when he says, "And that's not all"?

(A) He will give directions to the tourist center.
(B) He will introduce an additional feature of the tour.
(C) He will offer a discount on some products.
(D) He will go to a restaurant for dinner.

94 What should listeners do to make a reservation?

(A) Visit a website
(B) Talk to a representative in person
(C) Fill out a form
(D) Contact the business

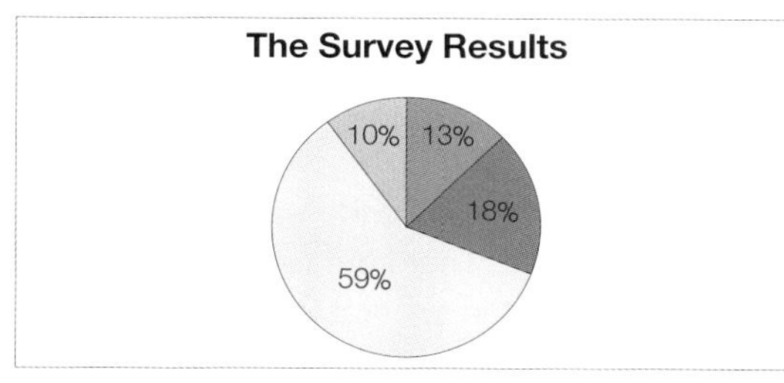

Employee Directory	
Name	Extension
Martha Chang	05
Lawrence Hwang	13
Debra Avery	22
Gwen McCoy	56

95 What merchandise does the speaker's company sell?
(A) Home appliances
(B) Office equipment
(C) Motor vehicles
(D) Cleaning products

96 What does the speaker say about the market research group?
(A) They put together a product manual.
(B) They designed new products.
(C) They researched a competing brand.
(D) They conducted a customer survey.

97 Look at the graphic. Which survey item accounts for 59 percent?
(A) Competitive prices
(B) Product quality
(C) Free shipping
(D) Customer reviews

98 What is the main purpose of the message?
(A) To respond to an inquiry
(B) To request a document
(C) To provide contact information
(D) To explain a new policy

99 What is mentioned about Debra Avery?
(A) She is on a business trip.
(B) She works in the payroll department.
(C) She reviews expense reports.
(D) She runs her own business.

100 Look at the graphic. Which extension will the listener probably dial?
(A) 05
(B) 13
(C) 22
(D) 56

This is the end of the Listening test. Turn to Part 5 in your test book.

GO ON TO THE NEXT PAGE

▶정답 및 해설 P176

LISTENING TEST

In the Listening test, you will be asked to demonstrate how well you understand spoken English. The entire Listening test will last approximately 45 minutes. There are four parts, and directions are given for each part. You must mark your answers on the separate answer sheet. Do not write your answers in your test book.

PART 1

Directions: For each question in this part, you will hear four statements about a picture in your test book. When you hear the statements, you must select the one statement that best describes what you see in the picture. Then find the number of the question on your answer sheet and mark your answer. The statements will not be printed in your test book and will be spoken only one time.

Example

Statement (C), "The man is working on a painting," is the best description of the picture, so you should select answer (C) and mark it on your answer sheet.

1

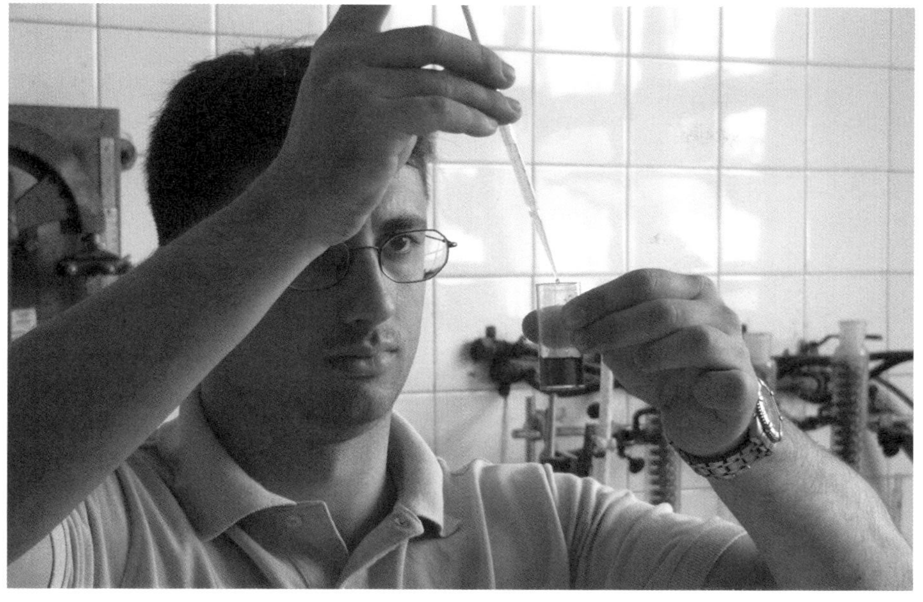

2

Test 09

GO ON TO THE NEXT PAGE

3

4

5

6

Test 09

GO ON TO THE NEXT PAGE

PART 2

Directions: You will hear a question or statement and three responses spoken in English. They will not be printed in your test book and will be spoken only one time. Select the best response to the question or statement and mark the letter (A), (B), or (C) on your answer sheet.

7 Mark your answer on your answer sheet.

8 Mark your answer on your answer sheet.

9 Mark your answer on your answer sheet.

10 Mark your answer on your answer sheet.

11 Mark your answer on your answer sheet.

12 Mark your answer on your answer sheet.

13 Mark your answer on your answer sheet.

14 Mark your answer on your answer sheet.

15 Mark your answer on your answer sheet.

16 Mark your answer on your answer sheet.

17 Mark your answer on your answer sheet.

18 Mark your answer on your answer sheet.

19 Mark your answer on your answer sheet.

20 Mark your answer on your answer sheet.

21 Mark your answer on your answer sheet.

22 Mark your answer on your answer sheet.

23 Mark your answer on your answer sheet.

24 Mark your answer on your answer sheet.

25 Mark your answer on your answer sheet.

26 Mark your answer on your answer sheet.

27 Mark your answer on your answer sheet.

28 Mark your answer on your answer sheet.

29 Mark your answer on your answer sheet.

30 Mark your answer on your answer sheet.

31 Mark your answer on your answer sheet.

PART 3

Directions: You will hear some conversations between two or more people. You will be asked to answer three questions about what the speakers say in each conversation. Select the best response to each question and mark the letter (A), (B), (C), or (D) on your answer sheet. The conversations will not be printed in your test book and will be spoken only one time.

32 What is the man trying to locate?
(A) A folder
(B) A telephone number
(C) A manual
(D) A photocopier

33 What is the man scheduled to do this afternoon?
(A) Introduce a new employee
(B) Interview a job candidate
(C) Meet with a client
(D) Speak to a manager

34 What does the woman offer to do?
(A) Ask a coworker
(B) E-mail a résumé
(C) Reschedule an interview
(D) Find a document

---

35 What are the speakers mainly discussing?
(A) A company policy
(B) A coffee machine
(C) A recipe for cooking
(D) A new business

36 What does the woman not want to do?
(A) Work overtime
(B) Wait in line
(C) Work out regularly
(D) Take the subway in the morning

37 What will start next week?
(A) A coffee-brewing class
(B) A construction project
(C) The sale of breakfast menu items
(D) A series of professional workshops

38 What will the speakers probably do on Monday?
(A) Share a taxi
(B) Attend a meeting
(C) Finish a report
(D) Check a schedule

39 Why does the man want to take the train?
(A) His car is being repaired.
(B) Train fares are not expensive.
(C) He will not be stuck in traffic.
(D) It is more comfortable than the bus.

40 What will the man probably do next?
(A) Reserve tickets
(B) Go to the station
(C) Review some notes
(D) Call a travel agency

---

41 What event are the speakers planning to attend?
(A) An art exhibit
(B) A music concert
(C) A theater performance
(D) A corporate function

42 How did the woman learn about the event?
(A) From an article
(B) From a colleague
(C) From a brochure
(D) From a close friend

43 What does the woman suggest?
(A) Watching a different show
(B) Going for a walk
(C) Parking in a garage
(D) Reading a newspaper

GO ON TO THE NEXT PAGE
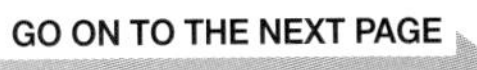

44 What are the speakers discussing?

(A) Purchasing some sporting goods
(B) Putting together an athletic team
(C) Changing the work hours
(D) Reserving some concert tickets

45 What does the woman usually do after work?

(A) Volunteer in the community
(B) Work out at the gym
(C) Take a course
(D) Do household chores

46 What does the man suggest?

(A) Sharing a ride to work
(B) Searching for another place
(C) Taking the woman out for dinner
(D) Meeting on a different day

---

47 Where most likely does the man work?

(A) At a recruiting agency
(B) At a financial company
(C) At a convention center
(D) At an interior design company

48 When will the speakers meet for an interview?

(A) Tuesday
(B) Wednesday
(C) Thursday
(D) Friday

49 What does the man ask the woman to do?

(A) Bring some work samples
(B) Contact a colleague
(C) Return a call
(D) Submit an application

50 What is the conversation mainly about?

(A) An installation manual
(B) An annual budget
(C) A missed deadline
(D) A meeting schedule

51 According to the man, why has he not finished his report?

(A) He has another assignment to complete.
(B) A purchase hasn't been approved.
(C) Some information hasn't been received.
(D) His coworker has been off sick.

52 What does the woman offer to do?

(A) Calculate some prices
(B) Extend a deadline
(C) Deliver a document
(D) Speak to a colleague

---

53 Who is the woman talking to?

(A) A real estate agent
(B) A park ranger
(C) An apartment janitor
(D) A photographer

54 What does the man say about the apartment?

(A) It is located on Royce Street.
(B) It has a nice view.
(C) It is fully furnished.
(D) It needs repairing.

55 What does the woman mean when she says, "I'd love that"?

(A) She would like to sign a contract.
(B) She would like to move into a new apartment.
(C) She would like to look at the property.
(D) She would like to leave the office early.

56 What is the man interested in doing?

(A) Purchasing a special carrier
(B) Taking a highway
(C) Reserving a ticket
(D) Transporting a bicycle

57 What does the woman suggest the man do?

(A) Avoid a specific time
(B) Receive a group discount
(C) Pay in cash
(D) Travel with a pet

58 What does the woman suggest about the bicycle racks?

(A) They can be reserved online.
(B) They were installed last year.
(C) They are provided only for the handicapped.
(D) They are available on a first come first served basis.

---

59 Why is the man at the pharmacy?

(A) To pick up some medication
(B) To apply for a position
(C) To get some directions
(D) To place an order

60 What does the man imply when he says, "But I'm not sure if it's a good idea"?

(A) He thinks that the quality of a service is poor.
(B) He is unsure of the effect of additional medicine.
(C) He cannot remember the name of a nurse.
(D) He does not know the dosage of a medication.

61 What does the woman suggest?

(A) Coming back later
(B) Using a different product
(C) Seeing a doctor
(D) Ordering online

62 Where do the speakers probably work?

(A) At an architectural firm
(B) At a hotel
(C) At a publishing company
(D) At a photo studio

63 Why does Luisa say, "What? Tomorrow morning"?

(A) She has missed a client meeting.
(B) She plans to take the day off tomorrow.
(C) She was not aware of a change in the schedule.
(D) She disagrees with her coworkers.

64 What will Luisa probably do tonight?

(A) Start a renovation
(B) Schedule a meeting
(C) Write a new contract
(D) Work overtime

GO ON TO THE NEXT PAGE

Wally's Fresh Catering	
Customer: Alyssa Kim Order Number: N00013	
Item	Quantity
Mixed Sandwich Platter	5 platters
Cheese & Olive Tray	3 trays
Lemonade	20 glasses
Dark Chocolate Cake	12 pieces

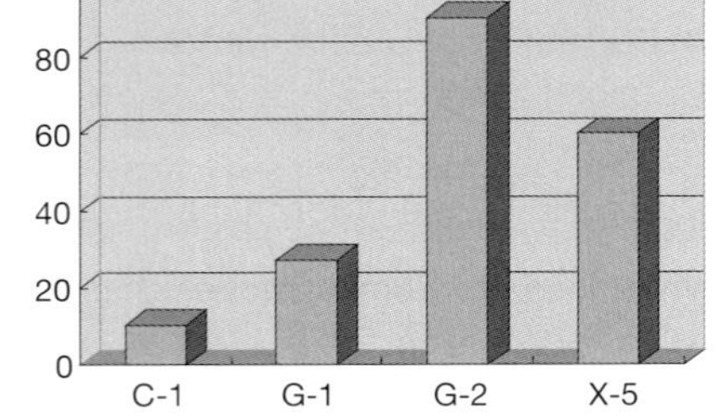

65 What are the speakers discussing?

(A) The details of a meeting
(B) The location of an office
(C) The price of an item
(D) The business hours of a restaurant

66 What does the woman mention about Wally's Fresh Catering?

(A) It offers a wide range of menu options.
(B) Its prices are reasonable.
(C) Many people are happy with its service.
(D) She has used the company before.

67 Look at the graphic. Which item will be eliminated from the order form?

(A) Mixed Sandwich Platter
(B) Cheese & Olive Tray
(C) Lemonade
(D) Dark Chocolate Cake

68 What are the speakers mainly discussing?

(A) Import and export regulations
(B) Concerns about the company's sales
(C) The launch of a new luxury sedan
(D) Safety regulations for automobiles

69 What problem is being discussed?

(A) Sales of bigger vehicles have decreased.
(B) The supply cannot meet the demand.
(C) The workers are on strike.
(D) Compact cars did not appeal to European customers.

70 Look at the graphic. Which car model does the woman ask the man to investigate?

(A) C-1
(B) G-1
(C) G-2
(D) X-5

PART 4

Directions: You will hear some talks given by a single speaker. You will be asked to answer three questions about what the speaker says in each talk. Select the best response to each question and mark the letter (A), (B), (C), or (D) on your answer sheet. The talks will not be printed in your test book and will be spoken only one time.

71 Who most likely is the speaker?

(A) A new waitress
(B) A restaurant manager
(C) A regular customer
(D) A food critic

72 What does the speaker say will happen tomorrow?

(A) A free beverage will be served.
(B) A jazz band will play.
(C) A restaurant will be inspected.
(D) A busy season will begin.

73 What will listeners most likely do next?

(A) Memorize menu items
(B) Prepare food
(C) Put on a uniform
(D) Sign a contract

74 What is the purpose of the broadcast?

(A) To interview a famous author
(B) To advertise a local music festival
(C) To inform listeners of a holiday
(D) To announce road repairs

75 What does the speaker recommend listeners should do?

(A) Purchase tickets online
(B) Leave early for an event
(C) Listen to a radio show
(D) Use a different road

76 What does the speaker mention about the subway?

(A) Service will be provided free of charge.
(B) An extra route will be added.
(C) The timetable has been revised.
(D) More frequent services have been demanded.

77 What is the report about?

(A) A construction company
(B) A marketing company
(C) A conference center
(D) A shopping mall

78 Why was the construction delayed?

(A) Equipment malfunction
(B) Poor weather conditions
(C) A series of strikes
(D) A lack of construction materials

79 What will the business provide for the first month?

(A) Gift certificates
(B) Reduced prices
(C) Shuttle services
(D) Meal vouchers

80 Why will the restaurant be closed until 5 P.M.?

(A) To celebrate the opening of the new building
(B) To host a private function
(C) To restock ingredients
(D) To train some employees

81 What news does the speaker mention about the restaurant?

(A) It is adding a new location.
(B) It is moving to a different city
(C) It is serving some exotic dishes.
(D) It is hiring a renowned chef.

82 What is offered at the new restaurant for free?

(A) Meal vouchers
(B) Wine tasting events
(C) Cooking classes
(D) Homemade cakes

GO ON TO THE NEXT PAGE

83 What change has the company recently made?

(A) It has adopted a strict recycling policy.
(B) It has moved to a more spacious office.
(C) It has replaced a service provider.
(D) It has hired additional employees.

84 What does the speaker mean when he says, "But it's going to be different with the new company"?

(A) Uncomfortable office furniture will be replaced soon.
(B) Problems regarding insufficient office space will be resolved.
(C) The company will purchase new office equipment.
(D) Employees will not need to do unnecessary paperwork.

85 What are listeners encouraged to do?

(A) Read a list
(B) E-mail a supplier
(C) Conserve paper
(D) Work overtime

---

86 What is the talk mainly about?

(A) Handling certain data
(B) Responding to complaints
(C) Training new employees
(D) Installing some software

87 What have some customers asked questions about?

(A) Who to speak to about technical difficulties
(B) When a scheduled update takes place
(C) Where to get a certificate issued
(D) How their information is protected

88 What are employees asked to refrain from?

(A) Viewing business contracts
(B) Reporting technical problems
(C) Copying restricted information
(D) Purchasing extra office supplies

89 Where is the talk most likely taking place?

(A) In a laboratory
(B) In a theater
(C) At a visitor's center
(D) At a festival

90 According to the speaker, what will listeners learn?

(A) How to read a sky map
(B) Where to sign up for a lecture
(C) How to use a telescope
(D) Where to find photos of the stars

91 For which information should listeners visit a website?

(A) Monthly stargazing information
(B) Some astronomical photographs
(C) Directions to the center
(D) Some research studies

---

92 What does the speaker mean when he says, "And it seems even worse now"?

(A) The maintenance office is closed.
(B) Heavy rains have caused a flood.
(C) A leak has gotten more serious.
(D) A burglar broke into his apartment.

93 What is the purpose of the message?

(A) To estimate the costs
(B) To inform of a procedure
(C) To schedule a repair
(D) To request advice

94 What is the speaker going to do?

(A) Protect some equipment
(B) Return a call
(C) Listen to a weather forecast
(D) Remove some furniture

Meeting Schedule	
Karen Park	10:00 a.m.
Santiago Juarez	11:00 a.m.
Lunch	12:00 p.m.
Liz Sacco	1:00 p.m.
Luke Smith	2:00 p.m.

95 Why is the speaker congratulating Luke?

(A) He has won an award.
(B) He has met a deadline.
(C) He has developed a new product.
(D) He has been promoted at work.

96 Look at the graphic. According to the revised schedule, who will give a presentation at 1 p.m. on Monday?

(A) Karen Park
(B) Santiago Juarez
(C) Liz Sacco
(D) Luke Smith

97 What is the topic of Karen's presentation?

(A) A marketing strategy
(B) A product launch
(C) A new advertisement
(D) A product budget

Item	Price	Quantity
Desktop PC	$450	3
Laptop Computer	$550	1
Monitor	$140	3
Keyboard	$15	3

98 In what department does the speaker work?

(A) Sales
(B) Shipping
(C) Purchasing
(D) Advertising

99 Look at the graphic. According to the speaker, what price will stay the same?

(A) $450
(B) $550
(C) $140
(D) $15

100 What will the speaker do on Monday?

(A) He will order some items.
(B) He will contact a store.
(C) He will install some equipment.
(D) He will revise a report.

This is the end of the Listening test. Turn to Part 5 in your test book.

GO ON TO THE NEXT PAGE

▶정답 및 해설 P198

LISTENING TEST

In the Listening test, you will be asked to demonstrate how well you understand spoken English. The entire Listening test will last approximately 45 minutes. There are four parts, and directions are given for each part. You must mark your answers on the separate answer sheet. Do not write your answers in your test book.

PART 1

Directions: For each question in this part, you will hear four statements about a picture in your test book. When you hear the statements, you must select the one statement that best describes what you see in the picture. Then find the number of the question on your answer sheet and mark your answer. The statements will not be printed in your test book and will be spoken only one time.

Example

Sample Answer

Statement (C), "The man is working on a painting," is the best description of the picture, so you should select answer (C) and mark it on your answer sheet.

1

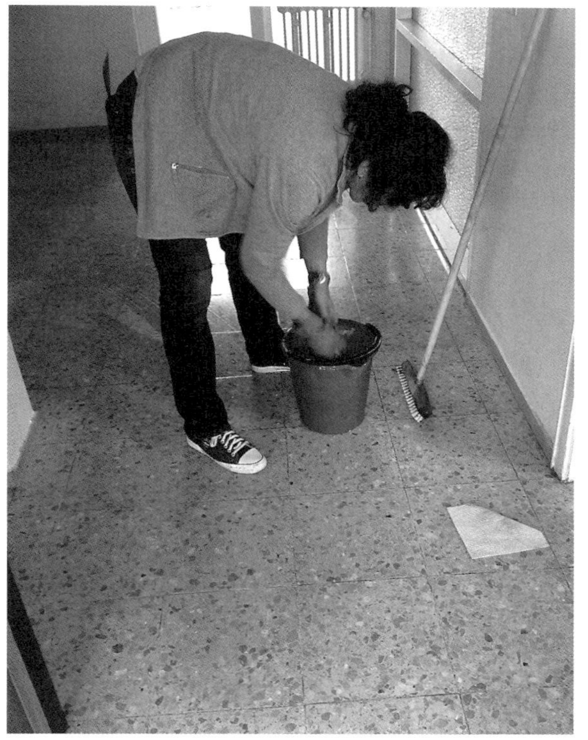

GO ON TO THE NEXT PAGE

3

4

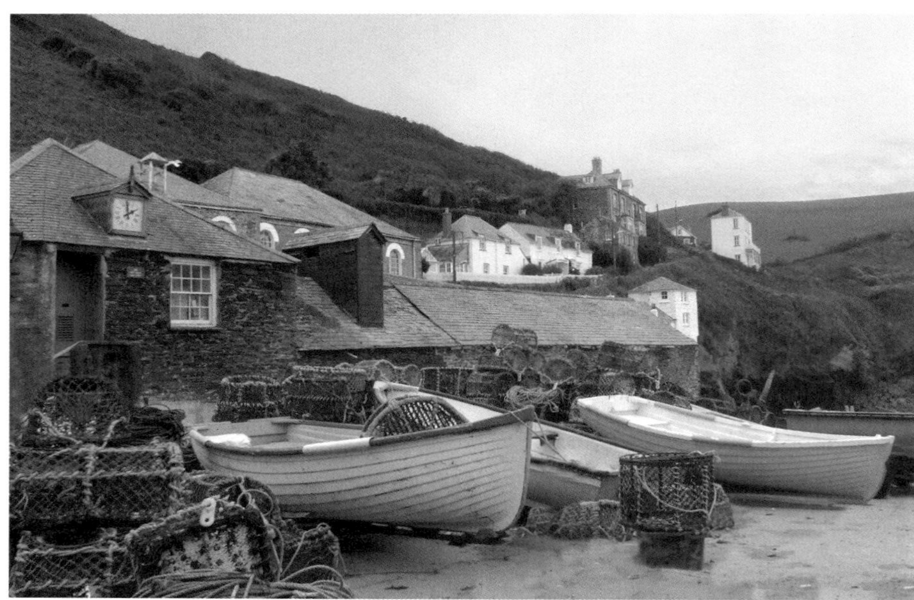

5

6

GO ON TO THE NEXT PAGE

PART 2

Directions: You will hear a question or statement and three responses spoken in English. They will not be printed in your test book and will be spoken only one time. Select the best response to the question or statement and mark the letter (A), (B), or (C) on your answer sheet.

7 Mark your answer on your answer sheet.

8 Mark your answer on your answer sheet.

9 Mark your answer on your answer sheet.

10 Mark your answer on your answer sheet.

11 Mark your answer on your answer sheet.

12 Mark your answer on your answer sheet.

13 Mark your answer on your answer sheet.

14 Mark your answer on your answer sheet.

15 Mark your answer on your answer sheet.

16 Mark your answer on your answer sheet.

17 Mark your answer on your answer sheet.

18 Mark your answer on your answer sheet.

19 Mark your answer on your answer sheet.

20 Mark your answer on your answer sheet.

21 Mark your answer on your answer sheet.

22 Mark your answer on your answer sheet.

23 Mark your answer on your answer sheet.

24 Mark your answer on your answer sheet.

25 Mark your answer on your answer sheet.

26 Mark your answer on your answer sheet.

27 Mark your answer on your answer sheet.

28 Mark your answer on your answer sheet.

29 Mark your answer on your answer sheet.

30 Mark your answer on your answer sheet.

31 Mark your answer on your answer sheet.

PART 3

Directions: You will hear some conversations between two or more people. You will be asked to answer three questions about what the speakers say in each conversation. Select the best response to each question and mark the letter (A), (B), (C), or (D) on your answer sheet. The conversations will not be printed in your test book and will be spoken only one time.

32 What are the speakers mainly discussing?
(A) A meeting agenda
(B) A new employee
(C) The relocation of a company
(D) A new software program

33 What are new employees required to do?
(A) Receive training
(B) Write sales reports
(C) Sign an agreement
(D) Finish a budget analysis

34 According to the man, what will happen on Monday?
(A) A meeting will be cancelled.
(B) A new colleague will be introduced.
(C) An office will be renovated.
(D) A training program will begin.

---

35 What is the conversation mainly about?
(A) A new play
(B) A charity concert
(C) A television show
(D) A tennis match

36 Who is Rebecca Green?
(A) A tennis player
(B) A TV show host
(C) An entertainer
(D) A business owner

37 What will the man probably do tonight?
(A) Purchase a ticket online
(B) Make dinner at home
(C) Watch a match on television
(D) Go to the movies

38 What type of business do the speakers work for?
(A) A supermarket
(B) A newspaper
(C) A restaurant
(D) A movie theater

39 What are the speakers mainly discussing?
(A) A critic's review
(B) An interview with an author
(C) A new menu selection
(D) A local food festival

40 What does the man expect to happen?
(A) They will hire more employees.
(B) A popular dish will sell out.
(C) The restaurant will be busier.
(D) They will raise their prices.

---

41 Who most likely is the woman?
(A) A job applicant
(B) A graphic designer
(C) An engineer
(D) A department head

42 What requirement of the job does the man mention?
(A) A college degree
(B) Relevant experience
(C) In-depth knowledge
(D) Good people skills

43 What does the man suggest the woman do?
(A) Attend an awards ceremony
(B) Contact a hiring manager
(C) Sign a contract
(D) Submit a document

GO ON TO THE NEXT PAGE

44 What does the woman want to do?

(A) Place an order
(B) Get directions to a store
(C) Examine some items
(D) Sign up for a subscription

45 Where most likely are the speakers?

(A) At a doctor's office
(B) At a café
(C) At a pharmacy
(D) At a community center

46 What does the man suggest?

(A) Completing a form
(B) Returning later
(C) Staying in the waiting room
(D) Seeing a doctor

---

47 What does the man imply when he says, "Yes! What a relief"?

(A) He can make a reservation for dinner tonight.
(B) A new subway line will start operating.
(C) He can make it to the dental clinic on time.
(D) He is glad to hear that his wallet has been found.

48 What does the man mention about the dentist's office?

(A) He works there.
(B) He found his wallet there.
(C) He had a check-up there today.
(D) It is located on Andrew Street.

49 What does the woman suggest the man do?

(A) Contact a restaurant
(B) Visit the woman's workplace
(C) Purchase a new wallet
(D) Order more business cards

50 What type of business do the speakers work for?

(A) A book store
(B) A florist shop
(C) A supermarket
(D) A restaurant

51 What does the man say helped sales?

(A) A local festival
(B) Good reviews from experts
(C) A special sale
(D) The nice weather

52 What will the man send the woman electronically?

(A) A copy of a license
(B) Some sales figures
(C) An updated brochure
(D) Pictures of a store

---

53 What type of business do the speakers probably work for?

(A) A manufacturing plant
(B) A community park
(C) A high school
(D) A fitness center

54 What is the man waiting for?

(A) Some fitness equipment
(B) A package from his family
(C) Confirmation from an instructor
(D) A list of mailing addresses

55 What does the woman ask the man to do?

(A) Send an e-mail
(B) Complete a schedule
(C) Go to the post office
(D) Finalize a contract

56 What does the man ask the woman to do?

(A) Test a system
(B) Attend a meeting
(C) Lead a session
(D) Order a computer

57 Why does the man need assistance?

(A) An extra session has been added.
(B) A deadline has to be met.
(C) A room has to be cleaned.
(D) A speaker will be unavailable.

58 What does the woman suggest?

(A) Having lunch together
(B) Registering for the session
(C) Contacting the manager
(D) Meeting to discuss plans

---

59 What are the speakers mainly discussing?

(A) An employment opportunity
(B) A new advertising campaign
(C) A colleague's salary
(D) A retirement plan

60 What type of company does the woman work for?

(A) A staffing agency
(B) An advertising firm
(C) An insurance company
(D) A catering company

61 What does the woman imply when she says, "There is no such thing as a free lunch"?

(A) She is willing to apply for the job.
(B) The position requires many years of experience.
(C) The job may pay well because it is demanding.
(D) She will review the job description.

62 What does the man say about Michael Carlson?

(A) He has lived in a foreign country.
(B) He has more experience than required.
(C) He does not want to travel often.
(D) He applied for several positions.

63 What does Sophia suggest doing?

(A) Building a new shopping center overseas
(B) Relocating the company's headquarters
(C) Recommending a candidate for another position
(D) Advertising job openings in a newspaper

64 What will happen in Hong Kong in two weeks?

(A) A phone interview will be conducted.
(B) A computer system will be upgraded.
(C) A construction project will begin.
(D) An annual event will be held.

GO ON TO THE NEXT PAGE

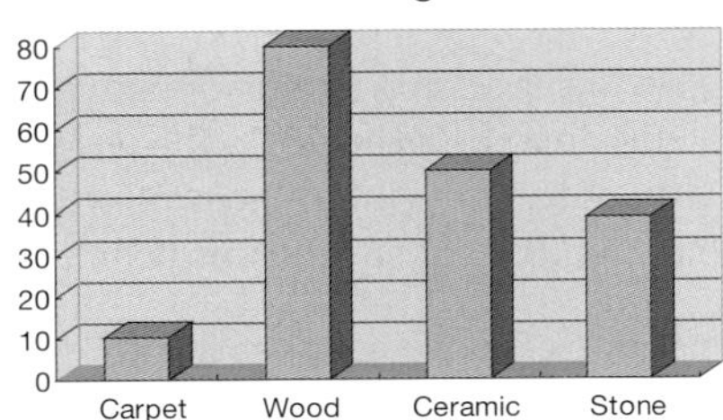

65 Which material is the best seller in the store?

(A) Bamboo
(B) Carpet
(C) Hardwood
(D) Ceramic

66 What does the man mention about bamboo flooring?

(A) It is easy to clean.
(B) It is environmentally friendly.
(C) It is affordable.
(D) It is durable.

67 Look at the graphic. Which material will the man investigate?

(A) Carpet
(B) Wood
(C) Ceramic
(D) Stone

Anne's Catering MENU		
Item	Tray for 20	Each Additional Tray
Spanish Salad	$100	$90
Chicken wings	$200	$180

68 What problem does the woman mention?

(A) A rain shower is forecast.
(B) Not many people have replied.
(C) A supplier has raised its prices.
(D) A restaurant does not accept reservations.

69 Look at the graphic. How much is it for the entire catering order?

(A) $100
(B) $200
(C) $300
(D) $480

70 What will the woman probably do next?

(A) Contact a catering company
(B) Pay a bill
(C) Call a party planner
(D) Cancel an event

PART 4

Directions: You will hear some talks given by a single speaker. You will be asked to answer three questions about what the speaker says in each talk. Select the best response to each question and mark the letter (A), (B), (C), or (D) on your answer sheet. The talks will not be printed in your test book and will be spoken only one time.

71 What kind of company is being advertised?
(A) A car dealership
(B) A clothing shop
(C) A new restaurant
(D) A furniture store

72 What is the purpose of the advertisement?
(A) To introduce a new car
(B) To announce a new location
(C) To promote a special sale
(D) To provide a free service

73 What does the speaker say about Best Dealership?
(A) It specializes in cars for families.
(B) It provides warranty service.
(C) It has opened another showroom.
(D) It opens only on weekends.

---

74 What did the listener recently order?
(A) A mini dress
(B) A computer
(C) A coffee table
(D) A refrigerator

75 What is the problem?
(A) An item is unavailable.
(B) A delivery is delayed.
(C) Some equipment is outdated.
(D) There is a mistake on the bill.

76 What does the speaker offer to do?
(A) Cancel an order
(B) Rent some tables
(C) Reserve some items
(D) Provide a discount

77 What is the main topic of the report?
(A) Music
(B) Weather
(C) Finance
(D) Traffic

78 Why is everybody leaving work early today?
(A) To attend a local festival
(B) To enjoy the good weather
(C) To avoid traffic jams
(D) To go on summer vacation

79 What event will begin tomorrow?
(A) A sporting event
(B) A ballet performance
(C) An annual festival
(D) A singing competition

---

80 Who is the intended audience of the talk?
(A) Business owners
(B) Local residents
(C) Soccer players
(D) Real estate agents

81 According to the speaker, what will be constructed?
(A) A hospital
(B) A community center
(C) A sports stadium
(D) A subway station

82 What does the speaker mention about some local businesses?
(A) They will provide financial support.
(B) They will host a charity banquet.
(C) They will attract more tourists.
(D) They have signed an agreement.

GO ON TO THE NEXT PAGE

83 Where does the speaker most likely work?

(A) At an accounting firm
(B) At a restaurant
(C) At a convention center
(D) At a radio station

84 Why does the speaker say, "So, let's make sure that's what they receive"?

(A) To encourage employees to provide excellent food and service
(B) To provide PA Accounting staff with a promotional gift
(C) To invite as many people as possible to an event
(D) To announce that the restaurant will receive an award

85 What will the listeners probably do next?

(A) Clean a dining room
(B) Start serving dinner
(C) Contact an accounting firm
(D) Check their work assignments

---

86 In what department does Adele most likely work?

(A) Human resources
(B) Advertising
(C) Accounting
(D) Engineering

87 Why does the speaker apologize?

(A) His report was overdue.
(B) His client complained about his work.
(C) He did not attend the meeting.
(D) He was late for the company event.

88 What does the speaker say he will do tonight?

(A) Examine a document
(B) Calculate sales figures
(C) Write up an agenda
(D) Speak with a client

89 Who is Dr. Jack Irwin?

(A) The CEO of the company
(B) A famous athlete
(C) A visiting consultant
(D) A heart surgeon

90 What is Dr. Jack Irwin's area of expertise?

(A) Chemistry
(B) Marketing
(C) Technology
(D) Healthcare

91 What does the woman imply when she says "So, please make every effort to be there"?

(A) Employees should be present at the party.
(B) Employees should be determined to reach a goal.
(C) Employees should work as a team.
(D) Employees should not be late for work.

---

92 Where does the speaker most likely work?

(A) At a clothing manufacturer
(B) At a fashion magazine
(C) At a shoe store
(D) At an advertising firm

93 What is special about the new merchandise?

(A) It has come down in price.
(B) It is popular in many countries
(C) It can be custom-made.
(D) It targets a specific age group.

94 What does the speaker suggest doing?

(A) Conducting a survey
(B) Changing advertising agencies
(C) Merging with a competitor
(D) Analyzing consumer preferences

Order Form			
Name: Kelly Hill Address: 511 King Street Telephone: 555-0078			
Item	Unit Price	Quantity	Color
Cotton Polo Shirt	$30	1	Green
	Discount coupon: 10% off Grand Total: $27		

95 What does the speaker say about Ms. Hill's order?

(A) A discount was applied to it.
(B) It has already been processed.
(C) She paid more than she owed.
(D) It does not include shipping costs.

96 Look at the graphic. According to the speaker, what information needs to be corrected?

(A) Item
(B) Quantity
(C) Color
(D) Discount rate

97 What is the listener asked to do?

(A) Select another item
(B) Visit a retail shop
(C) Check the inventory
(D) Confirm an order

Restaurant Inspection Checklist				
	Criteria	Grading		
		3	2	1
1	Toilet cleanliness			
2	Condition of kitchen equipment			
3	Condition of prepared foods			
4	Left-over food management			

98 Who most likely is the speaker?

(A) A chef
(B) A restaurant manager
(C) A marketing consultant
(D) An inspector

99 What did the speaker do to prepare for an inspection?

(A) Approved a budget
(B) Rearranged a dining room
(C) Conducted a customer survey
(D) Examined the dining facilities

100 Look at the graphic. What criterion should the wait staff try to improve on?

(A) Toilet cleanliness
(B) Condition of kitchen equipment
(C) Condition of prepared foods
(D) Left-over food management

Test 10

This is the end of the Listening test. Turn to Part 5 in your test book.

GO ON TO THE NEXT PAGE

▶정답 및 해설 P220

LISTENING TEST

In the Listening test, you will be asked to demonstrate how well you understand spoken English. The entire Listening test will last approximately 45 minutes. There are four parts, and directions are given for each part. You must mark your answers on the separate answer sheet. Do not write your answers in your test book.

PART 1

Directions: For each question in this part, you will hear four statements about a picture in your test book. When you hear the statements, you must select the one statement that best describes what you see in the picture. Then find the number of the question on your answer sheet and mark your answer. The statements will not be printed in your test book and will be spoken only one time.

Example

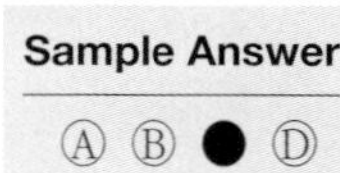

Sample Answer

Ⓐ Ⓑ ● Ⓓ

Statement (C), "The man is working on a painting," is the best description of the picture, so you should select answer (C) and mark it on your answer sheet.

1

2

Test 11

GO ON TO THE NEXT PAGE

3

4

5

6

Test 11

GO ON TO THE NEXT PAGE

PART 2

Directions: You will hear a question or statement and three responses spoken in English. They will not be printed in your test book and will be spoken only one time. Select the best response to the question or statement and mark the letter (A), (B), or (C) on your answer sheet.

7 Mark your answer on your answer sheet.

8 Mark your answer on your answer sheet.

9 Mark your answer on your answer sheet.

10 Mark your answer on your answer sheet.

11 Mark your answer on your answer sheet.

12 Mark your answer on your answer sheet.

13 Mark your answer on your answer sheet.

14 Mark your answer on your answer sheet.

15 Mark your answer on your answer sheet.

16 Mark your answer on your answer sheet.

17 Mark your answer on your answer sheet.

18 Mark your answer on your answer sheet.

19 Mark your answer on your answer sheet.

20 Mark your answer on your answer sheet.

21 Mark your answer on your answer sheet.

22 Mark your answer on your answer sheet.

23 Mark your answer on your answer sheet.

24 Mark your answer on your answer sheet.

25 Mark your answer on your answer sheet.

26 Mark your answer on your answer sheet.

27 Mark your answer on your answer sheet.

28 Mark your answer on your answer sheet.

29 Mark your answer on your answer sheet.

30 Mark your answer on your answer sheet.

31 Mark your answer on your answer sheet.

PART 3

Directions: You will hear some conversations between two or more people. You will be asked to answer three questions about what the speakers say in each conversation. Select the best response to each question and mark the letter (A), (B), (C), or (D) on your answer sheet. The conversations will not be printed in your test book and will be spoken only one time.

32 Where most likely are the speakers?
(A) In a factory
(B) In a store
(C) In a post office
(D) In a restaurant

33 What does the woman ask for?
(A) Directions to a clothing shop
(B) Proof of purchase
(C) An additional discount
(D) Merchandise in another color

34 What will the man probably do next?
(A) Go to the storage room
(B) Pay for a purchase
(C) Speak to his manager
(D) Send a package

35 What is the man doing now?
(A) Making a list of supplies
(B) Reading a magazine
(C) Packing his belongings
(D) Designing an invitation

36 When is the shipment expected to arrive?
(A) On Monday
(B) On Tuesday
(C) On Wednesday
(D) On Thursday

37 What is the man asked to do when he receives the package?
(A) Contact an assistant
(B) Place an order
(C) Pay a bill
(D) Call a delivery company

38 Who most likely is the woman?
(A) A bank clerk
(B) A parking attendant
(C) A local resident
(D) A real estate agent

39 What is the problem?
(A) A bank is closed for business.
(B) A man has forgotten his access code.
(C) A parking garage is currently full.
(D) A facility is exclusively for its residents.

40 What does the woman suggest the man do?
(A) Open a bank account
(B) Return the next day
(C) Use public transportation
(D) Go to a different location

41 What is the woman currently working on?
(A) A feature article
(B) A financial summary
(C) A survey report
(D) A cost estimate

42 What is the man supposed to do tomorrow?
(A) Calculate some figures
(B) Attend a meeting
(C) Watch a video
(D) Have a conference call

43 What information will the man give the woman later?
(A) The number of attendees
(B) The cost of an event
(C) The location of a meeting
(D) The time of a presentation

GO ON TO THE NEXT PAGE

44 What is the man calling about?

(A) An incomplete shipment
(B) A missing document
(C) An incorrect address
(D) A damaged product

45 What does the woman say caused the problem?

(A) Some items were not available.
(B) A mailing address was not correct.
(C) The order was sent from different places.
(D) A delivery truck broke down.

46 What does the woman say she will do?

(A) Contact a delivery company
(B) Cancel a bill
(C) Provide a coupon
(D) Find a number

---

47 Where most likely are the speakers?

(A) In a customer service department
(B) In a medical office
(C) In a furniture shop
(D) In a coffee shop

48 What is mentioned about Ms. Garcia?

(A) She has provided new contact information.
(B) She recently started working at a medical clinic.
(C) She has moved into a new house.
(D) She has an appointment with a doctor today.

49 What will the man probably do next?

(A) Find a document
(B) Contact a patient
(C) Repair a computer
(D) Make a reservation

50 Who most likely is the man?

(A) A reporter
(B) A factory worker
(C) A local entrepreneur
(D) A mayor

51 What goal does the man mention?

(A) Increasing employment
(B) Restoring old buildings
(C) Creating new car models
(D) Establishing an economic policy

52 What does the woman ask about?

(A) The number of new employees
(B) The opening date
(C) The cost of construction
(D) A building plan

---

53 What are the speakers mainly discussing?

(A) The location of a promotional event
(B) The opening of a new factory
(C) The shipment of some goods
(D) The cause of a power failure

54 What does the woman imply when she says, "Oh, I'm relieved to hear that"?

(A) She is happy that a delivery will arrive on time.
(B) She is satisfied with the quality of some products.
(C) She feels better after receiving treatment.
(D) She likes to hear other people's opinions.

55 According to the woman, what will happen next week?

(A) A factory tour
(B) A trade show
(C) A demonstration
(D) A promotional event

56 Why is the man calling?

(A) To report a billing mistake
(B) To request a copy of a receipt
(C) To provide a correct address
(D) To close a bank account

57 What change was made last month?

(A) Some new employees were hired.
(B) Wages were raised.
(C) A new line of products was added.
(D) Some new software was installed.

58 What does the woman offer to do?

(A) Send a letter of apology
(B) Open a new account
(C) Correct the mistake
(D) Offer a discount

---

59 What is the purpose of Mr. Kenta's call?

(A) To discuss a remodeling project
(B) To reschedule a meeting
(C) To arrange a trip
(D) To revise a contract

60 Why does the man say, "But would you mind taking my place"?

(A) To reschedule the meeting
(B) To ask the woman to finish a building plan
(C) To hold an event in another city
(D) To ask the woman to meet with the clients

61 What does the man say he will send the woman?

(A) A floor plan
(B) A list of suppliers
(C) A cost estimate
(D) A construction schedule

62 Who most likely is Ms. Quinn?

(A) A student
(B) A restaurant manager
(C) A guest lecturer
(D) A business owner

63 What does Ms. Quinn mean when she says, "Oh, that's very kind of you"?

(A) She is thankful for the invitation.
(B) She wants to use a specific kind of product.
(C) She needs to prepare for her lecture.
(D) She likes the village very much.

64 What does the man say about the restaurant?

(A) It serves Indian food.
(B) It has a great view.
(C) It is always crowded.
(D) It has opened recently.

GO ON TO THE NEXT PAGE

Satisfaction Rating by Age

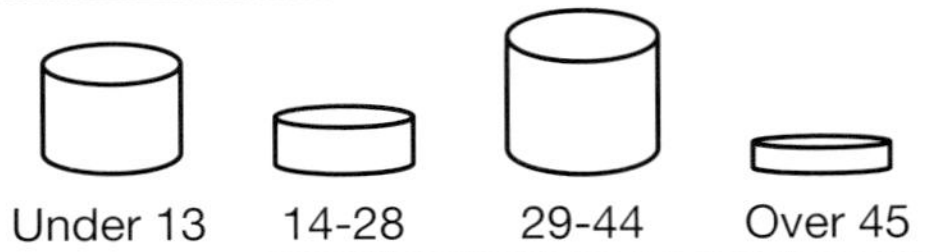

Under 13 | 14-28 | 29-44 | Over 45

65 Where do the speakers most likely work?

(A) At a research center
(B) At an art gallery
(C) At a fitness club
(D) At a community center

66 What are the speakers mainly discussing?

(A) A family membership
(B) Promoting a new program
(C) A schedule change
(D) The results of a recent survey

67 Look at the graphic. Which age group wants the center to offer more classes?

(A) Under 13
(B) 14-28
(C) 29-44
(D) Over 45

City Sights of NY		
	Adult	Senior/Student
Half Day City Tour	$60	$50
Full Day City Tour + Ferry	$100	$80

68 What is the man asking about?

(A) A sightseeing tour
(B) A concert schedule
(C) Directions to an attraction
(D) A famous artist

69 According to the woman, what is included in the full-day city tour?

(A) A museum tour
(B) A Broadway show
(C) A ferry ride
(D) A seafood lunch

70 Look at the graphic. How much will the man pay for a tour?

(A) $50
(B) $60
(C) $80
(D) $100

PART 4

Directions: You will hear some talks given by a single speaker. You will be asked to answer three questions about what the speaker says in each talk. Select the best response to each question and mark the letter (A), (B), (C), or (D) on your answer sheet. The talks will not be printed in your test book and will be spoken only one time.

71 Where does the speaker most likely work?
(A) At an airport lounge
(B) At a travel agency
(C) At an airline
(D) At a car rental agency

72 What is the woman calling about?
(A) A travel itinerary
(B) A boarding pass
(C) A piece of luggage
(D) A hotel reservation

73 When will the shipment arrive at the hotel?
(A) Today
(B) Tomorrow
(C) Next week
(D) In two weeks

74 Who is Earl Davis?
(A) A show host
(B) An interior designer
(C) A reporter
(D) A publisher

75 What will Mr. Davis discuss on the program?
(A) A critic's review
(B) Some art techniques
(C) Useful investment tips
(D) His recent book

76 What are the listeners invited to do?
(A) Register for a course
(B) Attend a fashion show
(C) Call in with questions
(D) Choose a color

77 Who most likely is the speaker?
(A) A car dealer
(B) A department director
(C) A factory manager
(D) A company president

78 What does the speaker say about the Zeta 500?
(A) It is faster than the previous model.
(B) It has a powerful engine.
(C) It has won an award.
(D) It is ready to be introduced.

79 What will Grace Lee discuss?
(A) An upcoming awards ceremony
(B) A manufacturing process
(C) A plan to unveil a new car
(D) A recent motor show

80 What is the purpose of the announcement?
(A) To collect old electronics equipment
(B) To promote a charity concert
(C) To thank local residents
(D) To celebrate an anniversary

81 What does the speaker imply when she says, "That's not all"?
(A) All local residents are invited to an event.
(B) Selected products in the store will be on sale.
(C) Participants will receive an additional bonus.
(D) A radio program will be broadcast on Sunday.

82 What will participants receive?
(A) A new television set
(B) Free shipping
(C) A confirmation document
(D) A discount coupon

GO ON TO THE NEXT PAGE

83 Where is the announcement most likely taking place?

(A) On a train
(B) At a bus terminal
(C) At an airport
(D) On a boat

84 What is the cause of the departure delay?

(A) A crew shortage
(B) A disabled train
(C) Foggy weather
(D) Flooded tracks

85 What are the listeners asked to do?

(A) Speak to the conductor
(B) View a lunch menu
(C) Conduct an inspection
(D) Take out their tickets

---

86 According to the speaker, what has Kyson-Vac done recently?

(A) They have revised an advertising campaign.
(B) They have merged with another manufacturer.
(C) They have released a new product.
(D) They have started a special promotion.

87 What are listeners encouraged to provide?

(A) Marketing strategies
(B) Product designs
(C) Survey results
(D) Work schedules

88 What are listeners asked to avoid?

(A) Implementing a new marketing campaign
(B) Contacting other suppliers
(C) Missing an important deadline
(D) Sharing confidential information

89 What is the main purpose of the talk?

(A) To describe a nature tour
(B) To give directions to a tower
(C) To recommend a travel agency
(D) To introduce a speaker

90 What are listeners not allowed to do?

(A) Take photographs
(B) Swim in some areas
(C) Explore the site alone
(D) Use cell phones

91 Why does the speaker say, "So, please watch your step"?

(A) To encourage them to enjoy the beautiful view
(B) To ask them to wear a life vest
(C) To tell them to look around the falls
(D) To warn them not to slip

---

92 According to the speaker, what is distinctive about the factory?

(A) It has the largest production facilities.
(B) It was built a long time ago.
(C) It has recently been renovated.
(D) It has a number of locations.

93 What will be distributed to the listeners?

(A) Safety gear
(B) Tour schedules
(C) Headphones
(D) Product samples

94 According to the speaker, what should be avoided during the tour?

(A) Exploring the factory alone
(B) Making noise
(C) Eating and drinking food
(D) Touching equipment

INVOICE			
Bill to:	Atkinson Industries 1130 Castlefield Ave. (064) 555-0887	Invoice Num: #00981 Due Date: 2016. 08. 31.	
Date	Item	Quantity	Balance
2016. 08. 05.	Shipping crate	200	$80

95 What is the speaker calling about?

(A) A manufacturing defect
(B) A late shipment
(C) A new contract
(D) A mistake on a bill

96 Look at the graphic. According to the speaker, what information is incorrect?

(A) Date
(B) Item
(C) Quantity
(D) Due date

97 What does the speaker request?

(A) A corrected invoice
(B) A price estimate
(C) An order number
(D) A full refund

Workshop Program

Presenter	Time
Mr. Woodbury	10:00 ~ 10:50
Ms. Roth	11:00 ~ 11:50
Lunch	12:00 ~ 12:50
Mr. Best	13:00 ~ 13:50
Ms. Levine	14:00 ~ 14:50

98 What kind of event is taking place?

(A) An annual conference
(B) A television show
(C) A cooking competition
(D) An awards ceremony

99 What is the problem?

(A) A food festival has been canceled.
(B) A venue has been changed.
(C) A presenter will arrive late.
(D) A flight is fully booked.

100 Look at the graphic. According to the revised schedule, who will be the day's first speaker?

(A) Mr. Woodbury
(B) Ms. Roth
(C) Mr. Best
(D) Ms. Levine

This is the end of the Listening test. Turn to Part 5 in your test book.

GO ON TO THE NEXT PAGE

▶정답 및 해설 P240

LISTENING TEST

In the Listening test, you will be asked to demonstrate how well you understand spoken English. The entire Listening test will last approximately 45 minutes. There are four parts, and directions are given for each part. You must mark your answers on the separate answer sheet. Do not write your answers in your test book.

PART 1

Directions: For each question in this part, you will hear four statements about a picture in your test book. When you hear the statements, you must select the one statement that best describes what you see in the picture. Then find the number of the question on your answer sheet and mark your answer. The statements will not be printed in your test book and will be spoken only one time.

Example

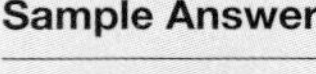

Statement (C), "The man is working on a painting," is the best description of the picture, so you should select answer (C) and mark it on your answer sheet.

1

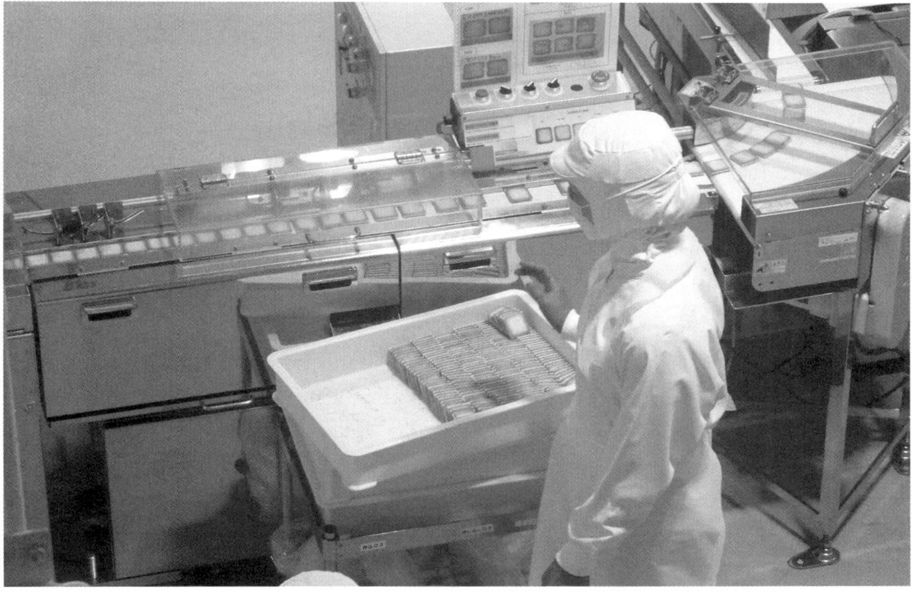

2

GO ON TO THE NEXT PAGE

3

4

5

6

Test 12

GO ON TO THE NEXT PAGE

PART 2

Directions: You will hear a question or statement and three responses spoken in English. They will not be printed in your test book and will be spoken only one time. Select the best response to the question or statement and mark the letter (A), (B), or (C) on your answer sheet.

7 Mark your answer on your answer sheet.

8 Mark your answer on your answer sheet.

9 Mark your answer on your answer sheet.

10 Mark your answer on your answer sheet.

11 Mark your answer on your answer sheet.

12 Mark your answer on your answer sheet.

13 Mark your answer on your answer sheet.

14 Mark your answer on your answer sheet.

15 Mark your answer on your answer sheet.

16 Mark your answer on your answer sheet.

17 Mark your answer on your answer sheet.

18 Mark your answer on your answer sheet.

19 Mark your answer on your answer sheet.

20 Mark your answer on your answer sheet.

21 Mark your answer on your answer sheet.

22 Mark your answer on your answer sheet.

23 Mark your answer on your answer sheet.

24 Mark your answer on your answer sheet.

25 Mark your answer on your answer sheet.

26 Mark your answer on your answer sheet.

27 Mark your answer on your answer sheet.

28 Mark your answer on your answer sheet.

29 Mark your answer on your answer sheet.

30 Mark your answer on your answer sheet.

31 Mark your answer on your answer sheet.

PART 3

Directions: You will hear some conversations between two or more people. You will be asked to answer three questions about what the speakers say in each conversation. Select the best response to each question and mark the letter (A), (B), (C), or (D) on your answer sheet. The conversations will not be printed in your test book and will be spoken only one time.

32 Why is the woman going to Australia?
(A) To attend a conference
(B) To visit her relatives
(C) To open a branch office
(D) To get a new job

33 What is the woman excited about?
(A) Working with the man
(B) Learning a foreign language
(C) Making new friends
(D) Travelling to another country

34 What does the man have to do by next Wednesday?
(A) Finalize the terms of an agreement
(B) Participate in a discussion
(C) Complete a financial report
(D) Make a flight reservation

---

35 What does the man ask the woman about?
(A) Business hours
(B) Directions to an office
(C) The name of a job applicant
(D) Information about the company

36 Where is Ms. Sullivan's office located?
(A) On the third floor
(B) On the eighth floor
(C) On the eleventh floor
(D) On the twentieth floor

37 What will the woman probably do next?
(A) Make a telephone call
(B) Prepare for an interview
(C) Go to another building
(D) Reserve a conference room

38 Where most likely are the speakers?
(A) In a clothing store
(B) In a restaurant
(C) In a warehouse
(D) In a paint shop

39 What is the problem with the woman's purchase?
(A) Its color
(B) Its size
(C) Its quality
(D) Its style

40 What does the man offer to do?
(A) Expedite a delivery
(B) Recommend another item
(C) Contact another store
(D) Provide a coupon

---

41 Why is the man worried?
(A) He missed a bus.
(B) He is late for a presentation.
(C) He cannot find meeting materials.
(D) He lost his briefcase.

42 What does the man ask the woman to do?
(A) Contact his assistant
(B) Reschedule a meeting
(C) Print out documents
(D) Set up some equipment

43 Where will the man probably go next?
(A) To his office
(B) To his car
(C) To a meeting room
(D) To a clothing store

GO ON TO THE NEXT PAGE

44 What did the woman do last week?

(A) Attended a marketing convention
(B) Visited an overseas branch
(C) Conducted a job interview
(D) Moved to another city

45 Which department do the speakers work in?

(A) Accounting
(B) Shipping
(C) Marketing
(D) Personnel

46 What is the woman going to do this afternoon?

(A) Prepare for a meeting
(B) Attend a seminar
(C) Speak to a colleague
(D) Read some e-mail

---

47 What does the man want to do?

(A) Purchase a gift
(B) Send a package
(C) Check in some luggage
(D) Book a flight ticket

48 What is the problem?

(A) A passport is lost.
(B) A flight ticket is unavailable.
(C) The man is sick.
(D) The weather is bad.

49 When will the man leave?

(A) At 7:00 a.m.
(B) At 8:00 a.m.
(C) At noon
(D) At 1:00 p.m.

50 Who most likely is the man?

(A) A tenant
(B) A home builder
(C) A designer
(D) A real estate agent

51 What does the woman say about the apartment?

(A) It is fully furnished.
(B) It is conveniently located.
(C) The rent is reasonable.
(D) The living room needs repairs.

52 What does the woman mean when she says, "That's more than I was hoping to spend"?

(A) The apartment is unnecessarily large.
(B) She has spent a lot of money on furniture.
(C) The rent is more expensive than she expected.
(D) She does not have time to think.

---

53 Why was the shipment delayed?

(A) A payment was not made.
(B) The delivery address was wrong.
(C) The manufacturer was understaffed.
(D) Some products were not available.

54 What did the supplier provide?

(A) A complimentary ticket
(B) A similar product
(C) Special delivery
(D) A reduced price

55 What will the man probably do next?

(A) Contact some customers
(B) Make some repairs
(C) Order some parts
(D) Use different parts

56 What is the man calling about?

(A) Moving into a new apartment
(B) Taking some lessons
(C) Opening a new business
(D) Buying a musical instrument

57 What information does the woman give the man?

(A) Directions to the store
(B) Rental fees
(C) A phone number
(D) Business hours

58 What will the man probably do next?

(A) Call a shop
(B) Request a product
(C) Provide contact information
(D) Rent a room

---

59 Who most likely is the man?

(A) A photographer
(B) A reporter
(C) A sales representative
(D) A tour guide

60 What does the man imply when he says, "Yeah, weren't they good"?

(A) He would like to visit the attractions with the woman.
(B) Many tourists have a good time in the city.
(C) He is satisfied with the work of the photographer.
(D) Many people like the photographs.

61 Why is the woman going to the City Museum?

(A) To take a tour
(B) To conduct an interview
(C) To participate in an event
(D) To view some artwork

62 What problem does the woman mention?

(A) A manager is unavailable.
(B) An item is not fresh.
(C) A shopping cart is broken.
(D) A product is spilled on the floor.

63 Why does the store manager say, "I can't believe it broke again"?

(A) The store sign has been damaged.
(B) The same problem has occurred again.
(C) Some items were recalled.
(D) An employee was late for work again.

64 What will Adam probably do next?

(A) Call a supplier
(B) Cancel an order
(C) Examine a package
(D) Clean a spill

GO ON TO THE NEXT PAGE

Planet Fitness Club	
EX Class	Trainer
Cycling	Morgan
Muscle Conditioning	Kyle
Zumba Dance	Amanda
Cardio Kick	Trevor

65 Why is the woman at the fitness club?

(A) To cancel a membership
(B) To provide some feedback
(C) To learn about exercise classes
(D) To participate in a competition

66 Why does the woman prefer private lessons?

(A) She is highly motivated to work out regularly.
(B) There is no wait for exercise machines.
(C) Her work schedule is quite irregular.
(D) She has worked at the gym before.

67 Look at the graphic. Which trainer does the woman want to learn from?

(A) Morgan
(B) Kyle
(C) Amanda
(D) Trevor

Red Tag SALE SAVE 50% OFF EVERYTHING IN THE SHOWROOM!		
	Regular Price	Sale Price
Diamond Bracelet	$500	$250
Genuine Ruby Bracelet	$300	$150

68 What was advertised in the newspaper?

(A) A job opening
(B) A fashion show
(C) A musical performance
(D) A half-off sale

69 What is the purpose of the woman's visit to Rome?

(A) To attend a conference
(B) To purchase some jewelry
(C) To open a business
(D) To write an article

70 Look at the graphic. How much will the woman pay for a bracelet?

(A) $150
(B) $250
(C) $300
(D) $500

PART 4

Directions: You will hear some talks given by a single speaker. You will be asked to answer three questions about what the speaker says in each talk. Select the best response to each question and mark the letter (A), (B), (C), or (D) on your answer sheet. The talks will not be printed in your test book and will be spoken only one time.

71 Who most likely is the speaker?
(A) An event organizer
(B) A university student
(C) A hotel clerk
(D) A dance teacher

72 What does the speaker agree to do?
(A) To make a donation
(B) To teach a class
(C) To lead a workshop
(D) To host an exhibit

73 What does the speaker request?
(A) Directions to a center
(B) Use of a special room
(C) A list of attendees
(D) Additional funding

---

74 What are the listeners encouraged to do?
(A) Sign up for a membership
(B) Take a tour of the farm
(C) Provide excellent service
(D) Order groceries online

75 What can listeners receive today?
(A) A shopping bag
(B) Meal vouchers
(C) Farm produce
(D) A membership card

76 Why should listeners go to the service desk?
(A) To request a catalog
(B) To complete a form
(C) To pay for goods
(D) To return items

77 Where most likely is the announcement being made?
(A) At a farewell party
(B) At a conference
(C) At a job fair
(D) At a sales meeting

78 According to the speaker, what has changed?
(A) The location of a party
(B) The number of participants
(C) The time of an event
(D) The guest lecturer

79 What will be available to listeners at the reception desk?
(A) Light snacks and beverages
(B) A city map
(C) Directions to a banquet center
(D) A revised schedule

---

80 What is the purpose of the talk?
(A) To explain the new payroll system
(B) To introduce a new employee
(C) To describe a change in the work schedule
(D) To welcome a company executive

81 What are employees asked to do starting tomorrow?
(A) Work overtime to meet a deadline
(B) Wear a security badge at all times
(C) Enter some data into the computer
(D) Attend a training session

82 Why would an employee contact Erica Yamada?
(A) To schedule some repair work
(B) To ask for a department code
(C) To request some instructions
(D) To explain an accounting error

GO ON TO THE NEXT PAGE

83 Where does Mr. King work?
(A) At a research lab
(B) At a university
(C) At a hospital
(D) At a government office

84 What does the speaker mean when she says, "But he turned the program around"?
(A) Mr. King worked hard to revive the program.
(B) The program was not well organized.
(C) Mr. King used to work at an investment firm.
(D) The school offers a variety of programs.

85 What will probably happen next?
(A) Students will ask questions.
(B) Refreshments will be served.
(C) An award will be presented.
(D) Music will be played.

---

86 Who is William Tate?
(A) A film director
(B) An actor
(C) An archeologist
(D) A movie-goer

87 According to the speaker, what did William do in Peru?
(A) He visited relatives.
(B) He selected shooting places.
(C) He attended a history class.
(D) He learned a foreign language.

88 What are listeners invited to do?
(A) Watch a movie
(B) Attend a party
(C) Ask questions
(D) Offer fashion advice

89 What is the purpose of the talk?
(A) To explain a reimbursement system
(B) To close a company event
(C) To assign a new task
(D) To remind employees of a change

90 What does the speaker mean when he says, "Changes will be in effect starting tomorrow"?
(A) The new measurements will be more effective.
(B) Employees cannot use paper forms any more.
(C) A deadline must be met by tomorrow.
(D) Employees can request extra days off.

91 Why should employees contact Sylvia?
(A) To inquire about training
(B) To reschedule a meeting
(C) To request office supplies
(D) To hand in a report

---

92 Who is the speaker addressing?
(A) News reporters
(B) Sports coaches and league staff
(C) Business owners
(D) Sporting goods store employees

93 What does the speaker want to do?
(A) Solicit sponsors
(B) Write an article
(C) Revise an advertisement
(D) Donate money

94 What can businesses gain from their sponsorship?
(A) They can reduce their operating costs.
(B) They can advertise their brands.
(C) They can be invited to a local event.
(D) They can get a free newspaper subscription.

Monk Printing Price List (Business Card)		
Basic	Single-sided	$20
	Double-sided	$35
Premium	Single-sided	$40
	Double-sided	$55

95 Why does the speaker mention Mr. Harrison?

(A) He has worked as a sales representative for years.
(B) He is in charge of ordering office supplies.
(C) He recommended the printing company.
(D) He cannot afford a premium service.

96 Look at the graphic. What type of card stock did the speaker choose?

(A) Basic single-sided
(B) Basic double-sided
(C) Premium single-sided
(D) Premium double-sided

97 What does the speaker want to do by the end of the week?

(A) Check a sample copy of his business card
(B) Purchase an item at a discounted price
(C) Meet with an international client
(D) Order from a recommended company

List of Moving Companies	
Company	Price Quote
1. Best Movers	$5,000
2. GTA Moving Co.	$10,000
3. Smart Movers	$7,000
4. Cargo Professionals	$3,500

98 What does the speaker mention about the new office?

(A) It has an impressive view.
(B) It is located close to a subway station.
(C) It is more spacious than the old one.
(D) It is opening on the 23rd of May.

99 What are employees asked to do?

(A) Submit a document
(B) Compare two moving companies
(C) Turn off office equipment
(D) Pack their belongings

100 Look at the graphic. Which moving company has been hired?

(A) Best Movers
(B) GTA Moving Co.
(C) Smart Movers
(D) Cargo Professionals

This is the end of the Listening test. Turn to Part 5 in your test book.

GO ON TO THE NEXT PAGE

ANSWER SHEET

응시일자 : 년 월 일

수험번호						

성명	한글	
	한자	
	영자	

좌석번호
Ⓐ Ⓑ Ⓒ Ⓓ Ⓔ
① ② ③ ④ ⑤ ⑥ ⑦

Actual Test 1

LISTENING (Part I~IV)

NO.	ANSWER				NO.	ANSWER				NO.	ANSWER				NO.	ANSWER				NO.	ANSWER			
	A	B	C	D		A	B	C	D		A	B	C	D		A	B	C	D		A	B	C	D
1	Ⓐ	Ⓑ	Ⓒ	Ⓓ	21	Ⓐ	Ⓑ	Ⓒ		41	Ⓐ	Ⓑ	Ⓒ	Ⓓ	61	Ⓐ	Ⓑ	Ⓒ	Ⓓ	81	Ⓐ	Ⓑ	Ⓒ	Ⓓ
2	Ⓐ	Ⓑ	Ⓒ	Ⓓ	22	Ⓐ	Ⓑ	Ⓒ		42	Ⓐ	Ⓑ	Ⓒ	Ⓓ	62	Ⓐ	Ⓑ	Ⓒ	Ⓓ	82	Ⓐ	Ⓑ	Ⓒ	Ⓓ
3	Ⓐ	Ⓑ	Ⓒ	Ⓓ	23	Ⓐ	Ⓑ	Ⓒ		43	Ⓐ	Ⓑ	Ⓒ	Ⓓ	63	Ⓐ	Ⓑ	Ⓒ	Ⓓ	83	Ⓐ	Ⓑ	Ⓒ	Ⓓ
4	Ⓐ	Ⓑ	Ⓒ	Ⓓ	24	Ⓐ	Ⓑ	Ⓒ		44	Ⓐ	Ⓑ	Ⓒ	Ⓓ	64	Ⓐ	Ⓑ	Ⓒ	Ⓓ	84	Ⓐ	Ⓑ	Ⓒ	Ⓓ
5	Ⓐ	Ⓑ	Ⓒ	Ⓓ	25	Ⓐ	Ⓑ	Ⓒ		45	Ⓐ	Ⓑ	Ⓒ	Ⓓ	65	Ⓐ	Ⓑ	Ⓒ	Ⓓ	85	Ⓐ	Ⓑ	Ⓒ	Ⓓ
6	Ⓐ	Ⓑ	Ⓒ	Ⓓ	26	Ⓐ	Ⓑ	Ⓒ		46	Ⓐ	Ⓑ	Ⓒ	Ⓓ	66	Ⓐ	Ⓑ	Ⓒ	Ⓓ	86	Ⓐ	Ⓑ	Ⓒ	Ⓓ
7	Ⓐ	Ⓑ	Ⓒ		27	Ⓐ	Ⓑ	Ⓒ		47	Ⓐ	Ⓑ	Ⓒ	Ⓓ	67	Ⓐ	Ⓑ	Ⓒ	Ⓓ	87	Ⓐ	Ⓑ	Ⓒ	Ⓓ
8	Ⓐ	Ⓑ	Ⓒ		28	Ⓐ	Ⓑ	Ⓒ		48	Ⓐ	Ⓑ	Ⓒ	Ⓓ	68	Ⓐ	Ⓑ	Ⓒ	Ⓓ	88	Ⓐ	Ⓑ	Ⓒ	Ⓓ
9	Ⓐ	Ⓑ	Ⓒ		29	Ⓐ	Ⓑ	Ⓒ		49	Ⓐ	Ⓑ	Ⓒ	Ⓓ	69	Ⓐ	Ⓑ	Ⓒ	Ⓓ	89	Ⓐ	Ⓑ	Ⓒ	Ⓓ
10	Ⓐ	Ⓑ	Ⓒ		30	Ⓐ	Ⓑ	Ⓒ		50	Ⓐ	Ⓑ	Ⓒ	Ⓓ	70	Ⓐ	Ⓑ	Ⓒ	Ⓓ	90	Ⓐ	Ⓑ	Ⓒ	Ⓓ
11	Ⓐ	Ⓑ	Ⓒ		31	Ⓐ	Ⓑ	Ⓒ		51	Ⓐ	Ⓑ	Ⓒ	Ⓓ	71	Ⓐ	Ⓑ	Ⓒ	Ⓓ	91	Ⓐ	Ⓑ	Ⓒ	Ⓓ
12	Ⓐ	Ⓑ	Ⓒ		32	Ⓐ	Ⓑ	Ⓒ	Ⓓ	52	Ⓐ	Ⓑ	Ⓒ	Ⓓ	72	Ⓐ	Ⓑ	Ⓒ	Ⓓ	92	Ⓐ	Ⓑ	Ⓒ	Ⓓ
13	Ⓐ	Ⓑ	Ⓒ		33	Ⓐ	Ⓑ	Ⓒ	Ⓓ	53	Ⓐ	Ⓑ	Ⓒ	Ⓓ	73	Ⓐ	Ⓑ	Ⓒ	Ⓓ	93	Ⓐ	Ⓑ	Ⓒ	Ⓓ
14	Ⓐ	Ⓑ	Ⓒ		34	Ⓐ	Ⓑ	Ⓒ	Ⓓ	54	Ⓐ	Ⓑ	Ⓒ	Ⓓ	74	Ⓐ	Ⓑ	Ⓒ	Ⓓ	94	Ⓐ	Ⓑ	Ⓒ	Ⓓ
15	Ⓐ	Ⓑ	Ⓒ		35	Ⓐ	Ⓑ	Ⓒ	Ⓓ	55	Ⓐ	Ⓑ	Ⓒ	Ⓓ	75	Ⓐ	Ⓑ	Ⓒ	Ⓓ	95	Ⓐ	Ⓑ	Ⓒ	Ⓓ
16	Ⓐ	Ⓑ	Ⓒ		36	Ⓐ	Ⓑ	Ⓒ	Ⓓ	56	Ⓐ	Ⓑ	Ⓒ	Ⓓ	76	Ⓐ	Ⓑ	Ⓒ	Ⓓ	96	Ⓐ	Ⓑ	Ⓒ	Ⓓ
17	Ⓐ	Ⓑ	Ⓒ		37	Ⓐ	Ⓑ	Ⓒ	Ⓓ	57	Ⓐ	Ⓑ	Ⓒ	Ⓓ	77	Ⓐ	Ⓑ	Ⓒ	Ⓓ	97	Ⓐ	Ⓑ	Ⓒ	Ⓓ
18	Ⓐ	Ⓑ	Ⓒ		38	Ⓐ	Ⓑ	Ⓒ	Ⓓ	58	Ⓐ	Ⓑ	Ⓒ	Ⓓ	78	Ⓐ	Ⓑ	Ⓒ	Ⓓ	98	Ⓐ	Ⓑ	Ⓒ	Ⓓ
19	Ⓐ	Ⓑ	Ⓒ		39	Ⓐ	Ⓑ	Ⓒ	Ⓓ	59	Ⓐ	Ⓑ	Ⓒ	Ⓓ	79	Ⓐ	Ⓑ	Ⓒ	Ⓓ	99	Ⓐ	Ⓑ	Ⓒ	Ⓓ
20	Ⓐ	Ⓑ	Ⓒ		40	Ⓐ	Ⓑ	Ⓒ	Ⓓ	60	Ⓐ	Ⓑ	Ⓒ	Ⓓ	80	Ⓐ	Ⓑ	Ⓒ	Ⓓ	100	Ⓐ	Ⓑ	Ⓒ	Ⓓ

1. 사용 필기구 : 컴퓨터용 연필(연필을 제외한 사인펜, 볼펜 등은 사용 절대 불가)
2. 잘못된 필기구 사용과 〈보기〉의 올바른 표기 이외의 잘못된 표기로 한 경우에는 당 위원회의 OMR기기가 판독한 결과에 따르며 그 결과는 본인 책임입니다. 1개의 정답만 골라 아래의 올바른 표기대로 정확히 표기하여야 합니다.
   〈보기〉 올바른 표기 : ● 잘못된 표기 : ⊘ ✖ ◍
3. 답안지는 컴퓨터로 처리되므로 훼손하시면 안 되며, 상단의 타이밍마크(▌▌▌▌)부분을 찢거나, 낙서 등을 하면 본인에게 불이익이 발생할 수 있습니다.

Actual Test 2

LISTENING (Part I~IV)

NO.	ANSWER				NO.	ANSWER				NO.	ANSWER				NO.	ANSWER				NO.	ANSWER			
	A	B	C	D		A	B	C	D		A	B	C	D		A	B	C	D		A	B	C	D
1	Ⓐ	Ⓑ	Ⓒ	Ⓓ	21	Ⓐ	Ⓑ	Ⓒ		41	Ⓐ	Ⓑ	Ⓒ	Ⓓ	61	Ⓐ	Ⓑ	Ⓒ	Ⓓ	81	Ⓐ	Ⓑ	Ⓒ	Ⓓ
2	Ⓐ	Ⓑ	Ⓒ	Ⓓ	22	Ⓐ	Ⓑ	Ⓒ		42	Ⓐ	Ⓑ	Ⓒ	Ⓓ	62	Ⓐ	Ⓑ	Ⓒ	Ⓓ	82	Ⓐ	Ⓑ	Ⓒ	Ⓓ
3	Ⓐ	Ⓑ	Ⓒ	Ⓓ	23	Ⓐ	Ⓑ	Ⓒ		43	Ⓐ	Ⓑ	Ⓒ	Ⓓ	63	Ⓐ	Ⓑ	Ⓒ	Ⓓ	83	Ⓐ	Ⓑ	Ⓒ	Ⓓ
4	Ⓐ	Ⓑ	Ⓒ	Ⓓ	24	Ⓐ	Ⓑ	Ⓒ		44	Ⓐ	Ⓑ	Ⓒ	Ⓓ	64	Ⓐ	Ⓑ	Ⓒ	Ⓓ	84	Ⓐ	Ⓑ	Ⓒ	Ⓓ
5	Ⓐ	Ⓑ	Ⓒ	Ⓓ	25	Ⓐ	Ⓑ	Ⓒ		45	Ⓐ	Ⓑ	Ⓒ	Ⓓ	65	Ⓐ	Ⓑ	Ⓒ	Ⓓ	85	Ⓐ	Ⓑ	Ⓒ	Ⓓ
6	Ⓐ	Ⓑ	Ⓒ	Ⓓ	26	Ⓐ	Ⓑ	Ⓒ		46	Ⓐ	Ⓑ	Ⓒ	Ⓓ	66	Ⓐ	Ⓑ	Ⓒ	Ⓓ	86	Ⓐ	Ⓑ	Ⓒ	Ⓓ
7	Ⓐ	Ⓑ	Ⓒ		27	Ⓐ	Ⓑ	Ⓒ		47	Ⓐ	Ⓑ	Ⓒ	Ⓓ	67	Ⓐ	Ⓑ	Ⓒ	Ⓓ	87	Ⓐ	Ⓑ	Ⓒ	Ⓓ
8	Ⓐ	Ⓑ	Ⓒ		28	Ⓐ	Ⓑ	Ⓒ		48	Ⓐ	Ⓑ	Ⓒ	Ⓓ	68	Ⓐ	Ⓑ	Ⓒ	Ⓓ	88	Ⓐ	Ⓑ	Ⓒ	Ⓓ
9	Ⓐ	Ⓑ	Ⓒ		29	Ⓐ	Ⓑ	Ⓒ		49	Ⓐ	Ⓑ	Ⓒ	Ⓓ	69	Ⓐ	Ⓑ	Ⓒ	Ⓓ	89	Ⓐ	Ⓑ	Ⓒ	Ⓓ
10	Ⓐ	Ⓑ	Ⓒ		30	Ⓐ	Ⓑ	Ⓒ		50	Ⓐ	Ⓑ	Ⓒ	Ⓓ	70	Ⓐ	Ⓑ	Ⓒ	Ⓓ	90	Ⓐ	Ⓑ	Ⓒ	Ⓓ
11	Ⓐ	Ⓑ	Ⓒ		31	Ⓐ	Ⓑ	Ⓒ		51	Ⓐ	Ⓑ	Ⓒ	Ⓓ	71	Ⓐ	Ⓑ	Ⓒ	Ⓓ	91	Ⓐ	Ⓑ	Ⓒ	Ⓓ
12	Ⓐ	Ⓑ	Ⓒ		32	Ⓐ	Ⓑ	Ⓒ	Ⓓ	52	Ⓐ	Ⓑ	Ⓒ	Ⓓ	72	Ⓐ	Ⓑ	Ⓒ	Ⓓ	92	Ⓐ	Ⓑ	Ⓒ	Ⓓ
13	Ⓐ	Ⓑ	Ⓒ		33	Ⓐ	Ⓑ	Ⓒ	Ⓓ	53	Ⓐ	Ⓑ	Ⓒ	Ⓓ	73	Ⓐ	Ⓑ	Ⓒ	Ⓓ	93	Ⓐ	Ⓑ	Ⓒ	Ⓓ
14	Ⓐ	Ⓑ	Ⓒ		34	Ⓐ	Ⓑ	Ⓒ	Ⓓ	54	Ⓐ	Ⓑ	Ⓒ	Ⓓ	74	Ⓐ	Ⓑ	Ⓒ	Ⓓ	94	Ⓐ	Ⓑ	Ⓒ	Ⓓ
15	Ⓐ	Ⓑ	Ⓒ		35	Ⓐ	Ⓑ	Ⓒ	Ⓓ	55	Ⓐ	Ⓑ	Ⓒ	Ⓓ	75	Ⓐ	Ⓑ	Ⓒ	Ⓓ	95	Ⓐ	Ⓑ	Ⓒ	Ⓓ
16	Ⓐ	Ⓑ	Ⓒ		36	Ⓐ	Ⓑ	Ⓒ	Ⓓ	56	Ⓐ	Ⓑ	Ⓒ	Ⓓ	76	Ⓐ	Ⓑ	Ⓒ	Ⓓ	96	Ⓐ	Ⓑ	Ⓒ	Ⓓ
17	Ⓐ	Ⓑ	Ⓒ		37	Ⓐ	Ⓑ	Ⓒ	Ⓓ	57	Ⓐ	Ⓑ	Ⓒ	Ⓓ	77	Ⓐ	Ⓑ	Ⓒ	Ⓓ	97	Ⓐ	Ⓑ	Ⓒ	Ⓓ
18	Ⓐ	Ⓑ	Ⓒ		38	Ⓐ	Ⓑ	Ⓒ	Ⓓ	58	Ⓐ	Ⓑ	Ⓒ	Ⓓ	78	Ⓐ	Ⓑ	Ⓒ	Ⓓ	98	Ⓐ	Ⓑ	Ⓒ	Ⓓ
19	Ⓐ	Ⓑ	Ⓒ		39	Ⓐ	Ⓑ	Ⓒ	Ⓓ	59	Ⓐ	Ⓑ	Ⓒ	Ⓓ	79	Ⓐ	Ⓑ	Ⓒ	Ⓓ	99	Ⓐ	Ⓑ	Ⓒ	Ⓓ
20	Ⓐ	Ⓑ	Ⓒ		40	Ⓐ	Ⓑ	Ⓒ	Ⓓ	60	Ⓐ	Ⓑ	Ⓒ	Ⓓ	80	Ⓐ	Ⓑ	Ⓒ	Ⓓ	100	Ⓐ	Ⓑ	Ⓒ	Ⓓ

4. 감독관의 확인이 없거나 시험 종료 후에 답안 작성을 계속할 경우 시험 무효 처리됩니다.

*서약 내용을 읽으시고 확인란에 반드시 서명하십시오.

서 약	확 인
본인은 TOEIC 시험 문제의 일부 또는 전부를 유출하거나 어떠한 형태로든 타인에게 누설 공개하지 않을 것이며 인터넷 또는 인쇄물 등을 이용해 유포하거나 참고 자료로 활용하지 않을 것입니다. 또한 TOEIC 시험 부정 행위 처리 규정을 준수할 것을 서약합니다.	

ANSWER SHEET

응시일자 :　　　년　　　월　　　일

수험번호						

성명	한글	
	한자	
	영자	

좌석번호
Ⓐ Ⓑ Ⓒ Ⓓ Ⓔ ① ② ③ ④ ⑤ ⑥ ⑦

Actual Test 3

LISTENING (Part I~IV)

NO.	ANSWER				NO.	ANSWER				NO.	ANSWER				NO.	ANSWER				NO.	ANSWER			
	A	B	C	D		A	B	C	D		A	B	C	D		A	B	C	D		A	B	C	D
1	Ⓐ	Ⓑ	Ⓒ	Ⓓ	21	Ⓐ	Ⓑ	Ⓒ		41	Ⓐ	Ⓑ	Ⓒ	Ⓓ	61	Ⓐ	Ⓑ	Ⓒ	Ⓓ	81	Ⓐ	Ⓑ	Ⓒ	Ⓓ
2	Ⓐ	Ⓑ	Ⓒ	Ⓓ	22	Ⓐ	Ⓑ	Ⓒ		42	Ⓐ	Ⓑ	Ⓒ	Ⓓ	62	Ⓐ	Ⓑ	Ⓒ	Ⓓ	82	Ⓐ	Ⓑ	Ⓒ	Ⓓ
3	Ⓐ	Ⓑ	Ⓒ	Ⓓ	23	Ⓐ	Ⓑ	Ⓒ		43	Ⓐ	Ⓑ	Ⓒ	Ⓓ	63	Ⓐ	Ⓑ	Ⓒ	Ⓓ	83	Ⓐ	Ⓑ	Ⓒ	Ⓓ
4	Ⓐ	Ⓑ	Ⓒ	Ⓓ	24	Ⓐ	Ⓑ	Ⓒ		44	Ⓐ	Ⓑ	Ⓒ	Ⓓ	64	Ⓐ	Ⓑ	Ⓒ	Ⓓ	84	Ⓐ	Ⓑ	Ⓒ	Ⓓ
5	Ⓐ	Ⓑ	Ⓒ	Ⓓ	25	Ⓐ	Ⓑ	Ⓒ		45	Ⓐ	Ⓑ	Ⓒ	Ⓓ	65	Ⓐ	Ⓑ	Ⓒ	Ⓓ	85	Ⓐ	Ⓑ	Ⓒ	Ⓓ
6	Ⓐ	Ⓑ	Ⓒ	Ⓓ	26	Ⓐ	Ⓑ	Ⓒ		46	Ⓐ	Ⓑ	Ⓒ	Ⓓ	66	Ⓐ	Ⓑ	Ⓒ	Ⓓ	86	Ⓐ	Ⓑ	Ⓒ	Ⓓ
7	Ⓐ	Ⓑ	Ⓒ		27	Ⓐ	Ⓑ	Ⓒ		47	Ⓐ	Ⓑ	Ⓒ	Ⓓ	67	Ⓐ	Ⓑ	Ⓒ	Ⓓ	87	Ⓐ	Ⓑ	Ⓒ	Ⓓ
8	Ⓐ	Ⓑ	Ⓒ		28	Ⓐ	Ⓑ	Ⓒ		48	Ⓐ	Ⓑ	Ⓒ	Ⓓ	68	Ⓐ	Ⓑ	Ⓒ	Ⓓ	88	Ⓐ	Ⓑ	Ⓒ	Ⓓ
9	Ⓐ	Ⓑ	Ⓒ		29	Ⓐ	Ⓑ	Ⓒ		49	Ⓐ	Ⓑ	Ⓒ	Ⓓ	69	Ⓐ	Ⓑ	Ⓒ	Ⓓ	89	Ⓐ	Ⓑ	Ⓒ	Ⓓ
10	Ⓐ	Ⓑ	Ⓒ		30	Ⓐ	Ⓑ	Ⓒ		50	Ⓐ	Ⓑ	Ⓒ	Ⓓ	70	Ⓐ	Ⓑ	Ⓒ	Ⓓ	90	Ⓐ	Ⓑ	Ⓒ	Ⓓ
11	Ⓐ	Ⓑ	Ⓒ		31	Ⓐ	Ⓑ	Ⓒ		51	Ⓐ	Ⓑ	Ⓒ	Ⓓ	71	Ⓐ	Ⓑ	Ⓒ	Ⓓ	91	Ⓐ	Ⓑ	Ⓒ	Ⓓ
12	Ⓐ	Ⓑ	Ⓒ		32	Ⓐ	Ⓑ	Ⓒ	Ⓓ	52	Ⓐ	Ⓑ	Ⓒ	Ⓓ	72	Ⓐ	Ⓑ	Ⓒ	Ⓓ	92	Ⓐ	Ⓑ	Ⓒ	Ⓓ
13	Ⓐ	Ⓑ	Ⓒ		33	Ⓐ	Ⓑ	Ⓒ	Ⓓ	53	Ⓐ	Ⓑ	Ⓒ	Ⓓ	73	Ⓐ	Ⓑ	Ⓒ	Ⓓ	93	Ⓐ	Ⓑ	Ⓒ	Ⓓ
14	Ⓐ	Ⓑ	Ⓒ		34	Ⓐ	Ⓑ	Ⓒ	Ⓓ	54	Ⓐ	Ⓑ	Ⓒ	Ⓓ	74	Ⓐ	Ⓑ	Ⓒ	Ⓓ	94	Ⓐ	Ⓑ	Ⓒ	Ⓓ
15	Ⓐ	Ⓑ	Ⓒ		35	Ⓐ	Ⓑ	Ⓒ	Ⓓ	55	Ⓐ	Ⓑ	Ⓒ	Ⓓ	75	Ⓐ	Ⓑ	Ⓒ	Ⓓ	95	Ⓐ	Ⓑ	Ⓒ	Ⓓ
16	Ⓐ	Ⓑ	Ⓒ		36	Ⓐ	Ⓑ	Ⓒ	Ⓓ	56	Ⓐ	Ⓑ	Ⓒ	Ⓓ	76	Ⓐ	Ⓑ	Ⓒ	Ⓓ	96	Ⓐ	Ⓑ	Ⓒ	Ⓓ
17	Ⓐ	Ⓑ	Ⓒ		37	Ⓐ	Ⓑ	Ⓒ	Ⓓ	57	Ⓐ	Ⓑ	Ⓒ	Ⓓ	77	Ⓐ	Ⓑ	Ⓒ	Ⓓ	97	Ⓐ	Ⓑ	Ⓒ	Ⓓ
18	Ⓐ	Ⓑ	Ⓒ		38	Ⓐ	Ⓑ	Ⓒ	Ⓓ	58	Ⓐ	Ⓑ	Ⓒ	Ⓓ	78	Ⓐ	Ⓑ	Ⓒ	Ⓓ	98	Ⓐ	Ⓑ	Ⓒ	Ⓓ
19	Ⓐ	Ⓑ	Ⓒ		39	Ⓐ	Ⓑ	Ⓒ	Ⓓ	59	Ⓐ	Ⓑ	Ⓒ	Ⓓ	79	Ⓐ	Ⓑ	Ⓒ	Ⓓ	99	Ⓐ	Ⓑ	Ⓒ	Ⓓ
20	Ⓐ	Ⓑ	Ⓒ		40	Ⓐ	Ⓑ	Ⓒ	Ⓓ	60	Ⓐ	Ⓑ	Ⓒ	Ⓓ	80	Ⓐ	Ⓑ	Ⓒ	Ⓓ	100	Ⓐ	Ⓑ	Ⓒ	Ⓓ

1. 사용 필기구 : 컴퓨터용 연필(연필을 제외한 사인펜, 볼펜 등은 사용 절대 불가)
2. 잘못된 필기구 사용과 〈보기〉의 올바른 표기 이외의 잘못된 표기로 한 경우에는 당 위원회의 OMR기기가 판독한 결과에 따르며 그 결과는 본인 책임입니다. 1개의 정답만 골라 아래의 올바른 표기대로 정확히 표기하여야 합니다.
   〈보기〉 올바른 표기 : ●　　　잘못된 표기 : ✓ ⊗ ◍
3. 답안지는 컴퓨터로 처리되므로 훼손하시면 안 되며, 상단의 타이밍마크(▌▌▌▌)부분을 찢거나, 낙서 등을 하면 본인에게 불이익이 발생할 수 있습니다.

Actual Test 4

LISTENING (Part I~IV)

NO.	ANSWER				NO.	ANSWER				NO.	ANSWER				NO.	ANSWER				NO.	ANSWER			
	A	B	C	D		A	B	C	D		A	B	C	D		A	B	C	D		A	B	C	D
1	Ⓐ	Ⓑ	Ⓒ	Ⓓ	21	Ⓐ	Ⓑ	Ⓒ		41	Ⓐ	Ⓑ	Ⓒ	Ⓓ	61	Ⓐ	Ⓑ	Ⓒ	Ⓓ	81	Ⓐ	Ⓑ	Ⓒ	Ⓓ
2	Ⓐ	Ⓑ	Ⓒ	Ⓓ	22	Ⓐ	Ⓑ	Ⓒ		42	Ⓐ	Ⓑ	Ⓒ	Ⓓ	62	Ⓐ	Ⓑ	Ⓒ	Ⓓ	82	Ⓐ	Ⓑ	Ⓒ	Ⓓ
3	Ⓐ	Ⓑ	Ⓒ	Ⓓ	23	Ⓐ	Ⓑ	Ⓒ		43	Ⓐ	Ⓑ	Ⓒ	Ⓓ	63	Ⓐ	Ⓑ	Ⓒ	Ⓓ	83	Ⓐ	Ⓑ	Ⓒ	Ⓓ
4	Ⓐ	Ⓑ	Ⓒ	Ⓓ	24	Ⓐ	Ⓑ	Ⓒ		44	Ⓐ	Ⓑ	Ⓒ	Ⓓ	64	Ⓐ	Ⓑ	Ⓒ	Ⓓ	84	Ⓐ	Ⓑ	Ⓒ	Ⓓ
5	Ⓐ	Ⓑ	Ⓒ	Ⓓ	25	Ⓐ	Ⓑ	Ⓒ		45	Ⓐ	Ⓑ	Ⓒ	Ⓓ	65	Ⓐ	Ⓑ	Ⓒ	Ⓓ	85	Ⓐ	Ⓑ	Ⓒ	Ⓓ
6	Ⓐ	Ⓑ	Ⓒ	Ⓓ	26	Ⓐ	Ⓑ	Ⓒ		46	Ⓐ	Ⓑ	Ⓒ	Ⓓ	66	Ⓐ	Ⓑ	Ⓒ	Ⓓ	86	Ⓐ	Ⓑ	Ⓒ	Ⓓ
7	Ⓐ	Ⓑ	Ⓒ		27	Ⓐ	Ⓑ	Ⓒ		47	Ⓐ	Ⓑ	Ⓒ	Ⓓ	67	Ⓐ	Ⓑ	Ⓒ	Ⓓ	87	Ⓐ	Ⓑ	Ⓒ	Ⓓ
8	Ⓐ	Ⓑ	Ⓒ		28	Ⓐ	Ⓑ	Ⓒ		48	Ⓐ	Ⓑ	Ⓒ	Ⓓ	68	Ⓐ	Ⓑ	Ⓒ	Ⓓ	88	Ⓐ	Ⓑ	Ⓒ	Ⓓ
9	Ⓐ	Ⓑ	Ⓒ		29	Ⓐ	Ⓑ	Ⓒ		49	Ⓐ	Ⓑ	Ⓒ	Ⓓ	69	Ⓐ	Ⓑ	Ⓒ	Ⓓ	89	Ⓐ	Ⓑ	Ⓒ	Ⓓ
10	Ⓐ	Ⓑ	Ⓒ		30	Ⓐ	Ⓑ	Ⓒ		50	Ⓐ	Ⓑ	Ⓒ	Ⓓ	70	Ⓐ	Ⓑ	Ⓒ	Ⓓ	90	Ⓐ	Ⓑ	Ⓒ	Ⓓ
11	Ⓐ	Ⓑ	Ⓒ		31	Ⓐ	Ⓑ	Ⓒ		51	Ⓐ	Ⓑ	Ⓒ	Ⓓ	71	Ⓐ	Ⓑ	Ⓒ	Ⓓ	91	Ⓐ	Ⓑ	Ⓒ	Ⓓ
12	Ⓐ	Ⓑ	Ⓒ		32	Ⓐ	Ⓑ	Ⓒ	Ⓓ	52	Ⓐ	Ⓑ	Ⓒ	Ⓓ	72	Ⓐ	Ⓑ	Ⓒ	Ⓓ	92	Ⓐ	Ⓑ	Ⓒ	Ⓓ
13	Ⓐ	Ⓑ	Ⓒ		33	Ⓐ	Ⓑ	Ⓒ	Ⓓ	53	Ⓐ	Ⓑ	Ⓒ	Ⓓ	73	Ⓐ	Ⓑ	Ⓒ	Ⓓ	93	Ⓐ	Ⓑ	Ⓒ	Ⓓ
14	Ⓐ	Ⓑ	Ⓒ		34	Ⓐ	Ⓑ	Ⓒ	Ⓓ	54	Ⓐ	Ⓑ	Ⓒ	Ⓓ	74	Ⓐ	Ⓑ	Ⓒ	Ⓓ	94	Ⓐ	Ⓑ	Ⓒ	Ⓓ
15	Ⓐ	Ⓑ	Ⓒ		35	Ⓐ	Ⓑ	Ⓒ	Ⓓ	55	Ⓐ	Ⓑ	Ⓒ	Ⓓ	75	Ⓐ	Ⓑ	Ⓒ	Ⓓ	95	Ⓐ	Ⓑ	Ⓒ	Ⓓ
16	Ⓐ	Ⓑ	Ⓒ		36	Ⓐ	Ⓑ	Ⓒ	Ⓓ	56	Ⓐ	Ⓑ	Ⓒ	Ⓓ	76	Ⓐ	Ⓑ	Ⓒ	Ⓓ	96	Ⓐ	Ⓑ	Ⓒ	Ⓓ
17	Ⓐ	Ⓑ	Ⓒ		37	Ⓐ	Ⓑ	Ⓒ	Ⓓ	57	Ⓐ	Ⓑ	Ⓒ	Ⓓ	77	Ⓐ	Ⓑ	Ⓒ	Ⓓ	97	Ⓐ	Ⓑ	Ⓒ	Ⓓ
18	Ⓐ	Ⓑ	Ⓒ		38	Ⓐ	Ⓑ	Ⓒ	Ⓓ	58	Ⓐ	Ⓑ	Ⓒ	Ⓓ	78	Ⓐ	Ⓑ	Ⓒ	Ⓓ	98	Ⓐ	Ⓑ	Ⓒ	Ⓓ
19	Ⓐ	Ⓑ	Ⓒ		39	Ⓐ	Ⓑ	Ⓒ	Ⓓ	59	Ⓐ	Ⓑ	Ⓒ	Ⓓ	79	Ⓐ	Ⓑ	Ⓒ	Ⓓ	99	Ⓐ	Ⓑ	Ⓒ	Ⓓ
20	Ⓐ	Ⓑ	Ⓒ		40	Ⓐ	Ⓑ	Ⓒ	Ⓓ	60	Ⓐ	Ⓑ	Ⓒ	Ⓓ	80	Ⓐ	Ⓑ	Ⓒ	Ⓓ	100	Ⓐ	Ⓑ	Ⓒ	Ⓓ

4. 감독관의 확인이 없거나 시험 종료 후에 답안 작성을 계속할 경우 시험 무효 처리됩니다.

*서약 내용을 읽으시고 확인란에 반드시 서명하십시오.

서　약	확 인
본인은 TOEIC 시험 문제의 일부 또는 전부를 유출하거나 어떠한 형태로든 타인에게 누설 공개하지 않을 것이며 인터넷 또는 인쇄물 등을 이용해 유포하거나 참고 자료로 활용하지 않을 것입니다. 또한 TOEIC 시험 부정 행위 처리 규정을 준수할 것을 서약합니다.	

ANSWER SHEET

응시일자 : 년 월 일

수험번호						

성명	한글	
	한자	
	영자	

좌석번호
Ⓐ Ⓑ Ⓒ Ⓓ Ⓔ ① ② ③ ④ ⑤ ⑥ ⑦

Actual **Test 5**

LISTENING (Part I~IV)

NO.	ANSWER				NO.	ANSWER				NO.	ANSWER				NO.	ANSWER				NO.	ANSWER			
	A	B	C	D		A	B	C	D		A	B	C	D		A	B	C	D		A	B	C	D
1	Ⓐ	Ⓑ	Ⓒ	Ⓓ	21	Ⓐ	Ⓑ	Ⓒ		41	Ⓐ	Ⓑ	Ⓒ	Ⓓ	61	Ⓐ	Ⓑ	Ⓒ	Ⓓ	81	Ⓐ	Ⓑ	Ⓒ	Ⓓ
2	Ⓐ	Ⓑ	Ⓒ	Ⓓ	22	Ⓐ	Ⓑ	Ⓒ		42	Ⓐ	Ⓑ	Ⓒ	Ⓓ	62	Ⓐ	Ⓑ	Ⓒ	Ⓓ	82	Ⓐ	Ⓑ	Ⓒ	Ⓓ
3	Ⓐ	Ⓑ	Ⓒ	Ⓓ	23	Ⓐ	Ⓑ	Ⓒ		43	Ⓐ	Ⓑ	Ⓒ	Ⓓ	63	Ⓐ	Ⓑ	Ⓒ	Ⓓ	83	Ⓐ	Ⓑ	Ⓒ	Ⓓ
4	Ⓐ	Ⓑ	Ⓒ	Ⓓ	24	Ⓐ	Ⓑ	Ⓒ		44	Ⓐ	Ⓑ	Ⓒ	Ⓓ	64	Ⓐ	Ⓑ	Ⓒ	Ⓓ	84	Ⓐ	Ⓑ	Ⓒ	Ⓓ
5	Ⓐ	Ⓑ	Ⓒ	Ⓓ	25	Ⓐ	Ⓑ	Ⓒ		45	Ⓐ	Ⓑ	Ⓒ	Ⓓ	65	Ⓐ	Ⓑ	Ⓒ	Ⓓ	85	Ⓐ	Ⓑ	Ⓒ	Ⓓ
6	Ⓐ	Ⓑ	Ⓒ	Ⓓ	26	Ⓐ	Ⓑ	Ⓒ		46	Ⓐ	Ⓑ	Ⓒ	Ⓓ	66	Ⓐ	Ⓑ	Ⓒ	Ⓓ	86	Ⓐ	Ⓑ	Ⓒ	Ⓓ
7	Ⓐ	Ⓑ	Ⓒ		27	Ⓐ	Ⓑ	Ⓒ		47	Ⓐ	Ⓑ	Ⓒ	Ⓓ	67	Ⓐ	Ⓑ	Ⓒ	Ⓓ	87	Ⓐ	Ⓑ	Ⓒ	Ⓓ
8	Ⓐ	Ⓑ	Ⓒ		28	Ⓐ	Ⓑ	Ⓒ		48	Ⓐ	Ⓑ	Ⓒ	Ⓓ	68	Ⓐ	Ⓑ	Ⓒ	Ⓓ	88	Ⓐ	Ⓑ	Ⓒ	Ⓓ
9	Ⓐ	Ⓑ	Ⓒ		29	Ⓐ	Ⓑ	Ⓒ		49	Ⓐ	Ⓑ	Ⓒ	Ⓓ	69	Ⓐ	Ⓑ	Ⓒ	Ⓓ	89	Ⓐ	Ⓑ	Ⓒ	Ⓓ
10	Ⓐ	Ⓑ	Ⓒ		30	Ⓐ	Ⓑ	Ⓒ		50	Ⓐ	Ⓑ	Ⓒ	Ⓓ	70	Ⓐ	Ⓑ	Ⓒ	Ⓓ	90	Ⓐ	Ⓑ	Ⓒ	Ⓓ
11	Ⓐ	Ⓑ	Ⓒ		31	Ⓐ	Ⓑ	Ⓒ		51	Ⓐ	Ⓑ	Ⓒ	Ⓓ	71	Ⓐ	Ⓑ	Ⓒ	Ⓓ	91	Ⓐ	Ⓑ	Ⓒ	Ⓓ
12	Ⓐ	Ⓑ	Ⓒ		32	Ⓐ	Ⓑ	Ⓒ	Ⓓ	52	Ⓐ	Ⓑ	Ⓒ	Ⓓ	72	Ⓐ	Ⓑ	Ⓒ	Ⓓ	92	Ⓐ	Ⓑ	Ⓒ	Ⓓ
13	Ⓐ	Ⓑ	Ⓒ		33	Ⓐ	Ⓑ	Ⓒ	Ⓓ	53	Ⓐ	Ⓑ	Ⓒ	Ⓓ	73	Ⓐ	Ⓑ	Ⓒ	Ⓓ	93	Ⓐ	Ⓑ	Ⓒ	Ⓓ
14	Ⓐ	Ⓑ	Ⓒ		34	Ⓐ	Ⓑ	Ⓒ	Ⓓ	54	Ⓐ	Ⓑ	Ⓒ	Ⓓ	74	Ⓐ	Ⓑ	Ⓒ	Ⓓ	94	Ⓐ	Ⓑ	Ⓒ	Ⓓ
15	Ⓐ	Ⓑ	Ⓒ		35	Ⓐ	Ⓑ	Ⓒ	Ⓓ	55	Ⓐ	Ⓑ	Ⓒ	Ⓓ	75	Ⓐ	Ⓑ	Ⓒ	Ⓓ	95	Ⓐ	Ⓑ	Ⓒ	Ⓓ
16	Ⓐ	Ⓑ	Ⓒ		36	Ⓐ	Ⓑ	Ⓒ	Ⓓ	56	Ⓐ	Ⓑ	Ⓒ	Ⓓ	76	Ⓐ	Ⓑ	Ⓒ	Ⓓ	96	Ⓐ	Ⓑ	Ⓒ	Ⓓ
17	Ⓐ	Ⓑ	Ⓒ		37	Ⓐ	Ⓑ	Ⓒ	Ⓓ	57	Ⓐ	Ⓑ	Ⓒ	Ⓓ	77	Ⓐ	Ⓑ	Ⓒ	Ⓓ	97	Ⓐ	Ⓑ	Ⓒ	Ⓓ
18	Ⓐ	Ⓑ	Ⓒ		38	Ⓐ	Ⓑ	Ⓒ	Ⓓ	58	Ⓐ	Ⓑ	Ⓒ	Ⓓ	78	Ⓐ	Ⓑ	Ⓒ	Ⓓ	98	Ⓐ	Ⓑ	Ⓒ	Ⓓ
19	Ⓐ	Ⓑ	Ⓒ		39	Ⓐ	Ⓑ	Ⓒ	Ⓓ	59	Ⓐ	Ⓑ	Ⓒ	Ⓓ	79	Ⓐ	Ⓑ	Ⓒ	Ⓓ	99	Ⓐ	Ⓑ	Ⓒ	Ⓓ
20	Ⓐ	Ⓑ	Ⓒ		40	Ⓐ	Ⓑ	Ⓒ	Ⓓ	60	Ⓐ	Ⓑ	Ⓒ	Ⓓ	80	Ⓐ	Ⓑ	Ⓒ	Ⓓ	100	Ⓐ	Ⓑ	Ⓒ	Ⓓ

Actual **Test 6**

LISTENING (Part I~IV)

NO.	ANSWER				NO.	ANSWER				NO.	ANSWER				NO.	ANSWER				NO.	ANSWER			
	A	B	C	D		A	B	C	D		A	B	C	D		A	B	C	D		A	B	C	D
1	Ⓐ	Ⓑ	Ⓒ	Ⓓ	21	Ⓐ	Ⓑ	Ⓒ		41	Ⓐ	Ⓑ	Ⓒ	Ⓓ	61	Ⓐ	Ⓑ	Ⓒ	Ⓓ	81	Ⓐ	Ⓑ	Ⓒ	Ⓓ
2	Ⓐ	Ⓑ	Ⓒ	Ⓓ	22	Ⓐ	Ⓑ	Ⓒ		42	Ⓐ	Ⓑ	Ⓒ	Ⓓ	62	Ⓐ	Ⓑ	Ⓒ	Ⓓ	82	Ⓐ	Ⓑ	Ⓒ	Ⓓ
3	Ⓐ	Ⓑ	Ⓒ	Ⓓ	23	Ⓐ	Ⓑ	Ⓒ		43	Ⓐ	Ⓑ	Ⓒ	Ⓓ	63	Ⓐ	Ⓑ	Ⓒ	Ⓓ	83	Ⓐ	Ⓑ	Ⓒ	Ⓓ
4	Ⓐ	Ⓑ	Ⓒ	Ⓓ	24	Ⓐ	Ⓑ	Ⓒ		44	Ⓐ	Ⓑ	Ⓒ	Ⓓ	64	Ⓐ	Ⓑ	Ⓒ	Ⓓ	84	Ⓐ	Ⓑ	Ⓒ	Ⓓ
5	Ⓐ	Ⓑ	Ⓒ	Ⓓ	25	Ⓐ	Ⓑ	Ⓒ		45	Ⓐ	Ⓑ	Ⓒ	Ⓓ	65	Ⓐ	Ⓑ	Ⓒ	Ⓓ	85	Ⓐ	Ⓑ	Ⓒ	Ⓓ
6	Ⓐ	Ⓑ	Ⓒ	Ⓓ	26	Ⓐ	Ⓑ	Ⓒ		46	Ⓐ	Ⓑ	Ⓒ	Ⓓ	66	Ⓐ	Ⓑ	Ⓒ	Ⓓ	86	Ⓐ	Ⓑ	Ⓒ	Ⓓ
7	Ⓐ	Ⓑ	Ⓒ		27	Ⓐ	Ⓑ	Ⓒ		47	Ⓐ	Ⓑ	Ⓒ	Ⓓ	67	Ⓐ	Ⓑ	Ⓒ	Ⓓ	87	Ⓐ	Ⓑ	Ⓒ	Ⓓ
8	Ⓐ	Ⓑ	Ⓒ		28	Ⓐ	Ⓑ	Ⓒ		48	Ⓐ	Ⓑ	Ⓒ	Ⓓ	68	Ⓐ	Ⓑ	Ⓒ	Ⓓ	88	Ⓐ	Ⓑ	Ⓒ	Ⓓ
9	Ⓐ	Ⓑ	Ⓒ		29	Ⓐ	Ⓑ	Ⓒ		49	Ⓐ	Ⓑ	Ⓒ	Ⓓ	69	Ⓐ	Ⓑ	Ⓒ	Ⓓ	89	Ⓐ	Ⓑ	Ⓒ	Ⓓ
10	Ⓐ	Ⓑ	Ⓒ		30	Ⓐ	Ⓑ	Ⓒ		50	Ⓐ	Ⓑ	Ⓒ	Ⓓ	70	Ⓐ	Ⓑ	Ⓒ	Ⓓ	90	Ⓐ	Ⓑ	Ⓒ	Ⓓ
11	Ⓐ	Ⓑ	Ⓒ		31	Ⓐ	Ⓑ	Ⓒ		51	Ⓐ	Ⓑ	Ⓒ	Ⓓ	71	Ⓐ	Ⓑ	Ⓒ	Ⓓ	91	Ⓐ	Ⓑ	Ⓒ	Ⓓ
12	Ⓐ	Ⓑ	Ⓒ		32	Ⓐ	Ⓑ	Ⓒ	Ⓓ	52	Ⓐ	Ⓑ	Ⓒ	Ⓓ	72	Ⓐ	Ⓑ	Ⓒ	Ⓓ	92	Ⓐ	Ⓑ	Ⓒ	Ⓓ
13	Ⓐ	Ⓑ	Ⓒ		33	Ⓐ	Ⓑ	Ⓒ	Ⓓ	53	Ⓐ	Ⓑ	Ⓒ	Ⓓ	73	Ⓐ	Ⓑ	Ⓒ	Ⓓ	93	Ⓐ	Ⓑ	Ⓒ	Ⓓ
14	Ⓐ	Ⓑ	Ⓒ		34	Ⓐ	Ⓑ	Ⓒ	Ⓓ	54	Ⓐ	Ⓑ	Ⓒ	Ⓓ	74	Ⓐ	Ⓑ	Ⓒ	Ⓓ	94	Ⓐ	Ⓑ	Ⓒ	Ⓓ
15	Ⓐ	Ⓑ	Ⓒ		35	Ⓐ	Ⓑ	Ⓒ	Ⓓ	55	Ⓐ	Ⓑ	Ⓒ	Ⓓ	75	Ⓐ	Ⓑ	Ⓒ	Ⓓ	95	Ⓐ	Ⓑ	Ⓒ	Ⓓ
16	Ⓐ	Ⓑ	Ⓒ		36	Ⓐ	Ⓑ	Ⓒ	Ⓓ	56	Ⓐ	Ⓑ	Ⓒ	Ⓓ	76	Ⓐ	Ⓑ	Ⓒ	Ⓓ	96	Ⓐ	Ⓑ	Ⓒ	Ⓓ
17	Ⓐ	Ⓑ	Ⓒ		37	Ⓐ	Ⓑ	Ⓒ	Ⓓ	57	Ⓐ	Ⓑ	Ⓒ	Ⓓ	77	Ⓐ	Ⓑ	Ⓒ	Ⓓ	97	Ⓐ	Ⓑ	Ⓒ	Ⓓ
18	Ⓐ	Ⓑ	Ⓒ		38	Ⓐ	Ⓑ	Ⓒ	Ⓓ	58	Ⓐ	Ⓑ	Ⓒ	Ⓓ	78	Ⓐ	Ⓑ	Ⓒ	Ⓓ	98	Ⓐ	Ⓑ	Ⓒ	Ⓓ
19	Ⓐ	Ⓑ	Ⓒ		39	Ⓐ	Ⓑ	Ⓒ	Ⓓ	59	Ⓐ	Ⓑ	Ⓒ	Ⓓ	79	Ⓐ	Ⓑ	Ⓒ	Ⓓ	99	Ⓐ	Ⓑ	Ⓒ	Ⓓ
20	Ⓐ	Ⓑ	Ⓒ		40	Ⓐ	Ⓑ	Ⓒ	Ⓓ	60	Ⓐ	Ⓑ	Ⓒ	Ⓓ	80	Ⓐ	Ⓑ	Ⓒ	Ⓓ	100	Ⓐ	Ⓑ	Ⓒ	Ⓓ

1. 사용 필기구 : 컴퓨터용 연필(연필을 제외한 사인펜, 볼펜 등은 사용 절대 불가)
2. 잘못된 필기구 사용과 〈보기〉의 올바른 표기 이외의 잘못된 표기로 한 경우에는 당 위원회의 OMR기기가 판독한 결과에 따르며 그 결과는 본인 책임입니다. 1개의 정답만 골라 아래의 올바른 표기대로 정확히 표기하여야 합니다.
   〈보기〉 올바른 표기 : ● 잘못된 표기 : ✓ ✗ ◍
3. 답안지는 컴퓨터로 처리되므로 훼손하시면 안 되며, 상단의 타이밍마크(▮▮▮▮)부분을 찢거나, 낙서 등을 하면 본인에게 불이익이 발생할 수 있습니다.
4. 감독관의 확인이 없거나 시험 종료 후에 답안 작성을 계속할 경우 시험 무효 처리됩니다.

*서약 내용을 읽으시고 확인란에 반드시 서명하십시오.

서 약	확 인
본인은 TOEIC 시험 문제의 일부 또는 전부를 유출하거나 어떠한 형태로든 타인에게 누설 공개하지 않을 것이며 인터넷 또는 인쇄물 등을 이용해 유포하거나 참고 자료로 활용하지 않을 것입니다. 또한 TOEIC 시험 부정 행위 처리 규정을 준수할 것을 서약합니다.	

ANSWER SHEET

응시일자 : 년 월 일

수험번호						

성명	한글	
	한자	
	영자	

좌석번호
Ⓐ Ⓑ Ⓒ Ⓓ Ⓔ ① ② ③ ④ ⑤ ⑥ ⑦

Actual **Test 7**

LISTENING (Part I~IV)

NO.	ANSWER				NO.	ANSWER				NO.	ANSWER				NO.	ANSWER				NO.	ANSWER			
	A	B	C	D		A	B	C	D		A	B	C	D		A	B	C	D		A	B	C	D
1	Ⓐ	Ⓑ	Ⓒ	Ⓓ	21	Ⓐ	Ⓑ	Ⓒ		41	Ⓐ	Ⓑ	Ⓒ	Ⓓ	61	Ⓐ	Ⓑ	Ⓒ	Ⓓ	81	Ⓐ	Ⓑ	Ⓒ	Ⓓ
2	Ⓐ	Ⓑ	Ⓒ	Ⓓ	22	Ⓐ	Ⓑ	Ⓒ		42	Ⓐ	Ⓑ	Ⓒ	Ⓓ	62	Ⓐ	Ⓑ	Ⓒ	Ⓓ	82	Ⓐ	Ⓑ	Ⓒ	Ⓓ
3	Ⓐ	Ⓑ	Ⓒ	Ⓓ	23	Ⓐ	Ⓑ	Ⓒ		43	Ⓐ	Ⓑ	Ⓒ	Ⓓ	63	Ⓐ	Ⓑ	Ⓒ	Ⓓ	83	Ⓐ	Ⓑ	Ⓒ	Ⓓ
4	Ⓐ	Ⓑ	Ⓒ	Ⓓ	24	Ⓐ	Ⓑ	Ⓒ		44	Ⓐ	Ⓑ	Ⓒ	Ⓓ	64	Ⓐ	Ⓑ	Ⓒ	Ⓓ	84	Ⓐ	Ⓑ	Ⓒ	Ⓓ
5	Ⓐ	Ⓑ	Ⓒ	Ⓓ	25	Ⓐ	Ⓑ	Ⓒ		45	Ⓐ	Ⓑ	Ⓒ	Ⓓ	65	Ⓐ	Ⓑ	Ⓒ	Ⓓ	85	Ⓐ	Ⓑ	Ⓒ	Ⓓ
6	Ⓐ	Ⓑ	Ⓒ	Ⓓ	26	Ⓐ	Ⓑ	Ⓒ		46	Ⓐ	Ⓑ	Ⓒ	Ⓓ	66	Ⓐ	Ⓑ	Ⓒ	Ⓓ	86	Ⓐ	Ⓑ	Ⓒ	Ⓓ
7	Ⓐ	Ⓑ	Ⓒ		27	Ⓐ	Ⓑ	Ⓒ		47	Ⓐ	Ⓑ	Ⓒ	Ⓓ	67	Ⓐ	Ⓑ	Ⓒ	Ⓓ	87	Ⓐ	Ⓑ	Ⓒ	Ⓓ
8	Ⓐ	Ⓑ	Ⓒ		28	Ⓐ	Ⓑ	Ⓒ		48	Ⓐ	Ⓑ	Ⓒ	Ⓓ	68	Ⓐ	Ⓑ	Ⓒ	Ⓓ	88	Ⓐ	Ⓑ	Ⓒ	Ⓓ
9	Ⓐ	Ⓑ	Ⓒ		29	Ⓐ	Ⓑ	Ⓒ		49	Ⓐ	Ⓑ	Ⓒ	Ⓓ	69	Ⓐ	Ⓑ	Ⓒ	Ⓓ	89	Ⓐ	Ⓑ	Ⓒ	Ⓓ
10	Ⓐ	Ⓑ	Ⓒ		30	Ⓐ	Ⓑ	Ⓒ		50	Ⓐ	Ⓑ	Ⓒ	Ⓓ	70	Ⓐ	Ⓑ	Ⓒ	Ⓓ	90	Ⓐ	Ⓑ	Ⓒ	Ⓓ
11	Ⓐ	Ⓑ	Ⓒ		31	Ⓐ	Ⓑ	Ⓒ		51	Ⓐ	Ⓑ	Ⓒ	Ⓓ	71	Ⓐ	Ⓑ	Ⓒ	Ⓓ	91	Ⓐ	Ⓑ	Ⓒ	Ⓓ
12	Ⓐ	Ⓑ	Ⓒ		32	Ⓐ	Ⓑ	Ⓒ	Ⓓ	52	Ⓐ	Ⓑ	Ⓒ	Ⓓ	72	Ⓐ	Ⓑ	Ⓒ	Ⓓ	92	Ⓐ	Ⓑ	Ⓒ	Ⓓ
13	Ⓐ	Ⓑ	Ⓒ		33	Ⓐ	Ⓑ	Ⓒ	Ⓓ	53	Ⓐ	Ⓑ	Ⓒ	Ⓓ	73	Ⓐ	Ⓑ	Ⓒ	Ⓓ	93	Ⓐ	Ⓑ	Ⓒ	Ⓓ
14	Ⓐ	Ⓑ	Ⓒ		34	Ⓐ	Ⓑ	Ⓒ	Ⓓ	54	Ⓐ	Ⓑ	Ⓒ	Ⓓ	74	Ⓐ	Ⓑ	Ⓒ	Ⓓ	94	Ⓐ	Ⓑ	Ⓒ	Ⓓ
15	Ⓐ	Ⓑ	Ⓒ		35	Ⓐ	Ⓑ	Ⓒ	Ⓓ	55	Ⓐ	Ⓑ	Ⓒ	Ⓓ	75	Ⓐ	Ⓑ	Ⓒ	Ⓓ	95	Ⓐ	Ⓑ	Ⓒ	Ⓓ
16	Ⓐ	Ⓑ	Ⓒ		36	Ⓐ	Ⓑ	Ⓒ	Ⓓ	56	Ⓐ	Ⓑ	Ⓒ	Ⓓ	76	Ⓐ	Ⓑ	Ⓒ	Ⓓ	96	Ⓐ	Ⓑ	Ⓒ	Ⓓ
17	Ⓐ	Ⓑ	Ⓒ		37	Ⓐ	Ⓑ	Ⓒ	Ⓓ	57	Ⓐ	Ⓑ	Ⓒ	Ⓓ	77	Ⓐ	Ⓑ	Ⓒ	Ⓓ	97	Ⓐ	Ⓑ	Ⓒ	Ⓓ
18	Ⓐ	Ⓑ	Ⓒ		38	Ⓐ	Ⓑ	Ⓒ	Ⓓ	58	Ⓐ	Ⓑ	Ⓒ	Ⓓ	78	Ⓐ	Ⓑ	Ⓒ	Ⓓ	98	Ⓐ	Ⓑ	Ⓒ	Ⓓ
19	Ⓐ	Ⓑ	Ⓒ		39	Ⓐ	Ⓑ	Ⓒ	Ⓓ	59	Ⓐ	Ⓑ	Ⓒ	Ⓓ	79	Ⓐ	Ⓑ	Ⓒ	Ⓓ	99	Ⓐ	Ⓑ	Ⓒ	Ⓓ
20	Ⓐ	Ⓑ	Ⓒ		40	Ⓐ	Ⓑ	Ⓒ	Ⓓ	60	Ⓐ	Ⓑ	Ⓒ	Ⓓ	80	Ⓐ	Ⓑ	Ⓒ	Ⓓ	100	Ⓐ	Ⓑ	Ⓒ	Ⓓ

1. 사용 필기구 : 컴퓨터용 연필(연필을 제외한 사인펜, 볼펜 등은 사용 절대 불가)
2. 잘못된 필기구 사용과 〈보기〉의 올바른 표기 이외의 잘못된 표기로 한 경우에는 당 위원회의 OMR기기가 판독한 결과에 따르며 그 결과는 본인 책임입니다. 1개의 정답만 골라 아래의 올바른 표기대로 정확히 표기하여야 합니다.
   〈보기〉 올바른 표기 : ● 잘못된 표기 : ⊘ ✖ ◍
3. 답안지는 컴퓨터로 처리되므로 훼손하시면 안 되며, 상단의 타이밍마크(❙❙❙❙)부분을 찢거나, 낙서 등을 하면 본인에게 불이익이 발생할 수 있습니다.

Actual **Test 8**

LISTENING (Part I~IV)

NO.	ANSWER				NO.	ANSWER				NO.	ANSWER				NO.	ANSWER				NO.	ANSWER			
	A	B	C	D		A	B	C	D		A	B	C	D		A	B	C	D		A	B	C	D
1	Ⓐ	Ⓑ	Ⓒ	Ⓓ	21	Ⓐ	Ⓑ	Ⓒ		41	Ⓐ	Ⓑ	Ⓒ	Ⓓ	61	Ⓐ	Ⓑ	Ⓒ	Ⓓ	81	Ⓐ	Ⓑ	Ⓒ	Ⓓ
2	Ⓐ	Ⓑ	Ⓒ	Ⓓ	22	Ⓐ	Ⓑ	Ⓒ		42	Ⓐ	Ⓑ	Ⓒ	Ⓓ	62	Ⓐ	Ⓑ	Ⓒ	Ⓓ	82	Ⓐ	Ⓑ	Ⓒ	Ⓓ
3	Ⓐ	Ⓑ	Ⓒ	Ⓓ	23	Ⓐ	Ⓑ	Ⓒ		43	Ⓐ	Ⓑ	Ⓒ	Ⓓ	63	Ⓐ	Ⓑ	Ⓒ	Ⓓ	83	Ⓐ	Ⓑ	Ⓒ	Ⓓ
4	Ⓐ	Ⓑ	Ⓒ	Ⓓ	24	Ⓐ	Ⓑ	Ⓒ		44	Ⓐ	Ⓑ	Ⓒ	Ⓓ	64	Ⓐ	Ⓑ	Ⓒ	Ⓓ	84	Ⓐ	Ⓑ	Ⓒ	Ⓓ
5	Ⓐ	Ⓑ	Ⓒ	Ⓓ	25	Ⓐ	Ⓑ	Ⓒ		45	Ⓐ	Ⓑ	Ⓒ	Ⓓ	65	Ⓐ	Ⓑ	Ⓒ	Ⓓ	85	Ⓐ	Ⓑ	Ⓒ	Ⓓ
6	Ⓐ	Ⓑ	Ⓒ	Ⓓ	26	Ⓐ	Ⓑ	Ⓒ		46	Ⓐ	Ⓑ	Ⓒ	Ⓓ	66	Ⓐ	Ⓑ	Ⓒ	Ⓓ	86	Ⓐ	Ⓑ	Ⓒ	Ⓓ
7	Ⓐ	Ⓑ	Ⓒ		27	Ⓐ	Ⓑ	Ⓒ		47	Ⓐ	Ⓑ	Ⓒ	Ⓓ	67	Ⓐ	Ⓑ	Ⓒ	Ⓓ	87	Ⓐ	Ⓑ	Ⓒ	Ⓓ
8	Ⓐ	Ⓑ	Ⓒ		28	Ⓐ	Ⓑ	Ⓒ		48	Ⓐ	Ⓑ	Ⓒ	Ⓓ	68	Ⓐ	Ⓑ	Ⓒ	Ⓓ	88	Ⓐ	Ⓑ	Ⓒ	Ⓓ
9	Ⓐ	Ⓑ	Ⓒ		29	Ⓐ	Ⓑ	Ⓒ		49	Ⓐ	Ⓑ	Ⓒ	Ⓓ	69	Ⓐ	Ⓑ	Ⓒ	Ⓓ	89	Ⓐ	Ⓑ	Ⓒ	Ⓓ
10	Ⓐ	Ⓑ	Ⓒ		30	Ⓐ	Ⓑ	Ⓒ		50	Ⓐ	Ⓑ	Ⓒ	Ⓓ	70	Ⓐ	Ⓑ	Ⓒ	Ⓓ	90	Ⓐ	Ⓑ	Ⓒ	Ⓓ
11	Ⓐ	Ⓑ	Ⓒ		31	Ⓐ	Ⓑ	Ⓒ		51	Ⓐ	Ⓑ	Ⓒ	Ⓓ	71	Ⓐ	Ⓑ	Ⓒ	Ⓓ	91	Ⓐ	Ⓑ	Ⓒ	Ⓓ
12	Ⓐ	Ⓑ	Ⓒ		32	Ⓐ	Ⓑ	Ⓒ	Ⓓ	52	Ⓐ	Ⓑ	Ⓒ	Ⓓ	72	Ⓐ	Ⓑ	Ⓒ	Ⓓ	92	Ⓐ	Ⓑ	Ⓒ	Ⓓ
13	Ⓐ	Ⓑ	Ⓒ		33	Ⓐ	Ⓑ	Ⓒ	Ⓓ	53	Ⓐ	Ⓑ	Ⓒ	Ⓓ	73	Ⓐ	Ⓑ	Ⓒ	Ⓓ	93	Ⓐ	Ⓑ	Ⓒ	Ⓓ
14	Ⓐ	Ⓑ	Ⓒ		34	Ⓐ	Ⓑ	Ⓒ	Ⓓ	54	Ⓐ	Ⓑ	Ⓒ	Ⓓ	74	Ⓐ	Ⓑ	Ⓒ	Ⓓ	94	Ⓐ	Ⓑ	Ⓒ	Ⓓ
15	Ⓐ	Ⓑ	Ⓒ		35	Ⓐ	Ⓑ	Ⓒ	Ⓓ	55	Ⓐ	Ⓑ	Ⓒ	Ⓓ	75	Ⓐ	Ⓑ	Ⓒ	Ⓓ	95	Ⓐ	Ⓑ	Ⓒ	Ⓓ
16	Ⓐ	Ⓑ	Ⓒ		36	Ⓐ	Ⓑ	Ⓒ	Ⓓ	56	Ⓐ	Ⓑ	Ⓒ	Ⓓ	76	Ⓐ	Ⓑ	Ⓒ	Ⓓ	96	Ⓐ	Ⓑ	Ⓒ	Ⓓ
17	Ⓐ	Ⓑ	Ⓒ		37	Ⓐ	Ⓑ	Ⓒ	Ⓓ	57	Ⓐ	Ⓑ	Ⓒ	Ⓓ	77	Ⓐ	Ⓑ	Ⓒ	Ⓓ	97	Ⓐ	Ⓑ	Ⓒ	Ⓓ
18	Ⓐ	Ⓑ	Ⓒ		38	Ⓐ	Ⓑ	Ⓒ	Ⓓ	58	Ⓐ	Ⓑ	Ⓒ	Ⓓ	78	Ⓐ	Ⓑ	Ⓒ	Ⓓ	98	Ⓐ	Ⓑ	Ⓒ	Ⓓ
19	Ⓐ	Ⓑ	Ⓒ		39	Ⓐ	Ⓑ	Ⓒ	Ⓓ	59	Ⓐ	Ⓑ	Ⓒ	Ⓓ	79	Ⓐ	Ⓑ	Ⓒ	Ⓓ	99	Ⓐ	Ⓑ	Ⓒ	Ⓓ
20	Ⓐ	Ⓑ	Ⓒ		40	Ⓐ	Ⓑ	Ⓒ	Ⓓ	60	Ⓐ	Ⓑ	Ⓒ	Ⓓ	80	Ⓐ	Ⓑ	Ⓒ	Ⓓ	100	Ⓐ	Ⓑ	Ⓒ	Ⓓ

4. 감독관의 확인이 없거나 시험 종료 후에 답안 작성을 계속할 경우 시험 무효 처리됩니다.

*서약 내용을 읽으시고 확인란에 반드시 서명하십시오.

서 약	확 인
본인은 TOEIC 시험 문제의 일부 또는 전부를 유출하거나 어떠한 형태로든 타인에게 누설 공개하지 않을 것이며 인터넷 또는 인쇄물 등을 이용해 유포하거나 참고 자료로 활용하지 않을 것입니다. 또한 TOEIC 시험 부정 행위 처리 규정을 준수할 것을 서약합니다.	

ANSWER SHEET

응시일자 : 년 월 일

수험번호						

성명	한글	
	한자	
	영자	

좌석번호
Ⓐ Ⓑ Ⓒ Ⓓ Ⓔ ① ② ③ ④ ⑤ ⑥ ⑦

Actual Test 9

LISTENING (Part I~IV)

NO.	ANSWER A B C D	NO.	ANSWER A B C D	NO.	ANSWER A B C D	NO.	ANSWER A B C D	NO.	ANSWER A B C D
1	Ⓐ Ⓑ Ⓒ Ⓓ	21	Ⓐ Ⓑ Ⓒ	41	Ⓐ Ⓑ Ⓒ Ⓓ	61	Ⓐ Ⓑ Ⓒ Ⓓ	81	Ⓐ Ⓑ Ⓒ Ⓓ
2	Ⓐ Ⓑ Ⓒ Ⓓ	22	Ⓐ Ⓑ Ⓒ	42	Ⓐ Ⓑ Ⓒ Ⓓ	62	Ⓐ Ⓑ Ⓒ Ⓓ	82	Ⓐ Ⓑ Ⓒ Ⓓ
3	Ⓐ Ⓑ Ⓒ Ⓓ	23	Ⓐ Ⓑ Ⓒ	43	Ⓐ Ⓑ Ⓒ Ⓓ	63	Ⓐ Ⓑ Ⓒ Ⓓ	83	Ⓐ Ⓑ Ⓒ Ⓓ
4	Ⓐ Ⓑ Ⓒ Ⓓ	24	Ⓐ Ⓑ Ⓒ	44	Ⓐ Ⓑ Ⓒ Ⓓ	64	Ⓐ Ⓑ Ⓒ Ⓓ	84	Ⓐ Ⓑ Ⓒ Ⓓ
5	Ⓐ Ⓑ Ⓒ Ⓓ	25	Ⓐ Ⓑ Ⓒ	45	Ⓐ Ⓑ Ⓒ Ⓓ	65	Ⓐ Ⓑ Ⓒ Ⓓ	85	Ⓐ Ⓑ Ⓒ Ⓓ
6	Ⓐ Ⓑ Ⓒ Ⓓ	26	Ⓐ Ⓑ Ⓒ	46	Ⓐ Ⓑ Ⓒ Ⓓ	66	Ⓐ Ⓑ Ⓒ Ⓓ	86	Ⓐ Ⓑ Ⓒ Ⓓ
7	Ⓐ Ⓑ Ⓒ	27	Ⓐ Ⓑ Ⓒ	47	Ⓐ Ⓑ Ⓒ Ⓓ	67	Ⓐ Ⓑ Ⓒ Ⓓ	87	Ⓐ Ⓑ Ⓒ Ⓓ
8	Ⓐ Ⓑ Ⓒ	28	Ⓐ Ⓑ Ⓒ	48	Ⓐ Ⓑ Ⓒ Ⓓ	68	Ⓐ Ⓑ Ⓒ Ⓓ	88	Ⓐ Ⓑ Ⓒ Ⓓ
9	Ⓐ Ⓑ Ⓒ	29	Ⓐ Ⓑ Ⓒ	49	Ⓐ Ⓑ Ⓒ Ⓓ	69	Ⓐ Ⓑ Ⓒ Ⓓ	89	Ⓐ Ⓑ Ⓒ Ⓓ
10	Ⓐ Ⓑ Ⓒ	30	Ⓐ Ⓑ Ⓒ	50	Ⓐ Ⓑ Ⓒ Ⓓ	70	Ⓐ Ⓑ Ⓒ Ⓓ	90	Ⓐ Ⓑ Ⓒ Ⓓ
11	Ⓐ Ⓑ Ⓒ	31	Ⓐ Ⓑ Ⓒ	51	Ⓐ Ⓑ Ⓒ Ⓓ	71	Ⓐ Ⓑ Ⓒ Ⓓ	91	Ⓐ Ⓑ Ⓒ Ⓓ
12	Ⓐ Ⓑ Ⓒ	32	Ⓐ Ⓑ Ⓒ Ⓓ	52	Ⓐ Ⓑ Ⓒ Ⓓ	72	Ⓐ Ⓑ Ⓒ Ⓓ	92	Ⓐ Ⓑ Ⓒ Ⓓ
13	Ⓐ Ⓑ Ⓒ	33	Ⓐ Ⓑ Ⓒ Ⓓ	53	Ⓐ Ⓑ Ⓒ Ⓓ	73	Ⓐ Ⓑ Ⓒ Ⓓ	93	Ⓐ Ⓑ Ⓒ Ⓓ
14	Ⓐ Ⓑ Ⓒ	34	Ⓐ Ⓑ Ⓒ Ⓓ	54	Ⓐ Ⓑ Ⓒ Ⓓ	74	Ⓐ Ⓑ Ⓒ Ⓓ	94	Ⓐ Ⓑ Ⓒ Ⓓ
15	Ⓐ Ⓑ Ⓒ	35	Ⓐ Ⓑ Ⓒ Ⓓ	55	Ⓐ Ⓑ Ⓒ Ⓓ	75	Ⓐ Ⓑ Ⓒ Ⓓ	95	Ⓐ Ⓑ Ⓒ Ⓓ
16	Ⓐ Ⓑ Ⓒ	36	Ⓐ Ⓑ Ⓒ Ⓓ	56	Ⓐ Ⓑ Ⓒ Ⓓ	76	Ⓐ Ⓑ Ⓒ Ⓓ	96	Ⓐ Ⓑ Ⓒ Ⓓ
17	Ⓐ Ⓑ Ⓒ	37	Ⓐ Ⓑ Ⓒ Ⓓ	57	Ⓐ Ⓑ Ⓒ Ⓓ	77	Ⓐ Ⓑ Ⓒ Ⓓ	97	Ⓐ Ⓑ Ⓒ Ⓓ
18	Ⓐ Ⓑ Ⓒ	38	Ⓐ Ⓑ Ⓒ Ⓓ	58	Ⓐ Ⓑ Ⓒ Ⓓ	78	Ⓐ Ⓑ Ⓒ Ⓓ	98	Ⓐ Ⓑ Ⓒ Ⓓ
19	Ⓐ Ⓑ Ⓒ	39	Ⓐ Ⓑ Ⓒ Ⓓ	59	Ⓐ Ⓑ Ⓒ Ⓓ	79	Ⓐ Ⓑ Ⓒ Ⓓ	99	Ⓐ Ⓑ Ⓒ Ⓓ
20	Ⓐ Ⓑ Ⓒ	40	Ⓐ Ⓑ Ⓒ Ⓓ	60	Ⓐ Ⓑ Ⓒ Ⓓ	80	Ⓐ Ⓑ Ⓒ Ⓓ	100	Ⓐ Ⓑ Ⓒ Ⓓ

1. 사용 필기구 : 컴퓨터용 연필(연필을 제외한 사인펜, 볼펜 등은 사용 절대 불가)
2. 잘못된 필기구 사용과 〈보기〉의 올바른 표기 이외의 잘못된 표기로 한 경우에는 당 위원회의 OMR기기가 판독한 결과에 따르며 그 결과는 본인 책임입니다. 1개의 정답만 골라 아래의 올바른 표기대로 정확히 표기하여야 합니다.
   〈보기〉 올바른 표기 : ● 잘못된 표기 : ✔ ✖ ▨
3. 답안지는 컴퓨터로 처리되므로 훼손하시면 안 되며, 상단의 타이밍마크(▮▮▮▮)부분을 찢거나, 낙서 등을 하면 본인에게 불이익이 발생할 수 있습니다.

Actual Test 10

LISTENING (Part I~IV)

NO.	ANSWER A B C D	NO.	ANSWER A B C D	NO.	ANSWER A B C D	NO.	ANSWER A B C D	NO.	ANSWER A B C D
1	Ⓐ Ⓑ Ⓒ Ⓓ	21	Ⓐ Ⓑ Ⓒ	41	Ⓐ Ⓑ Ⓒ Ⓓ	61	Ⓐ Ⓑ Ⓒ Ⓓ	81	Ⓐ Ⓑ Ⓒ Ⓓ
2	Ⓐ Ⓑ Ⓒ Ⓓ	22	Ⓐ Ⓑ Ⓒ	42	Ⓐ Ⓑ Ⓒ Ⓓ	62	Ⓐ Ⓑ Ⓒ Ⓓ	82	Ⓐ Ⓑ Ⓒ Ⓓ
3	Ⓐ Ⓑ Ⓒ Ⓓ	23	Ⓐ Ⓑ Ⓒ	43	Ⓐ Ⓑ Ⓒ Ⓓ	63	Ⓐ Ⓑ Ⓒ Ⓓ	83	Ⓐ Ⓑ Ⓒ Ⓓ
4	Ⓐ Ⓑ Ⓒ Ⓓ	24	Ⓐ Ⓑ Ⓒ	44	Ⓐ Ⓑ Ⓒ Ⓓ	64	Ⓐ Ⓑ Ⓒ Ⓓ	84	Ⓐ Ⓑ Ⓒ Ⓓ
5	Ⓐ Ⓑ Ⓒ Ⓓ	25	Ⓐ Ⓑ Ⓒ	45	Ⓐ Ⓑ Ⓒ Ⓓ	65	Ⓐ Ⓑ Ⓒ Ⓓ	85	Ⓐ Ⓑ Ⓒ Ⓓ
6	Ⓐ Ⓑ Ⓒ Ⓓ	26	Ⓐ Ⓑ Ⓒ	46	Ⓐ Ⓑ Ⓒ Ⓓ	66	Ⓐ Ⓑ Ⓒ Ⓓ	86	Ⓐ Ⓑ Ⓒ Ⓓ
7	Ⓐ Ⓑ Ⓒ	27	Ⓐ Ⓑ Ⓒ	47	Ⓐ Ⓑ Ⓒ Ⓓ	67	Ⓐ Ⓑ Ⓒ Ⓓ	87	Ⓐ Ⓑ Ⓒ Ⓓ
8	Ⓐ Ⓑ Ⓒ	28	Ⓐ Ⓑ Ⓒ	48	Ⓐ Ⓑ Ⓒ Ⓓ	68	Ⓐ Ⓑ Ⓒ Ⓓ	88	Ⓐ Ⓑ Ⓒ Ⓓ
9	Ⓐ Ⓑ Ⓒ	29	Ⓐ Ⓑ Ⓒ	49	Ⓐ Ⓑ Ⓒ Ⓓ	69	Ⓐ Ⓑ Ⓒ Ⓓ	89	Ⓐ Ⓑ Ⓒ Ⓓ
10	Ⓐ Ⓑ Ⓒ	30	Ⓐ Ⓑ Ⓒ	50	Ⓐ Ⓑ Ⓒ Ⓓ	70	Ⓐ Ⓑ Ⓒ Ⓓ	90	Ⓐ Ⓑ Ⓒ Ⓓ
11	Ⓐ Ⓑ Ⓒ	31	Ⓐ Ⓑ Ⓒ	51	Ⓐ Ⓑ Ⓒ Ⓓ	71	Ⓐ Ⓑ Ⓒ Ⓓ	91	Ⓐ Ⓑ Ⓒ Ⓓ
12	Ⓐ Ⓑ Ⓒ	32	Ⓐ Ⓑ Ⓒ Ⓓ	52	Ⓐ Ⓑ Ⓒ Ⓓ	72	Ⓐ Ⓑ Ⓒ Ⓓ	92	Ⓐ Ⓑ Ⓒ Ⓓ
13	Ⓐ Ⓑ Ⓒ	33	Ⓐ Ⓑ Ⓒ Ⓓ	53	Ⓐ Ⓑ Ⓒ Ⓓ	73	Ⓐ Ⓑ Ⓒ Ⓓ	93	Ⓐ Ⓑ Ⓒ Ⓓ
14	Ⓐ Ⓑ Ⓒ	34	Ⓐ Ⓑ Ⓒ Ⓓ	54	Ⓐ Ⓑ Ⓒ Ⓓ	74	Ⓐ Ⓑ Ⓒ Ⓓ	94	Ⓐ Ⓑ Ⓒ Ⓓ
15	Ⓐ Ⓑ Ⓒ	35	Ⓐ Ⓑ Ⓒ Ⓓ	55	Ⓐ Ⓑ Ⓒ Ⓓ	75	Ⓐ Ⓑ Ⓒ Ⓓ	95	Ⓐ Ⓑ Ⓒ Ⓓ
16	Ⓐ Ⓑ Ⓒ	36	Ⓐ Ⓑ Ⓒ Ⓓ	56	Ⓐ Ⓑ Ⓒ Ⓓ	76	Ⓐ Ⓑ Ⓒ Ⓓ	96	Ⓐ Ⓑ Ⓒ Ⓓ
17	Ⓐ Ⓑ Ⓒ	37	Ⓐ Ⓑ Ⓒ Ⓓ	57	Ⓐ Ⓑ Ⓒ Ⓓ	77	Ⓐ Ⓑ Ⓒ Ⓓ	97	Ⓐ Ⓑ Ⓒ Ⓓ
18	Ⓐ Ⓑ Ⓒ	38	Ⓐ Ⓑ Ⓒ Ⓓ	58	Ⓐ Ⓑ Ⓒ Ⓓ	78	Ⓐ Ⓑ Ⓒ Ⓓ	98	Ⓐ Ⓑ Ⓒ Ⓓ
19	Ⓐ Ⓑ Ⓒ	39	Ⓐ Ⓑ Ⓒ Ⓓ	59	Ⓐ Ⓑ Ⓒ Ⓓ	79	Ⓐ Ⓑ Ⓒ Ⓓ	99	Ⓐ Ⓑ Ⓒ Ⓓ
20	Ⓐ Ⓑ Ⓒ	40	Ⓐ Ⓑ Ⓒ Ⓓ	60	Ⓐ Ⓑ Ⓒ Ⓓ	80	Ⓐ Ⓑ Ⓒ Ⓓ	100	Ⓐ Ⓑ Ⓒ Ⓓ

4. 감독관의 확인이 없거나 시험 종료 후에 답안 작성을 계속할 경우 시험 무효 처리됩니다.

＊서약 내용을 읽으시고 확인란에 반드시 서명하십시오.

서 약	확 인
본인은 TOEIC 시험 문제의 일부 또는 전부를 유출하거나 어떠한 형태로든 타인에게 누설 공개하지 않을 것이며 인터넷 또는 인쇄물 등을 이용해 유포하거나 참고 자료로 활용하지 않을 것입니다. 또한 TOEIC 시험 부정 행위 처리 규정을 준수할 것을 서약합니다.	

ANSWER SHEET

응시일자 :　　년　　월　　일

수험번호						

성명	한글	
	한자	
	영자	

좌석번호
Ⓐ Ⓑ Ⓒ Ⓓ Ⓔ ① ② ③ ④ ⑤ ⑥ ⑦

Actual **Test 11**

LISTENING (Part I~IV)

NO.	A	B	C	D	NO.	A	B	C	D	NO.	A	B	C	D	NO.	A	B	C	D	NO.	A	B	C	D
1	Ⓐ	Ⓑ	Ⓒ	Ⓓ	21	Ⓐ	Ⓑ	Ⓒ		41	Ⓐ	Ⓑ	Ⓒ	Ⓓ	61	Ⓐ	Ⓑ	Ⓒ	Ⓓ	81	Ⓐ	Ⓑ	Ⓒ	Ⓓ
2	Ⓐ	Ⓑ	Ⓒ	Ⓓ	22	Ⓐ	Ⓑ	Ⓒ		42	Ⓐ	Ⓑ	Ⓒ	Ⓓ	62	Ⓐ	Ⓑ	Ⓒ	Ⓓ	82	Ⓐ	Ⓑ	Ⓒ	Ⓓ
3	Ⓐ	Ⓑ	Ⓒ	Ⓓ	23	Ⓐ	Ⓑ	Ⓒ		43	Ⓐ	Ⓑ	Ⓒ	Ⓓ	63	Ⓐ	Ⓑ	Ⓒ	Ⓓ	83	Ⓐ	Ⓑ	Ⓒ	Ⓓ
4	Ⓐ	Ⓑ	Ⓒ	Ⓓ	24	Ⓐ	Ⓑ	Ⓒ		44	Ⓐ	Ⓑ	Ⓒ	Ⓓ	64	Ⓐ	Ⓑ	Ⓒ	Ⓓ	84	Ⓐ	Ⓑ	Ⓒ	Ⓓ
5	Ⓐ	Ⓑ	Ⓒ	Ⓓ	25	Ⓐ	Ⓑ	Ⓒ		45	Ⓐ	Ⓑ	Ⓒ	Ⓓ	65	Ⓐ	Ⓑ	Ⓒ	Ⓓ	85	Ⓐ	Ⓑ	Ⓒ	Ⓓ
6	Ⓐ	Ⓑ	Ⓒ	Ⓓ	26	Ⓐ	Ⓑ	Ⓒ		46	Ⓐ	Ⓑ	Ⓒ	Ⓓ	66	Ⓐ	Ⓑ	Ⓒ	Ⓓ	86	Ⓐ	Ⓑ	Ⓒ	Ⓓ
7	Ⓐ	Ⓑ	Ⓒ		27	Ⓐ	Ⓑ	Ⓒ		47	Ⓐ	Ⓑ	Ⓒ	Ⓓ	67	Ⓐ	Ⓑ	Ⓒ	Ⓓ	87	Ⓐ	Ⓑ	Ⓒ	Ⓓ
8	Ⓐ	Ⓑ	Ⓒ		28	Ⓐ	Ⓑ	Ⓒ		48	Ⓐ	Ⓑ	Ⓒ	Ⓓ	68	Ⓐ	Ⓑ	Ⓒ	Ⓓ	88	Ⓐ	Ⓑ	Ⓒ	Ⓓ
9	Ⓐ	Ⓑ	Ⓒ		29	Ⓐ	Ⓑ	Ⓒ		49	Ⓐ	Ⓑ	Ⓒ	Ⓓ	69	Ⓐ	Ⓑ	Ⓒ	Ⓓ	89	Ⓐ	Ⓑ	Ⓒ	Ⓓ
10	Ⓐ	Ⓑ	Ⓒ		30	Ⓐ	Ⓑ	Ⓒ		50	Ⓐ	Ⓑ	Ⓒ	Ⓓ	70	Ⓐ	Ⓑ	Ⓒ	Ⓓ	90	Ⓐ	Ⓑ	Ⓒ	Ⓓ
11	Ⓐ	Ⓑ	Ⓒ		31	Ⓐ	Ⓑ	Ⓒ		51	Ⓐ	Ⓑ	Ⓒ	Ⓓ	71	Ⓐ	Ⓑ	Ⓒ	Ⓓ	91	Ⓐ	Ⓑ	Ⓒ	Ⓓ
12	Ⓐ	Ⓑ	Ⓒ		32	Ⓐ	Ⓑ	Ⓒ	Ⓓ	52	Ⓐ	Ⓑ	Ⓒ	Ⓓ	72	Ⓐ	Ⓑ	Ⓒ	Ⓓ	92	Ⓐ	Ⓑ	Ⓒ	Ⓓ
13	Ⓐ	Ⓑ	Ⓒ		33	Ⓐ	Ⓑ	Ⓒ	Ⓓ	53	Ⓐ	Ⓑ	Ⓒ	Ⓓ	73	Ⓐ	Ⓑ	Ⓒ	Ⓓ	93	Ⓐ	Ⓑ	Ⓒ	Ⓓ
14	Ⓐ	Ⓑ	Ⓒ		34	Ⓐ	Ⓑ	Ⓒ	Ⓓ	54	Ⓐ	Ⓑ	Ⓒ	Ⓓ	74	Ⓐ	Ⓑ	Ⓒ	Ⓓ	94	Ⓐ	Ⓑ	Ⓒ	Ⓓ
15	Ⓐ	Ⓑ	Ⓒ		35	Ⓐ	Ⓑ	Ⓒ	Ⓓ	55	Ⓐ	Ⓑ	Ⓒ	Ⓓ	75	Ⓐ	Ⓑ	Ⓒ	Ⓓ	95	Ⓐ	Ⓑ	Ⓒ	Ⓓ
16	Ⓐ	Ⓑ	Ⓒ		36	Ⓐ	Ⓑ	Ⓒ	Ⓓ	56	Ⓐ	Ⓑ	Ⓒ	Ⓓ	76	Ⓐ	Ⓑ	Ⓒ	Ⓓ	96	Ⓐ	Ⓑ	Ⓒ	Ⓓ
17	Ⓐ	Ⓑ	Ⓒ		37	Ⓐ	Ⓑ	Ⓒ	Ⓓ	57	Ⓐ	Ⓑ	Ⓒ	Ⓓ	77	Ⓐ	Ⓑ	Ⓒ	Ⓓ	97	Ⓐ	Ⓑ	Ⓒ	Ⓓ
18	Ⓐ	Ⓑ	Ⓒ		38	Ⓐ	Ⓑ	Ⓒ	Ⓓ	58	Ⓐ	Ⓑ	Ⓒ	Ⓓ	78	Ⓐ	Ⓑ	Ⓒ	Ⓓ	98	Ⓐ	Ⓑ	Ⓒ	Ⓓ
19	Ⓐ	Ⓑ	Ⓒ		39	Ⓐ	Ⓑ	Ⓒ	Ⓓ	59	Ⓐ	Ⓑ	Ⓒ	Ⓓ	79	Ⓐ	Ⓑ	Ⓒ	Ⓓ	99	Ⓐ	Ⓑ	Ⓒ	Ⓓ
20	Ⓐ	Ⓑ	Ⓒ		40	Ⓐ	Ⓑ	Ⓒ	Ⓓ	60	Ⓐ	Ⓑ	Ⓒ	Ⓓ	80	Ⓐ	Ⓑ	Ⓒ	Ⓓ	100	Ⓐ	Ⓑ	Ⓒ	Ⓓ

Actual **Test 12**

LISTENING (Part I~IV)

NO.	A	B	C	D	NO.	A	B	C	D	NO.	A	B	C	D	NO.	A	B	C	D	NO.	A	B	C	D
1	Ⓐ	Ⓑ	Ⓒ	Ⓓ	21	Ⓐ	Ⓑ	Ⓒ		41	Ⓐ	Ⓑ	Ⓒ	Ⓓ	61	Ⓐ	Ⓑ	Ⓒ	Ⓓ	81	Ⓐ	Ⓑ	Ⓒ	Ⓓ
2	Ⓐ	Ⓑ	Ⓒ	Ⓓ	22	Ⓐ	Ⓑ	Ⓒ		42	Ⓐ	Ⓑ	Ⓒ	Ⓓ	62	Ⓐ	Ⓑ	Ⓒ	Ⓓ	82	Ⓐ	Ⓑ	Ⓒ	Ⓓ
3	Ⓐ	Ⓑ	Ⓒ	Ⓓ	23	Ⓐ	Ⓑ	Ⓒ		43	Ⓐ	Ⓑ	Ⓒ	Ⓓ	63	Ⓐ	Ⓑ	Ⓒ	Ⓓ	83	Ⓐ	Ⓑ	Ⓒ	Ⓓ
4	Ⓐ	Ⓑ	Ⓒ	Ⓓ	24	Ⓐ	Ⓑ	Ⓒ		44	Ⓐ	Ⓑ	Ⓒ	Ⓓ	64	Ⓐ	Ⓑ	Ⓒ	Ⓓ	84	Ⓐ	Ⓑ	Ⓒ	Ⓓ
5	Ⓐ	Ⓑ	Ⓒ	Ⓓ	25	Ⓐ	Ⓑ	Ⓒ		45	Ⓐ	Ⓑ	Ⓒ	Ⓓ	65	Ⓐ	Ⓑ	Ⓒ	Ⓓ	85	Ⓐ	Ⓑ	Ⓒ	Ⓓ
6	Ⓐ	Ⓑ	Ⓒ	Ⓓ	26	Ⓐ	Ⓑ	Ⓒ		46	Ⓐ	Ⓑ	Ⓒ	Ⓓ	66	Ⓐ	Ⓑ	Ⓒ	Ⓓ	86	Ⓐ	Ⓑ	Ⓒ	Ⓓ
7	Ⓐ	Ⓑ	Ⓒ		27	Ⓐ	Ⓑ	Ⓒ		47	Ⓐ	Ⓑ	Ⓒ	Ⓓ	67	Ⓐ	Ⓑ	Ⓒ	Ⓓ	87	Ⓐ	Ⓑ	Ⓒ	Ⓓ
8	Ⓐ	Ⓑ	Ⓒ		28	Ⓐ	Ⓑ	Ⓒ		48	Ⓐ	Ⓑ	Ⓒ	Ⓓ	68	Ⓐ	Ⓑ	Ⓒ	Ⓓ	88	Ⓐ	Ⓑ	Ⓒ	Ⓓ
9	Ⓐ	Ⓑ	Ⓒ		29	Ⓐ	Ⓑ	Ⓒ		49	Ⓐ	Ⓑ	Ⓒ	Ⓓ	69	Ⓐ	Ⓑ	Ⓒ	Ⓓ	89	Ⓐ	Ⓑ	Ⓒ	Ⓓ
10	Ⓐ	Ⓑ	Ⓒ		30	Ⓐ	Ⓑ	Ⓒ		50	Ⓐ	Ⓑ	Ⓒ	Ⓓ	70	Ⓐ	Ⓑ	Ⓒ	Ⓓ	90	Ⓐ	Ⓑ	Ⓒ	Ⓓ
11	Ⓐ	Ⓑ	Ⓒ		31	Ⓐ	Ⓑ	Ⓒ		51	Ⓐ	Ⓑ	Ⓒ	Ⓓ	71	Ⓐ	Ⓑ	Ⓒ	Ⓓ	91	Ⓐ	Ⓑ	Ⓒ	Ⓓ
12	Ⓐ	Ⓑ	Ⓒ		32	Ⓐ	Ⓑ	Ⓒ	Ⓓ	52	Ⓐ	Ⓑ	Ⓒ	Ⓓ	72	Ⓐ	Ⓑ	Ⓒ	Ⓓ	92	Ⓐ	Ⓑ	Ⓒ	Ⓓ
13	Ⓐ	Ⓑ	Ⓒ		33	Ⓐ	Ⓑ	Ⓒ	Ⓓ	53	Ⓐ	Ⓑ	Ⓒ	Ⓓ	73	Ⓐ	Ⓑ	Ⓒ	Ⓓ	93	Ⓐ	Ⓑ	Ⓒ	Ⓓ
14	Ⓐ	Ⓑ	Ⓒ		34	Ⓐ	Ⓑ	Ⓒ	Ⓓ	54	Ⓐ	Ⓑ	Ⓒ	Ⓓ	74	Ⓐ	Ⓑ	Ⓒ	Ⓓ	94	Ⓐ	Ⓑ	Ⓒ	Ⓓ
15	Ⓐ	Ⓑ	Ⓒ		35	Ⓐ	Ⓑ	Ⓒ	Ⓓ	55	Ⓐ	Ⓑ	Ⓒ	Ⓓ	75	Ⓐ	Ⓑ	Ⓒ	Ⓓ	95	Ⓐ	Ⓑ	Ⓒ	Ⓓ
16	Ⓐ	Ⓑ	Ⓒ		36	Ⓐ	Ⓑ	Ⓒ	Ⓓ	56	Ⓐ	Ⓑ	Ⓒ	Ⓓ	76	Ⓐ	Ⓑ	Ⓒ	Ⓓ	96	Ⓐ	Ⓑ	Ⓒ	Ⓓ
17	Ⓐ	Ⓑ	Ⓒ		37	Ⓐ	Ⓑ	Ⓒ	Ⓓ	57	Ⓐ	Ⓑ	Ⓒ	Ⓓ	77	Ⓐ	Ⓑ	Ⓒ	Ⓓ	97	Ⓐ	Ⓑ	Ⓒ	Ⓓ
18	Ⓐ	Ⓑ	Ⓒ		38	Ⓐ	Ⓑ	Ⓒ	Ⓓ	58	Ⓐ	Ⓑ	Ⓒ	Ⓓ	78	Ⓐ	Ⓑ	Ⓒ	Ⓓ	98	Ⓐ	Ⓑ	Ⓒ	Ⓓ
19	Ⓐ	Ⓑ	Ⓒ		39	Ⓐ	Ⓑ	Ⓒ	Ⓓ	59	Ⓐ	Ⓑ	Ⓒ	Ⓓ	79	Ⓐ	Ⓑ	Ⓒ	Ⓓ	99	Ⓐ	Ⓑ	Ⓒ	Ⓓ
20	Ⓐ	Ⓑ	Ⓒ		40	Ⓐ	Ⓑ	Ⓒ	Ⓓ	60	Ⓐ	Ⓑ	Ⓒ	Ⓓ	80	Ⓐ	Ⓑ	Ⓒ	Ⓓ	100	Ⓐ	Ⓑ	Ⓒ	Ⓓ

1. 사용 필기구 : 컴퓨터용 연필(연필을 제외한 사인펜, 볼펜 등은 사용 절대 불가)
2. 잘못된 필기구 사용과 〈보기〉의 올바른 표기 이외의 잘못된 표기로 한 경우에는 당 위원회의 OMR기기가 판독한 결과에 따르며 그 결과는 본인 책임입니다. 1개의 정답만 골라 아래의 올바른 표기대로 정확히 표기하여야 합니다.
   〈보기〉 올바른 표기 : ●　　잘못된 표기 : ⊘ ⊗ ▨
3. 답안지는 컴퓨터로 처리되므로 훼손하시면 안 되며, 상단의 타이밍마크(▌▌▌▌)부분을 찢거나, 낙서 등을 하면 본인에게 불이익이 발생할 수 있습니다.
4. 감독관의 확인이 없거나 시험 종료 후에 답안 작성을 계속할 경우 시험 무효 처리됩니다.

*서약 내용을 읽으시고 확인란에 반드시 서명하십시오.

서　약	확 인
본인은 TOEIC 시험 문제의 일부 또는 전부를 유출하거나 어떠한 형태로든 타인에게 누설 공개하지 않을 것이며 인터넷 또는 인쇄물 등을 이용해 유포하거나 참고 자료로 활용하지 않을 것입니다. 또한 TOEIC 시험 부정 행위 처리 규정을 준수할 것을 서약합니다.	

나혼자 끝내는 토익 PART 1~4

신토익 실전12회

이주은 지음

정답 및 해설

넥서스

Actual Test 1

PART 1

본책 p.12

1 (C)	2 (B)	3 (B)	4 (A)	5 (B)	6 (D)

PART 2

본책 p.16

7 (A)	8 (B)	9 (B)	10 (C)	11 (A)	12 (B)
13 (C)	14 (C)	15 (A)	16 (C)	17 (B)	18 (A)
19 (B)	20 (C)	21 (B)	22 (C)	23 (A)	24 (B)
25 (A)	26 (B)	27 (A)	28 (A)	29 (B)	30 (B)
31 (C)					

PART 3

본책 p.17

32 (B)	33 (C)	34 (B)	35 (A)	36 (D)	37 (B)
38 (C)	39 (A)	40 (D)	41 (C)	42 (A)	43 (B)
44 (B)	45 (C)	46 (A)	47 (B)	48 (D)	49 (C)
50 (C)	51 (B)	52 (A)	53 (A)	54 (A)	55 (D)
56 (A)	57 (B)	58 (D)	59 (B)	60 (D)	61 (A)
62 (B)	63 (C)	64 (A)	65 (B)	66 (B)	67 (A)
68 (A)	69 (B)	70 (C)			

PART 4

본책 p.21

71 (D)	72 (C)	73 (A)	74 (B)	75 (C)	76 (A)
77 (C)	78 (A)	79 (D)	80 (C)	81 (B)	82 (D)
83 (B)	84 (A)	85 (C)	86 (B)	87 (A)	88 (D)
89 (A)	90 (C)	91 (D)	92 (A)	93 (B)	94 (D)
95 (A)	96 (B)	97 (C)	98 (A)	99 (C)	100 (D)

PART 1

1 (A) A woman is leaning back on a bench.
미W (B) There is an unoccupied chair on the sidewalk.
(C) The bicycle is propped against the wall.
(D) A woman is gesturing with her hand.

(A) 여자가 벤치에 등을 기대어 있다.
(B) 보도에 아무도 앉지 않은 의자가 있다.
(C) 자전거가 벽에 받쳐져 있다.
(D) 여자가 손짓을 하고 있다.

여자가 등을 기대며 깊숙이 앉아 있으나 벤치가 아니라 그냥 의자이며 의자에는 이미 여자가 앉아 있으므로 (A), (B) 모두 옳지 않다. 손에 휴대폰으로 보이는 것을 들고 있을 뿐 별다른 손짓을 보이지는 않으므로 정답은 (C)이다.

lean back 등을 기대다 prop against 받치다, 떠받치다 gesture 손짓이나 몸짓을 하다

2 (A) They are walking their bicycles.
영M (B) They are wearing the same uniform.
(C) They are wheeling a cart.
(D) They are having a competitive race.

(A) 사람들이 자전거를 끌며 걸어가고 있다.
(B) 사람들이 같은 유니폼을 입고 있다.
(C) 사람들이 카트를 밀고 있다.
(D) 사람들이 레이스 대회에 참여하고 있다.

모든 사람들이 똑같은 옷을 입고 운동용 사이클을 타고 있다. 행동 자체보다는 옷차림에 출제 포인트를 맞춘 문제이다.

walk one's bicycle 자전거를 끌며 걷다 wheel 바퀴 달린 것을 밀다, 끌다 competitive 경쟁적인

3 (A) He is using a hose to water his plants.
영W (B) He is utilizing a machine with handles.
(C) He is driving a tractor over rows of crops.
(D) He is collecting leaf samples in a bucket.

(A) 그는 식물에 물을 주려고 호스를 이용하고 있다.
(B) 그는 손잡이가 있는 기계를 이용하고 있다.
(C) 그는 여러 줄의 농작물 위로 트랙터를 운전하고 있다.
(D) 그는 양동이에 나뭇잎 샘플을 모으고 있다.

모자를 깊이 눌러 쓴 남자가 기계의 손잡이를 양손에 쥐고 일을 하고 있다. 트랙터는 멀리 주차되어 있으니 (C)는 오답이다.

water 물을 주다 utilize 활용하다, 이용하다 handle 손잡이 row 줄, 열 crop 농작물 collect 모으다, 수집하다 bucket 양동이

4 (A) They are heading in the same direction.
미M (B) They are waiting to board a subway car.
(C) Some people are lined up on a bridge.
(D) The train is approaching the platform.

(A) 사람들이 같은 방향으로 가고 있다.
(B) 사람들이 지하철을 타려고 기다리는 중이다.
(C) 몇몇은 다리에서 줄을 서 있다.
(D) 기차가 플랫폼에 다가가고 있다.

기차 플랫폼으로 보이는 곳에서 사람들이 등을 보이며 모두 같은 방향으로 걸어가고 있다. 어느 방향으로 가고 있으므로 기다리는 것이라고 보기 어려우며 줄을 서 있는 것도 아니다.

head 특정 방향으로 가다 direction 방향 subway car 지하철, 전철 board 승차하다, 탑승하다 line up 줄을 서다 approach 접근하다

5 (A) A man is working in an outdoor café.
미W (B) The man's work area is outdoors in the shade.
(C) A man is searching through his drawer.
(D) The man's tools are scattered on the floor.

(A) 남자가 야외 카페에서 일하고 있다.
(B) 남자의 작업장이 야외 그늘에 있다.
(C) 남자는 서랍을 뒤지고 있다.
(D) 남자의 도구들은 바닥에 흩어져 있다.

도구를 쥐고 작업을 하고 있는 남자의 작업장은 대부분 공간이 그늘져 있으며 바닥에 보이는 것을 도구라고 단정 짓기 어렵다.

outdoor 야외의 outdoors 야외에서, 옥외에서 in the shade 응달에서, 그늘에서 search 찾다 drawer 서랍 scatter 흩어지게 하다

6 (A) The framed pictures are positioned upside down.
영M (B) A man is turning on the lamp.
(C) The door of the room has been left open.
(D) A round mirror has been fixed on the wall.

(A) 그림 액자가 거꾸로 위치해 있다.
(B) 남자가 램프를 켜고 있다.
(C) 방문이 열려 있다.
(D) 둥근 모양의 거울이 벽에 고정되어 있다.

전등이 켜진 방안의 사물 배치를 잘 설명한 선택지를 골라야 한다. 뒤쪽에 있는 거울에 초점이 맞춰진 (D)가 정답이다. 사람이나 문은 보이지 않으므로 (B), (C)는 오답이다.

framed picture 액자에 넣은 그림 position 위치에 두다, 배치하다 upside down 거꾸로 turn on 켜다 left open 열린 채 round 둥근 fix 고정시키다

PART 2

7 What's the weather like today?
미W (A) It's overcast and cold.
미M (B) I like it too.
(C) After the weather update.

오늘 날씨가 어떤가요?
(A) 구름이 끼고 춥습니다.
(B) 저도 그게 좋아요.
(C) 일기 예보 후에요.

날씨를 물을 때 what's the weather like?라는 표현은 필수적으로 암기해 두자. What 의문문 중에서 빈출 암기 표현이다.

overcast 흐린, 구름 낀 weather update 일기 예보

8 Where is the noise coming from?
영M (A) He is from Italy.
미W (B) From the construction outside.
(C) Yes, I can hear it.

이 소음은 어디에서 오는 거죠?
(A) 그는 이탈리아 출신이에요.
(B) 바깥 공사장에서요.
(C) 네, 잘 들립니다.

where 의문문으로 소음의 출처를 물었으므로 (B)가 가장 자연스럽다.

noise 소음 construction 공사장

9 Will your parents be visiting you next month?
영W (A) I visited Chicago last month.
영M (B) I think so.
(C) Yes, by tomorrow.

부모님이 다음 달에 당신을 방문하시죠?
(A) 저는 지난달에 시카고를 방문했어요.
(B) 그럴 거예요.
(C) 네, 내일까지요.

Yes/No 의문문으로 부모님이 방문을 하실지 여부를 물었으므로 그렇다고 답한 (B)가 정답이 된다. I think so는 Yes 대신 사용되는 표현으로 외워 두고, I think so의 단어를 하나씩 해석하는 일이 없도록 하자.

10 Can I use your pen?
영M (A) I have other plans.
미W (B) She'll be back.
(C) Oh, it's out of ink.

당신의 펜을 써도 될까요?
(A) 저는 다른 계획이 있어요.
(B) 그녀는 돌아올 거예요.
(C) 아, 잉크가 떨어졌네요.

요청 의문문으로 상대방의 펜을 써도 되는지 물었으므로 잉크가 떨어져서(out of ink) 못 쓴다고 답한 (C)가 정답이다. (A)는 pen과 발음이 비슷한 plan을 사용한 유사 발음 함정이다.

out of ~이 떨어진

11 Who is available to give the opening speech?
미M (A) Professor Johnson can do it.
영M (B) Yes, please keep it open.
(C) Thank you very much.

누가 개회사를 할 시간이 되나요?
(A) Johnson 교수님이 할 수 있어요.
(B) 네, 열어 놓아 주세요.
(C) 정말 감사합니다.

질문의 키워드는 who로, 개회사를 할 수 있는 사람이 누구인지 물었으므로 정답은 (A)가 맞다. 의문사 의문문에는 Yes나 No로 시작되는 (B)와 같은 보기는 오답임을 반드시 기억해 두자.

opening speech 개회사

12 How do I get to the Crystal Hotel from the airport?
미W (A) It is not very far.
영W (B) You can take the shuttle bus.
(C) Try the hotel restaurant.

공항에서 Crystal 호텔까지 어떻게 가면 되나요?
(A) 그렇게 멀지 않습니다.
(B) 셔틀 버스를 타시면 돼요.
(C) 호텔 레스토랑을 가보세요.

의문사 how와 함께 'get to + 장소'가 나오면 그 장소까지 가는 교통수단 혹은 길 안내를 묻는 질문이다. 여기서는 호텔까지 가는 방법을 물었으므로 정답은 (B)가 맞다.

get to + 장소 ~에 가다

13 Are we meeting the architect in his office or ours?
영M (A) That sounds good.
미W (B) Nice to meet you.
(C) Our office, I think.

우리는 건축가를 그의 사무실에서 만나나요 아니면 우리 사무실이요?
(A) 좋습니다.
(B) 만나서 반갑습니다.
(C) 우리 사무실인 것 같아요.

선택 의문문으로 선택 사항은 his office(그의 사무실) 혹은 ours(우리 사무실)이다. 정답은 우리 사무실이라고 답한 (C)이다.

14 Do you have a used copy of this novel?
미M (A) No, the copier is out of order.
미W (B) Sometime next month.
(C) Not at the moment.

이 소설의 중고 서적이 있으신가요?
(A) 아니오, 복사기는 고장입니다.
(B) 다음 달 언제쯤이요.
(C) 지금은 없어요.

Yes/No 여부로 묻고 있는 것은 do you have '~이 있는지 여부'이다. used copy는 중고 서적이라는 의미로 쓰인 것이니 혼동하지 않도록 하자. (C)는 지금은 중고책이 없다는 뜻이므로 정답으로 자연스럽다. (A)는 copy와 발음이 비슷한 copier를 사용한 유사 발음 함정이 된다.

used copy 중고 서적 out of order 고장 난 at the moment 지금은

15 영W 미M Mr. Carlson, shouldn't these documents be filed today?
(A) Yes, could you do that?
(B) I've already seen it.
(C) No, he didn't.

Carlson 씨, 이 서류들은 오늘 정리되어야 하지 않나요?
(A) **네, 당신이 해 주시겠어요?**
(B) 전 그것을 이미 봤습니다.
(C) 아니요, 그는 하지 않았습니다.

질문의 핵심은 서류들이 정리되어야 하지 않는가이다. (A)의 Yes는 정리가 필요하다는 의미이며, 상대방에게 해 달라는 말로 끝을 맺고 있다.

be filed 정리되다

16 미W 영M You attended that conference last year, didn't you?
(A) Yes, I met her.
(B) It was yesterday.
(C) Which one?

작년에 그 컨퍼런스에 참석하셨죠, 그렇지 않나요?
(A) 네, 전 그녀를 만났어요.
(B) 그건 어제였어요.
(C) **어떤 거요?**

Yes/No 여부를 묻는 질문으로 that conference에 참석했었는지를 물었으므로 Which one?(어떤 컨퍼런스를 말하는 것이냐)으로 되물은 (C)가 정답이다. 여기서 one은 대명사로 앞에서 나왔던 명사를 받는다. 이 경우 conference를 받고 있으므로 Which conference?라고 되묻는 것과 동일하다.

17 미M 미W Why did you book a hotel room so far in advance?
(A) It was a nice trip.
(B) So I could get an early bird discount.
(C) Right behind us.

왜 호텔 룸을 이렇게 일찍 예약하셨죠?
(A) 좋은 여행이었어요.
(B) **조기 예약 할인을 받을 수 있거든요.**
(C) 바로 우리 뒤에요.

호텔 예약을 그렇게 일찍 한 이유가 무엇인지 물었으므로 조기 예약 할인을 받기 위해서라고 답한 (B)가 정답이다.

book 예약하다 so far (강조의 의미) 그렇게 in advance 사전에, 미리 early bird discount 사전 예약 할인, 조기 할인

18 영W 미M Please tell Ms. Holmes that I stopped by while she was out.
(A) Can I take a message for you?
(B) Keep going straight.
(C) She will leave soon.

Holmes 씨에게 그녀가 없을 때 제가 다녀갔다고 전해 주세요.
(A) **메시지를 받아 드릴까요?**
(B) 쭉 앞으로 가세요.
(C) 그녀는 곧 떠날 겁니다.

평서문의 내용이 Holmes 씨에게 본인이 다녀갔다는 사실을 전해 달라는 것이었으므로 메시지를 남기겠냐고 되물은 (A)가 가장 자연스러운 답이 된다.

stop by ~에 들르다 take a message 메시지를 받다 go straight 직진하다

19 미M 미W Why don't you join us on the planning committee?
(A) Because it is too far away.
(B) I wish I could, but I am very busy.
(C) They decided not to go.

기획 위원회에 가입하시는 게 어때요?
(A) 너무 멀기 때문에요.
(B) **그러고 싶지만, 전 너무 바빠요.**
(C) 그들은 안 가기로 결정했어요.

Why don't you는 제안의 의미이므로 위원회에 가입하는 게 어떤지를 권하는 것이다. 그러므로 너무 바쁘다고 거절한 (B)가 정답이 된다. Why don't you/we?는 '~ 하실래요?'라고 암기하고, why를 따로 해석하는 일이 없도록 하자.

planning committee 기획 위원회

20 영M 영W Where is the awards banquet going to be held this year?
(A) We need a larger office space.
(B) The bank is closed.
(C) You should ask Ken.

올해는 시상식 연회가 어디에서 열리게 되나요?
(A) 우리는 더 큰 사무실 공간이 필요해요.
(B) 그 은행은 문을 닫았어요.
(C) **Ken에게 물어 보시는 게 좋겠어요.**

올해의 시상식이 열리는 장소가 질문의 포인트이므로 사무 공간에 대해 얘기한 (A)는 오답이고 Ken에게 물어보라고 답한 (C)는 정답이 된다. 제3자의 이름, 직위가 언급되면서 그 사람에게 물어보라는 유형의 답변은 '천하무적 정답' 형태로 어떤 질문과 만나도 정답이 될 확률이 매우 높다.

awards banquet 시상식 연회 be held 열리다

21 미M 영M Mr. Ashan from the headquarters paid us a visit two days ago.
(A) About 500 dollars.
(B) Really? What did he say about our facilities?
(C) I visited there too.

본사 소속의 Ashan 씨가 2주일 전에 우리를 방문했어요.
(A) 500달러 정도요.
(B) **진짜요? 그가 우리 시설물에 대해 뭐라고 했나요?**
(C) 저도 거기에 방문했었어요.

정보를 알려주는 평서문으로 본사의 누군가가 방문했었다고 했으므로 시설물에 대해 뭐라고 얘기했는지를 되묻는 (B)가 가장 자연스러운 답변이다.

headquarters 본사 pay a visit 방문하다 facilities 시설물

22 영M 미W How can I reach you if the air conditioner breaks down again?
(A) I need some fresh air.
(B) You can take the train.
(C) Call me on my mobile phone.

에어컨이 또 고장 나면 당신에게 어떻게 연락을 취하죠?
(A) 전 신선한 공기가 필요해요.
(B) 기차를 타시면 됩니다.
(C) **제 휴대 전화로 전화하세요.**

의문사 how와 함께 reach + 사람/장소 등이 쓰이면 '~에게 연락을 취하다'는 의미로 쓰일 수 있다. 즉, 질문에서 상대방에게 연락 방법에 대해 묻고 있으므로 휴대전화로 연락하라고 말한 (C)가 정답이 된다.

reach 연락하다 break down 고장 나다 mobile phone 휴대 전화

23 I think the procedure for requesting technical help is
미W way too complicated.
미M (A) It will be revised soon.
(B) He used to be a technician.
(C) Let's take the highway.

기술적인 도움을 요청하는 절차가 너무 복잡한 것 같습니다.
(A) 그건 곧 수정될 거예요.
(B) 그는 예전에 기술자였어요.
(C) 고속 도로를 탑시다.

문제점에 대해 얘기하는 평서문으로 '절차가 복잡하다'는 것이 핵심이 된다. 정답은 곧 수정이 될 거라며 해결책을 제시한 (A)가 가장 자연스러운 답이 된다.

procedure 절차 technical help 기술적인 도움 complicated 복잡한 revise 수정하다 highway 고속 도로

24 What's the exact number of registered users of our
영W website?
영M (A) Fill out the registration form.
(B) Well, I'll have to count.
(C) The number 10 bus goes into the city.

우리 웹 사이트에 등록한 사용자가 정확하게 몇 명입니까?
(A) 등록 양식을 채워 주세요.
(B) 음, 세어봐야 하겠는데요.
(C) 10번 버스가 도시 안으로 들어갑니다.

단순히 what 질문이 아닌 what is the number, 즉 숫자가 무엇인지 묻는 how many 질문이 된다. 사용자의 수를 물었을 때 세어봐야 알겠다고 답한 (B)가 자연스러운 정답이다.

exact 정확한 registered user 등록한 사용자

25 Can you make it to the party tonight or do you have
미M too much work to do?
미W (A) I think I'll be able to come.
(B) It is too cold to eat outside.
(C) Yes, it is working now.

당신은 오늘 밤 파티에 올 수 있나요 아니면 할 일이 너무 많은가요?
(A) 갈 수 있을 것 같아요.
(B) 야외에서 밥을 먹기에는 너무 춥네요.
(C) 네, 그것은 지금 작동합니다.

선택 의문문으로 파티에 올 수 있는지 혹은 일이 많아서 못 오는지를 묻고 있으므로 갈 수 있다고 답한 (A)가 정답이다.

make it to ~에 가다

26 Who is the keynote speaker at the dedication of the
영W new community park?
미M (A) I work at the community center.
(B) Nobody I've heard of.
(C) It is located near my office.

누가 새로운 지역 공원의 개장식의 기조 연설자입니까?
(A) 저는 커뮤니티 센터에서 일해요.
(B) 누구인지 못 들었어요.
(C) 그건 제 사무실 옆에 있어요.

질문의 핵심은 who is the keynote speaker까지이다. 기조 연설자에 대해 물었을 때 아직 누구인지 못 들었다고 답한 (B)가 정답이 된다.

keynote speaker 기조 연설자 dedication 개장식

27 Would you be interested in a van instead?
영M (A) Oh, I've already rented a car.
미W (B) So, how long will it take?
(C) It wasn't that interesting.

대신 밴에 관심이 있으신가요?
(A) 오, 전 이미 차를 빌렸습니다.
(B) 그래서, 얼마나 걸릴까요?
(C) 그렇게 흥미롭지 않았습니다.

제안의 의도를 가진 would you be interested in 표현을 정확하게 암기해 놓는다. 밴에 관심이 있느냐는 것은 밴을 사거나 빌리고 싶은지를 묻는 질문이므로 이미 다른 차를 빌려서 관심이 없다고 답한 (A)가 정답이 된다. (C)는 interesting을 이용한 오류로, 주어 it에 연결되는 명사가 없으므로 주어 오류이며 시제 역시 잘못 사용된 시제 오류 함정이기도 하다.

be interested in ~에 관심이 있다 instead 대신에 rent 빌리다 interesting 흥미로운

28 Our company's profits increased by 20 percent in
미W the last year.
영W (A) We'll need more employees soon.
(B) For more than 20 years.
(C) Because they are financially unstable.

우리 회사의 수익이 작년에 20 퍼센트 증가했습니다.
(A) 곧 직원들이 더 필요하겠네요.
(B) 20년 이상 동안요.
(C) 그들은 재정적으로 불안정하기 때문입니다.

평서문의 내용이 회사의 수익이 작년에 늘었다는 것이므로 곧 사람들이 더 필요하겠다고 답한 (A)가 가장 자연스럽다.

profits 수익 financially 재정적으로 unstable 불안정한

29 Would you rather buy this blue tie?
미M (A) I'll paint the walls in gray.
미W (B) That would go well with my black suit.
(C) On the shelf.

차라리 이 파란색 넥타이를 사시겠어요?
(A) 벽들을 회색으로 칠할래요.
(B) 내 검은색 정장과 잘 어울리겠어요.
(C) 선반 위에요.

질문의 요지는 파란색 넥타이를 사겠냐는 것으로 (B)의 검은색 정장과 잘 어울리겠다는 것은 질문에 대해 Yes라고 답하는 의미가 된다.

30 Don't we usually get paid on the 20th of every
영M month?
미W (A) No, it is not a well-paying job.
(B) Yes, if it is not a holiday.
(C) Maybe next time.

우리는 보통 매달 20일에 급여를 받지 않나요?
(A) 아니오, 그것은 보수가 높은 일자리가 아니에요.
(B) 네, 공휴일이 아니면요.
(C) 아마도 다음 기회에요.

Yes/No 여부로 확인하고자 하는 것은 매달 20일에 월급을 받는지이다. 정답의 Yes는 20일에 받는다는 뜻으로, if it is not a holiday(공휴일이 아닌 경우에는) 그렇다고 답한 (B)가 정답이다.

get paid 급여를 받다 well-paying job 보수가 좋은 직업

31 That was the best movie I've ever seen.
영W (A) Sit wherever you like.
영M (B) We're moving to a larger office.
(C) I've seen better ones.

그건 제가 본 영화 중에 최고였어요.
(A) 앉고 싶은 곳에 앉으세요.
(B) 우리는 더 넓은 사무실로 이전합니다.
(C) 전 더 재미있는 것도 봤어요.

이 평서문의 요지는 특정 영화에 대한 의견이다. 최고였다고 말했고 상대방은 더 나은 것도 봤다고 말하며 반대되는 의견을 내고 있는 (C)가 자연스러운 정답이 된다.

PART 3

Questions 32-34 refer to the following conversation. 미M 미W

M Hi, I'm here for my 3 o'clock appointment with Dr. Howard.
W Oh, you must be Mr. Boe. I'm very sorry but Dr. Howard is not available right now. I left you a message about the schedule change this morning, but apparently you didn't get it.
M No, I haven't had a chance to check my messages yet. Is there any problem?
W Actually Dr. Howard had to perform an emergency operation at the general hospital. So he won't be available today. Can I reschedule you for tomorrow afternoon at the same time?

남 안녕하세요. Howard 선생님과 3시 약속 때문에 왔습니다.
여 아, Boe 씨로군요. 죄송하지만 Howard 선생님께서는 지금 안 계십니다. 아침에 스케줄 변경에 대해서 메시지를 남겼었는데 받지 못하신 것 같군요.
남 못 받았어요. 아직 메시지를 확인할 기회가 없었거든요. 문제가 있나요?
여 실은 Howard 선생님께서 종합 병원에서 응급 수술에 들어가셔야 했어요. 그래서 오늘은 시간이 안 됩니다. 내일 오후 같은 시간으로 예약을 다시 잡아 드릴까요?

apparently 보아 하니 have a chance to ~할 기회를 갖다 general hospital 종합 병원 reschedule 일정을 바꾸다

32 Who is the man speaking to?
(A) A doctor
(B) A receptionist
(C) A sales person
(D) A patient

남자는 누구와 이야기하는가?
(A) 의사
(B) 접수원
(C) 영업 사원
(D) 환자

여자가 누구인지 유추하는 질문이다. 접수원(receptionist)이 하는 일을 알면 굉장히 쉽게 풀 수 있는 질문이다. 접수원은 보통 의사나 임원 등의 스케줄 관리 업무를 하고 빌딩의 안내 데스크 등에서 손님이 왔을 때 처음 응대 하는 업무를 한다. 위의 대화는 의사가 지금 없다는 내용을 말했을 때 정답을 (B)로 선택할 수 있다.

33 According to the woman, why is Dr. Howard unavailable now?
(A) He is out of town.
(B) He has been hospitalized.
(C) He is performing an operation.
(D) He is completing a research paper.

여자에 따르면 Howard 선생님은 왜 지금 자리에 없는가?
(A) 지방에 갔다.
(B) 입원해 있다.
(C) 수술을 하고 있다.
(D) 연구 논문을 마치고 있다.

여자 대사에게 정답이 나온다는 것을 염두에 두고 듣자. Howard 선생님이 안 계신다고 하면서 종합 병원에서 응급 수술을 하러 갔다고 했으므로 정답은 (C)가 된다.

34 What does the woman suggest the man do?
(A) Complete a patient form
(B) Return the next day
(C) Find another doctor
(D) Buy some medication

여자는 남자에게 무엇을 하라고 권하는가?
(A) 환자 양식 작성하기
(B) 다음 날 다시 오기
(C) 다른 의사 찾기
(D) 약 구입하기

여자가 남자에게 내일 같은 시간으로 시간 변경을 해줄지(Can I reschedule you for tomorrow afternoon at the same time?) 물었으므로 내일 다시 오라는 의미가 된다. 정답은 (B)이다.

Questions 35-37 refer to the following conversation. 영M 미W

M Have you tried the new restaurant on Elm Street?
W You mean Spicy Thai House? Well, I haven't been there yet, but I heard the food is great. Apparently the chef is from Thailand so they serve authentic Thai cuisine there.
M That's wonderful. Christina and I are going there for lunch tomorrow. Do you want to join us?
W Sure, thanks. Should I meet you at one in the lobby?
M Let's make it at 12:30.

남 Elm Street에 새로 생긴 레스토랑에 가 보신 적 있어요?
여 Spicy Thai House 말씀이신가요? 음, 아직 가 보지는 못했지만, 음식은 맛있다고 들었어요. 듣자 하니 요리사가 태국 출신이어서 정통 태국 음식을 제공한다고 하더라고요.
남 잘됐네요. Christina와 제가 내일 점심을 먹으러 갈 건데 함께 가실래요?
여 좋아요, 감사해요. 1시에 로비에서 만날까요?
남 12시 30분으로 하죠.

apparently 듣자 하니, 보아 하니 authentic 정통의, 진짜의

35 What are the speakers mainly discussing?
(A) A new restaurant
(B) An outdoor market
(C) A foreign culture
(D) A travel destination

화자들은 무엇에 대해서 주로 이야기하는가?
(A) 새로운 레스토랑
(B) 야외 시장
(C) 외국 문화
(D) 여행 목적지

대화의 주제는 도입부에 언급이 된다. 남자가 여자에게 새로 생긴 레스토랑에 가봤는지(Have you tried the new restaurant on Elm Street?)물었으므로 정답은 (A)가 된다.

36 What is mentioned about the restaurant?
(A) The chef has won an award.
(B) It is located near the office.
(C) The ingredients are fresh.
(D) It serves authentic Thai food.

레스토랑에 대해 언급된 것은 무엇인가?
(A) 요리사가 상을 받은 적이 있다.
(B) 사무실 근처에 위치해 있다.
(C) 재료가 신선하다.
(D) 정통 태국 음식을 제공한다.

레스토랑에 대해 언급된 것 중 보기와 일치하는 내용은 the chef is from Thailand so they serve authentic Thai cuisine(요리사가 태국 출신으로 정통 타이 음식을 낸다)이라는 것이므로 정답은 (D)이다.

37 What time will the speakers probably meet tomorrow?
(A) At noon
(B) At 12:30 p.m.
(C) At 1:00 p.m.
(D) At 1:30 p.m.

화자들은 내일 몇 시에 만날 것 같은가?
(A) 정오
(B) 오후 12시 30분
(C) 오후 1시
(D) 오후 1시 30분

여자가 1시에 만날지 물었을 때 남자가 Let's make it at 12:30(12시 30분에 만나자)라고 했으므로 정답은 (B)가 맞다.

Questions 38-40 refer to the following conversation. 미W 미M

W Do you know where I can find some more ink cartridges? I need to make some copies for my presentation but the copy machine seems to be out of ink.
M Have you checked in the supply cabinet next to Karen's desk? All the office supplies should be stored in there.
W I already checked the cabinet but I didn't find any ink cartridges.
M Hmm... why don't you check with Karen? She takes care of supplies and she might know where they are.

여 잉크 카트리지가 어디에 더 있는지 아세요? 발표에 쓸 복사를 해야 하는데 복사기에 잉크가 떨어졌어요.
남 Karen의 책상 옆에 있는 물품 수납장 안은 찾아보셨나요? 모든 사무 물품들은 다 거기에 보관됩니다.
여 이미 그 수납장은 확인했는데 잉크 카트리지는 찾지 못했어요.
남 흠… Karen에게 물어보지 그래요? 그녀가 물품을 관리하니까 어디 있는지 알 겁니다.

ink cartridge 잉크 카트리지 out of ~이 없는 store 보관하다 cabinet 수납장 check with ~에게 물어보다 take care of 관리하다, 처리하다

38 What does the woman need to do?
(A) Attend a presentation
(B) Meet a deadline
(C) Make some copies
(D) Find a telephone number

여자는 무엇을 해야 하는가?
(A) 발표에 참석하기
(B) 마감 맞추기
(C) 복사하기
(D) 전화번호 찾기

여자가 발표 때문에 복사를 해야 한다(I need to make some copies for my presentation)고 했으므로 정답은 (C)이다.

39 What problem does the woman mention?
(A) A copier is out of ink.
(B) A delivery is late.
(C) Some equipment is broken.
(D) A coworker is not available.

여자는 어떤 문제에 대해 언급하는가?
(A) 복사기에 잉크가 떨어졌다.
(B) 배달이 늦었다.
(C) 기기가 고장 났다.
(D) 동료가 자리에 없다.

여자의 문제는 복사를 해야 하는데 복사기가 out of ink인 상황이므로 정답은 (A)이다.

40 What does the man suggest the woman do?
(A) Call a technician
(B) Pack some boxes

(C) Purchase some supplies
(D) Ask another colleague

남자는 여자에게 무엇을 하라고 제안하는가?
(A) 기술자 부르기
(B) 박스 포장하기
(C) 비품 구매하기
(D) 다른 동료에게 물어보기

남자가 Why don't you check with Karen?이라면서 Karen에게 물어보는 게 어떻겠냐고 했으므로 정답은 (D)가 된다. 보통 이름, 직위 등은 coworker, colleague와 같은 말로 패러프레이징된다.

Questions 41-43 refer to the following conversation. (영W) (미M)

W Hi, Arthur. I'm working on the schedule for next month and I was wondering if you could take the evening shift next month. I know you prefer to work in the morning but we're a little understaffed at night.
M Well, I go to school during the evenings to finish my degree. But my class just ended, so I'll be happy to work in the evenings next month.
W Thank you, Arthur. We have large orders to fill next month so the production line will be a lot busier. But I'm sure things will go smoothly because we have skilled workers like you on our team.

여 안녕하세요, Arthur. 제가 다음 달 스케줄 작업을 하고 있는데 혹시 다음 달에 저녁 근무를 해 주실 수 있을까 해서요. 당신이 오전에 일하는 걸 선호하는 것은 알지만 우리가 저녁에 사람이 부족해서요.
남 음, 저는 학위를 마치기 위해서 저녁에는 학교에 가요. 그렇지만 제 수업이 막 끝나서, 다음 달은 기꺼이 저녁에 일하도록 하겠습니다.
여 고마워요, Arthur. 다음 달에 만들어야 할 큰 주문 건들이 많이 있어서 생산 라인이 더 바빠질 텐데요. 그렇지만 우리 팀에 당신처럼 실력 있는 직원들이 있으니 일이 수월하게 진행될 거라고 확신합니다.

work on ~에 대한 작업을 하다 evening shift 저녁 근무조 degree 학위 fill an order 주문을 채우다, 주문 들어온 것을 만들다 go smoothly 잘 진행되다

41 What are the speakers mainly discussing?
(A) Building renovations
(B) Hiring temporary workers
(C) A work schedule
(D) An evening class

화자들은 주로 무엇에 대해서 말하고 있는가?
(A) 건물 보수 공사
(B) 임시 직원들을 고용하는 것
(C) 근무 스케줄
(D) 저녁 수업

대화의 주제를 찾는 질문이다. 여자가 다음 달 스케줄 작업을 하고 있다(I'm working on the schedule for next month)고 했으므로 근무 스케줄에 대한 대화이다.

42 What problem does the woman mention?
(A) Lack of staff
(B) An equipment malfunction
(C) A missed deadline
(D) Insufficient work space

여자는 어떤 문제점에 대해 언급하는가?
(A) 직원 부족
(B) 기계 오작동
(C) 시한 초과된 마감
(D) 부족한 근무 공간

여자 대사에서 언급되는 문제점을 노려 듣자. 다음 달 저녁 근무를 해달라고 부탁하면서 we're a little understaffed at night(저녁에 일손이 부족하다)이라고 했으므로 정답은 (A)가 된다.

43 According to the woman, why will the production line be busier next month?
(A) A few employees have resigned.
(B) Large orders have been placed.
(C) A deadline has been moved up.
(D) Some workers are on vacation.

여자에 따르면, 다음 달에는 생산 라인이 왜 더 바빠질 것인가?
(A) 직원 몇 명이 그만두었다.
(B) 큰 주문 건이 들어왔다.
(C) 마감이 당겨졌다.
(D) 직원 몇 명이 휴가 중이다.

질문을 통해 다음 달 생산 라인이 바쁠 것임을 미리 염두에 두고 해당 이유를 노려 듣자. We have large orders to fill next month라며 그래서 바빠질 것이라고 했으므로 정답은 (B)가 된다. '주문을 채우다'라고 말할 때 fill an order라고 표현함을 암기해 두자.

Questions 44-46 refer to the following conversation. (영M) (영W)

M Hey, what's all the fuss about in the meeting room?
W Oh, you should check this out. They just set up the display of the new desks and chairs we're getting.
M Are we getting new office furniture? I didn't know that. Well, I'm pretty happy with the desk and chair I have now.
W You'll change your mind once you see them. The new chairs are an especially big improvement. They provide great support for your lower back. Just get in there and try one out.

남 저기요, 회의실에 이게 다 무슨 소란이죠?
여 아, 이것 좀 보세요. 우리가 새로 받게 될 책상과 의자들을 전시해 두었어요.
남 우리가 새로운 사무 가구를 받게 되나요? 전 몰랐어요. 음, 저는 지금 제가 쓰고 있는 책상과 의자에 만족하거든요.
여 일단 보시면 생각이 바뀔 거예요. 특히 새 의자들은 엄청 좋아졌어요. 허리를 정말 잘 받쳐 주거든요. 일단 저 안에 들어가서 한 번 앉아 보세요.

fuss 소란, 야단법석 check out 확인하다 set up 설치하다 be happy with ~에 만족하다 improvement 향상, 개선, 좋아진 것 try out ~을 체험해보다, 해보다

44 What is happening in the meeting room?
(A) Some improvements are being made.
(B) Some furniture is on display.
(C) A fashion show is being held.
(D) A meeting is in progress.

회의실에서 무슨 일이 일어나고 있는가?
(A) 개선이 이루어지고 있다.
(B) 가구들이 진열되어 있다.
(C) 패션쇼가 열리고 있다.
(D) 미팅이 진행 중이다.

질문의 키워드는 meeting room과 happen이다. They just set up the display of the new desks and chairs we're getting에서 새로운 책상과 의자들의 진열을 해 놓았다고 했으므로 정답은 (B)가 된다.

45 What does the man say about his desk and chair?
(A) They are not comfortable.
(B) They are broken.
(C) They are fine.
(D) They are brand new.

남자는 그의 책상과 의자에 대해서 뭐라고 말하는가?
(A) 편안하지 않다.
(B) 고장 났다.
(C) 좋다.
(D) 새것이다.

남자의 대사에서 본인의 책상과 의자에 대해서 언급하는 부분을 집중해 듣는 것이 포인트이다. I'm pretty happy with the desk and chair I have now(현재 책상과 의자에 만족한다)라고 했으므로 정답은 (C)이다.

46 What does the woman say about the new chairs?
(A) They are better than the old ones.
(B) They cost a lot of money.
(C) They are colorful.
(D) They are durable.

여자가 새 의자에 대해서 뭐라고 하는가?
(A) 예전 것보다 더 좋다.
(B) 많은 돈이 든다.
(C) 색상이 다양하다.
(D) 내구성이 좋다.

여자가 새 의자가 많은 개선이 이루어졌다고(The new chairs are an especially big improvement) 했으므로 정답은 (A)이다.

Questions 47-49 refer to the following conversation. (미W) (미M)

W Excuse me. I'd like to go to Nathan Philips Square. Will this bus take me there?
M No, it won't. You are actually on the wrong side of the street to catch west-bound buses. You will have to take the same number 80 bus, but on the opposite side of the road. It goes west to Nathan Philips Square.
W Oh, I see. Thank you for your help.
M You're welcome. You will see a pharmacy around the corner when you cross the street. And the bus stop you need is right next to it.

여 실례합니다. 저는 Nathan Philips 광장에 가고 싶은데요. 이 버스가 거기 가나요?
남 아니요, 안 갑니다. 실은 서쪽 방향으로 가는 버스를 타는데 길의 반대쪽에 서 계세요. 똑같이 80번 버스를 타시되 길의 맞은편에서 타셔야 합니다. 그건 Nathan Philips 광장 방향 서쪽으로 갑니다.
여 아, 그렇군요. 도와주셔서 감사합니다.
남 천만에요. 길을 건너시면 모퉁이에 약국이 보일 겁니다. 찾으시는 버스 정류장은 바로 그 옆입니다.

square 광장 west-bound 서쪽 방향의

47 Who most likely is the man?
(A) A pharmacist
(B) A bus driver
(C) A store clerk
(D) A security guard

남자는 누구일 것 같은가?
(A) 약사
(B) 버스 기사
(C) 상점 점원
(D) 경비원

남자의 직업을 찾는 문제로, 문제의 힌트는 도입부부터 찾아야 한다. 여자가 남자에게 어떤 광장에 가는데 이 버스가 가는지 물었고 남자는 안 간다고 했으므로 정답은 (B)이다.

48 What problem does the man mention?
(A) The woman does not have a ticket.
(B) The street is being repaired.
(C) The traffic light is broken.
(D) The bus goes in the opposite direction.

남자는 어떤 문제점을 언급하는가?
(A) 여자는 표가 없다.
(B) 도로가 수리 중이다.
(C) 신호등이 고장이다.
(D) 버스는 반대 방향으로 간다.

남자 대사에게 언급되는 문제점으로 여자가 원하는 버스는 길 건너편에서 타야 한다고 했으므로 정답은 (D)가 된다. the wrong side of the street(도로의 잘못된 방향)에 있다고 했고 the opposite side of the road(도로의 맞은편)으로 가야 한다고 했던 표현들을 기억해 두자.

49 What will the woman probably do next?
(A) Look at a map
(B) Get another ticket
(C) Cross the street
(D) Buy some medication
여자는 다음에 무엇을 할 것 같은가?
(A) 지도 보기
(B) 다른 표 사기
(C) 길 건너기
(D) 약 사기

향후 행동을 묻는 질문으로 대화의 후반부에 단서가 있다. You will see a pharmacy around the corner when you cross the street(일단 길을 건너면 약국이 보일 거다)이라고 했으므로 정답은 (C)이다.

Questions 50-52 refer to the following conversation. 미W 영M

W Hello. I'm here to pick up the computer I ordered through your website, but I forgot to bring my order form. Is that a problem?
M No, that's okay. With our customer database, we can locate your order using your telephone number rather than your order number.
W Oh, that's convenient. My number is 555-0378. I ordered the computer two days ago. Is it ready to be picked up?
M I have your information right here. Umm... yes, it is ready. And I see you paid with your credit card in advance. So, please wait here for a minute. I'll go get it for you.

여 안녕하세요. 저는 웹 사이트상에서 주문한 컴퓨터를 가지러 왔는데요. 주문서를 가져오는 것을 깜빡했습니다. 문제가 될까요?
남 아니요, 괜찮습니다. 저희 고객 데이터로는 주문 번호보다는 전화번호로 주문 내역을 찾을 수 있거든요.
여 아, 그거 편리하네요. 제 전화번호는 555-0378입니다. 이틀 전에 컴퓨터를 주문했었는데요. 지금 가져갈 준비가 되었나요?
남 여기 당신의 정보가 있네요. 음… 네, 준비되었습니다. 그리고 미리 신용 카드로 결제하신 것으로 나오네요. 여기서 잠시만 기다리세요. 갖고 오겠습니다.

order form 주문서 locate 찾다 in advance 미리

50 What did the woman forget to bring?
(A) A broken computer
(B) An original receipt
(C) An order form
(D) A user manual
여자는 무엇을 가져오는 것을 잊었는가?
(A) 고장 난 컴퓨터
(B) 영수증 원본
(C) 주문서
(D) 사용자 설명서

세부 사항 질문이므로 순발력 있게 여자가 깜빡 잊은 것을 포착해야 한다. I forgot to bring my order form에서 주문서를 잊어버렸음을 알 수 있으므로 정답은 (C)이다.

51 What does the woman mean when she says, "Oh, that's convenient"?
(A) The store is located close to a subway station.
(B) She does not have to remember her order number.
(C) A free delivery service is provided.
(D) She can purchase an item online.
여자가 "아, 그거 편리하네요"라고 말한 의미는 무엇인가?
(A) 가게가 지하철역과 가까이에 위치해 있다.
(B) 여자가 주문 번호를 기억할 필요가 없다.
(C) 무료 배송 서비스가 제공된다.
(D) 여자가 상품을 온라인으로 구입할 수 있다.

해당 표현 자체는 무엇인가가 편리하다는 의미이므로 앞뒤 문맥을 통해 정확한 의미를 파악해야 한다. 주문서를 깜빡 한 여자에게 괜찮다고 하며 전화번호로 물건을 찾을 수 있다고 했으므로(we can locate your order using your telephone number rather than your order number), 여자가 굳이 주문번호를 외울 필요가 없어서 편리하다는 의미이다.

52 What will the man probably do next?
(A) Bring some merchandise
(B) Make a telephone call
(C) Go to the cashier
(D) Write down some information
남자는 다음에 무엇을 할 것 같은가?
(A) 상품 가져오기
(B) 전화하기
(C) 계산대로 가기
(D) 정보 적기

남자가 후반부에 주문한 컴퓨터를 I'll go get it for you(가서 갖고 오겠다)라고 했으므로 정답은 (A)가 된다.

Questions 53-55 refer to the following conversation. 영W 미M

W Hi, my name is Rhonda Trump and I'm calling about my luggage. I flew in from New York on flight 803 this morning and your airline lost my checked suitcase. Could you see if my suitcase has been located yet?
M One moment, Ms. Trump. Yes, we've found your luggage. If you give me the address of your hotel, I'll have it delivered to you by 4 o'clock.
W I'm staying at the Millennium Hotel on Nathan Road, but can I get the bag earlier? I have an important business meeting to attend at 2 and I don't have a proper outfit to wear.
M Don't worry, Ms. Trump. I'll be sure to get your luggage to you before the meeting.

여 안녕하세요. 저는 Ronda Trump이고 짐 때문에 전화했어요. 저는 오늘 아침에 뉴욕에서 803항공편을 통해 들어왔는데요, 그쪽 항공사에서 제가 맡긴 여행 가방을 분실했어요. 가방을 찾았는지 확인해 주시겠습니까?
남 잠시만요, Trump 씨. 네, 손님의 짐을 찾았습니다. 호텔 주소를 알려 주시면 제가 4시까지 보내 드릴게요.
여 전 Nathan Road에 있는 Millennium 호텔에 투숙하고 있습니다만, 가방을 좀 더 일찍 받을 수 있을까요? 제가 2시에 중요한 미팅에 참석해야 하는데, 입고 갈 적당한 옷이 없네요.
남 문제없습니다, Trump 씨. 미팅 전에 짐을 보내 드리겠습니다.

luggage 짐 flew (fly의 과거형) 비행기를 타다 checked (비행기를 탈 때) 맡긴, 부친 locate 찾다 proper 적절한, 적당한 outfit 의상, 옷

53 Why is the woman calling?
(A) To inquire about a missing item
(B) To book a hotel room
(C) To cancel a flight
(D) To make travel arrangements
여자는 왜 전화를 하는가?
(A) 없어진 물건에 대해 문의하기 위하여
(B) 호텔 방을 예약하기 위하여
(C) 항공편을 취소하기 위하여
(D) 여행 준비를 하기 위하여

전화 대화에서의 목적은 I'm calling to + V, I'm calling about 등의 힌트 표현과 함께 언급된다. 도입부에 여자가 I'm calling about my luggage라고 말하면서 항공사에서 짐을 잃어버렸다고 했으므로 정답은 (A)가 된다. flight가 들린다고 해서 (C)로 선택하는 실수는 하지 않도록 하자.

54 What does the woman say she will do in the afternoon?
(A) Go to a meeting
(B) Finalize an agreement
(C) Review a travel itinerary
(D) Stay in a hotel
여자는 오후에 무엇을 할 것이라고 말하는가?
(A) 회의에 가기
(B) 계약 마무리하기
(C) 여행 여정 검토하기
(D) 호텔에 머물기

질문의 키워드는 in the afternoon이다. 여자가 2시에 참석할 중요한 미팅이 있다고 했으므로 정답은 (A)이다. 조심할 부분은 in the afternoon이 at 2로 바꿔 표현되는 것을 놓치지 않아야 한다는 것이다.

55 What does the man agree to change?
(A) The location of an event
(B) A project deadline
(C) A holiday destination
(D) A delivery time
남자는 무엇을 변경하기로 동의하는가?
(A) 행사의 장소
(B) 프로젝트 마감 시간
(C) 휴가 목적지
(D) 배송 시간

세부 사항 질문으로 남자가 변경에 동의하는 내용이 있을 것을 미리 파악해두자. 여자가 짐을 좀 더 일찍 받을 수 있는지 요청했고, 남자가 이에 동의하며 미팅 전에 가방을 보내주기로 했으므로 정답은 (D)가 된다. 문맥을 이해하여 변경되는 것이 delivery time이란 점을 파악해야 하는 고난도 문제이다.

Questions 56-58 refer to the following conversation. 영M 영W

M Hello, Ms. Salvador. I asked to meet with you because I've decided to leave my job here to move to Boston.
W I'm surprised to hear that. You've done a great job as a police reporter. What made you decide to leave our company?
M Well, I've loved working here at The Daily Newspaper. It's been a privilege to be a part of such a distinguished newspaper company. But I want to live closer to my family and friends now and I've been offered a job in Boston.
W We'll certainly miss you a lot, Michael. I wish you the best of luck with your new job.

남 여보세요, Salvador 씨. 제가 보스턴으로 이사를 가게 되어 이곳 직장을 떠나기로 결정했기 때문에 뵙자고 요청을 드렸습니다.
여 조금 놀랐습니다. 당신은 경찰 전문 기자로서 일을 훌륭하게 해줬는데요. 무엇 때문에 우리 회사를 그만두기로 결정하셨나요?
남 음, 저는 여기 Daily Newspaper에서 일하는 것을 좋아했습니다. 이런 유명한 신문사의 일원으로 함께 할 수 있어서 영광이었습니다. 그러나 전 가족과 친구들과 가까이에 살고 싶고, 또 보스턴에서 일도 제안 받았습니다.
여 당신을 많이 그리워할 거예요 Michael. 새 직장에서도 행운을 빌겠습니다.

leave one's job 일을 그만두다 do a great job 일을 잘하다 police reporter 경찰 전문 기자 privilege 특권, 영광 distinguished 유명한, 성공한

56 Why did the man want to talk to the woman?
(A) To announce his resignation
(B) To make some suggestions
(C) To request vacation days
(D) To discuss a new project
남자는 왜 여자와 얘기하고 싶었는가?
(A) 그의 사직을 알리기 위하여
(B) 몇몇 제안을 하기 위하여
(C) 휴가를 요구하기 위하여
(D) 새로운 프로젝트에 대해 얘기하기 위하여

남자 대사에서 미팅을 요청한 이유를 찾자. because I've decided to leave my job here to move to Boston에서 남자는 직장을 그만둔다는 이야기를 하기 위해서 여자를 만났다는 것을 알 수 있다.

57 What type of company do the speakers probably work for?
(A) A theater company
(B) A newspaper
(C) A financial firm
(D) A police force

어떤 종류의 회사에서 화자는 일할 것 같은가?
(A) 극단
(B) 신문사
(C) 금융 회사
(D) 경찰서

화자의 직장을 유추하는 질문으로 남자의 업무, 직업 등이 힌트이다. 여자가 남자에게 You've done a great job as a police reporter(경찰 전문 기자로서 훌륭하게 일해 왔다)라고 했으므로 정답은 (B)이다.

58 What does the man say about Boston?
(A) He was born there.
(B) It has many newspaper companies.
(C) It is popular with tourists.
(D) His family and friends live there.
남자는 보스턴에 관하여 무엇을 말하는가?
(A) 그는 거기서 태어났다.
(B) 그곳에는 신문사가 많이 있다.
(C) 그곳은 관광객에게 인기가 많다.
(D) 그의 가족과 친구가 거기 산다.

보스턴에 대해서 여러 가지가 언급되었으나 보기와 일치하는 것은 보스턴으로 이사 가는 이유가 가족과 친구들과 가까이 살고 싶어서라고 밝혔던 부분이 된다. 정답은 (D)이다.

Questions 59-61 refer to the following conversation with three speakers. (미M) (영M) (영W)

M1 Thank you for coming, Valerie and Ron. We have to think about mailing out invitations for the next photo exhibition. How many people should we invite?
M2 Well, I think we should only invite our regular customers for the opening ceremony. It was just too crowded at our last opening. People were too bunched together and couldn't see any of the photos properly.
W You have a point there, Ron. But we sold most of the photos on that first day. I'm just worried that sales may go down with fewer guests.
M2 How about we invite art critics as well? Their reviews will bring in more people during the rest of the exhibition.
W That's a good idea, Ron. We'll still be able to sell a lot of photos that way.

남1 와 주셔서 감사합니다, Valerie와 Ron. 우리가 다음번 사진전을 위한 초대장을 발송해야 합니다. 몇 명이나 초대하는 게 좋을까요?
남2 음, 제 생각에는 오픈 행사에 단골 고객들만 초대하는 것이 좋을 것 같아요. 지난번 오픈 때에는 너무 붐볐거든요. 사람들이 너무 붙어 있어서 제대로 사진을 볼 수가 없었어요.
여 좋은 지적이네요, Ron. 그렇지만 우리는 첫날에 대부분의 사진을 팔았어요. 고객이 적으면 판매도 줄어들까 걱정이 됩니다.
남2 그럼 예술 평론가들도 초대하는 게 어떨까요? 그들의 평론이 나머지 전시 기간에 사람들을 더 불러 모을 수 있을 거예요.
여 좋은 생각이에요, Ron. 그렇게 하면 여전히 사진을 많이 판매할 수 있겠네요.

regular customer 단골 고객 bunch together 서로 붙어 있다 art critic 예술 평론가

59 What are the speakers mainly discussing?
(A) Mailing costs
(B) Preparations for an event
(C) Negative reviews
(D) Sales of a new book
화자들은 무엇을 주로 얘기하고 있는가?
(A) 우편 비용
(B) 행사 준비
(C) 부정적 논평
(D) 신간 서적의 판매

주제를 묻는 질문으로 도입부에 사진전에 대한 초대장을 발송해야 한다고 했으므로 행사를 준비하는 것에 대한 대화이다.

60 What does the woman mean when she says, "You have a point there, Ron"?
(A) She organized the last opening.
(B) Ron has made a mistake.
(C) They need a larger space.
(D) The last event was overcrowded.
여자가 "좋은 지적이네요, Ron"이라고 말한 의미는 무엇인가?
(A) 그녀가 마지막 오프닝을 준비했었다.
(B) Ron이 실수했다.
(C) 그들은 더 큰 공간이 필요하다.
(D) 지난 행사는 지나치게 혼잡했다.

남자가 지난 행사 때 너무 혼잡했다는 문제점을 지적했을 때 "You have a point there, Ron"이라고 말한 것이므로 남자의 지적에 동의한다는 뜻이다. 그러므로 정답은 (D)이다.

61 What does Ron suggest doing?
(A) Inviting local critics
(B) Advertising in the local newspaper
(C) Printing more brochures
(D) Sending out more invitations
Ron는 무엇을 할 것을 제안하는가?
(A) 지역 비평가를 초대하는 것
(B) 지역 신문사에 광고하는 것
(C) 안내 책자를 더 인쇄하는 것
(D) 초대장을 더 발송하는 것

3인 대화이므로 Ron이라는 이름을 놓치지 않도록 하자. 지역 평론가들도 초청을 하자(How about we invite art critics as well?)고 제안했으므로 정답은 (A)이다.

Questions 62-64 refer to the following conversation and floor plan. (미W) (미M)

W Bruno, could you take a quick look at the room assignments for our relocation before you leave today? I know you need to leave for a meeting soon, but I'd like to have it finalized before I meet with the sales staff at 4 p.m.

M Right. You're supposed to let them know about the floor plan layout at the meeting today. So, what exactly are we looking at?

W Well, Offices 2 and 4, the two largest offices, are assigned to the sales people and you've been given the office with the big window next to the staff lounge.

M Okay, it looks good. So that means the office in the middle is for you, right?

W Yes. That way I can be close to both you and the sales teams.

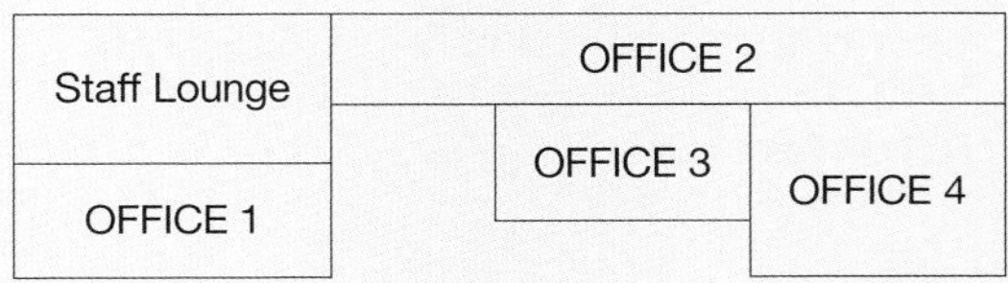

여 Bruno, 오늘 퇴근하시기 전에 우리 사무실 이전용 배치도를 좀 봐 주시겠어요? 미팅 때문에 곧 나가셔야 하는 거 알지만 전 오늘 오후 4시 영업부 직원과의 미팅에 가기 전에 이걸 마무리하고 싶어서요.

남 그래요. 오늘 미팅 때 배치도에 대해서 직원들에게 알려 주기로 되어 있죠. 그래서 정확히 뭘 보면 되는 거죠?

여 음, 가장 큰 2번과 4번 사무실은 영업 사원들에게 배정을 했고 당신은 직원 휴게실 옆 창문이 큰 사무실을 받으셨어요.

남 네, 좋아 보이네요. 그러면 이 중간에 있는 사무실이 당신 거죠, 맞죠?

여 네. 이렇게 하면 저는 당신과 영업팀 둘 다와 가깝게 있을 수 있어요.

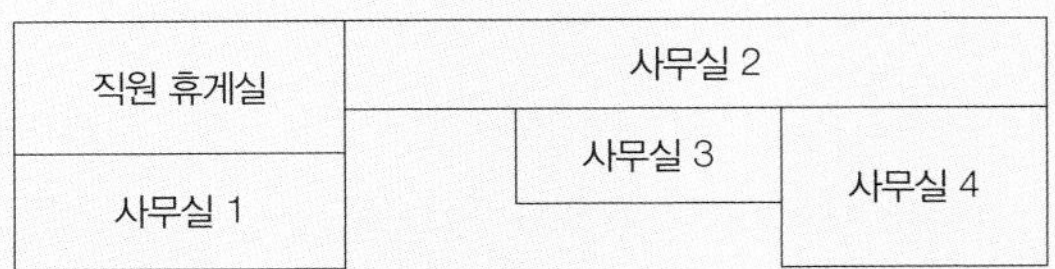

take a look at 살펴보다 room assignments 사무실 배치도 relocation 이전 finalize 마무리하다 floor plan layout 평면 배치도

62 What does the woman ask the man to do?
(A) Lease office space
(B) Review the room assignments
(C) Submit a sales report
(D) Purchase some office furniture

여자는 남자에게 무엇을 하라고 요청하는가?
(A) 사무실 공간을 빌리라고
(B) 사무실 배치도를 검토하라고
(C) 판매 보고서를 제출하라고
(D) 사무용 가구를 구매하라고

여자가 could you take a quick look at the room assignments(사무실 배치도를 봐달라)라고 했으므로 정답은 (B)가 된다.

63 Who will the woman meet with later today?
(A) Marketing experts
(B) The company president
(C) Sales staff
(D) An architect

오늘 나중에 여자는 누구를 만나는가?
(A) 마케팅 전문가
(B) 회사 사장
(C) 영업팀 직원
(D) 건축가

세부 사항 질문이므로 여자가 만날 사람에 집중하여 듣는다. 사무실 배치도를 마무리하고 싶다고 하며 before I meet with the sales staff at 4 p.m.(오후 4시에 있을 영업부 직원과의 미팅 전에)이라고 했으므로 여자는 이따가 영업팀 직원들을 만날 것임을 알 수 있다.

64 Look at the graphic. Which office has been assigned to the man?
(A) Office 1
(B) Office 2
(C) Office 3
(D) Office 4

시각 정보를 보시오. 남자에게 어느 사무실이 할당되었는가?
(A) 사무실 1
(B) 사무실 2
(C) 사무실 3
(D) 사무실 4

남자에게 배정된 사무실을 미리 염두에 두고 대화 내용을 듣는다. 사무실 2번과 4번은 판매팀에게 배정되었고, 남자는 staff lounge 옆의 사무실로 배정되었다고 했으므로 정답은 (A)이다.

Questions 65-67 refer to the following conversation and list. (미W) (영M)

W Hello, my name is Alicia Donovan. I'm calling about a fax machine that I ordered from your shop a week ago. Why has it not arrived yet?
M Sorry for the inconvenience. Let me check your account first. Could you give me your order number please?
W I don't have it right now. Could you search the account with my name?
M Sure, it's Alicia Donovan, right? Here it is. You ordered one fax machine six days ago and you paid $300 with your credit card. Oh, you'll be glad to hear that the price of the model you ordered has gone up recently. It is now $330.
W I guess I got lucky. By the way, when can I expect the delivery?
M According to our shipping records, your order will arrive this afternoon.

Price list (Fax Machines)	
Item	Price
Paramount Fax Machine	$250
MP Fax Machine	$300
Neon Fax Machine	$350
Priority Fax Machine	$400

여 안녕하세요, 저는 Alicia Donovan입니다. 제가 일주일 전에 당신네 가게에서 주문한 팩스기 때문에 전화를 드리는데요. 왜 아직 도착이 안 되고 있나요?
남 불편을 드려 죄송합니다. 제가 당신의 계정을 먼저 살펴볼게요. 주문 번호를 불러주시겠습니까?
여 지금 없는데요. 제 이름으로 계정을 찾아봐 주실 수 있나요?
남 알겠습니다, Alicia Donovan이시죠? 여기 있네요. 팩스기 한 대를 6일 전에 주문하셨고 300달러를 신용 카드로 지불하셨네요. 주문하신 그 모델의 가격이 최근에 올랐다는 사실은 들으시면 기쁘실 것 같네요. 이제는 330달러거든요.
여 제가 운이 좋았던 것 같네요. 그나저나 배달이 언제쯤 올까요?
남 저희 배송 기록에 따르면 오늘 오후에는 도착할 거예요.

가격표 (팩스기)	
상품	가격
Paramount 팩스기	250달러
MP 팩스기	300달러
Neon 팩스기	350달러
Priority 팩스기	400달러

account (고객의) 계정 go up (가격이) 오르다 shipping records 배송 기록

65 Why is the woman calling?
(A) To update contact information
(B) To inquire about a shipment
(C) To place an order
(D) To cancel an appointment

여자는 왜 전화를 하는가?
(A) 연락 정보를 업데이트 하려고
(B) 배송에 관하여 문의하려고
(C) 주문하려고
(D) 약속을 취소하려고

도입부 여자 대사에서 정답을 찾자. 주문한 팩스기 때문에 전화하고 있는데 왜 배송이 아직 안 오는지 물었으므로 정답은 (B)이다.

66 Look at the graphic. Which model did the woman order a week ago?
(A) Paramount Fax Machine
(B) MP Fax Machine
(C) Neon Fax Machine
(D) Priority Fax Machine

시각 정보를 보시오. 여자는 일주일 전에 어떤 모델을 주문했는가?
(A) Paramount Fax Machine
(B) MP Fax Machine
(C) Neon Fax Machine
(D) Priority Fax Machine

여자가 6일 전에 팩스기를 한 대 주문하고 300달러를 지불했다고 했으므로 정답은 (B)이다. 그 이후 해당 모델의 가격이 인상되었다는 언급이 있었으나 여자의 주문 내역과는 관계가 없다.

67 According to the man, when will the order arrive?
(A) Today
(B) Tomorrow
(C) In two days
(D) In a week

남자에 따르면, 주문은 언제 도착할 것인가?
(A) 오늘
(B) 내일
(C) 이틀 후에
(D) 일주일 후에

주문이 도착할 시점은 your order will arrive this afternoon(오늘 오후)이므로 today로 패러프레이징된다. 정답은 (A)이다.

Questions 68-70 refer to the following conversation and list.
영M 미W

M Jane, the presentation you gave this morning was excellent. The cost-cutting measures you suggested sounded very feasible. So, I'd like to you to make your report more comprehensive for myself and the other department directors.
W Okay, Mr. Hastings. But how soon do you need it? I'm currently working on the cost-benefit analysis for the sales department. And I'm supposed to present it to Ms. Larson by Thursday.
M Hmm... I was hoping to have the report for the directors' meeting on Thursday. I'll tell you what! I'll contact Ms. Larson, the sales manager, and ask her to give you an extension on that assignment. This report should be your top priority because the company president will see it as well.
W Okay, Mr. Hastings. I'll get on it right away.

Employee Directory	
Name	Extension
Beth Hall	55
Jonathan Hastings	9
Sandra Larson	23
Melody Wong	15

남 Jane, 오늘 아침에 한 발표가 매우 훌륭했어요. 제안했던 비용 절감 정책이 굉장히 실현 가능하게 들렸거든요. 그래서 그 보고서를 저와 다른 부서장들을 위해서 좀 더 종합적으로 만들어 줬으면 합니다.
여 알겠습니다, Hastings 씨. 그런데 얼마나 빨리 필요하세요? 저는 지금 판매 부서에서 원한 손익 분석표를 작업하고 있었거든요. Larson 씨에게 목요일까지 제출하기로 되어 있어서요.
남 흠… 저는 목요일 부서장 미팅 전에 그 보고서를 받아 보고 싶어요. 이렇게 하죠! 제가 판매 부장인 Larson 씨에게 연락해서 그 업무에 대해서는 마감 연장을 해 달라고 요청하죠. 사장님께서도 보실 것이기 때문에 이 보고서가 당신의 최우선 업무여야 합니다.
여 알겠습니다, Hastings 씨. 지금 당장 착수하겠습니다.

직원 전화번호부	
이름	내선번호
Beth Hall	55
Jonathan Hastings	9
Sandra Larson	23
Melody Wong	15

cost-cutting 비용을 절감하는 measure 정책 feasible 실현 가능한 extension 연장 top priority 최우선 순위 get on 착수하다

68 What does the man say about the presentation?
(A) The woman did a good job on it.
(B) The company president attended it.
(C) It contained incorrect information.
(D) It took a lot of time.

남자는 발표에 관하여 무엇을 말하는가?
(A) 여자가 발표를 잘 했다.
(B) 회사 사장이 발표에 참석했다.
(C) 발표에 부정확한 정보가 포함되었다.
(D) 발표는 오랜 시간이 걸렸다.

남자의 대사에서 presentation이 언급되는 부분을 잘 듣자. 여자에게 발표가 훌륭했다(the presentation you gave this morning was excellent)고 했으므로 정답은 (A)가 된다.

69 Why is the woman concerned?
(A) She is not good at analyzing data.
(B) She has to finish another assignment.
(C) She is unavailable to attend a meeting.
(D) She will be on a business trip.

여자는 왜 염려를 하는가?
(A) 자료 분석을 잘하지 못한다.
(B) 다른 업무를 끝내야 한다.
(C) 회의에 참석할 시간이 없다.
(D) 출장에 가야 한다.

남자가 맡긴 업무에 대해 얼마나 빨리 필요한지(But how soon do you need it?) 되물으면서 현재 다른 업무를 하고 있다고 했으므로 정답은 (B)가 맞다.

70 Look at the graphic. What extension will the man most likely call?
(A) 55
(B) 9
(C) 23
(D) 15

시각 정보를 보시오. 남자는 어떤 내선 번호로 전화를 할 것 같은가?
(A) 55
(B) 9
(C) 23
(D) 15

남자는 판매 부서장인 Larson 씨에게 연락을 취하겠다고 했으므로 전화번호부상의 23번으로 전화를 할 것이다.

PART 4

Questions 71-73 refer to the recorded message. (영W)

Hello. This recorded message is to notify all residents that we will be doing maintenance work on the plumbing system this weekend. Water supplies for the apartment complex will be shut off at 9 a.m. on Saturday. The work will be finished on Saturday evening and water will be available again by Sunday morning. To avoid being inconvenienced, please make sure you prepare enough water to use for the day. Thank you.

안녕하세요. 이 녹음된 메시지는 전 주민들에게 이번 주에 배관 보수 작업이 있음을 알리기 위한 것입니다. 아파트 단지의 물 공급은 토요일 오전 9시에 끊길 것입니다. 작업은 토요일 저녁에 끝날 것이고 물은 일요일 아침부터 다시 사용할 수 있습니다. 불편을 피하기 위해서는 하루 동안 사용할 충분한 물을 준비해 놓으세요. 감사합니다.

notify 알리다 maintenance work 보수 작업 plumbing system 배관 시스템 water supplies 물 공급 shut off 끊다

71 What type of work is scheduled?
(A) Software testing
(B) Computer upgrades
(C) Telephone system replacement
(D) Plumbing maintenance

어떤 종류의 공사가 잡혀 있는가?
(A) 소프트웨어 테스트
(B) 컴퓨터 업그레이드
(C) 전화시스템 교체
(D) 배관 보수

도입부의 메시지 목적에서 배관 보수 공사가 있을 것임을 주민들에게 알렸으므로 정답은 (D)가 된다.

72 When will the work be completed?
(A) On Monday
(B) On Friday
(C) On Saturday
(D) On Sunday

공사는 언제 완료될 것인가?
(A) 월요일
(B) 금요일
(C) 토요일
(D) 일요일

요일이 한 개 이상 언급되므로 정확하게 '공사 완료 시점'을 찾아야 한다. The work will be finished on Saturday evening라고 했으므로 정답은 (C)이다. (D)는 물 공급이 다시 이루어지는 시점이므로 답이 될 수 없다.

73 What are listeners encouraged to do?
(A) Store water
(B) Speak to the manager
(C) Prepare for a presentation
(D) Return a phone call

청자들은 무엇을 하라는 권고를 받는가?
(A) 물 저장하기
(B) 매니저에게 이야기하기
(C) 발표 준비하기
(D) 답신 전화하기

Please로 시작하는 권고 표현이 힌트가 된다. please make sure you prepare enough water to use for the day에서 하루 동안 쓸 물을 준비해 두라고 했으므로 정답은 (A)가 맞다.

Questions 74-76 refer to the following announcement. (미M)

Here's a special offer from Fiesta Electronics. Everybody knows that Fiesta Electronics has the lowest prices in town. But now through Sunday, we're offering an additional 20% off on our complete line of laptop computers. So hurry! This special offer will only last until Sunday. And when you purchase one of our laptop computers, you will receive a complimentary laptop computer bag. Come visit us today! We're located in the Pearl Shopping District, just off Highway 22.

Fiesta Electronics로부터의 특별한 혜택이 여기 있습니다! 모든 사람들이 Fiesta Electronics가 우리 동네에서 가장 싸다는 것을 알고 있죠. 그러나 지금부터 일요일까지, 모든 노트북 컴퓨터에 대해 추가로 20퍼센트를 더 할인해 드립니다. 그러니 서두르세요! 이 특가 혜택은 오직 일요일까지만 유지됩니다. 그리고 노트북 컴퓨터를 사시면, 무료로 노트북 컴퓨터 가방도 받게 됩니다. 오늘 저희를 방문해 주세요! 저희는 22번 고속 도로에서 나오자마자 Pearl Shopping District에 있습니다!

special offer 특가 혜택 additional 추가의 complimentary 무료의, 공짜의 just off + 장소 바로 옆에

74 What type of business is being advertised?
(A) A grocery store
(B) An electronics store
(C) A clothing store
(D) A photography studio

어떤 종류의 업체가 광고되는가?
(A) 식료품점
(B) 가전제품 상점
(C) 옷 가게
(D) 사진 스튜디오

광고되는 업체는 도입부에서 찾자. 업체명 Fiesta Electronics로부터 가전제품 가게임을 알 수 있고 컴퓨터를 할인한다고 했으니 정답은 (B)가 된다.

75 What will happen on Sunday?
(A) A new product will be released.
(B) A store will be relocated.
(C) A special offer will end.
(D) A business will be closed.

일요일에 무슨 일이 있을 것인가?
(A) 신제품이 출시될 것이다.
(B) 상점이 이전할 것이다.

(C) **특별 혜택이 끝날 것이다.**
(D) 사업체가 문을 닫을 것이다.

질문의 키워드인 Sunday를 놓치지 말고 듣자. 특가 혜택이 지금부터 일요일까지라고 했고 또 한 번 This special offer will only last until Sunday(일요일까지만 혜택이 제공된다)라고 했으므로 정답은 (C)가 맞다.

76 What is offered free of charge?
(A) Laptop cases
(B) Home delivery
(C) Computer software
(D) Refreshments

무엇이 무료로 제공되는가?
(A) **노트북 컴퓨터 케이스**
(B) 가정 배달
(C) 컴퓨터 소프트웨어
(D) 다과

질문의 키워드인 free of charge(공짜)인 것을 놓치지 말자. 컴퓨터를 사는 분께는 컴퓨터 가방을 무료로 받을 수 있다고 했으므로 정답은 (A)가 된다.

Questions 77-79 refer to the following announcement. 미W

Ladies and gentlemen, this is Julia Murray and I'm your chief flight attendant. On behalf of Captain Leigh and the entire crew, welcome aboard Flight 701, with non-stop service from Seattle to Paris. Our flight will take off shortly, so please make sure that your seat backs and tray tables are in their full upright position. Also, please fasten your seat belts and turn off any of your portable electronic devices during take-off. Thank you.

신사 숙녀 여러분, 저는 여러분의 수석 승무원인 Julia Murray입니다. Leigh 기장님과 전체 승무원을 대신하여, 시애틀에서 파리까지 가는 직행편인 701호기에 탑승하신 것을 환영합니다. 우리 항공기는 곧 이륙을 할 것이니 좌석 등받이와 트레이를 똑바로 세워 원래의 자리대로 놓아 주십시오. 또한 안전벨트를 착용해 주시고 가지고 계신 어떤 휴대용 가전 기기도 이륙 중에는 꺼 주십시오. 감사합니다.

on behalf of ~를 대신해서 non-stop 직행의 in full upright position 원래의 똑바른 자세로 portable 휴대가 가능한 take-off 이륙

77 Who most likely is the speaker?
(A) The captain
(B) A mechanic
(C) A flight attendant
(D) An airport employee

화자는 누구일 것 같은가?
(A) 기장
(B) 기계공
(C) **승무원**
(D) 공항 직원

도입부에 화자가 자기소개를 하는 this is Julia Murray and I'm your chief flight attendant에서 승무원임을 알 수 있다.

78 Which city is the flight departing from?
(A) Seattle
(B) London
(C) Paris
(D) Singapore

비행기는 어느 도시에서 떠나는가?
(A) **시애틀**
(B) 런던
(C) 파리
(D) 싱가포르

세부 사항을 묻는 질문이므로 순발력 있게 출발지를 고르자. 비행기가 from Seattle to Paris라고 했으므로 시애틀을 출발해서 파리로 가는 것이 된다. 정답은 (A)이다.

79 What are passengers asked to do during take-off?
(A) Listen to a weather forecast
(B) Sit back and enjoy the view
(C) Speak to a flight attendant
(D) Turn off electronic devices

승객들은 이륙 중에 무엇을 하라고 요청 받는가?
(A) 일기 예보를 경청하라고
(B) 뒤로 기대 앉아 경치를 즐기라고
(C) 승무원과 이야기하라고
(D) **전자 기기를 끄라고**

이륙 중에 할 내용으로 보기와 일치하는 것은 turn off any of your portable electronic devices during take-off이다. 모든 전자 기기를 끄라고 했으므로 정답은 (D)가 된다.

Questions 80-82 refer to the following talk. 영M

Thank you all for coming to see our new fitness center. My name is Harry Jones. As the center's manager, I'll be leading today's tour. In addition to our new state-of-the-art equipment, we offer a wide range of fitness, martial arts, and yoga classes. And we offer free nutrition classes to our members, which no other centers do. So if you become a member, you can learn many tips for a healthy diet for free. Okay, just one more thing before we begin our tour. As an added bonus, if you decide to join today, you can get 10 percent off the cost of any membership plan you choose.

저희 새로운 피트니스 센터에 와 주셔서 감사합니다. 저는 Harry Jones입니다. 센터의 매니저로서 제가 오늘의 투어를 진행하겠습니다. 최신의 장비뿐 아니라, 저희는 다양한 종류의 운동, 무술, 요가 수업을 제공합니다. 그리고 다른 센터에서는 하지 않는 무료 영양 수업을 회원들에게 제공합니다. 그래서 여러분은 회원이 되시면 건강한 식이요법에 대한 많은 팁들을 무료로 배울 수 있습니다. 좋습니다, 투어 시작 전에 한 가지만 더 알려 드리겠습니다. 추가적인 보너스로서 오늘 가입을 결정하시면, 어떤 멤버십을 선택하시든 10퍼센트 할인을 해 드리겠습니다.

lead a tour 투어를 진행하다 in addition to ~뿐만 아니라 a wide range of 다양한 martial arts 무술 for free 공짜로

80 Who most likely are the listeners?
(A) Yoga teachers
(B) Center managers
(C) Prospective members
(D) Engineers

청자들은 누구일 것 같은가?
(A) 요가 강사
(B) 센터 매니저
(C) 잠재 회원
(D) 엔지니어

듣는 사람들을 유추하는 질문으로 화자가 본인을 피트니스 센터 매니저라고 밝힌 후, 센터의 투어를 진행하겠다고 하는 점, 센터의 수업 등에 대해 설명하는 점 등에서 듣는 이들은 잠재 회원들임을 알 수 있다.

81 What special service does the fitness center offer?
(A) A cooking demonstration
(B) Some nutrition tips
(C) A charity concert
(D) A free shuttle bus

피트니스 센터는 무슨 특별 서비스를 제공하는가?
(A) 요리 시연
(B) 영양 관련 조언
(C) 자선 연주회
(D) 무료 셔틀 버스

여러 가지 운동 관련 수업과 더불어 we offer free nutrition classes to our members, which no other centers do(다른 센터에서는 제공하지 않는 무료 영양 수업을 제공한다)라고 했으므로 정답은 (B)가 맞다.

82 What will listeners probably do next?
(A) Sell tickets
(B) Complete a survey
(C) Reduce prices
(D) Go on a tour

청자들은 다음에 무엇을 할 것 같은가?
(A) 티켓을 판다.
(B) 설문지를 완성한다.
(C) 가격을 할인해 준다.
(D) 투어를 한다.

투어 시작 전에 마지막 공지 사항을 전달하겠다(just one more thing before we begin our tour)고 말한 것에서, 담화가 끝난 후에는 투어를 시작하게 될 것임을 알 수 있다. (C)는 할인을 해주는 쪽은 청자들이 아니기 때문에 정답이 될 수 없다.

Questions 83-85 refer to the following excerpt from a meeting.
영W

Good morning everyone. My name is Angela Taylor, the manager of human resources. I'd like to welcome you all to BT Manufacturing. The first item on the agenda today is how to report your work hours. Since we use an online reporting system, you can enter your hours through the company's website. You can find step-by-step instructions in the orientation packet you received earlier. Be sure to read it carefully. It is important to remember that you must report to your manager before you enter your hours whenever you work overtime. It is important because you will not get paid for the extra hours unless you notify your manager first.

좋은 아침입니다, 여러분. 저는 인사부장 Angela Taylor입니다. 여러분 모두 BT Manufacturing에 입사한 것을 환영합니다. 오늘 첫 번째 안건은 근무 시간을 기록하는 방법입니다. 우리는 온라인 기록 시스템을 사용하기 때문에, 여러분은 회사의 웹 사이트를 통해서 근무 시간을 입력할 수 있습니다. 자세한 설명서는 아까 받으신 오리엔테이션 자료집에서 보실 수 있습니다. 반드시 꼼꼼하게 읽어 보십시오. 언제든 초과 근무를 할 때에는 시간을 입력하기 전에 여러분의 매니저에게 반드시 보고해야 한다는 것을 기억해 두십시오. 매니저에게 먼저 알리지 않으면 초과 근무에 대해 수당을 받을 수 없기 때문에 중요합니다.

work hours 근무 시간 step-by-step instructions 단계별 상세 설명서 work overtime 초과 근무하다, 야근하다 get paid for ~에 대해 수당을 받다

83 Who most likely are the listeners?
(A) Department heads
(B) New employees
(C) Raw material suppliers
(D) News reporters

청자들은 누구일 것 같은가?
(A) 부서장
(B) 새로운 직원
(C) 원자재 공급자
(D) 뉴스 기자

듣는 사람들을 유추하는 질문으로 화자가 본인을 인사부장으로 소개하며 I'd like to welcome you all to BT Manufacturing이라고 말했을 때 듣는 사람들은 새롭게 입사한 신입 사원들임을 유추할 수 있다. 정답은 (B)이다.

84 What does the speaker mean when she says, "Be sure to read it carefully"?
(A) Employees should know how to report their work hours.
(B) Employees should not be late for work.
(C) Employees should set up an account.
(D) Employees should receive an orientation packet.

화자가 "반드시 꼼꼼하게 읽어 보십시오"라고 말한 의미는 무엇인가?
(A) **직원은 근무 시간 보고하는 방법을 알아야 한다.**
(B) 직원은 직장에 늦으면 안 된다.
(C) 직원은 계정을 설치해야 한다.
(D) 직원은 오리엔테이션 자료를 받아야 한다.

해당 표현 전에 근무 시간 보고 방법에 대해 설명하면서 You can find step-by-step instructions in the orientation packet(자세한 설명서는 오리엔테이션 자료집에 있다)이라고 했으므로 직원들이 내용을 숙지하여 근무 시간 보고 방법을 잘 알고 있어야 한다는 의미이다. 그러므로 정답은 (A)가 맞다.

85 In what situation, should employees notify their manager?
(A) When they are injured
(B) When they forget a password
(C) When they work extra hours
(D) When their computers are broken

직원들은 어떤 상황에서, 그들의 매니저에게 알려야 하는가?
(A) 다쳤을 때
(B) 비밀번호를 잊었을 때
(C) **초과 근무를 할 때**
(D) 컴퓨터가 고장일 때

you must report to your manager before you enter your hours whenever you work overtime에서 초과 근무 시에는 반드시 매니저에게 알려야 한다는 것을 알 수 있다. 정답은 (C)이다.

Questions 86-88 refer to the following announcement. (미M)

This announcement is for all employees. As most of you already know, a cafeteria opened on the top floor on Monday. Management, of course, highly encourages you to visit the cafeteria as often as possible. But first, I'd like to clarify the confusion over the cost of meals. The cafeteria is open to the public as well but there are differences in price between employees and regular customers. All of our staff members, including part-timers, are entitled to a 20% discount on any meals excluding beverages. In addition, if you decide to buy a set of 20 meal vouchers, you'll get an extra 10% off.

이 공지는 전 직원에게 해당됩니다. 이미 아시는 것처럼, 월요일에 구내식당이 맨 위층에 문을 열었습니다. 경영진들은, 당연히, 여러분들이 자주 방문할 것을 권고합니다. 그러나 먼저, 식사 비용에 대한 혼동을 명확히 정리해 드리려고 합니다. 구내식당은 일반 대중에게도 문을 열지만, 직원과 일반 손님 간에는 가격 차이가 있습니다. 파트타임 근무자를 포함한 우리 회사 전 직원들은 음료를 제외한 어떤 식사든지 20퍼센트 할인을 받을 자격이 주어집니다. 게다가 여러분이 20개의 식사 쿠폰을 구입하면, 10퍼센트의 추가 할인을 받을 수 있습니다.

management 경영진 clarify 명확하게 하다 confusion 혼동 be entitled to ~의 자격이 된다 voucher 쿠폰

86 What is the speaker discussing?
(A) A revised company policy
(B) A staff restaurant
(C) A coupon book
(D) A healthy diet

화자는 무엇에 대해 논의하는가?
(A) 수정된 회사 정책
(B) **직원 구내식당**
(C) 쿠폰북
(D) 건강한 식이요법

담화의 주제를 묻는 질문으로 도입부에 새로 문을 연 cafeteria(구내식당)에 대한 공지라는 내용을 듣고 정답을 (B)로 선택한다.

87 According to the speaker, what are employees confused about?
(A) Difference in cost
(B) A facility's opening date
(C) Benefits of the membership
(D) Medical insurance

화자에 따르면, 직원은 무엇에 관해 혼동하는가?
(A) **가격의 차이**
(B) 시설물의 개업일
(C) 멤버십의 혜택
(D) 의료 보험

질문의 키워드는 confused이다. 화자가 clarity the confusion이라고 언급하는 부분이 정답 단서로, 식사 비용에 관한 혼동이 있어 이를 바로잡겠다고 했으므로 정답은 (A)가 된다.

88 What does the speaker say employees can do?
(A) Request a breakfast menu
(B) Receive a discount on drinks
(C) Take time off after a meal
(D) Purchase meal coupons

화자는 직원들이 무엇을 할 수 있다고 말하는가?
(A) 아침 메뉴 요청하기
(B) 음료에 대해 할인 받기
(C) 식사 후에 휴식 취하기
(D) **식사 쿠폰 구매하기**

직원들이 할 수 있는 사항이 몇 가지 언급되므로 일치하는 것을 정답으로 선택한다. 20개의 식사 쿠폰을 구매하여 추가 할인을 받을 수 있다고 했으므로 정답은 (D)가 된다. (B)는 함정으로 직원들이 20퍼센트 할인을 받을 수 있지만 음료수는 제외한다(except beverages)고 했으므로 답이 될 수 없다.

Questions 89-91 refer to the following instructions. (영M)

I called this meeting to discuss the contract with our raw material supplier, Modesta. I'm not sure if we should continue to hire them for the future construction projects. I'm concerned that they seem too focused on providing cheap materials rather than good quality steel plates. As you know, quality is more important for us than price. **But here's the thing.** If we decide to end our business relationship with Modesta right now, we'll have to pay a penalty to terminate the current contract. To avoid paying the penalty, we could just see out the contract until its completion. But there will be complaints about the quality of the supplies for the time being. So I'd like to hear your suggestions on this matter.

제가 오늘의 미팅을 소집한 이유는 우리 원자재 공급업체인 Modesta와의 계약 건에 대해 이야기하기 위함입니다. 우리가 앞으로의 공사 프로젝트에 그들을 계속 고용하는 것이 좋을지 잘 모르겠습니다. 저는 그들이 좋은 품질의 철판보다는 저렴한 자재를 제공하는 것에만 너무 초점을 맞추고 있어 걱정입니다. 아시다시피, 우리에게는 가격보다 품질이 더 중요합니다. **그런데 문제는 이것입니다.** 만약 우리가 Modesta와의 사업 관계를 지금 당장 끝내려고 하면 현재의 계약을 끝내는 것에 대한 위약금을 내야만 합니다. 위약금을 피하기 위해서는 종료 시점까지 그냥 계약을 유지할 수도 있습니다. 그러나 당분간은 자재의 품질에 대한 불평이 계속 있을 것입니다. 그래서 저는 이 문제에 대해 여러분의 제안을 들어보고 싶습니다.

raw material 원자재　focus on ~에 집중하다　steel plate 철판　business relationship 사업 관계　pay a penalty 위약금을 내다　terminate a contract 계약을 끝내다　see out 끝까지 이어가다　completion 종료　for the time being 당분간

89 What problem does the speaker mention about Modesta?
(A) Their focus on low price
(B) Their poor customer service
(C) Their staffing problems
(D) Their request to renew a contract

화자는 Modesta에 관하여 어떤 문제를 언급하는가?
(A) 낮은 가격에 초점을 맞추는 것
(B) 그들의 형편없는 고객 서비스
(C) 그들의 인력 충원 문제
(D) 계약을 갱신하자는 그들의 요구

질문을 통해 미리 Modesta와 문제가 있다는 것을 염두에 두자. they seem too focused on providing cheap materials(그들이 싼 자재를 제공하는 데에 너무 초점을 맞춘다)라고 했으므로 정답은 (A)이다.

90 Why does the speaker say, "But here's the thing"?
(A) To hand out a document to listeners
(B) To change the subject
(C) To point out a problem to think about
(D) To recommend another supplier

화자는 왜 "그런데 문제는 이것입니다"라고 말하는가?
(A) 청자들에게 서류를 나누어 주기 위하여
(B) 주제를 바꾸기 위하여
(C) 생각해 볼 문제점을 언급하기 위하여
(D) 다른 공급업체를 추천하기 위하여

해당 표현은 보통 문제점을 제시할 때 쓰이는 것으로 앞뒤 문맥을 통해 정확히 어떤 의미인지 파악하자. 공급업체가 품질보다 가격에 집중하는 것이 문제라고 지적한 후 "But here's the thing"라고 말하며, 계약 관계를 지금 당장 끝내면 위약금이 발생한다고 했으므로 화자는 생각해 볼 문제점에 대해 언급하기 위해서 해당 표현을 쓴 것이다. 정답은 (C)가 맞다.

91 What are the listeners encouraged to do?
(A) Design a new product
(B) Meet a deadline
(C) Deal with customer complaints
(D) Come up with ideas

청자들은 무엇을 할 것을 권고 받는가?
(A) 신제품을 디자인하라고
(B) 마감 시간을 지키라고
(C) 고객 불평을 처리하라고
(D) 아이디어를 생각해 보라고

공급업체와 관련된 문제점을 언급한 후에 So I'd like to hear your suggestions on this matter(이 사안에 대한 여러분의 제안을 듣고 싶다)라고 했으므로 정답은 (D)가 된다.

Questions 92-94 refer to the following announcement. (영W)

Good morning everyone, next Monday evening, the new office photocopier will be delivered. This new machine has printing, copying, scanning and faxing capabilities all-in-one. I believe that without a doubt it will facilitate essential office tasks and help us reduce costs. When it is delivered, it'll take a couple of hours to install and conduct a trial run to make sure everything is working fine. Since we can't do it during office hours, I'd like to ask if some of you could volunteer to stay late and monitor the installation on Monday. Of course you'll get paid for the overtime worked. Thank you.

여러분 좋은 아침입니다. 다음 주 월요일 저녁에, 새로운 사무용 복사기가 배송될 것입니다. 이 새로운 기계에는 인쇄, 복사, 스캐닝 그리고 팩스 기능이 모두 포함되어 있습니다. 이 기계가 필수적인 사무 업무를 빠르게 하고 비용을 줄이는 데 도움을 줄 것이라고 확신합니다. 이것이 배송되면, 설치를 하고 잘 작동되는지 시험 작동을 해보는 데 두어 시간 정도가 걸릴 것입니다. 근무 시간 중에 그것을 할 수는 없기 때문에, 여러분 중 몇 명이 월요일에 야근을 자원해서 설치 감독을 해 줄 수 있는지 알고 싶습니다. 당연히 초과근무 시간에 따른 수당은 받게 될 것입니다. 감사합니다.

capability 기능　all-in-one (두 가지 이상의 기능이) 모두 하나로 된　without a doubt 의심할 여지없이　facilitate 용이하게 하다　essential 필수적인　reduce 줄이다　conduct 실행하다　trial run 시험 운행, 시험 작동　stay late 야근하다　monitor 감독하다　get paid 급여를 받다

92 What is the main topic of the announcement?
(A) An equipment installation
(B) A building inspection
(C) A corporate acquisition
(D) Orientation for new employees

공지의 주제는 무엇인가?
(A) 기계 설치
(B) 건물 검사
(C) 기업 인수
(D) 신입사원을 위한 오리엔테이션

주제는 담화의 도입부에 등장하는 경우가 대부분이다. new office photocopier가 배송될 것이라고 언급한 부분에서 정답은 이미 (A)로 압축된다. 특히 다른 보기는 정답 가능성이 없으므로 빠른 속도로 정답을 처리하자.

93 What benefit does the new machine have?
(A) It consumes less power.
(B) It can be used for multiple purposes.
(C) It prints 20% more documents per hour.
(D) Free installation is offered.

새로운 기계는 어떤 이점을 가지는가?
(A) 적은 전력을 소모한다.
(B) 다목적으로 사용될 수 있다.
(C) 시간당 20퍼센트의 문서를 더 인쇄한다.
(D) 무료 설치가 제공된다.

세부 사항 질문으로 보기는 미리 파악해 두고 일치하는 정보를 빠르게 선택할 수 있어야 한다. This new machine has printing, copying, scanning and faxing capabilities all-in-one에서 여러 기능이 한 기계에 들어 있다고 했으므로 이를 다목적으로 이용될 수 있다고 바꿔 표현한 (B)가 정답이 된다.

94 What does the speaker ask some listeners to do?
(A) Consult a supervisor
(B) Go over a manual
(C) Install new machinery
(D) Work overtime

화자는 청자들에게 무엇을 하라고 요청하는가?
(A) 상사와 의논하라고
(B) 설명서를 검토하라고
(C) 새로운 기계장치를 설치하라고
(D) 시간 외 근무를 하라고

화자가 요청한 내용은 I'd like to ask if some of you could volunteer to stay late and monitor the installation on Monday에서 단서를 잡는다. 야근해서 설치 과정을 감독해 줄 것을 요청하고 있으므로 stay late를 work overtime으로 바꿔 표현한 (D)를 정답으로 선택한다.

Questions 95-97 refer to the following message and schedule. 미W

Thank you for coming everyone. Please take a look at the schedule for the health education event our community center is planning to host next month. This is just the first draft so chances are there will be some changes made to it. And that's exactly what we're going to discuss today. You can make any suggestions you wish about the event. One of the things I suggest is that we have a food tasting after the easy recipes session. Because Karen will demonstrate each recipe for the participants, it makes sense to have them sample the food afterwards. The event will be more interactive that way and we won't be short on time if we move on to the panel discussion right after Karen's session.

Spring 2016 **Event Schedule**	
Simple Diet Tips (Cindy)	1:00 ~ 1:50
Easy Recipes (Karen)	2:00 ~ 2:50
Coffee Break	3:00 ~ 3:30
Panel Discussion	4:30 ~ 5:50

모두 참석해 주셔서 감사합니다. 다음 달에 우리 커뮤니티 센터가 개최할 예정인 건강 교육 행사의 스케줄 표를 봐주세요. 초안이기 때문에 변경 사항이 발생하게 될 수 있는데요. 그것이 바로 오늘 우리가 논의해야 할 부분이기도 합니다. 이 행사에 대해서 제안 사항이 있으면 얼마든지 해주시면 됩니다. 제가 제안하고 싶은 한 가지는 쉬운 레시피 수업 후에 음식 시식을 하자는 것입니다. Karen이 참가자들을 위해 각 레시피의 시연을 보여줄 것이기 때문에 그 후에 음식을 맛볼 수 있도록 하는 게 맞을 것 같습니다. 그러면 행사도 더 참여적일 것 같고 Karen의 세션 후에 바로 패널 토론으로 넘어간다면 시간이 부족하지도 않을 것입니다.

Spring 2016 행사 스케줄	
간단한 다이어트 팁 (Cindy)	1:00 ~ 1:50
쉬운 레시피 (Karen)	2:00 ~ 2:50
휴식 시간	3:00 ~ 3:30
패널 토론	4:30 ~ 5:50

draft 초안 food tasting 음식 시식 demonstrate 시연하다 sample food 음식을 맛보다 short on ~이 부족하다 interactive 상호적인, 참여적인 that way 그렇게 하면 coffee break 휴식 시간

95 What event does the community center plan?
(A) A health education event
(B) A cooking competition
(C) A seminar on home schooling
(D) A community festival

커뮤니티 센터는 어떤 행사를 계획하는가?
(A) 건강 교육 행사
(B) 요리 대회
(C) 홈 스쿨에 관한 세미나
(D) 지역 사회 축제

담화를 시작하면서 우리 커뮤니티 센터가 다음 달에 개최하려는 건강 교육 행사(the health education event)에 대한 이야기를 하자고 했으므로 정답은 (A)가 된다.

96 What does the speaker suggest?
(A) Bringing home-made desserts
(B) Adding a food tasting session
(C) Inviting some experts for a discussion
(D) Sharing ideas for recipes

화자는 무엇을 제안하는가?
(A) 집에서 만든 디저트를 가져오는 것
(B) 음식 시식 순서를 추가하는 것
(C) 토론을 할 몇몇 전문가를 초청하는 것
(D) 조리법을 위한 아이디어를 공유하는 것

행사의 스케줄에 대한 제안을 하겠다고 언급하며 we have a food tasting after the easy recipes session(쉬운 레시피 순서 다음에 시식을 갖자)이라고 했으므로 정답은 (B)가 맞다.

97 Look at the graphic. What does the speaker want to remove from the schedule?
(A) Simple diet tips
(B) Easy recipes
(C) Coffee break
(D) Panel discussion

시각 정보를 보시오. 화자는 무엇을 스케줄로부터 빼기를 원하는가?
(A) 간단한 다이어트 팁
(B) 쉬운 레시피
(C) 휴식 시간
(D) 패널 토론

화자의 제안 사항을 잘 듣자. 쉬운 레시피 수업 후에는 음식 시식을 하자고 제안하면서 그 후에는 시간이 부족하지 않도록 바로 패널 토론으로 넘어가자고 했으므로 휴식 시간을 빼기를 원하는 것이다. 정답은 (C)이다.

Questions 98-100 refer to the following message and list. 영M

Hello, Ms. O'Hara. I'm returning your call concerning your request for a change to the price estimate I sent you earlier today. Originally you wanted to ship a package to Vancouver by sea and you chose Quick Delivery Company. But I understand you want to airmail your package now, because you want it delivered to the recipient by Friday at the latest. That is no problem. So, I'm going to revise the price estimate accordingly and send it to you as soon as possible. Please note that the same delivery company you chose also offers airmail delivery, but it costs $30 more. I'm going to check if the measurements of the package are correct, then I'll send you a new price quote. Thank you for choosing our company and feel free to contact us at 555-3550 if you have any questions. Thank you.

Price Estimate	
Type	**Package**
Weight	5kg
Length	20cm
Width	20cm
Height	6cm
Delivery option	Quick Delivery Co.
Total Estimate of Charges: $60.00	

안녕하세요 O'Hara 씨. 제가 아까 보내 드렸던 가격 견적서에 변경을 요청하셨기에 그것과 관련하여 다시 전화드립니다. 원래는 Quick Delivery Company를 통해 배편으로 소포를 밴쿠버로 보내시길 원하셨죠. 그러나 지금은 수신자에게 아무리 늦어도 금요일까지 배달을 해야 하기 때문에, 소포를 항공우편으로 보내시길 원하는 것이죠. 문제없습니다. 그러면, 제가 가격 견적서를 이에 맞게 수정해서 최대한 빨리 보내드리겠습니다. 당신이 선택한 같은 업체가 항공 우편 배송도 제공하지만 30달러가 더 든다는 것은 알아두세요. 제가 소포의 수치가 정확한지 확인을 한 후에 새 견적서를 보내도록 하겠습니다. 저희 회사를 선택해 주셔서 감사하고 질문이 있으시면 언제든지 저에게 555-3550로 전화 주세요. 감사합니다.

가격 견적서	
종류	**Package**
무게	5kg
길이	20cm
넓이	20cm
높이	6cm
배송 업체	Quick Delivery Co.
총 견적 금액 : 60.00달러	

concerning ~와 관련해서 by sea 해상으로, 배편으로 airmail 항공 우편 recipient 수신자 accordingly 그에 맞도록 measurement 수치 price quote 가격 견적서

98 What did Ms. O'Hara request?
(A) A change to a price estimate
(B) Her travel schedule
(C) A new telephone number
(D) Information on a cruise

O'Hara 씨는 무엇을 요청했는가?
(A) 가격 견적서에 관한 변경
(B) 그녀의 여행 일정
(C) 새로운 전화번호
(D) 선박 여행에 관한 정보

메시지의 도입부에 답신 전화를 하는 이유로 가격 견적서에 변형사항을 요청(your request for a change to the price estimate)했기 때문이라고 했으므로 정답은 (A)가 된다.

99 Why does Ms. O'Hara want a package delivered by airmail?
(A) It is inexpensive.
(B) It is reliable.
(C) It is fast.
(D) It is popular.

O'Hara 씨는 왜 항공 우편으로 소포를 보내길 원하는가?
(A) 싸다.
(B) 믿을 수 있다.
(C) 빠르다.
(D) 인기가 많다.

질문의 키워드는 airmail로 항공 우편을 원하는 이유는 because you want it delivered to the recipient by Friday at the latest(늦어도 금요일까지는 수신자가 배달을 받기를 원해서)라고 했으므로 정답은 (C)이다.

100 Look at the graphic. According to the speaker, what information will be revised?
(A) Weight
(B) Height
(C) Delivery option
(D) Total charges

시각 정보를 보시오. 화자에 따르면, 무슨 정보가 수정되는가?
(A) 무게
(B) 높이
(C) 배송 업체
(D) 총 청구 금액

기존 견적서의 내용 중에서 수정되는 것이 무엇인지 묻는 질문으로 해상 우편에서 항공 우편으로 변경하면서 업체는 변경되지 않지만 금액이 30달러가 추가된다고 했으므로, 변경될 정보는 (D) Total charges가 된다.

Actual Test 2

PART 1

본책 p.24

1 (C)	2 (B)	3 (A)	4 (C)	5 (C)	6 (D)

PART 2

본책 p.28

7 (C)	8 (C)	9 (B)	10 (B)	11 (A)	12 (C)
13 (A)	14 (B)	15 (A)	16 (C)	17 (B)	18 (A)
19 (B)	20 (C)	21 (A)	22 (B)	23 (A)	24 (C)
25 (A)	26 (B)	27 (C)	28 (A)	29 (A)	30 (C)
31 (C)					

PART 3

본책 p.29

32 (C)	33 (D)	34 (B)	35 (B)	36 (C)	37 (A)
38 (B)	39 (C)	40 (A)	41 (A)	42 (C)	43 (B)
44 (D)	45 (A)	46 (C)	47 (A)	48 (D)	49 (B)
50 (A)	51 (B)	52 (D)	53 (D)	54 (A)	55 (B)
56 (C)	57 (D)	58 (C)	59 (C)	60 (A)	61 (D)
62 (A)	63 (C)	64 (D)	65 (A)	66 (C)	67 (C)
68 (A)	69 (C)	70 (A)			

PART 4

본책 p.33

71 (C)	72 (A)	73 (C)	74 (A)	75 (B)	76 (D)
77 (C)	78 (A)	79 (D)	80 (B)	81 (B)	82 (D)
83 (D)	84 (B)	85 (B)	86 (D)	87 (B)	88 (C)
89 (C)	90 (D)	91 (B)	92 (D)	93 (A)	94 (C)
95 (B)	96 (A)	97 (C)	98 (D)	99 (B)	100 (A)

PART 1

1 (A) The woman is securing the bag.
미W (B) The woman is gazing out at the scenery.
(C) The woman is going down the road.
(D) The woman is buttoning up her shirt.

(A) 여자가 가방을 고정시키고 있다.
(B) 여자가 풍경을 바라보고 있다.
(C) 여자가 길을 따라 가고 있다.
(D) 여자가 셔츠의 단추를 잠그고 있다.

여자가 헬멧을 쓰고 자전거를 타고 있다. 앞쪽의 모습을 알 수 없어 풍경을 바라보고 있는지 확신할 수는 없지만 길을 따라 계속 가고 있는 것은 분명하므로 정답은 (C)이다. 가방은 이미 자전거 뒤에 고정되어 있으므로 현재 진행형을 써서 진행 상태를 나타내는 (A)는 오답이다.

secure 단단히 고정시키다 gaze out 응시하다, 바라보다 down the road 길 따라 계속 button up 단추를 잠그다

2 (A) The branches of the trees are being trimmed.
영M (B) The man is inspecting one of the plants.
(C) A man is watering some plants.
(D) A farmer is harvesting his crops.

(A) 나뭇가지들이 손질되고 있다.
(B) 남자가 식물 중 하나를 살펴보고 있다.
(C) 남자가 식물에 물을 주고 있다.
(D) 농부가 작물을 수확하고 있다.

사방이 나무와 밭인 곳에서 남자가 과수원의 나무를 자세히 살펴보고 있다. 이처럼 무언가를 자세히 보는 경우 examine이나 inspect가 어김없이 등장한다는 것을 명심하자. 도구를 이용해 나뭇가지를 손질하는 것은 아니므로 (A)는 오답이다.

branch 가지 trim 손질하다 inspect 점검하다, 검사하다, 사찰하다 water 물을 주다 harvest 수확하다 crop 농작물

3 (A) The man is staring at the monitor.
미M (B) The man is putting on protective glasses.
(C) The man is working on a document.
(D) The man is placing files under a table.

(A) 남자가 모니터를 응시하고 있다.
(B) 남자가 보호 안경을 쓰는 중이다.
(C) 남자가 문서 작업을 하고 있다.
(D) 남자가 테이블 아래에 파일을 두고 있다.

녹음실처럼 보이는 곳에서 남자가 컴퓨터 모니터를 보고 있다. 남자가 안경을 쓰고 있기는 하지만 지금 안경을 쓰고 있는 동작을 하고 있지는 않으므로 (B)는 오답이다.

stair at 응시하다, 빤히 보다 work on a document 문서 작업을 하다 place 두다

4 (A) Some people are exchanging their business cards.
영W (B) A woman is getting into a train.
(C) Light fixtures line the ceiling.
(D) A door is being used by some people.

(A) 사람들이 명함을 주고받고 있다.
(B) 한 여자가 기차에 오르고 있다.
(C) 조명 기구가 천장에 늘어서 있다.
(D) 문이 사람들에 의해 이용되고 있다.

천장에 일렬로 달린 조명이 켜져 있으므로 정답은 (C)이다. 지하철에 문이 열려 있는데 타거나 내리는 사람은 없으므로 문이 사람들에 의해 이용된다고 볼 수 없다.

exchange 바꾸다, 교환하다 business card 명함 get into ~에 타다 light fixture 조명 기구 line 줄을 세우다, 늘어서다 ceiling 천장

5 (A) Some vegetables are being sorted.
미W (B) A woman is packing items into a grocery bag.
(C) The different fruits have been grouped.
(D) Various packaged items are on sale.

(A) 채소들이 분류되고 있다.
(B) 여자가 물건을 쇼핑백에 싸고 있다.
(C) 여러 가지 과일들이 분류되어 있다.
(D) 다양한 포장 물건들이 할인 중이다.

시장에서 과일과 야채를 파는 가게로 보이는 곳이다. 과일과 야채는 이미 종류별로 나눠져 있으므로 지금 사람이 분류하고 있다는 (A)는 오답이다.

pack 싸다, 꾸리다, 챙기다 group 무리를 지어 나누다, 분류하다 package 포장하다 on sale 할인 중인

6 (A) A fence is being repaired.
영M (B) Signs have been taken down from the post.
(C) The structures are reflected in the lake.
(D) The road is empty at the moment.

(A) 울타리가 수리 중이다.
(B) 표지판들이 기둥에서 치워졌다.
(C) 구조물들이 호수에 비친다.
(D) 도로는 지금 비어 있다.

기차 건널목으로 보이는 곳에 진입 금지 표시는 없지만 사람은 보이지 않는다. 완료된 동작을 나타내는 (B)가 정답이 되려면 표지판들이 기둥 아래쪽에 있고 기둥에는 뜯긴 흔적들이 보여야 한다. 참고로 tear down은 건물이나 담을 부수고 허무는 행위를, take down은 해체하여 치우는 상황을 의미한다.

fence 울타리, 담 sign 표지판 take down 해체하여 치우다 post 기둥 structure 구조물 reflect 반영하다, 반사하다 at the moment 현재, 지금

PART 2

7 Where is the guest speaker staying?
미W (A) Next month, I guess.
영M (B) To Seattle.
(C) At a nearby hotel.

초청 연사는 어디에 머물 것인가?
(A) 다음 달일 거예요.
(B) 시애틀로요.
(C) 근처 호텔이요

의문사 where와 함께 동사 staying이 꼭 해석해야 하는 키워드이다. 머물 장소를 물었으므로 정답은 (C)이다.

nearby 근처의

8 Would you like some dessert?
미M (A) The party was fun.
미W (B) Let's go there.
(C) No thanks. I'm full.

디저트 좀 드시겠어요?
(A) 파티는 재밌었어요.
(B) 거기에 갑시다.
(C) 사양할게요. 전 배가 불러요.

디저트를 먹겠냐는 제안이었으므로 배가 부르다며 거절한 (C)가 정답이다.

9 Who wrote this editorial?
미M (A) An online tutorial.
영W (B) I have no idea.
(C) He is the new editor.

누가 이 사설을 썼나요?
(A) 온라인 사용서입니다.
(B) 잘 모르겠어요.
(C) 그가 새로운 편집자랍니다.

누가 썼는지를 묻는 질문에 I don't know, I have no idea와 같은 모르겠다는 표현은 충분히 정답이 된다.

editorial 사설 tutorial (온라인 상의) 사용 지침 프로그램

10 What color did you paint your house?
영W (A) It went very well.
영M (B) I chose sky blue.
(C) Call her now.

집은 어떤 색으로 페인트칠했나요?
(A) 그건 매우 진행이 잘 되었어요.
(B) 전 하늘색을 골랐어요.
(C) 지금 그녀에게 전화하세요.

어떤 색깔을 선택했는지 물었으므로 색깔을 말해준 (B)가 정답이 된다.

11 How many computers will you need for your
미W demonstration?
영W (A) At least fifteen.
(B) At a university in Germany.
(C) She will be there too.

시연에 쓸 컴퓨터가 몇 대나 필요하신가요?
(A) 적어도 15대요.
(B) 독일의 한 대학에서요.
(C) 그녀도 거기에 올 것입니다.

질문의 핵심이 컴퓨터 대수(how many computers)를 묻는 것이므로 정답은 (A)가 된다.

demonstration 시연

12 Is Mr. Green in today?
미W (A) An important client.
미M (B) Maybe tomorrow afternoon.
(C) Yes, would you like to speak with him?

Green 씨 오늘 계신가요?
(A) 중요한 고객입니다.
(B) 아마도 내일 오후요.
(C) 네, 통화하시겠습니까?

보통 '주어+be in'은 '~가 (사무실에) 있다, 출근했다'는 의미가 된다. 그러므로 정답으로는 통화할 것인지 묻는 (C)가 가장 자연스럽다.

13 Who does this coat belong to?
영W (A) Oh, it's mine.
영M (B) To the manager's office.
(C) This shirt is made of cotton.

이 코트는 누구 것인가요?
(A) 아, 제 것입니다.
(B) 매니저의 사무실로.
(C) 이 셔츠는 면으로 만든 겁니다.

의문사 who 의문문으로 코트의 주인이 누구인지 물었으므로 정답은 (A)이다.

belong to ~의 것이다 be made of ~으로 만들어지다

14 That's the seafood restaurant we're looking for, isn't it?
미M (A) No, I'll look at it later.
미W (B) Yes, it's the one with the red front door.
(C) I just had dinner.

저곳이 우리가 찾고 있는 해산물 레스토랑이죠, 그렇지 않나요?
(A) 아니요, 나중에 보겠습니다.
(B) 네, 빨간 앞문이 있는 곳이요.
(C) 저는 막 저녁을 먹었습니다.

Yes/No 질문으로 that(저것)이 the seafood restaurant (그 해산물 레스토랑)인지 여부를 묻고 있으므로 긍정으로 답하고 부연 설명으로 정문이 빨간 곳이라고 답한 (B)가 정답이다.

later 나중에 front 앞쪽의

15 This dress will have to be dry-cleaned.
미W (A) How much will it cost?
영M (B) The stairs are still wet.
(C) At a shopping center.

이 원피스는 드라이클리닝을 해야 돼요.
(A) 돈이 얼마나 들까요?
(B) 계단이 여전히 젖었어요.
(C) 쇼핑센터에서요.

옷을 드라이클리닝해야 한다는 말에 대해 그 비용을 물은 (A)가 가장 적절한 정답이 된다. (B)과 (C)는 문맥에서 완전히 벗어난 보기들이다.

stairs 계단

16 Didn't you go to the seminar on management skills
미M last night?
영W (A) I'd love to come along next time.
(B) They look the same.
(C) Yes, it was very informative.

어젯밤에 경영 기술에 관한 세미나에 가지 않으셨어요?
(A) 다음번에는 저도 같이 가고 싶어요.
(B) 그것들은 똑같아 보여요.
(C) 네, 매우 유용했어요.

질문의 핵심은 어제 세미나에 갔었는지 여부이다. 우선 긍정으로 답하고 세미나가 유용했다고 부연 설명한 (C)가 정답이다. (A)는 시제 오류이다.

management skills 경영 기술 come along 같이 가다 informative 유용한, 정보가 많은

17 If you have any questions about the new policy, just
영M let me know.
미W (A) Drop me off at the police station.
(B) Thank you, I will.
(C) In office 231.

새 정책에 대해 질문이 있으시면, 저에게 알려 주세요.
(A) 경찰서에서 내려 주세요.
(B) 감사합니다, 그럴게요.
(C) 231호 사무실에서요.

이 평서문의 의도는 호의를 제공하는 것으로 질문이 있으면 말해달라고 했으므로 호의에 대해 감사를 표하는 (B)가 정답이 된다.

drop off 내려주다 police station 경찰서

18 Would you like me to work on the renovation
영W project?
영M (A) Yes, you can work with Chris and his team members.
(B) The hotel needs remodeling.
(C) She doesn't like to work overtime.

제가 이 보수 프로젝트 작업을 할까요?
(A) 네, Chris와 그의 팀원들과 함께 작업하세요.
(B) 그 호텔은 리모델링을 해야 됩니다.
(C) 그녀는 야근하길 원하지 않아요.

would you like me to (제가 …해 드릴까요)는 제안의 표현이므로 반드시 암기해 두자. (B)는 renovation과 유사어인 remodeling을 이용한 함정이고 (C)는 주어 오류이며 내용도 문맥상 맞지 않는다.

work overtime 야근하다

19 Where can I find more information about the job
미M openings?
미W (A) No, not so much.
(B) You should visit our company's website.
(C) They were successful applicants.

일자리에 대한 정보는 어디에서 더 찾을 수 있을까요?
(A) 아니요, 그렇게 많지 않아요.
(B) 우리 회사 웹 사이트를 방문해 보세요.
(C) 그들은 합격한 지원자들입니다.

의문사 where 질문으로 일자리 정보를 찾을 수 있는 장소이므로 정답은 (B) 회사의 웹 사이트가 가장 적절하다.

job opening 일자리 successful applicant 합격한 지원자

20 Are you going to hire a new marketing manager or
영M promote Mr. Klein?
영W (A) He is the division manager.
(B) It shows higher employment numbers.
(C) We should hire someone with fresh ideas.

새로운 마케팅 부장을 고용할 건가요 아니면 Klein 씨를 승진시킬 건가요?
(A) 그는 부서장입니다.
(B) 그것은 더 높은 고용 지수를 보여 주죠.
(C) 참신한 아이디어를 가진 누군가를 고용하는 게 좋겠어요.

선택 의문문으로 새로운 사람을 고용하는 것과 기존 직원을 승진시키는 것이 선택 사항이다. 정답은 참신한 아이디어를 가진 사람을 고용하자고 말한 (C)이다.

promote 승진시키다 division manager 부서장 employment number 고용 지수

21 Why isn't the presentation in the main meeting room?
미M (A) It is already taken.
영W (B) Everyone was present.
(C) About safety regulations.

발표가 왜 대회의장에서 열리지 않는 건가요?
(A) 이미 사용 중입니다.
(B) 모두 출석했어요.
(C) 안전 규정에 관해서요.

발표 장소가 왜 대회의장이 아닌지를 물었으므로 it is already taken (이미 누군가에 의해 사용되고 있다)이라고 답한 (A)가 정답이다.

be present 출석한 safety regulations 안전 규정

22 Would you like to put the lamp in this room or the
영M other one?
미W (A) You can find some in the storage room.
(B) I'm still deciding which room to put it in.
(C) It should arrive today.

이 램프를 이 방에 놓으실래요 아니면 다른 방이요?
(A) 창고에서 더 찾을 수 있습니다.
(B) 아직도 어떤 방에다 놓을지 결정하고 있어요.
(C) 그건 오늘 도착할 겁니다.

선택 의문문으로 선택 사항은 this room 혹은 the other one (다른 방)이다. 둘 중 하나를 선택하지는 않았지만 아직 결정을 못 내렸다고 한 (B)가 정답이 된다. 특히 질문에 대해 '아직 결정이 안 되었다'는 표현은 정답률이 매우 높으니 반드시 암기하자.

storage room 창고

23 Have you seen today's paper?
영M (A) Jerry was reading it in the lounge.
영W (B) Send it to Mr. Gatlin.
(C) I can finish it by tomorrow.

오늘 신문을 보셨나요?
(A) **Jerry가 휴게실에서 읽고 있었는데요.**
(B) Gatlin 씨에게 보내세요.
(C) 내일까지는 그걸 끝낼 수 있어요.

Have you seen은 목적어의 행방을 묻는 질문이다. 신문의 행방을 물었으므로 Jerry가 휴게실에서 읽고 있었다고 답한 (A)가 정답이 된다.

lounge 휴게실

24 We should finish unpacking these boxes before we
미M leave.
미W (A) I'm leaving town next week.
(B) It is in the lobby.
(C) Okay, we're almost done.

퇴근하기 전에 이 박스들을 다 풀어 놓는 게 좋겠어요.
(A) 전 다음 주에 도시를 떠납니다.
(B) 그것은 로비에 있어요.
(C) **좋아요, 거의 다 했어요.**

조동사 should는 제안, 권고의 의미이므로 박스 푸는 것을 다 끝내자는 제안에 대해서 수락하며 거의 끝났다고 답한 (C)가 정답이다.

unpack 풀다 leave town (지방, 다른 도시 등으로) 떠나다

25 Where do you think is better to hold the press
영M conference, in the conference room or somewhere
영W else?
(A) I'll see if the Seoul Hotel is available.
(B) The annual conference will be held in Seattle.
(C) I want to try something different.

기자 회견을 어디서 여는 게 좋을까요, 컨퍼런스 룸이요 아니면 다른 곳이요?
(A) **Seoul 호텔이 이용 가능한지 알아볼게요.**
(B) 그 연례 컨퍼런스는 시애틀에서 열릴 겁니다.
(C) 다른 것을 시도해 보고 싶어요.

선택 의문문으로 기자 회견을 열 장소가 컨퍼런스 룸인지 다른 곳인지 묻고 있다. 기자 회견 장소로 Seoul 호텔을 확인해 보겠다고 답한 (A)는 자연스러운 정답이 된다.

hold 열다, 개최하다 press conference 기자 회견

26 Could you look over the budget report when you get
미W a chance?
영M (A) Tuesday would be best.
(B) I have some free time now.
(C) Yes, it happened by chance.

시간 되실 때 이 예산 보고서를 검토해 주시겠어요?
(A) 화요일이 가장 좋습니다.
(B) **지금 시간이 됩니다.**
(C) 네, 우연히 그렇게 되었어요.

요청 의문문으로 보고서를 검토해 달라고 했으므로 지금 볼 시간이 된다고 수락한 (B)가 정답이 된다.

get a chance 기회를 갖다 by chance 우연히

27 Would you mind turning off your computer?
미M (A) Actually I'm taking the day off.
미W (B) To install new software.
(C) I need to save this file first.

컴퓨터를 좀 꺼 주시겠습니까?
(A) 실은 제가 오늘 휴가입니다.
(B) 새로운 소프트웨어를 설치하기 위해서요.
(C) **이 파일을 먼저 저장해야 합니다.**

요청 의문문으로 would you mind를 사용하였다. 컴퓨터를 꺼 달라는 요청에 휴가라고 답한 (A)는 어색하고, 파일 먼저 저장하겠다고 한 (C)가 자연스러운 정답이다.

take a day off 하루를 쉬다

28 Doesn't the gas station stay open until 10 p.m.?
영W (A) Yes, I believe so.
미M (B) Open the window a crack.
(C) I need 10 of them.

이 주유소는 저녁 10시까지 문을 열지 않나요?
(A) **네, 그럴 거예요.**
(B) 창문을 조금만 열어 주세요.
(C) 그것 10개가 필요합니다.

Yes/No 여부로 묻는 핵심은 이 주유소가 10시까지 영업을 하는지 여부이고 그렇다라고 답한 (A)가 정답이 된다. I think so는 '그렇다'고 해석되며 Yes와 같은 뜻이다.

gas station 주유소 crack 약간의 틈

29 Why did Samantha leave without her laptop?
영M (A) Oh no, she must've forgotten it.
미W (B) Did you find her computer?
(C) It comes with a manual.

Samantha는 왜 노트북 컴퓨터 없이 갔나요?
(A) **저런, 그녀는 깜빡 잊은 게 틀림없어요.**
(B) 그녀의 컴퓨터를 찾았나요?
(C) 그건 사용설명서가 딸려 나옵니다.

Samantha가 컴퓨터 없이 간 이유가 무엇인지 물었으므로 그녀의 컴퓨터를 찾았냐고 묻는 (B)는 매우 어색하다. 깜빡 잊은 것 같다고 답한 (A)가 정답이다.

come with ~이 함께 나오다

30 Would you prefer to see me tomorrow or the day
미W after tomorrow?
미M (A) I left right after the show.
(B) It should be delivered today.
(C) Thursday would be best for me.

저와 내일 만나는 게 더 좋으신가요 아니면 모레요?
(A) 저는 쇼가 끝나자마자 떠났어요.
(B) 그것은 오늘 배송될 것입니다.
(C) **목요일이 제일 좋습니다.**

선택 의문문으로 약속 시간이 내일이 좋은지 모레가 좋은지 물었으므로 목요일이 좋다는 (C)가 정답이다. (A)는 시제 오류이다.

the day after tomorrow 모레

31 The shopping bags we got from the supermarket
영M are made from recycled materials.
영W (A) I've come up with a new advertising campaign.
(B) It is located in the trendy shopping district.
(C) Yes, I noticed that.

그 슈퍼마켓에서 받은 쇼핑백은 재활용품으로 만들어졌어요.
(A) 저는 새로운 광고를 생각해 냈어요.
(B) 그것은 최신 쇼핑 구역 내에 위치해 있어요.
(C) 네, 저도 눈치챘어요.

쇼핑백이 재활용품으로 만들어진 것이란 말에 대해 자신도 알고 있었다고 답한 (C)가 정답이 된다. (B)는 shopping이 반복 사용되어 혼동을 주는 반복 어휘 함정이다.

recycled materials 재활용된 용품 trendy 최신 유행의 shopping district 쇼핑 구역 notice 알다, 알아채다

PART 3

Questions 32-34 refer to the following conversation. 미W 미M

W Hello, Adele's Landscaping Company. This is Bronte speaking.
M Hi, this is Clint Walker, the manager of the Phoenix Hotel. I'm calling because the flower gardens around our hotel need some maintenance work. Could someone from your company come by to have a look at the property?
W Absolutely. I can visit the hotel tomorrow morning if that's convenient for you.
M Okay, that sounds good. And I'd like to get a cost estimate as soon as possible.

여 여보세요, Adele's Landscaping Company의 Bronte입니다.
남 안녕하세요, 저는 피닉스 호텔의 매니저, Clint Walker입니다. 호텔 주변의 꽃 정원에 관리가 필요해서 전화합니다. 당신의 회사에서 누가 오셔서 저희 현장을 한 번 봐 주실 수 있나요?
여 물론입니다. 괜찮으시다면 내일 아침에 제가 호텔로 방문할 수 있습니다.
남 네, 좋습니다. 그리고 저는 가능한 한 빨리 가격 견적서를 받고 싶어요.

come by ~에 들르다, 방문하다 property 부동산, 건물 cost estimate 가격 견적서

32 Where does the woman most likely work?
(A) At a hotel
(B) At a florist shop
(C) At a landscaping company
(D) At a construction company

여자는 어디에서 일할 것 같은가?
(A) 호텔
(B) 꽃 가게
(C) 조경 회사
(D) 건축 회사

여자의 직장을 유추하는 질문으로 도입부에 여자가 전화를 받으면서 Adele's Landscaping Company라고 회사의 이름을 언급했던 부분이 단서이다. landscaping company는 조경 회사이므로 정답은 (C)이다.

33 What is the purpose of the man's call?
(A) To make a complaint
(B) To promote a special event
(C) To order some flowers
(D) To request some landscaping work

남자의 전화의 목적은 무엇인가?
(A) 불평하기 위하여
(B) 특별 이벤트를 홍보하기 위하여
(C) 꽃을 주문하기 위하여
(D) 조경 작업을 요청하기 위하여

남자는 호텔 주변 꽃 정원에 조경 관리가 필요해서(the flower gardens around our hotel need some maintenance work) 전화했다고 했으므로 정답은 (D)이다.

34 What does the man ask for as soon as possible?
(A) A list of companies
(B) A price estimate
(C) An appointment
(D) A corrected bill

남자는 무엇을 가능한 한 빨리 요청하는가?
(A) 회사들의 리스트
(B) 가격 견적서
(C) 약속
(D) 정정된 계산서

질문의 키워드는 as soon as possible이다. I'd like to get a cost estimate as soon as possible에서 가격 견적서를 가능한 한 빨리 받고 싶음을 알 수 있으므로 정답은 (B)이다.

Questions 35-37 refer to the following conversation. 영M 미W

M Cynthia, I think you should move your car off the street. The parking regulations are more strictly enforced now so you might get a fine for illegal parking.
W Oh, I didn't know about that. My car has been there for almost two hours now. What am I going to do?
M You'd better move your car into the parking garage near our office building right now. There are also several parking lots around here.
W Okay I will. Could you delay the meeting for a few minutes? I'll be right back.

남 Cynthia, 도로에서 차를 옮기시는 게 좋을 것 같아요. 요즘 주차 규정이 더 엄격하게 시행되고 있어서 불법 주차에 대한 벌금을 받을 수도 있거든요.
여 아, 전 그걸 몰랐네요. 차를 거기에 세운 지 거의 2시간이 다 되어 가요. 어쩌면 좋죠?
남 우리 사무실 건물 옆의 주차장으로 차를 당장 옮기시는 게 좋겠어요. 또 이 근처에 주차장이 몇 군데 더 있어요.
여 알겠어요, 그렇게 할게요. 회의를 잠시만 연기해 줄 수 있을까요? 바로 돌아오겠습니다.

parking regulations 주차 규정 be enforced (법, 규정 등이) 시행되다
illegal parking 불법 주차

35 What are the speakers talking about?
(A) An office complex
(B) Parking rules
(C) A new manager
(D) A community park

화자들은 무엇에 대해서 이야기하고 있는가?
(A) 사무실 단지
(B) 주차 규칙
(C) 새로운 매니저
(D) 지역 공원

대화의 주제는 도입부부터 집중하여 풀자. 도로에서 차를 옮기는 것이 좋겠다고 말하며 The parking regulations are more strictly enforced now(주차 규정이 더 엄격하게 시행되고 있다)라고 했으므로 주제는 (B)이다.

36 What does the man suggest the woman do?
(A) Purchase a new car
(B) Go for a walk
(C) Move a vehicle
(D) Check building regulations

남자는 여자에게 무엇을 하라고 제안하는가?
(A) 새로운 차 구입하기
(B) 산책하기
(C) 차량 옮기기
(D) 건축 규정 확인하기

남자는 주차장으로 차를 옮기는 게 좋겠다(You'd better move your car into the parking garage)고 했으므로 정답은 (C)이다.

37 What does the woman ask the man to do?
(A) Postpone a meeting
(B) Find a parking garage
(C) Recommend a mechanic
(D) Contact a moving company

여자는 남자에게 무엇을 하도록 요청하는가?
(A) 회의를 연기하기
(B) 주차장 찾기
(C) 기계공 추천하기
(D) 이삿짐 회사에 연락하기

여자의 대사에서 요청 표현을 주의 깊게 듣자. Could you delay the meeting for a few minutes?(미팅을 미뤄 달라)라고 했으므로 정답은 (A)이다. delay와 postpone은 동의어이다.

Questions 38-40 refer to the following conversation. 영W 미M

W Excuse me. Are you waiting for the City Hall-bound bus? I think I'm a little late but I hope I didn't miss the one at 9 o'clock.
M No, you didn't miss it. All the buses are a few minutes behind schedule this morning. I just heard the announcement about it.
W Oh, that's a relief. I should still get to work on time then. I have a very important meeting to attend this morning and I don't want to keep my team members waiting.

여 실례합니다. 시청 행 버스를 기다리고 계신가요? 제가 조금 늦었는데 그래도 9시 버스를 놓치진 않았으면 좋겠네요.
남 아니오, 놓치지 않으셨어요. 오늘 아침에 모든 버스가 다 일정보다 늦어지고 있어요. 방금 그것에 대한 공지를 들었거든요.
여 아, 다행이네요. 그럼 시간에 맞게 직장에 갈 수 있겠어요. 제가 오늘 아침에 참석해야 하는 중요한 미팅이 있어서 팀원들을 기다리게 하고 싶지 않거든요.

relief 안도 keep -ing 계속 ~하게 하다

38 Where is the conversation most likely taking place?
(A) In an office
(B) At a bus stop
(C) In a warehouse
(D) At a ticket office

대화는 어디에서 일어날 것 같은가?
(A) 사무실
(B) 버스 정류장
(C) 창고
(D) 매표소

대화의 장소를 유추하는 질문으로 여자가 남자에게 버스를 기다리는 중인지 물었으므로(Are you waiting for the City Hall-bound bus?) 정답은 (B)임을 알 수 있다.

39 How did the man learn about the delay?
(A) By speaking to a ticket agent
(B) By checking a schedule
(C) By hearing an announcement
(D) By reading a notice

남자는 어떻게 지연에 대해 알게 되었는가?
(A) 표 판매원과 얘기를 함으로써
(B) 스케줄 표를 확인함으로써
(C) 안내를 들음으로써
(D) 공지를 읽음으로써

남자 대사에서 지연에 대해 언급되는 부분을 집중한다. 오늘 아침에 모든 버스가 지연된다고 언급하면서 방금 안내 방송을 들었다(I just heard the announcement about it)고 했으므로 정답은 (C)가 된다.

40 Why is the woman pleased?
(A) She will arrive at work on time.
(B) There is no traffic jam.
(C) A bus fare has come down in price.
(D) She can purchase a ticket.

여자는 왜 기뻐하는가?
(A) 그녀는 시간에 맞춰 직장에 도착할 것이다.
(B) 교통 체증이 없다.
(C) 버스 운임이 내렸다.
(D) 그녀는 표를 구매할 수 있다.

여자가 what a relief(다행이네요)라고 말하며 I should still get to work on time then(시간에 맞춰 직장에 도착할 수 있겠다)이라고 했으므로 정답은 (A)가 된다.

Questions 41-43 refer to the following conversation. 영W 영M

W Hi, Mack. What would you like to have for lunch today? I'm actually having a craving for Turkish food.
M Really? I want to have Turkish food too! Oh, I know a good restaurant on Augusta Avenue. It's just a five minute walk from our office and the food there is delicious.
W Oh, you're talking about Doner Kebab House, aren't you? I just love that place. I always get the chicken plate there. It's a little expensive but the portions are large.
M Yeah, they give a generous serving of meat. Maybe we should share a chicken plate. Should I meet you downstairs at noon?
W Okay, I'll see you then.

여 안녕하세요, Mack. 오늘 점심은 뭘 먹고 싶으세요? 터키 음식이 너무 먹고 싶어요.
남 진짜요? 저도 터키 음식이 먹고 싶어요! Augusta Avenue에 좋은 레스토랑을 알아요. 우리 사무실에서 걸어서 5분 거리이고 음식이 정말 맛있어요.
여 아, Doner Kebab House 얘기하시는 거 맞죠? 저도 거기 레스토랑 정말 좋아해요. 거기서 항상 치킨 플레이트를 먹죠. 약간 비싸긴 해도 양이 많아요.
남 그래요, 정말 고기 양을 푸짐하게 주죠. 우리 치킨 플레이트 하나를 나눠 먹어도 좋겠어요. 정오에 아래층에서 만날까요?
여 좋습니다. 그때 봐요.

feel like ~을 하고 싶다 craving 갈망, (특정 음식이)당기는 것 a five minute walk 걸어서 5분 거리 portion (음식 1인분의) 양 a generous serving of ~의 푸짐한 양

41 What are the speakers discussing?
(A) A food craving
(B) Travel arrangements
(C) International chefs
(D) A newly opened restaurant

화자들은 무엇에 대해 얘기하고 있는가?
(A) 음식 갈망
(B) 여행 준비
(C) 국제적인 요리사
(D) 새로 문 연 레스토랑

대화의 주제는 도입부에서 점심 메뉴에 대한 얘기를 하며 I'm actually having a craving for Turkish food(터키 음식이 너무 먹고 싶다)라고 하므로 정답을 (A)로 선택한다.

42 What does the woman like about the chicken plate?
(A) The atmosphere
(B) The price
(C) The portion
(D) The location

여자는 치킨 플레이트에 대해 무엇이 좋다고 하는가?
(A) 분위기
(B) 가격
(C) 음식 양
(D) 위치

여자 대사에서 치킨 플레이트에 대해 언급된 부분에 집중하자. 여러 가지 언급된 내용 중에서 보기와 일치하는 것은 가격은 비싸지만 but the portions are large양이 많다고 한 부분이다. 정답은 (C)이다.

43 When will the speakers meet?
(A) At 11:45 a.m.
(B) At 12:00 p.m.
(C) At 12:15 p.m.
(D) At 1:00 p.m.

화자들은 언제 만날 것인가?
(A) 오전 11:45
(B) 오후 12:00
(C) 오후 12:15
(D) 오후 1:00

남자가 Should I meet you downstairs at noon?(정오에 만나자)이라고 했고 여자도 좋다고 했으므로 정답은 (B)이다.

Questions 44-46 refer to the following conversation. 미M 미W

M Hello, this is the technical support team.
W Hi. This is Debra Han from accounting. I've been trying to access my e-mail, but I keep getting an error message. It says that my password is incorrect but I am sure I'm using the correct one. What should I do?
M Well, in that case, the easiest thing to do would be to reset your password. I'd like to help you with that right now, but I won't be available until 3 p.m. How about I stop by your office at 3?
W Okay. I have a meeting scheduled for 3:30 so please don't be late.

남 여보세요, 기술 지원팀입니다.
여 안녕하세요, 회계부의 Debra Han입니다. 제가 이메일을 보려고 하는데 에러 메시지가 계속 나옵니다. 제 비밀번호가 맞지 않다고 하는데 전 정확한 번호를 사용하고 있거든요. 어떻게 해야 할까요?
남 음, 그런 경우에는, 가장 쉬운 해결책은 비밀번호를 재설정하는 것입니다. 지금 당장 도와 드리고 싶지만 전 오후 3시에나 시간이 됩니다. 3시에 제가 당신의 사무실로 들르면 어떨까요?
여 좋아요. 전 3시 30분에 미팅이 있으니 늦지 말아 주세요.

technical support team 기술 지원팀 incorrect 부정확한 reset 재설정하다

44 What is the woman having trouble with?
(A) A printer
(B) A delivery
(C) A security pass
(D) A password

여자는 무엇에 관한 어려움을 겪고 있는가?
(A) 프린터 기기
(B) 배송
(C) 보안 출입증
(D) 암호

여자 대사에서 이메일 접속이 안 된다고 하며 비밀번호가 틀리다(It says that my password is incorrect)는 에러 메시지를 받는다고 했으므로 정답은 (D)이다.

45 How does the man say he will solve the problem?
(A) By changing a password
(B) By upgrading software
(C) By calling technical support
(D) By inspecting a building

남자는 어떻게 문제를 해결해 줄 것이라고 말하는가?
(A) 암호를 바꿈으로써
(B) 소프트웨어를 업그레이드함으로써
(C) 기술지원부에 전화를 함으로써
(D) 건물을 조사함으로써

남자는 가장 쉬운 방법은 비밀번호를 재설정하는 것이라고 했으므로 정답을 (A)로 선택한다.

46 What will the man do at 3 o'clock?
(A) Replace a computer
(B) Find a telephone
(C) Visit an office
(D) Review an instruction manual

남자는 3시에 무엇을 할 것인가?
(A) 컴퓨터 교체하기
(B) 전화번호 찾기
(C) 사무실 방문하기
(D) 사용 설명서 검토하기

질문의 키워드는 3 o'clock이다. 남자가 3시에 시간이 된다고 말하며 3시에 사무실로 방문하면 어떻겠냐(How about I stop by your office at 3)고 했고 여자도 수락했으므로 정답은 (C)가 된다.

Questions 47-49 refer to the following conversation. 미W 미M

W Mark, did you hear the morning news report?
M No, I was in a meeting with the clients from China. What did I miss?
W The city council finally approved the plan to widen Freeway 302. The construction will take about 6 months, but once it's done, traffic on the freeway won't be as congested as it is now.
M Wow, that's good news. You know I always take Freeway 302 to get to work. When the widening project is over, my commute will be a lot better than it is now.

여 Mark, 오늘 아침 뉴스 들으셨어요?
남 아니오, 전 중국에서 온 고객과 회의 중이었습니다. 제가 무엇을 놓쳤죠?
여 시의회에서 드디어 302번 고속 도로를 넓히자는 안을 승인해 주었어요. 공사는 6개월 정도 걸릴 것이지만, 일단 끝나면 고속 도로 교통이 지금처럼 많이 막히지는 않을 거예요.
남 와, 그거 좋은 소식이네요. 전 출근할 때 항상 302번 고속 도로를 타거든요. 확장 공사가 끝나면, 제 통근은 지금보다 훨씬 더 좋아지겠네요.

approve 승인하다 widen 넓히다, 확장하다 freeway 고속 도로 congested 막히는 widening project 확장 프로젝트 commute 통근

47 Why was the man unable to hear the news report?
(A) He had a meeting with some clients.
(B) There was too much noise.
(C) He woke up late in the morning.
(D) His radio was out of order.

남자는 왜 뉴스 보도를 들을 수 없었는가?
(A) 그는 고객들과 회의를 했다.
(B) 소음이 심했다.
(C) 그는 아침에 늦게 일어났다.
(D) 그의 라디오가 고장 났다.

여자가 남자에게 아침 뉴스를 들었냐고 물었을 때 No, I was in a meeting with the clients from China(중국에서 온 고객과 미팅 중이어서 못 들었다)라고 했으므로 정답은 (A)이다.

48 What is the subject of the news report?
(A) A sales meeting
(B) A company policy
(C) A traffic accident
(D) A council decision

뉴스 보도의 주제는 무엇인가?
(A) 영업 회의
(B) 회사 정책
(C) 교통사고
(D) 의회 결정

뉴스의 내용은 The city council finally approved the plan to widen Freeway 302(시의회가 고속 도로 확장 계획을 승인했다)라는 것으로 정답은 (D)가 된다.

49 What does the man imply when he says, "Wow, that's good news"?
(A) He will share a ride with the woman.
(B) He will experience less traffic congestion.
(C) A construction project will be cancelled.
(D) His work will be finished on time.

남자가 "와, 그거 좋은 소식이네요"라고 말한 의도는 무엇인가?
(A) 그는 여자와 차를 함께 탈 것이다.
(B) 그는 교통 혼잡을 덜 겪을 것이다.
(C) 건설 프로젝트는 취소될 것이다.
(D) 그의 업무가 시간 안에 끝날 것이다.

고속 도로 확장 뉴스에 대해서 "Wow, that's good news"라고 말한 뒤 공사가 끝나면 통근이 더 좋아질 것이라고 했으므로 정답은 (B)가 된다.

Questions 50-52 refer to the following conversation. (영W) (영M)

W Hello. I'd like three tickets for admission to the theme park. And I was also wondering if you offer discounts for children.

M Yes, for children under six, admission is free and for children between seven and ten, admission is 5 dollars. But if you visit our theme park frequently, we also have a one-year membership for only 50 dollars.

W Thank you for the information. We're visiting from out of town though. So I'll just get tickets for two adults and one 5 dollar ticket for my son.

M Sure thing. That'll be 25 dollars in total.

여 안녕하세요. 테마 파크 입장권 3매를 사고 싶습니다. 혹시 아이들을 위한 할인을 제공하는지도 궁금합니다.

남 네, 6세 미만의 아이들에게는 입장료가 무료이고, 7세부터 10세 어린이들은 입장료가 5달러입니다. 그렇지만 저희 테마 파크를 자주 방문하신다면, 일 년 회원권을 50달러에 이용 가능합니다.

여 알려 주셔서 감사해요. 그런데 저희는 다른 지역에서 방문 중이라서요. 그럼, 어른 표 2장과 제 아들을 위한 5달러짜리 표를 한 장 살게요.

남 알겠습니다. 총액은 25달러입니다.

admission 입장권 theme park 테마 파크, 놀이 공원 frequently 자주 from out of town 다른 지역으로부터

50 Where is the conversation most likely taking place?
(A) At an amusement park
(B) At a movie theater
(C) At a sports center
(D) At a museum

대화는 어디에서 일어나고 있는 것 같은가?
(A) 놀이 공원
(B) 영화관
(C) 스포츠 센터
(D) 박물관

대화의 장소를 유추하는 질문으로 theme park의 입장권을 구입하고 싶다고 했으므로 이곳은 놀이공원이 된다.

51 What does the woman ask about?
(A) Special events
(B) Discounts for children
(C) Directions to a gift shop
(D) Weather conditions

여자는 무엇에 대해 묻는가?
(A) 특별 이벤트
(B) 아이들을 위한 할인
(C) 선물 가게에 가는 길
(D) 날씨 상태

여자는 어린이를 위한 할인을 제공하는지 물었으므로 정답은 (B)가 된다.

52 What additional information does the man give?
(A) A guided tour
(B) An event for children
(C) Business hours
(D) Benefits of a membership

남자는 무슨 추가 정보를 제공하는가?
(A) 가이드 투어
(B) 아이들을 위한 행사
(C) 영업시간
(D) 회원의 혜택

남자 대사에서 언급되는 정보 중에서 보기와 일치되는 것은 we also have a one-year membership for only 50 dollars(일 년짜리 회원권을 저렴한 금액에 살 수 있다)라는 것이므로 정답은 (D)이다.

Questions 53-55 refer to the following conversation with three speakers. (미W) (미M) (영W)

W1 You guys know about the training classes all new employees are required to take?

M Oh, yes. My manager mentioned something about it. He suggested I take the course on marketing strategies.

W2 I'm sorry, but I'm not following. What classes are you talking about?

W1 Oh, it's mandatory for you too, Stacey. The training classes are offered online so you can take them anywhere and at any time. It is possible to take them during working hours too.

W2 Oh, that's great. How do we register for them?

M We can just go to the company's website and click on the employee training tab. Let me go online now. There's a good explanation of the whole registration process here. Check this out, Stacey.

여1 여러분은 모든 신입 사원들이 들어야 하는 교육 수업에 대해 알고 계세요?

남 아, 네. 저의 매니저가 그것에 대한 얘기를 했었어요. 그는 저에게 마케팅 전략에 대한 수업을 들으라고 제안해 줬습니다.

여2 죄송한데 저는 무슨 말인지 모르겠어요. 무슨 수업에 대해 얘기하시는 거예요?

여1 아, 당신에게도 필수 사항이에요, Stacey. 교육 수업은 온라인으로 제공되기 때문에 아무 때나 어디서든 들을 수가 있어요. 게다가 근무 시간에 듣는 것도 가능합니다.

여2 아, 그거 좋은데요. 저희가 어떻게 등록을 하면 되죠?

남 회사 웹 사이트로 가서 직원 교육 탭을 클릭하시면 됩니다. 제가 지금 접속을 해 볼게요. 모든 등록 절차에 대해서 자세한 설명이 되어 있네요. 이거 한번 보세요, Stacey.

mandatory 필수의 working hours 근무시간 registration process 등록 절차

53 What are the speakers mainly discussing?
(A) A new manager
(B) Employee benefits
(C) A project deadline
(D) Training classes

화자들은 주로 무엇에 대해 얘기하는가?
(A) 새로운 매니저
(B) 사원 혜택
(C) 프로젝트 마감
(D) 교육 수업

대화의 주제는 도입부에 언급된 신입 사원 모두가 들어야 하는 training classes로 정답은 (D)이다.

54 What does Stacey mean when she says, "I'm sorry but I'm not following"?
(A) She was not aware of the training classes.
(B) She wants to discuss another subject.
(C) She is an expert on marketing strategies.
(D) She is sorry about being late for work.

Stacey가 "죄송한데 저는 무슨 말인지 모르겠어요"라고 말한 의미는 무엇인가?
(A) 그녀는 교육 수업에 대해 모르고 있었다.
(B) 그녀는 다른 주제에 대해 얘기하길 원한다.
(C) 그녀는 마케팅 전략의 전문가이다.
(D) 그녀는 직장에 지각한 것에 미안해한다.

해당 표현인 I'm not following의 원래 의미는 "저는 이해가 안 됩니다"라는 뜻이다. 신입 사원들이 필수적으로 들어야 하는 트레이닝 수업에 대한 이야기를 하자 Stacey가 "I'm sorry but I'm not following"라고 말했으므로 정답은 (A)가 된다.

55 How can new employees register for the classes?
(A) By speaking to a manager
(B) By visiting a website
(C) By completing a form
(D) By upgrading software

신입 사원들은 어떻게 수업에 등록할 수 있는가?
(A) 매니저에게 말함으로써
(B) 웹 사이트를 방문함으로써
(C) 양식을 작성함으로써
(D) 소프트웨어를 업그레이드 시킴으로써

세부 정보를 묻는 질문으로 등록 방법을 집중해서 듣자. 어떻게 등록해야 하는지 질문을 했을 때, We can just go to the company's website(웹 사이트에 들어가서 할 수 있다)라고 했으므로 정답은 (B)이다.

Questions 56-58 refer to the following conversation. 영W 미M

W Hello. I'm calling about the curtains I recently purchased from your shop. I bought them to cover my bedroom windows but they are too small. The measurements I gave you must've been wrong. Can I exchange them for a larger size?
M If you want to exchange the curtains, you have two options – either you can return them to one of our nearby branches, or you can send them back to us by courier.
W I prefer the courier service. Can I pick up my new curtains at a store near my house?
M If you give me your address and the item code, I'll check our inventory and let you know which store is closest to you.

여 여보세요. 당신의 상점에서 최근에 구매한 커튼에 관하여 전화드려요. 침실 창문을 가리기 위해서 그것들을 구입했는데 사이즈가 너무 작습니다. 제가 드렸던 치수가 잘못된 것 같아요. 더 큰 사이즈로 그것들을 교환할 수 있을까요?
남 커튼을 교환하고 싶으시다면, 두 가지의 선택 사항이 있습니다 – 저희의 상점 중 가까운 곳에 반납을 해주시거나 또는 택배 서비스를 이용해서 저희에게 다시 보내 주시는 것입니다.
여 택배 서비스가 더 좋아요. 제 집과 가까운 지점에서 새 커튼을 가져올 수 있을까요?
남 저에게 당신의 집 주소와 상품코드를 알려 주시면, 재고를 조사해 보고 어떤 상점이 가장 가까운지 알려 드리겠습니다.

purchase 구매하다 measurement 치수 exchange 교환하다 curtain 커튼 option 선택 사항 branch 지점 by courier 택배로, 배달로 item code 상품 코드 stock 재고

56 What is the problem with the curtains?
(A) They are too dark.
(B) They look unattractive.
(C) They are the wrong size.
(D) They are out of stock.

커튼에 대한 문제는 무엇인가?
(A) 너무 어둡다.
(B) 외형이 아름답지 않다.
(C) 잘못된 사이즈이다.
(D) 품절이다.

세부 사항 질문으로 키워드는 curtains로 부정적인 내용에 집중한다. 커튼을 침실 창문용으로 구입했다고 밝힌 후, they are too small이라고 말했으므로 사이즈가 맞지 않는 것이 문제이다. 정답은 (C)이다.

57 What does the woman decide to do?
(A) Call for a brochure
(B) Request a refund
(C) Take measurements again
(D) Send a package by parcel

여자는 무엇을 하기로 결정하는가?
(A) 안내 책자를 요청하기로
(B) 환불을 요청하기로
(C) 치수를 다시 측정하기로
(D) 소포로 물건을 보내기로

세부 사항 질문으로 여자 대사에서 최종적으로 선택하는 사항이 정답이 된다. 물건을 교환하기 위한 방법으로 직접 지점에 방문하는 것과 택배를 통하는 것이 언급되었고, 여자는 택배를 선택했으므로 정답은 (D)가 된다. 택배와 관련된 어휘인 by courier, send, by parcel 등을 함께 암기해 두자.

58 What does the man offer to check?
(A) Where to mail a shipment
(B) How to pay an additional fee
(C) Whether a product is available
(D) When a process will be completed

남자는 무엇을 확인해 주겠다고 하는가?
(A) 배송을 보낼 곳
(B) 추가 요금을 지불하는 방법
(C) 상품이 구입 가능한지 여부
(D) 과정이 완료되는 시점

대화의 후반부에 주소와 상품코드를 알려주면 재고를 확인하겠다(I'll check our inventory)고 했고, 이를 상품이 구입 가능한(available)지 확인하겠다고 바꿔 표현한 (C)가 정답이 된다.

Questions 59-61 refer to the following conversation. (영M) (미W)

M Hi, Samantha. How's it going with your new florist shop?
W Well, business has been pretty weak for the last 3 months. I think it is because I relied only on word of mouth referrals at the beginning. So now I'm going to increase online advertising and start offering repeat customers more benefits.
M That's a good idea. I think it's time for a more aggressive approach which will bring you more business. Oh, actually I can help you out too. My company is planning an annual function for all employees. And I'd be happy to suggest that we hire your shop to prepare the flower arrangements.
W Oh, thank you very much for your help, Kyle.

남 안녕하세요, Cate, 당신의 새로운 꽃 가게는 어떻게 되고 있나요?
여 음, 사업이 지난 3개월 동안 좀 저조했습니다. 제가 초반에 입소문 추천에만 의존해서 그런 것 같아요. 그래서 이제는 온라인 광고도 늘리려고 하고 단골 고객들에게는 더 많은 혜택을 제공하기 시작하려고요.
남 좋은 생각이네요. 지금은 고객을 더 많이 늘릴 수 있는 좀 더 공격적인 접근을 해야 할 것 같습니다. 아, 실은 저도 도울 수 있을 것 같아요. 저희 회사에서 직원들을 위해 연례 행사를 계획하고 있어요. 그리고 제가 꽃 장식을 준비하는 데 당신의 가게를 고용하자고 기꺼이 추천해 드릴게요.
여 아, 도와주셔서 정말 감사합니다, Kyle.

florist shop 꽃 가게 rely on ~에 의존하다 word of mouth 입 소문 referral 추천 repeat customer 단골 고객 aggressive approach 공격적인 접근 function 행사 flower arrangements 꽃 장식

59 What type of business does the woman own?
(A) An advertising agency
(B) An online game company
(C) A florist shop
(D) A catering company

여자는 어떤 종류의 사업을 소유하고 있는가?
(A) 광고 회사
(B) 온라인 게임 회사
(C) 꽃 가게
(D) 출장 뷔페 회사

남자가 여자에게 당신의 꽃 가게가 어떻게 되고 있는지(How's it going with your new florist shop?)물었으므로 정답은 (C)이다.

60 What does the woman say about her business?
(A) It has been unprofitable.
(B) It is adding a branch.
(C) It has hired a new advertising agent.
(D) It has a bad reputation.

여자는 그녀의 사업에 관해서 뭐라고 말하는가?
(A) 수익을 내지 못했다.
(B) 지점을 추가로 낼 것이다.
(C) 새로운 광고 업체를 고용했다.
(D) 평판이 안 좋다.

여자 대사에서 본인의 사업에 대한 언급한 부분은 business has been pretty weak for the last 3 months로 사업이 3개월 동안 저조했다는 내용이므로 정답은 (A)이다. 지문의 pretty weak는 (A)에서 unprofitable로 패러프레이징되었다.

61 What does the man offer to do?
(A) Bring his acquaintances
(B) Help prepare flower arrangements
(C) Review a contract
(D) Recommend the woman's business

남자는 무엇을 해 주겠다고 하는가?
(A) 그의 지인 데려오기
(B) 꽃 장식 준비하는 것 도와주기
(C) 계약서 검토하기
(D) 여자의 사업체 추천하기

남자가 회사의 행사에 대해 언급하면서 And I'd be happy to suggest that we hire your shop(당신의 가게를 고용하자고 제안하겠다)이라고 했으므로 정답은 (D)가 된다.

Questions 62-64 refer to the following conversation with three speakers. (미W) (영M) (미M)

W Hi. I'm looking for a color printer. Could you recommend one for me?
M1 Certainly. This is our latest model, The XG-200. Its color resolution has been greatly improved from the previous version and it prints very fast. I think you're going to like it.
W Okay, and how much does it cost?
M1 It costs 380 dollars.
W Hmm... do you have anything that's more affordable? My budget is only 300 dollars.
M1 Well, we also have last year's model, The XG-100. It is a little slower but costs only 290 dollars. I'm not sure if we have any more of that model in stock though. Hey Steven, do we have any XG-100 printers available at the moment?
M2 Yes we do. But there are only two units left because all of last year's models are 10 percent off right now.
W Oh, that's great. I'll take one.

여 안녕하세요. 컬러 인쇄기를 찾고 있습니다. 한 개 추천해 주실 수 있을까요?
남1 그럼요. 최신 모델인 XG-200입니다. 컬러 해상도가 지난 모델에 비해 크게 향상되었고 인쇄 속도가 매우 빠릅니다. 만족하실 겁니다.
여 좋네요. 얼마인가요?
남1 380달러입니다.
여 흠… 더 저렴한 것도 있으신가요? 예산이 300달러라서요.
남1 음, 작년 모델인 XG-100도 있습니다. 이건 조금 느리지만 290달러밖에 하지 않습니다. 그런데 우리가 재고를 가지고 있는지는 잘 모르겠어요. 이봐요 Steven, XG-100프린터기가 지금 남은 게 있나요?
남2 네, 있습니다. 그런데 지금 작년 모델들은 10퍼센트 할인을 하기 때문에 딱 두 대밖에 남지 않았어요.
여 아, 좋네요. 제가 하나 사겠습니다.

color resolution 컬러 해상도 previous 이전의 affordable 저렴한 budget 예산 in stock 재고가 있는

62 What is mentioned about The XG-200?
(A) It is the newest model.
(B) It is slower than the previous model.
(C) It is the most expensive model.
(D) It comes in different colors.

XG-200에 관하여 무엇이 언급되는가?
(A) 가장 최신 모델이다.
(B) 이전 모델보다 느리다.
(C) 가장 비싼 모델이다.
(D) 여러 색깔로 나온다.

질문의 키워드는 XG-200으로 지문에서 The XG-200가 가장 최신 모델이라고(This is our latest model, The XG-200) 했으므로 정답은 (A)가 된다.

63 What is the woman's concern?
(A) She prefers a faster printer.
(B) A product is unavailable right now.
(C) Her budget is limited.
(D) She has to go back to her office.

여자는 무엇에 대해 염려하는가?
(A) 그녀는 더 빠른 프린터를 선호한다.
(B) 상품이 지금 구매 가능하지 않다.
(C) 그녀의 예산은 제한적이다.
(D) 그녀는 사무실에 돌아가야 한다.

여자가 보다 affordable(저렴한) 모델을 찾으면서 My budget is only 300 dollars(나의 예산은 300달러뿐이다)라고 했으므로 정답은 (C)가 된다.

64 What advantage does Steven mention about last year's models?
(A) Free shipping is provided.
(B) They are lightweight.
(C) Self-installation is easy.
(D) They have come down in price.

Steven은 작년 모델에 대해서 어떤 장점을 언급하는가?
(A) 무료 배송이 제공된다.
(B) 무게가 가볍다.
(C) 설치가 쉽다.
(D) 가격이 내렸다.

3인 대화로 Steven이라는 이름을 놓치지 않고 듣는 것이 중요하다. 작년 모델 프린터에 대해서 10퍼센트의 할인을 제공한다고 했으므로 정답은 (D)가 된다.

Questions 65-67 refer to the following conversation and notice.
영W 미M

W Excuse me. I saw my name on the 'overdue' list at the check-out counter. Apparently I haven't returned an item to your library but I can't remember what it is. Could you check it for me? My name is Lisa Reston.
M Hold on a second please. Well, according to our record, you currently have a copy of *Psychology in the Workplace*. You checked it out on March 11th and it is 10 days overdue.
W Oh, you're right. I completely forgot about it. I'll make sure to return it and pay the fine tomorrow. Can I check these two books out now?
M You can do that after the overdue fine has been taken care of. But I can put them aside for you for tomorrow evening if you want.

Library Check-out Policy
- 4 items at a time
- Books = 2 weeks
- Magazines and videos = 1-3 days
- Fines = 5 cents per day

여 실례합니다. 제가 카운터 옆에 '기한 초과' 리스트에서 제 이름을 봤는데요. 보아하니 제가 도서관에서 빌린 물건을 반납하지 않은 것 같은데 무엇인지 기억이 안 나네요. 확인을 좀 해 주시겠어요? Lisa Reston입니다.
남 잠시만 기다리세요. 음, 저희 기록에 따르면, 현재 〈직장에서의 심리학〉이란 책을 한 권 가지고 계시네요. 3월 11일에 책을 빌려 가셨고 10일간 연체가 되었습니다.
여 아, 맞습니다. 완전히 잊고 있었어요. 내일 반드시 반납하고 연체료를 내겠습니다. 이 책 두 권을 지금 빌릴 수 있을까요?
남 기한 초과 벌금이 처리된 후에 빌리실 수 있습니다. 원하신다면 내일 저녁까지 제가 이 책들을 따로 보관해 두겠습니다.

도서관 대출 정책
- 한 번에 4개 품목까지
- 책 = 2주일
- 매거진과 비디오 = 1–3일
- 벌금 = 하루에 5센트

overdue list 연체 리스트 apparently 보아하니 fine 벌금 put aside 따로 떼어두다

65 What problem does the woman mention?
(A) She has an overdue item.
(B) Her library card has expired.
(C) She cannot find a book.
(D) The library is about to close.

여자는 무슨 문제를 언급하는가?
(A) 그녀는 연체 품목이 있다.
(B) 그녀의 대출 카드가 만료되었다.
(C) 그녀는 책을 찾을 수가 없다.
(D) 도서관이 문을 닫기 직전이다.

여자가 언급한 문제는 I saw my name on the 'overdue' list(연체 리스트에서 본인 이름을 봤다)라는 것이므로 정답은 (A)이다.

66 Look at the graphic. How much will the woman have to pay for the overdue book tomorrow?
(A) 5 cents
(B) 15 cents
(C) 55 cents
(D) 2 dollars

시각 정보를 보시오. 여자는 내일 연체된 책에 대해 얼마를 지불해야만 하는가?
(A) 5센트
(B) 15센트
(C) 55센트
(D) 2달러

표에 따르면 연체료는 하루에 5센트이고, 대화 내용에서 it is 10 days overdue(책은 열흘 간 연체되었다)라고 했으며 여자는 내일 연체료를 내겠다고 했으므로 내일 여자가 내야만 하는 금액은 55센트가 된다.

67 What does the man offer to do?
(A) Revise a policy
(B) Find a magazine
(C) Reserve some books
(D) Arrange a meeting

남자는 무엇을 해 주겠다고 하는가?
(A) 방침 수정하기
(B) 잡지 찾기
(C) 책 따로 두기
(D) 회의 준비하기

남자가 여자를 위해 해 주겠다고 하는 일은 I can put them aside for you for tomorrow evening(여자가 빌리려는 책을 내일 저녁까지 따로 보관해 두겠다)이므로 정답은 (C)가 맞다.

Questions 68-70 refer to the following conversation and chart.
미W 영M

W Hey, Ted. People are showing a lot of interest in the career development program we're developing. I was browsing the company's website last night and noticed that there's a lot of interest in our workshops.

M Oh, that's great. How many people have registered so far?

W About eighty. I think we will need a larger space than the meeting room.

M I think so too. Maybe we should use the main conference hall at the headquarters. That will accommodate more than a hundred people. And we could record each workshop and post the video clips on the company's website. That way the workshops can be viewed online as well.

W That's a brilliant idea. And... we need to revise the workshop schedule. The first and last workshops need to be switched. So the day's first workshop will be social media by Ellie Morris. Could you update the schedule on the website?

Schedule	
Workshop	**Time**
Job Maintenance	10:00 a.m.
Dealing with Change	11:00 a.m.
Lunch	12:00 p.m.
Self Esteem	1:00 p.m.
Social Media	2:00 p.m.

여 이봐요, Ted. 사람들이 우리가 개발 중인 경력 개발 프로그램에 많은 관심을 보여 주고 있어요. 제가 어젯밤에 회사 웹 사이트를 둘러 봤는데 우리 워크숍에 관심들이 많더군요.

남 아, 그거 잘됐네요. 얼마나 많은 사람들이 이제까지 등록했죠?

여 대략 80명이요. 회의실보다는 더 큰 공간이 필요할 것 같아요.

남 저도 그렇게 생각합니다. 우리 본사에 있는 메인 컨퍼런스 홀을 이용하는 게 좋을 수도 있겠어요. 거기는 100명 이상 수용할 수 있으니까요. 그리고 각 워크숍을 촬영해서 그 동영상을 회사 웹 사이트에 올리면 어떨까요. 그렇게 하면 워크숍을 온라인으로도 볼 수 있으니까요.

여 정말 훌륭한 아이디어네요. 그리고… 우리는 워크숍 스케줄을 수정해야 해요. 첫 번째 그리고 마지막 워크숍은 바꾸어야 해요. 그러니까 그날의 첫 번째 워크숍은 Ellie Morris에 의한 소셜 미디어가 되는 거죠. 웹 사이트에 스케줄을 업데이트 해주시겠어요?

스케줄	
워크숍	**시간**
직업 유지	오전 10시
변화에 대응하기	오전 11시
점심	정오
자존감	오후 1시
소셜 미디어	오후 2시

career development 경력 개발 accommodate 수용하다 update 수정하다

68 What are the speakers mainly discussing?
(A) The upcoming workshops
(B) A company policy
(C) Online shopping
(D) Some Internet tools

화자들은 주로 무엇에 대해 토론하고 있습니까?
(A) 다가오는 워크숍
(B) 회사 정책
(C) 온라인 쇼핑
(D) 인터넷 도구

주제를 묻는 질문으로 도입부부터 집중력을 발휘하자. 화자들이 준비하고 있는 경력 개발 프로그램에 사람들이 많은 관심을 보이고 있다고 했고 워크숍 신청 인원에 대해 얘기하므로 정답은 (A)가 맞다.

69 What does the man suggest?
(A) Inviting the company CEO
(B) Viewing some photos online
(C) Using a larger space
(D) Changing the seating arrangement

남자는 무엇을 제안하는가?
(A) 회사 CEO를 초대하는 것
(B) 온라인에서 사진을 보는 것
(C) 더 큰 공간을 사용하는 것
(D) 좌석 배열을 바꾸는 것

남자의 대사에서 정답을 찾는다. Maybe we should use the main conference hall at the headquarters(회사 본사의 컨퍼런스 홀을 이용하자)라고 하면서 100명 이상 수용할 수 있다고 했으므로 정답은 (C)가 된다.

70 Look at the graphic. According to the woman, which workshop will now be held last?
(A) Job Maintenance
(B) Dealing with Change
(C) Self Esteem
(D) Social Media

시각 정보를 보시오. 여자에 따르면, 어떤 워크숍이 마지막으로 열릴 것인가?
(A) 직업 유지
(B) 변화에 대응하기
(C) 자존감
(D) 소셜 미디어

스케줄 변경과 관련해서 The first and last workshops need to be switched(첫 번째와 마지막의 워크숍이 바뀌어야 한다)라고 했으므로 정답은 (A)이다.

PART 4

Questions 71-73 refer to the following message. 미W

Hello, Dr. Lee. This is Emma Clark from human resources. I'm trying to schedule interviews for the research assistant you want to hire. I'm thinking of conducting the first interview on Tuesday afternoon if that's convenient for you. I asked you to be there because you are the director of the research lab, but if you are busy that day, could you recommend another researcher from your department? I've already put together a list of questions for the applicants. Please let me know if Tuesday afternoon works for you. Thank you.

안녕하세요, Lee 박사님. 저는 인사부의 Emma Clark입니다. 당신이 고용하기 원하셨던 연구 보조를 뽑기 위한 인터뷰의 일정을 잡고 있는데요. 괜찮으시다면 화요일 오후에 첫 인터뷰를 진행하려고 합니다. 당신이 연구 실험실의 감독이기 때문에 참석해 달라고 요청을 드렸었는데, 만약 그날 바쁘시다면, 같은 부서의 다른 연구원을 추천해 주실 수 있으십니까? 지원자들을 위한 질문 리스트는 이미 준비해 두었습니다. 그럼 화요일 오후가 괜찮으신지 알려 주세요. 감사합니다.

research assistant 연구 보조 put together만들다 applicant 지원자

71 Which department does the speaker most likely work in?
(A) Marketing
(B) Research and Development
(C) Human resources
(D) Customer service

화자는 어느 부서에서 일할 것 같은가?
(A) 마케팅
(B) 연구와 개발
(C) 인사부
(D) 고객 서비스

말하는 사람의 부서를 찾는 문제이므로 This is Emma Clark from human resources에서 인사부 소속임을 알 수 있다.

72 What is the purpose of the message?
(A) To schedule an interview
(B) To request a document
(C) To introduce a new employee
(D) To invite a keynote speaker

메시지의 목적은 무엇인가?
(A) 면접의 일정을 잡기 위하여
(B) 문서를 요청하기 위하여
(C) 새로운 직원을 소개하기 위하여
(D) 기조 연설자를 초대하기 위하여

화자가 인터뷰에 대해 언급하면서 I'm thinking of conducting the first interview on Tuesday afternoon(첫 번째 인터뷰를 화요일 오후에 하고 싶다)이라고 했으므로 정답은 (A)가 된다.

73 What has already been prepared?
(A) A meeting room
(B) A user manual
(C) A list of questions
(D) A security badge

무엇이 이미 준비되었는가?
(A) 회의실
(B) 사용자 설명서
(C) 질문 리스트
(D) 보안 배지

질문의 키워드는 already, prepare이다. 화자가 I've already put together a list of questions for the applicants에서 이미 질문 리스트를 만들어 놓았음을 알 수 있으므로 정답은 (C)가 된다.

Questions 74-76 refer to the following announcement. (미M)

Good evening shoppers! Venus Clothing Shop will be closing in 30 minutes. Please take your items and proceed to the check-out line. Don't forget that all women's hats are 10 percent off today and you can find them in the women's section on the first floor. The customer service counter is now closed so please direct all questions to the store manager. Finally, I'm pleased to announce that our operating hours will be extended starting next weekend. Our new hours will be from 10 a.m. to 10 p.m., from Tuesday to Sunday and we will be closed on Mondays. Thank you for shopping with us and we look forward to seeing you again.

안녕하세요, 쇼핑객 여러분! Venus Clothing Shop은 30분 후에 문을 닫습니다. 물건을 가지고 계산대로 가주시기 바랍니다. 오늘은 모든 여성용 모자가 10퍼센트 할인이 되고 1층 여성복 매장에서 찾으실 수 있습니다. 고객 서비스 카운터는 지금 문을 닫았으므로 모든 질문은 매장 매니저에게 해 주십시오. 마지막으로, 저희 영업시간이 다음 주말부터 연장된다는 것을 알려 드립니다. 새로운 영업시간은 화요일부터 일요일까지 오전 10시부터 오후 10시까지이며 매주 월요일은 문을 닫습니다. 저희 매장에서 쇼핑을 해주셔서 감사드리며 또 뵙기를 바랍니다.

proceed to ~로 가다 check-out line 계산대 operating hours 영업시간 extend 연장시키다

74 What is the purpose of the announcement?
(A) To announce the closing of a store
(B) To introduce a new line of products
(C) To explain a new refund policy
(D) To direct shoppers to the service desk

공지의 목적은 무엇인가?
(A) 상점의 폐장을 알리려고
(B) 새로운 제품을 소개하려고
(C) 새로운 환불 정책을 설명하려고
(D) 쇼핑객들을 서비스 데스크로 안내하려고

공지의 도입부에 상점이 30분 후에 문을 닫는다고 했으므로 정답은 (A)가 된다.

75 Where can shoppers find the sale items?
(A) Next to the checkout counters
(B) In the women's section
(C) In the children's section
(D) Near the event hall

쇼핑객은 어디에서 할인 품목을 찾을 수 있는가?
(A) 계산대의 옆
(B) 여성복 매장
(C) 어린이 매장
(D) 이벤트 홀 근처

질문의 키워드인 sale items에 집중하자. 여성용 모자가 10퍼센트 할인된다고 하며 1층 여성복 매장에서 찾을 수 있다(you can find them in the women's section on the first floor)고 했으므로 정답은 (B)가 된다.

76 What change will be implemented next weekend?
(A) A special sale will be held.
(B) A new manager will be hired.
(C) The store will have more stock.
(D) Business hours will be extended.

다음 주말에 어떤 변화가 실행될 것인가?
(A) 특별 세일이 열릴 것이다.
(B) 새로운 매니저가 고용될 것이다.
(C) 상점에는 재고가 늘어날 것이다.
(D) 영업시간이 연장될 것이다.

마지막 공지 사항으로 다음 주말부터 영업시간이 연장될 것(our operating hours will be extended starting next weekend)이라고 했으므로 정답은 (D)가 된다.

Questions 77-79 refer to the following radio broadcasting. (영W)

Good evening. You're listening to KAT 89.5. This is Mia Yang, the host of 'Healthy Life'. Tonight, I'll be speaking with leading health experts about daily exercise, diet and the latest medical developments. You will learn a lot of new things that can improve your life! After the discussion, our listeners will be invited to call in with questions and comments. So stay tuned for 'Healthy Life'. I'll be back at 8 o'clock right after the local news.

안녕하세요. 여러분은 KAT 89.5를 듣고 있습니다. 저는 'Healthy Life'의 진행자 Mia Yang입니다. 오늘 밤, 선두적인 건강 전문가들과 매일 할 수 있는 운동, 식이요법, 그리고 신약 개발에 대한 이야기를 나눌 것입니다. 여러분의 삶을 향상시킬 수 있는 많은 새로운 것들을 배우게 될 겁니다. 토론 후에는 청취자들이 질문과 의견이 있으면 전화하실 수 있습니다. 그러니 'Healthy Life'에 주파수를 고정해 주세요. 지역 뉴스가 끝나고 8시에 다시 돌아오겠습니다.

leading 선두적인 health expert 건강 전문가 call in (라디오 방송국 등으로)전화하다 stay tuned 주파수를 고정하다

77 What is the topic of the talk show?
(A) Fashion
(B) Finance
(C) Health
(D) Politics

토크 쇼의 주제는 무엇인가?
(A) 패션
(B) 재무
(C) 건강
(D) 정치

쇼의 이름이 'Healthy Life'이고 건강 전문가들과 운동, 식이요법 등의 이야기를 나눈다고 했으므로 정답은 (C)이다.

78 What are listeners invited to do?
(A) Join a discussion with experts
(B) Order a subscription
(C) Leave their contact information
(D) Take a tour of the radio station

청취자는 무엇을 하도록 초대되는가?
(A) 전문가들과의 토론에 참여하기
(B) 정기 구독을 신청하기
(C) 연락처를 남겨 놓기
(D) 라디오 방송국의 투어하기

청취자들은 will be invited to call in with questions and comments(질문과 코멘트를 가지고 전화하라)라고 했으므로 정답은 (A)가 된다.

79 What will listeners hear next?
(A) A traffic update
(B) A commercial
(C) The weather forecast
(D) A news report

청취자들은 다음에 무엇을 들을 것인가?
(A) 교통 정보
(B) 광고 방송
(C) 일기 예보
(D) 뉴스 보도

다음에 이어질 방송에 대한 정보는 마지막에 등장한다. I'll be back at 8 o'clock right after the local news(지역 뉴스 후에 다시 돌아오겠다)라고 했으므로 다음 방송은 뉴스이다.

Questions 80-82 refer to the following excerpt from a meeting. 영M

Hi, Ms. Carter. This is Peter Bell from the Municipal Licensing & Standards Office calling about the restaurant licensing procedures. You called earlier and asked whether your restaurant needed to pass an inspection before opening? Yes, it does. Two certified inspectors from our office will visit your restaurant to make sure that the kitchen and other areas are safe and clean. The inspection takes about three hours and if your restaurant receives a passing grade, a license will be mailed to you within a week. And please note that the license must be renewed annually. If you have any further questions, please give me a call.

안녕하세요, Carter씨. Municipal Licensing & Standards Office의 Peter Bell이며 레스토랑 허가증 발급 절차 관련해서 전화드립니다. 아까 전화를 주셔서 레스토랑을 열기 전에 검사를 통과할 필요가 있는지 물으셨죠? 네, 그렇습니다. 우리 사무실에서 두 명의 전문 검사관이 당신의 레스토랑을 방문하여 부엌과 다른 공간들이 안전하고 깨끗한지 확인하게 될 것입니다. 검사는 약 3시간 정도 걸리고 귀하의 레스토랑이 통과 점수를 받으면 일주일 내로 허가증이 당신에게 우편으로 보내집니다. 그리고 허가증은 일 년마다 갱신되어야 한다는 것 기억해 주세요. 더 질문이 있으시면, 전화 주십시오.

licensing procedure 허가증 발급 절차 certified inspector 자격증을 갖춘 검사관 passing grade 통과 점수 renew 갱신하다

80 What is the purpose of the message?
(A) To schedule a visit
(B) To discuss the licensing procedures
(C) To explain the results of an inspection
(D) To request a document

메시지의 목적은 무엇인가?
(A) 방문의 일정을 잡으려고
(B) 허가증 발급 절차에 대해 얘기하려고
(C) 검사의 결과에 대해 설명하려고
(D) 문서를 요구하려고

메시지의 목적은 도입부에서 찾자. calling about the restaurant licensing procedures에서 정답은 (B)임을 바로 알 수 있다.

81 What does the speaker mean when he says, "Yes, it does"?
(A) The process takes a long time.
(B) An inspection is required to open a restaurant.
(C) Inspectors are available to visit the restaurant.
(D) There is a fee for the service.

화자가 "네, 그렇습니다"라고 말한 의미는 무엇인가?
(A) 절차는 장시간이 걸린다.
(B) 레스토랑을 열기 위해서는 검사가 필요하다.
(C) 검사관들은 레스토랑을 방문할 시간이 된다.
(D) 서비스를 위한 요금이 있다.

"그렇다"라고 말한 의도는 해당 표현의 앞에 나온다. you asked whether your restaurant needed to pass an inspection before opening?(레스토랑을 열기 전에 검사 통과가 필요한지 물었죠?)이라고 묻고는 "Yes, it does"라고 했으므로 정답은 (B)가 된다.

82 What does the speaker say about renewing a license?
(A) A fee must be paid first.
(B) Staff training is required.
(C) The renewal form is available online.
(D) It must be done every year.

화자는 허가증 갱신에 관하여 무엇을 말하는가?
(A) 요금은 먼저 지불되어야 한다.
(B) 직원 교육이 요구된다.
(C) 갱신 신청서는 온라인에서 이용 가능하다.
(D) 그것은 매년 행해져야 한다.

질문의 키워드는 renewing a license이다. And please note that the license must be renewed annually(허가증 갱신은 매년 이루어져야만 한다)라고 했으므로 정답은 (D)이다.

Questions 83-85 refer to the following introduction. 미M

Thank you for coming to today's training session. We're going to focus on modern day marketing strategies today. As you know, sales here at Blue Beverage Company have grown steadily for the last three years. And of course we want to keep the trend going. That's why we've invited a special guest speaker tonight. Let me introduce Mike Anderson, a leading expert in modern day marketing techniques and consumer behavior. Mr. Anderson is famous for his unique marketing model called 'The Vault' and he will be discussing how to apply these techniques to our products with us in the marketing team. Now, please give Mr. Anderson a very warm welcome.

오늘의 교육에 와 주셔서 감사합니다. 우리는 오늘 현대의 마케팅 전략에 초점을 맞출 것입니다. 아시다시피, 이곳 Blue Beverage Company의 판매는 지난 3년 동안 꾸준히 성장했습니다. 그리고 당연히 우리는 계속 그렇게 되길 원합니다. 그것이 바로 오늘 밤 특별 초청 연사를 모신 이유입니다. 현대 사회의 마케팅 기술과 소비자 행동 분야의 선두적인 전문가이신 Mike Anderson을 소개합니다. Anderson 씨는 독특한 마케팅 모델인 'The Vault'로 유명하신데 이 기술들을 어떻게 우리 제품에 적용시킬 수 있을지에 대해서 우리 마케팅 팀원들과 함께 이야기를 나눌 것입니다. 이제, Anderson 씨에게 큰 박수를 보내 주세요.

focus on ~에 초점을 맞추다 consumer behavior 소비자 행동 unique 독특한, 특별한 apply 적용시키다

83 What does the speaker mention about Blue Beverage Company?
(A) They have won an award.
(B) They will hire additional employees.
(C) They have developed a new product.
(D) Their sales have increased.

화자는 Blue Beverage Company에 관하여 무엇을 언급하는가?
(A) 그들은 상을 받았다.
(B) 그들은 추가 직원을 고용할 것이다.
(C) 그들은 신제품을 개발했다.
(D) 그들의 판매는 증가했다.

Blue Beverage Company라는 회사 이름을 미리 확인해 두고 듣자. sales here at Blue Beverage Company have grown steadily for the last three years(판매가 3년간 꾸준히 올랐다)라고 했으므로 정답은 (D)가 된다.

84 Who is Mike Anderson?
(A) A quality control expert
(B) A marketing expert
(C) A department head
(D) A sales representative

Mike Anderson은 누구인가?
(A) 품질 관리 전문가
(B) 마케팅 전문가
(C) 부서장
(D) 영업 직원

Mike Anderson이라는 이름이 언급되는 부분에 직업도 함께 등장한다. Mike Anderson, a leading expert in modern day marketing techniques라고 했으므로 마케팅 전문가임을 알 수 있다.

85 What will Mr. Anderson discuss?
(A) His recent book
(B) His marketing techniques
(C) His educational background
(D) His hard times

Anderson 씨는 무엇을 토론할 것인가?
(A) 최근 책
(B) 마케팅 기술
(C) 교육 배경
(D) 어려운 시기

그의 독특한 마케팅 모델을 언급하며 우리 제품에 어떻게 이 techniques를 적용시킬지 논의할 것이라고 했으므로 정답은 (B)가 된다.

Questions 86-88 refer to the following introduction. (영W)

Ladies and gentlemen, let me introduce our last speaker of the 11th Annual Gathering of News Journalists, Mr. Gregory Bateman. Mr. Bateman started his career as a police reporter covering local crimes for the Western News. And in just two years, he has risen to editor-in-chief. Today, he'll be discussing the public interest surrounding news stories. Before Mr. Bateman delivers his talk, I'd kindly ask everyone to attend the reception afterwards. It will provide you with a great opportunity to mingle with fellow members of the News Journalists' Association. And now, please give a warm round of applause for Mr. Bateman.

신사 숙녀 여러분, 11번째 뉴스 언론인 연례 모임의 마지막 연사인 Gregory Bateman 씨를 소개합니다. Bateman 씨는 Western News 사에서 지역 범죄를 다루는 경찰 취재원으로 그의 경력을 시작했습니다. 그리고 단 2년 후에, 그는 편집장으로 승진이 되었습니다. 오늘, 그는 뉴스를 둘러싼 대중의 관심에 대해서 이야기를 할 것입니다. Bateman 씨가 연설을 시작하기 전에, 여러분 모두 연설 후에 연회에 참석해 주실 것을 부탁드립니다. 이 행사는 뉴스 언론인 협회의 다른 동료 회원들과 어울릴 수 있는 좋을 기회를 제공할 것입니다. 자 이제, Bateman 씨에게 큰 박수를 주십시오.

police reporter 경찰 취재원 cover (기사를) 취재하다, 다루다 crime 범죄 rise 오르다, 승진하다 public interest 대중의 관심 deliver a talk 연설을 하다 afterwards 후에 fellow 동료 association 협회

86 What is the purpose of the talk?
(A) To discuss a current social issue
(B) To report a local crime
(C) To present an award
(D) To introduce a speaker

담화의 목적은 무엇인가?
(A) 현재의 사회 문제에 대해 논의하려고
(B) 지역 범죄를 보고하려고
(C) 상을 수여하려고
(D) 연사를 소개하려고

담화의 목적은 도입부에 보통 등장하므로 let me introduce you to our last speaker에서 바로 연사를 소개하기 위한 목적임을 알 수 있다.

87 Who is Gregory Bateman?
(A) A professor
(B) A news writer
(C) A policeman
(D) A politician

Gregory Bateman은 누구인가?
(A) 교수
(B) 뉴스 기자
(C) 경찰관
(D) 정치가

세부 사항 질문으로 키워드인 Gregory Bateman이 언급되는 부분 앞이나 뒤에 직업에 대한 정보가 항상 함께 나온다. 이름을 언급한 후 그가 경찰 취재원으로서의 경력을 시작했다는 부분에서 정답을 (B)로 선택한다. 혹시라도 police reporter(경찰 취재원)를 듣고 (C) A policeman으로 잘못 선택하는 일이 없도록 주의하자.

88 What will the audience most likely do after the talk?
(A) Enroll in a course
(B) Join an association
(C) Participate in a reception
(D) Register for a seminar

청중은 담화 후에 무엇을 할 것 같은가?
(A) 수업 과정에 등록하기
(B) 협회에 가입하기
(C) 연회에 참석하기
(D) 세미나 신청하기

세부 사항 질문으로 키워드는 after the talk이다. 지문에서는 afterwards로 키워드가 바뀌 표현된 것을 기억해 두자. I'd like to ask everyone to attend the reception afterwards 부분에서 연설 후 열리는 연회에 청중이 참석할 것이라고 파악할 수 있다. 정답은 (C)이다.

Questions 89-91 refer to the following talk. (미W)

I called this marketing meeting to assign everyone with a new task. But first I'd like to share some good news. It is with great pleasure that I can announce that this has been the most profitable year in the history of ZT Electronics. **It is all because of everyone here.** The company's profits have increased by 20% since last year thanks to your hard work. And we're planning to release our new smart phone, the Scorpion 7, on September 1st, which we have high hopes for. Now Chris Harrison will tell you more about the marketing strategies you will use to attract customers to purchase the Scorpion 7. Please come up to the stage, Chris. And could somebody dim the lights for his presentation please?

제가 이 마케팅 회의를 소집한 이유는 여러분에게 새로운 업무를 배정해 주기 위함입니다. 그러나 먼저 좋은 소식을 알려 드리겠습니다. 올해가 ZT Electronics 역사상 가장 높은 수익을 올린 해였다는 것을 발표하게 되어 기쁩니다. **이것은 모두 여러분 덕분입니다.** 여러분들이 열심히 일하신 덕분에 작년부터 한 해 동안 회사의 수익은 20퍼센트 증가하였습니다. 그리고 많은 기대를 하고 있는 우리의 새로운 스마트폰 the Scorpion 7의 출시를 9월 1일로 계획하고 있습니다. 이제 Chris Harrison 씨가 여러분이 the Scorpion 7을 구입하도록 고객들을 끌어 올 마케팅 전략에 대해서 더 얘기를 할 것입니다. Chris, 무대 앞으로 나와 주세요. 그리고 누가 그의 발표를 위해서 조명을 낮춰 주시겠습니까?

profitable 수익성이 좋은 thanks to ~ 덕분에 dim the lights 조명을 줄이다

89 Who most likely are the listeners?
(A) Sales representatives
(B) Store customers
(C) Marketing staff
(D) Magazine reporters

청자들은 누구일 것 같은가?
(A) 판매 사원
(B) 매장 고객
(C) 마케팅 직원
(D) 잡지 기자

도입부에 화자가 I called this marketing meeting이라고 말했을 때 듣는 사람들은 마케팅 회의에 참석한 마케팅 직원들임을 알 수 있다.

90 What does the speaker mean when she says, "It is all because of everyone here"?
(A) Employees have developed a new product.
(B) Employees have organized tonight's event.
(C) Employees are able to multi-task.
(D) Employees have helped the company succeed.

화자가 "이것은 모두 여러분 덕분입니다"라고 말한 의미는 무엇인가?
(A) 직원들은 신제품을 개발했다.
(B) 직원들은 오늘 밤의 행사를 주관했다.
(C) 직원들은 여러 가지 일을 동시에 할 수 있다.
(D) 직원들은 회사가 성공하도록 도왔다.

해당 표현 전에 올해가 가장 수익이 높은 해(the most profitable year)였다고 말한 후 "It is all because of everyone here(여기 있는 여러분들 덕분이다)"라고 했으므로 정답은 (D)가 된다.

91 What will the company do on September 1st?
(A) Open a branch overseas
(B) Launch a new product
(C) Conduct a marketing survey
(D) Celebrate an anniversary

회사는 9월 1일에 무엇을 할 것인가?
(A) 해외 지점을 연다.
(B) 신제품을 출시한다.
(C) 마케팅 설문조사를 한다.
(D) 기념일을 축하한다.

질문의 키워드는 September 1st이다. 새로운 스마트폰의 출시를 9월 1일로 계획하고 있다고 했으므로 정답은 (B)가 된다.

Questions 92-94 refer to the following excerpt from a meeting. 미M

I've called this budget meeting to assign everyone a very important job. But first, let me remind everybody that the budget report including the forecasts for next quarter is due in just five days. Although our company's profits have increased steadily over the past two quarters, there has been a massive increase in spending as well. So I'd like you to come up with some new, effective ways to cut costs. I'm going to incorporate the best cost-cutting measures into the final budget and present it to the CEO on August 28th. I look forward to hearing your creative ideas at our next meeting in two days.

저는 여러분에게 아주 중요한 업무를 배정하기 위해 이 예산 회의를 소집했습니다. 그러나 먼저 다음 분기의 추정치를 포함하는 예산안이 5일 후면 마감이라는 것을 상기시켜 드립니다. 우리 회사의 수익은 지난 두 분기 동안 꾸준히 증가해 왔음에도 불구하고, 지출 역시 큰 폭의 증가가 있었습니다. 따라서 비용을 줄일 수 있는 새롭고 효과적인 방법을 생각해 보셨으면 합니다. 저는 가장 잘된 비용 절감 조치를 최종 예산안에 포함할 것이고 그것을 8월 28일에 CEO에게 발표할 것입니다. 이틀 후에 있을 다음 미팅에서 여러분의 창의적인 아이디어를 기대하겠습니다.

budget 예산 assign 배정하다 forecast 추정 금액 quarter 분기 massive 엄청난 spending 지출 cut costs 비용을 줄이다 cost-cutting measure 비용 절감 조치 look forward to 기대하다 creative 창의적인

92 What is the purpose of the meeting?
(A) To forecast the weather
(B) To discuss a problem
(C) To evaluate employees
(D) To assign a task

회의의 목적은 무엇인가?
(A) 날씨를 예측하기 위하여
(B) 문제에 대해 토론하기 위하여
(C) 직원을 평가하기 위하여
(D) 업무를 배정하기 위하여

회의의 목적을 가장 직접적으로 명시한 부분은 도입부의 I've called this budget meeting to assign everyone a very important job이다. 중요한 업무를 배정하기 위해서 미팅을 소집했다고 했으므로 정답은 (D)이 된다. forecast는 수치, 예산 등의 예측이라는 뜻도 있기 때문에 그 단어만 듣고 (A)로 답을 선택하는 일은 없어야 하겠다.

93 What does the speaker want to do?
(A) Reduce expenditures
(B) Boost profits
(C) Postpone a deadline
(D) Interview an applicant

화자는 무엇을 하길 원하는가?
(A) 비용 줄이기
(B) 이익 증가시키기
(C) 마감 미루기
(D) 지원자 면접 보기

화자가 청자에게 요청했던 내용이 I'd like you to come up with some new, effective ways to cut costs이므로 화자는 비용 절감을 원하는 것을 알 수 있다. 정답은 (A)이다.

94 What will happen on August 28th?
(A) A merger will be discussed.
(B) The CEO will be appointed.
(C) A meeting will take place.
(D) A product will be demonstrated.

8월 28일에 무엇이 일어날 것인가?
(A) 합병이 논의될 것이다.
(B) CEO가 임명될 것이다.
(C) 회의가 열릴 것이다.
(D) 제품이 시연될 것이다.

세부 사항 질문으로 on August 28th가 키워드이다. 화자가 final budget(최종 예산안)을 완성하여 28일날 CEO에게 발표할 것이라고 했으므로 정답은 미팅이 열릴 것이라고 바꿔 표현한 (C)가 된다.

Questions 95-97 refer to the following message and schedule. 미W

Thank you all for volunteering to help with the arrangements for the company's awards banquet. Firstly, the location has been decided. We're going to hold this year's event at the Lakeshore Convention Hall because they have agreed to offer a 5% discount. Now we have to decide which catering company to hire. We have narrowed down the list to four caterers. Many of you probably know Daniel Catering because we hired them for last year's event. Their prices were very good but the quality of their food was not very satisfactory. This year I think we should try another caterer that offers better food and great service. This company's price seems high compared to the others, but it is known for its gourmet food and its well trained staff. Although it's our most expensive option, I think we should give this company a try.

List of Catering Companies

Company	Price Quote
1. Daniel Catering	$3,000
2. Rose Catering	$4,500
3. The Lazy Gourmet	$7,000
4. Christine Catering	$3,500

회사의 시상식 연회를 준비하는 데 도와주기로 자원해 주셔서 감사합니다. 첫째로 장소가 결정되었습니다. 우리는 올해의 행사를 Lakeshore Convention Hall에서 열 것이고 그들은 5퍼센트 할인을 제공해 주기로 했습니다. 이제 어떤 출장 뷔페 업체를 고용할지 결정해야 합니다. 4개의 업체로 리스트를 줄여 놓았는데요. 많은 분들이 작년에 우리가 고용했었던 Daniel Catering은 아실 겁니다. 그들은 가격이 매우 좋았지만 음식의 질은 만족스럽지 못했습니다. 올해는 더 좋은 음식과 서비스를 제공하는 다른 업체를 시도해 보는 게 좋을 것 같습니다. 이 회사의 가격은 다른 회사들과 비교해서 높아 보이지만, 그러나 이곳은 고급 음식과 잘 훈련된 직원들로 유명합니다. 비록 가장 가격이 비싼 회사이지만, 이 회사를 한 번 써보는 게 좋을 것 같습니다.

출장 뷔페 업체 리스트

회사	가격 견적
1. Daniel Catering	3,000달러
2. Rose Catering	4,500달러
3. The Lazy Gourmet	7,000달러
4. Christine Catering	3,500달러

volunteer 자원하다 narrow down 줄이다 satisfactory 만족스러운
gourmet food 고급 음식 give a try 시도해 보다

95 What event will the company hold?
(A) A retirement party
(B) An awards banquet
(C) A press conference
(D) An annual convention

회사는 무슨 행사를 열 것인가?
(A) 은퇴 파티
(B) 시상식 연회
(C) 기자 회견
(D) 연례 컨벤션

도입부에 회사의 awards banquet을 준비하는 내용이 나왔으므로 정답은 (B)가 된다.

96 What does the speaker mention about Daniel Catering?
(A) The food was not good.
(B) The service was excellent.
(C) The price was expensive.
(D) The employees are well trained.

화자는 Daniel Catering에 관하여 무엇을 언급하는가?
(A) 음식이 좋지 않았다.
(B) 서비스가 우수했다.
(C) 가격이 비쌌다.
(D) 직원들이 잘 훈련되었다.

업체의 이름을 먼저 파악해 두고 듣자. 작년에 고용했던 업체가 Daniel Catering으로 가격은 매우 좋지만 음식의 질이 not satisfactory(만족스럽지 않았다)라고 했으므로 정답은 (A)이다.

97 Look at the graphic. Which company does the speaker want to hire?
(A) Daniel Catering
(B) Rose Catering
(C) The Lazy Gourmet
(D) Christine Catering

시각 정보를 보시오. 화자는 어떤 회사를 고용하기 원하는가?
(A) Daniel Catering
(B) Rose Catering
(C) The Lazy Gourmet
(D) Christine Catering

표를 참고하며 내용을 듣는다. 이 업체는 it's our most expensive option(가장 비싼 선택 사항)이지만 음식과 직원이 훌륭하니 고용하자고 했으므로 정답은 가장 견적 비용이 비싼 (C)가 정답이다.

Questions 98-100 refer to the following message and list. 영M

As most of you know, our Asian city tour packages have sold very well during the last year and that is the main reason for the increase in our travel agency's annual profits. In fact, the Seoul City Tours were the most popular, especially for customers in their 20s and 30s because there are a lot fun things to do day and night in Seoul. So we're planning to add more Korean city tours, such as one to Busan. On the other hand, we might have to reduce the number of tours in this city considering the poor sales results on this chart. But before we make a final decision, I'd like you to look into why the sales of tour packages in this city decreased so dramatically last year.

Sales of Asia City Tours

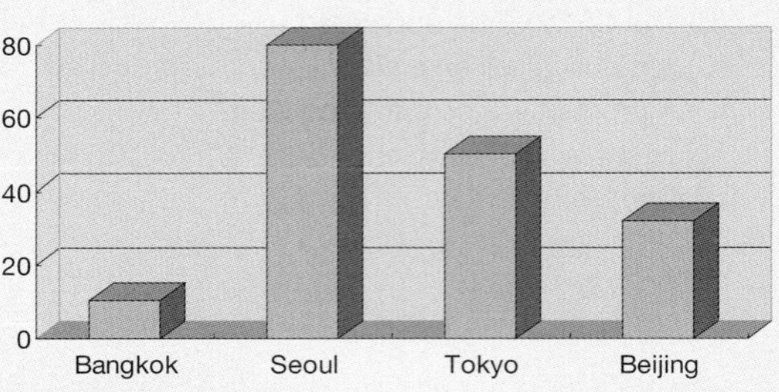

많은 분들이 알겠지만, 우리 아시아 도시 투어 패키지 상품은 작년 동안 잘 팔렸고 그것이 우리 여행사의 연례 수익 증가의 주 요인이었습니다. 사실 서울 도시 투어가 특기 20대와 30대의 고객들에게 가장 인기가 많았고 이는 서울에는 밤낮으로 즐길 거리가 많기 때문인 것 같습니다. 그래서 우리는 부산과 같은 한국 도시 투어를 더 추가하려고 합니다. 반면에, 차트상의 안 좋은 판매 결과를 고려해볼 때 이 도시의 투어는 줄어야 할 것 같습니다. 그렇지만 최종 결정을 내리기 전에 여러분께서 작년에 이 도시의 패키지 투어가 이렇게 갑자기 줄어든 원인을 조사해 주시길 바랍니다.

아시아 도시 패키지 판매

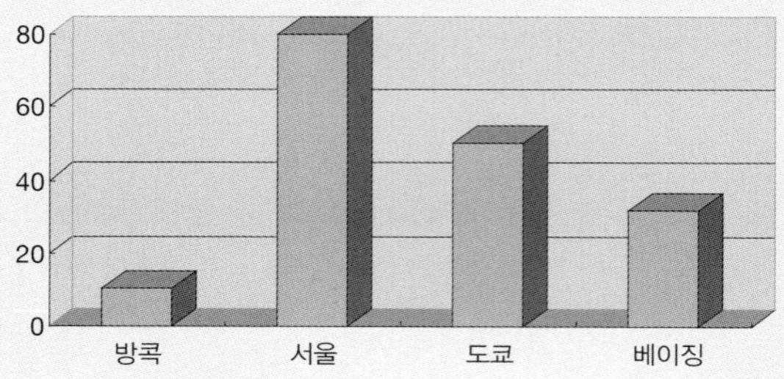

annual profits 연례 수익 considering ~을 고려해 볼 때 make a final decision 최종 결정을 내리다 dramatically 큰 폭으로, 엄청나게

98 What is responsible for the increase in the company's profits?
(A) The company's new web site
(B) The decreased cost of operations

(C) Cheaper flight tickets
(D) Sales of city tours
무엇이 회사의 이익 증가의 원인이 되는가?
(A) 회사의 새로운 웹 사이트
(B) 줄어든 운영 비용
(C) 더 싼 항공 티켓
(D) 도시 투어의 판매

도입부에 아시아 도시 투어 패키지의 판매가 좋았다고 언급하면서 그것이 수익 증가의 주요 원인이었다고 했으므로 정답은 (D)가 된다.

99 According to the speaker, why do customers like Seoul?
(A) It is safe to travel around the city.
(B) They can enjoy the city day and night.
(C) There are many inexpensive hotels.
(D) It is easy to use public transportation.
화자에 따르면, 고객들은 왜 서울을 좋아하는가?
(A) 도시를 여행하는 것이 안전하다.
(B) 도시를 밤낮으로 즐길 수 있다.
(C) 저렴한 호텔들이 많이 있다.
(D) 대중교통의 이용이 쉽다.

서울 도시 투어가 20대, 30대에게 가장 인기가 좋은 이유로 밤낮으로 즐길 거리가 많기 때문이라고(because there are a lot fun things to do day and night in Seoul) 했으므로 정답은 (B)가 된다.

100 Look at the graphic. What city will the listeners investigate?
(A) Bangkok
(B) Seoul
(C) Tokyo
(D) Beijing
시각 정보를 보시오. 청자들은 어떤 도시를 조사할 것인가?
(A) 방콕
(B) 서울
(C) 도쿄
(D) 베이징

차트 상으로 매우 수익이 안 좋은 도시에 대해서 왜 급격히 판매가 떨어졌는지 조사해 보라고 했으므로 가장 수익이 낮은 방콕을 조사할 것임을 알 수 있다.

Actual Test 3

PART 1

본책 p.36

1 (D)	2 (B)	3 (B)	4 (B)	5 (A)	6 (C)

PART 2

본책 p.40

7 (B)	8 (C)	9 (A)	10 (C)	11 (B)	12 (B)
13 (A)	14 (C)	15 (A)	16 (B)	17 (C)	18 (C)
19 (A)	20 (B)	21 (B)	22 (A)	23 (B)	24 (C)
25 (B)	26 (A)	27 (B)	28 (C)	29 (C)	30 (A)
31 (B)					

PART 3

본책 p.41

32 (C)	33 (A)	34 (D)	35 (B)	36 (D)	37 (A)
38 (C)	39 (A)	40 (C)	41 (A)	42 (D)	43 (D)
44 (B)	45 (D)	46 (C)	47 (C)	48 (B)	49 (D)
50 (C)	51 (A)	52 (D)	53 (B)	54 (C)	55 (B)
56 (B)	57 (C)	58 (A)	59 (B)	60 (C)	61 (C)
62 (A)	63 (C)	64 (B)	65 (D)	66 (C)	67 (A)
68 (C)	69 (B)	70 (A)			

PART 4

본책 p.45

71 (C)	72 (D)	73 (A)	74 (C)	75 (D)	76 (A)
77 (A)	78 (C)	79 (A)	80 (C)	81 (D)	82 (B)
83 (B)	84 (B)	85 (A)	86 (C)	87 (A)	88 (B)
89 (D)	90 (B)	91 (A)	92 (B)	93 (B)	94 (D)
95 (C)	96 (D)	97 (B)	98 (D)	99 (A)	100 (C)

PART 1

1 (A) The same caps are being given to the soldiers.
미W (B) Some men are paving the road.
(C) One of the men is buttoning up his uniform.
(D) Some men are saluting in a parade.

(A) 같은 모자들이 군인들에게 주어지고 있다.
(B) 어떤 남자들이 도로를 포장하고 있다.
(C) 남자 한 명이 제복의 단추를 잠그고 있다.
(D) 어떤 남자들이 행진을 하며 경례를 하고 있다.

사진 속에 군인으로 보이는 남자들이 행진을 하고 있으며, 그중 일부는 경례를 하고 있다. 오답에서도 도로, 군인, 제복 등 사진에서 볼 수 있는 어휘가 다양하게 등장하였으므로 관련 어휘는 모두 익혀 두자.

cap 모자 salute (거수) 경례를 하다 pave the road 도로를 포장하다 button up 단추로 꽉 잠그다 uniform 제복, 군복, 교복 in a parade 행군을 하며, 행진하며

2 (A) He is talking on the phone.
영M (B) His arms are resting on a desk.
(C) He is sitting on a sofa.
(D) He is taking off his jacket.

(A) 남자가 전화로 얘기를 하고 있다.
(B) 남자의 팔이 책상 위에 있다.
(C) 남자가 소파에 앉아 있다.
(D) 남자가 재킷을 벗고 있다.

남자가 테이블 위에 팔을 두고 노트북의 화면을 보고 있다. 전화나 소파는 보이지 않고 재킷은 입고 있는 상태이다.

rest ~에 받치다, 기대다 take off 벗다, 출발하다

3 (A) A car is being lifted at the side of the street.
미M (B) The road is shaded by some trees.
(C) Some leaves are scattered on the ground.
(D) Cars are parked side by side.

(A) 차가 길 한 쪽에서 들어 올려지고 있다.
(B) 나무로 인해 도로에 그늘이 졌다.
(C) 나뭇잎들은 바닥에 흩어져 있다.
(D) 자동차들이 나란히 주차되어 있다.

도로에 차 한 대가 달리는 중인지 멈춘 상태인지 알 수 없다. 도로가 나무로 인해 그늘져 있으므로 정답은 (B)이다. 사진 묘사에서는 그늘진 상황을 묘사하는 문제가 종종 등장한다.

lift 들어 올리다 shade 그늘지게 하다 scatter 흩어지다 side by side 나란히

4 (A) She is hanging up the phone.
미W (B) The scene is captured on her screen.
(C) She is hanging some pictures.
(D) A group of people are clapping their hands.

(A) 여자가 전화를 끊고 있다.
(B) 풍경이 여자의 화면에 포착되었다.
(C) 여자가 사진을 걸고 있다.
(D) 한 무리의 사람들이 손뼉을 치고 있다.

휴대폰으로 정면의 무언가를 찍고 있으며, 휴대폰의 화면에 그 모습이 보이는 사진이다. 사진에서 유추할 수 있는 여러 어휘들이 등장하는데 오답이라도 눈여겨보자.

hang up 전화를 끊다 scene 광경, 장면 capture 포착하다, 담다 hang 걸다 clap one's hands 손뼉을 치다

5 (A) Some folk disguises are on display.
영M (B) Some toys are being shown on a screen.
(C) A man is trying on a mask.
(D) Costumes are being stored in a closet.

(A) 전통적인 변장 도구들이 진열되어 있다.
(B) 장난감 몇 개가 화면에 나타나고 있다.
(C) 남자가 마스크를 써 보고 있다.
(D) 분장 도구가 벽장에 보관되는 중이다.

이 문제의 핵심은 바로 mask를 직접 언급하지 않는 선택지 중에서 정답을 찾는 것이다. mask라는 익숙한 단어가 등장한 (C)는 사람이 등장하여 오답이다. mask를 folk disguise로 달리 표현한 정답 (A)에 주목하자.

folk 민속의, 전통의 disguise 변장, 변장 도구 on display 진열 중인 try on 시험 삼아 해 보다 mask 가면 costume 분장, 의상 store 저장하다, 보관하다 closet 벽장

6 (A) A drawer has been stocked with supplies.
영W (B) Cabinets are positioned at the corner of the room.
(C) A room is filled with some equipment.
(D) Some jars are arranged on the counter.

(A) 서랍이 비품들로 채워져 있다.
(B) 캐비닛은 방의 모퉁이에 있다.
(C) 방은 장비로 가득하다.
(D) 항아리가 작업대에 배열되어 있다.

실험실로 보이는 방에 도구들이 보이고 있다. (D)가 오답인 이유는 사진에서 보이는 병들과 테이블을 각각 jar, counter라고 보기 어렵기 때문이다.

drawer 서랍　be stocked with ~로 가득 차다　supplies 비품　position 위치시키다　be filled with ~로 가득하다　jar 항아리, 단지　arrange 정리하다, 배열하다　counter 작업대

PART 2

7 Who is responsible for overseeing the construction project?
영M (A) It is a little behind schedule.
미W (B) Mr. Evans, I think.
(C) It was constructed last year.

누가 공사 프로젝트를 감독하는 책임자이죠?
(A) 일정보다 약간 뒤처져 있습니다.
(B) Evans 씨일 겁니다.
(C) 그것은 작년에 지어졌어요.

의문사 who 의문문으로 공사의 책임자를 물었으므로 이름으로 답해 준 (B)가 정답이다

be responsible for ~의 책임을 맡다　oversee 감독하다　behind schedule 일정보다 뒤처진

8 So, when would you like to meet?
미W (A) Yes, I would.
미M (B) About 12 hours.
(C) How about Friday?

그래서 언제 만나고 싶으세요?
(A) 네, 그렇습니다.
(B) 12시간 정도요.
(C) 금요일은 어떠세요?

의문사 when 질문으로 언제 만날지 물었으므로 금요일이라고 답한 (C)가 정답이다. (B)의 12 hours는 기간의 의미로 how long에 대한 답이다.

9 How many interns are we going to hire?
영M (A) One for each department.
미W (B) For international calls.
(C) Through the agency.

몇 명의 인턴을 고용할 건가요?
(A) 각 부서당 한 명이요.
(B) 국제 전화용입니다.
(C) 중개사를 통해서요.

질문의 핵심은 how many interns, 즉 인턴의 인원이다. 그러므로 부서당 한 명이라고 답한 (A)가 정답이다.

10 Can we pay the fare on the train?
미M (A) You are not late.
영W (B) Fairly small.
(C) Yes, we can.

기차에서 요금을 낼 수 있을까요?
(A) 당신은 늦지 않았어요.
(B) 꽤 작습니다.
(C) 네, 가능해요.

Yes/No 여부를 묻는 질문으로 기차에서 요금을 내도 되는지에 대해 그렇다고 답한 (C)가 정답이 된다. (B)는 fare와 발음이 비슷한 fairly를 이용한 유사 발음 함정이다.

fare (버스, 기차 등의) 요금　fairly 꽤

11 Where did you put the latest fashion magazines?
미W (A) No, you keep it.
영M (B) They are on my desk.
(C) Oh, I'm very interested in fashion.

가장 최신 패션 잡지들은 어디에 두었나요?
(A) 아니요, 당신 가지세요.
(B) 내 책상 위에 있어요.
(C) 오, 저는 패션에 매우 관심이 많아요.

의문사 where 질문으로 잡지를 어디에 두었는지 물었으므로 정답은 (B)가 된다.

latest 최신의

12 Could you please make 10 copies of this letter?
영W (A) Yes, they are.
미M (B) Sure, no problem.
(C) With sugar please.

이 편지를 10부 복사해 주시겠어요?
(A) 네, 그것들은 그렇습니다.
(B) 그럼요, 문제없습니다.
(C) 설탕과 함께요.

복사를 해 달라는 요청 의문문이므로 흔쾌히 수락하는 (B)가 정답이다. 요청에 수락하는 표현으로 sure, no problem 등이 대표적이다.

make a copy 복사를 하다

13 What is the name of the dental clinic down the street?
영M (A) I believe it is called Meza Dental Clinic.
영W (B) Dr. Hopkins and his assistant.
(C) It is quite fast.

길 아래에 있는 치과의 이름이 뭐죠?
(A) Meza Dental Clinic일 거예요.
(B) Hopkins 박사님과 비서요.
(C) 꽤 빠르네요.

치과의 이름을 묻는 질문으로 (A)가 정답이다. (B)는 Dr. Hopkins처럼 clinic (병원)을 들었을 때 연상되는 단어를 이용한 연상어 함정이다.

dental clinic 치과　it is called ~라고 불리다

14 Why has the shipment been delayed?
미W (A) It came from the manager.
미M (B) I hope not.
(C) The package was lost in transit.

배송은 왜 지연이 되었나요?
(A) 이건 매니저로부터 왔어요.
(B) 그렇지 않기를 바랍니다.
(C) 운송 중에 소포를 분실했습니다.

질문의 핵심이 배송 지연의 이유이므로 운송 중에 소포를 분실했기 때문이라고 답한 (C)가 정답이다. (A)는 의문사 where에 대한 답이다.

shipment 배송 be lost 분실되다 in transit 수송 중에, 운송 중에

15 Will you take the train or drive to Baltimore?
영M (A) I'll go by train.
미W (B) With Cynthia.
(C) We just passed the exit ramp.

볼티모어에 기차 타고 가나요 아님 운전하나요?
(A) 기차로 갈 것입니다.
(B) Cynthia와 함께요.
(C) 출구를 방금 지나쳤어요.

선택 사항은 교통수단으로 기차와 운전이었으므로 기차를 타고 갈 것이라고 답한 (A)가 정답이다.

pass 지나치다 exit ramp (고속 도로 등의) 출구

16 These muffins are delicious, aren't they?
영W (A) At the bakery next door.
영M (B) Yes, I like the blueberry ones.
(C) That's very kind of you.

이 머핀은 맛있네요, 그렇지 않나요?
(A) 옆집 베이커리에서요.
(B) 네, 저는 블루베리 머핀을 좋아해요.
(C) 정말 친절하시네요.

Yes/No 여부를 묻는 질문으로 머핀이 맛있는지 묻고 있다. 긍정으로 답하고 그중에서도 블루베리 머핀이 좋다고 답한 (B)가 정답이다.

17 Will Mr. Macy be arriving tomorrow afternoon?
미M (A) He missed my presentation.
미W (B) Probably in Mexico.
(C) Yes, he'll be here by 4.

Macy 씨가 내일 오후에 도착하나요?
(A) 그는 제 발표에 오지 않았어요.
(B) 아마도 멕시코요.
(C) 네, 그는 4시까지 여기 올 겁니다.

내일 오후 도착이 맞는지 Yes/No 여부를 묻고 있으므로 긍정으로 답한 후 좀 더 세부적으로 4시까지 도착한다고 답한 (C)가 정답이다.

18 How many days off do we get this year?
영W (A) Six employees showed up at the meeting.
영M (B) Okay, I'll do it.
(C) Same as last year, I believe.

올해 휴가를 며칠 받게 되죠?
(A) 6명의 직원이 미팅에 왔어요.
(B) 좋아요, 그렇게 할게요.
(C) 작년하고 같을 거예요.

올해 휴가가 며칠인지 물었고 작년과 동일하다고 답한 (C)가 정답이다. (A)는 직원의 숫자에 대해 말했으므로 오답이다.

day off 휴가 show up 등장하다, 나타나다, 참석하다

19 Do you want me to drive you to the airport?
미W (A) Thanks, but I already have a ride.
영M (B) It departs in two hours.
(C) I took the train.

공항까지 태워다 드릴까요?
(A) 고맙지만 전 이미 탈 게 있어요.
(B) 그것은 두 시간 후에 떠납니다.
(C) 저는 기차를 탔어요.

상대방에게 태워다 줄 것을 제안한 것에 대해 사양한 (A)가 정답이 된다.

a ride 탈 것, 차량 depart 떠나다

20 When did you learn about Sonia's transfer?
미M (A) Mr. Han is the supervisor.
영W (B) Just now.
(C) I go to school every day.

Sonia의 전근에 대해 언제 알았죠?
(A) Han 씨가 감독관이에요.
(B) 지금 막이요.
(C) 저는 매일 학교에 갑니다.

질문의 핵심은 when으로 just now (지금 막)라고 답한 (B)가 정답이다.

transfer 전근 supervisor 감독, 상사

21 Could you work the booth at the trade fair
영W tomorrow?
미W (A) Yes, he's fairly good with machines.
(B) I'm afraid I won't be able to.
(C) It was working yesterday.

내일 무역 박람회 부스에서 일해 줄 수 있나요?
(A) 네, 그는 기계를 꽤 잘 다뤄요.
(B) 갈 수가 없을 것 같아요.
(C) 그건 어제 작동됐어요.

박람회 부스에서 일해 줄 수 있는지 물어보고 있다. (B)는 박람회에 갈 수 없다는 의미로 요청에 대해 거절하는 답이 되므로 정답이다.

booth 부스 trade fair 무역 박람회 be good with ~을 잘 다루다

22 Who did you just speak to?
미M (A) It was Alice, my coworker.
영W (B) I'd like that.
(C) No, you didn't.

누구와 이야기를 나눴나요?
(A) 제 동료 Alice요.
(B) 그거 좋습니다.
(C) 아니요, 당신은 안 했어요.

질문의 핵심은 who이므로 이름으로 답해 준 (A)가 정답이다.

23 Would you like me to water your plants while you
미W are gone?
미M (A) Yes, show me your business plan.
(B) I'd appreciate that.
(C) Okay, I'll go there.

당신이 없는 동안에 제가 화분에 물을 줄까요?
(A) 네, 당신의 사업 계획서를 보여 주세요.
(B) 그럼 감사하죠.
(C) 좋습니다. 그곳에 갈게요.

would you like me to(~해 드릴까요)라는 제안의 표현이 사용되었다. 화분에 물을 줄지 물었고 그럼 고맙겠다고 답한 (B)가 정답이다. (A)는 질문과 관계없는 business plan에 대한 얘기를 하고 있다.

water 물을 주다 plant 화분 appreciate ~에 감사하다

24 It is supposed to be very cold this weekend.
영W (A) The old one is broken.
영M (B) This week or next week.
(C) Maybe we should stay home.

이번 주말은 매우 추울 거예요.
(A) 낡은 것은 고장 났어요.
(B) 이번 주 혹은 다음 주요.
(C) 우리는 집에 있는 게 좋겠어요.

평서문의 내용은 날씨에 대한 것으로 추울 것이라고 했으므로 집에 머무는 게 낫겠다고 답한 (C)가 가장 자연스럽다.

25 Why did you decide to apply for this position?
영M (A) They've already made a decision.
미W (B) I have work experience in this field.
(C) It was a challenging job.

왜 이 직업에 지원하기로 결정했나요?
(A) 그들은 이미 결정을 내렸습니다.
(B) 저는 이 분야에 근무 경력이 있습니다.
(C) 그것은 힘든 직업이었어요.

일자리 지원 이유가 질문의 핵심이므로 관련 경력이 있기 때문이라고 답한 (B)가 가장 좋은 답이다.

apply for ~에 지원하다 make a decision 결정을 내리다 work experience 근무 경력 field 분야 challenging 어려운

26 Friday's jazz concert hasn't sold out yet, has it?
영W (A) Only two seats are left at the back.
영M (B) I really enjoyed the performance.
(C) No, I prefer Thursdays.

금요일 재즈 콘서트는 매진되지 않았죠, 그렇죠?
(A) 뒤에 2개 좌석만 남아 있어요.
(B) 전 공연을 정말 즐겁게 봤어요.
(C) 아니요, 전 목요일이 더 좋아요.

질문의 핵심은 콘서트 매진 여부이다. 이에 대해 뒷좌석이 2개 남았다고 답한 (A)가 정답이다. (B)는 시제 오류이다.

sold out 매진되다 at the back 뒤편에

27 Are accommodations available for visiting
미M professors?
미W (A) She works at Carleton University.
(B) Yes, at the hotel next door.
(C) No, other basic commodities.

초청 교수들을 위한 숙박 시설이 준비되어 있습니까?
(A) 그녀는 Carleton 대학교에서 일합니다.
(B) 네, 옆에 호텔에요.
(C) 아니요, 다른 기본 물건들이요.

숙박 시설이 준비되었는지 여부를 Yes/No로 묻고 있으므로 그렇다고 답한 (B)가 정답이다. (A)는 professor를 들었을 때 연상되는 university를 이용한 함정이다.

visiting professor 초청 교수 basic commodities 기본 물건, 기본 품목

28 The medical research center is accessible by public
영W transportation.
미W (A) About thirteen researchers work there.
(B) An efficient security system.
(C) That must be very convenient.

그 의학 연구 센터는 대중교통으로 갈 수 있어요.
(A) 약 13명의 연구원들이 거기에서 일해요.
(B) 효율적인 보안 시스템이요.
(C) 그거 아주 편리하겠네요.

평서문 내용의 핵심은 연구 센터가 대중교통을 이용해서 갈 수 있다는 것이므로 편리하겠다고 답한 (C)가 가장 자연스럽다. 다른 선택지들은 문맥상 동떨어져 있다.

be accessible by ~을 통해 접근할 수 있다 convenient 편리한

29 Haven't you had your black-and-white copier fixed
영M yet?
미W (A) I've made 20 copies.
(B) No, she faxed us this letter.
(C) You mean my color copier?

흑백 복사기를 다 고치지 않았나요?
(A) 저는 20부 복사했어요.
(B) 아니요, 그녀가 이 편지를 팩스로 보냈어요.
(C) 제 컬러 복사기 말씀하시는 건가요?

상대방의 흑백 복사기를 다 고쳤는지 묻고 있다. 이에 대해 컬러 복사기를 말하는 것이냐고 정정해 준 (C)가 정답이 된다. (A)는 유사 발음 함정이고 (B) 역시 fix와 유사 발음인 fax를 이용한 함정이다.

30 Do you know how many invitations we need to send
영W out?
영M (A) Definitely more than 50.
(B) We didn't invite Ms. Wilson.
(C) An annual event.

우리가 몇 장의 초대장을 발송해야 하는지 아세요?
(A) 50개 이상인 건 확실해요.
(B) 우리는 Wilson 씨를 초대하지 않았어요.
(C) 연례 행사요.

질문의 핵심은 how many invitations이다. 몇 부를 보낼지 물었으므로 50부 이상이라고 답한 (A)가 정답이 된다.

invitation 초대장 send out 발송하다

31 Our department's sales projections were too
미M optimistic for this month.
미W (A) I had too much work to do.
(B) I know. Business was not as good as we expected.
(C) The projector is not working properly.

이번 달 우리 부서의 판매 예상치가 지나치게 낙관적이었어요.
(A) 전 할 일이 너무 많았어요.
(B) 맞아요. 판매가 예상만큼 좋지가 않았죠.
(C) 그 프로젝터는 제대로 작동이 안 되네요.

평서문의 내용은 판매 예상치가 너무 긍정적이었다는 것으로 즉, 예상보다 판매가 저조했다는 의미가 된다. 그러므로 판매가 예상만큼 좋지 않았다고 답한 (B)가 정답이다.

sales projections 판매 예상 수치 optimistic 긍정적인 projector 프로젝터 properly 제대로

PART 3

Questions 32-34 refer to the following conversation. 영M 영W

M Debbie, have you seen the movie showing at the Golden Moon Cinema? It's a comedy starring Abigail Heyns.
W No I haven't, but I read some reviews about it online. Most of the reviews said that it was really funny.
M Yeah, it's really popular right now. I actually tried to get tickets but they were all sold out. I was so disappointed.
W I heard the cinema has added more showings of the film. Why don't you check their website to see if you can buy tickets now?

남 Debbie, Golden Moon Cinema에서 상영 중인 영화를 보셨나요? Abigail Heyns가 주연인 코미디 영화인데요.
여 아니요, 못 봤어요. 그렇지만 온라인에서 후기는 읽어 봤어요. 대부분의 후기들이 정말 재미있다고 하더군요.
남 네, 요즘 진짜 인기가 많아요. 실은 저도 표를 구하려고 했었는데 다 매진이더군요. 정말 실망했었어요.
여 영화관에서 그 영화의 상영을 늘렸다고 들었어요. 웹 사이트에서 지금 티켓을 살 수 있는지 다시 확인해 보지 그러세요?

starring 주연인 sold out 매진되다 showing 상영

32 What are the speakers mainly discussing?
(A) A comic book
(B) A musical performance
(C) A comedy film
(D) A famous actor

화자들은 주로 무엇에 대해 이야기하는가?
(A) 만화책
(B) 음악 공연
(C) 코미디 영화
(D) 유명한 배우

대화의 주제는 도입부에서 찾자. 남자가 여자에게 영화를 봤는지 물어보면서 It's a comedy starring Abigail Heyns라고 했으므로 영화에 대한 대화임을 알 수 있다.

33 Why was the man disappointed?
(A) Tickets were unavailable.
(B) The cinema was closed.
(C) Performers have changed.
(D) A colleague was busy.

남자는 왜 실망했는가?
(A) 표를 살 수가 없었다.
(B) 영화관이 닫혔다.
(C) 공연자들이 바뀌었다.
(D) 동료가 바빴다.

남자 대사에서 실망했다는 내용이 나왔을 때 I actually tried to get tickets but they were all sold out(티켓을 사려고 했지만 매진이었다)이라고 했으므로 정답은 (A)가 된다.

34 What does the woman suggest the man do?
(A) Watch another movie
(B) Go to the cinema early
(C) Speak to a ticket agent
(D) Try getting tickets again

여자는 남자에게 무엇을 할 것을 권하는가?
(A) 다른 영화 보기
(B) 영화관에 일찍 가기
(C) 표 판매원에게 말하기
(D) 표를 다시 사보기

여자 대사에서 정답을 찾는다. 남자가 표가 매진이라고 했을 때 극장에서 추가 상영을 한다고 말하며 Why don't you check their website to see if you can buy tickets now?(지금 웹 사이트에서 표를 구할 수 있는지 다시 확인해 보라)라고 했으므로 정답은 (D)이다.

Questions 35-37 refer to the following conversation. 미W 미M

W Is the copy machine still out of order?
M Yes. I asked the maintenance department this morning to fix it and they promised to have it working by tomorrow morning.
W Tomorrow morning? But I have to make copies for my presentation at 3. Is there any other place where I can make copies?
M Hmm... I think there is a print shop across the street. Why don't you go there and try?

여 복사기는 아직 고장인가요?
남 네, 아침에 유지보수 부서에 고쳐 달라고 요청을 했고 내일 아침까지는 작동시켜 주겠다고 약속을 했어요.
여 내일 아침이요? 그렇지만 저는 3시에 있을 발표 때문에 복사를 해야 하거든요. 제가 복사를 할 수 있는 다른 장소가 있을까요?
남 흠… 길 건너편에 인쇄소가 있는 것 같아요. 그곳에 가서 해 보시면 어떨까요?

35 What is the woman's problem?
(A) She is unable to work overtime.
(B) She cannot make copies.
(C) She is not prepared for an interview.
(D) She has to go on a business trip.

여자의 문제는 무엇인가?
(A) 초과 근무를 할 수 없다.
(B) 복사를 할 수 없다.
(C) 면접을 볼 준비가 안 되었다.
(D) 출장을 가야 한다.

여자가 복사기가 여전히 고장인지 물으면서 발표에 쓸 복사를 해야 한다고 했으므로 정답은 (B)이다.

36 What is the woman supposed to do at 3 o'clock?
(A) Go shopping
(B) Visit the headquarters
(C) Meet with a client
(D) Give a presentation

여자는 3시에 무엇을 하기로 되어 있는가?
(A) 쇼핑을 간다.
(B) 본사를 방문한다.

(C) 고객을 만난다.
(D) **발표를 한다.**

질문의 키워드인 3시를 놓치지 말자. 여자는 복사를 해야 한다고 말하며 3시에 발표가 있다고 했으므로 정답은 (D)가 된다.

37 What will the woman probably do next?
(A) Go to a print shop
(B) Reschedule a meeting
(C) Request some help
(D) Contact another department

여자는 다음에 무엇을 할 것 같은가?
(A) **인쇄소에 간다.**
(B) 회의의 일정을 바꾼다.
(C) 도움을 요청한다.
(D) 다른 부서에 연락한다.

향후 행동에 대한 단서는 대화의 후반부에서 확인할 수 있다. 남자가 there is a print shop across the street(길 건너편에 인쇄소가 있다)라고 하며 그곳에 가서 복사를 해 보는 게 어떠냐고 했고 여자는 인쇄소에 갈 것이다. 그러므로 정답은 (A)이다.

Questions 38-40 refer to the following conversation. (영M) (미W)

M Good morning. This is my first time at your bank, and I'd like to open a savings account. Can you help me?
W Certainly. If you are not currently a CIT Bank customer, we'll need to see your photo identification. Did you bring your passport or driver's license with you?
M Yes, here's my passport.
W Thank you. Now please fill out this application form while I make a copy of your passport. I'll be right back.

남 좋은 아침이에요. 전 이 은행은 처음인데 저축 계좌를 만들고 싶습니다. 도와주시겠어요?
여 그럼요. 현재 CIT 은행 고객이 아니시라면, 사진이 있는 신분증을 보여 주셔야 합니다. 여권이나 운전 면허증을 가져 오셨나요?
남 네, 제 여권이 여기 있어요.
여 감사합니다. 이제 제가 여권을 복사하는 동안에 이 신청 양식을 채워주시면 됩니다. 곧 돌아오겠습니다.

savings account 저축 계좌 photo identification 사진이 부착된 신분증
application form 신청 양식 make a copy of ~의 사본을 만들다

38 Where most likely are the speakers?
(A) At a post office
(B) At a coffee shop
(C) At a bank
(D) At a grocery store

화자들은 어디에 있을 것 같은가?
(A) 우체국
(B) 커피숍
(C) **은행**
(D) 식료품점

대화 장소를 유추하는 질문으로 남자가 open a savings account(저축 계좌를 만들고 싶다)고 했을 때 정답을 (C)로 선택한다.

39 What document does the man present?
(A) A passport
(B) A driver's license
(C) An application form
(D) A bank statement

남자는 어떤 문서를 제시하는가?
(A) **여권**
(B) 운전 면허증
(C) 신청 양식
(D) 은행 내역서

여권이나 운전 면허증을 제시해 달라고 요청을 받았을 때 여권이 여기 있다(here's my passport)고 했으므로 정답은 (A)이다.

40 What will the man probably do next?
(A) Make copies
(B) Take a photograph
(C) Complete a form
(D) Go to the lobby

남자는 다음에 무엇을 할 것 같은가?
(A) 사본 만들기
(B) 사진 찍기
(C) **양식 작성하기**
(D) 로비에 가기

대화의 후반부에는 남자와 여자의 향후 행동이 둘 다 언급되므로 정확하게 남자가 할 일을 정답으로 연결하자. 여자가 복사하는 동안 신청 양식을 채워 달라고 했으므로 남자는 양식을 작성할 것이다. 정답은 (C)이다.

Questions 41-43 refer to the following conversation. (미M) (영W)

M Hi Missy. It's Pablo. My train has been delayed because of railroad maintenance. So I won't be able to make it to the meeting this afternoon. Can we reschedule it for later this week?
W Oh, I'm sorry to hear that, but sure, we can meet another day. When do you expect to be back at the office?
M I'm not exactly sure when the work will be completed but I'm hoping to get on the train sometime tomorrow. So I'd say I should be back at the office by Wednesday morning.
W Okay. I'm available on Wednesday morning or any time on Thursday. I'm taking the day off on Friday though.

남 안녕하세요 Missy. Pablo입니다. 제 기차가 철도 보수 때문에 지연이 되었어요. 그래서 오늘 오후 미팅에 참석하지 못할 것 같습니다. 이번 주 후반으로 일정을 조절할 수 있을까요?
여 오, 안타깝네요. 그렇지만 알겠습니다. 다른 날에 만나죠. 언제쯤 사무실로 돌아오실 것 같나요?
남 공사가 정확하게 언제 끝날지 모르겠지만 내일은 기차에 탈 수 있기를 바라고 있어요. 그래서 수요일 오전까지는 사무실로 돌아갈 수 있을 것 같아요.
여 좋아요. 전 수요일 오전이나 목요일 아무 때나 시간이 됩니다. 그렇지만 금요일에는 휴무에요.

railroad maintenance 철도 보수 reschedule 일정을 바꾸다 take a day off 하루를 쉬다

41 What is the cause of the delay?
(A) Maintenance work
(B) Insufficient funds
(C) A labor shortage
(D) Weather conditions

지연의 원인은 무엇인가?
(A) 보수 공사
(B) 부족한 기금
(C) 인력 부족
(D) 기상 조건

세부 정보를 찾는 질문으로 지연에 대한 언급과 함께 원인이 언급될 것이다. My train has been delayed because of railroad maintenance(철로의 보수 공사 때문에 지연됐다)라고 했으므로 정답은 (A)가 된다.

42 Why is the man calling?
(A) To reserve a train ticket
(B) To ask for a timetable
(C) To change seats
(D) To postpone a meeting

남자는 왜 전화를 하는가?
(A) 기차표를 예약하려고
(B) 시간표를 요청하려고
(C) 좌석을 바꾸려고
(D) 회의를 연기하려고

남자가 기차 지연을 언급하면서 미팅의 일정을 다른 날로 미뤘으면 좋겠다고 했으므로 정답은 (D)가 된다.

43 When does the woman say she will be unavailable?
(A) On Tuesday
(B) On Wednesday
(C) On Thursday
(D) On Friday

여자는 언제 그녀가 시간이 없다고 말하는가?
(A) 화요일
(B) 수요일
(C) 목요일
(D) 금요일

여자가 수요일과 목요일은 시간이 된다고 했고 I'm taking the day off on Friday though에서 금요일에는 휴가라고 했으므로 정답은 (D)이다.

Questions 44-46 refer to the following conversation. (영M) (영W)

M Ms. Sanders, I was wondering if I can take a day off next week. I still have some vacation days left.
W Well, the thing is, a second inspection is scheduled for Wednesday next week and I'd like you to be here that day. As you know, it is very important for us to pass the inspection this time.
M Oh, of course, Ms. Sanders. I forgot about the safety inspection. I'm sorry. I'll take my vacation afterwards.

남 Sanders 씨, 제가 다음 주에 휴가를 쓸 수 있는지 궁금해서요. 휴가 일수가 아직 남아 있거든요.
여 음, 문제는, 두 번째 검사가 다음 주 수요일로 일정이 잡혀 있고 당신이 그날 꼭 있었으면 해요. 아시다시피, 이번에는 검사를 통과하는 것이 무척 중요하거든요.
남 아, 당연하죠, Sanders 씨. 제가 안전 검사에 대해서 깜빡 잊었네요. 죄송합니다. 휴가는 이후에 가도록 하겠습니다.

inspection 검사 afterwards 이후에

44 What does the man want to do?
(A) Select a vacation destination
(B) Take some time off work
(C) Submit an expense report
(D) Leave for the day

남자는 무엇을 하고 싶어 하는가?
(A) 휴가지 정하기
(B) 일 쉬기
(C) 비용 보고서 제출하기
(D) 퇴근하기

남자가 도입부에 I was wondering if I can take a day off next week(다음 주에 하루를 쉬어도 되는지)라고 했으므로 정답은 (B)가 된다.

45 What is scheduled for next Wednesday?
(A) A company picnic
(B) A business trip
(C) A department meeting
(D) A safety inspection

다음 주 수요일에 어떤 일정이 잡혀 있는가?
(A) 회사 피크닉
(B) 출장
(C) 부서 회의
(D) 안전 검사

질문의 키워드는 next Wednesday(다음 주 수요일)이다. 여자가 다음 주 수요일에 두 번째 검사가 잡혀 있다고 했으므로 정답은 (D)가 된다.

46 What does the man agree to do?
(A) Cancel a flight ticket
(B) Contact an inspector
(C) Postpone his vacation
(D) Fill in for a coworker

남자가 무엇을 하는 것에 동의하는가?
(A) 비행 표를 취소하는 것
(B) 검사관에게 연락하는 것
(C) 자신의 휴가를 연기하는 것
(D) 동료를 대신하는 것

남자가 I'll take my vacation afterwards라고 말하며 검사를 마치고 나서 휴가를 가겠다고 했으므로 정답은 (C)가 된다.

Questions 47-49 refer to the following conversation. 미W 미M

W Have you finished the final assignment for our communication skills course?

M No, I've been too busy. I haven't even read the course material yet. I don't think I can finish it by the deadline. How's yours coming along?

W Well, I'm having the same problem. We are supposed to submit it by the end of the week, right?

M Yes. Maybe we should ask the instructor for an extension. I'll write him an e-mail to see if he will let us hand it in by Monday.

여 커뮤니케이션 기술 수업의 마지막 과제를 다 끝내셨나요?

남 아니오, 너무 바빴어요. 아직 수업 자료도 읽어보지 못했어요. 마감까지 끝낼 수 없을 것 같아요. 당신 것은 어떻게 되고 있어요?

여 음, 저도 같은 문제를 갖고 있어요. 우리가 과제를 이번 주 말까지 제출하기로 되어 있는 거 맞죠?

남 네. 강사에게 마감 연장을 부탁해 보는 게 좋을 것 같아요. 제가 그에게 이메일을 써서 우리가 월요일까지 제출해도 되는지 물어볼게요.

course material 수업 자료 come along 진행 되다 hand in 제출하다

47 What are the speakers discussing?
(A) Communicating by e-mail
(B) Addressing employee concerns
(C) Completing a course assignment
(D) Registering for a professional seminar

화자들은 무엇을 토론하고 있는가?
(A) 이메일을 통한 의사소통
(B) 직원 걱정거리를 처리하는 것
(C) 수업 과제를 끝내는 것
(D) 전문 세미나를 신청하는 것

대화의 도입부에 Have you finished the final assignment에서 최종 과제를 다 끝냈는지 묻고 있으므로 정답은 (C)로 선택한다.

48 What does the woman imply when she says, "Well, I'm having the same problem"?
(A) She wants the man to help her with a project.
(B) She won't be able to finish her assignment on time.
(C) She has been out of town.
(D) She will report to a new director.

여자가 "음, 저도 같은 문제를 갖고 있어요"라고 말한 의도는 무엇인가?
(A) 그녀는 남자가 프로젝트를 도와주길 원한다.
(B) 그녀는 제때 과제를 끝낼 수가 없을 것이다.
(C) 그녀는 다른 곳에 가 있다.
(D) 그녀는 새로운 부서장에게 보고할 것이다.

해당 표현의 앞뒤 문맥을 통해 정답을 찾자. 남자가 마감까지 과제를 끝낼 수 없다고 했을 때 여자가 "Well, I'm having the same problem"이라고 말한 것이므로 여자 역시 마감을 맞출 수 없다는 뜻이 된다. 정답은 (B)가 된다.

49 What will the man probably do next?
(A) Speak to a colleague
(B) Train some staff
(C) Confirm an appointment
(D) Request an extension

남자는 다음에 무엇을 할 것 같은가?
(A) 동료와 이야기하기
(B) 직원들 훈련시키기
(C) 약속 시간 확인하기
(D) 마감 연장 요청하기

남자가 대화의 후반부에 I'll write him an e-mail to see if he will let us hand it in by Monday(강사에게 이메일을 써서 월요일까지 제출해도 되는지 물어보겠다)라고 했으므로 정답은 (D)가 된다.

Questions 50-52 refer to the following conversation. 영M 미W

M Excuse me. Could you tell me where I can find a map of the museum? It is my first time here.

W Sure. There is an information desk by the main entrance and you can pick up a map there. Are you looking for something in particular?

M Yes, I'm trying to find the technology exhibit where I can see robots.

W Oh, that exhibit is being held on the third floor. But you should go to the information desk and check the museum directory to see exactly where it is. As you can see, the layout of the museum is complicated and it is very crowded today.

남 실례합니다. 어디서 박물관 지도를 찾을 수 있는지 알려 주시겠어요? 여기가 처음이라서요.

여 물론이지요. 입구 옆에 안내소가 있는데 거기서 지도를 가져가시면 됩니다. 특별히 찾고 계신 게 있나요?

남 네, 로봇들을 볼 수 있는 기술 전시회를 찾고 있습니다.

여 아, 그 전시회는 3층에서 열려요. 그렇지만 안내 데스크로 가서 정확하게 어디인지 박물관 안내판에서 확인을 하시는 게 좋아요. 보시다시피, 박물관의 배치도가 복잡하고 오늘 많이 붐비니까요.

main entrance 정문 in particular 특별하게 technology exhibit 기술 전시회 museum directory 박물관 배치도 complicated 복잡한

50 Where most likely are the speakers?
(A) At a public library
(B) At a school
(C) At a museum
(D) At a shopping mall

화자들은 어디에 있을 것 같은가?
(A) 공공 도서관
(B) 학교
(C) 박물관
(D) 쇼핑몰

장소를 유추하는 질문으로 대화의 도입부에 박물관의 지도를 찾는 내용을 듣고 정답은 (C)로 선택할 수 있다.

51 What is the man trying to locate?
(A) A robot exhibit
(B) A ticket office
(C) An exit
(D) An art show

남자는 무엇을 찾고 있는가?
(A) 로봇 전시회
(B) 매표소
(C) 출구
(D) 예술 전시

여자가 특별히 찾고 있는 게 있냐고 물었을 때 I'm trying to find the technology exhibit where I can see robots(로봇을 볼 수 있는 기술 전시회를 찾고 있다)라고 했으므로 정답은 (A)이다.

52 What does the woman suggest the man do?
(A) Purchase a special gift
(B) Use an elevator
(C) Take a guided tour
(D) Find out the location of an event

여자는 남자에게 무엇을 하라고 권하는가?
(A) 특별한 선물 사기
(B) 엘리베이터 이용하기
(C) 가이드 투어 하기
(D) 행사의 위치 알아보기

여자 대사에 정답이 있는 질문이다. 여자가 남자에게 안내 데스크로 가서 check the museum directory to see exactly where it is(정확히 전시회가 어디인지 배치도를 확인하라)라고 했으므로 정답은 (D)가 된다.

Questions 53-55 refer to the following conversation. (영W) (미M)

W Hi, I know I'm a little late but can I still get on the plane? It took me a long time to get here by bus because of a traffic jam on the way.

M I'm afraid no one can board the plane anymore. The gate is already closed.

W Oh no. I really have to get on this flight. Otherwise, I'll miss my connecting flight in Dallas too.

M I'm sorry to hear that. But there is nothing I can do. Our airline has another flight that leaves for Dallas at 6 p.m. Do you want me to see if I can get you a seat on that flight?

여 안녕하세요. 제가 좀 늦었는데 아직 비행기에 탈 수 있나요? 오는 길에 교통 체증 때문에 버스로 여기까지 오는 데 너무 오래 걸렸어요.

남 죄송하지만 더 이상 아무도 탑승할 수가 없습니다. 게이트가 이미 닫혔거든요.

여 오, 안 돼요. 전 정말 이 비행기에 타야만 합니다. 댈러스에서 연결 항공편도 놓치게 될 거라서요.

남 안타깝습니다. 그러나 제가 할 수 있는 일이 없네요. 우리 항공사에 댈러스로 가는 오후 6시 비행기가 또 있어요. 그 항공편에 자리가 있는지 확인을 해 볼까요?

connecting flight 연결 항공편

53 Where most likely are the speakers?
(A) At a bus stop
(B) In an airport
(C) In a car
(D) At a taxi stand

화자들은 어디에 있는 것 같은가?
(A) 버스 정류소
(B) 공항
(C) 차 안
(D) 택시 승차장

여자가 교통 체증 때문에 늦었다고 말하면서 아직 비행기에 탈 수 있는지를 물었으므로 대화 장소는 공항임을 알 수 있다. 정답은 (B)이다.

54 What is the woman concerned about?
(A) Losing some luggage
(B) Locating a terminal
(C) Missing a connecting flight
(D) Changing seats

여자는 무엇에 대해 염려하는가?
(A) 수화물을 잃는 것
(B) 터미널을 찾는 것
(C) 연결 항공편을 놓치는 것
(D) 좌석을 바꾸는 것

여자가 비행기를 놓치면 안 된다고 하면서 댈러스에서 연결 항공편까지 놓치게 된다고 했으므로 정답은 (C)가 된다.

55 What does the man mean when he says, "But there is nothing I can do"?
(A) The flight for Dallas is fully booked.
(B) He cannot let the woman get on the flight.
(C) The woman has to leave the airport.
(D) He cannot help the woman find her gate.

남자가 "그러나 제가 할 수 있는 일이 없네요"라고 말한 의미는 무엇인가?
(A) 댈러스행 비행기는 완전히 예약되었다.
(B) 그는 여자를 비행기에 태울 수가 없다.
(C) 여자는 공항을 떠나야만 한다.
(D) 그는 여자가 게이트를 찾는 것을 도울 수 없다.

보통 도울 수가 없을 때 하는 표현이다. 여자가 비행기에 꼭 타야 한다고 하며 연결 항공편까지 놓칠 수 있다고 했을 때, "그러나 제가 할 수 있는 일이 없네요"라고 답한 것이므로 여전히 여자를 비행기에 태울 수 없다는 뜻이 된다.

Questions 56-58 refer to the following conversation. (영M) (영W)

M Natalie, welcome to Alton Chemical Company. I'm happy to have you on board as a new assistant technician in our chemical lab. This morning you're going to have orientation with human resources. And then you will start training with your mentor, Mark Lathem. Do you have any questions?

W Yes, could you tell me more about what kind of laboratory equipment I'll be using?

M Well, you'll get to use a variety of machines. We recently purchased some new up-to-date equipment that you might not be used to. But don't worry. Mark will walk you through everything step-by-step.

W Okay. Thank you very much for your time, Mr. Bergmann.

남 Natalie, Alton Chemical 사에 온 걸 환영합니다. 당신이 우리 화학 실험실 보조 기사로 들어오게 되어서 정말 기쁩니다. 오늘 아침에 인사부와 오리엔테이션을 할 거예요. 그러고 나서 당신의 멘토인 Mark Lathem과 교육을 시작할 겁니다. 질문이 있으신가요?

여 네, 제가 어떤 종류의 실험실 장비를 사용할지에 대해서 좀 더 얘기해 주시겠습니까?

남 음, 다양한 기계들을 사용하게 될 겁니다. 최근에 최신 장비를 구매했는데 그것은 당신이 사용하기에 익숙하지 않을 수도 있어요. 그렇지만 걱정 마세요. Mark가 전부 하나씩 설명해 줄 것입니다.

여 알겠습니다. 시간을 내 주셔서 감사합니다, Bergmann 씨.

have on board 신입으로 받게 되다 assistant technician 보조 기사 up-to-date 최신의 walk through 자세히 설명하다, 익히도록 단계별로 보여 주다

56 Who most likely is the woman?
(A) A human resources manager
(B) A laboratory technician
(C) A factory worker
(D) A sales representative

여자는 누구일 것 같은가?
(A) 인사부 매니저
(B) 실험실 기술자
(C) 공장 직원
(D) 영업 사원

여자의 직업을 유추하는 질문으로 남자가 입사를 환영하면서 as a new assistant technician (새로운 보조 기사로서)일하게 되었다고 했으므로 여자는 (B) 실험실 기술자이다.

57 What does the woman want to know about?
(A) The position that she will be working in
(B) The type of clients that she will be working with
(C) The kind of equipment that she will be using
(D) The instructions that she will follow

여자는 무엇에 대해 알고 싶어 하는가?
(A) 그녀가 일하게 될 직위
(B) 그녀가 일할 고객의 유형
(C) 그녀가 사용할 장비의 종류
(D) 그녀가 따라야 할 지시사항

여자 대사에서 남자에게 질문한 부분을 찾아 듣자. could you tell me more about what kind of laboratory equipment I'll be using?(어떤 종류의 장비를 이용하게 될지 더 알려 달라)이라고 했으므로 정답은 (C)가 된다.

58 What does the man say the company did recently?
(A) Purchased some laboratory equipment
(B) Trained some new technicians
(C) Revised a company policy
(D) Relocated to a different building

남자는 회사가 최근에 무엇을 했다고 말하는가?
(A) 실험실 장비를 구매했다.
(B) 새로운 기술자들을 훈련시켰다.
(C) 회사 정책을 수정했다.
(D) 다른 건물로 이전했다.

최근에 회사에서 한 일은 We recently purchased some new up-to-date equipment, 즉 최신 장비를 구매한 것이므로 정답은 (A)이다.

Questions 59-61 refer to the following conversation. (미M) (미W)

M Hi Diana, I just heard about your promotion. Congratulations! I think you're going to make a great corporate trainer, although we'll miss you a lot here in health insurance. Is it true that you've already set up your first seminar series on sales strategies?

W Oh thanks Larry. That's right. You know I have been an insurance agent for over 15 years. Now I have quite a few effective sales methods to share, such as how to build trust, and how to use online social networks for free advertising, etc. I'm pretty excited to start teaching.

M Great. I'm so looking forward to your first training series. When is it scheduled to begin?

W In two weeks, on August 3rd. I hope I see you there.

남 안녕하세요 Diana, 당신의 승진 소식을 방금 들었어요. 축하합니다! 여기 건강 보험부서에서는 당신을 매우 그리워하겠지만, 당신이 훌륭한 기업체 교육 담당자가 될 거라고 생각해요. 이미 판매 전략에 대한 첫 세미나 시리즈를 준비하셨다는 게 사실인가요?

여 감사해요 Larry. 네 맞아요. 아시다시피 제가 15년 넘게 보험 대리인으로 일했잖아요. 이제 사람들에게 알려줄 효과적인 영업 방법이 좀 있어요. 예를 들어 어떻게 신뢰를 쌓을 수 있는지, 온라인 커뮤니티를 통해 무료로 광고 효과를 누릴 수 있는지 등이요. 가르치는 걸 시작하게 되어 신 나요.

남 잘됐네요. 당신의 첫 교육 시리즈가 정말 기대됩니다. 그건 언제 시작되나요?

여 2주 후 8월 3일에요. 그때 볼 수 있으면 좋겠어요.

promotion 승진 corporate trainer 기업 교육 담당자 seminar series 세미나 (교육) 시리즈 sales strategy 영업 전략 insurance agent 보험 대리인 sales method 영업 방법 share 나누다

59 Why does the man congratulate the woman?
(A) She has won an employee award.
(B) She has been promoted.
(C) She has been transferred overseas.
(D) She has started teaching at a university.

남자는 왜 여자에게 축하하는가?
(A) 그녀는 직원 상을 받았다.
(B) 그녀는 승진되었다.
(C) 그녀는 해외로 전근되었다.
(D) 그녀는 대학에서 가르치기 시작했다.

세부 사항 질문으로 남자 대사에서 congratulate란 키워드가 언급되는 부분에서 정답을 찾자. I just heard about your promotion. Congratulations에서 여자의 승진 사실을 듣고 축하하고 있음을 알 수 있으므로 정답은 (B)가 된다.

60 Where most likely do the speakers work?
(A) At an auto dealership
(B) At an advertising agency
(C) At an insurance firm
(D) At a university

화자들은 어디에서 일할 것 같은가?
(A) 자동차 판매 대리점
(B) 광고 대행사
(C) 보험사
(D) 대학

화자들의 직장을 유추하는 질문으로 회사의 이름, 업무 내용 등에서 유추할 수 있다. 이 지문의 경우 동료에게 승진을 축하하면서, here in health insurance(여기 건강보험부에서)라고 했을 때 보험사라는 것을 알 수 있다. 정답은 (C)이다.

61 What is the topic of the seminar series?
(A) Public speaking
(B) Event planning
(C) Sales techniques
(D) Product development

세미나 시리즈의 주제는 무엇인가?
(A) 대중 연설
(B) 행사 기획
(C) 영업 기술
(D) 제품 개발

세부 사항 질문으로 키워드는 seminar series이고, 주제는 보통 전치사 on(~에 관한)과 함께 언급된다는 점을 활용해서 문제를 풀자. 남자의 첫 번째 대사 중, seminar series on sales strategies로부터 영업 전략에 관한 세미나임을 알 수 있고, 그 이후에도 영업 방법을 알려줄 것이라고 했으므로 정답은 (C)가 된다.

Questions 62-64 refer to the following conversation with three speakers. (영W) (미W) (영M)

W1 Yuki, I see on the calendar that we have a meeting with the director next week. Do you know what he wants to talk about with us?
W2 We're going to discuss the budget. Management has asked each department to think of ways to reduce operating expenses, so we are to come up with methods we can use here in the payroll department.
M I don't think there is much that we can do here in payroll though. I mean we are not the main source of high expenditures in the company, don't you think Yuki?
W2 You're right, Ron. But there are some easy things we can do around here, like turning off the printers and copiers at the end of the day to save electricity.
M Right. We can save paper by printing on both sides of each sheet as well.

여1 Yuki, 다음 주에 부장님과 미팅이 있는 것으로 달력에 표시가 되어 있는데요. 혹시 그가 무슨 얘기를 하고 싶어 하는지 아세요?
여2 우리는 예산에 관해 이야기할 겁니다. 경영진이 각 부서에 비용을 절감하는 방법을 생각해 보라고 했고, 그래서 우리는 여기 급여 정산 부서에서 활용할 수 있는 방법을 생각해 볼 예정이거든요.
남 여기 급여 정산 부서가 크게 할 수 있이 없는 것 같아요. 제 말은 우리가 회사 내에서 비용을 많이 사용하는 부서가 아니잖아요. 그렇게 생각 안 해요, Yuki?
여2 맞습니다, Ron. 그렇지만 우리가 주변에서 쉽게 할 수 있는 일들이 있어요. 전기를 아끼기 위해서 하루가 끝나면 프린터와 인쇄기를 끄는 것처럼요.
남 맞아요. 양면 복사를 해서 종이를 아낄 수도 있겠네요.

management 경영진 operating expenses 운영 비용 come up with 생각해내다 high expenditures 높은 비용 electricity 전기

62 What will be discussed at an upcoming meeting?
(A) How to reduce costs
(B) Which office equipment supplier to hire
(C) Where to hold a company event
(D) How to meet sales goals

다가오는 회의에서 무엇이 토론될 것인가?
(A) 비용을 삭감하는 방법
(B) 어느 사무용품 공급업체를 고용할지
(C) 회사 행사를 어디서 열지
(D) 영업 목표를 달성하는 방법

대화의 시작에서 미팅에서 어떤 내용을 이야기할지 물었고 경영진의 지시로 비용을 절감하는 방법에 대한 논의를 할 것이라고 했으므로 정답은 (A)이다.

63 Which department do the speakers work in?
(A) Accounting
(B) Sales
(C) Payroll
(D) Shipping

화자들은 어떤 부서에서 일할 것 같은가?
(A) 회계
(B) 판매
(C) 급여 정산
(D) 배송

두 번째 여자가 여기 급여 부서에서 비용 절감을 위해 우리가 할 수 있는 일이 있다고 했으므로 정답은 (C)가 된다.

64 What does Yuki suggest?
(A) Completing a budget report
(B) Turning off some office equipment
(C) Attending a board meeting
(D) Buying a new printer

Yuki는 무엇을 제안하는가?
(A) 예산 보고서 끝낼 것
(B) 사무기기 끌 것
(C) 이사 회의에 참석할 것
(D) 새로운 프린터 구입할 것

3인 대화로 이름을 잘 파악하는 것이 좋다. Yuki라는 이름은 대화의 도입부부터 계속 언급이 되었다. 비용 절감 방법으로 전기를 줄이기 위해 프린터와 복사기를 끄자고 제안했으므로 정답은 (B)가 된다.

Questions 65-67 refer to the following conversation and list.
영W 영M

W Frank, Ms. Brown called again to complain about the delay in shipping. She ordered a red dress ten days ago that she wanted to wear at a Christmas party, but it hasn't arrived yet.
M I know all deliveries tend to be behind schedule at this time of the year, but taking ten days is unusual. Have you checked with XDL Delivery Service?
W I just did. Apparently their computer system went down a few days ago and they lost some data including that of Ms. Brown.
M Uh, that's absurd! It is already December 20th and the order should've been delivered to Ms. Brown two days ago.
W I know. They were really apologetic. And they said they would offer their XDL Premier Service, which is overnight delivery, for the price of a standard delivery. We originally selected standard delivery to ship Ms. Brown's order but we don't have to pay the difference.
M Okay. Please call Ms. Brown now and let her know that she'll get her dress by tomorrow.

XDL DELIVERY SERVICE	
Delivery Type	Price
Standard Delivery	$50
Next Working Day	$70
XDL Premier	$120
Next Day Evening	$75

여 Frank, Brown 씨가 또 전화를 해서 배송 지연에 대해 불평을 했습니다. 그녀는 빨간 원피스를 크리스마스 파티에 입기 위해서 열흘 전에 주문을 했는데 아직도 도착하지 않았어요.
남 모든 배송이 매년 이맘때 지연이 되는 건 알지만 열흘이 걸리는 것은 이상하네요. XDL Delivery Service와는 확인을 해 봤나요?
여 네, 방금요. 보아하니 그들의 컴퓨터 시스템이 며칠 전에 다운이 됐는데 Brown 씨의 데이터를 포함해 기록이 일부 없어졌다고 합니다.
남 어, 그건 황당한 일이네요! 이미 12월 20일이고 주문은 이틀 전에 Brown 씨에게 배송이 되었어야 했어요.
여 압니다. 그들은 정말 미안해했고요. 그들의 익일 배송인 XDL Premier Service를 일반 배송 비용에 해 주기로 했습니다. 우리는 원래 일반 배송으로 Brown 씨의 주문품을 배송하기로 선택했었는데, 이제 차액을 낼 필요가 없는 것이죠.
남 알겠습니다. Brown 씨에게 지금 전화를 해서 그녀가 원피스를 내일까지는 받게 될 것이라고 알려 주세요.

XDL 배달 서비스	
배송 종류	금액
일반 배송	50달러
다음 영업일 배송	70달러
XDL 프리미어 배송	120달러
다음 날 저녁 배송	75달러

behind schedule 일정보다 늦는　at this time of the year 일 년 중 이맘때　absurd 말도 안 되는　apologetic 미안해하는, 사과하는　overnight delivery 익일 배송, 다음 날 배송　difference 차액

65 What is the purpose of Ms. Brown's call?
(A) To request a catalog
(B) To arrange a party
(C) To order some clothing
(D) To make a complaint

Brown 씨의 전화 목적은 무엇인가?
(A) 카탈로그를 요구하려고
(B) 파티를 준비하려고
(C) 의류를 주문하려고
(D) 불평을 하려고

Brown 씨의 이름을 염두에 두고 풀자. Ms. Brown called again to complain 부분을 통해 불평을 하기 위해서 전화했음을 알 수 있다.

66 What is the cause of the delivery delay?
(A) An increased number of orders
(B) A missing document
(C) A system malfunction
(D) A shortage of delivery men

배송 지연의 원인은 무엇인가?
(A) 주문의 증가
(B) 없어진 문서
(C) 시스템 오작동
(D) 배달원의 부족

배송이 지연된 원인으로 업체의 컴퓨터 시스템이 다운되면서 데이터가 분실되었다고 했으므로 정답은 (C)가 맞다.

67 Look at the graphic. How much will the company pay for the delivery?
(A) $50
(B) $70
(C) $120
(D) $75

시각 정보를 보시오. 회사는 얼마를 배송에 대해 지불할 것인가?
(A) 50달러
(B) 70달러
(C) 120달러
(D) 75달러

원래 선택한 배송은 standard delivery(일반 배송)이었고 업체의 실수로 지연이 되어 XDL Premier로 배달을 해 주기로 된 점을 파악하자. 여자가 but we don't have to pay the difference(우리가 차액을 지불할 필요는 없다)고 말했으므로 회사는 배송에 대해서 standard delivery에 대한 비용을 지불할 것이다. 정답은 (A)가 된다.

Questions 68-70 refer to the following conversation and chart.
영M 미W

M Good morning. I'm looking for a new car and I'd really like to get something that's fuel efficient.
W Sure. Many people are looking for a car that gives great mileage these days. This fuel efficiency chart will give you a good comparison of the different models we have. As you can see, our latest model, The Maxton, has an excellent fuel efficiency rating. It is fully automatic and it seats six comfortably. It is on display right here, so feel free to take a look at it.
M Oh, I really like the exterior design of this car. But it is a little too big for my liking. Do you have anything that is a little smaller but is still fuel efficient?
W Actually we do. This one here is probably what you are looking for. The exterior of this car is very much like the Maxton, but it is smaller in size. And its fuel efficiency rating is even higher than the Maxton. What do you think?
M Wow, this is the perfect car for me! Can I take it for a test drive?

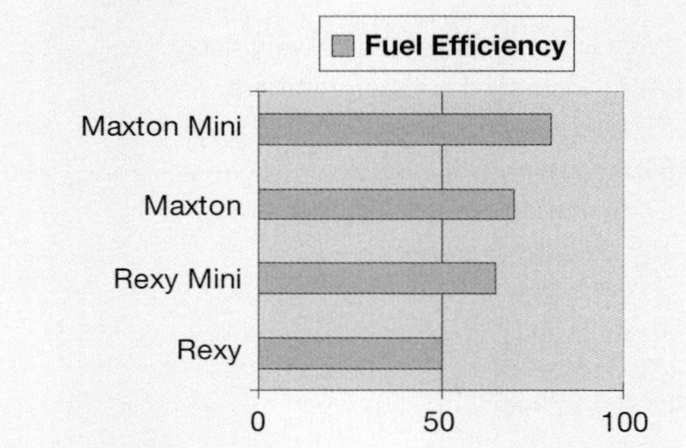

남 안녕하세요. 새 차를 찾고 있는데요, 연료 효율이 높은 것을 사고 싶어요.
여 물론이지요. 많은 분들이 요즘은 연료 효율이 높은 차를 찾습니다. 이 연료 효율 분석표를 보시면 각기 다른 모델들의 비교가 잘 될 것입니다. 저희 최신 모델인 Maxton은 높은 등급의 연료 효율을 받았습니다. 오토매틱이고 여섯 명이 편안하게 탈 수 있지요. 바로 여기에 진열이 되어 있으니 마음껏 살펴보세요.
남 아, 이 차의 외부 디자인은 정말 마음에 드네요. 그러나 제가 평소 좋아하는 것보다는 크기가 너무 커요. 조금 작으면서도 여전히 연료 효율이 높은 모델도 있나요?
여 여기 있습니다. 여기 이 제품이 당신이 찾는 것일 것 같네요. 외형은 Maxton과 매우 비슷하지만, 크기 면에서 더 작습니다. 그리고 연료 효율 등급 역시 Maxton보다 더 높습니다. 어떠세요?
남 와, 이 차가 저에게 완벽하네요! 제가 시운전을 해봐도 될까요?

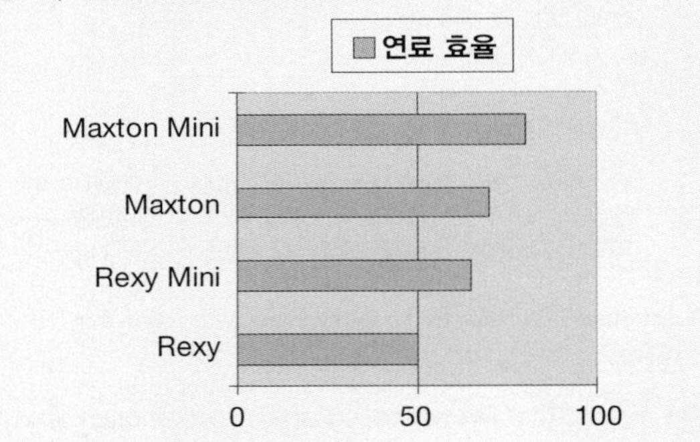

fuel efficient 연료 효율이 좋은 give great mileage 거리가 많이 나오는(= 연료 효율이 높은) for my liking 평소 내가 좋아하는 정도 exterior 외형

68 What is the man mainly looking for in a car?
(A) Safety features
(B) A powerful engine
(C) Fuel economy
(D) A discounted price

남자는 차에서 무엇을 주로 찾는가?
(A) 안전성
(B) 강력한 엔진
(C) 연료 효율
(D) 할인된 가격

남자가 새 차를 찾고 있다고 말하며 I'd really like to get something that's fuel efficient(연료 효율이 높은 차를 사고 싶다)라고 했으므로 정답은 (C)가 된다.

69 What does the man like about the Maxton?
(A) Its size
(B) Its design
(C) Its automatic transmission
(D) Its comfortable seating

남자는 Maxton에 대해서 무엇을 좋아하는가?
(A) 크기
(B) 디자인
(C) 자동 변속 장치
(D) 안락한 좌석

차의 모델인 Maxton을 기억해 두고 내용을 듣자. 남자는 I really like the exterior design of this car(이 차의 디자인이 매우 마음에 든다)라고 했으므로 정답은 (B)가 된다.

70 Look at the graphic. Which car model will the man take for a test drive?
(A) The Maxton Mini
(B) The Maxton
(C) The Rexy Mini
(D) The Rexy

시각 정보를 보시오. 남자는 어느 차 모델을 시운전하기 원하는가?
(A) Maxton Mini
(B) Maxton
(C) Rexy Mini
(D) Rexy

Maxton에 대해서 외형은 마음에 들지만 사이즈가 크다고 했고 이에 여자가 추천한 모델은 외형은 Maxton과 비슷하면서 크기가 작고 연료 효율은 더 높다고 했으므로 차트에서 연료 효율이 Maxton보다 높은 Maxton Mini에 대해 이야기 하고 있음을 알 수 있다. 남자가 이 차의 시운전을 원했으므로 정답은 (A)이다.

PART 4

Questions 71-73 refer to the following message. 미W

Hello, my name is Brooke Bennett and I'm calling about the swimming lessons you offer at the community center. A friend of mine has been taking a class that Ms. Hoff teaches for a few months now and he is really happy with the way she teaches. I'd like to sign up for the swimming class on Wednesday nights, but I want to find out who will be teaching that class first. Could you please call me back to let me know who the instructor for that class is? I can't find that information on your website. My number is 555-1090. Thank you.

안녕하세요, 저는 Brooke Bennett이고 커뮤니티 센터에서 제공하는 수영 수업 때문에 전화를 드립니다. 제 친구 한 명이 몇 달 동안 Hoff 씨가 가르치는 수업을 듣고 있는데 그녀의 수업 방식에 매우 만족을 하더군요. 저는 수요일 저녁마다 하는 수영 수업을 등록하고 싶은데요, 먼저 그 수업을 가르치는 분이 누구인지 알고 싶습니다. 그 수업의 강사가 누구인지 저에게 답신 전화를 해 주시겠어요? 웹 사이트에서는 그 정보를 찾을 수가 없네요. 제 전화번호는 555-1090입니다. 감사합니다.

sign up for 등록하다 call back 답신 전화하다

71 What kind of class is the speaker interested in?
(A) Yoga
(B) Computer programming
(C) Swimming
(D) Public speaking

화자는 어떤 종류의 수업에 관심이 있는가?
(A) 요가
(B) 컴퓨터 프로그래밍
(C) 수영
(D) 연설

메시지의 목적을 언급할 때 I'm calling about the swimming lessons(수영 수업과 관련해서 전화했다)라고 했으므로 정답은 (C)이다.

72 How did the speaker learn about the class?
(A) She saw a schedule online.
(B) She has taken the class before.
(C) It was advertised in a newspaper.
(D) It was recommended by a friend.

화자는 수업에 대해 어떻게 알게 되었는가?
(A) 그녀는 온라인으로 시간표를 봤다.
(B) 그녀는 전에 이 수업을 들었다.
(C) 그것은 신문에 광고되었다.
(D) 그것은 친구에 의해 추천되었다.

화자는 수영 수업에 대해서 친구가 몇 달 동안 특정 선생님이 가르치는 수업을 듣고 있고 수업 방식에 매우 만족해한다고 했으므로 친구로부터 알게 된 것이다. 정답은 (D)가 된다.

73 What information does the speaker request?
(A) The name of an instructor
(B) The starting date of a class
(C) The cost of a program
(D) The location of the center

화자는 어떤 정보를 요청하는가?
(A) 강사의 이름
(B) 수업의 시작 날짜
(C) 프로그램의 비용
(D) 센터의 위치

화자는 등록을 원하지만 그 전에 우선 I want to find out who will be teaching that class(그 수업을 누가 가르치는지 알고 싶다)라고 했으므로 정답은 (A)이다.

Questions 74-76 refer to the following radio advertisement. 미M

Are you planning on taking a trip? When it comes to traveling by train, Porter Railways is your best option! We provide service to more cities around the country than any other intercity rail company. Starting in May, we will be adding more frequent service to our three most popular destinations. You can enjoy comfortable travel at an affordable price with Porter Railways because our fares are just half the price of air travel. To see the revised schedule for May, visit our website at www.porterrailways.com.

여행을 가려고 계획하십니까? 기차 여행에 관한 한 Porter Railways가 최고의 선택입니다! 우리는 다른 어떤 도시 간 철도 회사보다 더 많은 도시로 가는 서비스를 제공합니다. 5월부터 저희는 가장 인기 많은 세 곳의 목적지에 더 자주 서비스를 추가하려고 합니다. 저희 요금은 비행기 여행의 절반밖에 안 되기 때문에 여러분은 저희 Porter Railways에서 더 저렴한 금액으로 편안한 여행을 즐길 수 있습니다. 5월의 바뀐 스케줄을 보기 위해서는 저희 웹 사이트인 www.porterrailways.com으로 방문해 주세요.

when it comes to ~에 관한 한 intercity 도시간의 air travel 항공 여행

74 What is being advertised?
(A) A vacation destination
(B) Local attractions
(C) Train service
(D) A bus tour
무엇이 광고되고 있는가?
(A) 휴가 목적지
(B) 지역의 명소
(C) 기차 서비스
(D) 버스 투어

광고되는 것은 도입부에서부터 찾아 듣는 것이 중요하다. 기차 여행에 관한 한 Porter Railways가 최고의 선택이라고 했으므로 정답은 (C)이다.

75 What is mentioned about the cost of traveling with Porter Railways?
(A) It is discounted for senior citizens.
(B) It has recently been reduced.
(C) It is more expensive during the peak season.
(D) It is cheaper than taking a plane.
Porter Railways와 여행하는 비용에 대해 무엇이 언급되는가?
(A) 노인에게 할인이 된다.
(B) 최근에 내려갔다.
(C) 성수기 중에 더 비싸다.
(D) 비행기를 타는 것보다 싸다.

질문의 키워드는 the cost of traveling with Porter Railways로 기차 운임에 대해 언급된 것을 찾는 것이 질문의 포인트이다. our fares are just half the price of air travel(우리 운임은 항공 여행의 절반 가격이다)이라고 했으므로 정답은 (D)이다.

76 Why should listeners visit the company's website?
(A) To view an updated timetable
(B) To book a ticket online
(C) To see a city map
(D) To sign up for a membership
청자들은 왜 회사의 웹 사이트를 방문해야 하는가?
(A) 개정된 시간표를 보려고
(B) 표를 온라인으로 예약하려고
(C) 도시 지도를 보려고
(D) 회원제를 신청하려고

질문의 키워드는 the company's website로 5월의 바뀐 스케줄을 확인하기 위해서는 웹 사이트를 방문하라고 했으므로 정답은 (A)이다.

Questions 77-79 refer to the following announcement. (영W)

Okay everyone. Before we start setting tables for the lunch customers, I have an announcement. Our famous spinach lasagna will not be available for lunch today. The latest shipment of spinach hasn't arrived yet since the delivery truck broke down on its way here. As you know, many of our repeat customers come especially for the lasagna. So make sure you let every customer know that it is not on the menu as soon as you seat them. It will be back on the menu for dinner though because we're getting the shipment in a couple of hours. Okay, let's get started with our preparations.

좋습니다, 여러분. 점심 고객을 위한 테이블을 준비하기에 앞서, 공지사항이 있습니다. 우리의 유명한 시금치 라자냐는 오늘 점심 때 주문이 불가능합니다. 배달 트럭이 오늘 길에 고장 나서 마지막 시금치의 배송이 아직 도착을 안 했기 때문입니다. 아시다시피, 단골 고객 중 많은 분들이 이 라자냐를 위해서 옵니다. 그러니 반드시 모든 고객들이 자리에 앉자마자 이 음식은 메뉴에 없다는 사실을 알려 주세요. 그리고 두어 시간 후면 배송을 받기 때문에 저녁 메뉴에는 다시 올라갑니다. 좋습니다. 다들 준비를 시작해 주십시오.

spinach 시금치 break down 고장 나다 repeat customer 단골 고객 get started with ~을 시작하다

77 Who most likely are the listeners?
(A) Restaurant employees
(B) Truck drivers
(C) Lunch customers
(D) Vegetable suppliers
청자들은 누구일 것 같은가?
(A) 레스토랑 직원
(B) 트럭 운전사
(C) 점심 고객
(D) 채소 공급업체

화자가 청자들에게 Before we start setting tables for the lunch customers(점심 고객들을 위해 테이블을 세팅하기에 앞서) 공지가 있다고 했으므로 청자들은 레스토랑 직원들이다.

78 What is the problem?
(A) A restaurant sign has been damaged.
(B) Some staff members called in sick.
(C) A popular dish is not available.
(D) A shipment was sent to the wrong address.
문제는 무엇인가?
(A) 레스토랑 간판이 손상되었다.
(B) 일부 직원이 아파서 결근한다고 전화했다.
(C) 인기 있는 요리가 주문 가능하지 않다.
(D) 배송은 틀린 주소로 보내졌다.

공지의 내용이 Our famous spinach lasagna will not be available for lunch today(오늘 인기 많은 라자냐가 주문이 불가능하다)라는 것이었으므로 정답은 (C)이다.

79 What will happen in a couple of hours?
(A) A delivery will arrive.
(B) A restaurant will be closed.
(C) Staff will start serving lunch.
(D) A new dish will be created.
두어 시간 후에 무슨 일이 있을 것인가?
(A) 배달이 도착할 것이다.
(B) 레스토랑은 문을 닫을 것이다.
(C) 직원은 점심을 제공하기 시작할 것이다.
(D) 새로운 메뉴가 만들어질 것이다.

질문의 키워드는 in a couple of hours이다. we're getting the shipment in a couple of hours(두어 시간 후에 배송될 것)라고 했으므로 정답은 (A)이다.

Questions 80-82 refer to the following broadcasting. 영M

This is the weather forecast. I'm Ryan Chang at KGB Radio Broadcasting. The weather here in the north of the country has been beautiful this past week, with blue skies and warm temperatures. But our seven day run of perfect weather is about to end. There is a 70% chance of rain tonight and overnight temperatures will drop to a low of 10 degrees Celsius. It's going to be rainy and chilly tomorrow morning as well. So don't forget your umbrella and bring a jacket with you. Stay tuned to KGB for a traffic update.

일기 예보입니다. 저는 KGB Radio Broadcasting의 Ryan Chang 입니다. 여기 북쪽 지역의 날씨는 지난 한 주 동안 파란 하늘과 따뜻한 기온으로 매우 좋았습니다. 그러나 7일간의 완벽한 날씨는 이제 곧 끝나게 됩니다. 오늘 밤 70퍼센트 강수 확률이 있고 밤사이 최저 기온이 섭씨 10도까지 내려갈 것입니다. 내일 아침에도 비가 오고 쌀쌀할 것입니다. 그러니 잊지 말고 우산을 챙기시고 재킷을 가져가세요. 교통 방송을 위해 KGB로 주파수를 고정해 주세요.

temperature 기온 chance of rain 비 올 확률 overnight 밤 동안의 degree 도 Celsius 섭씨 stay tuned 주파수를 고정하다

80 Who most likely is the speaker?
(A) A taxi driver
(B) A magazine editor
(C) A radio reporter
(D) A police officer
화자는 누구일 것 같은가?
(A) 택시 운전사
(B) 잡지 편집자
(C) 라디오 기자
(D) 경찰관

화자가 일기 예보에서 본인을 I'm Ryan Chang at KGB Radio Broadcasting라고 밝혔으므로 정답은 (C)이다.

81 How long has the weather been nice?
(A) For one day
(B) For three days
(C) For five days
(D) For seven days
얼마 동안 날씨가 좋았는가?
(A) 1일
(B) 3일
(C) 5일
(D) 7일

The weather here in north of the country has been beautiful this past week에서 지난 한 주 동안 날씨가 좋았다고 했으므로 정답은 7일 동안이 된다.

82 What are listeners advised to do?
(A) Buy a new jacket
(B) Bring an umbrella
(C) Leave home early
(D) Use public transportation
청자들은 무엇을 하라는 조언을 받는가?
(A) 새 재킷 사기
(B) 우산 가져가기
(C) 집에서 일찍 나가기
(D) 대중교통 이용하기

내일 아침도 비가 오고 쌀쌀하다고 한 후 우산을 잊지 말라(don't forget your umbrella)고 했으므로 정답은 (B)가 된다.

Questions 83-85 refer to the following excerpt from a meeting. 영W

I'd like to make an important announcement to everyone here at the company. Starting next week, the company's pay cycle will change from a monthly schedule to a bi-weekly one. We've already installed the new payroll system that enables us to convert to a bi-weekly schedule. You will be receiving a memo that describes the new schedule in more detail. It should answer any questions you have. If you have any further questions though, please contact the payroll department for assistance. I hope everything will go smoothly next week.

회사의 전 직원들에게 중요한 공지를 하려고 합니다. 다음 주부터, 회사의 급여 사이클이 월급제에서 2주에 한번 급여를 받는 것으로 바뀌게 됩니다. 저희는 이미 새로운 급여 정산 시스템을 설치하여 2주마다 한 번씩 급여를 받는 스케줄로 전환할 수 있도록 하였습니다. 여러분 모두 보다 자세하게 급여 시스템을 설명해 놓은 메모를 받게 될 것입니다. 이것이 여러분이 궁금할 만한 질문에 답을 해 줄 것입니다. 만약 질문이 더 있다면 급여 정산 부서에 연락하여 도움을 요청하세요. 다음 주에 모든 일들이 잘 진행되기를 바랍니다.

pay cycle 급여제 bi-weekly 2주일에 한 번씩 convert to ~으로 전환하다 in more detail 더 자세하게 go smoothly 잘 진행되다

83 What is the purpose of the talk?
(A) To explain plans for a company merger
(B) To announce a new pay schedule
(C) To say farewell to a colleague
(D) To provide a conference schedule
대화의 목적은 무엇인가?
(A) 회사 합병을 위한 계획을 설명하려고
(B) 새로운 급여 스케줄을 알리려고

(C) 동료에게 작별 인사를 하려고
(D) 컨퍼런스 스케줄을 제공하려고

도입부에 the company's pay cycle will change, 즉 회사의 급여 사이클이 바뀌는데 월급제에서 2주일에 한 번씩으로 바뀐다고 했으므로 정답은 (B)가 된다.

84 When will the change take effect?
(A) This week
(B) Next week
(C) In two weeks
(D) In a month

변경 사항은 언제 효력이 발생하는가?
(A) 이번 주
(B) 다음 주
(C) 2주 후
(D) 한 달 후

급여 스케줄이 변경되는 것이 다음 주부터(Starting next week) 시작된다고 했으므로 정답은 (B)이다. 시작 시점을 묻는 질문의 힌트어로 starting, beginning 등이 가장 많이 나오므로 반드시 암기해 두자.

85 What does the speaker mean when she says, "It should answer any questions you have"?
(A) Employees should go over the memo carefully.
(B) All questions should be directed to the manager.
(C) A questionnaire will be sent to employees.
(D) The article should be easy to understand.

화자가 "이것이 여러분이 궁금할 만한 질문에 답을 해 줄 것입니다" 라고 말한 의미는 무엇인가?
(A) 직원들은 메모를 주의 깊게 검토해야 한다.
(B) 모든 질문은 매니저에게 보내져야 한다.
(C) 설문지가 직원들에게 보내질 것이다.
(D) 기사는 이해하기 쉬울 것이다.

새로운 급여 스케줄에 대해서 You will be receiving a memo that describes the new schedule in more detail(더 자세한 설명을 메모를 통해 받게 될 것이다)이라고 한 후 It should answer any questions you have(이것이 여러분이 궁금할 만한 질문에 답을 해 줄 것이다)라고 했으므로 정답은 (A)가 된다.

Questions 86-88 refer to the following excerpt from a meeting. 미M

Good morning, members of the Advisory Board of Action for Animals. The first item on the agenda today is to nominate a new member to the board. We have two strong candidates to consider, the first of which is Dr. Clifford Olson. Dr. Olson has been a renowned veterinarian for over 30 years and has also worked as the director of our volunteer animal rescue program for 10 years. He has played a key role in rescuing and rehabilitating abandoned animals. He said that his interest in becoming a board member is to promote our volunteer programs by offering well-organized training methods to others. Before we move on to our second candidate, please take some time to review Dr. Olson's application.

안녕하세요, Action for Animals의 자문 위원회 여러분. 오늘의 의제 중 첫 번째 항목은 새로운 위원을 후보자로 추천하는 것입니다. 우리는 고려해야 할 두 분의 강력한 지원자가 있는데, Clifford Olson 박사가 그 중 첫 후보입니다. Olson 박사는 30년 이상 유명한 수의사로써 일해 왔고 또한 지난 10년간 우리 동물 구조 자원 프로그램의 책임자로 일했습니다. 그는 버려진 동물을 구조하고 건강을 회복시키는 데 핵심적인 역할을 해왔습니다. 그가 자문 위원이 되는데 관심이 있는 이유는 잘 조직화된 훈련을 제공함으로써 자원 프로그램의 질을 향상시키기 위함이라고 밝혔습니다. 우리가 두 번째 후보로 넘어가기 전에, 시간을 갖고 Olson 박사의 지원서를 살펴봐 주십시오.

advisory board 자문 위원회 agenda 안건 nominate 후보를 지명하다, 등록하다 applicant 지원자 renowned 저명한, 유명한 veterinarian 수의사 rescue 구조 play a key role in ~에서 핵심적인 역할을 수행하다 rehabilitate (건강을) 회복시키다 abandoned 버려진 promote 향상시키다 well-organized 잘 짜여진, 잘 조직된 move on to ~로 넘어가다 take some time 시간을 갖다

86 What is the purpose of the meeting?
(A) To present an award
(B) To explain a new policy
(C) To discuss some candidates
(D) To introduce a new board member

회의의 목적은 무엇인가?
(A) 상을 수여하려고
(B) 새로운 정책을 설명하려고
(C) 후보자에 대해 토론하려고
(D) 새로운 임원을 소개하려고

목적에 대한 언급을 보통 도입부에서 찾을 수 있다. 안건의 첫 번째 항목으로 '새로운 자문 위원의 후보 지명을 하는 것(to nominate a new member to the board)'이라고 했으므로 정답은 (C)가 된다. 아직 새로운 멤버가 결정된 것이 아니므로 (D)는 오답 함정이 된다.

87 What does Clifford Olson do?
(A) He cares for sick animals.
(B) He plans the annual budget.
(C) He advises local businesses on financial matters.
(D) He contributes articles to a medical journal.

Clifford Olson은 무엇을 하는 사람인가?
(A) 그는 아픈 동물을 보살핀다.
(B) 그는 연간 예산을 계획한다.
(C) 그는 재정 문제에 대해 지역 사업체에게 조언을 한다.
(D) 그는 의학 저널에 글을 기고한다.

세부 사항 질문으로 Clifford Olson이라는 이름을 잘 숙지하고 이 사람에 대해 언급되는 내용 중 보기와 일치하는 것을 고른다. Olson 박사는 30년간 수의사로 일해오고 있다고 했으므로 정답은 (A)이다. 지문의 Veterinarian이라는 직업이 보기에서는 care for sick animals라고 바꿔 표현되었다.

88 What will listeners most likely do next?
(A) Interview the candidates
(B) Examine the credentials of an applicant
(C) Register for a training program
(D) Hear from the recipient of an award

청자들은 다음에 무엇을 할 것 같은가?
(A) 후보자를 인터뷰한다.
(B) 지원자의 자격을 검토한다.

(C) 훈련 프로그램에 등록한다.
(D) 수상자로부터 연설을 듣는다.

향후 행동에 대한 단서는 보통 후반부에 주어지는데, 두 번째 후보로 넘어가기 전에 Olson 박사의 지원서류를 살펴봐 달라고 했으므로 정답은 (B)가 된다. 면접을 본다는 언급을 없었으므로 (A)는 답이 될 수 없다.

Questions 89-91 refer to the following message. 미W

Hi, this is Judy Thorne. I just wanted to let you know that I've finished the report you asked for and I left it on your desk. I analyzed the company's shipping costs and made some suggestions on how to reduce them. For example, by transporting products by truck, we can reduce shipping expenses by 20%. Of course there is a downside. It takes a little longer and can be more affected by weather or road conditions. But the savings are worth it. As you know, I'm supposed to present this information at the next department meeting. So could you look it over and give me some feedback? Thanks for your help. Talk to you later.

안녕하세요, Judy Thorne입니다. 요청하셨던 보고서를 다 끝내서 당신의 책상 위에 올려 놓았다는 것을 알려 드립니다. 회사의 배송 비용을 분석해서 이를 줄이기 위한 방법을 몇 가지 제안해 놓았습니다. 예를 들어, 상품으로 트럭으로 운송함으로써 우리는 배송 비용을 20퍼센트 줄일 수 있습니다. 물론 단점도 있습니다. 시간이 좀 더 오래 걸리고 도로 상태나 날씨에 따라 영향을 받을 수가 있습니다. 그러나 절약된 금액을 볼 때 그럴 만한 가치가 있습니다. 아시듯이, 제가 이 정보를 다음 부서 미팅 때 발표를 하기로 되어 있습니다. 그러니 한 번 읽어보시고 피드백을 주실 수 있을까요? 도움을 주셔서 감사합니다. 나중에 뵙겠습니다.

analyze 분석하다 shipping costs 배송 비용 transport 운송하다
downside 단점 savings 절약된 금액

89 What is the purpose of the telephone message?
(A) To apologize for a late shipment
(B) To schedule a meeting
(C) To ask about a new project
(D) To explain a report

전화 메시지의 목적은 무엇인가?
(A) 늦은 배송에 대해 사과하려고
(B) 회의의 일정을 잡으려고
(C) 새로운 프로젝트에 대해 물어보려고
(D) 보고서에 대해 설명하려고

도입부에 화자는 청자가 요청한 보고서를 다 끝냈고 책상 위에 올려 놓았다고 했으며 이에 대한 세부 내용을 얘기했으므로 메시지의 목적은 보고서에 대한 이야기를 하기 위함이다.

90 What does the speaker mean when she says, "But the savings are worth it"?
(A) She needs to do additional research.
(B) Transporting by truck is a better option for the company.
(C) It is better to send packages by express mail.
(D) Meeting deadlines is the most important thing.

화자가 "그러나 절약된 금액을 볼 때 그럴 만한 가치가 있습니다"라고 말한 의미는 무엇인가?
(A) 그녀는 추가 연구를 할 필요가 있다.
(B) 트럭으로 운송을 하는 게 회사를 위한 더 나은 선택이다.
(C) 빠른 우편으로 소포를 보내는 것이 낫다.
(D) 마감 시간을 지키는 것이 가장 중요한 일이다.

해당 표현에 앞서 트럭으로 제품을 운송하는 것을 제안하면서 비용상의 장점과 시간상의 단점을 언급한 후에, "But the savings are worth it"이라고 했으므로 아낄 수 있는 금액을 생각하면 단점을 보완한다는 의미이므로 정답은 (B) 트럭 배송이 회사에게 더 득이 된다는 것이다.

91 What does the speaker ask the listener to do?
(A) Review a report
(B) Change procedures
(C) Attend a presentation
(D) Develop a new product

화자는 청자에게 무엇을 해 달라고 요청하는가?
(A) 보고서 검토하기
(B) 절차 바꾸기
(C) 발표에 참석하기
(D) 신제품 개발하기

화자의 요청 표현을 놓치지 말고 듣자. could you look it over and give me some feedback에서 보고서를 검토하고 피드백을 달라고 요청하고 있으므로 정답은 (A)이다.

Questions 92-94 refer to the following excerpt from a meeting. 영W

Before we end today's marketing meeting, I'd like to make an important announcement. According to the revised company policy on client meetings, whenever you are away from the office to meet with a client, you need to notify Linda, our assistant manager. Detailed information about the meeting, such as where it will take place, which client you will meet with, and when you'll be back, must be stated. So, from now on, I'd like you to complete the new out-of-office meeting forms and submit them directly to Linda before you leave the office. She'll post them on the bulletin board in the main office, so it will keep all of us in marketing up to date on all on-going projects.

오늘의 마케팅 회의를 끝내기 전에, 중요한 공지가 있습니다. 고객 미팅과 관련해 수정된 회사 정책에 따르면, 고객을 만나기 위하여 당신이 사무실 밖으로 나가는 경우에는 언제나 부팀장인 Linda에게 알려 주어야 합니다. 회의에 관한 세부 정보인 어디서 회의가 열리는지, 어떤 고객을 만나는지, 그리고 언제 사무실로 복귀하는지 등이 반드시 명시되어야 합니다. 따라서, 이제부터는 여러분이 사무실을 떠나기 전에 이 외부 미팅 양식을 완성하여 Linda에게 직접 제출해 주시길 바랍니다. 그녀가 메인 사무실의 게시판에 그걸 붙여 둘 것이고, 이로 인해 마케팅 팀 전원은 진행 중인 프로젝트에 대해 최신 정보를 알 수 있을 것입니다.

revised 수정된 notify 알리다 assistant manager 부팀장, 대리 out-of-office meeting 외부 미팅 bulletin board 게시판 up to date 최신의 on-going 진행 중인

92 Who is the intended audience of the talk?
(A) Department heads
(B) Marketing staff
(C) Office equipment suppliers
(D) International clients
담화의 의도된 청중은 누구인가?
(A) 부서장
(B) 마케팅 직원
(C) 사무용품 공급업체
(D) 해외 고객

청자를 유추하는 질문으로 가장 단순하지만 확실한 유추 포인트는 도입부에 언급된, Before we end today's marketing meeting이다. 오늘의 마케팅 미팅에 참석해 있는 사람들이 청자들이므로 답은 (B)가 된다.

93 What is the purpose of the talk?
(A) To welcome a company executive
(B) To explain a company policy
(C) To announce a special promotion
(D) To summarize some survey results
담화의 목적은 무엇인가?
(A) 회사 임원을 환영하려고
(B) 회사 정책을 설명하려고
(C) 특별 승진을 발표하려고
(D) 조사 결과를 요약하려고

담화의 목적은 대부분 도입부에 언급이 된다. According to the revised company policy on client meetings(고객 미팅과 관련된 수정된 회사 정책에 따르면)라고 언급했으므로 정답은 (B)가 된다.

94 According to the speaker, what will Linda do?
(A) Prepare copies of a sales report
(B) Contact some suppliers
(C) Evaluate employees' performance
(D) Post some information
화자에 따르면, Linda는 무엇을 할 것인가?
(A) 판매 보고서의 사본을 준비한다.
(B) 공급업체에게 연락한다.
(C) 직원들의 성과를 평가한다.
(D) 정보를 게시한다.

직원들이 양식을 제출해서 Linda에게 제출하면 Linda는 게시판에 그 양식을 붙여 놓을 것이라고 했으므로 정답은 (D)가 된다.

Questions 95-97 refer to the following message and schedule.
미M

Hello. This is Kevin Hwang calling from Exposures Photography at 1120 Main Street. I just placed a lunch order for me and my colleagues on your website. But I want to make a slight change to the order. I forgot to add extra cheese to the burgers, so can you please make them double-cheese burgers. And could you please remove the last item from our order? One of my coworkers wanted to have it for dessert but apparently she changed her mind. Sorry for the inconvenience. And just to confirm, the lunch should be delivered to our office by noon. We have an important meeting with international clients at one o'clock. Thank you very much.

Lunch Order Form

Item	Quantity	Cost
Burger	3	$3.50
French Fries	2	$1.50
Coke	3	$1.00
Frozen Yogurt	1	$1.50

안녕하세요. Main Street 1120번지에 있는 Exposures Photography의 Kevin Hwang입니다. 제가 방금 웹 사이트를 통해 저와 저의 동료들을 위한 점심을 주문했는데 그 주문을 변경하고 싶습니다. 버거에 치즈 추가하는 것을 깜빡했는데 더블 치즈 버거로 변경해 주십시오. 그리고 주문서의 마지막 품목을 빼 주시겠습니까? 제 동료 중 한 명이 디저트로 먹겠다고 했으나 생각을 바꾼 것 같습니다. 불편을 드려 죄송합니다. 그리고 점심은 정오까지 저희 사무실로 배달이 돼야 한다는 것을 다시 한 번 확인해 드립니다. 저희는 1시 정각에 해외 고객들과 중요한 미팅이 있거든요. 감사합니다.

점심 주문서

품목	수량	금액
버거	3	3.50달러
감자튀김	2	1.50달러
콜라	3	1.00달러
후로즌 요거트	1	1.50달러

make a change 변경을 하다 add 추가하다 remove 빼다, 제거하다 apparently 보아하니

95 What is the purpose of the message?
(A) To inquire about costs
(B) To get directions to a restaurant
(C) To change an order
(D) To ask about business hours
메시지의 목적은 무엇인가?
(A) 비용에 관하여 문의하려고
(B) 레스토랑에 가는 길을 알려고
(C) 주문을 변경하려고
(D) 영업시간에 대해 물어보려고

메시지의 도입부에 점심 주문을 이미 했다고 밝히며 But I want to make a slight change to the order(주문을 변경하고 싶다)라고 했으므로 정답은 (C)가 된다.

96 Look at the graphic. Which item will not be delivered by noon?
(A) Burger
(B) French fries
(C) Coke
(D) Frozen yogurt
시각 정보를 보시오. 정오까지 어느 품목이 배달되지 않을 것인가?
(A) 햄버거
(B) 감자 튀김
(C) 콜라
(D) 후로즌 요구르트

시각 정보를 활용해서 세부 정보를 파악하는 유형으로 주문을 변경할 때 주문서의 마지막 품목을 취소해 달라고 했으므로 frozen yogurt는 배달이 되지 않을 것임을 알 수 있다.

97 What is scheduled at 1 o'clock?
(A) A training session
(B) A meeting with clients
(C) An international event
(D) A video conference

1시 정각에 무엇이 잡혀 있는가?
(A) 교육
(B) 고객과의 회의
(C) 국제적인 행사
(D) 화상 회의

질문의 키워드는 1시 정각으로 We have an important meeting with international clients at one o'clock이라고 했으므로 정답은 (B)가 맞다. (C)는 international이라는 단어만을 이용한 함정이 된다.

Questions 98-100 refer to the following message and list. 영W

Thank you for coming to the marketing meeting on such short notice. I'll get straight to the point. Could you first take a look at this chart? Since we launched our online newspaper service, there has been an increase in the number of subscribers from these two age groups. It shows that many customers prefer to read news online nowadays. And that's why we need to continue developing more useful applications for our readers. One thing that worries me though is that the subscription rate of this age group has decreased slightly each year. That means we have to create something new and exciting to target younger consumers like them. I'd like you to do some research on this age group. We need to find out what their interests are and what they are looking for in a newspaper. Okay. We're going to have another meeting about this next Monday.

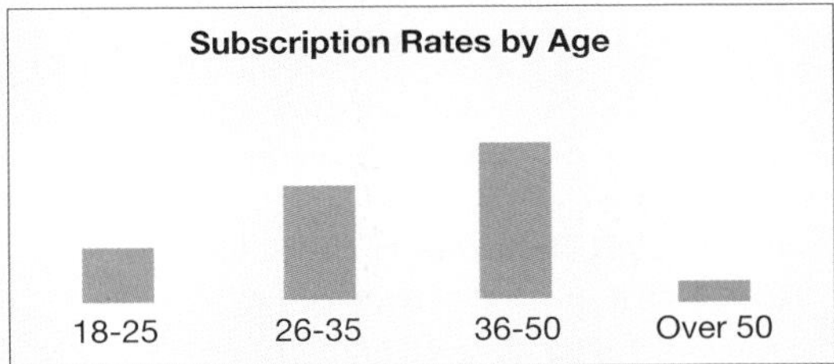

갑작스러운 요청에도 마케팅 미팅에 참석해 주셔서 감사합니다. 바로 요점으로 들어가겠습니다. 우선 차트를 살펴봐 주시겠습니까? 우리가 온라인 뉴스를 출시한 이후로 이 두 연령대의 구독자 수가 증가했습니다. 이것은 요즘에는 많은 고객들이 온라인으로 뉴스를 읽는 것을 선호한다는 것을 보여줍니다. 그리고 그것이 우리가 계속해서 우리 독자들을 위해 더 유용한 애플리케이션을 개발해야 하는 이유입니다. 그런데 한 가지 염려스러운 것은 이 연령대 그룹의 구독률이 매년 조금씩 줄어들고 있다는 것입니다. 이것은 우리가 이들과 같은 젊은 소비자들을 목표로 하는 보다 새롭고 신 나는 뭔가를 개발해야 한다는 것입니다. 저는 여러분께서 이 연령대 그룹에 대한 조사를 해 주시길 바랍니다. 그들의 관심사가 무엇인지 그리고 신문에서 그들이 원하는 것이 무엇인지를 알아야 합니다. 이것에 대한 다음 미팅은 다음 주 월요일에 갖도록 하겠습니다.

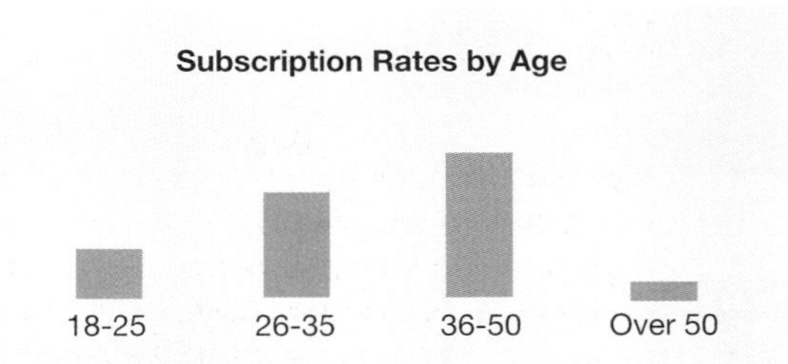

get straight to the point 바로 요점으로 넘어가다 subscriber 구독자

98 Why does the company want to develop online applications?
(A) The company can save money on advertising.
(B) Online sales have decreased.
(C) They are inexpensive to develop.
(D) Customers prefer to read news online.

회사는 왜 온라인 애플리케이션을 개발하고 싶어 하는가?
(A) 회사가 광고에 드는 돈을 아낄 수 있다.
(B) 온라인 판매가 줄었다.
(C) 개발하기가 저렴하다.
(D) 고객이 온라인으로 뉴스 읽는 것을 선호한다.

It shows that many customers prefer to read news online nowadays(온라인으로 뉴스 읽는 것을 좋아한다)라고 언급한 후, 그것이 애플리케이션을 개발해야 하는 이유라고 했으므로 정답은 (D)가 맞다.

99 Look at the graphic. Which age group will the listeners look into?
(A) 18-25
(B) 26-35
(C) 36-50
(D) Over 59

시각 정보를 보시오. 청자들은 어떤 연령대를 조사할 것인가?
(A) 18-25세
(B) 26-35세
(C) 36-50세
(D) 59세 이상

구독률이 가장 낮은 그룹은 59세 이상이지만 화자는 we have to create something new and exciting to target younger consumers like them(젊은 고객층을 타깃으로 하는 새롭고 나는 뭔가를 개발해야 한다)이라고 했고 그들이 원하는 것이 무엇인지 조사하라고 했으므로 구독률이 저조한 두 그룹 중에서 조사될 연령대는 (A)가 된다.

100 What is scheduled for next Monday?
(A) A software upgrade
(B) A job interview
(C) A department meeting
(D) A political debate

다음 월요일에 무엇이 있을 것인가?
(A) 소프트웨어 업그레이드
(B) 취업 면접
(C) 부서 회의
(D) 정치 토론

질문의 키워드는 next Monday로 We're going to have another meeting about this next Monday(한 번의 미팅이 더 있을 것이다)라고 했으므로 정답은 (C)가 된다.

Actual Test 4

PART 1

본책 p.48

1 (D)	2 (B)	3 (C)	4 (B)	5 (A)	6 (D)

PART 2

본책 p.52

7 (B)	8 (C)	9 (C)	10 (C)	11 (A)	12 (A)
13 (C)	14 (C)	15 (B)	16 (B)	17 (B)	18 (C)
19 (A)	20 (B)	21 (B)	22 (A)	23 (C)	24 (A)
25 (C)	26 (A)	27 (B)	28 (C)	29 (B)	30 (B)
31 (C)					

PART 3

본책 p.53

32 (B)	33 (C)	34 (D)	35 (D)	36 (D)	37 (A)
38 (D)	39 (C)	40 (B)	41 (A)	42 (D)	43 (C)
44 (C)	45 (D)	46 (D)	47 (C)	48 (A)	49 (B)
50 (A)	51 (C)	52 (B)	53 (A)	54 (B)	55 (C)
56 (C)	57 (B)	58 (D)	59 (C)	60 (C)	61 (D)
62 (C)	63 (A)	64 (D)	65 (C)	66 (B)	67 (B)
68 (B)	69 (D)	70 (A)			

PART 4

본책 p.57

71 (B)	72 (D)	73 (B)	74 (C)	75 (A)	76 (B)
77 (D)	78 (B)	79 (D)	80 (C)	81 (D)	82 (B)
83 (B)	84 (C)	85 (A)	86 (D)	87 (A)	88 (B)
89 (A)	90 (C)	91 (C)	92 (A)	93 (C)	94 (C)
95 (D)	96 (A)	97 (C)	98 (D)	99 (A)	100 (B)

PART 1

1 미M
(A) A customer is selecting a product to buy.
(B) Some papers are being removed from the counter.
(C) All the drawers have been left open.
(D) The shelves are fully stocked with items.

(A) 손님이 살 물건을 고르고 있다.
(B) 종이들이 카운터에서 치워지고 있다.
(C) 모든 서랍들은 열려 있다.
(D) 선반들이 모두 물건으로 가득 차 있다.

약국의 선반으로 보이는 곳에 물건이 가득 차 있으므로 정답은 (D)이다. 아래쪽의 서랍은 닫혀 있으므로 (C)는 오답이다.

select 고르다 product 제품 remove 제거하다 shelves 선반, 책장 item 물품

2 영W
(A) A car is passing close to the man.
(B) A man is holding an advertising sign.
(C) A man is greeting some customers.
(D) A man is installing a sign.

(A) 자동차가 남자 가까이에 지나가고 있다.
(B) 남자가 광고판을 들고 있다.
(C) 남자가 손님들을 맞이하고 있다.
(D) 남자가 표지판을 설치하고 있다.

도로에서 한 남자가 식당 음식을 알리는 광고판을 들고 있다. 지나가는 차가 없고 그냥 표지판을 들고 있을 뿐이므로 (B)를 제외한 나머지는 모두 오답이다.

close to ~에 가까운 hold 들다, 쥐다 advertising 광고 greet 맞다, 환영하다 install 설치하다

3 영M
(A) They are cleaning some computer monitors.
(B) They are looking at each other.
(C) They are doing some work at their desks.
(D) One man is answering the phone.

(A) 사람들이 컴퓨터 모니터를 청소하고 있다.
(B) 사람들이 서로를 보고 있다.
(C) 사람들이 책상에서 일을 하고 있다.
(D) 한 남자가 전화를 받고 있다.

마주 향하는 자세로 앉은 두 남자가 책상에서 일을 하고 있으므로 정답은 (C)이다. 둘의 시선은 모두 컴퓨터를 향하고 있으므로 서로를 보고 있다고 표현하긴 어렵다.

answer the phone 전화를 받다

4 미W
(A) The railing is being repaired.
(B) Some paintings line the hallway.
(C) Pieces of furniture sit along the walls.
(D) The corridor has many decorative features.

(A) 난간을 수리하고 있다.
(B) 그림들이 복도에 늘어서 있다.
(C) 가구들이 벽을 따라 놓여 있다.
(D) 복도에는 많은 장식적인 특징이 있다.

좁은 복도에 그림이 몇 점 걸려 있고 가구는 보이지 않는다. 복도에 걸린 그림 몇 점 외에는 다른 특징이 없으므로 (D)는 정답이 되기 어렵다. 사진을 '걸다'라는 뜻의 hang을 쓰지 않고 같은 높이에 나란히 있는 모습에 line을 쓴 (B)가 정답이다.

railing 난간, 철책 line 늘어서다 hallway 복도 corridor 복도, 회랑 decorative 장식의 feature 특징

5 미M
(A) Some people have their sleeves rolled up.
(B) Audience members are applauding the musicians.
(C) Some people are reaching for a knob.
(D) A man is pointing to another man.

(A) 일부 사람들이 소매를 걷어 올렸다.
(B) 관객들이 연주자들에게 박수를 치고 있다.
(C) 일부 사람들이 문고리를 향해 손을 뻗고 있다.
(D) 한 남자가 다른 남자를 가리키고 있다.

악기를 연주하는 남자들이 셔츠의 소매를 걷어 올린 모습이다. 관객들은 보이지 않으므로 (B)는 오답이다.

roll up 소매나 바지를 걷다 applaud 박수를 치다 knob 문이나 서랍에 달린 동그란 손잡이 point to ~를 가리키다

6 영W
(A) Some people are jogging on a path.
(B) A path runs through the woods.
(C) A lane has been blocked for maintenance work.
(D) Some cars are lined up near a building.

(A) 일부 사람들이 길에서 조깅을 하고 있다.

(B) 길이 숲을 가로지르고 있다.
(C) 한 차로가 유지 보수 작업으로 막혀 있다.
(D) 자동차들이 건물 근처에 일렬로 세워져 있다.

건물 사이에 나무가 몇 그루 있고 차들이 일렬로 주차되어 있으므로 정답은 (D)이다. 나무가 몇 그루 있기는 하지만 이곳을 woods라고 보기는 어렵다. 따라서 (B)는 오답이다.

path 작은 길　lane 도로, 길, 차선　be blocked 막혀 있다
maintenance work 유지 보수 작업　line up 일렬로 세우다

PART 2

07 Who bought the donuts?
미W (A) They cost a lot.
미M (B) My secretary did.
(C) With coffee.

누가 도넛을 샀습니까?
(A) 그것들은 가격이 비쌉니다.
(B) 제 비서가요.
(C) 커피와 함께요.

의문사 who가 주어로 쓰여 누가 도넛을 샀는지 질문했으므로 비서가 샀다고 답한 (B)가 정답이다. (A)는 가격이 비싸다고 했으므로 오답이고, (C)는 도넛을 들었을 때 연상되는 coffee를 이용한 오답이다.

cost (값, 비용이) 들다

08 Where's your office located?
영M (A) For two hours.
미W (B) No, I don't.
(C) On King Street.

당신의 사무실은 어디에 있습니까?
(A) 2시간 동안요.
(B) 아니오, 전 안 합니다.
(C) King Street요.

의문사 where 질문으로 사무실을 묻고 있으므로 길 이름으로 답한 (C)가 정답이다. (A)는 기간을 나타내므로 의문사 how long에 알맞은 답이고, (B)의 경우 의문사 의문문에 대해서 Yes/No로 답할 수 없기 때문에 무조건 오답이 된다.

be located (~에) 위치해 있다

09 Is the software the latest version?
미M (A) Yes, he's the developer.
미W (B) Not lately.
(C) I believe so.

그 소프트웨어는 최신 버전입니까?
(A) 네, 그는 개발자입니다.
(B) 최근에는 아닙니다.
(C) 그럴 거예요.

Yes/No 여부를 묻는 질문으로 주어 the software가 주격 보어 the latest version인지를 묻는 것이므로 (C)가 정답이다. I believe so, I think so 등의 표현은 '그런 것 같다'의 의미로 Yes 대신 쓸 수 있는 표현이므로, 의문사 없는 의문문의 정답으로 자주 등장한다.

latest 최신의　developer 개발자　lately 최근에

10 What movie is playing at the cinema?
영W (A) I prefer to stay home.
영M (B) Actually we're lost.
(C) A new comedy.

어떤 영화가 영화관에서 상영되고 있습니까?
(A) 집에 있는 게 더 좋아요.
(B) 실은 우리가 길을 잃었습니다.
(C) 새로운 코미디요.

의문사 what 질문으로 what이 형용사로 쓰이는 경우로, 명사가 뒤따르고 해석은 '어떤 ~'라고 한다. 상영 중인 영화를 묻는 것이 질문의 포인트이므로 영화의 종류로 답한 (C)가 정답이다.

play 공연되다　cinema 영화관　be lost 길을 잃다

11 How's the new database software working?
미W (A) It's a lot faster.
영W (B) For an hour and a half.
(C) I walk every day.

새로운 데이터 베이스 소프트웨어는 어떻게 작동하나요?
(A) 훨씬 더 빠릅니다.
(B) 1시간 반 동안이요.
(C) 전 매일 걷습니다.

의문사 how 질문으로 주어 the new database software에 대한 상태를 묻는 것이 질문의 핵심이다. 정답은 소프트웨어가 더 빠르게 작동된다고 답한 (A)이다. (C)는 질문 속의 working과 발음이 유사한 walk를 사용한 함정이 된다.

work (기계, 장비 등이) 작동하다　a lot (비교급을 강조할 때) 훨씬 더

12 Why did Clara change her mind about the plan?
영M (A) Because the new techniques were quite costly.
미W (B) No, I don't mind.
(C) Let's see how it goes.

Clara는 왜 계획에 대한 생각을 바꿨나요?
(A) 신기술이 비용이 많이 들어서요.
(B) 아니오, 전 괜찮아요.
(C) 그것이 어떻게 되는지 봅시다.

의문사 why 질문으로 Clara가 계획에 대한 생각을 바꾼 이유를 묻고 있으므로 비용이 많이 들기 때문이라고 답한 (A)가 정답이다. 의문사 의문문에 (B)처럼 Yes/No로 답할 수 없으므로 오답 소거를 해야 하고 (C)의 Let's는 제안할 때 쓰는 표현이므로 어울리지 않는다.

change one's mind ~의 생각을 바꾸다　costly 비싼　mind 꺼리다

13 Would you like me to order lunch for you?
미M (A) There's a café by the hair salon.
영W (B) It is 35 dollars.
(C) Yes, a cheese burger and coke, please.

당신을 위해 점심을 주문해 드릴까요?
(A) 미용실 옆에 카페가 있습니다.
(B) 35달러입니다.
(C) 네, 치즈 버거와 콜라로 부탁해요.

상대방에게 호의를 제공하는 질문으로 Would you like me to V ~? 를 반드시 외워 두고 해석은 '제가 V를 해 드릴까요?'라고 한다. 정답은 상대방의 호의를 Yes로 받고 주문할 점심 메뉴를 추가로 덧붙인 (C)가 정답이다. (A)는 lunch를 들었을 때 연상되는 단어 café를 이용한 함정이고, (B)는 how much처럼 가격을 묻는 질문에 대한 답이다.

14 This winter coat needs to be repaired.
영M (A) It's supposed to snow now.
미W (B) Does it come in green too?
(C) Oh, what's wrong with it?

이 겨울 외투를 수선해야겠어요.
(A) 이제 눈이 올 거예요.
(B) 그것은 녹색으로도 나오나요?
(C) 오, 무슨 문제가 있죠?

평서문 유형으로 겨울 코트를 수선해야 한다는 것이 요지이므로 무슨 문제가 있냐고 되묻는 (C)가 가장 자연스러운 답변이 된다. (A)는 날씨에 대한 정보를 주고 있으므로 오답이고 (B)는 상품이 녹색으로 나오는지 묻고 있으므로 문맥에서 벗어난 답변이 된다.

repair 수리하다, 수선하다 come in (상품이 특정 색상, 사이즈로) 나오다

15 When should we do the gardening in the back-yard?
영W (A) Write on the front.
미M (B) How about now?
(C) That's what I thought.

우리가 언제 뒤뜰의 정원 손질을 하는 게 좋을까요?
(A) 앞면에 쓰십시오.
(B) 지금은 어때요?
(C) 그것이 제가 생각한 바입니다.

의문사 when 질문으로 정원 손질을 하기 좋은 시점이 언제인지 묻고 있는데 '지금'은 어떠냐고 되묻는 (B)가 가장 자연스러운 답변이 된다. 질문의 back-yard의 연상어 오류로 (A) front가 쓰였고, (C)는 보통 제안에 대한 긍정 답변으로 쓰이는 표현으로 '나도 그 생각을 했다'는 의미이다.

gardening 정원 손질 back-yard 뒤뜰

16 It's a three-day conference.
미W (A) The hotel has a shuttle service.
영W (B) That'll fit our schedule.
(C) I enjoyed it a lot.

컨퍼런스는 3일간 열립니다.
(A) 그 호텔에는 셔틀 서비스가 있습니다.
(B) 우리 스케줄에 잘 맞겠네요.
(C) 전 그게 아주 좋았어요.

평서문 유형으로 컨퍼런스가 3일짜리라는 정보를 주는 것이 요지이다. (B)에서는 일정이 스케줄과 잘 맞을 것이라고 답했으므로 가장 자연스러운 답변이 된다. (A)는 컨퍼런스의 장소로 떠올릴 수 있는 hotel을 이용한 오답 함정이 되고, (C)는 아직 열리지도 않은 컨퍼런스를 이미 즐겼다고 답하고 있으므로 시제 오류의 함정이 된다.

conference 대규모 회의, 학회 fit (일정 등이) 잘 맞다

17 What do you think of our new company logo?
미M (A) She's good at that.
미W (B) It looks a little too simple.
(C) We already have, thanks.

새로운 회사 로고에 대해서 어떻게 생각하세요?
(A) 그녀는 그것을 잘합니다.
(B) 좀 너무 단순한 것 같습니다.
(C) 저희는 이미 했어요, 감사합니다.

의문사 what 질문 중 암기가 필요한 관용 표현이다. What do you think of/about은 상대방의 의견/견해를 묻는 질문으로 '~에 대해 어떻게 생각하세요?'라고 해석한다. 회사의 새 로고에 대한 의견/견해를 말한 것은 (B)이다. (A)는 주어 오류 함정이고, (C)는 제안에 대한 거절 표현이므로 문맥에서 매우 벗어난 답변이 된다.

be good at ~을 잘하다 simple 단순한

18 Wouldn't you like me to prepare an extra copy?
영W (A) Thanks to Ms. Vonn.
영M (B) No, you can have another cup.
(C) We'll need ten more.

여분의 사본을 준비해 드릴까요?
(A) Vonn 씨 덕분에요.
(B) 아니오, 한 잔 더 드셔도 됩니다.
(C) 우리는 10부 더 필요할 것 같습니다.

제공 의문문 유형으로 Would/wouldn't you like me to는 '제가 ~해 드릴까요?'라고 호의를 제공할 때 쓰는 표현이다. 상대방의 제공에 대해 호의를 받아들이거나 거절하는 것이 정답이 되는데, (C)에서는 10부가 더 필요하다며 도움을 받아들이고 있으므로 정답이 된다. (B)는 질문 속의 extra와 의미가 같은 another를 이용한 연상어 오류이다.

prepare 준비하다 extra 여분의 thanks to ~ 덕분에

19 Why hasn't the Out-of-Order sign been put up yet?
미W (A) I'm making one now.
미M (B) He's on a business trip.
(C) A nice present.

'고장' 표지판은 왜 아직도 붙여지지 않았나요?
(A) 지금 하나 만들고 있는 중이에요.
(B) 그는 출장 중입니다.
(C) 좋은 선물이네요.

의문사 why 질문으로 고장 표지판이 아직도 안 붙여진 이유를 물었기 때문에 아직 표지판이 완성되지 않았다고 답한 (A)가 정답이 된다. (B)는 주어 오류로 정답이 될 수 없다.

Out-of-Order sign 고장 표지판 on a business trip 출장 중인

20 Where can I find more paper?
영M (A) Print it in color, please.
영W (B) Check the supply cabinet.
(C) The bank is in Macao.

제가 어디에서 종이를 더 찾을 수 있을까요?
(A) 그걸 칼라로 인쇄해 주세요.
(B) 물품 수납장을 살펴보세요.
(C) 그 은행은 마카오에 있습니다.

의문사 where 질문으로 종이가 있는 곳을 물었으므로 정답은 (B)가 된다. (C)의 Macao는 지명으로 의문사 where에는 해당하나 이 질문에서는 함정으로 사용되었다.

in color 칼라로 supply 물품 cabinet 수납장

21 Which of the receptionists is working today?
미M (A) It is working now.
영M (B) Susie, I think.
(C) At two o'clock.

오늘은 어떤 접수원이 근무하나요?

(A) 그것은 이제 작동합니다.
(B) Susie일 거예요.
(C) 2시 정각에요.

의문사 which 질문이나 which of the receptionists(접수원 중 누구)라고 정확하게 해석하면 의문사 who 질문이 된다는 것을 파악할 수 있다. 누구인지 묻는 질문에 Susie라는 사람 이름으로 답한 (B)가 정답이 된다. 질문 속의 working은 '근무하다'는 의미이고 (A)의 working은 주어가 it이므로 '작동하다'는 의미로 해석된다.

receptionist 접수원 work 일하다, 작동하다

22 Could you fax us the receipts by the end of today?
영W (A) I'll do it right now.
미M (B) Sorry, he couldn't fix it.
(C) Make two copies please.

오늘까지 영수증을 저희에게 팩스로 보내 줄 수 있으신가요?
(A) 지금 바로 하겠습니다.
(B) 죄송하지만, 그가 그걸 고칠 수 없었어요.
(C) 2부의 사본을 만들어 주세요.

요청 의문문 유형으로 상대방에게 요청하는 내용의 핵심이 영수증을 팩스로 보내 줄 수 있는지 여부이므로 당장 하겠다고 답한 (A)가 정답이 된다. (B)는 주어가 틀린 주어 오류 함정인데 fax와 발음이 비슷한 fix를 이용해 오답을 유도하는 형태이다. (C)는 fax를 들었을 때 연상되는 copy라는 단어를 이용한 연상어 오류이다.

fax 팩스를 보내다 receipt 영수증 fix 고치다 make a copy 사본을 만들다

23 I ran into the new accountant this morning.
미W (A) Maybe tomorrow.
영M (B) We ran out of paper.
(C) Really? I did too.

오늘 아침에 새로운 회계사와 우연히 마주쳤어요.
(A) 아마도 내일이요.
(B) 우리는 종이가 다 떨어졌습니다.
(C) 진짜요? 저도요.

평서문 유형으로 정확한 해석이 요구된다. 'run into + 사람'은 '~와 우연히 마주치다'는 의미로 아침에 새로운 회계사와 마주쳤다는 내용을 말했으므로 의미상 자연스러운 답변은 (C)이다. (A)는 this morning에 대한 연상어인 tomorrow를 이용한 함정이고, (B)는 동사 run이 들어가는 다른 표현 run out of(~이 다 떨어지다)를 이용한 함정이 된다.

run into ~와 우연히 마주치다 accountant 회계사 run out of ~이 다 떨어지다

24 How did the mechanic locate the faulty parts so
영M quickly?
영W (A) He is a skilled worker.
(B) It's a great location.
(C) Because of the weather.

그 기계공은 어떻게 결함 있는 부품을 그렇게 빨리 찾았나요?
(A) 그는 숙련된 직원이거든요.
(B) 좋은 위치네요.
(C) 날씨 때문에요.

의문사 how 질문으로 의역을 하면 감탄의 의도를 담고 있음을 파악할 수 있다. 기계공이 결함 부품을 빨리 찾아낸 것에 대한 놀라움의 표현이므로 가장 어울리는 답변은 (A)가 된다. (B)는 locate의 유사 발음인 location이 쓰인 오답이고, (C) 날씨 때문이라는 내용은 문맥에서 벗어나므로 오답 소거한다.

mechanic 기계 수리공 locate 찾다 faulty 결함 있는 part 부품
skilled 숙련된 location 위치

25 Shouldn't the printer be working by now?
미M (A) Look inside the tool box.
미W (B) I'll take the latest model.
(C) We're still waiting for a part.

인쇄기는 지금쯤 작동되어야 하지 않나요?
(A) 연장 박스 안을 보세요.
(B) 최신 모델로 할게요.
(C) 우린 아직도 부품을 기다리고 있어요.

Yes/No 여부를 묻는 질문으로 인쇄기가 지금은 작동되어야 하지 않는지, 즉 기계가 고쳐졌는지 여부를 물었으므로 해석상 부품이 없어서 고치지 못했다고 답한 (C)가 정답이 된다.

by now 지금쯤은 latest 최신의

26 When are you sending Ms. Williams our final
영W proposal?
미M (A) Right after I double-check the figures.
(B) Please leave it on my desk.
(C) No, I don't think so.

언제 Williams 씨에게 우리의 최종 제안서를 보낼 건가요?
(A) 수치를 한 번 더 검토한 직후에요.
(B) 그걸 제 책상에 두세요.
(C) 아니오, 그렇지 않을 거예요.

의문사 when 질문으로 최종 보고서를 보낼 시점이 언제인지 묻는 질문에 정확한 시점이 아닌 검토를 한 번 더 하고 나서라고 답한 (A)가 가장 자연스러운 답변이 된다. (B)는 책상 위에 놓으라는 where에 대한 답을 주었으므로 오답이고, (C)는 의문사 의문문에 No로 답변을 하므로 오답이 된다.

final 최종의 double-check 한 번 더 확인하다 leave 남기다, 두다

27 Have you signed up for the magazine subscription?
영M (A) A hundred page long article.
영W (B) No, I decided not to.
(C) Yes, they finally signed the agreement.

잡지 구독을 신청하셨나요?
(A) 100쪽 분량의 기사요.
(B) 아니오, 안 하기로 했어요.
(C) 네, 그들은 결국 계약서에 사인했어요.

Yes/No 여부를 묻는 질문으로 잡지 구독 신청 여부를 물었으므로 구독을 하지 않기로 결정했다고 답한 (B)가 정답이다. (A)는 magazine을 들었을 때 연상되는 단어 article을 이용한 오답이고, (C)는 sign이라는 동사를 반복 이용하여 함정을 주는 유형이다.

sign up for 등록하다, ~을 신청하다 subscription 구독 article 기사 finally 결국 agreement 계약서

28 Didn't you put together a list showing the database
미M you analyzed?
미W (A) It has increased dramatically.
(B) I've asked for one.
(C) Yes, and I already sent it to you.

당신이 분석한 데이터를 보여 주는 리스트를 만들지 않았나요?
(A) 그것은 급격하게 늘었어요.
(B) 제가 하나를 요청했어요.
(C) 네, 그리고 당신에게 벌써 보냈죠.

Yes/No 여부를 묻는 질문으로 핵심은 put together a list(리스트를 만들다)에 대한 사실 여부 확인이다. (C)에서 Yes(만들었다)라고 답한 후에 만든 리스트를 이미 보냈다고 부연 설명했으므로 가장 자연스러운 답변이다. (A)와 (B)는 리스트를 만들었는지 여부에 대한 어떠한 답도 주지 않으므로 정답이 될 수 없다.

put together (보고서, 리스트 등을) 만들다 analyze 분석하다 increase 증가하다 dramatically 급격하게, 극적으로

29 The next step is to have the invitations mailed out.
영W (A) The first one was better.
미M (B) Okay, I'll get in touch with Linda.
(C) I'm planning a birthday party.

다음 단계는 초대장을 우편으로 발송하는 것입니다.
(A) 처음 것이 더 나았습니다.
(B) 좋습니다, 제가 Linda에게 연락하겠습니다.
(C) 저는 생일 파티를 계획하고 있습니다.

평서문 유형으로 다음 업무는 초대장 발송이라고 정보를 주었고 이에 대해 Linda에게 연락을 취하겠다는 (B)를 들었을 때 Linda가 초대장 발송의 담당자임을 연결할 수 있어야 한다. 나머지 선택지들은 문맥상 벗어나므로 정답이 될 수 없다.

invitation 초대장 mail out 우편으로 발송하다 get in touch with ~와 연락을 취하다

30 Has anyone given you a tour of the office?
영M (A) We offer two types of package tours.
미W (B) Yes, the manager showed me around.
(C) I'll be busy then.

누가 당신에게 사무실 구경을 시켜줬나요?
(A) 저흰 두 종류의 패키지 투어를 제공합니다.
(B) 네, 매니저가 구경을 시켜줬어요.
(C) 전 그때 바쁠 거예요.

Yes/No 여부를 묻는 질문으로 사무실 구경을 시켜준 사람이 있는지를 물었으므로, 구체적으로 매니저가 주변을 보여 줬다고 답한 (B)가 정답이다. (A)는 tour가 들렸을 때 연상되는 package tours를 이용하여 오답을 유도하는 유형이며, (C)는 주어와 시제가 맞지 않는 답변이므로 오답 소거한다.

give ~ a tour ~에게 구경을 시켜 주다

31 Aren't we supposed to update the anti-virus
미M software regularly?
영W (A) Their database is pretty up-to-date.
(B) Free installation will be offered.
(C) Yes, it is the latest version though.

우리는 바이러스 퇴치 소프트웨어를 주기적으로 업데이트 하도록 되어 있지 않나요?
(A) 그들의 데이터는 꽤 최신입니다.
(B) 무료 설치가 제공될 것입니다.
(C) 네, 그런데 이게 최신 버전입니다.

Yes/No 여부를 묻는 질문으로 be supposed to 뒤에 등장하는 동사 update가 진짜 의미를 담고 있는 동사이다. 즉, 주기적인 업데이트가 행해져야 하는지 여부를 묻는 것이 핵심이므로 Yes라고 답한 후, 현재의 소프트웨어가 최신 버전이라고 덧붙여 준 (C)가 정답이 된다. (A)는 update와 발음이 유사한 up-to-date가 쓰인 오답이고, software를 들었을 때 연상되는 installation을 이용한 (C) 역시 연상어 오류이다.

be supposed to ~하도록 되어 있다 regularly 주기적으로 up-to-date 최신의 installation 설치

PART 3

Questions 32-34 refer to the following conversation. 미M 영W

M Hi, I'm here to sign up for a race-walking you're holding next month. I saw your poster and it said that I could come here to the community sports center. Who should I speak to?

W Originally we were planning to have registration here but it has been moved to the community college on Main Street, two blocks from here. We posted the new flyers with the corrected information but there must've been some old ones left. Sorry for the inconvenience.

M No problem. Actually my office is near the community college so I can stop by on my way back to work. By the way, could I get some extra leaflets with the accurate information? Some friends of mine are also interested.

남 안녕하세요. 다음 달 열리는 경보 대회에 등록하려고요. 이 주민 체육관으로 오면 된다고 적혀 있는 포스터를 봤거든요. 누구와 얘기해야 할까요?

여 원래는 등록을 이곳에서 받으려고 했으나 여기에서 두 블록 떨어진 메인 가의 전문대로 옮겼습니다. 저희가 정정된 정보가 있는 전단을 붙였는데 아마도 예전 것이 남아 있었나 보네요. 불편을 드려 죄송합니다.

남 괜찮아요. 실은 제 사무실이 그 전문대와 가까이 있어서 회사로 돌아가는 길에 들르면 됩니다. 그나저나, 그 바뀐 정보가 들어 있는 여분의 전단을 얻을 수 있을까요? 제 친구들 몇 명도 관심이 있거든요.

race-walking 경보 originally 원래 flyer (광고, 안내용) 전단 corrected 수정된, 정정된 inconvenience 불편 stop by ~에 들르다 on one's way to ~에 가는 길에 leaflet (광고, 안내용) 전단 accurate 정확한

32 Why did the man visit the community sports center?
(A) To report a lost item
(B) To participate in an event
(C) To volunteer for a carnival
(D) To ask for directions

남자는 왜 주민 체육관을 방문했는가?
(A) 분실된 물건을 신고하려고
(B) 행사에 참가하려고
(C) 카니발에 자원 봉사하려고
(D) 길 안내를 요청하려고

도입부 남자의 대사 I'm here to sign up for a race-walking에서 경보 대회 신청 목적임을 알 수 있고 정답 표현은 participate in an event로 패러프레이징되었다.

33 What is the man instructed to do?
(A) Enroll in a college course
(B) Exercise on a regular basis
(C) Go to another place
(D) Distribute some flyers

남자는 무엇을 하도록 지시받는가?
(A) 대학 과정에 등록하기
(B) 주기적으로 운동하기
(C) 다른 장소로 가기
(D) 전단지 배부하기

남자가 지시를 받는 내용은 여자가 지시하는 내용이므로 정답은 여자 대사에 있다. 원래의 등록 장소는 커뮤니티 센터였으나 전문대로 변경되었다는 여자의 대사에서 남자가 해야 할 일은 (C)임을 확인한다.

34 What does the man ask for?
(A) A city map
(B) A registration form
(C) A list of participants
(D) Updated information
남자는 무엇을 요청하는가?
(A) 도시 지도
(B) 등록 용지
(C) 참가자 명단
(D) 개정된 정보

남자 대사에서 요청 표현과 함께 leaflets with the accurate information을 추가로 달라고 했으므로 정답은 (D)가 된다. 정답의 타이밍은 남자 대사에서 Could I라는 요청 표현이 등장할 때 잡는다.

Questions 35-37 refer to the following conversation. 미W 미M

W Hey, Dennis, I'm working on the flower decorations for the company banquet tomorrow night. But, I can't find any lilies.
M There are none left in the store because we didn't receive any deliveries yesterday.
W Oh no. The client requested white and yellow lilies, and I can't finish the decorations without them.
M Well, Let me call our shop on Broadway and ask them if they can send us the flowers we need.

여 Dennis, 지금 내일 밤 있을 회사 연회에 쓸 꽃 장식을 만들고 있는데요, 백합을 하나도 찾을 수가 없어요.
남 우리가 어제 배송을 받지 못했기 때문에 가게에는 남는 게 하나도 없죠.
여 어쩌죠. 고객이 흰색과 노란색 백합을 요청해서 그것들이 없이는 이 장식을 마칠 수가 없어요.
남 음, 제가 브로드웨이 가에 있는 우리 상점에 전화해서 그들이 그 꽃을 보내 줄 수 있는지 알아볼게요.

work on ~에 대한 작업을 하다 flower decorations 꽃 장식 banquet 연회 lily 백합 request 요청하다

35 Where most likely do the speakers work?
(A) At a delivery company
(B) At a jewelry shop
(C) At a party planning firm
(D) At a florist shop
화자들은 어디에서 일할 것 같은가?
(A) 배송 회사
(B) 보석상
(C) 파티 기획사
(D) 꽃 가게

직장을 묻는 질문은 화자들의 업무 내용으로부터 유추한다. 도입부 여자 대사에서 working on the flower decorations를 듣고 꽃 장식을 만드는 곳은 꽃 가게임을 유추할 수 있다.

36 What problem does the woman mention?
(A) A client complained about the service.
(B) A party has been postponed.
(C) A delivery was late.
(D) Some work has not been completed.
여자는 어떤 문제점을 언급하는가?
(A) 고객이 서비스에 관하여 불평을 했다.
(B) 파티가 연기되었다.
(C) 배달이 늦었다.
(D) 업무가 완료되지 않았다.

여자가 언급하는 문제점은 반드시 여자 대사에서 공략한다. I can't finish the decorations without them을 듣고 진행 중인 업무를 끝낼 수 없는 것이 문제임을 알 수 있다. 부정적인 표현 I can't finish 등과 함께 문제점이 언급된다는 것을 기억하자.

37 Why will the man make a phone call?
(A) To request more supplies
(B) To cancel an order
(C) To apologize for a mistake
(D) To confirm the address
남자는 왜 전화를 걸 것인가?
(A) 물품을 더 요청하려고
(B) 주문을 취소하려고
(C) 잘못에 대해 사과하려고
(D) 주소를 확인하려고

남자 대사에서 전화를 하겠다는 let me call이 들리고, 우리가 필요한 꽃을 보내 줄 수 있는지 알아본다는 부분에서 (A)가 정답임을 알 수 있다.

Questions 38-40 refer to the following conversation. 영M 영W

M Hi, I'm calling because the safe in my room seems to be broken. The lock doesn't open when I dial the combination. Could you send someone to fix it?
W I'm sorry for the inconvenience. I'll send someone from housekeeping. What's your room number?
M It's room 1804. Could you do it right away please? I'm leaving for a conference in a minute. And I'd rather not leave my room with a broken safe. I just put my valuables in it.

남 여보세요, 제 방의 금고가 고장 나서 전화드립니다. 다이얼로 비밀번호를 돌렸을 때 자물쇠가 열리지 않네요. 누군가를 보내서 고쳐 주시겠습니까?
여 불편을 드려 죄송합니다. 제가 객실 관리부에서 사람을 보내겠습니다. 객실 번호가 어떻게 되시죠?
남 1804호입니다. 지금 바로 해주실 수 있을까요? 컨퍼런스 때문에 곧 나가야 하는데 금고가 망가진 채로 방을 나가고 싶지 않아서요. 귀중품을 방금 그 안에 넣어 두었거든요.

safe 금고 broken 망가진 lock 자물쇠 combination (자물쇠를 열 수 있는) 번호 right away 당장 valuables 귀중품

38 What problem does the man report?
(A) He's locked out of his room.
(B) The Internet connection is not working.
(C) A window is stuck.
(D) A safe is broken.
남자는 무슨 문제를 보고하는가?
(A) 그가 방문을 밖에서 잠가서 안으로 들어갈 수 없다.
(B) 인터넷 연결이 되질 않는다.
(C) 창문이 끼어서 열리지 않는다.
(D) 금고가 망가졌다.

남자의 문제점은 남자 대사에서 공략한다. 대화 도입부에 남자가 방 안의 금고가 고장 나서 전화를 한다는 부분이 정답이다. 부정어 broken이 문제점에 대한 단서가 된다.

39 What does the woman say she will do?
(A) Replace a device
(B) Do some errands
(C) Send a maintenance person
(D) Arrange for transportation
여자는 무엇을 할 것이라고 말하는가?
(A) 장비 교체하기
(B) 심부름 하기
(C) 수리 기사 보내기
(D) 교통편 준비하기

여자가 말하는 본인의 향후 행동이므로 여자 대사 중 I'll이 들렸을 때가 정답 타이밍이다. 객실 관리부에서 사람을 보내겠다고 했으므로 (C)가 정답이다.

40 Why does the man want the problem to be solved quickly?
(A) He cannot get into his room.
(B) He is storing some valuables.
(C) He is having some guests over.
(D) He has to catch a flight soon.
남자는 왜 문제가 빨리 해결되기를 원하는가?
(A) 그는 방안으로 들어갈 수가 없다.
(B) 그는 귀중품을 보관하고 있다.
(C) 그는 손님이 오기로 되어 있다.
(D) 그는 곧 비행기를 타야만 한다.

남자가 Could you do it right away please?라고 언급했을 때가 정답 타이밍이다. 망가진 금고를 둔 채로 방을 나갈 수 없고, 귀중품을 넣어 두었기 때문이라고 했으므로 정답은 (B)가 된다.

Questions 41-43 refer to the following conversation. 미M 영W

M Hi. Yesterday I made a reservation for dinner at 6 o'clock Saturday night, under the name of Andrew Myers.
W Hi, Mr. Myers. Yes, I can see on the list that you've booked a table for three for Saturday. Do you want to confirm your reservation?
M Actually, I'm calling to see if you could change the reservation from a party of three to six.
W Well, the restaurant's always very busy on Saturday night and we don't have any larger tables available until 7:30. Would you like to come then?

남 여보세요, 어제 제가 Andrew Myers 이름으로 토요일 밤 6시에 저녁 예약을 했습니다.
여 안녕하세요, Myers 씨. 네, 리스트에 당신이 토요일에 3인석 테이블을 예약했다고 확인됩니다. 예약을 확인하고 싶으세요?
남 실은, 그 예약을 3명에서 6명으로 바꿀 수 있는지 알아보려고 전화했어요.
여 음, 저희 레스토랑은 토요일 밤은 항상 매우 바쁘기 때문에 7시 30분이 되어야 더 큰 테이블이 이용 가능합니다. 그럼 그때 오시겠어요?

make a reservation 예약을 하다 under the name of (보통 예약 시) ~라는 이름으로 book 예약하다 a party of ~의 일행

41 Where does the woman work?
(A) At a restaurant
(B) At an airport
(C) At a hotel
(D) At a coffee shop
여자는 어디에서 일하는가?
(A) 레스토랑
(B) 공항
(C) 호텔
(D) 커피숍

여자의 직장을 유추하는 문제이다. 도입부에서 남자가 토요일 6시로 저녁 예약을 했다는 말을 여자에게 하고 있다는 사실에서 여자는 레스토랑 직원임을 바로 유추할 수 있다.

42 Why is the man calling?
(A) To book a hotel room
(B) To confirm a flight booking
(C) To ask for directions
(D) To change a reservation
남자는 왜 전화하는가?
(A) 호텔 방을 예약하려고
(B) 비행 예약을 확인하려고
(C) 길 안내를 요청하려고
(D) 예약을 바꾸려고

전화 목적을 묻는 질문의 답은 보통 도입부에 등장하지만, 여자가 예약 확인을 하기 위해 전화했는지 물었을 때 남자가 예약 인원을 3명에서 6명으로 바꾸고 싶다고 했으므로 기존의 예약을 변경하기 위한 목적인 (D)가 정답이 된다.

43 What alternative does the woman offer the man?
(A) Visiting on a different day
(B) Informing him if there is a cancellation
(C) Coming in at a later time
(D) Eating in an outdoor dining area
여자는 남자에게 어떤 대안을 제안하는가?
(A) 다른 날에 방문하는 것
(B) 취소가 있는 경우에 남자에게 알려 주는 것
(C) 더 늦은 시간에 오는 것
(D) 야외 식사 장소에서 먹는 것

세부 사항 문제로 키워드 alternative와 여자 대사에서 정답이 나올 것임을 미리 파악한다. 여자 대사에서 남자가 원하는 큰 테이블은 더 늦은 시간대에 이용 가능하다고 말한 후 Would you like to come then? 이라고 했을 때 더 늦은 시간대에 오라는 제안임을 알 수 있으며 정답은 (C)가 된다.

Questions 44-46 refer to the following conversation. 영M 미W

M Excuse me. Can I get some help with my medication? I have trouble selecting a proper pain killer for myself since there are so many different kinds on the shelves. I just don't know which would work best for me.

W I'd like to help but what I do here is stock the shelves. You'd better talk to one of our pharmacists. Go down the aisle and you'll see one at the back counter.

M Oh, actually I didn't see anybody at the counter when I was there just a minute ago.

W They might have gone into the back room to fill a prescription. I'll have them paged and tell them a customer's waiting right away.

남 실례합니다. 제 약과 관련해서 도움을 좀 받을 수 있을까요? 선반에 너무 많은 종류가 있어서 저한테 맞는 진통제를 고르기가 어렵네요. 어떤 것이 가장 효과가 있을지 모르겠어요.

여 도와 드리고 싶지만 저는 여기에서 선반에 재고를 채우는 일을 합니다. 우리 약사들 중 한 분에게 얘기하시는 것이 좋겠어요. 통로를 따라 가면 뒤쪽 카운터에 한 분이 계실 거예요.

남 실은 방금 전에 그곳에 있었는데 카운터에서 아무도 보질 못했는데요.

여 처방전 약을 짓기 위해 뒤쪽 사무실에 들어갔을지도 모르겠네요. 바로 호출해서 고객이 기다리신다고 전하겠습니다.

medication 약, 약품 have trouble -ing ~하는 데 어려움을 겪다 select 선택하다, 고르다 proper 적합한, 적절한 pain killer 진통제 work (약 등이) 효과가 있다 pharmacist 약사 aisle 통로 fill a prescription 처방전대로 약을 짓다 page 호출하다

44 What does the man want?

(A) A receipt for his purchase
(B) Directions to a drugstore
(C) A recommendation
(D) A reduced rate

남자는 무엇을 원하는가?

(A) 구매 영수증
(B) 약국으로 가는 방법
(C) 추천
(D) 할인된 가격

남자가 원하는 것은 남자 대사에서 공략한다. 대화의 도입 부분에 남자가 본인에게 맞는 진통제가 어떤 것인지 모르겠다고 말하는 부분에서 '약 추천'을 원한다는 것을 알 수 있으므로 정답은 (C)이다.

45 What does the woman suggest the man do?

(A) Get a prescription
(B) Try a new remedy
(C) Fill out a form
(D) Consult another employee

여자는 남자에게 무엇을 하라고 제안하는가?

(A) 처방전 받기
(B) 새로운 약 써 보기
(C) 양식 작성하기
(D) 다른 직원과 상담하기

여자의 대사에서 정답이 나오지만 선택지 중에서 남자가 할 일을 고르는 질문으로 여자 대사에서 상대방에게 제안을 할 때 쓰는 표현인 You'd better가 들릴 때 정답을 처리한다. You'd better talk to one of our pharmacists(약사 중 한 명에게 얘기하는 게 좋겠다)라고 했으므로 답은 (D)가 된다.

46 What will the woman most likely do next?

(A) Make an announcement
(B) Issue a coupon
(C) Offer a map
(D) Page a colleague

여자는 다음에 무엇을 할 것 같은가?

(A) 공지하기
(B) 쿠폰 발행하기
(C) 지도 제공하기
(D) 동료 호출하기

대화의 흐름과 연계하여 후반부에 정답이 나오는 향후 행동을 묻는 질문이다. 남자가 약사를 한 명도 보지 못했다는 상황에서 여자가 할 일은 I'll have them paged라는 말을 듣고 약사에게 호출을 할 것이라고 예상할 수 있다. 사역동사 have의 목적어로 them(=pharmacists)이 쓰였고 호출을 받는 대상이므로 과거분사 paged를 사용한 것이다. 토익 리스닝에 자주 등장하는 사역동사를 직청직해할 수 있도록 다시 한 번 문장 구조를 복습하자.

Questions 47-49 refer to the following conversation. 영W/미M

W Caleb, how do you like the new project management software? I heard it has scheduling tools which can be used to sequence project activities and assign dates.

M Actually it's very user-friendly. The instructions are so easy to follow that I'm already used to the program. But, it's still taking me some time to enter all the information on our current renovation projects into the computer.

W You know our new assistant is starting work on Thursday. If the program is not too complicated to use, why don't you train her to enter all the data? Then you can concentrate on the Boston Hotel renovation project.

여 Caleb, 새로운 프로젝트 관리 소프트웨어에 대해 어떻게 생각하세요? 제가 듣기로는 프로젝트 활동을 순서대로 배열하고 날짜를 배정하는 데 사용할 수 있는 스케줄링 기능이 있다고 하던데요.

남 실제로 사용이 매우 편리합니다. 설명을 따라 하기가 쉬워서 전 이미 그 프로그램에 익숙해졌어요. 그러나 현재 우리가 진행하는 리노베이션 프로젝트의 정보를 컴퓨터에 입력하는 일은 여전히 시간이 오래 걸립니다.

여 신입 조수가 목요일에 일을 시작하잖아요. 프로그램이 사용하기에 너무 복잡하지 않다면, 그녀가 데이터를 입력하도록 교육하면 어떨까요? 그러면 당신은 보스턴 호텔 리노베이션 프로젝트에 전념할 수 있을 겁니다.

sequence 순서대로 배열하다 user-friendly 사용이 쉬운 current 현재의 administrative assistant 행정 조수 complicated 복잡한 concentrate on ~에 집중하다

47 Where most likely do the speakers work?
(A) At a software company
(B) At a computer repair shop
(C) At an architectural firm
(D) At a travel agency
화자들은 어디에서 일할 것 같은가?
(A) 소프트웨어 회사
(B) 컴퓨터 수리점
(C) 건축 회사
(D) 여행사

화자의 직장을 유추하는 문제로 도입부에 보통 정답의 단서가 등장한다. 화자들의 업무 내용은 남자 대사 중 our current renovation projects를 들었을 때, 리노베이션을 하는 건축 회사로 유추할 수 있다.

48 What is the advantage of the new software?
(A) It is easy to use.
(B) It is reliable.
(C) It is inexpensive
(D) It is fast.
새로운 소프트웨어의 이점은 무엇인가?
(A) 사용하기 편하다.
(B) 믿을 수 있다.
(C) 저렴하다.
(D) 빠르다.

소프트웨어의 장점을 찾는 문제로 user-friendly, the instructions are easy to follow 등을 통해 (A)가 정답임을 알 수 있다.

49 What will happen on Thursday?
(A) A welcome reception will be held.
(B) A new employee will arrive.
(C) An expert will hold a seminar.
(D) A new task will be assigned.
목요일에 무엇이 일어날 것인가?
(A) 환영회가 열릴 것이다.
(B) 새로운 직원이 도착할 것이다.
(C) 전문가가 세미나를 열 것이다.
(D) 새로운 업무가 배정될 것이다.

질문 속의 힌트는 Thursday로, 새로운 조수가 목요일에 일을 시작한다는 부분에서 정답을 (B)로 선택한다.

Questions 50-52 refer to the following conversation. 미W 미M

W Hi, Peter. I heard you recently started your own catering company. How's it going?
M Um... It has been quite slow because we just depended on referrals from friends and acquaintances at the beginning. But now, I'm planning to post an on-line advertisement and provide regular customers with more benefits. I hope that it will bring us more business.
W I'm sure it will. And maybe I can help too. My company is planning a farewell party for my boss. I'd be happy to mention your company to the organizer and suggest we hire you to prepare food and drink.

여 안녕, 피터. 당신이 최근에 출장뷔페 업체를 시작했다는 소식을 들었어요. 어떻게 되어 가나요?
남 음… 사업 초기에 친구들과 지인들로부터 추천을 받는 것에만 의존해서인지 그동안 저조했어요. 그러나 이제, 온라인 광고를 올리고 단골 고객들에게는 더 많은 혜택을 주려고 합니다. 그것이 더 많은 고객을 불러오기를 바라고 있고요.
여 분명히 그럴 거예요. 그리고 저도 도울 수 있어요. 회사가 저의 상사를 위해 송별회를 계획하고 있는데 기획자에게 당신네 회사에 대해 얘기하고 음식과 음료 준비를 하는 데 당신을 고용하자고 제안할게요.

recently 최근에 catering company 출장 뷔페 업체 referral 추천 regular customer 단골 고객 farewell 작별 organizer (행사의) 기획자, 조직자

50 What kind of business does the man own?
(A) A catering service
(B) An advertising firm
(C) A marketing company
(D) A web design company
남자는 어떤 종류의 사업체를 소유하고 있는가?
(A) 출장 뷔페 업체
(B) 광고 회사
(C) 마케팅 회사
(D) 웹 디자인 회사

남자가 소유한 사업체를 묻는 질문으로 여자가 you recently started your own catering company라고 언급할 때 남자는 출장 뷔페 업체를 소유하고 있음을 확인한다.

51 What does the man say about his business?
(A) It will participate in a bid.
(B) It has hired an advertising agent.
(C) Its sales have been down.
(D) It is opening another branch.
남자는 그의 사업에 대해 뭐라고 말하는가?
(A) 입찰에 참여할 것이다.
(B) 광고 대리인을 고용했다.
(C) 매출이 저조했다.
(D) 다른 매장을 연다.

질문의 포인트는 남자가 본인의 사업에 대해 언급하는 내용이 정답이라는 점이다. 남자 대사에서 It has been quite slow라고 말했을 때 이미 판매가 저조했다는 답이 나온 것이므로 (C)를 정답으로 처리한다.

52 What does the woman offer to do?
(A) Help organize an event
(B) Recommend the man's business
(C) Arrange a meeting
(D) Write a review
여자는 무엇을 해 주겠다고 하는가?
(A) 행사 조직 돕기
(B) 남자의 업체 추천하기
(C) 회의 준비하기
(D) 후기 쓰기

여자가 남자를 위해서 해 주겠다고 언급하는 것이 정답이 된다. 그러므로 I'd be happy to(기꺼이 ~하겠다)라고 말하는 부분을 주의 깊게 듣는다. 남자의 업체를 고용하자는 제안을 하겠다고 했으므로 정답은 (B)이다.

Questions 53-55 refer to the following conversation. 미W 영M

W We have unloaded the last box from the truck, Mr. Carson. My team members are unpacking the pads used to protect your office furniture during the move.
M Oh, I appreciate all your hard work, Ms. Lopez. The move went smoothly as your team worked very efficiently.
W You're welcome. By the way, where would you like this last box to go? There's no label on it that says where it should go.
M Um... I think some extra office supplies are in it. Can you put it in the storage room at the end of the hall please?

여 Carson 씨, 트럭에서 마지막 상자를 내렸습니다. 저의 팀원들이 지금 이사 중에 사무용 가구를 보호하기 위해 사용했던 패드를 풀고 있습니다.
남 오, 열심히 일해 주셔서 감사합니다, Lopez 씨. 당신의 팀이 일을 효율적으로 해줘서 이사가 순조롭게 진행됐어요.
여 천만에요. 그나저나 이 마지막 박스는 어디에 둘까요? 어디에 놓으라는 라벨이 박스에 붙어 있지는 않네요.
남 음… 그 안에 여분의 사무용품이 있을 거예요. 그 박스를 복도 끝에 있는 창고 안에 넣어 주시겠어요?

unload (짐을) 내리다 unpack (짐을) 풀다 move 이사 go smoothly 순조롭게 진행되다 label 라벨 storage room 창고, 비품실

53 Where does the woman most likely work?
(A) At a moving company
(B) At a financial firm
(C) At an office supply store
(D) At a property development company
여자는 어디에서 일할 것 같은가?
(A) 이삿짐 회사
(B) 금융 회사
(C) 사무용품 상점
(D) 자산 개발 회사

여자의 업무 내용으로 직장을 유추하는 문제로 트럭에서 마지막 박스를 내렸다는 것과 이사 중 가구를 보호했다는 것을 통해 (A)가 정답임을 유추할 수 있다. 이삿짐 회사임을 유추할 수 있는 주요 키워드는 unloaded the last box from the truck, during the move 등이다.

54 What does the man imply when he says, "Oh, I appreciate all your hard work, Ms. Lopez"?
(A) He has received a discount.
(B) He is satisfied with his office relocation.
(C) He wants the woman to try harder.
(D) A renovation project is ahead of schedule.
남자가 "오, 열심히 일해주셔서 감사합니다, Lopez 씨"라고 말한 의도는 무엇인가?
(A) 그는 할인을 받았다.
(B) 그는 사무실 이전에 만족한다.
(C) 그는 여자가 좀 더 노력하기 원한다.
(D) 보수 프로젝트가 일정보다 빠르다.

특정 표현에 대한 화자의 의도를 묻는 질문으로 해당 표현의 앞뒤에서 문맥상의 단서를 찾자. 남자가 여자에게 열심히 일해 준 것에 감사를 표한 후, The move went smoothly as your team worked very efficiently라고 했으므로 정답은 (B)가 된다.

55 What does the woman ask the man about?
(A) How to get to a meeting room
(B) The cost of a special service
(C) Where to place a container
(D) The name of a company
여자는 남자에게 무엇에 관해 묻는가?
(A) 회의실에 가는 방법
(B) 특별 서비스의 비용
(C) 용기를 놓을 장소
(D) 회사의 이름

여자 대사에서 남자에게 질문하는 내용이 정답이 된다. 여자가 '마지막 박스는 어디에 둘까요?'라고 질문하는 부분을 (C) Where to place a container로 바꿔 표현했으므로 정답이다. box가 용기라는 의미의 container로 바꿔 표현된 점을 기억해 두자.

Questions 56-58 refer to the following conversation. 미M 미W

M Good morning. My name is James Ross and I'm the hiring manager at Humax. Thank you for your interest in Humax Incorporated. Take your time to look around our booth. And please let me know if you would like to know more about our job openings.
W Thank you Mr. Ross. I've recently completed my degree in psychology at Sheffield University. And I'm very interested in working in Human Resources. I saw on your website that you're now hiring people for Accounting, Sales and Personnel. How can I apply for the job?
M First, let me ask you a couple of questions. Have you had any relevant experience before?
W Yes, I had a winter internship last year at a Seattle-based headhunting firm. I enjoyed working with many different kinds of people.

남 안녕하세요. 저는 James Ross이고 Humax의 채용 담당자입니다. Humax 사에 관심을 가져 주셔서 감사합니다. 천천히 부스를 살펴보시고 저희 회사의 일자리에 관하여 더 알고 싶으시면 알려 주세요.
여 감사합니다 Ross 씨. 저는 최근에 셰필드 대학에서 심리학 학위를 받았습니다. 그리고 인사부에서 일하는 것에 관심이 있습니다. 회사의 웹 사이트에서 지금 회계, 영업, 인사부 채용을 한다는 광고를 보았습니다. 어떻게 지원을 할 수 있을까요?
남 먼저 제가 두 가지 질문을 드릴게요. 전에 관련된 경력을 쌓은 적이 있나요?
여 네, 작년 겨울에 시애틀에 본사를 둔 헤드헌팅 업체에서 인턴을 했습니다. 다양한 사람들과 함께 일하는 것이 매우 즐거웠습니다.

take one's time 시간을 (여유 있게) 가지다 job opening 일자리 degree 졸업 증서 Human Resources 인사부 Personnel 인사부 relevant experience 관련 경력

56 Why is the woman at the Humax booth?
(A) To attend a meeting
(B) To introduce a product
(C) To get more information
(D) To register for a lecture

여자는 왜 Humax 부스에 있는가?
(A) 회의에 참석하려고
(B) 제품을 소개하려고
(C) 정보를 더 얻으려고
(D) 강의에 등록하려고

질문을 통해 여자가 Humax 부스에 있다는 사실은 미리 파악해두고 그 이유에 집중한다. 도입부 남자의 대사에서 Humax 사의 job openings에 대해 궁금한 부분은 알려달라고 한 부분에서 여자는 일자리에 대해 더 알고자 Humax 부스에 갔음을 알 수 있다.

57 What has the woman recently done?
(A) Worked as a freelancer
(B) Obtained a diploma
(C) Demonstrated a product
(D) Relocated to a new city

여자는 최근에 무엇을 했는가?
(A) 프리랜서로 일했다.
(B) 졸업장을 받았다.
(C) 제품을 시연했다.
(D) 새로운 도시로 이전했다.

질문 속의 키워드인 woman, recently, done 등을 미리 파악해두자. 여자가 I've recently completed my degree in psychology라는 것으로 보아 최근 심리학 학위를 받았음을 알 수 있다.

58 What does the man want to know about?
(A) Relevant licenses
(B) The Interview process
(C) The location of the company
(D) Adequate work experience

남자는 무엇에 대해 알고자 하는가?
(A) 관련 면허
(B) 인터뷰 절차
(C) 회사의 위치
(D) 적절한 업무 경험

남자가 여자에게 질문하는 내용에서 정답을 처리한다. 남자가 여자에게 relevant experience(관련 경력)이 있는지를 물었으므로 이를 adequate work experience라고 바꿔 표현한 (D)가 정답이 된다.

Questions 59-61 refer to the following conversation. 미W 미M

W Hey Martin, Could you please lend me your laptop computer? I think I'm going to need it for my presentation later this afternoon.
M Oh, I thought you were presenting early this morning. Was it postponed?
W Yes. I had to put it off for a few hours because some of our team members were in a meeting with a client to discuss some contract terms. It went longer than expected, but they are on their way back to the office now. So we're meeting at 2 instead.
M Okay, that's no problem. But just remember one thing. Please make sure you log off the computer completely and bring it back to my office when you're finished with it. I'm leaving the office for a doctor's appointment now.

여 저기, Martin, 노트북 컴퓨터를 좀 빌려 주실 수 있나요? 오후에 제 발표 때 필요할 것 같아요
남 당신이 오늘 아침 일찍 발표를 한다고 생각했는데 연기되었나요?
여 네. 저의 팀원 몇몇이 계약서 조항에 대해 논의하기 위해 고객과 회의 중이라 몇 시간 연기해야 했어요. 회의가 예상보다 길어졌지만 지금 사무실로 돌아오는 길이라고 하네요. 그래서 대신 2시에 만나기로 했어요.
남 좋아요, 문제될 것 없죠. 그러나 한 가지는 기억해 주세요. 다 사용하신 후에 반드시 컴퓨터 완전히 로그오프 하시고 제 사무실로 다시 가져다 주세요. 저는 진료 예약 때문에 지금 사무실을 나갈 겁니다.

postpone 연기하다 put off 연기하다 contract terms 계약 조항

59 What does the woman ask permission to do?
(A) Enter a restricted area
(B) Extend a project deadline
(C) Use some equipment for a presentation
(D) Change the time of a meeting

여자는 무엇을 할 수 있는 허락을 요청하는가?
(A) 제한된 지역에 들어가기
(B) 프로젝트 마감 시간 연장하기
(C) 발표할 때 장비 사용하기
(D) 회의의 시간 바꾸기

질문을 통해 여자가 허락을 요청한다는 것은 미리 파악해 두고 여자의 대사에서 컴퓨터를 빌려줄 수 있는지 묻는 부분에서 (C)로 정답을 처리한다. 상대방에게 허가를 구할 때 자주 쓰이는 표현 중 하나로 Could you를 암기해 두자.

60 Why was the woman's presentation rescheduled?
(A) Some reports were incomplete.
(B) An event venue was unavailable.
(C) Some coworkers were in another meeting.
(D) There was a technical malfunction.

왜 여자의 발표는 일정이 변경되었는가?
(A) 일부 보고서가 불완전했다.
(B) 행사의 장소가 이용 불가능했다.
(C) 몇몇 동료가 다른 회의에 있었다.
(D) 기계 오작동이 있었다.

세부 사항 질문으로 여자의 발표 일정이 변경됐다는 사실을 미리 파악해 두고 이유에 집중하면서 듣는다. 질문의 reschedule이라는 어휘가 대화 속에서는 '연기되다'는 의미의 put off로 바뀌 표현되고, 그 이유를 because some of our team members were in a meeting with a client라고 했으므로 동료들이 고객과 미팅을 한 것이 발표 지연의 이유가 된다.

61 What does the man mean when he says, "Okay, that's no problem"?
(A) The woman should attend a meeting.
(B) The woman should make a reservation.
(C) The woman may leave work early.
(D) The woman may borrow his computer.

남자가 "좋아요, 문제될 것 없죠"라고 말한 의미는 무엇인가?
(A) 여자는 미팅에 참석해야 한다.
(B) 여자는 예약을 해야 한다.
(C) 여자는 일찍 퇴근해도 된다.
(D) 여자는 남자의 컴퓨터를 빌려도 된다.

특정 표현에 대한 화자의 의도를 묻는 신토익 유형으로 대화의 문맥을 이해하는 것이 중요하다. "That's no problem"은 상대방의 요청, 부탁 등에 대해 수락할 때 쓰이는 대표적인 표현으로, 대화의 도입부에 여자가 남자의 컴퓨터를 빌릴 수 있는지 물어본 것에 대한 답으로써 "Okay, that's no problem"이 쓰인 것이다. 따라서 정답은 (D)가 된다.

Questions 62-64 refer to the following conversation with three speakers. 영M 미W 미M

M Hi Denise and Mark, thank you for coming. Caroline just called in sick, so we're a little short-staffed this evening. I was wondering if one of you can fill in for her.
W Oh, I'm afraid I can't, Mr. Gaines. I take a business class after work on Tuesdays and Thursdays. But I'll be able to work extra hours tomorrow if you want me to.
M Oh I see. How about you, Mark?
M Well, I'd be happy to work overtime tonight. Should I just work in the main dining room?
M No, Bruce can handle that and I can help out if necessary. Could you work with Sophia to serve food to the guests in the banquet room? There will be a private party there.
M Sure, no problem. I'll go change into my uniform and help Sophia with the seating arrangement.

남1 안녕하세요 Denise, Mark, 와 주셔서 감사합니다. Caroline이 막 병가 신청을 해서 오늘 저녁에 우리가 일손이 부족하네요. 여러분 중 한 명이 그녀는 대신해 줄 수 있을까 해서요.
여 Gaines 씨, 죄송하지만 저는 안 될 것 같아요. 저는 매주 화요일과 목요일에는 퇴근 후에 비즈니스 수업을 듣거든요. 그렇지만 원하시면 내일 추가 근무를 할 수 있어요.
남1 아, 그렇군요. Mark는 어때요?
남2 음, 제가 오늘 밤 추가 근무를 기꺼이 하겠습니다. 메인 식당 홀에서 일하면 될까요?
남1 아니요, Bruce가 거기를 맡을 것이고 필요하면 제가 도울 것입니다. 당신은 Sophia와 함께 연회실에서 손님들에게 서빙을 해 주시겠어요? 그곳에서 프라이빗 파티가 있을 거예요.
남2 그럼요, 문제없습니다. 유니폼으로 갈아 입고 나서 Sophia가 좌석 배치하는 것을 돕겠습니다.

call in sick 병가 신청 전화를 하다 short-staffed 일손이 부족한 fill in for ~를 대신하다 work extra hours 추가 근무를 하다 work overtime 추가 근무를 하다 change into ~으로 갈아입다 seating arrangement 좌석 배치

62 What problem is being discussed?
(A) Some ingredients are missing.
(B) A class has been cancelled.
(C) An employee is out sick.
(D) A customer has complained.

어떤 문제점이 이야기 되고 있는가?
(A) 일부 재료가 없다.
(B) 수업이 취소되었다.
(C) 직원이 아파서 결근했다.
(D) 고객이 불평을 했다.

직원이 병가를 내서 일손이 부족하다고 언급하는 부분을 듣고 정답을 (C)로 선택한다. 동의어 표현에 해당하는 call in sick과 be out sick를 반드시 암기해 두자.

63 What does the woman mean when she says, "Oh, I'm afraid I can't, Mr. Gaines"?
(A) She cannot cover for her coworker.
(B) She has not made a reservation.
(C) She is unavailable to attend a meeting.
(D) She cannot reschedule an event.

여자가 "Gaines 씨, 죄송하지만 저는 안 될 것 같아요"라고 말한 의미는 무엇인가?
(A) 여자는 동료를 대신할 수 없다.
(B) 여자는 예약을 하지 못했다.
(C) 여자는 미팅에 참석할 시간이 없다.
(D) 여자는 행사의 일정을 바꿀 수 없다.

남자가 병가 낸 직원을 대신해 줄 수 있는지를 물었고 이에 대한 답으로서 Oh, I'm afraid I can't라고 말했으므로 정답은 (A)가 된다. '동료를 대신하다'는 의미로 fill in for와 cover for가 사용되었다.

64 What will Mark most likely do next?
(A) Prepare some food
(B) Contact a coworker
(C) Seat some customers
(D) Put on a uniform

Mark는 이후에 무엇을 할 것 같은가?
(A) 음식 준비하기
(B) 동료에게 연락하기
(C) 고객들 앉히기
(D) 유니폼 입기

3인 대화에서는 이름을 파악해 두는 것이 중요하다. Mark는 남자 대화자 중 한 명으로 대화의 마지막 부분에 I'll go change into my uniform이라며 유니폼으로 갈아 입겠다고 했으므로 정답은 (D)가 된다.

Questions 65-67 refer to the following conversation and list.
영M 영W

M Jennifer, we have a new researcher starting on Monday next week. And I need you to order a new desk for him.
W Sure, Mr. Parker. But did you know that our supplier has raised their prices recently?
M No. In that case, could you ask them if they have any alternative to the wooden desks we've been using?
W Oh, actually I have their price list right here with me. Well, our budget for each new employee is $400 maximum, right? As you can see, there are two desk options that are within our budget.
M OK, let's order the metal one then.

Material	Price
MDF	$250
metal	$380
Rubberwood	$420
Mahogan	$550

남 Jennifer, 다음 주 월요일에 새로운 연구원이 일을 시작합니다. 그래서 그를 위해 책상을 주문해 주셨으면 해요.
여 알겠습니다, Parker 씨. 그런데 최근에 우리 공급업체에서 가격을 올렸다는 걸 알고 계신가요?
남 아니요. 그런 경우라면, 우리가 이용해오던 나무 책상에 대한 대안이 있는지 물어봐 주시겠어요?
여 아, 실은 제가 가격표를 지금 가지고 있어요. 신입 사원 한 명에 대한 예산이 최대 400달러 맞죠? 보시다시피, 예산에 맞는 책상이 두 종류가 있어요.
남 좋아요, 그럼 저 철제 책상을 주문합시다.

재질	가격
MDF	250달러
철제	380달러
고무나무	420달러
마호가니	550달러

supplier 공급업체 alternative 대안 price list 가격표 budget 예산 option 선택 사항 within budget 예산에 맞는

65 What does the man ask the woman to do?
(A) Contact her supervisor
(B) Repair some equipment
(C) Order some office furniture
(D) Find a new supplier

남자는 여자에게 무엇을 하라고 요청하는가?
(A) 그녀의 상사에게 연락하기
(B) 장비 수리하기
(C) 사무 가구 주문하기
(D) 새로운 공급업체 찾기

남자 대사에서 여자에게 요청하는 내용을 파악하는 문제로 남자가 I need you to~(당신이 ~을 해 주길 바란다)라는 표현이 들렸을 때 정답은 책상을 주문해 주는 것임을 알 수 있다. 그러므로 (C)가 정답이다.

66 What problem does the woman mention?
(A) A product is out of stock.
(B) A vendor has increased its prices.
(C) A researcher has made a mistake.
(D) A budget proposal is incomplete.

여자는 어떤 문제점을 언급하는가?
(A) 상품이 재고가 없다.
(B) 공급업체가 가격을 인상했다.
(C) 연구원이 실수를 했다.
(D) 예산안이 완성되지 않았다.

여자의 대사에서 언급되는 부정적인 내용을 찾아 듣자. 책상을 주문해야 하는 상황에서 공급업체가 가격을 인상했다고 언급한 부분이 정답이 된다. (B)가 정답으로 대화 속의 supplier는 vendor로 바뀌 표현된 점을 기억하자.

67 Look at the graphic. How much will the speakers pay for a desk?
(A) $250
(B) $380
(C) $420
(D) $550

시각 정보를 보시오. 화자들은 책상에 얼마를 지불할 것인가?
(A) 250달러
(B) 380달러
(C) 420달러
(D) 550달러

시각 정보를 참고하여 문제를 푸는 신토익 유형이다. 해당 리스트의 내용을 미리 파악해 둔 후 리스트에서 화자들이 최종적으로 선택한 철제 책상의 리스트에서 확인하여 (B) 380달러를 정답으로 선택한다.

Questions 68-70 refer to the following conversation and directory. 미W 영M

W Hey Frank, did you hear that the plant manager is looking for someone to fill in for Pete Declan in the Production department? He is leaving the factory.

M Oh, really? Actually, I'm pretty interested in working on a production line myself. The work may be more challenging, but I can get paid more.

W That's right. Production line employees receive hazard pay in addition to their regular pay for performing hazardous duties. But I'm not sure about the exact pay rate.

M Me, neither. Hmm... I think I should talk to Mr. Graham about the open position in more detail. Do you know his extension?

W Wait. I'll look it up in the directory. Here, try this number.

M Thanks, Melissa. I owe you one.

Company Directory	
Name	Extension
Andrew Graham	1
Elizabeth White	9
Nora Wong	11
Tyler Chang	15

여 안녕 Frank, 공장 매니저가 생산 부서의 Pete Declan의 자리를 채우려고 사람 구한다는 거 들었어요? 그가 공장을 그만둔대요.

남 아, 진짜요? 실은 제가 생산라인에서 일하는 것에 관심이 있어요. 일은 좀 더 어려울 수 있지만 돈을 더 벌 수 있잖아요.

여 그건 맞아요. 생산라인 직원들은 봉급뿐만 아니라 위험한 업무를 하는 것에 대해 위험 수당을 받거든요. 그렇지만 정확한 시간당 급여는 잘 모르겠어요.

남 저도요. 흠… 제가 Graham 씨에게 이 공석에 대해서 더 자세하게 물어보는 게 좋겠어요. 그의 내선번호 알아요?

여 잠깐만요. 전화번호부에서 찾아볼게요. 여기, 이 번호로 해 보세요.

남 고마워요, Melisa. 제가 신세졌네요.

회사 전화번호부	
이름	내선번호
Andrew Graham	1
Elizabeth White	9
Nora Wong	11
Tyler Chang	15

production line 생산 라인 challenging 어려운, 힘든 get paid 급여를 받다 hazard pay 위험 수당 in addition to ~뿐만 아니라 hazardous duty 위험한 업무 pay rate 시간당 급여 in detail 자세하게 extension 내선번호

68 Which department is looking to fill a vacancy?
(A) Sales
(B) Production
(C) Human Resources
(D) Marketing

어떤 부서가 공석을 채우려고 하는가?
(A) 판매
(B) 생산
(C) 인사
(D) 마케팅

세부 사항 질문으로 질문을 읽고 특정 부서에 공석이 있다는 점을 미리 파악하자. 대화의 도입부에 공장 매니저가 Production department 직원을 대신할 사람을 찾고 있다고 했으므로 정답은 (B) 생산 부서가 된다. 'fill in for + 사람'은 '~를 대신하다' 의미로 자주 사용되므로 반드시 암기해 두자.

69 What does the woman say about production line workers?
(A) They have to wear protective gear.
(B) They are skilled workers.
(C) They are required to work overtime.
(D) They get paid well.

여자는 생산 라인 직원들에 대해서 뭐라고 하는가?
(A) 그들은 안전 장비를 착용해야만 한다.
(B) 그들은 숙련된 일꾼들이다.
(C) 그들은 초과 근무할 것이 요구된다.
(D) 그들은 급여를 많이 받는다.

여자의 대사에서 정답을 찾는 질문으로 키워드는 production line workers가 된다. 생산 라인 직원들은 월급뿐만 아니라 hazard pay(위험 수당)도 받는다고 언급했으므로 정답은 (D)가 된다.

70 Look at the graphic. What number will the man most likely call?
(A) 1
(B) 9
(C) 11
(D) 15

시각 정보를 보시오. 남자는 어떤 번호로 전화할 것 같은가?
(A) 1
(B) 9
(C) 11
(D) 15

시각 정보를 참고하여 문제를 푸는 신토익 유형이다. 남자가 대화 후에 전화할 번호를 찾는 질문으로 남자가 여자에게 Graham 씨의 내선번호를 묻는 부분에서 전화번호부를 참고한다. Andrew Graham의 내선번호는 1번이므로 정답은 (A)가 된다.

PART 4

Questions 71-73 refer to the following telephone message. (미M)

Hi Ms. Florence. This is Larry Conwell from Conwell Property. I'm calling about an apartment that I think you might be interested in. It has two bedrooms and a large kitchen and living room facing the river. It is fully furnished and the best part is that the bathroom has recently been renovated. I'd be happy to show you this property if you want. Please call me at 555-0879 to set up an appointment. Thank you.

안녕하세요 Florence 씨. Conwell Property의 Larry Conwell입니다. 당신이 관심을 보일만한 아파트에 관해서 전화를 드립니다. 침실 2개와 큰 부엌 겸 거실이 강을 바라보고 있습니다. 가구가 완비되어 있고 가장 좋은 점은 최근에 욕실이 수리 보수되었다는 것입니다. 원하신다면 기꺼이 이 집을 보여 드리겠습니다. 약속을 잡으시려면 555-0879로 저에게 전화를 주십시오. 감사합니다.

facing ~쪽을 향하는　be furnished 가구가 비치되다　property 부동산
set up (약속 등을) 잡다, 정하다

71 Where most likely does the speaker work?
(A) At a furniture store
(B) At a real estate agency
(C) At a moving company
(D) At an interior design firm

화자는 어디에서 일할 것 같은가?
(A) 가구점
(B) 부동산
(C) 이삿짐 회사
(D) 실내 디자인 회사

전화 메시지 유형에서 화자의 직장을 유추할 때는 도입 부분을 잘 듣자. 이름과 함께 본인의 소속을 from Conwell Property라고 밝히는 부분에서 property(부동산) 관련 회사임을 빠르게 유추할 수 있다.

72 What does the speaker mention about the property?
(A) It has a parking lot.
(B) It is not available.
(C) It is in a good location.
(D) It has a nice view.

화자는 해당 부동산에 관하여 무엇을 언급하는가?
(A) 주차장이 있다.
(B) 이용할 수 없다.
(C) 좋은 위치에 있다.
(D) 전망이 좋다.

해당 부동산에 대해 언급되는 내용은 모두 정답의 가능성이 있으므로 미리 보기의 내용을 읽어두고 일치하는 정보가 나오면 바로 정답으로 처리한다. a large kitchen and living room facing the river(강을 바라보는 부엌 겸 거실)가 있다는 부분이 a nice view로 바꿔 표현되었으므로 정답은 (D)이다.

73 What has recently been renovated?
(A) A balcony
(B) A bathroom
(C) A kitchen
(D) A bedroom

최근에 무엇이 개조되었는가?
(A) 발코니
(B) 욕실
(C) 부엌
(D) 침실

질문의 키워드인 recently, renovated에 집중하여 정답을 파악하는 세부 사항 문제이다. bathroom has recently been renovated, 즉 욕실이 최근 개조되었다고 들리는 부분을 순발력 있게 정답으로 처리한다.

Questions 74-76 refer to the following introduction. (영W)

Good evening, ladies and gentlemen. Welcome to Alexandria Library. This is the third in our series of lectures on effective tax strategies. Tonight, we're very lucky to have as a guest speaker, Adrianne McCoy. Ms. McCoy has worked as a tax specialist accountant for 17 years and she has recently published a book titled *Minimizing Taxes, Preserving Wealth.* Tonight, she's going to share with us simple tips and tools to minimize paying taxes and saving more money. But first, I'd like to let you know that today's lecture will be recorded and posted on our website. So if you want to listen to it again later, just visit the library's website at www.alexandrialibrary.com.

신사 숙녀 여러분, 안녕하세요. Alexandria 도서관에 오신 것을 환영합니다. 이것은 효과적인 세금 전략에 관한 강의 시리즈의 세 번째 강연입니다. 오늘 밤, 초청 연사이신 Adrianne McCoy를 모실 수 있게 되어 행운입니다. McCoy 씨는 세금 전문 회계사로서 17년간 일해 왔고, 최근에 〈Minimizing Taxes, Preserving Wealth〉라는 제목의 책을 출간하셨습니다. 오늘 밤, 그녀는 세금을 최소화하고 더 많은 돈을 저축할 수 있는 간단한 방법을 공유해 주실 겁니다. 그러나 우선, 오늘의 강의가 녹화되어 도서관 웹 사이트에 게시될 것임을 알려 드립니다. 따라서 나중에 다시 듣길 원하신다면, www.alexandrialibrary.com으로 도서관의 웹 사이트를 방문하십시오.

series of lectures 시리즈 강연　strategy 전략　specialist 전문가
accountant 회계사　minimize 최소화하다

74 Where is the event taking place?
(A) At a government office
(B) At a financial convention
(C) At a library
(D) At a job fair

행사는 어디에서 일어나고 있는가?
(A) 관공서
(B) 재무 컨벤션
(C) 도서관
(D) 직업 박람회

장소를 유추하는 질문으로 'welcome to + 장소'처럼 장소를 바로 알려 주는 힌트어는 반드시 암기하자.

75 What is the topic of the presentation?
(A) How to develop tax strategies
(B) How to travel on a small budget
(C) How to write a best-selling book
(D) How to plan for retirement
발표의 주제는 무엇입니까?
(A) 세금 전략 개발하는 방법
(B) 적은 예산으로 여행하는 방법
(C) 베스트셀러 책 쓰는 방법
(D) 은퇴를 위해 계획하는 방법

세부 사항 질문으로 질문의 키워드 presentation이 들릴 때 발표의 주제도 함께 나온다. 지문 중 our series of lectures on effective tax strategies처럼 '~에 관한'이라는 의미의 전치사 on이 붙고 주제가 나온다.

76 According to the speaker, what will be available online?
(A) A list of new publications
(B) A recording of the lecture
(C) Adrianne McCoy's columns
(D) Photographs of the event
화자에 따르면, 무엇이 온라인에서 이용 가능하게 될 것인가?
(A) 출간물의 명부
(B) 강의의 녹화
(C) Adrianne McCoy의 칼럼
(D) 행사의 사진

세부 사항 질문으로 질문의 키워드 online을 미리 파악해둔다. 오늘의 강연이 녹화되고 웹 사이트에 게시된다고 했으므로 정답은 (B)가 된다.

Questions 77-79 refer to the following excerpt from a meeting.
영M

Good morning everyone. I have an important reminder about tomorrow morning's fire evacuation drill for the entire factory. We hold fire drills every 6 months, but this time the regional safety inspectors will be present. Since your performance in a drill will be evaluated, it is extremely important that you follow the emergency guidelines exactly. Now, please take a close look at the evacuation plan we've handed out. Please make sure that you know which exit is nearest to your workstation and how to move there when you hear the alarm tomorrow.

안녕하세요 여러분. 내일 아침에 있을 공장 전체 화재 대피 훈련에 대한 중요한 공지 사항이 있습니다. 우리는 6개월에 한 번씩 화재 대피 훈련을 실시하는데 이번에는 지역 안전 감독관들이 참석을 하게 됩니다. 훈련 중 여러분의 수행 능력이 평가될 것이므로, 비상사태 지침을 정확하게 따르는 것이 매우 중요합니다. 이제, 나누어 드린 대피 계획을 면밀히 검토해 주십시오. 여러분의 작업장과 가장 가까운 출구가 어디인지 반드시 숙지하고 내일 경보를 들었을 때 어떻게 그 출구까지 갈 수 있는지 알아두십시오.

reminder 상기시켜주는 것 fire evacuation drill 화재 대피 훈련 regional 지역의 inspector 검사관, 감독관 performance 수행 extremely 매우 workstation 작업장

77 What will take place tomorrow morning?
(A) Installation of equipment
(B) A factory renovation
(C) An annual road clean-up
(D) An emergency drill
내일 아침에 무엇이 일어날 것인가?
(A) 장비의 설치
(B) 공장 보수 공사
(C) 연례 도로 대청소
(D) 비상 훈련

세부 사항 질문으로 tomorrow morning이라는 시점을 미리 파악해 둔다. 도입 부분에 tomorrow morning's fire evacuation drill이 언급되었을 때, 내일 아침에 화재 대피 훈련이 있을 것임을 알 수 있고 이를 an emergency drill로 바꿔 표현한 (D)가 정답이다.

78 According to the speaker, who will visit the factory?
(A) Electricians
(B) Inspectors
(C) Firefighters
(D) Union delegates
화자에 따르면, 누가 공장을 방문할 것인가?
(A) 전기 기사
(B) 검사관
(C) 소방관
(D) 조합 대표

세부 사항 질문으로 공장에 방문할 사람에 대한 정보를 순발력 있게 정답으로 연결하는 것이 핵심이 된다. 질문의 visit이란 단어는 '참석하다'는 의미의 be present로 바꿔 표현되면서 safety inspectors(안전 검사관)들이 언급됐으므로 정답은 (B)가 된다.

79 What are employees instructed to do?
(A) Complete a check list
(B) Distribute a manual
(C) Inspect some machines
(D) Read an evacuation plan
직원들은 무엇을 하라는 지시를 받는가?
(A) 검사 목록 완료하기
(B) 설명서 배부하기
(C) 기계 검사하기
(D) 대피 계획 읽기

화자의 대사 중 청자들에게 요청 혹은 권고하는 표현과 함께 정답의 단서가 나온다. 이 지문에서는 상대방에게 요청할 때 가장 자주 등장하는 please와 함께 take a close look at the evacuation plan(대피 계획을 면밀히 검토하라)이라고 했으므로 (D)가 정답이다.

Questions 80-82 refer to the following announcement. (미W)

Welcome to the Oakwood Theater. I'd like to inform you that tonight's special performance is the premiere of the new play written by the famous local playwright, Benjamin Han. In order to celebrate this special occasion, we invite the audience to the after-party, which will be held in the garden. All the actors, actresses and Mr. Han will be there to talk about the play with you. Now everybody, enjoy the show.

Oakwood 극장에 오신 것을 환영합니다. 오늘 밤의 특별 공연은 이 지역 출신의 유명한 극작가 Benjamin Han이 쓰신 새 연극의 초연임을 알려 드립니다. 이 특별 행사를 축하하기 위해서, 관객들을 정원에서 열리는 공연 후 파티에 초대합니다. 모든 배우, 여배우 및 Han 씨께서도 참석하여 여러분과 연극에 대한 이야기를 나눌 것입니다. 자 여러분, 이제 공연을 즐기세요.

premiere 초연, 첫 공연 playwright 극작가 celebrate 축하하다 occasion 행사 after-party 행사 후의 사교모임

80 Where does the announcement most likely take place?
(A) In a museum
(B) In a bookstore
(C) In a theater
(D) In a radio studio

공지는 어디에서 발생할 것 같은가?
(A) 박물관
(B) 서점
(C) 극장
(D) 라디오 스튜디오

장소를 유추하는 질문은 'welcome to + 장소'가 들릴 때 순발력 있게 정답을 처리한다. 장소가 Oakwood Theater이므로 정답은 (C)가 된다.

81 According to the speaker, who is Benjamin Han?
(A) A producer
(B) A conductor
(C) An actor
(D) A playwright

화자에 따르면, Benjamin Han은 누구인가?
(A) 프로듀서
(B) 지휘자
(C) 배우
(D) 극작가

질문 속에 이름을 키워드로 주고 직업을 선택하도록 하는 세부 사항 문제를 풀 때는 한 가지만 기억해 두자. 사람의 이름과 직업은 함께 언급되기 때문에 이름 전, 후에 반드시 직업이 따라 나온다. by the famous local playwright, Benjamin Han을 들었을 때 Benjamin Han의 직업은 playwright(극작가)임을 바로 알 수 있으므로 정답은 (D)이다.

82 What are listeners told to do after the show?
(A) Reserve a seat
(B) Speak with the performers
(C) Attend a meeting
(D) Watch a movie

청자들은 공연 후에 무엇을 하라고 요청받는가?
(A) 좌석 예약하기
(B) 공연자들과 대화하기
(C) 회의에 참석하기
(D) 영화 보기

질문의 키워드 after the show를 반드시 미리 파악해두자. 청중을 the after-party(행사 후 사교 모임)에 초대한다고 언급하고 그곳에 배우와 극작가들이 참석하여 연극에 대해 얘기 나눌 것이라 했으므로 정답은 (B)가 된다.

Questions 83-85 refer to the following introduction. (영M)

Ladies and Gentlemen, welcome to the 26th Annual IMC Marketing Conference. I'm sure this two-day conference will give you the opportunity to advance your career and acquire new skills in marketing and advertising. Our first presenter is Dr. Abigail Evans, a prominent marketing expert. Her talk today will focus on how to get your brand recognized by using a creative website and logo. She is going to explain a marketing strategy that will more effectively deliver clients. Following her talk, there will be a question and answer session. So please hold your questions until the end. Now everyone, please give Dr. Evans a warm welcome.

신사 숙녀 여러분, 26번째 연례 IMC 마케팅 컨퍼런스에 오신 것을 환영합니다. 저는 이틀간의 컨퍼런스가 여러분에게 마케팅 홍보 분야에서 새로운 스킬을 획득하고, 경력을 발전시킬 수 있는 기회를 제공하리라 확실합니다. 첫 번째 발표자는 저명한 마케팅 전문가 중 한 분이신 Abigail Evans 박사입니다. 오늘 연설은 창의적인 웹 사이트 및 로고를 사용해서 어떻게 여러분의 브랜드를 인식하게 만들 것인지에 대해 초점을 맞출 것입니다. 또한 고객을 효과적으로 창출하는 마케팅 전략에 대해 설명해 주실 겁니다. 연설 후에는 질의응답 시간이 있을 예정입니다. 그러니 그때까지 질문은 참아 주세요. 자 그럼 여러분, Evans 박사를 따뜻하게 환영해 주세요.

opportunity to ~하는 기회 advance 발전시키다 acquire 획득하다 presenter 발표자 prominent 저명한 expert 전문가 focus on ~에 초점을 맞추다 recognize 인식하다 creative 창의적인 deliver a client 고객을 창출하다 question and answer session 질의응답 시간 hold 보유하다, 가지고 있다

83 What kind of event is taking place?
(A) An opening ceremony
(B) An annual conference
(C) An awards dinner
(D) A company outing

어떤 종류의 행사가 일어나고 있는가?
(A) 개회식
(B) 연례 컨퍼런스
(C) 시상식 만찬
(D) 회사 야유회

도입 부분의 welcome to the 26th Annual IMC Marketing Conference를 들으면 연례 컨퍼런스가 열리고 있음을 알 수 있으므로 (B)가 정답이다.

84 What is Dr. Evans famous for?
(A) Receiving a prestigious award
(B) Having written a series of books
(C) Developing a successful marketing strategy
(D) Expanding her own business overseas

Evans 박사는 무엇으로 유명한가?
(A) 명망 있는 상을 받은 것
(B) 책 시리즈를 쓴 것
(C) 성공적인 마케팅 전략을 개발한 것
(D) 해외로 자신의 사업을 확장한 것

질문의 키워드는 Dr. Evans, famous를 들을 때 Evans 박사가 잘 알려진 이유를 노려 듣는다. 도입부에 초청 연사로 Dr. Evans가 언급되고 저명한(prominent) 마케팅 전문가 중 한 명으로 소개된 후 고객을 창출하는 마케팅 전략에 대해 강의하겠다고 했으므로 정답은 (C)이다.

85 What does the speaker mean when he says, "So please hold your questions until the end"?
(A) The audience should not interrupt the speaker.
(B) The audience should not leave their seats.
(C) The audience should applaud the speaker.
(D) The audience should answer some questions.

남자가 "그러니 그때까지 질문은 참아 주세요"라고 말한 의미는 무엇인가?
(A) 청중은 연사를 중단시키지 않아야 한다.
(B) 청중은 자리를 뜨지 않아야 한다.
(C) 청중은 연사에게 박수를 보내야 한다.
(D) 청중은 질문에 대답해야 한다.

화자의 의도를 묻는 신유형 질문이다. 해당 표현 바로 앞에 Following her talk, there will be a question and answer session을 통해 연설 후에는 질의 응답 시간이 있다는 것을 알 수 있다. 그러므로 화자가 그때까지(until then) 질문은 참아 달라고 말한 의도는 연설 중에는 질문으로 연사를 중단시키지 말라는 당부이므로 정답은 (A)이다.

Questions 86-88 refer to the following talk. 미M

I hope you all enjoyed your first self-defense martial arts class. During this three month program, we will cover all kinds of self-defense techniques, which are simple yet effective. Now, there's just one more thing we'd like you to do before you leave. I'm going to hand out a questionnaire, which is composed of 10 questions. Please fill it in and write your comments about the session. We value your feedback and any ideas you might have for future exercise classes. Also, we're starting to offer yoga and pilates classes starting next month. So if you would like to learn more about our new classes, please put your e-mail address on the form as well. We're going to send out the complete schedule for next month in a week.

여러분 모두 첫 호신 무술 수업이 즐거우셨기를 바랍니다. 이 3개월 프로그램 동안, 간단하지만 효과적인 온갖 종류의 호신 기술을 다루게 될 것입니다. 이제 여러분이 가시기 전에 한 가지 더 해주셔야 하는 일이 있습니다. 제가 10개의 질문으로 구성된 설문지를 나눠 드릴 것입니다. 그것을 채우시고 수업에 대한 의견을 써 주십시오. 저희는 여러분의 피드백과 앞으로의 수업에 대한 어떤 아이디어도 중요하게 생각합니다. 또한, 다음 달부터 저희가 요가와 필라테스 수업을 시작하게 됩니다. 그러니 새로운 수업에 대해서 더 알고 싶으시다면, 이 양식에 이메일 주소도 적어 주시기 바랍니다. 일주일 후에 다음 달 스케줄을 보내 드리겠습니다.

self-defense 자기 방어 martial arts 무술 effective 효과적인 hand out 나누어 주다 questionnaire 질문지, 설문지 fill in 기입하다, 입력하다

86 What have the listeners been learning?
(A) Writing techniques
(B) Advanced culinary skills
(C) Pencil drawing
(D) Martial arts for self defense

청자들은 무엇을 배우고 있는가?
(A) 글쓰기 기술
(B) 고급 요리 기술
(C) 연필화
(D) 호신 무술

지문의 첫 문장에서 청자들에게 your first self-defense martial arts class를 즐기셨기를 바란다고 했으므로, 청자들이 배우고 있는 것은 호신 무술 수업이 된다.

87 What are listeners asked to do?
(A) Complete a questionnaire
(B) Request a class schedule
(C) Exercise every day
(D) Apply for a membership

청자들은 무엇을 하도록 요청 받는가?
(A) 설문지 완성하기
(B) 강의 스케줄 요청하기
(C) 매일 운동하기
(D) 멤버십 신청하기

화자가 요청을 하는 내용을 고르는 질문으로 questionnaire (설문지)를 나눠주겠다고 한 후 Please fill it in이라고 요청하였으므로 설문지를 채우라는 것이 정답이 된다.

88 Why would listeners provide an e-mail address?
(A) To participate in a competition
(B) To receive some information
(C) To register for an exercise class
(D) To view some photos of an event

청자들은 왜 이메일 주소를 제공하겠는가?
(A) 대회에 참가하려고
(B) 정보를 받으려고
(C) 운동 수업에 등록하려고
(D) 행사의 사진을 보려고

질문 속의 키워드는 provide an e-mail address이고 이메일 주소를 달라는 내용이 나오면 그 이유가 주변에 등장하게 되어 있다. 여기서는 if 절로 단서를 붙여서, 우리의 새로운 수업에 대해서 더 알고 싶다면(if you would like to learn more about the new classes) 이메일 주소를 써 달라고 했으므로 정답은 (B)가 된다.

Questions 89-91 refer to the following telephone message. 영W

Hello, Mr. Hudson. This is Jenny Biles calling from TBI Bank. I received your inquiry about your enrollment in TBI's online banking service. Let me explain how it works. First, your activation code was just sent to your home address and you should receive it in the mail within five days. When you receive the code, you must enter it into our online banking system within 30 days. Then, you'll have full access to our online banking. In the meantime, you can set up a password on our website. It will give you immediate but limited access, allowing you to check your balances and bank statements. If you have any questions, please contact me at 555-8510. Thank you.

안녕하세요, Hudson 씨. TBI 은행의 Jenny Biles입니다. TBI의 온라인 은행 서비스 등록에 관한 귀하의 문의 사항을 잘 받았습니다. 어떻게 진행되는지 설명을 해 드릴게요. 고객님의 생성 코드가 집 주소로 막 보내졌고, 5일 안에 우편으로 받게 되실 겁니다. 코드를 받으시면, 반드시 30일 내에 저희 온라인 뱅킹 프로그램에 그것에 입력해 주셔야 합니다. 그러면, 온라인 뱅킹 업무에 대한 전체 권한을 얻게 됩니다. 그 동안 저희 웹 사이트에 비밀번호를 설정해 주세요. 그 비밀번호가 즉각적이지만 제한된 권한을 주어, 잔액과 은행 거래 내역을 조회할 수 있게 됩니다. 질문이 있으시면, 555-8510로 저에게 연락 주십시오. 감사합니다.

inquiry 문의 (사항) enrollment 등록, 신청 activation code 활성화 코드, 생성 코드 enter 입력하다 set up 만들다, 설정하다 immediate 즉각적인 limited 제한된 balance 잔액 bank statement 은행 거래 내역

89 What did Mr. Hudson ask about?
(A) Online banking enrollment
(B) A high-interest savings account
(C) Directions to the nearest branch
(D) A lost credit card

Hudson 씨는 무엇에 대해 문의했는가?
(A) 온라인 뱅킹 등록
(B) 고리 저축 예금
(C) 가장 가까운 지점에 가는 법
(D) 분실된 신용 카드

Hudson 씨가 문의한 내용을 묻는 질문으로 도입 부분에서 your inquiry about your enrollment in TBI's online banking service를 들었을 때 온라인 뱅킹 신청에 관한 문의임을 알 수 있다. 정답은 (A)가 된다.

90 What does the woman mean when she says, "Let me explain how it works"?
(A) She will assemble some equipment.
(B) She will send a repair person.
(C) She will offer detailed instructions.
(D) She will explain the hiring process.

여자가 "어떻게 진행되는지 설명을 해 드릴게요"라고 말한 의미는 무엇인가?
(A) 기기를 조립할 것이다.
(B) 수리 기사를 보낼 것이다.
(C) 상세한 안내를 제공할 것이다.
(D) 고용 절차를 설명할 것이다.

화자의 의도를 묻는 신유형 질문으로 해당 표현 주변에 단서가 있다. 첫 문장에서 온라인 뱅킹 신청에 관한 내용임을 할 수 있고 Let me explain how it works(어떻게 진행되는지 설명해 주겠다)라고 말한 후 순차적인 가입 방법을 설명하고 있으므로 정답은 (C)가 된다. 또한 Let me explain how it works라는 표현 자체가 상세한 설명을 하기 앞서 일반적으로 사용된다는 것을 암기해 두자.

91 What does the speaker say about a password?
(A) It must be updated every month.
(B) It is required to transfer funds.
(C) It can be used to check balances.
(D) It should be memorable.

화자는 비밀번호에 관하여 무엇을 말하는가?
(A) 매달 갱신되어야 한다.
(B) 돈을 이체할 때 요구된다.
(C) 잔액을 확인할 때 이용될 수 있다.
(D) 기억이 잘 나야 한다.

질문의 키워드인 password가 언급되는 주변에 정답이 있는 세부 사항 질문이다. password를 만들라는 언급과 함께 비밀번호로 잔액 확인과 은행 내역서 조회가 가능하다고 했으므로 정답은 (C)가 된다.

Questions 92-94 refer to the following talk and chart. 미M

Thank you for attending our first official meeting since I took on the role of sales director at Aqua Drinks Company. I'm glad that I have the opportunity to meet you all today. But first, we need to focus on the task at hand. Our last quarter's sales were the lowest ever. And as you can see from the chart, our major competitor ranked first with the largest market share at 42% for the first time last quarter and our company's market share was the second largest. In order to regain our No. 1 soft drink company title, I think we should release our new line of flavored lemonades earlier than scheduled. Originally, they weren't scheduled to come on the market until July 10th. But with increased productivity, we'll be able to move up the release date to June 20th. So everybody, let's do everything we can to make the launch a success.

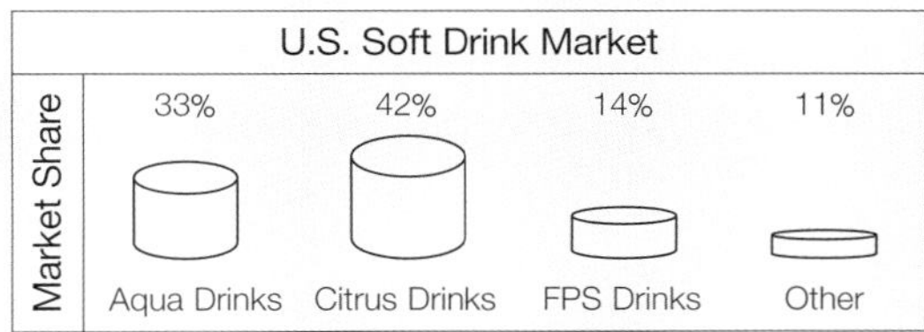

제가 Aqua Drinks 사의 영업 부서장을 맡은 후 첫 공식 회의에 참석해 주셔서 감사합니다. 오늘 여러분 모두를 만나게 되어 기쁩니다. 그러나 우선, 당장 급한 업무에 집중할 필요가 있습니다. 지난 분기의 판매는 지금까지 중에서 가장 낮았습니다. 그리고 차트에서 보시다시피, 주요 경쟁사는 지난 분기에 최초로 42퍼센트라는 시장 점유율로 1위를 차지하였고 우리의 시장 점유율은 2위였습니다. 다시 우리의 1위 청량음료 회사라는 타이틀을 되찾기 위해서는, 신상품인 레모네이드를 예정보다 일찍 출시하는 것이 좋을 것 같습니다. 원래는 7월 10일이 되어야 시장에 나올 예정이었지만 생산력 증가와 함께, 6월 20일로 출시 날짜를 앞당길 수 있을 것 같습니다. 자 여러분, 성공적인 출시를 하기 위해 모든 노력을 기울입시다.

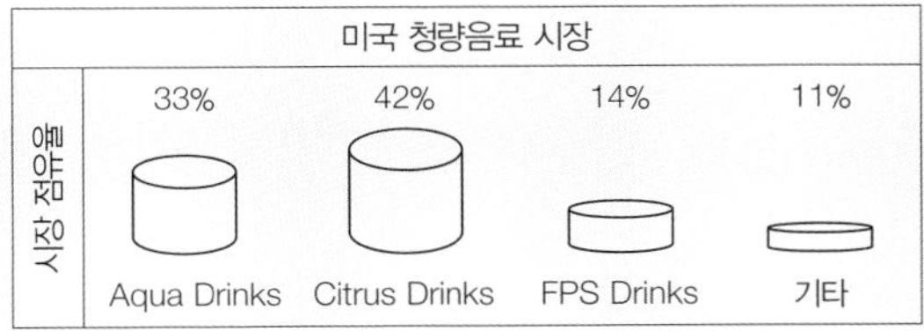

take on (일, 책임 등을) 맡다 official 공식적인 task 업무 at hand 가까운, 급한 competitor 경쟁자, 경쟁사 rank first 1위를 차지하다 market share 시장 점유율 for the first time 최초로 increased productivity 증가된 생산력 move up 앞당기다 release date 출시 날짜 launch 출시

92 Which department does the speaker work in?
(A) Sales
(B) Advertising
(C) Personnel
(D) Product development

화자는 어떤 부서에서 일하는가?
(A) 영업
(B) 광고
(C) 인사
(D) 상품 개발

화자의 부서를 묻는 질문으로 보통 도입부에 유추할 수 있는 근거가 제시된다. 화자가 sales director (영업 부서장)의 역할을 맡은 후 첫 공식 미팅이라고 했으므로 정답은 (A)임을 알 수 있다.

93 Look at the graphic. How much market share did the man's company have last quarter?
(A) 11%
(B) 14%
(C) 33%
(D) 42%

시각 정보를 보시오. 남자의 회사는 지난 분기에 얼마의 시장 점유율을 보였는가?
(A) 11퍼센트
(B) 14퍼센트
(C) 33퍼센트
(D) 42퍼센트

시각 정보를 이용하는 신유형 질문으로 키워드인 남자의 회사 시장 점유율을 놓치지 않고 듣는 것이 중요한 전략이 된다. our major competitor ranked first with the largest market share at 42% for the first time last quarter and our company's market share was the second largest를 통해 남자의 경쟁사는 점유율이 42퍼센트이고 남자의 회사는 두 번째로 높은 33퍼센트의 점유율을 차지했음을 알 수 있다.

94 According to the speaker, what will happen on June 20th?
(A) A merger will take place.
(B) The division head will get a promotion.
(C) A new product will be introduced.
(D) Employees will submit proposals.

화자에 따르면, 6월 20일에 무슨 일이 일어날 것인가?
(A) 합병이 일어날 것이다.
(B) 부서장이 승진될 것이다.
(C) 신제품이 소개될 것이다.
(D) 직원들이 제안서를 제출할 것이다.

질문의 키워드인 June 20th에 집중하여 정보를 듣자. we'll be able to move up the release date to June 20th를 듣고 6월 20일로 출시 날짜가 앞당겨졌음을 알 수 있고 정답은 (C)가 된다.

Questions 95-97 refer to the following talk and schedule. (미W)

Before we break for lunch at noon, I'd like to go over our afternoon agenda. First, Caitlin will present the field test results on our new image editing software at 1 o'clock sharp. So everybody, please be punctual. After Caitlin's presentation, we will split into small groups to discuss possible solutions to the negative feedback we received from some of the testers. Then we're going to have a quick coffee break at...... Uh-oh, I just noticed an error in your printed programs. It says that coffee break is scheduled at 1:30 and the group discussion is at 3. However, they are actually in reverse order. Group discussions will take place before the coffee break. Sorry about the mistake. And finally at 3:30, Douglas Park will briefly recap what we have discussed today.

Program	
Lunch	12:00–1:00
Caitlin Stewart	1:00–1:30
Coffee break	1:30–3:00
Group discussion	3:00–3:30
Douglas Park	3:30–4:00

정오에 점심 시간을 갖기 앞서, 오후 일정을 설명해 드리겠습니다. 먼저 1시 정각에 Catlin이 새로운 이미지 편집 소프트웨어에 대한 현장 테스트 결과를 발표할 것입니다. 그러니 여러분 반드시 시간을 엄수해 주세요. Catlin의 발표 후에, 우리는 소규모 그룹으로 나누어 상품 테스터들로부터 받은 부정적인 피드백에 대한 해결책을 논의할 것입니다. 그 다음에 잠깐의 휴식 시간이…… 오 저런, 여러분의 일정표에 실수가 있다는 걸 방금 보았네요. 일정표에는 휴식이 1시 30분으로 잡혀 있고 그룹 토론이 3시로 되어 있는데 사실은 거꾸로 되어야 합니다. 그룹 토론이 휴식보다 먼저 진행될 것입니다. 실수가 있어 죄송합니다. 그리고 마지막으로 3시 30분에, Douglas Park 씨가 오늘 우리가 논의했던 내용을 간단하게 요약해 줄 것입니다.

일정표	
점심	12:00–1:00
Caitlin Stewart	1:00–1:30
휴식	1:30–3:00
그룹 토론	3:00–3:30
Douglas Park	3:30–4:00

go over 검토하다, 설명하다 field test (상품의) 현장 테스트 sharp 정각에 punctual 시간을 지키는 split into ~으로 나누다 in reverse order 거꾸로 recap 요약하다

95 What are listeners asked to do at 1 o'clock?
(A) Provide feedback on a new product
(B) Break for lunch
(C) Analyze some data from customers
(D) Attend a presentation on time

청자들은 1시에 무엇을 하라고 요청받는가?
(A) 신상품에 대하여 피드백 주기
(B) 점심 시간 가지기
(C) 고객으로부터의 정보 분석하기
(D) 발표에 늦지 않게 참석하기

요청되는 것을 찾는 세부 사항 질문이므로 요청 표현과 1 o'clock에 집중하여 듣는다. 1시 정각에 Catlin이 발표를 할 것이라고 말한 후 please be punctual(시간을 엄수해 주세요)이라고 했으므로 정답은 (D)가 된다.

96 What does the speaker mention about small group discussions?
(A) Solutions will be discussed.
(B) Testers will be selected.
(C) Interviews will be conducted.
(D) Errors will be corrected.

화자는 소규모 그룹 토론에 대하여 무엇을 언급하는가?
(A) 해결책이 논의될 것이다.
(B) 테스터들이 선정될 것이다.
(C) 면접이 진행될 것이다.
(D) 오류가 정정될 것이다.

세부 사항 질문으로 키워드인 small group discussions에 대한 내용에 집중하여 정답을 고른다. small groups로 나누어 부정적인 평가에 대한 possible solutions를 논의할 것이라고 했으므로 정답은 (A)가 된다. 오답 보기의 경우, 정답 주변에 쓰인 testers, error 등의 단어를 이용한 함정이 된다.

97 Look at the program. When will listeners actually have a coffee break?
(A) At 1:00
(B) At 1:30
(C) At 3:00
(D) At 3:30

일정표를 보시오. 청자들은 실제로 언제 휴식 시간을 갖게 될 것인가?
(A) 1시
(B) 1시 30분
(C) 3시
(D) 3시 30분

시각 정보를 활용한 신토익 유형이다. 일정표에 실수가 있다는 부분을 집중하여 단서를 찾는다. 일정표에는 휴식이 1시 30분, 그룹 토론이 3시로 되어 있다고 언급한 후, However, they are actually in reverse order(실제로는 순서가 거꾸로이다)라고 정정했으므로 휴식은 3시에 갖게 된다. 정답은 (C)이다.

Questions 98-100 refer to the following message and list. (영W)

Hello, Mr. Sydney. This is Clara calling from Green Wise Landscaping. As you requested, I faxed our price list for bare root trees to you this morning. You said you were particularly interested in oak trees for your back yard but we carry many different types of oak trees and the prices vary. Our regular price for trees from 6 to 8 inches ranges from $30 to $60. However, you can get a 10% discount on all the items on the list right now except for the first one. You can also buy mature oak trees, which are larger than 10 feet, but they can start at $1000 or more. If you're interested in mature oak trees, please let me know. I'd be happy to send you another price list with that information.

Bare Root Prices		
Plant	Size	Price
Black Oak	6 in	$60
Chestnut Oak	6 in	$30
Bur Oak	8 in	$60
Red Oak	6 in	$30

안녕하세요 Sydney 씨. 저는 GreenWise Landscaping의 Clara입니다. 요청하신 것처럼, 저희 모종 나무 가격표를 아침에 팩스로 보내드렸습니다. 뒤뜰에 심을 떡갈나무에 특히 관심이 있다고 하셨는데 저희는 다양한 종류의 떡갈나무를 취급하고 있으며 가격이 다양합니다. 6인치에서 8인치 되는 나무의 경우 보통 가격이 30달러에서 60달러 정도입니다. 그러나 지금은 첫 번째 품목 외에는 리스트에 있는 전 품목에 대해서 10퍼센트 할인을 받을 수 있습니다. 10피트가 넘는 다 큰 떡갈나무 역시 구매할 수 있지만 가격이 1,000달러에서 시작해 더 오를 수 있습니다. 만약 다 자란 떡갈나무에 관심이 있으시다면, 저에게 알려 주세요. 그 정보가 들어 있는 다른 가격표를 보내 드리겠습니다.

모종 나무 가격		
식물	사이즈	가격
큰떡갈나무	6 in	60달러
떡갈밤나무	6 in	30달러
북미 중부 동부산 오크	8 in	60달러
북가시나무	6 in	30달러

bare root tree 묘목, 모종 나무 particularly 특히 carry ~을 취급하다 range from A to B 범위가 A에서 B까지이다 regular price 정가 mature 성숙한, 다 자란

98 What kind of business is the woman calling from?
(A) A delivery company
(B) An office supplies store
(C) A real estate agency
(D) A landscaping firm

여자는 어떤 종류의 업체로부터 전화하는가?
(A) 배달 회사
(B) 사무용품 상점
(C) 부동산
(D) 조경 회사

화자의 직장을 유추하는 질문으로 전화 메시지의 경우 도입부에 본인을 소개하는 부분에 정답의 힌트가 있다. This is Clara calling from GreenWise Landscaping을 통해 화자는 조경 회사 소속임을 알 수 있다. 소속을 나타낼 때 사용되는 전치사 from을 기억해 두자. 정답은 (D)이다.

99 Look at the graphic. Which oak tree has not gone down in price?
(A) Black
(B) Chestnut
(C) Bur
(D) Red

시각 정보를 보시오. 어떤 떡갈나무의 가격이 내려가지 않았는가?
(A) 큰떡갈나무
(B) 떡갈밤나무
(C) 북미 중부 동부산 오크
(D) 북가시나무

시각 정보를 활용한 신토익 유형으로 질문에서 가격이 내려가지 않은 떡갈나무의 종류를 물었으므로 할인과 관련된 표현에 집중해서 듣는다. 떡갈나무의 일반 가격을 언급한 후 리스트 상 첫 번째 품목 외에는 할인을 받을 수 있다고 했으므로(you can get a 10% discount on all the items on the list right now except for the first one) 가격이 낮아지지 않은 나무는 black oak가 된다. 정답은 (A)이다.

100 What should Mr. Sydney do if he is interested in mature oak trees?
(A) Send a price estimate
(B) Contact the company
(C) Plant some trees
(D) Apply for a membership

다 자란 떡갈나무에 관심이 있다면 Sydney 씨는 무엇을 해야 하는가?
(A) 가격 견적서 보내기
(B) 업체에 연락하기
(C) 나무 심기
(D) 멤버십 신청하기

세부 사항 질문으로 mature oak trees에 관심이 있을 경우에 해당하는 정보를 잘 듣는다. 다 자란 떡갈나무에 대한 가격을 언급한 후 이에 관심이 있다면 please let me know(내게 알려달라)라고 했으므로 정답은 (B)가 된다.

Actual Test 5

PART 1

본책 p.60

1 (D)	2 (A)	3 (A)	4 (C)	5 (C)	6 (C)

PART 2

본책 p.64

7 (C)	8 (A)	9 (C)	10 (A)	11 (A)	12 (A)
13 (B)	14 (A)	15 (B)	16 (A)	17 (C)	18 (C)
19 (A)	20 (B)	21 (A)	22 (C)	23 (B)	24 (B)
25 (B)	26 (A)	27 (C)	28 (A)	29 (B)	30 (A)
31 (C)					

PART 3

본책 p.65

32 (A)	33 (C)	34 (A)	35 (D)	36 (B)	37 (B)
38 (C)	39 (A)	40 (B)	41 (D)	42 (A)	43 (B)
44 (B)	45 (B)	46 (D)	47 (B)	48 (A)	49 (D)
50 (D)	51 (A)	52 (B)	53 (B)	54 (B)	55 (C)
56 (C)	57 (D)	58 (A)	59 (B)	60 (D)	61 (D)
62 (C)	63 (A)	64 (B)	65 (A)	66 (C)	67 (C)
68 (D)	69 (C)	70 (B)			

PART 4

본책 p.69

71 (C)	72 (A)	73 (A)	74 (B)	75 (D)	76 (A)
77 (A)	78 (C)	79 (A)	80 (C)	81 (D)	82 (A)
83 (B)	84 (A)	85 (C)	86 (D)	87 (B)	88 (D)
89 (C)	90 (A)	91 (B)	92 (B)	93 (B)	94 (D)
95 (B)	96 (A)	97 (D)	98 (B)	99 (C)	100 (B)

PART 1

1 (A) The people are baking some bread.
영M (B) Various pots are on display in a store.
(C) Some jars are stacked on the table.
(D) A table is covered with tablecloth.

(A) 사람들이 빵을 굽고 있다.
(B) 여러 가지 화분들이 상점에 진열되어 있다.
(C) 항아리들이 테이블 위에 쌓여 있다.
(D) 테이블이 테이블보로 덮여 있다.

야외 식당으로 유추되는 곳에 테이블 위에 테이블보가 덮인 채로 항아리, 화분, 빵이 놓여 있다. 빵은 이미 구워진 것으로 보이고 화분은 하나만 있다. 정직하게 사진에서 볼 수 있는 것만 판단하면 된다.

bake 굽다 various 다양한, 여러 가지의 pot 화분 on display 진열 중인 jar 항아리, 단지 stack 쌓다 be covered with ~로 덮여 있다 tablecloth 테이블보

2 (A) They are spending time together.
미W (B) They are exchanging their tools.
(C) The girl is handing a boy a shovel.
(D) A picnic bench lies folded on the ground.

(A) 사람들이 함께 시간을 보내고 있다.
(B) 사람들이 서로 도구를 교환하고 있다.
(C) 소녀가 소년에게 삽을 건네고 있다.
(D) 피크닉 벤치는 땅에 접힌 채로 놓여 있다.

모래사장에서 남자 아이와 여자 아이가 놀고 있다. 갖가지 도구들이 흩어져 있지만 서로 주고받고 있지는 않으며 소년 옆에 보이는 의자를 피크닉 벤치로 단정 지을 수 없고 접혀 있지도 않다.

exchange 교환하다, 바꾸다 hand 건네주다 shovel 삽 lie 눕다, 놓여 있다 folded 접힌

3 (A) The man's face is partially shaded.
미M (B) The man is closing the door of the car.
(C) The man is holding the door handle.
(D) The man is getting out of a vehicle.

(A) 남자의 얼굴이 일부만 그늘져 있다.
(B) 남자는 차문을 닫고 있다.
(C) 남자는 문손잡이를 잡고 있다.
(D) 남자는 차에서 내리고 있다.

남자가 팔을 차창에 걸치고 운전석에 앉아 있는데 얼굴은 약간 그늘져 있으므로 (A)가 정답이다. 우연인지 문제를 풀다 보면 그늘이 지거나 그림자가 생기는 상황이 정답인 경우가 많다. 참고로 handle의 정확한 뜻을 알아 두고 자동차의 운전대는 steering wheel임을 기억하자.

partially 부분적으로 shade 그늘지게 하다, 가리다 handle 손잡이 get out of ~에서 내리다, 나가다

4 (A) Some of the microphones are being put away.
영W (B) One of the men is giving a speech inside an auditorium.
(C) Some people on stage are facing the audience.
(D) One of the men has a microphone in his hand.

(A) 몇 대의 현미경이 치워지고 있다.
(B) 한 남자가 강당 안에서 연설을 하고 있다.
(C) 무대에 있는 사람들이 관객을 향하고 있다.
(D) 한 남자가 손에 마이크를 갖고 있다.

한 밴드가 무대에서 공연을 하고 있는데 마이크를 잡고 있는 사람은 없다. 연주를 하는 중이므로 연설을 한다고 보기 어렵고 무대에서 관객석을 향하고 있으므로 (C)가 가장 적절한 설명이다.

microphone 마이크 put away 치우다 give a speech 연설하다 auditorium 강당 stage 무대 face 향하다

5 (A) A man is feeding the horse.
미M (B) Police are assisting in directing traffic.
(C) There is a bystander near the horse.
(D) A horse is stopped at a traffic light.

(A) 남자가 말에게 먹이를 주고 있다.
(B) 경찰들이 교통정리에 도움을 주고 있다.
(C) 말 근처에 행인이 있다.
(D) 말은 신호등 앞에 멈춰 있다.

도심에서 경찰로 보이는 남자가 말을 탄 채로 멈춰 있는데 그 이유는 알 수가 없다. 말 앞쪽으로 다른 곳을 바라보는 행인이 보이므로 가장 적절한 설명은 (C)이다.

feed 먹이다, 먹을 것을 주다 direct traffic 교통정리를 하다 bystander 구경꾼, 행인 traffic light 신호등

6 (A) Some glasses have been left near the monitor.
영W (B) The worker is standing at a sink.
(C) The worker is using a tool on a plate.
(D) The worker is taking off her protective goggles.

(A) 유리잔 몇 개가 모니터 옆에 놓여 있다.
(B) 작업자가 싱크대에 서 있다.
(C) 작업자가 판 위에서 도구를 사용하고 있다.
(D) 작업자가 보호 안경을 벗고 있다.

공장으로 보이는 곳에서 작업자가 보호 안경을 쓰고 작업대 앞에 서 있다. 손에 작은 도구를 쥐고 일하는 중이므로 (C)가 가장 적절한 설명이다. (D)가 정답이 되려면 taking off 대신에 wearing이어야 한다.

plate 판, 접시, 그릇 take off 벗다, 제거하다 protective goggles 보호 안경

PART 2

7 Where is the board meeting being held?
미W (A) A budget report.
영M (B) At 2 o'clock.
(C) On the fifth floor.

이사회 회의는 어디에서 열리나요?
(A) 예산 보고서요.
(B) 2시에요.
(C) 5층에서요.

의문사 where 질문으로 회의가 열리는 장소에 대해 5층이라고 답한 (C)는 정답이고 장소에 대한 개념이 전혀 없는 (A)와 (B)는 답이 될 수 없다.

board meeting 이사회 회의 be held (행사가) 열리다

8 How many firms have you worked for?
미M (A) Just two.
미W (B) I'll look it up in a dictionary.
(C) As a freelancer.

얼마나 많은 회사에서 일해 보셨나요?
(A) 두 곳뿐입니다.
(B) 사전에서 그것을 찾아볼 것입니다.
(C) 프리랜서로요.

의문사 how many 질문으로 지금까지 일해 본 회사가 몇 곳인지를 묻고 있다. (A)처럼 숫자로만 답해주는 경우에는 당연히 정답이 된다. Just two (firms)처럼 회사가 뒤에 생략된 것이다.

firm 회사 freelancer 자유 계약자, 프리랜서

9 Where does Dr. Pullen keep the patient records?
영M (A) Twice a day.
영W (B) Yes, it's not locked.
(C) In the bottom drawer.

Pullen 박사는 어디에 환자 기록을 보관하나요?
(A) 하루에 두 번이요.
(B) 네, 그것은 잠기지 않았어요.
(C) 맨 아래 서랍에요.

의문사 where 질문으로 서류 보관 장소를 물었기 때문에 서랍이라고 답한 (C)가 가장 자연스럽다. (A)는 How often(빈도)을 묻는 질문에 대한 답이고 (B)는 where 의문문에 Yes라고 답하는 것 자체가 불가능하다.

keep 보관하다 patient record 환자 기록 drawer 서랍

10 Why don't we go to the Indian restaurant tonight?
미W (A) That sounds fine to me.
영M (B) Let's meet on Thursday.
(C) I e-mailed her already.

오늘 밤에 인도 음식점에 가는 게 어때요?
(A) 좋습니다.
(B) 목요일에 만납시다.
(C) 제가 그녀에게 이미 이메일을 보냈습니다.

Why don't we는 '~ 하시겠어요?'라는 의미의 제안 표현이다. 정답은 보통 제안에 대한 찬성 혹은 거절인데 (A)는 제안에 대한 찬성 표현으로 자주 등장한다. (B)는 tonight을 들었을 때 연상되는 Thursday를 이용한 오답이다.

11 When will the professor be leaving?
미M (A) This afternoon.
미W (B) For Toronto.
(C) A quite busy schedule.

교수님은 언제 떠나시나요?
(A) 오늘 오후에요.
(B) 토론토로요.
(C) 꽤 바쁜 일정입니다.

의문사 when 질문으로 떠나는 시점을 물었으므로 오늘 오후라고 답한 (A)가 정답이다. (B)처럼 '전치사 for + 행선지'가 쓰이면 '~로, ~행'이라고 해석되고 where에 대한 답이다.

professor 교수 quite 꽤

12 Can I help you, ma'am?
영M (A) Yes, I'm looking for a book called *Magic Tree*
영W *House*.
(B) Let's meet at the café.
(C) It's ten-thirty, sir.

부인, 제가 도와 드릴까요?
(A) 네, 〈Magic Tree House〉라는 책을 찾고 있습니다.
(B) 카페에서 만납시다.
(C) 10시 30분입니다.

도움을 제공하는 제공 의문문으로, 호의를 받아들이면서 세부적으로 도움을 요청한 (A)가 정답이다. (B)는 만날 장소를 언급했으므로 문맥상 벗어났고 (C)는 현재 시각을 알려주고 있으므로 탈락이다.

13 Did you reserve the concert ticket online or here at
미M the box office?
영M (A) It was too expensive.
(B) I did it on your website.
(C) We enjoy playing music.

온라인에서 콘서트 티켓을 예약하셨나요 혹은 여기 매표소에서 하셨나요?
(A) 그것은 너무 비쌌어요.
(B) 당신네 웹 사이트에서 했습니다.
(C) 우리는 음악 연주를 즐깁니다.

선택 의문문 질문으로 or 앞, 뒤에 언급된 선택 사항을 정확히 파악한다. 티켓 예약을 온라인으로 했는지 매표소에서 했는지를 물었으므로, 온라인을 on you website로 바꿔 표현한 (B)가 정답이다.

reserve 예약하다 box office 매표소 expensive 비싼

14 Do your tires need checking?
영W (A) I believe so.
미M (B) Yes, from working late.
(C) We can split the check.

당신의 타이어는 점검이 필요한가요?
(A) 그럴 겁니다.
(B) 네, 늦게까지 일해서요.
(C) 우리는 계산을 반씩 나눠서 해도 됩니다.

Yes/No 여부를 묻는 질문으로 주어를 your tires로 정확하게 파악한 후 점검이 필요한지 여부에 대한 답을 고른다. (A) I believe so는 Yes와 바꿔 쓸 수 있는 표현이므로 정답이다.
I believe so, I think so 등의 표현은 Yes 대신 쓸 수 있는 표현으로 암기하자.

check 점검하다, 계산서 split 나누다

15 What's the fastest way to the baseball stadium?
미M (A) The bus came late this morning.
미W (B) It's only a ten-minute walk from here.
(C) To reduce expenses.
야구 경기장에 가는 가장 빠른 방법은 무엇입니까?
(A) 오늘 아침에 버스가 늦게 왔어요.
(B) 여기서 걸어서 10분 거리입니다.
(C) 경비를 줄이려고요.

의문사 what 질문으로 경기장에 가는 빠른 방법을 물어봤기 때문에, 교통수단 등의 답을 예상할 수 있다. (B)는 해석상 걸어가면 10분 거리라는 뜻이지만 결국 걸어가는 것이 가장 빠르다는 답변으로 연결되므로 정답이다. (A)는 bus가 언급되어 혼돈을 주었고, to부정사로 답한 (C)는 why 질문에 대한 답이라는 점을 기억하자.

walk 도보 reduce 줄이다, 감소시키다 expense 비용

16 Won't the entire department be at the reception
영W tonight?
영M (A) Ronda can't make it.
(B) Yes, we enjoyed it entirely.
(C) At the Italian restaurant.
오늘 밤 연회에 전 부서 직원들이 참석하지 않나요?
(A) Ronda는 갈 수 없습니다.
(B) 네, 우리는 매우 즐거운 시간을 보냈어요.
(C) 이탈리안 음식점에서요.

Yes/No 여부를 묻는 질문으로 won't의 발음에 주의하자. entire department는 전체 부서 직원들이란 의미로 연회에 모두 참석하는지 여부를 묻는 것이다. Ronda는 갈 수 없다라고 답한 (A)는 결국 질문에 대해 No라고 답하는 것이므로 정답이다. (B)는 과거 시제로 답한 시제 오류 함정이고, (C)는 의문사 where에 대한 답이다.

entire 전체 reception 연회 make it (to 장소) ~에 가다

17 Why aren't the new employees here?
미W (A) I don't think so.
영W (B) Check the budget please.
(C) They are in a meeting.
왜 신입 사원들이 여기에 없나요?
(A) 아닌 것 같은데요.
(B) 예산안을 검토해 주세요.
(C) 그들은 회의 중입니다.

의문사 why 질문으로 신입 사원이 여기에 없는 이유를 물었으므로 회의 중이라고 답한 (C)가 정답이다. (A) I don't think so는 No와 바꿔 쓸 수 있는 표현으로 why 질문에 No로 답변할 수 없는 것처럼 I don't think so로도 답할 수 없다.

budget 예산, 예산안 in a meeting 회의 중인

18 How do I check books out of the local library?
미M (A) They won't be produced locally.
미W (B) We don't accept checks.
(C) You need to get a library card first.
지역 도서관에서 책을 어떻게 대여할 수 있나요?
(A) 그것들은 이 지역에서 생산되지 않습니다.
(B) 우리는 수표를 받지 않습니다.
(C) 도서관 카드를 먼저 만드셔야 합니다.

의문사 how 질문으로 책을 빌리는 방법을 물었으므로 도서관 카드를 받아야 한다고 답한 (C)가 정답이다. (A)는 local과 발음이 유사한 locally를 이용, (B)는 check이라는 단어를 반복 이용한 함정이다.

check out (책 등을) 빌리다, 대여하다 accept 받다, 받아들이다
check 수표

19 Mr. Woo's office is the first door on the left, isn't it?
영W (A) No, it's in the East Building.
영M (B) She's a famous writer.
(C) We didn't order two.
Woo 씨의 사무실은 왼쪽 첫 번째 문입니다, 그렇지 않나요?
(A) 아니오, 그것은 동관 건물에 있습니다.
(B) 그녀는 유명한 작가입니다.
(C) 우리는 두 개를 주문하지 않았어요.

Yes/No 여부를 묻는 부가의문문 형태이다. 사무실의 위치를 확인하는 질문으로, 다른 건물에 있다고 답해 준 (A)가 정답이다. (B)는 주어가 she로 쓰였기 때문에 주어 오류이고, (C)는 주문한 물건의 개수에 대해 말하고 있으므로 문맥에서 벗어났다.

on the left 왼쪽에 writer 작가

20 My motorcycle can be shipped to the United States,
미M can't it?
미W (A) They arrived from Seattle.
(B) Yes, we can help you with that.
(C) Enjoy your trip.
제 오토바이는 미국으로 배송될 수 있어요, 그렇지 않습니까?
(A) 그들은 시애틀로부터 도착했습니다.
(B) 네, 저희가 도와 드릴 수 있어요.
(C) 즐거운 여행 되십시오.

Yes/No 여부를 묻는 부가 의문문 형태로 오토바이가 다른 나라로 배송이 가능한지 여부를 묻고 있다. (B)에서 Yes(가능하다)라고 답한 후 우리가 도와주겠다고 덧붙였으므로 정답이 된다. (A)는 United States를 들었을 때 연상되는 Seattle을 이용한 함정이고, (C)는 질문에 대해서는 전혀 답을 주지 않으므로 오답이다.

motorcycle 오토바이 ship 배송하다, 보내다

21 Have you completed the monthly payroll report?
영W (A) Yes, I handed it in.
미M (B) We get paid bi-weekly.
(C) Travel expenditures.
월급 보고서를 완료하셨나요?
(A) 네, 제출했습니다.
(B) 우리는 2주일에 한 번 급여를 받습니다.
(C) 출장 경비요.

Yes/No 여부를 묻는 질문으로 키워드는 completed, report 이다. 보고서 완료 여부에 대한 답을 찾으면 되므로 이미 제출했다고 답한 (A)가 정답이다.

complete 완성하다 monthly 매월의, 한 달에 한번의 payroll 급여 정산금 hand in 제출하다 bi-weekly 2주일에 한번 expenditure 경비, 지출

22 Should we throw a birthday party for Linda at
미W Jackson's Steak House?
영M (A) I'd like a glass of wine with my steak.
(B) Where did you buy the cake?
(C) Yes, everybody loves that place.

Jackson's Steak House에서 Linda를 위한 생일파티를 여는 게 좋을까요?
(A) 스테이크와 함께 와인 한 잔을 하고 싶네요.
(B) 어디서 그 케이크를 샀나요?
(C) 네, 다들 그곳을 좋아하니까요.

조동사 should를 이용한 제안 의문문 형태로 특정 장소가 파티를 열기에 좋을 것인지 물었고 모두 좋아하는 장소라고 긍정의 답변을 주었으므로 (C)가 정답이 된다. (B)는 파티를 들었을 때 연상되는 cake를 이용한 오답이고, (A)는 와인을 주문/요청할 때 쓸 수 있는 표현으로 오답이다.

throw a party 파티를 열다

23 The design proposal is due on Thursday.
미W (A) Every Tuesday.
미M (B) I can finish it by then.
(C) Leave it on my desk.

디자인 제안서는 목요일에 마감입니다.
(A) 매주 화요일이요.
(B) 그때까지 그것을 완성할 수 있어요.
(C) 제 책상에 그것을 놔두세요.

평서문 유형으로 제안서의 마감일을 알리는 것이 이 평서문의 요지이다. (B)에서 마감까지 끝낼 수 있다고 했으니 정답이다. 앞서 나온 on Thursday를 by then으로 바꿔 표현한 것을 기억하자.

proposal 제안서 due 마감인 leave 남기다, 놓아 두다

24 Will this year's fashion show be held in Paris or New
영M York?
영W (A) It was a huge success.
(B) I haven't heard about it yet.
(C) Several new designers will attend.

올해 패션쇼는 파리에서 열리나요 아님 뉴욕에서 열리게 되나요?
(A) 엄청난 성공이었습니다.
(B) 아직 아무 얘기도 못 들었어요.
(C) 몇몇 신입 디자이너는 참석할 것입니다.

선택 의문문으로 쇼가 열리는 장소가 파리인지 뉴욕인지를 물었고 정답은 아무 얘기도 못 들어서 모른다고 답한 (B)가 된다. 천하무적 정답 형태로 어떤 질문과 만나도 '모르겠다'라고 답하면 정답의 가능성이 매우 높다는 사실을 기억하자.

be held (행사, 쇼 등이) 열리다 attend 참석하다

25? Isn't Melissa the president of the city planning
미M committee
영M (A) Yes, I'll have some.
(B) I heard that she resigned.
(C) Many tourist attractions.

Melissa가 도시 계획 위원회의 회장이 아닌가요?
(A) 네, 조금 먹을게요.
(B) 그녀는 사퇴했다고 들었어요.
(C) 많은 유명 관광지들이요.

Yes/No 여부를 묻는 질문으로 위원회의 회장이 Melissa인지 여부가 질문의 핵심이다. (B)에서 she(=Melissa)가 사임했다는 뜻은 이제 회장이 아니라는 No의 의미이므로 정답이 된다. (A)의 경우 Yes의 의미는 Melissa가 회장이 맞다는 의미인데, 그 후에 큰 성공이었다고 말하고 있어 문맥을 벗어났다.

resign 사임하다 tourist attraction 관광지

26 Can you move them all by yourself?
영M (A) I think I could use some help.
미W (B) It can't be folded.
(C) I already ate one.

당신은 그것들을 혼자서 옮길 수 있습니까?
(A) 약간의 도움이 필요할 것 같네요.
(B) 그것은 접을 수 없어요.
(C) 전 이미 한 개를 먹었어요.

Yes/No 여부를 묻는 질문으로 혼자 옮길 수 있는지를 물었을 때 I could use some help는 도움이 필요하다는 의미로 질문에 대한 No 답변이 성립된다. could use는 관용 표현으로 need(필요하다)라는 의미이다.

by oneself 혼자서 could use (=can use) 필요하다 fold 접다

27 Shouldn't the chairs we ordered have been delivered
영W by now?
미M (A) The banquet starts in an hour.
(B) We carry a wide selection of tables.
(C) Yes, let me call the shipping company.

우리가 주문한 의자들이 지금쯤이면 도착했어야 하지 않나요?
(A) 연회는 한 시간 후에 시작합니다.
(B) 저희는 다양한 종류의 테이블을 취급합니다.
(C) 네, 배송 업체에 전화해 보겠습니다.

Yes/No 여부를 묻는 질문으로 키워드는 chairs, delivered, by now이다. (C)는 지금쯤 의자가 도착했어야 한다는 의미로, 배송 업체에 확인 전화를 해 보겠다는 부연 설명이 자연스럽다.

by now 지금쯤에 banquet 연회 carry (상품, 물건)을 취급하다 shipping company 배송 업체

28 Would you like me to remind you to call Alan?
미M (A) That won't be necessary.
미W (B) I don't mind walking.
(C) On the fifth floor.

Alan에게 전화하라고 제가 상기시켜 드릴까요?
(A) 그럴 필요 없습니다.
(B) 전 걷는 것 괜찮아요.
(C) 5층에요.

상대방에게 호의를 제공하는 제공 의문문으로 would you like me to + V?를 통으로 암기해 두자. (A)는 호의를 거절할 때 쓰는 표현이므로 정답이 된다. 다른 거절 표현으로는 No thanks, That's not necessary 등이 있다. (B)는 remind와 발음이 유사한 mind를 이용한 오답 함정이다.

remind 상기시키다 necessary 필요한 mind 꺼리다, 싫어하다

29 Mindy finally advertised the new marketing position.
미W (A) It should be selling well.
영W (B) And a couple of people have already applied.
(C) He has a lot of experience.

Mindy가 드디어 새로운 마케팅직 광고를 올렸네요.
(A) 그건 잘 팔릴 거예요.
(B) 그리고 두어 명은 이미 지원을 했어요.
(C) 그는 경력이 많아요.

평서문 유형은 말의 요지를 파악하는 것이 중요하다. advertise a position은 구인 광고를 하다는 뜻이고 새로운 마케팅직의 구인 광고를 냈다고 했으므로, 이미 2명은 지원까지 했다고 답한 (B)가 가장 자연스러운 답변이 된다. (A)의 주어 it은 무엇을 가리키는지 알 수 없는 주어 오류이고, (C)의 주어 He 역시 마찬가지이다.

advertise 광고를 하다 position 직위 sell well (물건이) 잘 팔리다 apply 지원하다

30 Why didn't you request a receipt?
미M (A) I didn't realize I had to.
미W (B) An incorrect address.
(C) That's a good idea.

당신은 왜 영수증을 요청하지 않았나요?
(A) 해야 한다는 것을 몰랐어요.
(B) 부정확한 주소요.
(C) 좋은 아이디어네요.

이유를 묻는 why 의문문으로 영수증을 요청하지 않은 이유를 묻고 있으므로, 요청해야 한다는 것을 인식하지 못했다고 답한 (A)가 정답이 된다. (B)는 요청을 안 한 이유로 해석될 수 없으므로 오답이고, (C)는 제안문에 대한 승낙 표현으로 사용되는 표현이다.

request 요청하다 receipt 영수증 realize 깨닫다, 인식하다 incorrect 부정확한

31 The mechanics are here.
영W (A) It's so noisy outside.
영M (B) He can drive there.
(C) Show them where the broken-down car is.

정비 기사들이 왔습니다.
(A) 밖이 매우 시끄럽네요.
(B) 그가 거기까지 운전할 수 있어요.
(C) 고장 난 차가 어디 있는지 그들에게 알려 주세요.

평서문 유형으로 말의 요지는 정비 기사들이 도착했음을 알리는 것이다. 그러므로 고쳐야 할 차가 어디 있는지 알려주라고 답한 (C)가 가장 자연스러운 답변이다.

mechanic 정비 기사 noisy 시끄러운 broken-down 고장 난

PART 3

Questions 32-34 refer to the following conversation. 미W 영M

W Hi, Leon, I'm designing a cover for our new novel and I need your opinion. Do you have time to look at it?
M Sorry, Katie. I'm about to leave the office for the day. My parents are visiting me for the weekend and I need to be at the airport in an hour to pick them up.
W In an hour? You should hurry up to avoid the rush-hour traffic. I'll just ask Philip to look at it.

여 안녕하세요, Leon, 제가 새 소설 표지를 디자인하고 있는데 당신의 의견이 필요해요. 그걸 보실 시간이 있으세요?
남 미안해요, Katie. 막 퇴근을 하려던 참이었어요. 부모님께서 주말 동안 저를 만나러 오시는데 한 시간 후까지 공항으로 모시러 가야 하거든요.
여 한 시간 후요? 러시아워를 피하려면 서두르셔야 하겠네요. 그냥 Philip에게 봐 달라고 부탁할게요.

cover 표지 opinion 의견, 견해 pick up (사람) ~를 태우다, 데리러 가다 avoid 피하다 traffic 교통량, 교통체증

32 What is the woman currently working on?
(A) Designing a book cover
(B) Writing an article
(C) Planning an event
(D) Preparing for a presentation

여자는 현재 무엇을 작업 중인가?
(A) 책 표지 디자인
(B) 기사 작성
(C) 행사 계획
(D) 발표 준비

세부 사항 질문으로 여자가 작업 중인 업무에 집중한다. 대화의 도입부 여자 대사 I'm designing a cover for our new novel을 들었을 때 책 표지 디자인 작업 중임을 알 수 있다. 정답은 (A)이다.

33 Why is the man unable to help the woman?
(A) He has been caught in traffic.
(B) He is late for a doctor's appointment.
(C) He is picking up his relatives.
(D) He is leaving for Singapore.

남자는 왜 여자를 도울 수 없는가?
(A) 막히는 도로에 갇혔다.
(B) 진료 예약에 늦었다.
(C) 가족을 데리러 간다.
(D) 싱가포르로 떠난다.

why 질문 내용을 읽고 '남자는 여자를 도울 수 없다'는 내용을 미리 파악해둔다. 대화에서 여자가 도움을 요청하는 내용이 나오고 남자가 Sorry라고 답하면서 언급하는 이유를 정답으로 연결한다. 부모님을 데리러 공항에 가야 하기 때문이라고 말했고, 가족 구성원은 relatives로 바꿔 표현되므로 정답은 (C)가 된다. (A)는 대화 중 언급된 traffic을 이용하여 함정을 만든 것이다.

34 What does the woman say she will do?
(A) Speak to a coworker
(B) Read a manual
(C) Attend a conference
(D) Leave the office for the day

여자는 무엇을 할 것이라고 말하는가?
(A) 동료와 얘기하기
(B) 설명서 읽기
(C) 컨퍼런스에 참석하기
(D) 퇴근하기

여자의 향후 행동을 묻는 질문으로 여자의 대사에서 I'll just ask Philip to look at it을 들었을 때 Philip에게 요청할 것임을 알 수 있고, 동료의 이름은 보통 a coworker 혹은 a colleague로 바꿔 표현되므로 정답은 (A)이다.

Questions 35-37 refer to the following conversation. 미M 미W

M Hello, I'm calling to request a copy of my proof of employment. I'm applying for a new job, and the employer wants to see my employment history. Would you mind sending an official document to them?

W Not at all. In fact, I'll be able to process your request right away if you just let me know the mailing address of your employer. I'll make sure they receive the copy within a week.

M The problem is that they need it quite urgently to finalize the paperwork. Why don't you send it by express delivery? And I'll pay the extra charge.

남 여보세요. 저는 고용 증명서 한 부를 요청하기 위해 전화드렸어요. 새로운 직장에 지원하려고 하는데요, 고용주가 저의 고용 내력을 보고 싶어 합니다. 공식 서류를 그쪽으로 보내 주실 수 있나요?

여 그럼요. 사실, 당신의 고용주의 우편 주소를 알려 주신다면 지금 바로 처리해 드릴 수 있습니다. 그들이 일주일 안에 문서를 받도록 해 드리겠습니다.

남 문제는 그들이 서류 작업을 마무리하기 위해서 급하게 그 서류가 필요하다는 것입니다. 빠른 배송을 통해 보내 주시면 어떨까요? 제가 추가 비용을 지불하겠습니다.

request 요청하다 proof of ~에 대한 증거 employment 고용 employer 고용주 official 공식의 process 처리하다 within ~내에 urgently 급하게 finalize 마무리하다 paperwork 서류작업 express delivery 빠른 배송 charge 요금, 비용

35 What are the speakers mainly discussing?
(A) Submitting a résumé
(B) Rescheduling a meeting
(C) Selecting a company
(D) Obtaining a document

화자들은 무엇에 대해 논의하는가?
(A) 이력서를 제출하는 것
(B) 회의 일정을 조정하는 것
(C) 회사를 선정하는 것
(D) 문서를 받는 것

대화의 주제를 묻는 질문으로 도입부 I'm calling to를 들었을 때 전화의 목적을 확인할 수 있다. 고용을 입증하는 서류를 요청하기 위함이므로 proof of employment를 document로 바꿔 표현한 (D)가 정답이다.

36 What does the woman ask for?
(A) A certificate
(B) An address
(C) An order form
(D) A telephone number

여자는 무엇을 요구하는가?
(A) 증명서
(B) 주소
(C) 주문 용지
(D) 전화번호

반드시 여자 대사에서 여자가 요청하는 것을 정답으로 연결한다. if you just let me know the mailing address of your employer에서 고용주의 주소를 알려 달라고 요청하므로 정답은 (B)가 된다.

37 What does the man say he will do?
(A) Receive the package
(B) Pay for a special service
(C) Choose a payment option
(D) Enroll in a training course

남자는 무엇을 하겠다고 말하는가?
(A) 소포 받기
(B) 특별 서비스에 대한 비용 지불하기
(C) 지불 방법 고르기
(D) 교육 과정 등록하기

남자 대사에서 앞으로 하겠다고 언급된 내용을 노린다. 여자에게 빠른 배송 서비스로 보낼 것을 제안한 후 I'll pay the extra charge에서 추가 비용을 내겠다고 했으므로 정답은 (B)가 된다. express delivery는 special service로 바꿔 표현되었다.

Questions 38-40 refer to the following conversation. 영M 영W

M Samantha, I was thinking of getting some new reading material for the hair shop. The magazines in the waiting area have been there for a while now and our customers would really appreciate a change.

W Which reminds me, I read a magazine just the other day that had a useful article on hair treatment and styling. I think it would be good reading for the beauty shop, so I'll see if I can find it. I can't quite remember the title of it though.

M But you would recognize the magazine if you saw it, right? The bookstore just down the street has a lot of beauty magazines. Why don't you try looking for it there?

W You're right. If they have it, I'll buy a copy for you. Then, read some of the articles over and let me know what you think.

남 Samantha, 우리 헤어숍에 읽을거리를 새로 사 놓는 게 좋을 것 같아요. 대기실에 있는 잡지는 오랫동안 있었기 때문에 고객들도 변화를 원할 거고요.
여 그 얘기를 하니 생각나는 것이 있어요. 일전에 헤어 트리트먼트와 스타일링에 관한 좋은 정보가 있는 잡지를 읽었었어요. 그게 우리 뷰티숍에 잘 맞는 읽을거리가 될 것 같은데 한 번 찾아볼게요. 그런데 제목이 정확하게 기억나지 않아요.
남 그렇지만 그 잡지를 본다면 알아볼 수 있을 것 같나요? 바로 길가에 있는 서점에 뷰티 잡지가 많이 있어요. 그곳에서 찾아보는 게 어때요?
여 맞는 말이에요. 만약 그곳에 있다면 제가 한 권을 살게요. 그러면 기사들을 읽어본 후에 어떻게 생각하는지 얘기해 주세요.

reading material 읽을거리 appreciate 고맙게 생각하다, 인식하다, 진가를 알다 title 이름, 제목 read over ~을 꼼꼼히 읽어 보다

38 What idea does the man propose?
(A) Reading articles on beauty tips
(B) Changing the layout of the shop
(C) Getting new reading material
(D) Posting customer benefits online

남자는 무슨 아이디어를 제안하는가?
(A) 뷰티 조언에 관한 기사를 읽는 것
(B) 상점의 배치를 바꾸는 것
(C) 새로운 읽을거리를 사는 것
(D) 고객 혜택을 온라인에 게시하는 것

남자의 제안 사항을 묻는 질문으로 남자 대사에 정답이 있다. 대화의 도입부에 남자가 new reading material을 살 생각이라고 했으므로 정답은 (C)가 된다. (A)는 여자 대사에서 언급됐던 article, beauty tips 등의 어휘를 이용한 함정이 된다.

39 What did the woman forget?
(A) The name of a magazine
(B) The date of a meeting
(C) A list of new books
(D) A company's name

여자는 무엇을 잊었는가?
(A) 잡지의 이름
(B) 회의의 날짜
(C) 신간 서적의 리스트
(D) 회사 이름

여자가 잊은 것을 묻는 질문으로 여자 대사에서 I can't quite remember라고 말한 부분이 forgot과 같은 의미이다. 매거진의 title이 기억나지 않는다고 했으므로 정답은 (A)가 된다.

40 What does the man suggest the woman do?
(A) Read some articles
(B) Visit a bookstore
(C) Send out some coupons
(D) Sign up for a subscription

남자는 여자에게 무엇을 할 것을 제안하는가?
(A) 기사 읽기
(B) 서점에 방문하기
(C) 쿠폰 발송하기
(D) 구독 신청하기

남자가 여자에게 제안하는 내용은 남자 대사에서 답을 찾는다. 남자가 뷰티 잡지를 많이 취급하는 서점이 있음을 언급한 후에 그곳에서 잡지를 찾아보는 게 어떻겠냐고 제안했으므로 정답은 (B)가 된다. (A)는 여자가 남자에게 하라는 내용이므로 오답이 된다.

Questions 41-43 refer to the following conversation. (영M) (미W)

M Hello. This is John. You know I'm attending The National Film Director's Conference next month. And I was wondering if you could review the editing software I'm demonstrating. I've got feedback from some of my co-workers but I really need a second opinion on this.
W Do you mean the image editing software you developed? I think it works great. I especially like the fact that you've simplified the color adjusting process so it can be learned and used with ease.
M Right. I think that directors will be impressed when they actually see how conveniently they can make revisions to their films.
W Just make sure of one thing John. You should let the conference organizers know that you'll need about ten more laptops for the participants. That way they can experience your software firsthand.

남 여보세요, John입니다. 제가 다음 달에 National Film Director 컨퍼런스에 참석하는데, 제가 시연하게 될 편집 소프트웨어를 한 번 검토해 주실 수 있는지 궁금해서요. 저는 동료 몇 명의 피드백을 받았지만 또 다른 견해가 필요합니다.
여 당신이 개발한 그 이미지 편집 소프트웨어를 얘기하시는 건가요? 아주 잘 작동한다고 생각해요. 특히 색상 편집 과정을 간소화시켜서 쉽게 배우고 쓸 수 있다는 점이 좋습니다.
남 맞아요. 감독들이 얼마나 편리하게 영화를 편집할 수 있는지 본다면 매우 감명을 받을 거예요.
여 다만 한 가지만 명심하세요. 컨퍼런스 담당자들에게 참가자들이 쓸 수 있게 10대의 노트북이 더 필요하다고 말하는 게 좋겠어요. 그렇게 한다면 그들이 당신의 소프트웨어를 직접 경험해 볼 수 있을 테니까요.

demonstrate 시연하다, 선보이다 feedback 의견, 견해 second opinion 다른 사람의 견해 especially 특히 simplify 단순화하다 adjust 조절하다 with ease 쉽게 make a revision 수정하다, 편집하다 participant 참가자 firsthand 직접

41 Who most likely is the man?
(A) An editor
(B) A film director
(C) A conference organizer
(D) A software developer

남자는 누구일 것 같은가?
(A) 편집자
(B) 영화 감독
(C) 회의 담당자
(D) 소프트웨어 개발자

남자의 직업을 유추하는 질문으로 남자의 업무 내용에서 유추해야 정확하게 풀 수 있다. 남자 대사에서 the editing software I'm demonstrating에서 본인이 소프트웨어를 시연한다고 했고, 여자 대사에서 the image editing software you developed에서 상대방(남자)이 소프트웨어를 개발한 사람이라고 했으므로 정답은 (D)임을 알 수 있다. (B)의 경우 행사의 이름에 film director가 언급되었기 때문에 혼동을 줄 수 있는 단어 함정이 된다.

42 What is the man preparing for?
(A) A demonstration
(B) A movie
(C) An assessment report
(D) A product proposal

남자는 무엇에 대한 준비 중인가?
(A) 시연
(B) 영화
(C) 평가 보고서
(D) 제품 제안서

남자가 현재 업무 중인 내용을 찾는 것으로 도입부 남자 대사에서 컨퍼런스에 참석한다는 것과 그곳에서 소프트웨어를 시연한다는 것에서 demonstration을 준비하는 중임을 알 수 있다.

43 What does the woman recommend the man do?
(A) Test the software
(B) Request some equipment
(C) Register for the event in advance
(D) Ask a colleague

여자는 남자에게 무엇을 할 것을 추천하는가?
(A) 소프트웨어를 시험하는 것
(B) 장비를 요청하는 것
(C) 행사의 등록을 미리 하는 것
(D) 동료에게 물어보는 것

여자가 남자에게 권고하는 내용을 묻는 질문으로 답은 여자 대사에 있다. 상대방에게 권고할 때 자주 쓰이는 표현인 You should 부분이 정답의 단서가 된다. 컨퍼런스 담당자에게 10대의 노트북이 추가로 필요하다는 것을 말하라고 했고 이를 equipment(장비)를 요청하는 것으로 바꿔 표현한 (B)가 정답이 된다.

Questions 44-46 refer to the following conversation. 영W 미M

W Thomas, I think I need to get a new cell phone. I accidentally dropped my phone in the toilet and it won't turn on.
M Oh, I'm so sorry to hear that. But sometimes it turns back on and works fine when you dry it out completely. If you have already decided to get a new one, you should go to Dominique's Mobile. Their prices are reasonable and they provide the best after-sales service in town.
W That's good to hear. I think I'll go over there at lunchtime.
M When you go, don't forget to bring your old phone with you. You know, they might know how to save water-damaged cell phones.

여 Thomas, 저 휴대폰을 새로 사야 할 것 같아요. 실수로 변기에 전화기를 빠뜨렸는데 전화기가 켜지질 않아요.
남 저런, 안타깝네요. 그런데 가끔씩 전화기를 완전히 말리면 다시 켜지고 정상으로 작동하기도 해요. 만약 새것을 사기로 결정하셨다면, Dominique's Mobile로 가 보세요. 가격이 합리적이고 이 지역에서 가장 훌륭한 애프터 서비스를 해 주거든요.
여 좋은 정보네요. 점심 시간에 가 봐야겠어요.
남 그리고 가실 때, 이전 전화기를 가지고 가는 걸 잊지 마세요. 그들이 물에 젖은 휴대 전화를 살릴 수 있는 방법을 알 수도 있으니까요.

cell phone 휴대 전화(=mobile phone) accidentally 실수로 reasonable 합리적인 water-damaged 물에 의해 손상된

44 What problem does the woman mention?
(A) She does not know how to operate a machine.
(B) Her mobile phone is out of order.
(C) Her car has been damaged in an accident.
(D) She is late for an appointment.

여자는 어떤 문제점을 언급하는가?
(A) 그녀는 기계를 어떻게 다루는지 모른다.
(B) 그녀의 휴대 전화는 고장 났다.
(C) 그녀의 차는 사고로 손상되었다.
(D) 그녀는 약속에 늦었다.

여자 대사에서 언급되는 문제점을 찾는 질문이다. 도입부에 새 휴대 전화를 사야 한다는 말과 함께 I accidentally dropped my phone in the toilet and it won't turn on(실수로 전화기를 변기에 떨어뜨렸는데 켜지지 않는다)에서 정답은 (B)임을 알 수 있다.

45 What does the man suggest about Dominique's Mobile?
(A) Its employees are knowledgeable.
(B) Its after-sales service is excellent.
(C) It is conveniently located.
(D) It carries many kinds of cell phones.

남자는 Dominique's Mobile에 대해 무엇을 암시하는가?
(A) 직원들이 아는 게 많다.
(B) 애프터 서비스가 훌륭하다.
(C) 위치가 편리하다.
(D) 다양한 종류의 휴대 전화를 취급한다.

남자 대사에서 Dominique's Mobile이 언급되는 부분에서 정답의 단서를 찾자. 남자는 여자에게 Dominique's Mobile에 가 보라고 권고하면서 가격이 합리적인 것과 after-sales service가 좋은 것을 언급했으므로 정답은 (B)가 된다.

46 What is the woman advised to do?
(A) Leave the office early
(B) Call a supplier
(C) Speak to an expert
(D) Bring a device with her

여자는 무엇을 하라고 권고 받는가?
(A) 일찍 퇴근하기
(B) 공급업체에 전화하기
(C) 전문가에게 이야기하기
(D) 기기 가지고 가기

여자가 권고 받는 것을 찾는 질문이므로 정답은 남자 대사에 있다. 남자가 여자에게 don't forget to bring your old phone with you라고 말한 부분에서 정답은 (D)임을 알 수 있고, old phone을 device(기기)로 바꿔 표현한 것을 기억해 두자.

Questions 47-49 refer to the following conversation. 미W 미M

W Peter, were you able to ship the yellow curtains to the customer?

M No, not yet. I haven't received the shipping address from the sales office yet. I called them earlier today but nobody answered.

W Maybe they were out for lunch. Why don't you try calling them now? I'd like to get that information as soon as possible, so the curtains leave the warehouse today.

M Okay, I'll do it right away.

여 Peter, 고객에게 노란색 커튼을 배송하셨나요?

남 아니요, 아직이요. 영업 사무실로부터 배송 주소를 아직 못 받았어요. 아까 전화를 했는데 아무도 안 받더군요.

여 점심 먹으러 나갔었던 것 같네요. 지금 전화를 해보면 어때요? 커튼이 오늘 창고에서 나갈 수 있도록 최대한 빨리 그 정보를 받고 싶어요.

남 알겠습니다. 바로 해 볼게요.

shipping address 배송 주소 warehouse 창고

47 What are the speakers mainly discussing?
(A) A job opening
(B) A shipment of an order
(C) A conference call
(D) An e-mail address

화자들은 주로 무엇에 대한 이야기를 하는가?
(A) 일자리
(B) 주문의 배송
(C) 전화 회의
(D) 이메일 주소

대화의 주제를 묻는 질문으로 대화의 도입부에서 단서를 찾는다. 여자의 첫 대사 were you able to ship the yellow curtains to the customer?에서 고객에게 커튼을 배송했는지 물었으므로 정답은 (B)임을 알 수 있다.

48 What problem does the man mention?
(A) He does not know where to send an order.
(B) He cannot locate a missing document.
(C) Some items were sent to a wrong address.
(D) Some employees are out sick today.

남자는 어떤 문제점을 언급하는가?
(A) 그는 어디로 주문품을 보낼지 모른다.
(B) 그는 없어진 서류를 찾을 수 없다.
(C) 일부 상품이 잘못된 주소로 보내졌다.
(D) 일부 직원이 오늘 아파서 결근했다.

남자의 대사에서 언급된 문제점에 집중한다. 주문품을 배송하지 못한 이유로 영업팀이 아직 주소를 주지 않아서라고 했으므로 정답은 (A)가 된다.

49 What is the man asked to do now?
(A) Answer a customer's question
(B) Review some information
(C) Finish a project
(D) Contact another office

남자는 지금 무엇을 하라고 요청 받는가?
(A) 고객의 질문에 답하기
(B) 정보 검토하기
(C) 프로젝트 끝내기
(D) 다른 사무실에 연락하기

남자가 요청 받는 것을 묻는 질문이므로 정답은 여자의 대사에 있다. 여자가 남자에게 Why don't you try calling them now?(지금 그들에게 전화해보는 게 어때요?)라고 부탁한 부분이 정답이 되고, 문맥을 통해 them은 sales office라는 것을 알 수 있다. 정답은 (D)가 된다.

Questions 50-52 refer to the following conversation. 영M 영W

M Heidi, were you able to meet your monthly sales goal for last month? I only sold 50% of mine.

W I didn't reach my goal either. Since Lona Motors opened their showroom just across the street, we've lost a lot of customers. I heard their new compact cars have been very popular especially with female customers.

M I heard that too. Don't you think our company has to do something to attract customers? How about we start offering more flexible payment options?

W That's a great idea. Why don't you bring it up at the next sales meeting?

M I think I will. We really need to come up with better ideas to remain competitive and successful in this marketplace.

남 Heidi, 당신은 지난달에 세운 판매 목표치를 달성할 수 있었나요? 저는 50퍼센트밖에 판매하지 못했습니다.

여 저도 제 목표에 도달하지 못했어요. Lona Motors가 길 맞은편에 전시실을 개장한 후로, 많은 고객을 잃었어요. 그들의 새로 나온 소형차가 특히 여성 고객들에게 매우 인기가 많대요.

남 저도 들었어요. 우리 회사도 고객을 유치하기 위해 뭔가 해야만 한다고 생각하지 않으세요? 좀 더 융통성 있는 결제 방식을 제공하기 시작하면 어떨까요?

여 좋은 생각이네요. 다음번 영업부 미팅 때 그 얘기를 꺼내 보는 게 어때요?

남 그럴 생각입니다. 우리가 이 업계에서 계속 경쟁력을 갖추고 성공하려면 더 좋은 아이디어를 생각해 봐야 해요.

meet a goal 목표를 달성하다 reach a goal 목표에 도달하다 attract (사람을) 끌다, 유치하다 showroom 전시실 flexible 유연한, 융통성 있는 bring up (화제를) 꺼내다 come up with 생각해내다, 알다 competitive 경쟁력 있는

50 Who most likely are the speakers?
(A) Loan officers
(B) Factory workers
(C) Department heads
(D) Car dealers

화자들은 누구일 것 같은가?
(A) 대출 담당 직원
(B) 공장 근로자
(C) 부서장
(D) 자동차 영업 사원

화자들의 직업을 유추하는 질문으로 업무에 관한 내용과 회사 명칭 등에서 단서를 찾는다. 도입부에 영업 목표를 달성하는 부분과 경쟁사로 언급된 Lona Motors(자동차 회사), 그들의 소형차가 인기인 것 등에서 화자들은 차를 판매하는 사원들임을 유추할 수 있다.

51 What problem are the speakers discussing?
(A) Their company has been losing business.
(B) A competitor has won an award.
(C) Shipments have been delayed.
(D) Customers have complained about poor service

화자들은 어떤 문제점에 대해 토론하는가?
(A) 그들의 회사는 많은 고객을 잃고 있다.
(B) 경쟁사가 상을 받았다.
(C) 선적이 지연되었다.
(D) 고객들이 형편없는 서비스에 대해 불평했다.

문제점을 묻는 질문은 주제에 해당되기 때문에 도입 부분부터 문맥을 유지하며 듣는다. 여자 대사에서 경쟁사의 전시실이 개장한 이후로 we've lost a lot of customers라고 말한 부분이 정답이 된다. lose customers는 lose business라고 바꿔 표현할 수 있으니 암기해 두자.

52 What does the man suggest to solve the problem?
(A) Renovating a facility
(B) Offering flexible payment plans
(C) Hiring skilled workers
(D) Soliciting customer feedback

남자는 문제점을 해결하기 위해 무엇을 제안하는가?
(A) 시설물을 개조하는 것
(B) 융통성 있는 결제 방식을 제공하는 것
(C) 숙련된 직원을 고용하는 것
(D) 고객의 피드백 요청하는 것

남자의 대사에서 제안되는 내용을 노려 듣는다. 판매가 줄어든 것에 대해서 How about we start offering more flexible payment options?(융통성 있는 결제 방식을 제공하기 시작하면 어떨까요?)라고 했으므로 정답은 (B)가 된다.

Questions 53-55 refer to the following conversation. 미M 미W

M I'm calling about the amusement park's holiday hours. I heard that you'll be extending business hours during the long holidays.

W Yes, from tomorrow until the end of December, we'll be open until 11 p.m. every night. We're also having some special performances for children during that time.

M Oh, that sounds lovely. As a matter of fact, I'm planning to visit your theme park with my sons. Does it cost extra to watch a show?

W No, the price is included in the admission. And children under 5 are eligible for a discount. We're offering advance ticket sales on our website, so if you want to avoid long ticket lines, you might want to look into that.

남 이 놀이 공원의 휴일 영업시간 때문에 전화했어요. 긴 휴일 동안 영업시간을 연장할 것이라고 들었어요.

여 그렇습니다. 내일부터 12월 말까지, 매일 밤 11시까지 문을 엽니다. 또한 그 기간 동안 아이들을 위한 특별 공연을 할 것입니다.

남 오, 그거 좋네요. 실은, 제가 아들들과 함께 그 놀이공원을 방문할 예정이거든요. 쇼를 보려면 추가로 비용이 드나요?

여 아니요, 입장료에 포함되어 있습니다. 그리고 5세 이하 아이들은 할인을 받을 수 있습니다. 저희 웹 사이트에 사전 티켓 판매를 제공하오니, 티켓을 사려고 길게 줄을 서는 것을 피하시려면 그것을 살펴보시는 게 좋겠습니다.

amusement park 놀이 공원 holiday hours 휴일 영업시간 extend business hours 영업시간을 연장하다 special performance 특별 공연 cost 비용이 들다 be eligible for ~의 자격이 되다 admission 입장료 advance ticket sale 사전 티켓 판매 look into ~을 조사하다, 살펴보다

53 Why is the man calling?
(A) To request a website address
(B) To find out about extended hours
(C) To apply for membership
(D) To reserve some tickets

남자는 왜 전화를 하는가?
(A) 웹 사이트 주소를 요청하려고
(B) 연장된 영업시간에 대해 알아내려고
(C) 멤버십을 신청하려고
(D) 표를 예약하려고

전화의 목적은 보통 도입부에 나온다. 남자가 놀이 공원의 휴일 영업시간에 관해서 전화했다는 부분이 정답이 된다. I'm calling about과 같은 표현은 전화 목적을 말할 때 쓰는 표현이므로 정답의 단서가 된다.

54 What does the man imply when he says, "Oh, that sounds lovely"?
(A) The facilities stay open late.
(B) His children can have fun.
(C) Admission is free of charge.
(D) He enjoys outdoor activities.

남자가 "오, 그거 좋네요"라고 말한 의미는 무엇인가?
(A) 시설물이 늦게까지 문을 연다.
(B) 그의 아이들이 재미있게 보낼 수 있다.
(C) 입장료가 무료이다.
(D) 남자는 야외 활동을 즐긴다.

특정 표현에 대한 화자의 의도를 유추하는 신유형 질문으로, 해당 표현의 앞뒤에 단서가 있다. 놀이공원 직원이 아이들을 위한 특별 행사가 있을 거라는 정보를 줬을 때, 남자가 Oh, that sounds lovely라고 하며 아들들과 함께 방문할 계획이라고 밝혔으므로 남자의 의도는 아이들이 즐길 거리가 있어서 좋다는 의미가 된다. 정답은 (B)이다.

55 What does the woman suggest?
(A) Taking public transportation
(B) Visiting outdoor markets
(C) Purchasing tickets online
(D) Arriving early

여자는 무엇을 제안하는가?
(A) 대중교통을 이용하는 것
(B) 야외 시장을 방문하는 것
(C) 온라인으로 표를 구매하는 것
(D) 일찍 도착하는 것

여자가 제안하는 것을 묻는 질문으로 웹 사이트에서 사전 티켓 구매를 제공한다고 언급한 후 you might want to look into that에서 그것을 확인하는 게 좋겠다고 하므로 정답은 (C)가 된다. 상대방에게 제안하는 표현으로 you might want to + V를 반드시 암기하자.

Questions 56-58 refer to the following conversation. 미M 영W

M Hello, I'm calling to get some information about running a classified advertisement in your newspaper.

W Well, I'm glad you just called in time. We're currently offering a 50% discount on any print ad. But the special offer ends today.

M Oh, that's great. I'm planning to rent a summer house. I'd like to place a 25-word ad and have it run for 7 days. With the special deal, how much would that be?

W You'll pay only 30 dollars. That's just half the original price!

남 여보세요. 신문사에 광고를 내기 위한 정보를 얻으려고 전화했습니다.

여 다행히도 때 맞춰 전화를 주셨네요. 저희는 현재 어떤 인쇄 광고든지 50퍼센트 할인을 제공하고 있습니다. 그런데 이 특별 혜택은 오늘 종료됩니다.

남 아주 좋네요. 저는 여름 별장을 세놓을 계획이어서 25자 광고를 7일 동안 내고 싶습니다. 특가를 적용해서 얼마입니까?

여 30달러만 지불하시면 됩니다. 원가의 절반밖에 되지 않지요!

run an advertisement 광고를 내다 in time 때 맞춰, 제때에 special offer 특가, 특별 혜택 rent 세놓다 original price 원가

56 Where does the woman work?
(A) At a gym
(B) At a real estate agency
(C) At a newspaper
(D) At a printing company

여자는 어디에서 일하는가?
(A) 체육관
(B) 부동산
(C) 신문사
(D) 인쇄소

여자의 직장을 유추할 때 가장 확실한 근거 부분은 남자가 in your newspaper라고 말한 부분이다. 여자에게 '당신네 신문사에서'라고 말했으므로 여자가 일하는 곳은 신문사이다. 이처럼 유추 문제에서는 my, your와 같은 어휘를 잘 활용하면 쉽게 정답을 유추할 수 있다.

57 What does the woman say about the special deal?
(A) It is only for house owners.
(B) It includes a discounted subscription.
(C) It is provided annually.
(D) It will not be valid tomorrow.

여자는 특가에 관하여 뭐라고 말하는가?
(A) 주택 소유주들만을 위한 것이다.
(B) 할인 구독료를 포함한다.
(C) 일 년에 한 번씩 제공된다.
(D) 내일은 유효하지 않게 된다.

여자 대사에서 정답을 찾되, 질문의 키워드인 special deal에 관한 내용을 정답으로 연결한다. 여자가 50퍼센트 할인가를 언급한 후, 내일 그 혜택이 종료된다고 했으므로 정답은 (D)이다. discount라는 단어가 들린다고 해서 (B)를 선택한다면 단어 함정에 빠지는 것이다.

58 What does the man ask about the advertisement?
(A) The cost
(B) The period
(C) The word limit
(D) The seasonal change

남자는 광고에 관해서 무엇을 묻는가?
(A) 비용
(B) 기간
(C) 단어 제한
(D) 계절적 변동

남자 대사에서 질문으로 언급되는 것이 정답이므로 질문 형태를 잘 노려 듣는다. 남자가 특가를 적용하여 how much would that be?라고 질문하였으므로 정답은 (A)비용이 된다.

Questions 59-61 refer to the following conversation. 미W 영M

W Did you hear about the delay from the supplier? He said that the wooden shingles we ordered won't be delivered until next Monday because of a labor strike.

M **That's not good.** We promised Ms. Harrison to finish the roof of her house by the end of April. I'm worried because this delay might cause us to fall behind schedule.

W How about asking Ms. Harrison to allow us more time to finish the work?

M Okay, let me speak to her about it.

여 공급업체로부터 지연에 관하여 들으셨나요? 우리가 주문한 나무 지붕 판이 노동 파업 때문에 다음 주 월요일이 되어야 배달될 것이라고 하더군요.

남 **좋지 않네요.** 우리가 Harrison 씨에게 집 지붕 작업을 4월 말까지 마치겠다고 약속했잖아요. 이 지연으로 인해 일정보다 늦게 될까 걱정이 됩니다.

여 Harrison 씨에게 작업을 완료할 시간을 더 요청하는 건 어떨까요?

남 좋아요. 제가 그녀와 이야기해 보겠습니다.

delay 지연, 연기 wooden shingles 나무로 된 지붕 판 labor strike 노동 파업 behind schedule 일정보다 뒤처진

59 Who most likely are the speakers?
(A) Building inspectors
(B) Home builders
(C) Personnel employees
(D) Professional gardeners

화자들은 누구일 것 같은가?
(A) 건물 조사관
(B) 주택 건축업자
(C) 인사부 직원
(D) 전문 정원사

화자들의 직업을 유추하는 질문으로 어떤 업무에 대한 얘기가 나오는지 집중한다. 건축 자재를 주문했다는 것과 Harrison 씨의 새 집 공사에 대해 얘기할 때 house builders로 유추할 수 있다. 정답은 (B)이다.

60 What does the man mean when he says, "That's not good"?
(A) A budget might not be approved.
(B) Some materials are out of stock.
(C) Heavy rains are forecast.
(D) A project might not be finished on time.

남자가 "좋지 않네요"라고 말한 의미는 무엇인가?
(A) 예산이 승인되지 않을지도 모른다.
(B) 일부 자재의 재고가 없다.
(C) 호우가 예보되어 있다.
(D) 프로젝트가 제때 끝나지 않을 수 있다.

특정 표현에 대한 화자의 의도를 묻는 신유형 질문으로, 해당 표현의 앞뒤에 단서가 있다. 나무 지붕 판의 배송이 늦어진다는 얘기를 듣고 남자가 That's not good(좋지 않네요)이라고 하였고, 고객에게 집을 4월말까지 끝내기로 약속했다고 하므로 정답은 (D)임을 유추할 수 있다.

61 What do the speakers decide to do?
(A) Purchase from another supplier
(B) Cancel an order
(C) Hire more workers
(D) Contact a client

화자들은 무엇을 하기로 결정하는가?
(A) 다른 공급자에게서 구입하기
(B) 주문 취소하기
(C) 인부 더 고용하기
(D) 고객에게 연락하기

두 명의 화자가 최종 결정한 사항이 정답이 되므로, 여자가 마감 연장을 요청하라고 제안하고 남자가 이를 받아들여 고객에게 이야기해 보겠다는 부분에서 정답을 (D)로 선택한다.

Questions 62-64 refer to the following conversation with three speakers. 영W 미M 미W

W1 Welcome to Agra Indian Cuisine. How are you doing tonight, folks?
M Fine, thank you. This is my first time at your restaurant and I like the atmosphere very much.
W1 Thank you sir. Do you have any questions about the menu?
M Well, yes. I don't know much about Indian food. What would you recommend for a light dinner?
W1 Well, We have delicious tandoori chicken, which is traditional Indian barbecued chicken. And as you can see on the menu, we have many kinds of tasty curries you can choose from.
M They all look good. By the way, can you handle spicy food, Lisa?
W2 Of course I can. In fact, I'd like to try this hot chicken curry.
W1 Oh, that's an excellent choice. It's one of the most popular dishes at our restaurant and it comes with our famous garlic naan bread and home-made salad.

여1 Adra Indian Cuisine에 오신 걸 환영합니다. 오늘 저녁 어떻게 보내고 계신가요, 여러분?
남 좋습니다. 감사합니다. 이 레스토랑에 처음 왔는데 분위기가 매우 좋네요.
여1 감사합니다. 메뉴에 대해서 질문 있으신가요?
남 네. 제가 인도 음식에 대해 잘 몰라서요. 가벼운 저녁식사로 무엇을 추천해 주시겠어요?
여1 음, 맛있는 탄두리 치킨이 있는데요, 인도 전통의 바비큐 치킨이에요. 그리고 메뉴에서 보시다시피, 선택하실 수 있는 카레의 종류가 매우 다양하게 있습니다.
남 전부 다 맛있어 보이네요. 그나저나 Lisa, 매운 음식 먹을 수 있어요?
여2 그럼요 물론이죠. 사실 전 이 매운 치킨 카레를 먹어 보고 싶어요.
여1 오, 훌륭한 선택이세요. 이건 저희 레스토랑에서 가장 인기 많은 음식 중 하나인데 저희 유명한 갈릭 난과 홈메이드 샐러드가 함께 나옵니다.

cuisine 음식 folks (일반적인) 사람들, 여러분 atmosphere 분위기 handle 다루다 come with ~이 함께 나오다

62 What does the man like about the restaurant?
(A) Food
(B) Wait staff
(C) Atmosphere
(D) Location

남자는 레스토랑에 대해 무엇을 좋아하는가?
(A) 음식
(B) 종업원
(C) 분위기
(D) 위치

세부 사항 질문으로 남자 대사에서 레스토랑에 대해 언급하는 것을 잘 듣는다. 남자가 I like the atmosphere very much라고 말한 부분에서 순발력 있게 정답을 (C)로 선택한다. atmosphere은 분위기라는 뜻으로 어떤 장소의 실내 장식과 조명 등을 포함하는 분위기를 가리킨다.

63 What does Lisa imply when she says, "Of course I can"?
(A) She enjoys spicy food.
(B) She can cook Indian food.
(C) She feels hungry.
(D) She does not need help.

Lisa가 "그럼요 물론이죠"라고 말한 의도는 무엇인가?
(A) 여자는 매운 음식을 즐긴다.
(B) 여자는 인도 음식을 만들 수 있다.
(C) 여자는 배가 고프다.
(D) 여자는 도움이 필요하지 않다.

특정 표현에 대한 화자의 의도를 유추하는 신유형 질문으로, 해당 표현의 앞뒤에 단서가 있다. 남자의 질문 can you handle spicy food?(매운 음식 먹을 수 있어요?)에 대한 답으로 Of course I can(그럼요 물론이죠)이라고 말한 것이고 이어 매운 치킨 카레를 주문한 것으로 미루어 여자는 매운 음식을 즐긴다고 짐작할 수 있다. 정답은 (A)이다.

64 What is served with the hot chicken curry?
(A) Steamed rice
(B) Bread and salad
(C) A beverage
(D) Grilled vegetables

매운 치킨 카레와 함께 제공되는 것은 무엇인가?
(A) 밥
(B) 빵과 샐러드
(C) 음료
(D) 구운 채소

세부 사항 질문으로 핵심어인 hot chicken curry가 언급되는 부분을 주의 깊게 듣자. hot chicken curry에 대해 it comes with our famous garlic naan and home-made salad(갈릭 난과 홈메이드 샐러드가 함께 나온다)라고 했으므로 정답은 (B)가 된다.

Questions 65-67 refer to the following conversation and schedule. 영W 영M

W This year, our museum has planned a weekly lecture series on architecture since many people have shown a lot of interest in this area. Here's the tentative program I've prepared.

M It looks good. But did you check with all the lecturers about the schedule?

W No, not all of them. I confirmed the timetable with Mr. McKean and Ms. Rivers by phone this morning. I couldn't talk to Dr. Brown myself because he is in Mexico on business right now. However, his assistant confirmed that he would be available anytime between March 27th and April 10th.

M That's good. What about Ms. Witt? Did you get through to her too?

W No. I tried several times, but for some reason I couldn't reach her.

M Ms. Witt is invited to the Annual Architects' Conference as the keynote speaker this year, which takes place on Friday, April 7th. So I think she might be too busy on April 6th. Why don't we switch the times for the last two speakers?

W Sure, no problem. I'll revise the program accordingly.

The 2016 Architecture Series @ Evans Museum		
Thursday, March 15	5:00-6:00 p.m.	Anthony McKean
Thursday, March 22	5:00-6:00 p.m.	Joan Rivers
Thursday, March 29	5:00-6:00 p.m.	Richard Brown
Thursday, April 6	5:00-6:00 p.m.	Sophia Witt

여 올해는 우리 미술관에서 건축에 관한 시리즈 강연을 매주 계획했는데 사람들이 이 분야에 관심을 많이 보였기 때문입니다. 여기 제가 준비한 잠정적인 프로그램입니다.

남 좋아 보이네요. 그런데 이 스케줄에 대해 모든 강연자들과 확인은 했어요?

여 아니오, 모두 다는 아닙니다. McKean 씨와 Rivers 씨와는 아침에 전화로 스케줄을 확인했습니다. Brown 박사님은 지금 멕시코에 출장 중이어서 직접 통화하지는 못했어요. 그러나 그의 비서가 3월 27일부터 4월 10일까지는 시간이 되신다고 확인해 주셨고요.

남 잘됐네요. Witt 씨는 어떻게 되었나요? 그녀와도 연락이 닿았나요?

여 아니오. 몇 번 전화를 했는데 무슨 이유인지 연락이 안 되었어요.

남 Witt 씨는 올해의 연례 건축가 컨퍼런스에 기조 연설가로 초청을 받았어요. 그 행사는 4월 7일 금요일에 열리죠. 그래서 제 생각에 4월 6일에는 그녀가 너무 바쁠 수 있을 것 같네요. 마지막 두 명의 연사들의 순서를 바꾸면 어떨까요?

여 좋습니다. 문제없습니다. 그럼 말씀대로 프로그램을 변경하겠습니다.

Evans Museum에서의 2016년 건축 강연		
3월 15일 목요일	오후 5:00–6:00	Anthony McKean
3월 22일 목요일	오후 5:00–6:00	Joan Rivers
3월 29일 목요일	오후 5:00–6:00	Richard Brown
4월 6일 목요일	오후 5:00–6:00	Sophia Witt

lecture series 시리즈 강연 show interest in ~에 관심을 보이다 tentative 잠정적인 get through to ~와 연락이 닿다 reach ~에게 연락하다 switch (순서를) 바꾸다

65 Who are the speakers?
(A) Museum employees
(B) News reporters
(C) Event planners
(D) Local artists

화자들은 누구인가?
(A) 박물관 직원
(B) 뉴스 기자
(C) 행사 기획자
(D) 지역 예술가

화자들의 관계를 유추하는 유형으로 보통 도입부부터 단서가 나온다. 여자가 our museum에서 특정 행사를 준비했다고 언급한 부분에서 화자들은 같은 박물관에서 일하는 동료 사이임을 알 수 있으므로 정답은 (A)이다.

66 What problem does the woman mention?
(A) She cannot participate in a class discussion.
(B) She has misplaced her passport.
(C) She is unable to contact one of the speakers.
(D) She is unavailable to give a speech.

여자는 어떤 문제점을 언급하는가?
(A) 수업 토론에 참여할 수 없다.
(B) 여권을 잃어버렸다.
(C) 연사 중 한 명과 연락을 취할 수 없다.
(D) 연설을 할 수 없다.

순발력 있게 정답을 처리하기 위해서는 선택지를 미리 읽어 두는 것이 필수인 세부 사항 질문이다. 여자 대사에 집중하여 4명의 연사 중 한 명과는 연락이 안 된다고 언급한 No. I tried several times but for some reason, I couldn't reach her에서 정답을 (C)로 선택한다. 누구에게 연락을 하다는 의미로 쓰인 get through to, reach, contact 등을 함께 암기하자.

67 Look at the graphic. According to the speakers, whose lecture will now be held last?
(A) Anthony McKean
(B) Joan Rivers
(C) Richard Brown
(D) Sophia Witt

시각 정보를 보시오. 화자들에 따르면, 이제 누구의 강연이 마지막에 열릴 것인가?
(A) Anthony McKean
(B) Joan Rivers
(C) Richard Brown
(D) Sophia Witt

시각 정보 연계 유형으로 마지막 연설이 누가 될지에 집중하여 대화를 듣자. 연설 스케줄과 관련해 Why don't we switch the times for the last two speakers?라고 마지막 두 명의 시간을 바꾸자고 제안했고 여자는 이에 동의했으므로 마지막 연사는 (C) Richard Brown이 된다. 정답에 앞서 언급된 정보, 예를 들어 Brown 박사는 스케줄이 융통성이 있고 Witt 씨는 해당일에 바쁠 것이라는 문맥 등을 파악하면서 듣는다면 시각 정보를 좀 더 정확하게 활용할 수 있다.

Questions 68-70 refer to the following conversation and leaflet.
미W 영M

W There are still many things that need to be done before the opening of our new restaurant on Friday. How are the preparations coming along, David?
M Well, I have a 3 o'clock meeting with Chef Marco to decide on the main dishes and desserts. Have you taken a look at the sample leaflet from the printers? I need your approval to get it printed.
W Okay, I'm looking at it now. Um... David, I think there's a misprint in here. Our new restaurant is located on Kings Avenue, not Park Avenue. But it says here, Park Avenue.
M Really? Oh-uh, you're right. But I'm glad you found that error before we start printing it. I'll call the printing company and correct the mistake right away.
W Hold on. Let me double check it first.

GRAND OPENING **Kitchen 105 Burger** New Location	
Where? 5301 Park Ave. Sacramento	When? Friday, November 28th
(916) 555–3890	

여 금요일에 있는 새 레스토랑 오프닝 전에 할 일이 아직도 많아요. 준비는 어떻게 진행되고 있나요, David?
남 음, 주방장 Marco와 3시에 미팅을 갖고 주 메뉴와 디저트를 결정하기로 했어요. 인쇄소에서 온 전단지 샘플은 보셨나요? 그걸 인쇄하려면 당신의 승인이 필요해요.
여 네, 지금 보고 있어요. 어… David, 여기 인쇄 실수가 있는 것 같은데요. 우리 레스토랑은 Kings Avenue에 위치해 있지 Park Avenue가 아니잖아요. 그런데 여기에는 Park Avenue라고 되어 있네요.
남 정말요? 이런, 당신 말이 맞네요. 그렇지만 인쇄를 시작하기 전에 그 실수를 발견해서 다행이에요. 제가 바로 인쇄소에 전화해서 실수를 정정하도록 할게요.
여 잠깐만요. 제가 먼저 한 번 더 확인하고요.

GRAND OPENING **Kitchen 105 Burger** 새로운 지점	
어디서? 5301 Park Ave. Sacramento	언제? 금요일 11월 28일
(916) 555–3890	

leaflet 전단지 approval 승인 misprint 인쇄상의 실수 printer 인쇄소, 인쇄업자

68 What are the speakers mainly discussing?
(A) A dinner reservation
(B) A meeting with clients
(C) A delivery of supplies
(D) Preparations for an event

화자들은 주로 무엇에 대해 이야기하는가?
(A) 저녁 식사 예약
(B) 고객과의 미팅
(C) 물품 배달
(D) 행사를 위한 준비

대화의 주제는 보통 도입부에서 단서를 찾을 수 있다. 여자가 새 레스토랑의 개점에 대해 이야기하면서 preparations(준비 사항들)는 어떻게 진행되는지 물었으므로 정답은 (D)가 된다.

69 Look at the graphic. According to the speakers, which information is incorrect?
(A) The name of a restaurant
(B) The opening date
(C) The address of a business
(D) The telephone number

시각 정보를 보시오. 화자들에 따르면, 어떤 정보가 부정확한가?
(A) 레스토랑의 이름
(B) 개점 날짜
(C) 업체의 주소
(D) 전화번호

시각 정보를 활용해서 답의 단서를 찾는 신토익 유형으로 잘못된 정보에 집중하여 대화를 듣는다. 여자가 레스토랑의 위치에 대해 길 이름이 잘못 인쇄되었다고 언급한 부분에서 정답을 (C)로 선택한다.

70 What does the woman say she will do next?
(A) Contact the printers
(B) Review printed material
(C) Make an appointment
(D) Find an address

여자는 다음에 무엇을 하겠다고 하는가?
(A) 인쇄소에 연락하기
(B) 인쇄물 검토하기
(C) 약속 잡기
(D) 주소 찾기

여자의 향후 행동을 묻는 세부 사항 질문으로 단서는 대화의 후반부에 있다. 남자가 인쇄소에 전화를 하겠다고 했을 때, 여자가 마지막에 Let me double check it first(제가 먼저 다시 한 번 확인하고요)라고 말한 부분이 정답이다. it은 앞서 언급된 leaflet(전단지)을 의미하므로 정답은 (B)가 되며 printed material(인쇄물)로 바꾸어 표현된 점을 기억해 두자.

PART 4

Questions 71-73 refer to the following advertisement. 영M

Are you looking for the best fitness facilities in town? Then BMC Fitness Center is for you. The facilities have been fully renovated with state-of-the-art fitness equipment and a top-quality stereo system. We're open 24 hours, 7 days a week. And this month only, we're offering a variety of memberships at a discounted price. So don't miss out on this great opportunity! For more information, please give us a call at 521-7070.

이 지역 최고의 피트니스 시설을 찾고 있으세요? 그러면 BMC Fitness Center가 당신을 위한 곳입니다. 이곳은 최신식 운동 장비와 최상급 스테레오 시스템으로 완전히 개조되었습니다. 저희는 일주일에 7일 24시간 내내 문을 엽니다. 그리고 이번 달에만 할인된 가격으로 다양한 멤버십을 제공하고 있습니다. 그러니 이 엄청난 기회를 놓치지 마세요. 더 자세한 정보를 원하시면, 521-7070으로 전화 주십시오.

state-of-the-art 최신의, 최근의 top-quality 최고 품질의 miss out 놓치다

71 What business is being advertised?
(A) An office supply store
(B) A delivery service
(C) A fitness center
(D) An electronics store

어떤 사업체가 광고되고 있는가?
(A) 사무용품 상점
(B) 배달 업체
(C) 피트니스 센터
(D) 전자제품 상점

광고되는 업체에 대한 정보는 도입부에 있다. 첫 문장인 Are you looking for the best fitness facilities in town?(최고의 피트니스 시설을 찾으세요?)에서 바로 정답을 (C)로 선택한다.

72 What service is now available?
(A) A reduced price
(B) An online registration system
(C) A renovated swimming pool
(D) Extended business hours

어떤 서비스가 지금 이용 가능한가?
(A) 할인된 가격
(B) 온라인 등록 시스템
(C) 개조된 수영장
(D) 연장된 영업시간

세부 사항 질문으로 혜택을 언급하는 부분에 집중한다. 이번 달에만 다양한 멤버십을 할인된 가격으로 제공한다는 부분에서 정답을 (A)로 선택한다.

73 How can listeners get a discount?
(A) By becoming a member
(B) By presenting a coupon
(C) By calling the center
(D) By doing exercise at night

청자들은 어떻게 할인을 받을 수 있는가?
(A) 멤버가 됨으로써
(B) 쿠폰을 제시함으로써
(C) 센터에 전화를 함으로써
(D) 밤에 운동을 함으로써

세부 사항 질문으로 discount가 언급되는 부분에서 할인을 얻는 방법을 노려 듣는다. we're offering a variety of memberships at a discounted price에서 멤버십이 할인가로 제공된다고 했으므로, 멤버십을 신청하면 할인 혜택을 누릴 수 있음을 확인한다. 주의 사항은 같은 문장에서 72번과 73번의 정답이 동시에 나오므로, 질문 속의 키워드를 놓치지 않도록 주의해야 한다.

Questions 74-76 refer to the following radio announcement. 미W

Once again, this year, Radio Cape Appledale is proud to sponsor the 2nd Annual Cape Appledale Singing Contest. If you think you are a good singer, this competition may be just the place for you to showcase your talent. It is open to soloists, duets, or groups of all ages and categories, including classical, jazz, and pop. The winners of each category will be given the chance to perform on stage at the spring carnival. The competition takes place between 10 a.m. to 4 p.m. on Friday, March 10th at the Appledale Community Center. Entries must be submitted by February 28th through the station's website at www.radiocapeappledale.org.

올해 다시 한 번 Radio Cape Appledale이 제2회 연례 Cape Appledale 노래 경연대회를 후원하게 되어 자랑스럽게 생각합니다. 당신이 훌륭한 가수라고 생각하신다면, 이 대회야말로 당신의 재능을 보여줄 수 있는 장이 될 수 있습니다. 모든 연령의 솔로, 듀엣, 그룹과 클래식, 재즈와 팝을 포함하는 모든 장르가 열려 있습니다. 각 카테고리의 우승자는 봄 축제에서 무대 공연을 할 기회가 주어질 것입니다. 대회는 3월 10일 금요일, Appledale 지역 문화 회관에서 오전 10시부터 오후 4시까지 진행됩니다. 참가 신청은 2월 28일까지 방송국 웹사이트 www.radiocapeappledale.org에 제출해 주셔야만 합니다.

competition 경쟁, 대회 showcase 보여 주다 talent 재능 perform 공연하다 take place 열리다, 발생하다 entry 참가 신청

74 Who is the Cape Appledale Singing Contest intended for?
(A) Writers
(B) Vocalists
(C) Painters
(D) Photographers

Cape Appledale 노래 경연 대회는 누구를 위해 의도되었는가?
(A) 작가
(B) 가수
(C) 화가
(D) 사진사

세부 사항 질문으로 대회가 누구를 대상으로 하는지를 묻는다. 도입부 대회의 이름, the 2nd Annual Cape Appledale Singing Contest를 들었을 때 노래 대회임을 알 수 있다. 정답은 (B)이다.

75 What will the winners of the event receive?
(A) A convertible car
(B) A musical instrument
(C) A cash prize
(D) A chance to sing on stage

행사의 우승자들은 무엇을 받을 것인가?
(A) 오픈 카
(B) 악기
(C) 현금 상품
(D) 무대에서 노래할 기회

세부 사항 질문으로 키워드인 winners에 집중하여 듣는다. The winners of each category가 언급되고 봄 축제에서 무대 공연할 기회가 주어진다고 했으므로 정답은 (D)가 된다.

76 What should interested listeners do by February 28th?
(A) Submit an entry form online
(B) Read the rules for the competition
(C) Learn from a vocal trainer
(D) Tune in to a radio station

관심 있는 청취자는 2월 28일까지 무엇을 해야 하는가?
(A) 온라인으로 참가 신청서 제출하기
(B) 대회 규칙 읽어 보기
(C) 보컬 트레이너로부터 배우기
(D) 라디오 방송에 주파수 맞추기

세부 사항 질문으로 질문의 키워드인 February 28th에 집중한다. 참가 신청이 2월 28일까지 웹 사이트를 통해서만 제출될 수 있다고 했으므로 정답은 (A)가 된다. Through the station's website가 online으로 바꿔 표현된 점을 기억하자.

Questions 77-79 refer to the following recorded message. 미M

Thanks for calling Flagstaff Tea Ware Museum. The museum is located in the center of the city, right next to City Hall. It displays a large collection of antique tea ware, including delicate china sets. Our current exhibition features traditional tea ceremonies and tea ware from all around the world. And we also provide visitors with hands-on experience of the tea ceremonies. The museum is open Tuesday to Saturday, from 9 A.M. to 6 P.M. If you would like to speak to one of our employees, please stay on the line.

Flagstaff Tea Ware Museum에 전화 주셔서 감사합니다. 이 박물관은 시청 바로 옆, 도시의 중심에 위치해 있습니다. 섬세한 자기 세트를 포함하여 다양한 앤티크 차 다기를 전시하고 있습니다. 현재 전시회에서는 전통적인 다도 및 전 세계의 차 상품을 특별 전시하고 있습니다. 또한 방문객들에게 다도를 실제로 경험할 기회를 제공하고 있습니다. 박물관은 화요일부터 토요일까지, 오전 9시부터 오후 6시까지 문을 엽니다. 직원 중 한 명과 통화하기를 원하신다면 전화를 끊지 말고 기다리세요.

be located 위치하다 in the center of ~의 중심에 antique 골동품 tea ware 차 도구 delicate 섬세한, 연약한 china 자기 (그릇) feature 특징으로 삼다 tea ceremony 다도 hands-on 직접 해 보는 stay on the line 전화를 끊지 않고 대기하다

77 Where is the museum located?
(A) In the middle of the city
(B) A block from City Hall
(C) Next to a tea shop
(D) Across from the Chinese Embassy

박물관은 어디에 위치해 있는가?
(A) 도시의 한가운데
(B) 시청에서 한 블록 떨어진 곳
(C) 차 상점 옆
(D) 중국 대사관에서 맞은편

세부 사항 질문으로 박물관의 위치에 집중한다. The museum is located in the center of the city가 정답의 근거로 (A)를 선택한다. 그 후에 언급된 right next to City Hall을 듣고 들리는 단어 함정인 (B)를 선택하는 일이 없도록 하자.

78 What does the exhibition feature?
(A) Sculptures
(B) Silverware
(C) Tea ceremonies
(D) Antique furniture

전시회는 무엇을 특별 전시하는가?
(A) 조각상
(B) 은 식기
(C) 다도
(D) 골동 가구

세부 사항 질문으로 키워드 feature에 집중한다. 현재의 전시를 소개하면서 traditional tea ceremonies를 특별 전시한다고 언급했으므로 정답은 (C)가 된다.

79 Why would listeners stay on the line?
(A) To talk to a staff member
(B) To reserve a ticket
(C) To get directions
(D) To leave a message

청자들은 왜 전화를 끊지 않고 기다릴 것인가?
(A) 직원과 얘기하려고
(B) 표를 예매하려고
(C) 길 안내를 받으려고
(D) 메시지를 남기려고

세부 사항 질문으로 키워드 stay on the line이 언급되는 부분에 정답의 단서가 등장한다. If you would like to speak to one of our employees(직원 중 한 명과 얘기하시길 원한다면)라고 단서를 붙인 후 전화를 끊지 말고 기다리라고 했으므로 정답은 (A)가 된다.

Questions 80-82 refer to the following telephone message. (영W)

Hello, this message is for Mr. Kyle Dobson. This is Kathy Chang from Freshy Catering. I've received the online order for your business lunch meeting scheduled for tomorrow at 1 p.m. I just need to know some more details, which you forgot to indicate on the form. We offer two lunch options – cold and hot. Cold lunches include salads, sandwiches and wraps, whereas hot lunches include hot entrées, stone baked pizza and toasted sandwiches. Could you call me back and let me know which option you'd like? If you'd like to see pictures of our menu, they are available on our website. Please get back to me by 4 this afternoon, so we can start the food preparation. Thank you.

여보세요, 이 메시지는 Kyle Dobson 씨에게 남기는 것입니다. 저는 Freshy Catering의 Kathy Chang입니다. 내일 오후 1시에 잡힌 당신의 사업상 오찬 회의를 위한 온라인 주문서를 받았습니다. 당신이 주문 양식에 표시하는 것을 깜빡 잊은 몇 가지 세부 사항을 알고자 합니다. 저희는 점심 메뉴를 2가지 제공합니다-차가운 것과 따뜻한 것이요. 찬 점심은 샐러드, 샌드위치 및 랩이 포함되는 반면 따뜻한 점심은 더운 메인 요리와, 돌에 구운 피자 및 구운 샌드위치를 포함합니다. 어떤 종류를 선호하는지 저에게 다시 전화를 해주시겠습니까? 메뉴의 사진을 보고 싶으시면, 웹 사이트에서 보실 수 있습니다. 오늘 오후 4시까지 답신을 주시면, 음식 준비를 시작할 수 있습니다. 감사합니다.

online order 온라인 주문 indicate 표시하다 food preparation 음식 준비

80 Where does the caller work?
(A) At an event planning firm
(B) At a local restaurant
(C) At a catering company
(D) At a convention center

전화하는 사람은 어디서 일하는가?
(A) 이벤트 기획사
(B) 지역 레스토랑
(C) 출장 음식 업체
(D) 컨벤션 센터

메시지에서 화자에 대한 정보는 도입부 자신을 소개하는 부분에 나온다. This is Kathy Chang from Freshy Catering처럼 이름과 함께 전치사 from 뒤에 소속을 밝히는데 업체의 이름에 catering이 있는 것으로 볼 때 출장 음식 업체가 정답이다.

81 What problem does the caller mention?
(A) An incorrect price was charged.
(B) An event will be delayed.
(C) Requested items are unavailable.
(D) An order form is not complete.

전화하는 사람은 어떤 문제점을 언급하는가?
(A) 부정확한 가격이 부과되었다.
(B) 행사는 연기될 것이다.
(C) 요청된 물건은 이용이 불가능하다.
(D) 주문 양식이 완료되지 않았다.

문제점은 보통 주제의 역할을 하므로 도입부부터 문맥을 잡는 것이 중요하다. 온라인 주문을 받았으나 상대방이 표시하는 것을 잊은(forgot to indicate) 세부 사항을 알아야 한다고 말하므로 정답은 주문지가 완벽히 채워지지 않았다는 뜻의 (D)가 된다.

82 According to the speaker, what should the listener do by 4 o'clock?
(A) Call the business
(B) Cancel an order
(C) Pay a bill online
(D) Speak to a supervisor

화자에 따르면, 청자는 4시까지 무엇을 해야 하는가?
(A) 업체에 전화하기
(B) 주문 취소하기
(C) 온라인으로 계산서 지불하기
(D) 상사와 얘기하기

세부 사항 질문으로 키워드 4 o'clock에 집중한다. 전체 문맥상 두 가지 런치 메뉴 중 하나를 선택해 달라고 했고, 오후 4시까지는 get back to me(나에게 답신 전화를 달라)라고 했으므로 정답은 (A)가 된다.

Questions 83-85 refer to the following talk. (미M)

Good morning everyone. Welcome to Margo Plastics. My name is Nick Clegg and I'm the facilities supervisor. As new assembly line workers, you'll be spending most of your time in the production areas we've just entered. However, I'd like to show you the other facilities at the factory. Our first stop will be the technical service department, which is located in the south wing. To enter the building, you'll need to present your photo ID at the entrance. So please get that ready.

여러분 안녕하세요. Margo Plastics에 오신 걸 환영합니다. 저는 Nick Clegg이고 시설 감독관입니다. 새로운 조립라인 신입 직원으로서, 당신은 우리가 지금 막 들어온 생산 구역에서 대부분의 시간을 보내게 될 것입니다. 그러나 저는 여러분에게 공장의 다른 시설물들도 보여 드리고 싶습니다. 첫 번째로 들를 곳은 남쪽 별관에 위치해 있는 기술 서비스 부서입니다. 건물에 들어가기 위해서 입구에서 사진이 부착된 신분증을 제시해야만 합니다. 그럼 신분증을 준비해 주십시오.

assembly line 조립 라인 spend one's time 시간을 보내다 production area 생산 구역 facility 시설물 wing 별관 entrance 입구

83 Who is the speaker addressing?
(A) International clients
(B) Production workers
(C) Factory managers
(D) University students

화자는 누구에게 이야기하는가?
(A) 해외 고객
(B) 생산 노동자
(C) 공장 매니저
(D) 대학생

청자가 누구인지 묻는 질문으로 질문 속에 speaker라는 단어를 보고 화자를 묻는 것으로 착각하지 않도록 하자. 청자에 대한 단서는 As new assembly line workers, you'll be이다. 전치사 as는 직업/신분을 나타낼 때 자주 쓰이므로 기억해 두자. 이 경우는 청자들의 신분이 조립라인 직원들임을 알 수 있다.

84 According to the speaker, where will the listener go next?
(A) To a different building
(B) To the assembly floor
(C) To a manufacturing plant
(D) To a training room

화자에 따르면, 청취자는 다음에 어디로 갈 것인가?
(A) 다른 건물
(B) 조립라인 층
(C) 생산 공장
(D) 교육실

세부 사항 질문으로 담화가 끝난 후에 갈 곳을 묻는다. 단서는 Our first stop will be가 들리고 남쪽 별관에 있는 다른 부서에 간다고 언급했으므로 정답은 (A)가 된다. The south wing이 a different building으로 바꿔 표현된 점을 기억해 두자.

85 What does the speaker mean when he says, "please get that ready"?
(A) Employees should read a document.
(B) Employees should unlock a door.
(C) Employees should have their identification handy.
(D) Employees should be prepared for a test.

화자가 "그것을 준비해 주세요"라고 말한 의도가 무엇인가?
(A) 직원들은 서류를 읽어야 한다.
(B) 직원들은 문을 열어야 한다.
(C) 직원들은 신분증을 꺼내기 쉽게 준비해야 한다.
(D) 직원들은 시험에 대비해야 한다.

화자의 의도를 묻는 해당 표현 앞에 단서가 있다. 빌딩에 들어가기 위해서는 photo ID(사진이 있는 신분증)를 제시해야 한다고 말한 후, please get that ready라고 한 것은 신분증을 준비하라는 의미가 된다. 정답은 (C)이고 have ~ handy라는 표현은 '~을 꺼내기 쉽게 두다'는 의미로 암기해 두자.

Questions 86-88 refer to the following talk. 영W

Today, I'd like to clarify a couple things about the company's business travel policies. Your travel expenses will be reimbursed only if your trip is approved by your department head in advance. If you're planning on a business trip, you should get authorization from your manager at least one week prior to your departure. And please remember to keep all the receipts for accommodations, meals and transportation during your trip. Unless you submit those original documents to accounting, the company won't be able to reimburse you.

오늘 저는 회사의 출장 정책에 대해서 몇 가지 사항을 명확하게 하려고 합니다. 여러분의 출장 경비는 여러분의 부서장이 사전에 승인을 해준 출장에 대해서만 환급을 받게 됩니다. 출장을 계획하고 있다면, 매니저로부터 적어도 출발 일주일 전에는 승인을 받아야만 합니다. 그리고 출장 중에 숙박, 식사 및 교통수단에 쓰인 모든 영수증을 반드시 보관해 주십시오. 회계 부서에 원본을 제출해 주시지 않는 한 회사는 환급해 드리지 않습니다.

clarify 명확하게 하다 business travel policy 출장 정책 expense 경비, 비용 reimburse 배상하다, 환급하다 department head 부서장 authorization 승인, 허가 at least 적어도 prior to ~전에 accommodations 숙박

86 What is the purpose of the talk?
(A) To suggest a cost-cutting measure
(B) To clarify the parking regulations
(C) To revise the hiring process
(D) To describe a company policy

대화의 목적은 무엇입니까?
(A) 비용 절감 대책을 제안하려고
(B) 주차 규정을 분명히 하려고
(C) 고용 절차를 변경하려고
(D) 회사 정책에 대해 설명하려고

담화의 목적은 도입부에 명확하게 밝히는 경우가 대부분이다. 회사의 출장 정책에 대해 명확하게 하고 싶은 것이 있다고 했으므로 정답은 (D)이다. clarify라는 동사만 듣고 (B)를 선택한다면 주차에 대한 내용은 언급되지 않았으므로 오답 함정에 빠진 것이 된다.

87 What are employees encouraged to do in advance?
(A) Confirm the travel itinerary
(B) Request permission for travel
(C) Submit a progress report
(D) Meet a project deadline

직원들은 사전에 무엇을 할 것을 권고 받는가?
(A) 출장 일정 확인하기
(B) 출장에 대한 승인 요청하기
(C) 경과 보고서 제출하기
(D) 프로젝트 마감 맞추기

세부 사항 질문으로 키워드 in advance를 통해 사전에 할 일로 언급되는 것에 집중한다. 사전에 승인된 출장에 대해서만 회사가 환급을 해준다고 말한 후, 적어도 1주일 전에는 매니저에게 출장 승인을 받으라고 했으므로 정답은 (B)가 된다. in advance가 a week prior to와 바꿔 쓰인 것을 암기해 두자.

88 What are employees asked to submit?
(A) Personal information
(B) A revised price list
(C) An original product proposal
(D) Expense receipts

직원들은 무엇을 제출할 것을 요청 받는가?
(A) 개인 정보
(B) 수정된 가격표
(C) 제품 제안서 원본
(D) 경비 영수증

세부 사항 질문으로 화자가 요청하는 내용에 집중한다. 정답 근거 문장은 Unless절이 사용되어 원본 영수증을 제출하지 않으면 회사는 환급을 하지 않는다고 했으므로, 원본 영수증을 제출하면 환급을 받을 수 있다는 의미가 된다. 정답은 (D)이다.

Questions 89-91 refer to the following advertisement. (미W)

Harris-Moore, your number one supplier of high-end home furniture, is now having a special winter sale on all our products! In addition to offering the best selection and lowest prices, we guarantee your satisfaction. We'll provide you with a full refund including any delivery fees, if you are not happy with your purchase and wish to return it. And what's more, you can even create your own furniture. If you're looking for something unique for your home, simply visit our website at www.harrismoore.com. You can choose from any of our furniture and then customize it to suit your style. There are many kinds of fabrics and leathers you can choose from at our online store.

여러분의 넘버원 최고급 가구 공급업체인 Harris-Moore가 지금 전 제품에 대해 특별 겨울 세일을 진행하고 있습니다! 최고의 제품을 최저의 가격으로 제공할 뿐 아니라, 귀하의 만족을 보장해 드립니다. 구입하신 물건에 만족하지 못해서 환불하기로 결정하신다면, 귀하는 배송비를 포함한 전액을 환불해 드립니다. 그뿐만 아니라, 귀하만의 가구를 만드실 수도 있습니다. 집에 놓을 뭔가 독특한 것을 찾고 계시다면, 그냥 www.harrismoore.com로 방문해 주시면 됩니다. 저희 가구 중에 선택하신 후 귀하의 스타일에 맞도록 주문 제작하세요. 온라인 매장에는 귀하가 선택할 수 있는 많은 종류의 천과 가죽이 있습니다.

supplier 공급업체 guarantee 보장하다 full refund 전액 환불 what's more 그뿐만 아니라 unique 독특한 customize ~을 주문 제작하다 suit ~에 맞추다 leather 가죽

89 What type of business is being advertised?
(A) A house repair shop
(B) A delivery company
(C) A furniture supplier
(D) An office supply store

어떤 종류의 사업이 광고되고 있는가?
(A) 주택 수리 업체
(B) 배달 업체
(C) 가구 공급업자
(D) 사무용품 상점

광고되는 업체는 광고의 도입부부터 언급된다. 첫 문장 Harris-Moore, your number one supplier of high-end home furniture에서 가구를 공급하는 업체임을 알 수 있다.

90 What does the woman mean when she says, "And what's more"?
(A) She will add another important point.
(B) She wants to know more about the company.
(C) She has forgotten a word.
(D) She will introduce a new line of merchandise.

여자가 "그뿐만 아니라"라고 말한 의미가 무엇인가?
(A) 여자는 다른 중요한 요점을 덧붙일 것이다.
(B) 여자는 회사에 대해 더 알고 싶다.
(C) 여자는 단어를 까먹었다.
(D) 여자는 신상품을 소개할 것이다.

특정 표현에 대한 화자의 의도를 묻는 신토익 유형 질문으로 해당 표현 what's more(그뿐만 아니라) 이후에 상품을 주문 제작도 할 수 있다는 추가 정보를 알려 주는 것에서 정답은 (A)임을 알 수 있다.

91 What can customers do online?
(A) Exchange items
(B) Customize a product
(C) Participate in an event
(D) Request a catalog

고객은 온라인으로 무엇을 할 수 있는가?
(A) 물건 교환하기
(B) 제품 주문 제작하기
(C) 행사에 참여하기
(D) 카탈로그를 요청하기

세부 사항 질문으로 online으로 할 수 있는 것에 집중한다. 웹 사이트를 방문해서 customize it(제품을 주문 제작할 수 있다)이라고 했으므로 정답은 (B)가 된다. Just visit our website라고 힌트어가 나오면 집중해서 듣는 것이 중요하다.

Questions 92-94 refer to the following talk. (영M)

Ladies and Gentlemen, welcome to the grand reopening of FIC Concert Hall. As you can see, the concert hall has undergone an amazing transformation over the past 2 years and it's now ready to meet the needs of a savvy 21st century audience. The auditorium's iconic dome is still intact but with some upgrades to the acoustics, the overall sound quality has been improved dramatically. Now everyone, in just 10 minutes the Metropolitan Orchestra will be performing at its new home for the first time. So please join us for this special event. And after the performance, please pick up a brochure for our upcoming shows on your way out.

신사 숙녀 여러분, FIC Concert Hall의 재오픈 행사에 오신 것을 환영합니다. 보시다시피, 이 콘서트홀은 지난 2년 동안 엄청난 변신을 했고 이제 똑똑한 21세기 관객들의 요청에 부합할 준비가 되었습니다. 이 공연장의 상징인 돔 천장은 본래 그대로 유지되어 있지만 음향 장치는 개선되어서, 전반적인 음질이 크게 향상되었습니다. 이제 10분 후에 Metropolitan Orchestra가 새로운 보금자리에서 최초로 공연을 하게 됩니다. 그러니 이 특별한 순간에 저희와 함께 해 주십시오. 그리고 공연이 끝난 후에는 나가는 길에 향후 공연에 대한 안내 책자를 가져가 주십시오.

undergo 겪다, 진행하다 transformation 변신, 탈바꿈 savvy 정통한, 박식한 auditorium 강당, 객석 iconic 상징이 되는 dome 돔, 반구형 지붕 intact 온전히 보존된 acoustics 음향 시설 sound quality 음질 dramatically 극적으로 upcoming 다가오는

92 What is the purpose of the event?
(A) To introduce a local musician
(B) To celebrate the reopening of a concert hall
(C) To congratulate the purchaser of a building
(D) To recognize the contribution of an employee

행사의 목적은 무엇인가?
(A) 지역 음악가를 소개하려고
(B) 콘서트홀의 재오픈을 축하하려고
(C) 건물의 구입자를 축하하려고
(D) 직원의 공헌을 인정해 주려고

행사가 열리는 이유는 도입부에 밝혀지는 경우가 대부분이다. welcome to the grand reopening of FIC Concert Hall에서 순발력 있게 정답을 (B)로 선택한다.

93 Who will perform at the event?
(A) A famous vocalist
(B) A symphony orchestra
(C) A dance group
(D) A world-class artist

누가 행사에서 공연할 것인가?
(A) 유명한 가수
(B) 관현악단
(C) 댄스 그룹
(D) 세계적인 예술가

세부 정보를 찾는 질문으로 공연이 언급될 때를 잘 노려 듣는다. 10분 후에 Metropolitan Orchestra's performance가 있을 것이라고 했으므로 정답은 (B)가 된다.

94 What is suggested about the brochure?
(A) It is only for members.
(B) It is available at the information desk.
(C) It lists the names of performers.
(D) It contains upcoming events.

팸플릿에 관하여 무엇이 암시되는가?
(A) 회원들만을 위한 것이다.
(B) 안내 데스크에 준비되어 있다.
(C) 공연자의 이름이 나열되어 있다.
(D) 다가오는 공연을 포함한다.

brochure가 언급되는 부분에서 일치되는 정보를 찾는 세부 사항 문제이다. 마지막 부분에 안내 책자를 가져가라고 하며 for our upcoming shows라고 했으므로 정답은 (D)가 된다. show와 event는 바꿔 쓸 수 있는 패러프레이징 어휘이다.

Questions 95-97 refer to the following telephone message and list. 영W

Hello, this is Eleanor Jackson calling from Eastbay Athletic Wear. I placed an online order yesterday for some of the items we'd run out of. The order number is C00129. I'm calling to make a change to my order if it hasn't been shipped out yet. I requested 10 white T-shirts but I'd like to make it 30. They've been selling very quickly since the summer sale began. Also, I'd like to remove the first item from my order form. Customers are only looking for summer wear because of the hot weather. Oh, and as I have indicated, you can deliver the rest of the order to our store at 3319 Bay Street. If you have any questions, please give me a call. Thank you very much.

PCA Clothing Order Form
Customer: Eleanor Jackson
Order Number: C00129

Item	Color	Quantity
Zip-up hoodie	Yellow	20
T-shirt	White	10
Polo shirt	White	10
Swim shorts	Red	5

안녕하세요, 저는 Eastbay Athletic Wear에서 전화드리는 Eleanor Jackson입니다. 제가 어제 재고가 떨어진 상품들을 온라인으로 주문을 했고 주문번호는 C00129입니다. 그런데 만약 상품이 아직 배송되지 않았으면 주문을 변경하려고 전화했어요. 흰색 티셔츠 10개를 요청했었는데 30개로 변경하고 싶습니다. 여름 세일이 시작된 후로 그 제품이 빨리 팔리고 있어서요. 또한 주문서의 첫 번째 상품은 취소하고 싶습니다. 더운 날씨 때문에 고객들이 여름 상품들만 찾고 있어서요. 아, 그리고 이미 알려 드린 대로, 나머지 주문품은 저희 가게인 Bay Street 3319번지로 배달해 주시면 됩니다. 문의 사항이 있으시면, 전화 주세요. 정말 감사합니다.

PCA 의류 주문 양식
고객: Eleanor Jackson 주문 번호: C00129

상품	색상	개수
후드 집업	노란색	20
티셔츠	흰색	10
폴로 셔츠	흰색	10
수영복 반바지	빨간색	5

athletic wear 스포츠 의류 run out 다 떨어지다 summer wear 여름 의류 indicate 나타내다

95 Why is the speaker calling?
(A) To book a venue
(B) To change an order
(C) To request some information
(D) To give directions to a store

화자는 왜 전화하는가?
(A) 장소를 예약하려고
(B) 주문을 변경하려고
(C) 정보를 요청하려고
(D) 상점까지 길 안내를 해 주려고

메시지의 목적을 묻는 질문으로 I'm calling to 뒤에 보통 목적이 나온다. 도입부에 주문을 이미 했다는 내용을 파악한 후, I'm calling to make a change to my order에서 주문 변경이 목적임을 알 수 있다. 정답은 (B)이다.

96 Look at the graphic. Which item will be removed from the order?
(A) Zip-up hoodie
(B) T-shirt
(C) Polo shirt
(D) Swim shorts

시각 정보를 보시오. 어떤 상품이 주문서에서 취소될 것인가?
(A) 후드 집업
(B) 티셔츠
(C) 폴로 셔츠
(D) 수영복 반바지

시각 정보를 활용해서 답의 단서를 찾는 신토익 유형으로 주문서에서 취소될 품목에 집중한다. I'd like to remove the first item on my order form을 통해 주문서의 첫 번째 품목이 취소될 것임을 알 수 있다. 정답은 (A)이다.

97 What additional information does the speaker provide?
(A) What time a store closes
(B) How a payment should be made
(C) What date a sale begins on
(D) Where a business is located

화자는 어떤 추가 정보를 제공하는가?
(A) 몇 시에 상점이 문을 닫는지
(B) 어떻게 지불이 되어야 하는지
(C) 며칠에 세일이 시작하는지
(D) 어디에 업체가 위치해 있는지

주문 변경에 대한 언급 후 추가로 제공되는 정보는 you can deliver the rest of the order to our store at 3319 Bay Street으로 상점의 주소를 알려 주는 부분이 된다. 그러므로 정답은 (D)이며 다른 선택지들은 화자에 의해 전혀 언급되지 않았다.

Questions 98-100 refer to the following excerpt from a meeting and chart. 영M

I called this marketing meeting today, to share some good news with you. A few months ago, some of you suggested that we diversify our sales channels to increase sales. So we started selling our new laundry detergent, Green 7X, through some television shopping networks. I just received last month's sales figures and they look pretty good, as the total sales of Green 7X have risen by 30%. Many home shoppers, who have purchased our product more than once, especially like the fact that it is an eco-friendly detergent. The most surprising thing is which age group Green 7X is the most popular with. Damian, I'd like you to analyze why this age group is so interested in green detergents. Hopefully we can come up with some new marketing strategies based on that information.

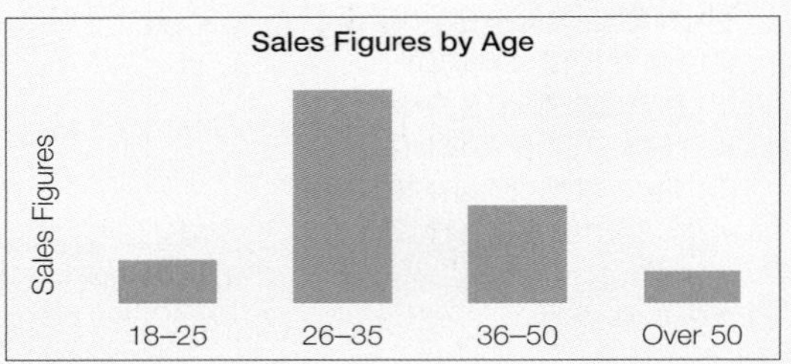

오늘 이 마케팅 미팅을 소집한 것은 여러분과 좋은 소식을 나누기 위함입니다. 몇 달 전에, 여러분 중 몇 명이 판매 증가를 위해 판매 채널을 다양화시켜야 한다고 제안했었죠. 그래서 신상품 세탁 세제인 Green 7X를 텔레비전 쇼핑 방송을 통해 팔기 시작했습니다. 제가 막 지난달의 판매 수치를 받았는데 Green 7X의 총 판매가 30퍼센트 오르는 등 성과가 좋습니다. 우리 상품을 한 번 이상 구매한 홈 쇼핑 고객들은 특히 이 제품이 친환경 세제라는 점을 마음에 들어 합니다. 가장 놀라운 것은 Green 7X가 어떤 연령대에 가장 인기가 좋은가입니다. Damian, 왜 이 연령대가 친환경 세제에 그렇게 관심이 많은지 분석을 해주세요. 그 정보를 기반으로 우리가 새로운 마케팅 전략을 세울 수 있기를 바랍니다.

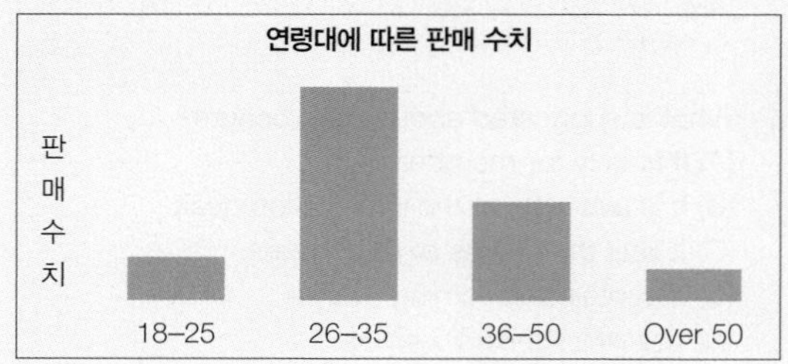

diversify 다양화하다 sales channel 판매 채널 detergent 세제 eco-friendly 친환경적인 age group 연령대 green 친환경의 come up with 생각하다, 떠올리다

98 Who is the speaker addressing?
(A) Department heads
(B) Marketing staff
(C) Regular customers
(D) Environmentalists

화자는 누구에게 말하는가?
(A) 부서장
(B) 마케팅 직원
(C) 단골 고객
(D) 환경운동가

청자를 묻는 대표적인 질문으로 화자를 묻는 질문으로 착각하지 말자. 도입부의 Today I called this marketing meeting to share some good news with you(좋은 소식을 나누기 위해 마케팅 회의를 소집했다)에서 듣는 이들은 마케팅 직원들임을 유추할 수 있다. 정답은 (B)이다.

99 According to the speaker, what did the company start?
(A) Expanding its business overseas
(B) Producing energy-efficient appliances
(C) Selling products on TV shopping channels
(D) Offering a free delivery service

화자에 따르면, 회사는 무엇을 시작했는가?
(A) 해외로 사업을 확장하는 것
(B) 에너지 효율이 높은 가전제품을 생산하는 것
(C) 홈쇼핑 채널에서 상품을 판매하는 것
(D) 무료 배송 서비스를 제공하는 것

세부 사항 질문이므로 키워드인 '회사가 시작한 것'에 주목하여 듣자. we started selling our new laundry detergent, Green 7X, through some television shopping networks 부분에서 텔레비전 쇼핑 방송을 통해 새로운 세제를 팔기 시작했음을 알 수 있다. 정답은 (C)이다.

100 Look at the graphic. Which age group is Damian asked to look into?
(A) 18-25
(B) 26-35
(C) 36-50
(D) Over 50

시각 정보를 보시오. Damian은 어떤 연령대를 조사하라고 요청받는가?
(A) 18–25세
(B) 26–35세
(C) 36–50세
(D) 50세 이상

시각 정보를 활용해서 답의 단서를 찾는 신토익 유형으로 화자가 Damian에게 요청하는 내용과 시각 정보를 연결하는 것이 포인트가 된다. 화자는 Damian에게 이 연령대에서 인기가 많은 이유를 분석해 달라고 요청했으므로 그래프에서 가장 높은 판매 수치를 보인 26–35세가 정답이 된다.

Actual Test 6

PART 1

본책 p.72

1 (A)	2 (B)	3 (A)	4 (A)	5 (C)	6 (A)

PART 2

본책 p.76

7 (B)	8 (A)	9 (B)	10 (A)	11 (A)	12 (A)
13 (C)	14 (B)	15 (A)	16 (B)	17 (C)	18 (C)
19 (B)	20 (C)	21 (A)	22 (C)	23 (A)	24 (A)
25 (B)	26 (C)	27 (B)	28 (C)	29 (B)	30 (C)
31 (C)					

PART 3

본책 p.77

32 (A)	33 (C)	34 (C)	35 (A)	36 (D)	37 (B)
38 (D)	39 (C)	40 (A)	41 (A)	42 (C)	43 (D)
44 (D)	45 (C)	46 (B)	47 (D)	48 (A)	49 (B)
50 (B)	51 (D)	52 (A)	53 (D)	54 (A)	55 (C)
56 (B)	57 (A)	58 (C)	59 (B)	60 (D)	61 (C)
62 (A)	63 (C)	64 (B)	65 (A)	66 (C)	67 (D)
68 (A)	69 (C)	70 (A)			

PART 4

본책 p.81

71 (B)	72 (C)	73 (D)	74 (B)	75 (D)	76 (C)
77 (B)	78 (D)	79 (C)	80 (B)	81 (A)	82 (D)
83 (C)	84 (A)	85 (C)	86 (A)	87 (B)	88 (D)
89 (C)	90 (D)	91 (A)	92 (D)	93 (B)	94 (A)
95 (D)	96 (C)	97 (A)	98 (C)	99 (B)	100 (A)

PART 1

1 (A) The man is trimming some shrubs.
미M (B) The man is holding a broomstick.
(C) The ladder is leaning against a vertical wall.
(D) The man is ascending a staircase.

(A) 남자가 관목을 손질하고 있다.
(B) 남자가 긴 빗자루를 쥐고 있다.
(C) 사다리는 수직 벽에 기대어져 있다.
(D) 남자가 계단을 올라가고 있다.

남자가 사다리에 걸터앉아 우거진 관목을 기구로 손질하고 있는 모습이다. 손에 쥔 것의 이름을 알 수 없지만 빗자루가 아닌 것은 확실하고 사다리가 벽에 기대어져 있는 상황도 아니다. 토익에서 나무나 정원을 손질하는 상황이 자주 나오니 관련 어휘를 알아 두자.

trim 다듬다, 손질하다 shrub 관목 hold 잡다, 쥐다 broomstick 긴 빗자루 lean against ~에 기대다 vertical 수직의 ascend 오르다 staircase 계단

2 (A) Some people are marching through the street.
영W (B) Traffic is running in several lanes.
(C) The pedestrian crosswalk is being painted.
(D) Cars are parked at the side of the street.

(A) 사람들이 거리에서 행진하고 있다.
(B) 차량들이 여러 차선으로 지나가고 있다.
(C) 횡단보도가 칠해지는 중이다.
(D) 차들이 길 옆쪽에 주차되어 있다.

횡단보도 앞에 사람들이 신호가 바뀌기를 기다리고 있고 차들은 여러 차선으로 지나가는 중이다. 차들이 달리는 중이지 주차된 상황은 아니므로 (D)는 오답이다.

march 행진하다 traffic 교통, 차량 lane 도로, 차선 pedestrian crosswalk 횡단보도

3 (A) They are jogging on a road.
영M (B) They are driving away from the garage.
(C) They are working together.
(D) They are walking on a ranch.

(A) 사람들이 도로에서 조깅을 하고 있다.
(B) 사람들이 차고에서 차를 몰고 떠나고 있다.
(C) 사람들이 함께 일하고 있다.
(D) 사람들이 목장에서 걷고 있다.

도로에서 군인으로 보이는 두 명의 남자가 조깅을 하고 있다. 한 명은 배낭을 메고 있지만 선택지에서 가방에 대한 언급은 없다. 발음이 비슷한 work와 walk를 이용한 전통적인 함정이 아직도 종종 등장하니 주의해야 한다.

drive away 차를 몰고 떠나다 garage 차고, 주차장 ranch 목장

4 (A) The water has been left running.
미W (B) Some glasses have been placed near the sink.
(C) More dishes are being added into a sink.
(D) A woman is using a towel to wipe off the kitchen worktop.

(A) 물이 틀어져 있다.
(B) 유리잔 몇 개가 싱크대 근처에 놓여 있다.
(C) 더 많은 그릇이 싱크대 안에 더해지고 있다.
(D) 여자가 부엌 조리대를 닦기 위해 타월을 쓰고 있다.

싱크대에 아직 설거지하기 전의 그릇들이 잔뜩 담겨 있고 물이 틀어져 있는 모습이다. 사람이 전혀 보이지 않으므로 사람이 언급되면 무조건 오답이 되며 유리잔 또한 보이지 않는다. (C)가 옳은 설명이 되려면 그릇을 들고 있고 싱크대 위에 더 갖다 놓는 동작이 진행 중이어야 하므로 역시 사람이 필요하다.

run 액체를 흐르게 하다 place 두다, 놓다 add 더하다 wipe off 닦아내다 worktop 조리대

5 (A) The bricks are being removed.
미M (B) Some curtains have been closed.
(C) A woman is wiping the window.
(D) A woman is watering the potted plants.

(A) 벽돌들이 치워지고 있다.
(B) 커튼이 쳐져 있다.
(C) 여자가 창문을 닦고 있다.
(D) 여자가 화분에 물을 주고 있다.

화분이 놓여 있는 창가에서 여자가 창문을 닦고 있다. 커튼은 걷혀져 있으므로 (B)는 오답이다. 무언가를 닦고 있는 모습에서 자주 등장하는 표현인 wipe, wipe off는 꼭 익혀 두자.

brick 벽돌 remove 제거하다, 없애다 wipe 닦다 water 물을 주다 potted plant 화분

6 (A) Some people are facing the same direction.
영M (B) Lights on the ceiling have been turned off.
(C) The speaker is distributing some notebooks.
(D) Some people are greeting each other.

(A) 일부 사람들이 같은 방향을 향하고 있다.
(B) 천장에 조명들이 꺼져 있다.
(C) 연사는 공책을 나눠 주고 있다.
(D) 일부 사람들이 서로 인사하고 있다.

등을 보이고 있는 사람이 마이크를 들고 뭔가를 말하고 있는데 나머지 사람들은 앉아서 이를 듣고 있다. 듣는 이들은 이 연사를 바라보고 있으므로 '같은 방향으로 향하다'라는 표현이 정확하다. 사진에서는 동작 자체 외에도 시선이나 몸이 향하고 있는 방향을 언급할 때가 많다.

face 향하다, 바라보다 direction 방향 lights 조명 turn off 끄다 speaker 연사 distribute 나눠주다, 분배하다 greet 인사하다

PART 2

7 When is the entrée being served?
영M (A) To the table.
미W (B) Very shortly.
(C) 20 dollars.

주 요리는 언제 나오나요?
(A) 테이블로요.
(B) 금방이요.
(C) 20달러입니다.

의문사 when 질문으로 시점에 대한 정보가 없는 (A)와 (C)는 오답 소거해야 한다. shortly는 '곧'이라는 의미로 when의 정답이 될 수 있다.

entree 주 요리 shortly 곧

8 How do you usually get to work?
미W (A) I take the train.
미M (B) For an hour.
(C) It's on Main Street.

보통 직장에 어떻게 가시나요?
(A) 기차를 탑니다.
(B) 1시간 동안이요.
(C) 메인 가에 있습니다.

의문사 how와 함께 'get to+장소'가 쓰이면 '~에 가는 방법'이라는 의미이다. 직장에 가는 교통수단을 물었으므로 정답은 (A)가 된다.

work 직장

9 Who's organizing the budget meeting?
영M (A) As soon as possible.
영W (B) Nathan is.
(C) It'll be on the third floor.

누가 예산 회의를 준비하고 있나요?
(A) 가능한 한 빨리요.
(B) Nathan이요.
(C) 3층에 있을 것입니다.

의문사 who 질문으로 사람 이름으로 답을 말해준 (B)가 정답이 된다. (A)는 의문사 when 질문에 대한 답이고 (C)는 의문사 where 질문에 대한 답이다.

organize 준비하다, 조직하다 as soon as possible 가능한 한 빨리

10 Has the mechanic fixed your car yet?
미M (A) He just finished.
미W (B) My card is not valid.
(C) That's fair.

정비 기사가 당신 차를 다 고쳤나요?
(A) 그가 지금 막 끝냈습니다.
(B) 제 카드는 유효하지 않아요.
(C) 공평하네요.

Yes/No 여부를 묻는 질문으로 정비공이 차를 고쳤는지 여부를 묻고 있으므로, 방금 다 끝냈다고 답한 (A)가 정답이다. (B)는 car와 유사 발음인 card를 이용한 함정이고, (C)는 문맥에서 완전히 벗어났으므로 정답이 될 수 없다.

mechanic 정비공, 수리공 fix 고치다 valid 유효한 fair 공평한, 공정한

11 Is the convenience store open 24 hours?
미W (A) Yes, all year round.
영M (B) I already had breakfast.
(C) No, she works the morning shift.

그 편의점은 24시간 문을 여나요?
(A) 네, 1년 내내요.
(B) 이미 아침을 먹었습니다.
(C) 아니오, 그녀는 아침 근무를 합니다.

Yes/No 여부를 묻는 질문으로 주어는 편의점이고 24시간 문을 여는지에 대한 사실 여부가 포인트이다. (A)의 Yes는 '24시간 문을 연다'고 해석되고 all year round는 '일 년 내내'라는 뜻으로 정답이다. 반면, (C)의 No는 24시간 문을 열지 않는다고 해석되므로 주어가 she로 바뀌는 것은 주어 오류 함정으로 보아야 한다.

convenience store 편의점 all year round 일 년 내내 morning shift 아침 근무, 아침 교대조

12 How often does the number 85 bus come?
미M (A) Every 15 minutes.
영W (B) I'll go by train.
(C) At the main entrance.

85번 버스는 얼마나 자주 옵니까?
(A) 15분에 한 번씩이요.
(B) 전 기차로 가려고요.
(C) 정문에서요.

의문사 how often은 빈도를 묻는 질문이기 때문에 (A)가 정답이다. 보통 every Monday(매주 월요일), once a month(한 달에 한 번) 같은 표현들이 정답에 자주 등장한다.

every 매, ~마다 main entrance 정문

13 Where's the receipt for the parcel you sent?
영M (A) It begins on Wednesday.
미W (B) They have been sent abroad.
(C) I put it in the top drawer.

당신이 보낸 소포의 영수증은 어디 있나요?
(A) 그것은 수요일에 시작합니다.
(B) 그것들은 해외로 보내졌어요.
(C) 제가 맨 위 서랍 안에 넣어놨어요.

의문사 where 질문으로 요지는 '영수증이 어디 있는지'이다. 뒤에 나오는 parcel, you sent 등은 부수적인 정보일 뿐이므로 질문의 핵심을 정확하게 해석하자. 영수증의 위치에 대한 정보는 서랍에 있다고 답한 (C)이다. (B)의 경우 parcel을 듣고 연상할 수 있는 sent, abroad 등의 어휘들을 이용한 함정이 된다.

receipt 영수증 parcel 소포 abroad 해외로

14 Doesn't this job require financial management
미W experience?
미M (A) He's our new manager.
(B) Yes, along with a degree in business.
(C) It is ten times larger.

이 일자리는 재무 관리 경력을 요구하지 않나요?
(A) 그가 우리 새 매니저입니다.
(B) 맞아요, 비즈니스 학위도요.
(C) 열 배 더 큽니다.

Yes/No 질문으로 주어는 this job이다. 이 직업이 특정 경력을 요구하는지 물었으므로 정답 (B)의 Yes는 요구한다는 의미가 되고, 특정 분야의 학위도 함께 요구한다는 부연 설명이 된다. (A)는 주어 오류 함정이고, (C)는 크기에 대해 말하므로 문맥에서 벗어났다.

require 요구하다 financial management 재무 관리 along with ~와 함께 ten times 열 배

15 Will Anna be on vacation all next week?
영M (A) Yes, until the 20th.
영W (B) Taking the train is faster.
(C) A tourist attraction.

Anna는 다음 주 내내 휴가를 가나요?
(A) 네, 20일까지요.
(B) 기차를 타는 것이 더 빠릅니다.
(C) 관광지요.

Yes/No 여부를 묻는 질문으로 Anna가 다음 주에 휴가인지 여부를 확인하는 것이 질문의 핵심이다. (A)의 Yes는 휴가가 맞다는 뜻이고, 20일까지라고 부연 설명을 했으므로 정답이다. (B)와 (C)는 vacation이라는 단어를 들었을 때 연상되는 어휘를 이용한 함정이 된다.

on vacation 휴가 중인 tourist attraction 관광지

16 Why is the grocery store closed today?
미M (A) To the garage.
미W (B) They don't open on Sundays.
(C) Yes, for two days.

식료품 가게가 왜 오늘 문을 닫았나요?
(A) 차고로요.
(B) 그들은 일요일에 문을 열지 않아요.
(C) 네, 이틀 동안요.

의문사 why 질문으로 식료품 가게가 문을 열지 않은 적절한 이유를 찾는다. (B)는 일요일에는 항상 문을 열지 않는다는 의미로 정답이 된다. (A)는 의문사 where에 대한 정답이고 (C)는 Yes를 듣자마자 오답 소거한다.

grocery store 식료품 가게 garage 차고

17 When was the book review published?
영W (A) In the magazine.
미M (B) It was a best-seller in Europe.
(C) In August.

그 서평은 언제 출판되었습니까?
(A) 잡지에요.
(B) 유럽에서는 베스트셀러였어요.
(C) 8월이요.

질문의 핵심은 when(시점)이므로 정답은 (C)이다. (A)는 where에 대한 답변이고 (B) 역시 시점에 대해서는 전혀 언급되지 않아 정답이 될 수 없다.

book review 신간 서적에 대한 서평 publish 간행하다, 출판하다

18 How did the safety inspection go?
미M (A) Tomorrow at noon.
영M (B) All of the factory workers.
(C) Actually, it was postponed.

안전 검사는 어떻게 진행됐나요?
(A) 내일 정오에요.
(B) 모든 공장 인부들이요.
(C) 실은 연기되었어요.

지난 일의 결과/상태 등을 묻는 질문으로 How did+주어+go?를 암기해 두자. 검사의 진행이 어땠는지 묻는 것이 질문의 요지인데, 연기되어 검사를 하지 않았다고 답한 (C)가 정답이 된다.

safety inspection 안전 검사 postpone 연기하다

19 Alex has made a dinner reservation, hasn't he?
영W (A) I'd like something light for lunch.
미W (B) Yes, he just did it.
(C) Place it in the middle.

Alex가 저녁 예약을 했죠, 그렇지 않나요?
(A) 저는 점심은 가볍게 먹고 싶습니다.
(B) 네, 그가 지금 막 했어요.
(C) 그걸 중앙에 두세요.

예약을 완료했는지 묻는 Yes/No 질문으로, 지금 막 했다고 답한 (B)가 정답이다.

light 가벼운 place ~에 두다 in the middle 중앙에

20 What should I do with this pen after I use it?
영W (A) I used to work there.
미M (B) Not very much.
(C) Leave it with my secretary.

제가 이 펜을 사용한 후에 어떻게 하면 될까요?
(A) 저는 거기서 일했었어요.
(B) 많지 않아요.
(C) 제 비서에게 남겨 주세요.

What should I do ~ ?는 상대방의 지시를 바랄 때 쓰는 표현으로 암기해 두자. 펜을 다 쓴 후에 어떻게 하면 될지 묻고 있으므로 비서에게 남겨 달라고 한 (C)가 정답이다.

used to (과거에) ~했다 leave 남기다, 두다

21 Didn't you hear about Henry's promotion to vice
영M president?
미W (A) Yes, he really deserves it.
(B) I know Ms. Stratford.
(C) The company banquet.

당신은 Henry가 부사장으로 승진한 것에 대해서 못 들었나요?
(A) 들었어요, 그는 정말 자격이 충분하죠.

(B) 저는 Stratford 씨를 알아요.
(C) 회사 연회요.

Yes/No 여부를 묻는 부정 의문문 형태로 질문의 not은 해석상 제외하고 생각하는 것이 포인트이다. (A)의 Yes는 동사 hear에 대해 답하는 것이므로 '들었다'고 해석되며, Henry가 부사장이 될 자격이 충분하다는 부연 설명을 한 것이므로 정답이다.

promotion 승진 vice president 부사장 deserve 받을 만하다, 누릴 자격이 되다 banquet 연회

22 Which road is usually less congested?
영W (A) Jenny wrote it.
영M (B) Because of the car accident.
(C) Try Robson Avenue.

어느 도로가 보통 덜 막히나요?
(A) Jenny가 그것을 썼습니다.
(B) 차 사고 때문에요.
(C) Robson 로로 가보세요.

의문사 which 질문으로 어떤 도로가 덜 막히는지를 묻고 있으므로 특정 도로 이름으로 답해준 (C)가 정답이다. (A)는 road와 발음이 유사한 wrote을 이용한 함정이고, (B)는 막히는 이유를 말하고 있으므로 의문사 why에 대한 답이다.

congested 막히는, 정체되는 car accident 차 사고

23 What's your policy on refunds and exchanges?
미M (A) You need to pay the shipping charges.
미W (B) No, it is a non-refundable ticket.
(C) In 7 business days.

환불과 교환에 관한 그쪽 방침이 어떻게 되나요?
(A) 배송비를 지불하셔야 합니다.
(B) 아니오, 이것은 환불 불가 티켓입니다.
(C) 영업일로 7일 후에요.

의문사 what 질문으로 환불과 교환에 관한 정책이 무엇인지를 묻고 있다. 배송비를 부담하라고 정책의 내용을 말한 (A)가 정답이다. (B)처럼 No로 답변하는 것은 불가능하므로 오답 소거하고, (C)는 의문사 when에 대한 답이 된다.

policy 정책 refund 환불 exchange 교환 shipping charge 배송 비용 non-refundable 환불 불가능한 business day 영업일

24 I'm here for my 2 o'clock appointment.
영W (A) Could you fill out this form first?
미W (B) He answered my call.
(C) Before the doctor leaves.

2시 진료 때문에 왔습니다.
(A) 먼저 이 양식을 작성해 주시겠습니까?
(B) 그가 제 전화를 받았어요.
(C) 의사 선생님이 떠나기 전에요.

평서문 유형으로 대화의 상황을 떠올리며 의도를 파악하는 것이 중요하다. 약속을 미리 잡고 약속 장소에 왔다는 말을 하고 있으므로 대화의 상대방은 접수 담당자가 된다. (A)에서 양식을 먼저 작성해 달라는 답을 들었을 때 병원에서의 대화 상황이었음을 알 수 있다. (B)는 주어 오류 함정이고, (C)는 병원 상황과 연상되는 어휘 doctor를 사용한 함정이다.

fill out 작성하다 form 양식 answer a call 전화를 받다

25 Didn't we just pass the exit ramp?
영M (A) Please turn off the light.
미W (B) No, it's right up ahead.
(C) In the back of the store.

우리가 막 출구를 지나치지 않았나요?
(A) 불을 꺼 주세요.
(B) 아니오, 바로 앞에 있어요.
(C) 상점의 뒤쪽에요.

Yes/No 질문으로 출구를 지나쳤는지 여부를 물었고 질문의 not은 해석상 제외하므로 (B)의 No를 '지나치지 않았다'로 해석하고 exit ramp는 바로 앞에 있다는 부연 설명으로 연결한다. (A)는 ramp의 유사 발음인 lamp와 의미가 동일한 light를 사용한 연상어 함정이다.

pass 지나치다 exit ramp (고속 도로의) 출구, 나들목 up ahead 앞쪽에

26 Why don't you create your own website?
미M (A) Yes, I made it on time.
영W (B) By credit card.
(C) I don't think I need one.

당신만의 웹 사이트를 만드는 게 어떠세요?
(A) 네, 저는 시간 안에 해냈어요.
(B) 신용 카드로요.
(C) 필요 없을 것 같아요.

제안 의문문으로 웹 사이트를 만드는 게 어떠냐고 물었으므로 거절로 답변한 (C)가 정답이다. (A)는 문맥에서 벗어난 답으로 시제도 틀리게 사용되었고, (B)는 의문사 how에 대한 답이다.

create 만들다 own 자신의 make it ~을 해내다, 시간 맞춰 도착하다

27 The bus fare is going up next month, isn't it?
영W (A) No, keep going straight.
영M (B) Starting on Monday, I think.
(C) 40 dollars per day.

버스 요금이 다음 달에 오를 거예요, 그렇지 않나요?
(A) 아니오, 계속 똑바로 가세요.
(B) 월요일부터 시작될 거예요.
(C) 하루에 40달러요.

Yes/No 여부를 묻는 질문으로 주어는 bus fare (버스 요금)이다. 요금이 인상될 것인지 여부를 말해주는 것이 정답인데 (B)는 월요일부터 오른다고 말하고 있으므로 적절한 답이 된다. (C)는 how much에 대한 답으로 볼 수 있다.

bus fare 버스 요금 straight 똑바로 starting+시점 ~부터

28 Mr. Lion, can we meet the construction deadline by Wednesday?
미W (A) We're late for the meeting.
미M (B) Call him at extension 705.
(C) If we work overtime.

Lion 씨, 우리 수요일까지 공사 마감을 맞출 수 있을까요?
(A) 저희는 회의에 늦었습니다.
(B) 내선번호 705로 그에게 전화하세요.
(C) 우리가 초과 근무를 한다면요.

파트2에서 상대방의 이름을 부르는 것은 해석상 제외시킨다. 질문의 요지는 마감을 맞출 수 있는지 Yes/No 여부를 묻는 것이므로 초과 근무를 한다면 가능하다고 답한 (C)가 정답이고, 이렇게 if절 형태로 간접적으로 Yes/No 여부를 밝히는 형태는 반드시 기억해 두자.

meet a deadline 마감을 맞추다 extension 내선번호 work overtime 초과 근무하다

29 You can use my car until you get yours back from
영M the mechanic's.
영W (A) Some engine problems.
(B) I'd appreciate it very much.
(C) I'm flying to Sydney.

당신의 차를 정비소에서 가져올 때까지 제 차를 쓰셔도 됩니다.
(A) 엔진 문제가 좀 있어요.
(B) 정말 감사합니다.
(C) 비행기를 타고 시드니에 갑니다.

평서문 유형으로 상대방에게 호의를 제공하는 것이 요지이다. 제공에 대한 답변 형태는 상대방의 호의를 받거나 거절하는 것이므로, 감사하다며 호의를 받는 (B)가 정답이 된다. (A)는 car, mechanic's 등을 들었을 때 연상되는 engine problems를 사용한 연상어 오류이고, (C) 역시 car를 들었을 때 연상되는 flying을 사용한 함정이 된다.

get ~ back 되찾다 appreciate 고마워 하다

30 Do you want to present first or last?
미M (A) I'd prefer a window seat.
미W (B) In case she's late.
(C) I'll go first.

당신은 처음에 발표를 하시겠어요 아니면 마지막에 하시겠어요?
(A) 전 창가 좌석을 선호합니다.
(B) 그녀가 늦는 경우를 대비해서요.
(C) 제가 처음에 할게요.

Do you want to는 '~하시겠어요?'라는 의미이다. 발표 순서상 처음을 선호하는지, 마지막을 선호하는지 물었으므로 처음을 선택한 (C)가 정답이다. (A)는 선택 의문문과 어울리는 prefer란 어휘를 이용한 함정이고 (B)는 주어 오류이면서 문맥상 벗어난 답이다.

present 발표하다 prefer 선호하다 in case+절 ~한 경우를 대비하여

31 We create unique designs for company logos.
미W (A) Munich is a beautiful city.
영M (B) Sure, any time is fine.
(C) Do you have some samples?

우리는 회사 로고를 위해 독특한 디자인을 만듭니다.
(A) 뮌헨은 아름다운 도시입니다.
(B) 그럼요, 아무 때나 좋습니다.
(C) 샘플이 있으신가요?

평서문 유형으로 회사가 독특한 디자인을 만들어내는 곳이라고 말했으므로 샘플을 볼 수 있냐고 묻는 (C)가 정답이 된다. (A)는 unique와 발음이 유사한 Munich를 이용한 함정이고, (B)는 문맥상 벗어났으므로 오답으로 처리한다.

create 만들다 unique 독특한

PART 3

Questions 32-34 refer to the following conversation. 미M 영W

M Excuse me. I'd like to get one of the coats displayed in your show window. Does it come in grey, or anything other than black?
W Oh, that coat is also available in blue, but we're currently out of stock. The next shipment won't arrive until the day after tomorrow. Would you like me to reserve one for you when it arrives?
M Thank you but no. I wanted it as a birthday present for my wife today. Is there any other way to get one?
W In that case, you should go to the shop on Maple Street and see if they have one. But let me call them and ask if they have one in stock before you go over there.

남 실례합니다. 진열장에 전시되어 있는 코트 중 하나를 구입하고 싶은데요. 검은색 말고 회색이나 다른 색으로 나오나요?
여 아, 그 코트는 파란색이 가능하지만, 지금은 품절입니다. 다음 배송이 내일 모레가 되어야 도착합니다. 도착하면 당신을 위해 하나 따로 남겨놓을까요?
남 감사합니다만 됐습니다. 오늘 와이프의 생일 선물로 그걸 원했던 겁니다. 하나 구입할 수 있는 다른 방법이 있을까요?
여 그런 경우라면, Maple Street에 있는 매장에 하나 있는지 가 보시는 게 좋겠어요. 그러나 가시기 전에 제가 그쪽에 전화를 해서 재고가 하나 있는지 물어보겠습니다.

show window 진열장 come in (색상, 사이즈로) 나오다 out of stock 재고가 없는 the day after tomorrow 내일 모레 reserve 따로 남기다 in that case 그런 경우라면 in stock 재고가 있는

32 Where is the conversation most likely taking place?
(A) In a store
(B) At a shipping company
(C) In a warehouse
(D) On the street

대화는 어디서 이뤄지고 있는 것 같은가?
(A) 상점
(B) 배송 회사
(C) 창고
(D) 거리

대화의 장소를 유추하는 질문으로 대화의 도입부에 단서가 있다. 도입부에 남자가 코트를 구입하고 싶다고 하는 부분에서 바로 정답을 (A)로 선택한다.

33 What does the man not like about the product?
(A) The size
(B) The fabric
(C) The color
(D) The price

남자는 상품의 어떤 점을 좋아하지 않는가?
(A) 크기
(B) 직물
(C) 색깔
(D) 가격

세부 사항 질문으로 남자가 상품에 대해 좋아하지 않는 것에 집중한다. Does it come in grey, or anything other than black?에서 남자는 회색 혹은 다른 색상을 원하고 현재 보고 있는 상품은 검은색임을 파악할 수 있다. 따라서 정답은 (C)가 된다.

34 What will the woman probably do next?
(A) Visit a shop
(B) Speak to a manager
(C) Contact a store
(D) Wrap a gift

여자는 다음에 무엇을 할 것인가?
(A) 상점 방문하기
(B) 매니저에게 얘기하기
(C) 매장에 연락하기
(D) 선물 포장하기

여자의 향후 행동을 묻는 질문으로 정답의 단서는 후반부에 나온다. 여자의 대사에서 Let me가 들릴 때가 정답인데 앞서 언급됐던 상점에 전화해 보겠다고 했으므로 (C)가 적절하다.

Questions 35-37 refer to the following conversation. 영M 미W

M Hello, I'm calling from VPO Phone Service. We're offering local businesses a month-long trial of VPO Premium with unlimited international calling. Would you like to sign up for it today and take advantage of this special offer?

W It sounds like a good deal. And we do make a lot of international calls in the office. How much will it cost after the trial period?

M It will cost 30 dollars per month. And after the trial, you can cancel your premium service if you don't want to continue with it.

W I'd like to sign up, but not today because I'll be on a business trip until next Wednesday. Could you call me back on Thursday?

남 여보세요, VPO Phone Service에서 전화를 드립니다. 저희가 이 지역 업체들에게 한 달간 무료로 국제 전화를 무제한 사용할 수 있는 VPO Premium의 체험 혜택을 드리고 있습니다. 오늘 신청하셔서 특별 혜택을 이용해 보시겠습니까?

여 좋은 제안 같네요. 게다가 우리는 사무실에서 국제 전화를 많이 쓰거든요. 무료 사용 기간 후에는 얼마나 비용이 들죠?

남 매달 30달러입니다. 그리고 체험 기간 후에, 서비스를 유지하고 싶지 않다면 프리미엄 서비스를 취소하실 수 있습니다.

여 신청하고 싶지만 오늘은 아닙니다. 다음 주 수요일까지 출장을 가거든요. 목요일에 다시 전화 주시겠어요?

local business 지역 사업체 trial (상품의) 체험, 시험 사용 unlimited 무제한의 sign up for신청하다 take advantage of 이용하다, 활용하다

35 What is the man calling about?
(A) A free trial
(B) A job interview
(C) A mistake on the bill
(D) A magazine subscription

남자는 무엇에 관해서 전화하는가?
(A) 무료 체험
(B) 취업 면접
(C) 계산서의 실수
(D) 잡지 구독

남자의 전화 목적을 묻는 질문으로 도입부에서 정답의 단서를 찾는다. 남자가 한 달 동안 국제 전화를 무료로 사용하는 체험 혜택을 제공하고 있다고 말했으므로 정답은 (A)이다.

36 What does the woman ask about?
(A) The location of an event
(B) The status of an order
(C) The name of a provider
(D) The cost of a service

여자는 무엇에 관해서 질문하는가?
(A) 행사 장소
(B) 주문 상태
(C) 공급업체 이름
(D) 서비스 비용

체험 기간 후에 비용이 얼마나 들지 질문하는 부분에서 (D)로 정답을 선택한다. How much will it cost가 단서가 된다.

37 Why does the woman ask the man to call her back?
(A) To revise an estimate
(B) To sign up for a service
(C) To complain about a poor service
(D) To complete a form

여자는 왜 남자에게 다시 전화해 달라고 하는가?
(A) 견적을 수정하려고
(B) 서비스를 신청하려고
(C) 형편없는 서비스에 관하여 불평하려고
(D) 양식을 완성하려고

여자가 서비스 신청을 원하지만 오늘은 아니라고 한 이유가 출장을 가기 때문이었고, 출장 후에 다시 전화를 달라고 했으므로 정답은 (B) 서비스 신청을 하기 위해서이다. 질문의 키워드보다 정답 단서가 먼저 나오기 때문에 문맥을 유지해서 듣는 것이 중요한 포인트가 된다.

Questions 38-40 refer to the following conversation. 미W 미M

W Excuse me, how much do you charge here for parking per hour?

M We charge $6 per hour, but you can't park here at the moment because the area is full. A concert is scheduled to be held in one hour.

W Oh, no. I've been looking around to find a space for more than 30 minutes, but I couldn't find any. Is there anywhere around here I could go?

M Well, did you try the Jenkins bank? You can find it right on the corner of 5th Avenue. The parking is free there on weekends, though it's a bit far to walk from there.

여 실례합니다. 여기 한 시간 주차하는 데 요금이 얼마인가요?

남 한 시간에 6달러지만, 지금 주차장이 꽉 차서 주차하실 수 없습니다. 콘서트가 한 시간 뒤에 열릴 예정이어서요.

여 이런. 30분 넘게 주변에서 주차할 곳을 찾아다녔는데 전혀 안 보이더라고요. 여기 주변에 마땅한 곳이 있나요?

남 Jenkins 은행에 가 보셨나요? 5번가 모퉁이를 돌면 바로 있어요. 그 주차장이 주말에는 무료예요. 걸어가기에는 좀 멀지만요.

charge (요금을) 청구하다 be scheduled to ~하기로 예정되어 있다 realtor 부동산 중개인 parking attendant 주차장 안내원 facility (특정 목적용 장소나 건물 같은) 시설 parking permit 주차 허가증

38 Who most likely is the man?
(A) A taxi driver
(B) A bank guard
(C) A realtor
(D) A parking attendant

남자의 직업은?
(A) 택시 운전사
(B) 은행 경비원
(C) 부동산 중개인
(D) 주차 안내원

여자가 남자에게 주차 요금을 묻고 있고 다른 주차장을 안내하고 있으므로 남자의 직업은 (D)로 볼 수 있다.

39 What is the problem?
(A) The bank is closed.
(B) The woman doesn't have a parking ticket.
(C) The facility is full at the moment.
(D) The woman has lost her ticket.

무엇이 문제인가?
(A) 은행이 문을 닫았다.
(B) 여자가 주차권을 갖고 있지 않다.
(C) 시설이 현재 꽉 차 있다.
(D) 여자가 표를 잃어버렸다.

여자가 주차장에서 30분 넘게 주차할 곳을 찾았지만 찾지 못해서 남자가 다른 장소를 언급하고 있는 상황이므로 (C)가 가장 적절한 답이다.

40 What does the man suggest the woman do?
(A) Try a different location
(B) Buy a parking permit
(C) Return to the facility later
(D) Pay the fee by cash

남자가 여자에게 제안하는 것은?
(A) 다른 장소로 가 보기
(B) 주차 허가증을 구매하기
(C) 나중에 그 시설로 되돌아오기
(D) 현금으로 요금 지불하기

주차할 공간을 찾지 못한 여자에게 남자는 다른 곳을 가 보라고 제안하고 있으므로 (A)가 정답이다.

Questions 41-43 refer to the following conversation. 미W 미M

W Hello, this is Bella calling from Dr. Waylon's office. I just wanted to confirm your appointment with the doctor on Wednesday at 2 p.m.

M Oh, no. I completely forgot about it and scheduled a very important meeting that day. Is it possible to reschedule the appointment for Friday? Any time after noon would be fine.

W Let's see. Um... Dr. Waylon can see you on Friday at 1 p.m. Also, could you tell me what type of medical insurance coverage you have now? We need that information to keep our records up-to-date.

여 여보세요. Waylon 박사님 병원에서 전화드리는 Bella입니다. 수요일 오후 2시에 의사 선생님과 진료 예약하신 걸 확인하려고 전화 드렸습니다.

남 오, 어쩌죠. 제가 그걸 완전히 잊어버리고 그 날짜에 중요한 미팅을 잡았어요. 진료 예약을 금요일로 재조정하는 것이 가능할까요? 정오 이후에는 언제든 좋습니다.

여 한 번 볼게요. 음… Waylon 박사님은 금요일 오후 1시에 진료 보실 수 있습니다. 또 어떤 종류의 의료 보험을 가지고 있는지 지금 좀 알려 주시겠어요? 기록을 최신 정보로 업데이트 해야 합니다.

confirm 확인하다 reschedule 일정을 재조정하다 medical insurance coverage 의료 보험 up-to-date 최신의, 최근의

41 Who most likely is the woman?
(A) A receptionist
(B) An insurance salesperson
(C) A pharmacist
(D) A doctor

여자는 누구일 것 같은가?
(A) 접수 담당자
(B) 보험 판매원
(C) 약사
(D) 의사

여자의 직업을 유추하는 질문으로 여자의 도입부 대사를 집중해서 듣고 판단한다. 여자가 의사와의 진료 예약을 확인하고자 한다는 부분에서 (A)로 선택한다. 혹시라도 doctor라는 단어만 듣고 (D)를 선택하는 일이 없도록 하자. 환자와의 진료 예약을 확인하는 업무는 대표적인 receptionist의 업무이다.

42 What does the man want to do?
(A) Expedite a delivery
(B) Locate some documents
(C) Reschedule an appointment
(D) Speak to a doctor

남자는 무엇을 원하는가?
(A) 배송을 빠르게 하기
(B) 서류 찾기
(C) 예약 변경하기
(D) 의사와 이야기하기

남자 대사에서 남자가 원하는 일을 찾아 듣는다. Is it possible to reschedule the appointment for Friday?에서 진료 예약 날짜를 변경하고자 함을 알 수 있으므로 정답은 (C)가 된다.

43 What does the woman ask the man to do?
(A) Pay a bill in advance
(B) Fill out a set of questionnaires
(C) Bring his medical history form
(D) Provide his insurance information

여자는 남자에게 무엇을 해 달라고 요청하는가?
(A) 계산서 미리 지불하기
(B) 설문지 한 세트 작성하기
(C) 의료 기록 양식 가져오기
(D) 남자의 보험 정보 제공하기

남자가 요청을 받는 일을 물었으므로 정답은 여자 대사에서 나온다. 여자가 could you라는 요청 표현을 쓸 때 집중해서 정답을 캐치한다. 남자의 현재 의료보험이 어떤 것인지 물었으므로 정답은 (D)가 된다.

Questions 44-46 refer to the following conversation. 영W 영M

W Thank you for dropping by, Ron. I really want to say that you've done such a great job as our newspaper's economics reporter over the past 5 years. As you may know, we're planning to expand our international coverage. And I'd like to recommend you for the position based in Beijing. It's a year-long assignment and I think you'd be perfect for that job.

M Oh, thank you very much, Ms. Jones. It sounds like a huge opportunity but I need to discuss it with my wife before I make any decision. As you know, relocating to Beijing would be a big change.

W I understand. Why don't you take some time to think it over and talk to me when you make up your mind? Here's the specific description of the assignment. Read it over carefully and let me know if you have any more questions.

여 들러줘서 고마워요, Ron. 당신은 지난 5년 동안 우리 신문사의 경제부 기자로서 일을 정말 잘하셨다고 말하고 싶어요. 아시다시피, 우리는 해외 기사 보도를 확대하려고 계획 중이에요. 북경 근무 직책에 당신을 추천하고 싶어요. 1년간의 임무인데 당신이 적임자라고 생각합니다.

남 대단히 감사합니다. Jones 씨. 굉장한 기회인 것 같지만 결정을 내리기 전에 아내와 얘기를 나눠봐야 합니다. 아시다시피, 북경으로 이사를 가는 것은 큰 변화일 테니까요.

여 이해합니다. 시간을 가지고 심사숙고하신 후 결정을 내리면 얘기해 주시겠어요? 여기 업무에 대한 세부 설명이 있습니다. 주의 깊게 읽어 보고 질문이 있으면 알려 주세요.

drop by 들르다 do a great job 일을 잘하다 economics reporter 경제부 기자 expand 확대하다, 확장하다 coverage (뉴스) 보도 make a decision 결정을 내리다 think over 숙고하다

44 According to the woman, what change will the newspaper make?
(A) Another department will be added.
(B) A merger will take place.
(C) The headquarters will be moved.
(D) International coverage will increase.

여자에 의하면, 신문사는 어떤 변화를 갖게 되는가?
(A) 부서가 하나 추가될 것이다.
(B) 합병이 일어날 것이다.
(C) 본사가 이전될 것이다.
(D) 해외 기사 보도가 증가할 것이다.

세부 사항 질문으로 여자 대사에서 신문사에 있을 변화의 내용에 집중한다. international coverage(해외 기사 보도)를 확대하고 싶다고 했으므로 정답은 (D)이다. expand와 increase는 패러프레이징되니 반드시 암기하자.

45 What does the man say he needs to do?
(A) Rearrange the office
(B) Request detailed information
(C) Discuss with his spouse
(D) Contact his manager

남자는 무엇을 해야 한다고 말하는가?
(A) 사무실 다시 배치하기
(B) 세부 정보 요청하기
(C) 배우자와 논의하기
(D) 상사에게 연락하기

남자 대사에서 I need to가 들릴 때 놓치지 말고 정답을 캐치한다. 아내와 의논해야 한다고 했으므로 정답은 (C)로 선택하고, wife는 spouse(배우자)로 바꿔 표현됨을 기억하자.

46 What does the woman give the man?
(A) Flight tickets to Beijing
(B) Details of the work assignment
(C) A travel itinerary
(D) A deadline extension

여자는 남자에게 무엇을 주는가?
(A) 베이징 행 비행기 티켓
(B) 업무에 대한 세부 사항
(C) 출장 여정표
(D) 마감 연장

세부 사항 질문으로 여자가 Here's라고 할 때 뭔가를 남자에게 건네며 말하는 것이므로 집중한다. 업무의 세부 설명이라고 했으므로 정답은 (B)가 된다.

Questions 47-49 refer to the following conversation. (미W) (미M)

W Hi, Johnathan. How was the product testing on our new line of hiking boots last week?

M It went well actually. We had a group of 20 product testers evaluate the three types of boots. They tried them all out and liked the overall design. But some of them said they wouldn't wear the leather ones because they were too tight for hiking.

W I see. I'd like to hear more about the test results. How soon can you present them to the entire department?

M We're analyzing the data now. I think the final report will be completed by tomorrow. So why don't I show it to everyone at the staff meeting on Wednesday?

여 안녕하세요, Johnathan. 지난주에 있었던 신상품 등산 부츠의 상품 테스트는 어땠나요?

남 잘 진행됐습니다. 20명의 상품 평가자 그룹에게 세 가지 종류의 부츠를 평가하도록 했어요. 그들이 모두 착용해보았고 전반적인 디자인은 좋아했는데 그들 중 일부는 등산하기에 너무 타이트하기 때문에 가죽으로 된 제품은 신지 않을 것이라고 합니다.

여 그렇군요. 테스트 결과에 대해서 좀 더 알고 싶은데요. 얼마나 빨리 전체 부서에게 발표를 할 수 있으신가요?

남 지금 자료를 분석하고 있습니다. 최종 보고서는 내일까지 완료될 것 같으니 수요일 직원 회의 때 모든 분들께 보여 드리면 어떨까요?

hiking boots 등산 부츠 product tester 상품 평가자 evaluate 평가하다 try out 테스트해 보다 overall 전반적인 leather 가죽 entire department 전체 부서

47 Who did the man meet with last week?

(A) A product designer
(B) Sales representatives
(C) A company executive
(D) Product testers

남자는 지난주에 누구를 만났는가?

(A) 제품 디자이너
(B) 영업 사원
(C) 회사 임원
(D) 제품 평가자

세부 사항 질문으로 last week에 집중하여 정답을 캐치한다. 여자가 지난주 product testing(상품 테스트)이 어땠는지를 묻는 부분과 남자가 product testers(상품 평가자들)에게 상품 평가를 했다는 부분에서 정답이 (D)임을 알 수 있다.

48 What was the problem with one type of boots?

(A) Its material
(B) Its size
(C) Its price
(D) Its weight

부츠 중 한 종류는 무엇이 문제였는가?

(A) 소재
(B) 크기
(C) 가격
(D) 무게

질문의 스키밍을 통해 이미 부츠 중 한 종류에는 문제가 있음을 파악해 두고 부정적인 내용에 집중한다. 3가지 종류의 부츠가 있다고 했고, the leather ones(가죽 부츠)는 너무 타이트해서 등산용으로 맞지 않다고 했으므로 가죽이라는 소재가 문제임을 알 수 있다.

49 What will the man do on Wednesday?

(A) Meet with some volunteers
(B) Present some product information
(C) Collect some data from questionnaires
(D) Sign an agreement

남자는 수요일에 무엇을 할 것인가?

(A) 자원봉사자들 만나기
(B) 상품 정보 발표하기
(C) 설문지로부터 정보 수집하기
(D) 계약서에 서명하기

세부 사항 질문으로 남자가 Wednesday에 할 일로 언급한 내용은 '상품 테스트 결과를 직원 회의에서 모두에게 보여 주겠다'이므로 정답은 (B)로 선택한다.

Questions 50-52 refer to the following conversation. (영W) (미M)

W Ethan, I've got a favor to ask of you. I know we're supposed to give a demonstration on the new payroll software tomorrow morning, but Mr. Gordon wants me to go to Boston to meet with some clients on short notice. Can you do the presentation without me? I don't think I'll be back in time.

M I actually haven't finished my part of the presentation yet and we don't have to give the demonstration until next week. Why don't we just put it off for a week?

W **That's not a bad idea.** All right then, I'll call the payroll department and let them know about the schedule change.

여 Ethan, 부탁할 게 있어요. 우리가 내일 아침에 새로운 급여 정산 소프트웨어를 시연하기로 되어 있잖아요. 그런데 Gordon 씨께서 갑자기 제게 보스턴에 가서 고객을 만나라고 하세요. 저 없이 발표를 하실 수 있겠어요? 시간 안에 돌아오지 못할 것 같아요.

남 실은 제가 발표에서 맡은 부분을 아직 끝내지 못했고 우리는 다음 주에 시연을 해도 되잖아요. 일주일만 미루는 게 어떨까요?

여 **괜찮은 생각이네요.** 좋아요 그럼 급여 정산 부서에 전화해서 스케줄 변경에 대해 알릴게요.

favor 부탁 be supposed to ~하기로 되어 있다 demonstration 시연 payroll software 급여 정산 소프트웨어 on short notice 갑작스럽게 put off 연기하다

50 What are the speakers supposed to do tomorrow morning?

(A) Meet with some clients
(B) Give a demonstration
(C) Attend an international event
(D) Finish some product samples

화자들은 내일 아침에 무엇을 하기로 되어 있는가?
(A) 고객들과 미팅하기
(B) 시연하기
(C) 국제 행사에 참석하기
(D) 제품 샘플 완성하기

세부 사항 질문으로 키워드인 tomorrow morning을 노려 듣는다. 내일 아침에 give a demonstration(시연을 하기)이 있다고 했으므로 정답은 (B)이다.

51 Why is the woman asking the man a favor?
(A) She is leaving the company.
(B) She is not feeling well.
(C) She has planned a vacation.
(D) She has a scheduling conflict.
여자는 왜 남자에게 부탁을 하는가?
(A) 그녀는 회사를 그만 둔다.
(B) 그녀는 몸이 좋지 않다.
(C) 그녀는 휴가를 계획했다.
(D) 그녀의 일정이 겹친다.

세부 사항 질문으로 여자가 남자에게 부탁하는 이유를 정답으로 연결한다. 원래 시연이 잡혀 있는 시간에 고객과의 미팅을 해야 한다는 내용을 듣고 정답을 (D)으로 선택한다. 같은 시간대에 두 개 이상의 일정이 겹치는 경우를 영어로는 a scheduling conflict로 표현한다는 것을 반드시 암기해 두자.

52 What does the woman imply when she says, "That's not a bad idea"?
(A) She agrees to a delay.
(B) She wants to schedule a meeting.
(C) She will review some documents.
(D) She will ask another colleague for help.
여자가 "괜찮은 생각이네요"라고 말한 의도는 무엇인가?
(A) 여자는 지연에 동의한다.
(B) 여자는 미팅의 일정을 잡고 싶다.
(C) 여자는 서류를 검토할 것이다.
(D) 여자는 다른 동료에게 도움을 요청할 것이다.

화자의 의도를 묻는 신토익 유형으로 해당 표현의 전후 문맥을 파악하는 것이 포인트이다. 남자가 시연을 일주일만 미루자(put off)고 제안했을 때 여자가 That's not a bad idea(괜찮은 생각이네요)라고 답했고 스케줄 변경에 대해 다른 부서에 알리겠다고 했으므로 정답은 (A)가 된다.

Questions 53-55 refer to the following conversation. 영W 영M

W Hey, Eric. I noticed there are a lot of decorations in the back of your restaurant. Are you planning to have a reception tonight?
M Not really. They're all left over from last night's retirement party. I need to put them into storage for later and clean up the mess in the dining hall. Where do you think I can get some boxes?
W Well, you may want to check with Mary at the gift shop down the street. Ask her if she saves any after she unpacks shipments.
M That's a good idea. I'm about to go grocery shopping at Farmers' Market but I'll be sure to stop by the gift shop first on my way.

여 이봐요, Eric. 당신의 레스토랑 뒤편에 장식이 많이 있는 걸 봤어요. 오늘 밤에 연회를 계획하고 계신가요?
남 그렇진 않아요. 그건 어젯밤 은퇴 파티에서 남은 거예요. 나중에 쓸 수 있게 창고에 보관해 두고 식당의 지저분한 것들을 치워야만 해요. 어디에서 상자를 좀 얻을 수 있을까요?
여 음, 길 아래 선물 가게의 Mary와 얘기해 보시는 게 좋겠어요. 배송품을 풀고 나서 보관해 둔 게 있는지 물어보세요.
남 좋은 생각이네요. Farmers' Market으로 장을 보러 가려던 참이었는데 가는 길에 선물 가게부터 들러야겠어요.

decoration 장식품 reception 연회 put into storage 창고에 보관하다 unpack 포장을 풀다 stop by 들르다

53 Where does the man most likely work?
(A) At a supermarket
(B) At a gift shop
(C) At a party planning firm
(D) At a restaurant
남자는 어디에서 일할 것 같은가?
(A) 슈퍼마켓
(B) 선물 가게
(C) 파티 기획사
(D) 레스토랑

남자가 일하는 직장을 유추하는 질문으로 도입부 여자가 your restaurant에서 장식품들 봤다는 부분이 단서이다. 여자가 your restaurant라고 했으니 남자는 레스토랑에서 일하는 것이다.

54 Why does the man need boxes?
(A) To store some items
(B) To pack up an order
(C) To categorize files
(D) To move to a new place
남자는 왜 상자를 필요로 하는가?
(A) 물건을 저장하려고
(B) 주문품을 찾아오려고
(C) 파일을 분류하려고
(D) 새로운 장소로 이사하려고

남자가 box를 언급하는 부분을 잘 노려 듣는다. 남자가 남은 장식품을 보관해야 한다고 말하면서 어디서 박스를 얻을 수 있을지 물었으므로 정답은 (A)가 된다.

55 What will the man most likely do next?
(A) Buy groceries
(B) Call an acquaintance
(C) Talk to a store attendant
(D) Check the list

남자는 다음에 무엇을 할 것 같은가?
(A) 식료품 사기
(B) 지인에게 전화하기
(C) 상점 직원과 이야기하기
(D) 리스트 확인하기

남자의 향후 행동은 후반부를 주의 깊게 듣는다. 남자가 먼저 식료품을 사러 갈 것이라고 했으나 I'll be sure to stop by the gift shop first(선물 가게에 먼저 들러야겠다)라고 했으므로 정답은 (C)가 된다. 향후 행동은 사실 대화 후에 제일 먼저 할 일을 묻는 do first 질문으로 기억해 두자.

Questions 56-58 refer to the following conversation. 미W 영M

W Hey Tony, do you see the long line at the bakery? And there's only one cashier working at the desk.
M We have a meeting with some clients at 1, which means we only have 40 minutes to eat lunch. Would you like to try the taco truck near our office instead? That should be faster.
W That's a good idea. I heard that their prices are reasonable and their food is quite tasty too. But do you know if they accept credit cards? I don't have any cash on me.
M I don't think they accept any other forms of payment other than cash. But don't worry. Lunch is on me.
W Thanks Tony. I'll treat you next time.

여 Tony, 빵집에 저 긴 줄이 보이세요? 게다가 계산대에는 계산원이 한 명 밖에 없네요.
남 우리가 1시에 중요한 고객 미팅이 있고 그 말은 40분밖에는 점심 먹을 시간이 없다는 거죠. 대신 회사 근처에 있는 타코 트럭에 가 보실래요? 그 편이 더 빠를 거예요.
여 좋은 생각이에요. 거긴 가격이 적당하고 음식도 꽤 맛이 좋다고 들었어요. 그런데 그들이 신용 카드를 받는지 아시나요? 제가 현금이 없거든요.
남 현금 외에는 어떤 지불 수단도 받지 않을 텐데요. 걱정 마세요. 점심은 제가 낼게요.
여 고마워요 Tony. 다음번에는 제가 살게요.

cashier 현금 출납원 instead 대신에 reasonable 합리적인, 적당한 tasty 맛이 좋은 form of payment 지불 수단 treat 대접하다, 사다

56 What problem are the speakers discussing?
(A) Some clients will be arriving late.
(B) A store is overcrowded with people.
(C) Some merchandise is out of stock.
(D) A business is currently closed.

화자들은 어떤 문제점에 대해 이야기하고 있는가?
(A) 고객 몇 명이 늦게 도착할 것이다.
(B) 상점이 사람들로 지나치게 붐빈다.
(C) 일부 상품이 품절이다.
(D) 업체는 현재 문을 닫았다.

문제점을 묻는 질문은 주제와 관련되는 경우가 많아서 도입부에 주로 단서가 나온다. 빵집 앞에 사람들이 줄을 길게 서 있고 계산대에는 직원이 한 명뿐이라는 내용을 듣고 정답을 (B)로 선택한다.

57 What does the woman ask the man about?
(A) Payment options
(B) Directions to a shop
(C) The business hours
(D) His favorite food

여자는 남자에게 무엇에 대해 묻는가?
(A) 지불 수단
(B) 상점까지 가는 방법
(C) 영업시간
(D) 남자가 가장 좋아하는 음식

세부 사항 질문으로 반드시 여자 대사에서 질문 형태로 나오는 정보를 노려 듣는다. 여자가 do you know if they accept credit cards?에서 신용 카드를 받는지 묻고 있으므로 정답은 (A)가 된다. payment options는 현금, 신용 카드, 수표 등의 지불 수단을 총칭하는 표현으로 암기해 두자.

58 What does the man mean when he says, "Lunch is on me"?
(A) He wants to stop by a bank.
(B) He will lend her some money.
(C) He will buy her lunch.
(D) He wants to eat somewhere else.

남자가 "점심은 제가 낼게요"라고 말한 의미는 무엇인가?
(A) 남자는 은행에 들르고 싶다.
(B) 남자는 여자에게 돈을 빌려 줄 것이다.
(C) 남자는 여자에게 점심을 살 것이다.
(D) 남자는 다른 곳에서 식사하기를 원한다.

화자의 의도를 묻는 신토익 유형으로 해당 표현의 전후 문맥을 파악하는 것이 포인트이다. 여자는 현금이 없고 타코 트럭에서는 신용 카드를 받지 않는 상황에서 남자가 But don't worry. Lunch is on me라고 말한 의도는 점심을 사겠다는 의미이다. '(주어) be on me'는 사겠다는 표현으로 자주 사용되는데 이를 몰랐다 하더라도 문맥상 의도를 유추해 낼 수 있다. 여자가 다음번에 사겠다는 의미로 말한 I'll treat you next time도 외워 두자.

Questions 59-61 refer to the following conversation. 미W 미M

W Hi, this is Roberta Green. I checked out earlier this morning from room 1105 and I think I left my wrist watch behind either on the bathroom counter or on the night stand in the room.
M Hello, Ms. Green. Let me check that for you. Oh, it's already been turned in by the housekeeping staff. The lost and found office can store your watch in a locker until you're able to pick it up.
W Hmm. The thing is, I have to catch a 1 o'clock flight to Montreal and I'm already at the airport. Is there any way you can have it delivered to me? I'm willing to pay the shipping charge.

M Of course we can mail it to you, Ms. Green. And don't worry about the charge. It's our policy to pay the shipping costs to return lost items.

여 안녕하세요, Roberta Green입니다. 저는 오늘 아침에 1105실에서 체크아웃을 했는데 욕실 세면대나 침대 탁자 위에 시계를 놓고 온 것 같아요.
남 안녕하세요, Green 씨. 한 번 확인해 보겠습니다. 아, 그것은 시설 관리부 직원에 의해 이미 반납되었네요. 시계는 분실물 보관소 사무실의 보관함에서 당신이 가지러 올 때까지 보관해 드리겠습니다.
여 흠. 문제는 제가 1시에 몬트리올 행 비행기를 타야 해서 이미 지금 공항에 있다는 겁니다. 저에게 배송해 줄 수 있는 방법이 있을까요? 배송비는 기꺼이 지불할게요.
남 당연히 보내 드릴 수 있습니다, Green 씨. 비용은 염려하지 마세요. 분실된 품목을 돌려보낼 때 배송비를 지불하는 것이 저희의 정책입니다.

check out (호텔 객실에서) 나오다, 체크아웃하다 leave behind 두고 가다 turn in 반납하다 housekeeping (호텔 등의) 시설 관리부 lost and found office 분실물 보관소 be willing to 기꺼이 ~하다 policy 정책 return 돌려주다

59 Why is the woman calling?
(A) To reserve a hotel room
(B) To recover a missing item
(C) To confirm a departure time
(D) To ask about a job opening

여자는 왜 전화를 하는가?
(A) 호텔 방을 예약하려고
(B) 잃어버린 물건을 되찾으려고
(C) 출발 시간을 확인하려고
(D) 일자리에 관해서 물어보려고

도입부 여자 대사에서 전화 목적을 찾는 질문으로 I left my wrist watch behind에서 시계를 두고 갔고 그 물건을 찾기 위해 전화하는 걸 알 수 있다. 정답은 (B)이다.

60 Where most likely does the man work?
(A) At an airport
(B) At a subway station
(C) At a delivery service
(D) At a hotel

남자는 어디에서 일할 것 같은가?
(A) 공항
(B) 지하철 역
(C) 배달 회사
(D) 호텔

남자의 직장을 유추하는 질문으로 대화의 도입부에 여자가 남자에게 문의하는 내용에서 유추가 가능하다. 여자가 오늘 호텔 룸에서 체크아웃을 했고 소지품을 두고 나왔다고 했으므로 남자는 호텔에서 일하는 직원이다.

61 What does the man offer to do?
(A) Mail a receipt
(B) Provide contact information
(C) Pay for shipping
(D) Arrange for a ride

남자는 무엇을 해주겠다고 제안하는가?
(A) 영수증 보내 주기
(B) 연락 정보 제공하기
(C) 배송료 지불하기
(D) 탈것 준비하기

남자 대사에서 여자를 위해 해주겠다는 내용에 집중한다. 배송료를 내겠다는 여자에게 분실품을 돌려주기 위한 배송료를 내는 것이 호텔의 규정이라고 했으니 정답은 (C)가 된다.

Questions 62-64 refer to the following conversation with three speakers. (미M) (영W) (영M)

M1 Did you guys hear the news? Beginning today, the Lions Bridge will be closed for repairs.
W Yes, I just read about it in the newspaper. Road crews will be closing one lane of the Lions Bridge to do maintenance work at 9 p.m. every night. But all the lanes will reopen by 6 a.m. the following morning.
M2 Then we don't have to worry about traffic during the morning commute. Do you know how long it will take, Steve?
M1 Yes. Unless it rains or snows, the work will be finished within a week.
W I'm worried about night time congestion though. It's going to be pretty backed up in the evening leaving the city, since vehicles in both directions will have to share the one open lane.
M2 I know. Maybe I should take a rain check on the movie tonight. I hate being stuck in traffic after a long day of work.

남1 여러분 뉴스 들으셨어요? 오늘부터 Lion Bridge가 수리 때문에 폐쇄된다고 하네요.
여 네, 저도 신문에서 방금 읽었어요. 매일 밤 9시에 도로 작업자들이 Lion Bridge의 차선 하나를 봉쇄하고 수리 작업을 한대요. 그러나 다음 날 아침 6시까지는 전 차선이 다시 열린다고 해요.
남2 그럼 아침 출근 때 교통 체증은 걱정할 필요 없겠네요. 그게 얼마나 걸릴지 알아요, Steve?
남1 네, 비나 눈이 오지 않으면 작업은 일주일 안에 끝날 거예요.
여 그런데 저는 저녁 교통 체증이 걱정되네요. 양쪽 차선 차량들이 열린 한 차선을 번갈아 이용해야 하니 저녁 시간에 도시를 빠져나갈 때 꽤 막히겠어요.
남2 맞아요. 전 오늘 밤 영화는 다음으로 미뤄야겠어요. 하루 종일 일하고 막히는 차에 갇혀 있는 건 싫거든요.

road crew 도로 작업자 lane 차선 congestion 체증 be backed up (차량이)막히다 take a rain check on 다음 기회로 미루다 be stuck in traffic 교통 체증에 갇히다

62 What is scheduled to begin today?
(A) Some repair work
(B) A sporting event
(C) Building renovations
(D) A new theater production

오늘 무엇이 시작될 예정인가?
(A) **보수 공사**
(B) 스포츠 경기
(C) 건물 보수
(D) 새로운 무대 공연

세부 사항 질문으로 today라는 시점에 주목한다. Beginning today(오늘부터)이후 언급되었던 Lion Bridge의 보수 공사가 바로 정답이 된다.

63 According to Steve, what might delay the scheduled repairs?
(A) Special events
(B) Labor costs
(C) Changes in the weather
(D) Complaints from local residents

Steve에 따르면, 무엇이 예정된 보수를 연기할 수 있는가?
(A) 특별 행사
(B) 노동 임금
(C) **날씨의 변화**
(D) 지역 주민의 불평

질문의 the scheduled repairs는 다리 보수 공사를 가리키는 것으로 Steve의 대사에서 Unless it rains or snows(비나 눈이 오지 않는다면)이라는 단서를 정확히 캐치한다. 비나 눈이 오지 않는다면 일주일 내에 공사가 끝날 것이라고 했으므로, 공사를 미룰 수 있는 요소는 (C)가 된다.

64 Why is traffic congestion expected at night?
(A) Some road crews are off sick.
(B) A bridge is not fully open to traffic.
(C) Many people are attending an event.
(D) Several cars are involved in an accident.

왜 밤에 교통 체증이 예상되는가?
(A) 몇 명의 도로 작업자가 아파서 결근했다.
(B) **다리가 차량들에 완전히 열리지 않는다.**
(C) 많은 사람들이 행사에 참석한다.
(D) 여러 차량이 사고에 휘말렸다.

세부 사항 질문으로 밤에 막힐 것이라는 여자 대사에 집중하여 since vehicles in both directions will have to share the one open lane(양쪽 방향 차량들이 열린 한 차선을 번갈아 이용해야 하기 때문이다)이라는 부분을 정답으로 연결한다. 한 차선만 이용 가능하다는 것이 A bridge is not fully open to traffic으로 바꾸어 표현되었다.

Questions 65-67 refer to the following conversation and list.
미W 미M

W Larry, I've got a new price list from Stanley Electronics right here. Don't we need to order some more printers for next week's sale?

M Yes. We're running out of some of the models. Generally laser printers are the best-selling products in our store, so I think we should order the four models on this list in white, grey and black.

W But don't you think this premium model is too expensive? They cost $500 each and it only comes in black. Not many people will buy such an expensive model and we don't want to deal with unsold stock after the sale ends.

M Well, you have a point there. Let's order the other three models then. Could you ask the supplier if they offer a bulk discount?

W Sure, I'll give them a call right away.

Item	Price
MFC Laser Printer (Grey/Black)	$200
Concord Laser Printer (Grey/Black)	$220
SP Laser Printer (White/Black)	$300
Quantum Laser Printer (Black)	$500

여 Larry, Stanley Electronics로부터 새로 온 가격표를 제가 지금 갖고 있는데요. 다음 주 세일을 위해 프린터를 더 주문해야 하지 않나요?

남 네. 일부 모델의 재고가 떨어지고 있어요. 일반적으로 레이저 프린터가 우리 가게에서 제일 잘 팔리는 상품이니까 제 생각에는 이 리스트에 있는 4개의 모델 전부를 흰색, 회색, 검정색으로 주문하는 게 좋겠어요.

여 그렇지만 이 프리미엄 모델은 너무 비싸지 않나요? 한 개당 500달러이고 검정색만 나오잖아요. 이렇게 비싼 모델을 사려고 하는 사람들은 많지 않을 것이고 세일이 끝난 후에 안 팔린 재고를 처리하고 싶진 않아요.

남 당신 말이 일리가 있네요. 그럼 나머지 세 개의 모델만 주문하죠. 공급업체에게 혹시 대량 주문 할인을 제공하는지 물어봐 주시겠어요?

여 네, 바로 전화해 보겠습니다.

상품	가격
MFC Laser Printer (회색/검은색)	200달러
Concord Laser Printer (회색/검은색)	220달러
SP Laser Printer (흰색/검은색)	300달러
Quantum Laser Printer (검은색)	500달러

run out of 떨어지다 unsold stock 안 팔린 재고 bulk discount 대량 주문 할인

65 What will take place next week?
(A) A sale
(B) A meeting
(C) A convention
(D) A product demonstration

다음 주에 무슨 일이 있을 것인가?
(A) 세일
(B) 미팅
(C) 컨벤션
(D) 상품 시연

키워드인next week에 집중하여 듣고 next week's sale을 듣는 순간 순발력 있게 정답을 (A)로 처리하자.

66 What does the man suggest?
(A) Advertising the best-selling products
(B) Installing new software
(C) Ordering four different models of printers
(D) Requesting a price estimate

남자는 무엇을 제안하는가?
(A) 가장 잘 팔리는 제품을 광고하는 것
(B) 새로운 소프트웨어를 설치하는 것
(C) 4가지 종류의 프린터를 주문하는 것
(D) 가격 견적서를 요청하는 것

남자의 대사에서 I think we should라는 키워드와 함께 정답이 언급되었다. 리스트에 있는 4개의 모델 전부를 주문하자고 했으므로 정답은 (C)가 된다.

67 Look at the graphic. According to the speakers, which item will not be ordered?
(A) MFC Laser Printer
(B) Concord Laser Printer
(C) SP Laser Printer
(D) Quantum Laser Printer

시각 정보를 보시오. 화자들에 따르면, 어떤 제품이 주문되지 않을 것인가?
(A) MFC 레이저 프린터
(B) Concord 레이저 프린터
(C) SP 레이저 프린터
(D) Quantum 레이저 프린터

시각 정보를 활용하는 신토익 유형으로 대화의 문맥과 시각 정보를 연계하여 정답을 찾는다. 남자가 리스트에 있는 4개의 모델을 모두 주문하자고 제안했을 때 여자가 특정 모델에 대해 500달러로 비싸고 검은색만 출시된다는 이유를 들며 주문 대상에서 제외시켰으므로 최종적으로 주문하지 않을 모델은 Quantum 레이저 프린터가 된다. 정답은 (D)이다.

Questions 68-70 refer to the following conversation and cast list. 영M 영W

M Hi Carla, have you seen the stage director around? I need to talk to her about the stage sets.
W She's in her office meeting with the costume designer right now, but she'll be back soon. Oh, actually I wanted to check with you about the cast list. Did you finish putting it together?
M Yes, here it is.
W It looks good except that Max Clifford is going to play the main character instead of Roy Nichols. Mr. Nichols was recently injured in a car accident so unfortunately he won't be available.
M Oh, that's terrible news. I hope he recovers quickly.
W Same here. Could you revise the cast list by the end of today?
M Sure, no problem.

GOMES	directed by Audrey Woods
Cast in order of appearance:	
Gomes	Roy Nichols
Lady Howe	Rachel Campbell
Emily	Sarah Braid
Dr. Colin Dennis	James Leith

남 안녕하세요 Carla, 혹시 무대 감독님 보셨나요? 무대 장치와 관련해서 그녀와 이야기를 해야 하는데요.
여 지금 그녀의 사무실에서 의상 디자이너와 미팅 중인데 곧 돌아오실 겁니다. 아, 실은 출연자 명단 관련해서 당신과 확인을 하려고 했었어요. 출연자 명단은 다 만드셨나요?
남 네, 여기 있습니다.
여 Max Clifford가 Roy Nichols 대신에 주인공을 연기한다는 것 빼고는 다 좋네요. Nichols 씨는 최근에 차 사고로 부상을 입어서 안타깝게도 출연할 수가 없어요.
남 저런, 끔찍한 소식이네요. 그가 빨리 회복되기를 바랄게요.
여 저도요. 출연자 명단은 오늘까지 수정해 주시겠어요?
남 네, 문제없습니다.

GOMES	Audrey Woods 감독
출연진(출연 순서대로):	
Gomes	Roy Nichols
Lady Howe	Rachel Campbell
Emily	Sarah Braid
Dr. Colin Dennis	James Leith

stage director 무대 감독 stage set 무대 장치 costume 의상 cast list 출연자 명단 except 제외하고

68 Who is the man looking for?
(A) A stage director
(B) A costume designer
(C) A performer
(D) A repair person

남자는 누구를 찾고 있는가?
(A) 무대 감독
(B) 의상 디자이너
(C) 출연자
(D) 수리공

순발력을 요구하는 세부 사항 질문으로 남자가 찾고 있는 사람은 도입부 남자 대사 have you seen the stage director around?에서 바로 알 수 있다. 정답은 (A)이다.

69 Why is the stage director not available at the moment?
(A) She is working overseas.
(B) She is changing a flat tire.
(C) She is in a meeting.
(D) She is on vacation.

무대 감독은 지금 왜 시간이 없는가?
(A) 여자는 해외에서 일하고 있다.
(B) 여자는 펑크 난 타이어를 교체하고 있다.
(C) 여자는 미팅 중이다.
(D) 여자는 휴가 중이다.

무대 감독은 시간이 없는 상황임을 미리 인지하고 대화를 듣자. 감독은 의상 디자이너와 사무실에서 이야기를 나누고 있다고 했으므로 정답은 (C)가 된다. 질문의 at the moment는 대화 중에서는 right now로 바꿔 표현되었다.

70 Look at the graphic. According to the speakers, which character in the story will Max Clifford be playing?
(A) Gomes
(B) Lady Howe
(C) Emily
(D) Dr. Colin Dennis

시각 정보를 보시오. 화자들에 따르면, Max Clifford는 스토리상의 어떤 역할을 연기할 것인가?
(A) Gomes
(B) Lady Howe
(C) Emily
(D) Colin Dennis 박사

Max Clifford가 연기하게 될 배역을 시각 정보와 연계하여 듣자. Max Clifford is going to play the main character instead of Roy Nichols을 통해 Max Clifford는 Roy Nichols가 하려던 배역을 대신 연기하게 되었음을 알 수 있다. 그러므로 정답은 (A)가 된다.

PART 4

Questions 71-73 refer to the following news broadcast. 미M

Good morning everyone, this is Conner Jones with your local news. A spokesperson from the city council's planning committee stated this morning that the construction project on Huntsville Airport's new international terminal resumed last week. Although inclement weather conditions during winter delayed the construction, the new terminal will open on May 15th as scheduled, thanks to the crew members working overtime. Once the construction is complete, more flights from Huntsville Airport to major Asian cities will be available.

안녕하세요 여러분. 지역 뉴스의 Conner Jones입니다. 오늘 아침 도시계획위원회의 대변인이 Huntsville 공항의 새 국제 터미널 건설이 지난주 다시 시작했다고 말했습니다. 비록 겨울 동안의 혹독한 날씨로 공사가 지연되었지만, 초과 근무를 해 주신 공사 팀원들 덕분에 새 터미널은 5월 15일에 예정대로 문을 열 것입니다. 일단 건축이 완성되면, Huntsville 공항에서 아시아의 주요 도시로 가는 항공편은 더 많이 이용 가능해질 것입니다.

spokesperson 대변인 state 언급하다 resume 다시 시작하다, 재개하다 inclement 혹독한 delay 지연시키다 thanks to 덕분에

71 What construction project does the speaker mention?
(A) A community college
(B) An airport terminal
(C) An international financial center
(D) A shopping mall complex

화자는 어떤 건설 프로젝트를 언급하는가?
(A) 지역 전문대
(B) 공항 터미널
(C) 국제 금융 센터
(D) 복합 쇼핑몰

세부 사항 질문으로 construction에 집중하여 듣는다. the construction project on Huntsville Airport's new international terminal을 들었을 때 새롭게 지어지는 것은 국제 터미널임을 알 수 있다.

72 What is the cause of the delay?
(A) A shortage of funds
(B) Insufficient supplies
(C) Adverse weather conditions
(D) A series of strikes

지연의 원인은 무엇인가?
(A) 자금의 부족
(B) 부족한 물품
(C) 불리한 기상 조건
(D) 일련의 파업

세부 사항 질문으로 지연이 있었음을 미리 파악해두고 이유에 집중한다. Although inclement weather conditions during winter delayed the construction을 듣고 겨울 동안의 혹독한 날씨가 지연의 원인임을 파악할 수 있다. inclement weather는 adverse weather와 바꿔 표현될 수 있으므로 암기해 두자.

73 According to the speaker, what will be available when the project is finished?
(A) Reduced air fares
(B) Wider restaurant selection
(C) Complimentary drinks
(D) More frequent service

화자에 따르면, 프로젝트가 완성되면 무엇이 이용 가능해질 것인가?
(A) 인하된 항공료
(B) 더 많은 레스토랑 종류
(C) 무료 음료
(D) 더 빈번한 서비스

세부 사항 질문으로 키워드는 when the project is finished이다. 프로젝트가 끝나면 이용할 수 있는 것에 집중한다. Once the construction is complete라고 힌트어를 먼저 준 후에, 더 많은 비행편이 이용 가능해진다고 말했으므로 정답은 (D)가 된다. more flights는 more frequent service로 대체되었다.

Questions 74-76 refer to the following instruction. 영W

OK, Harry. Here's what I'd like you to do every day before the lab technicians arrive for work. Please double-check that each of the laboratories is equipped with all the necessary supplies. First take a close look at the supply list on the door of each room, and make sure everything on the list is on the shelves as well. If you find any missing item, check the supply cabinet in room 505 for extras. And when you are short of any supplies, please contact Jackson, and he'll place an order immediately.

자, Harry. 실험실 기술자들이 매일 출근하기 전에 당신이 했으면 하는 일이 있습니다. 실험실에 모든 필요한 물품이 갖춰져 있는지 한 번 더 확인해 주세요. 우선 각 방문에 붙어있는 물품 리스트를 꼼꼼히 살펴보시고, 리스트에 있는 물건이 모두 선반에 있는지 확인해 주세요. 없는 품목을 발견하시면, 505호에 있는 물품 보관함에 남은 것이 있는지 확인하세요. 그리고 어떤 물품이 부족할 때는 Jackson에게 연락해 주세요. 그러면 그가 즉시 주문을 해 줄 거예요.

lab technician 실험실 기술자 double-check 이중으로 확인하다, 한 번 더 확인하다 be equipped with 갖춰진 take a look at ~을 보다 be short of 부족한 place an order 주문하다

74 Where does the speaker most likely work?
(A) At a stationary store
(B) At a laboratory
(C) At a factory
(D) At a retail store

화자는 어디에서 일할 것 같은가?
(A) 사무용품 상점
(B) 실험실
(C) 공장
(D) 소매점

화자의 직장을 유추하는 질문으로 도입부에 보통 단서가 주어지므로 앞부분을 잘 듣자. 청자에게 the lab technicians arrive for work(실험실 기술자들이 출근하기 전에)라고 해야 할 일에 대해 설명하는 내용에서 이곳은 lab, 즉 laboratory임을 알 수 있다.

75 What is the listener asked to do?
(A) Confirm the payment status of invoices
(B) Evaluate the accuracy of the statement
(C) Monitor the progress of renovation
(D) Check the availability of supplies

청자는 무엇을 하도록 요청 받는가?
(A) 청구서의 지불 상태 확인하기
(B) 진술의 정확성 평가하기
(C) 보수의 진척 사항 감독하기
(D) 물품의 이용 가능 여부 확인하기

화자가 청자에게 요청하는 내용에 집중하여 듣고, please와 같이 요청할 때 사용되는 어휘가 들리면 정답을 처리할 준비를 하자. Please double-check that each of the laboratories is equipped with all the necessary supplies(각 실험실에 필요한 물품이 갖춰져 있는지를 확인하라)라고 했으므로 정답은 (D)가 된다.

76 Why should the listener contact Jackson?
(A) To have a key copied
(B) To request an order form
(C) To have some items ordered
(D) To help him with the inventory

청자는 왜 Jackson과 연락을 취해야 하는가?
(A) 열쇠를 복사하려고
(B) 주문 용지를 요청하려고
(C) 물품을 주문하려고
(D) 재고 정리를 도우려고

세부 사항 질문으로 반드시 키워드인 Jackson을 듣고 정답을 처리하자. Please contact Jackson이 들릴 때 집중하고 he'll place an order를 듣고 정답을 (C)로 선택한다.

Questions 77-79 refer to the following telephone message. 미W

Hello Ms. Harrison. This is Mia Choi calling from Sears Clothing. We've checked your on-line order form that you submitted this morning for a black mini-dress, product code 173. Unfortunately, that particular mini-dress is currently unavailable since the item has been in great demand for the last month. I know you were expecting to receive it by Tuesday but we won't get the next shipment until Thursday. We're very sorry for the inconvenience. But as soon as the item is back in stock, I will personally take care of your order. And I'll be sure to send your package by express mail, so you can receive your purchase by Friday. Thank you for your patience and understanding.

안녕하세요 Harrison 씨, Sears Clothing에서 전화드리는 Mia Choi입니다. 오늘 아침에 주문하신 상품번호 173, 검정 미니드레스의 온라인 주문서를 확인했습니다. 안타깝게도, 그 미니 드레스는 현재 없습니다. 지난달에 수요가 매우 많았거든요. 귀하가 화요일까지 그것을 받을 것으로 예상하고 있었다는 것을 알지만 목요일이 되어야 저희도 다음 배송을 받을 것 같습니다. 불편을 드려 대단히 죄송합니다. 그렇지만 다시 재고가 들어오자마자, 제가 직접 주문품을 처리하겠습니다. 빠른 우편으로 귀하의 물건을 금요일까지는 상품을 받을 수 있도록 하겠습니다. 인내심을 갖고 이해해 주셔서 감사합니다.

online order form 온라인 주문서 product code 상품 번호 unavailable 이용할 수 없는 in demand 수요가 있는 be back in stock 재고가 다시 차다 take care of 처리하다 patience 인내심

77 Why does the caller apologize?
(A) The online order system is not working.
(B) Some merchandise is out of stock.
(C) The sales price was incorrect.
(D) An item was shipped to the wrong place.

전화하는 사람은 왜 사과를 하는가?
(A) 온라인 주문 시스템이 작동하지 않는다.
(B) 일부 상품이 재고가 없다.
(C) 판매 가격이 부정확했다.
(D) 상품이 잘못된 장소에 발송되었다.

전화 메시지 유형으로 전화를 하는 사람이 사과한다는 점은 미리 기억해 두고 해당 내용을 노려 듣는다. 고객에게 주문한 상품이 재고가 없어 배송이 지연됨을 알리고 있으므로 정답은 (B)이다.

78 According to the speaker, when will the order be delivered to Ms. Harrison?
(A) On Tuesday
(B) On Wednesday
(C) On Thursday
(D) On Friday

화자에 따르면, 주문 상품은 언제 Harrison 씨에게 배송될 것인가?
(A) 화요일
(B) 수요일
(C) 목요일
(D) 금요일

세부 사항 질문으로 상품이 최종적으로 고객에게 도착하는 시점을 정답으로 연결해야 한다. 특히 배송 지연의 경우 원래 도착 예정일을 포함해 여러 요일이 언급되므로 정확하게 최종 도착 예상일을 노려 듣는다. 후반부에 빠른 배송으로 보내면 you can receive your purchase by Friday(금요일까지 받을 수 있다)라고 했으므로 정답은 (D)가 맞다.

79 What does the caller offer to do?
(A) Check the stockroom
(B) Recommend another product
(C) Ship an item by special delivery
(D) Provide a store credit

전화하는 사람은 무엇을 해주겠다고 하는가?
(A) 창고 확인하기
(B) 다른 상품 추천하기
(C) 빠른 배송으로 상품 보내기
(D) 상점 포인트 제공하기

전화하는 사람이 할 일을 골라야 하므로 I'll, Let me 등의 힌트어를 노려 듣는다. I'll be sure to send your package by express mail을 듣고 빠른 우편을 이용하여 상품을 보낼 것임을 확인한다.

Questions 80-82 refer to the following talk. (영M)

Welcome to Nuaka Organic Fruit Farm. Our tropical fruit tasting tour includes samples of 8 to 10 in-season fruits, such as mangoes, guava, tangerines and more. You're going to head out to the field and pick them on your own in a moment. But please don't forget to stop by the farm store to pick up a basket on your way out. You'll need one to carry the fruit you've harvested. If you need any help while you're in the field, please let any of our workers know. They're all wearing red t-shirts so that you'll be able to locate them easily. Now, let me show you how to pick each fruit. Some of them are quite delicate, so you need to know the correct technique.

Nuaka Organic Fruit Farm에 오신 것을 환영합니다. 저희 열대 과일 맛보기 투어는 망고, 구아바, 귤 등과 같은 제철 과일 여덟 개에서 열 개가 포함됩니다. 여러분은 곧 밭으로 나가서 직접 과일들을 따게 될 것입니다. 그렇지만 가시는 길에 농장 상점을 들러서 바구니를 가져가는걸 잊지 마세요. 딴 과일들을 나르기 위해 필요할 것입니다. 밭에서 일하는 동안에 도움이 필요하시면, 저희 직원에게 알려 주십시오. 여러분이 쉽게 찾을 수 있도록 그들은 모두 빨강 티셔츠를 입고 있습니다. 이제, 제가 각 과일을 어떻게 따는지 시범을 보여 드리겠습니다. 어떤 과일들은 다치기 쉽기 때문에 정확한 기술을 아셔야 합니다.

tasting 맛 보는 것, 음미 in-season 제철의 head 향하다 stop by 들르다 harvest 추수하다, 채취하다 locate 찾다 delicate 민감한, 부서지기 쉬운

80 What are listeners encouraged to get from the farm store?
(A) A bottle of water
(B) A basket
(C) A cart
(D) A pair of gloves

농장 상점으로부터 청자들은 무엇을 가져가도록 권고 받는가?
(A) 생수 한 병
(B) 바구니
(C) 손수레
(D) 장갑 한 켤레

세부 사항 질문으로 키워드인 farm store에 집중하자. please don't forget to stop by the farm store to pick up a basket가 정답 단서로 농장 상점에 들러서 바구니를 가져가라고 했으므로 정답은 (B)가 맞다.

81 According to the speaker, why are farm workers dressed in red?
(A) To be visible to the participants
(B) To feel a sense of belonging
(C) To harvest farm produce
(D) To give directions to the store

화자에 따르면, 농장 일꾼들은 왜 빨강 옷을 입고 있는가?
(A) 참가자의 눈에 잘 보이려고
(B) 소속감을 느끼게 하려고
(C) 농산물을 추수하려고
(D) 상점으로 가는 길을 안내하려고

세부 사항 질문으로 농장 일꾼들이 빨강 옷을 입고 있다는 내용을 파악하고 해당 내용을 들어야 한다. 도움이 필요하면 농장 일꾼들에게 알리라고 하면서 They're all wearing red t-shirts so that you'll be able to locate them easily(빨강 셔츠를 입은 이유가 쉽게 찾을 수 있도록 하기 위함)라고 했으니 정답은 (A)이다. To be visible to the participants는 so that you'll be able to locate them easily로 바꿔 표현되었다.

82 What will the speaker most likely do next?
(A) Serve refreshments
(B) Examine some products
(C) Distribute questionnaires
(D) Give a demonstration

화자는 다음에 무엇을 할 것 같은가?
(A) 다과 대접하기
(B) 상품 점검하기
(C) 질문지 배부하기
(D) 시연하기

화자의 향후 행동은 단서가 후반부에 등장한다. Now(이제)라고 말하며 주의를 환기시킨 후 let me show you how to pick each fruit라고 과일 따는 방법을 보여 주겠다고 했으므로 정답은 (D)이다. 향후 행동 질문의 힌트어는 now, first 등이 주로 쓰인다.

Questions 83-85 refer to the following telephone message. 영W

Hi, this is Barbara Kay calling for Samuel Brown. Yesterday, we met briefly at the seminar on effective communication skills. I think we must have accidentally taken each other's laptop computers since we both brought the same black LCB laptop. Luckily I did find your business card with your office number. I'm actually preparing for a marketing presentation scheduled for tomorrow morning, and all the necessary information is on my laptop. **So I really hope it is in your possession.** I'd like to trade the computers today if possible. Could you please call me on my mobile as soon as you can? My number is 077-529-0023. Thank you.

안녕하세요, 저는 Barbara Kay이고 Samuel Brown에게 전화를 드립니다. 어제, 우리가 효율적인 의사소통 기술에 관한 세미나에서 잠시 만났었죠. 제 생각에는 우리 둘 다 똑 같은 검정 LCB 노트북을 갖고 있었는데 실수로 상대방의 노트북을 가져간 것 같아요. 다행히 저는 당신의 사무실 전화번호가 있는 명함을 찾아냈습니다. 실은 제가 내일 아침에 있을 마케팅 발표를 준비 중인데요, 제 노트북에 필요한 모든 정보가 다 들어 있습니다. **그래서 당신이 그걸 가지고 있길 정말 바랍니다.** 가능하다면 컴퓨터를 오늘 교환하고 싶습니다. 저에게 최대한 빨리 휴대전화로 전화를 주시겠습니까? 제 번호는 077-529-0023입니다. 감사합니다.

effective communication skill 효과적인 의사소통 기술 accidentally 실수로, 우연히 carry 지니고 있다 business card 명함 in one's possession ~의 소유에 있다, ~가 지니고 있다 trade 교환하다

83 Where did the speaker meet Samuel Brown?
(A) At a trade fair
(B) At a business meeting
(C) At a seminar
(D) At a press conference

화자는 어디에서 Samuel Brown을 만났는가?
(A) 무역 박람회
(B) 사업상 회의
(C) 세미나
(D) 기자 회견

세부 사항 질문으로 화자가 Samuel Brown을 만났다는 사실은 스키밍으로 미리 파악해두고 장소에 집중하자. Yesterday, we met briefly at the seminar를 듣고 정답을 바로 seminar로 선택한다.

84 What is the purpose of the message?
(A) To exchange some devices
(B) To make a complaint
(C) To arrange for an event
(D) To apologize for being late

메시지의 목적은 무엇인가?
(A) 기기를 교환하려고
(B) 불만을 제기하려고
(C) 행사를 준비하려고
(D) 늦은 것에 대해 사과하려고

메시지를 남기는 목적을 찾는 질문으로 도입부부터 단서를 찾으며 듣자. 화자와 청자가 똑 같은 노트북을 가지고 있었고 실수로 컴퓨터가 바뀌었다고 언급한 부분과 연결하여 I'd like to trade the computers today if possible이라고 말한 부분이 목적이 된다. 정답은 (A)로 동사 trade는 exchange로 바꿔 표현되었고 computers는 devices로 패러프레이징되었다.

85 What does the speaker mean when she says, "So I really hope it is in your possession"?
(A) She would like to buy a new computer.
(B) She does not want to pay an extra fee.
(C) She hopes her computer hasn't gone missing.
(D) She wants to arrive at work on time.

화자가 "그래서 당신이 그걸 가지고 있길 정말 바랍니다"라고 말한 의미는 무엇인가?
(A) 여자는 새 컴퓨터를 사고 싶다.
(B) 여자는 추가 수수료를 내고 싶지 않다.
(C) 여자는 그녀의 컴퓨터가 없어지지 않았기를 바란다.
(D) 여자는 늦지 않게 회사에 도착하기 원한다.

해당 표현의 앞뒤에서 단서를 찾자. 여자가 준비한 발표 자료가 모두 컴퓨터에 있다고 한 후 So I really hope it is in your possession(당신이 그 컴퓨터를 가지고 있기 바란다)라고 했으므로 여자가 의미하는 바는 (C)가 된다.

Questions 86-88 refer to the following excerpt from a meeting. 영M

Good morning, council members. Welcome to our monthly meeting. The first item on our agenda is fixing the signs in our community park. Recently, there was an increase in the cost of labor and materials. As a result, the repair project has been put off because of lack of funds. In order to make up the shortage, I recommend that we use the significant proceeds from the community carnival for the repairs. If the majority of council members vote in favor of this proposal, we'll go forward with it. Now, please raise your hand if you agree on using carnival profits in this way.

안녕하세요, 자문 위원회 위원 여러분. 월례회의에 오신 것을 환영합니다. 안건에 있는 첫 번째 항목은 지역 공원의 표지판을 고치는 것입니다. 최근에, 인건비와 원자재 금액이 올랐습니다. 그 결과, 기금 부족으로 인해 수리 작업이 지연되어 왔습니다. 부족금을 채우기 위해서 지역 카니발에서 걷어들인 엄청난 수익금을 수리에 사용할 것을 제안합니다. 대다수의 위원들이 이 제안에 찬성으로 투표한다면, 그대로 진행할 것입니다. 자 이제, 카니발 수익을 이렇게 사용하는 것에 동의하시면, 손을 들어 주십시오.

council 의회, 자문 위원회 agenda 안건 cost of labor 인건비 material 자재 put off 연기하다 lack 부족 make up 보충하다 significant 엄청난 proceeds 수익금 the majority of 다수의 vote 투표하다 in favor of ~에 찬성하여, ~에 호의적으로 go forward with ~을 진행시키다 in this way 이 방법으로

86 What has been postponed?
(A) A maintenance project
(B) A monthly meeting
(C) A community event
(D) A charity concert

무엇이 연기되었는가?
(A) 수리 프로젝트
(B) 월례 회의
(C) 지역 행사
(D) 자선 콘서트

세부 사항 질문으로 연기된 것을 묻고 있다. 동사 postpone은 put off와 바꿔 쓸 수 있으므로 the repair project has been put off에서 정답을 (A)로 선택한다.

87 What does the speaker mention about the carnival?
(A) It attracted a record turnout.
(B) A large profit was made.
(C) Admission was free for children.
(D) It is an annual event.

화자는 카니발에 관해서 무엇을 언급하는가?
(A) 기록적인 숫자의 참석자를 유치했다.
(B) 큰 이윤이 남았다.
(C) 아이들에게 입장이 무료였다.
(D) 연중 행사이다.

세부 사항 질문으로 키워드 carnival이 언급되는 부분을 잘 듣자. the significant proceeds from the community carnival을 듣고 카니발에서 엄청난 수익금이 남았다는 것을 알 수 있다. 정답은 (B)이다.

88 What will listeners most likely do next?
(A) Attend an event
(B) Have a meal
(C) Receive a ballot
(D) Vote on a proposal

청자들은 다음에 무엇을 할 것 같은가?
(A) 행사에 참석하기
(B) 식사하기
(C) 투표 용지 받기
(D) 제안에 대해 투표하기

담화의 후반부를 잘 듣고 청자들이 다음에 무엇을 할지 연결한다. 카니발 수익금을 수리 프로젝트에 쓰는 것을 제안했고, 마지막에 now라며 주의를 환기시킨 후 찬성하는 사람은 손을 들라고 했으므로 정답은 (D)이다. (C)의 ballot은 투표 용지라는 의미인데 참가자들은 용지 없이 손을 들어 투표를 하므로 오답이 된다.

Questions 89-91 refer to the following announcement. 미M

Today, I have an important announcement to make. At the last board meeting, Brandon Engineering Company decided to implement a variety of green projects throughout the company. One of the easiest things you can do to participate, is carpooling with your co-workers to and from work. Not only will this help reduce carbon-dioxide emissions but it will also reduce your fuel expenses. Plus you can have a better parking space at work. That's right. The spaces close to the building will be reserved for car-pooling vehicles. So if you're interested, please contact Ronald Kim in human resources and let him know your home address. Based on your information, he will match you up with other employees.

오늘은 중요한 공지 사항을 발표하려고 합니다. 지난번 이사회의에서, Brandon Engineering Company는 다양한 친환경 프로젝트를 실시하기로 결정하였습니다. 여러분이 참여할 수 있는 가장 쉬운 프로젝트 중 하나는 출퇴근할 때 동료와 차를 함께 타는 것입니다. 이것은 이산화탄소 방출을 감소시킬 뿐 아니라 당신의 연료 경비를 감소시켜 줄 것입니다. 또한 직장에서 더 좋은 주차 공간도 가질 수 있습니다. 그렇습니다. 빌딩과 가까운 주차 공간이 카풀 차량을 위해 따로 배정될 것입니다. 자 이제 관심이 있는 분은, 인사부의 Ronald Kim에게 연락해서 여러분의 집 주소를 알려 주세요. 그 정보를 바탕으로, 그가 다른 직원들과 연결을 시켜 줄 것입니다.

board meeting 이사 회의 implement 실행하다 throughout 통틀어 to and from work 출퇴근할 때 reduce 줄이다 carbon-dioxide 이산화탄소 fuel expenses 연료비 close to ~와 가까운 based on ~을 토대로 match up with ~와 맞추어 주다, 짝지어 주다

89 What does the company encourage employees to do?
(A) Participate in a walking project
(B) Recycle office supplies
(C) Share rides to work
(D) Attend a conference

회사는 직원들에게 무엇을 하도록 권고하는가?
(A) 걷기 프로젝트에 참가하기
(B) 사무용품 재활용하기
(C) 출근할 때 차를 함께 타기
(D) 컨퍼런스에 참석하기

회사가 권고하는 것을 노려 듣고, One of the easiest things you can do to participate(참여할 수 있는 가장 쉬운 것 중 하나는)를 들었을 때 권고 사항이 언급될 것을 예상할 수 있어야 한다. 출퇴근 시 동료와 카풀을 하는 것이라고 했으므로 정답은 (C)가 된다.

90 What does the speaker mean when he says, "That's right"?
(A) He is interested in a new project.
(B) Expenses will be reimbursed.
(C) Employees should submit ideas.
(D) He emphasizes the benefit of reserved parking.

화자가 "그렇습니다"라고 말한 의미는 무엇인가?
(A) 남자는 새로운 프로젝트에 관심이 있다.
(B) 비용이 환급될 것이다.
(C) 직원들은 아이디어를 제출해야 한다.
(D) 남자는 지정 주차의 혜택을 강조한다.

화자의 의도를 파악하기 위해서는 해당 표현의 앞뒤 문맥을 파악하는 것이 중요하다. That's right(그렇습니다)라는 표현 전후로 car pool을 할 경우 혜택으로 지정 주차 공간이 제공됨을 말하고 있음으로 이를 강조하기 위한 표현으로 쓰인 경우이다. 정답은 (D)가 된다.

91 What information should interested employees provide?
(A) Their home address
(B) Their extension number
(C) Their medical history
(D) Their department code

관심 있는 직원은 어떤 정보를 제공해야 하는가?
(A) 집 주소
(B) 내선 번호
(C) 병력 기록
(D) 부서 코드

세부 사항 질문으로 신청을 하고 싶다면 Ronald Kim에게 전화해서 let him know your home address라고 했으니 집 주소를 제공해야 한다.

Questions 92-94 refer to the following talk. (미W)

Welcome to the two-day orientation program for new employees. As new assembly-line workers here at Apex Manufacturing, you'll learn about the company history and important policies over the next two days. It is mandatory that you attend all the sessions offered during the orientation. You will be permitted to use factory equipment after you receive a certificate of completion at the end of the program. Apex Manufacturing is committed to meeting the highest standards of workplace safety, which is reflected in our new employee training. Now, you can take a 10 minute break before the first session begins.

신입 사원을 위한 이틀간의 오리엔테이션 프로그램에 오신 것을 환영합니다. Apex Manufacturing의 새로운 조립라인 직원들로서, 여러분은 앞으로 이틀 동안 회사 역사와 중요한 정책들에 대해 배울 것입니다. 여러분은 오리엔테이션 동안에 주어지는 모든 수업에 필수적으로 참석해야 합니다. 프로그램이 끝날 때 수료증을 받게 될 것이고 그 이후에 공장 장비를 이용할 수 있게 허락됩니다. Apex Manufacturing은 가장 높은 수준의 작업장 안전 기준을 맞추기 위해 최선을 다하고 있고 이것이 신입사원 교육에 반영되어 있는 것입니다. 이제, 여러분은 첫 번째 수업이 시작되기 전에 10분간 휴식을 취하십시오.

92 Who most likely are the listeners?
(A) Factory managers
(B) Safety inspectors
(C) Company executives
(D) New assembly workers

청자들은 누구일 것 같은가?
(A) 공장 관리자
(B) 안전 검사관
(C) 회사 임원
(D) 새로운 조립라인 직원

청자를 유추하는 질문으로 직업을 유추할 때 가장 쉬운 힌트어는 전치사 as이다. As new assembly-line workers here at Apex Manufacturing, you'll을 듣고 you에 해당하는 청자들은 모두 새로운 조립라인 직원들임을 알 수 있다.

93 Why is the program mandatory for the listeners?
(A) To receive a promotion
(B) To operate some machinery
(C) To pass a test
(D) To set safety standards

프로그램이 청자들에게 필수적인 이유가 무엇인가?
(A) 승진을 하려고
(B) 장비를 작동시키려고
(C) 시험을 통과하려고
(D) 안전 기준을 정하려고

세부 사항 질문으로 청자들이 프로그램을 의무적으로 들어야 한다는 것은 미리 질문에서 파악해두고 해당 내용을 노려 듣자. 프로그램의 모든 session에 필수적으로 참석해야 한다고 언급한 후 수료증을 받은 후에 장비를 이용할 수 있도록 허가된다고 했으므로 정답은 (B)이다.

94 What will the listeners receive after finishing the sessions?
(A) A completion certificate
(B) A safety manual
(C) A team project
(D) A program schedule

청자들은 수업을 마친 후에 무엇을 받게 되는가?
(A) 수료 증서
(B) 안전 설명서
(C) 팀 프로젝트
(D) 프로그램 계획표

93번과 정답이 동시에 등장하는 고난도 질문으로, 질문 3개의 키워드는 동시에 염두에 두자. 세션을 모두 마친 후에 받는 것이 키워드로 after you receive a certificate of completion at the end of the program을 들었을 때 프로그램이 끝날 때 수료 증서를 받게 됨을 알 수 있다.

Questions 95-97 refer to the following telephone message and invoice. (영M)

Hello, this is Walter Mandela calling from Watson Manufacturing. I'm calling because there seems to be an error in the invoice we just received this morning. For the last two years, we've ordered 60 reels of copper wire every month. Well last month, we ordered only half that amount because our production was down. But we were still charged for an order of 60 according to this bill. I'm sure it is just a mistake, but I'd like to get a corrected statement as soon as possible so I can complete the payment by the due date. If you have any questions, please give me a call at 555-0982. Thank you.

INVOICE
Platt Supply   Bill to: Watson Manufacturing Company
Due date: 2016. 06. 15   Date: 2016. 05. 29

Date	Item	Quantity	Cost	Balance
2016. 05. 05	Copper Wire	60	$1.50 each	$90

안녕하세요. Watson Manufacturing에서 전화드리는 Walter Mandela입니다. 제가 전화한 건 오늘 아침에 받은 청구서에 오류가 있어 보여서요. 지난 2년 동안 저희는 매달 60릴의 구리선을 주문해 왔습니다. 그러나 지난달에는 생산이 저조했기 때문에 그 절반만 주문을 했습니다. 그런데 이 청구서에 따르면 여전히 60릴에 대해서 청구가 되어 있네요. 그냥 실수일 것이라 생각하지만 최대한 빨리 수정된 청구서를 받고 싶습니다. 그래서 만기일까지 지불을 해 드릴 수 있도록요. 질문이 있으시면, 555-0982로 전화 주세요. 감사합니다.

청구서
Platt Supply   청구 대상: Watson Manufacturing Company
만기 날짜: 2016. 06. 15   날짜: 2016. 05. 29

날짜	상품	양	금액	미납 금액
2016. 05. 05	구리선	60	개당 1.50달러	90달러

reel (끈, 줄이 감겨있는) 릴, 실패   copper wire 구리선   be charged 청구받다   corrected statement 정정된 청구서   due date 납부 만기일

95 What is the purpose of the message?
(A) To cancel an order
(B) To discuss a faulty product
(C) To expedite a delivery
(D) To report a billing problem

메시지의 목적은 무엇인가?
(A) 주문을 취소하려고
(B) 결함 상품에 대해 논의하려고
(C) 배송을 빠르게 하려고
(D) 청구서의 문제를 알리려고

메시지의 목적은 보통 도입부에 언급되고 특히 I'm calling because와 같은 표현이 들리면 그 부분에 답이 있다. invoice(청구서)에 오류가 있어 보인다고 했으므로 정답은 (D)가 된다.

96 Look at the graphic. What information is incorrect?
(A) Date
(B) Item
(C) Quantity
(D) Cost

시각 정보를 보시오. 어떤 정보가 부정확한가?
(A) 날짜
(B) 상품
(C) 양
(D) 금액

청구서상의 정보 중 잘못된 것을 찾는 문제로 화자가 청구서상의 error에 대해 언급하는 부분을 잘 듣자. 매달 60릴의 구리선을 주문했으나 지난달에는 we ordered only half that amount(절반만 주문을 했다)라고 언급했으므로 정답은 (C)가 된다. 총 금액이 잘못 청구된 것이지만 청구서상의 cost에는 한 개당 금액인 $1.50이 쓰여 있으므로 (D)는 정답이 될 수 없다.

97 What does the speaker request?
(A) A corrected invoice
(B) A deadline extension
(C) An updated catalog
(D) A telephone number

화자는 무엇을 요청하는가?
(A) 수정된 청구서
(B) 연장된 마감일
(C) 수정된 카탈로그
(D) 전화번호

화자의 요청 표현을 잘 노려 듣자. I'd like to get a corrected statement as soon as possible(최대한 빨리 고쳐진 청구서를 받고 싶다)이라고 했으므로 정답은 (A)가 된다. 청구서를 뜻하는 invoice, bill, statement 등은 같은 의미임을 기억해 두자.

Questions 98-100 refer to the following excerpt from a meeting and list. 미W

This is our first marketing meeting since we published our new thriller novel, *December*, a month ago. We've been promoting this book heavily and even author Neil Dawson has appeared on several TV shows to talk about his new novel. So far the book has been selling very well nationwide and in fact it has become the second best seller in thrillers. Josh Alexis's *Double Trouble* is the best-selling thriller of the month. But at the rate it's selling, I'm pretty sure our book will top the list next month. Also, we're teaming up with Waterstones Bookstore to host a book signing and Meet-the-Author event. Jeremy and his team are in charge of organizing the events but there is a lot of work to be done. So if you are not on a deadline and have time to volunteer, please let Jeremy know by the end of the day. Thank you for your help.

Best Sellers in Thrillers (March)
1. *Double Trouble* by Josh Alexis
2. *December* by Neil Dawson
3. *Curse of the Sahara* by Howard Stone
4. *Nineteen Sixty Four* by George Bourne

한 달 전에 새 스릴러 소설인 〈December〉를 출간한 이후 갖는 첫 번째 마케팅 회의입니다. 우리는 이 책을 크게 홍보해왔고 심지어 작가 Neil Dawson 씨도 여러 TV쇼에 본인의 책을 소개하기 위해서 출연했습니다. 현재까지 책은 전국적으로 매우 잘 팔리고 있고 스릴러 분야에서 2위를 했습니다. Josh Alexis의 〈Double Trouble〉이 이달의 베스트 스릴러이지만, 이 책이 팔리는 속도대로라면 다음 달에는 우리 책이 리스트에서 1위를 할 것이 틀림없습니다. 또한, 우리는 작가 사인회와 작가를 만나는 행사를 주최하기 위해서 Waterstones 서점과 협력하여 일하게 됩니다. Jeremy와 그의 팀이 이 행사를 준비하는 책임을 맡고 있지만 끝내야 할 일이 매우 많습니다. 그러니 여러분 중 현재 마감을 앞두고 있지 않거나 자원할 시간이 있는 분은 오늘까지 Jeremy에게 알려 주세요. 여러분의 도움에 감사합니다.

스릴러 분야 베스트셀러 (3월)
1. *Double Trouble* by Josh Alexis
2. *December* by Neil Dawson
3. *Curse of the Sahara* by Howard Stone
4. *Nineteen Sixty Four* by George Bourne

thriller novel 스릴러 소설 promote 홍보하다 author 작자 appear 출연하다 so far 현재까지 nationwide 전국적으로 top the list 리스트에서 1위에 오르다 team up with 팀을 이루다, 협력하다 book signing 작가 사인회

98 Where most likely does the speaker work?
(A) At a bookstore
(B) At a television station
(C) At a publishing firm
(D) At an advertising agency

화자는 어디에서 일할 것 같은가?
(A) 서점
(B) 텔레비전 방송국
(C) 출판사
(D) 광고 대행사

화자의 직업은 반드시 유추를 통해 풀어야 한다. 화자는 책을 출간하는 업무를 한다는 점에서 정답은 (C)가 된다. TV나 novel 등의 들리는 단어를 이용한 (A), (B) 등은 함정이 된다.

99 Look at the graphic. According to the speaker, which book will become the best seller in April?
(A) *Double Trouble*
(B) *December*
(C) *Curse of the Sahara*
(D) *Nineteen Sixty Four*

시각 정보를 보시오. 화자에 따르면, 4월에는 어떤 책이 베스트셀러가 될 것인가?
(A) 〈Double Trouble〉
(B) 〈December〉
(C) 〈Curse of the Sahara〉
(D) 〈Nineteen Sixty Four〉

주어진 베스트셀러 리스트는 March(3월)의 정보이므로 담화의 내용을 통해 April(4월)에 대한 정보를 파악한다. 책이 잘 팔려서 our book will top the list next month(다음 달에는 리스트에서 1위를 할 것이다)라고 말한 부분이 단서가 된다. 화자의 출판사에서 출간한 ***December***가 4월의 베스트셀러가 될 것임을 알 수 있다.

100 What are listeners asked to do?
(A) Help with some preparations
(B) Make travel arrangements
(C) Meet a project deadline
(D) Donate money to a charity

청자들은 무엇을 할 것을 요청 받는가?
(A) 준비 돕기
(B) 출장 준비하기
(C) 프로젝트 마감일 맞추기
(D) 자선 단체에 돈 기부하기

화자가 청자들에게 요청하는 내용은 개최 준비를 하는 행사에 할 일이 많으므로 마감일이 임박하지 않았거나 자원할 시간이 되는 사람들은 Jeremy에게 알리라는 부분이 된다. 직접적으로 help라는 단어가 쓰이지 않았으나 전후 문맥상 행사 준비를 도우라는 의미가 된다. 정답은 (A)이다.

Actual Test 7

PART 1

본책 p.84

1 (C)	2 (B)	3 (D)	4 (C)	5 (A)	6 (B)

PART 2

본책 p.88

7 (C)	8 (A)	9 (A)	10 (B)	11 (B)	12 (A)
13 (C)	14 (A)	15 (A)	16 (A)	17 (C)	18 (B)
19 (C)	20 (B)	21 (B)	22 (B)	23 (C)	24 (A)
25 (B)	26 (B)	27 (A)	28 (B)	29 (C)	30 (A)
31 (B)					

PART 3

본책 p.89

32 (A)	33 (C)	34 (B)	35 (A)	36 (A)	37 (B)
38 (B)	39 (A)	40 (C)	41 (A)	42 (C)	43 (D)
44 (B)	45 (C)	46 (D)	47 (B)	48 (B)	49 (A)
50 (B)	51 (C)	52 (A)	53 (B)	54 (C)	55 (D)
56 (B)	57 (B)	58 (D)	59 (C)	60 (A)	61 (D)
62 (C)	63 (A)	64 (C)	65 (A)	66 (B)	67 (D)
68 (A)	69 (B)	70 (C)			

PART 4

본책 p.93

71 (B)	72 (B)	73 (D)	74 (C)	75 (A)	76 (C)
77 (B)	78 (A)	79 (C)	80 (A)	81 (D)	82 (C)
83 (C)	84 (C)	85 (A)	86 (C)	87 (B)	88 (C)
89 (C)	90 (C)	91 (B)	92 (A)	93 (C)	94 (D)
95 (A)	96 (C)	97 (D)	98 (D)	99 (A)	100 (B)

PART 1

1 (A) Some people are sunbathing on the beach.
미M (B) Some girls are resting under the shade of trees.
(C) Buildings can be seen from an outdoor area.
(D) The scenery is reflected on the roof of a car.
(A) 몇몇 사람들이 해변에서 일광욕을 하고 있다.
(B) 몇몇 소녀들이 나무 그늘 아래에서 쉬고 있다.
(C) 건물들은 야외에서 보일 수 있다.
(D) 풍경이 자동차 지붕에 반사되었다.

높은 건물로 둘러싸인 도심의 공원에서 사람들이 쉬고 있다. (A)는 장소가 맞지 않고 (B)는 알 수 없는 내용이다.

sunbathe 일광욕을 하다 rest 쉬다 shade 그늘 outdoor 야외의 scenery 경치, 풍경 reflect 비추다, 반사하다

2 (A) A man is leaning against the wall.
영W (B) A man is exercising indoors.
(C) A man is on a balance beam.
(D) A man lies face down on the floor.
(A) 남자가 벽에 기대어 있다.
(B) 남자가 실내에서 운동하고 있다.
(C) 남자가 평균대 위에 있다.
(D) 남자가 바닥에 엎드려 있다.

남자의 물구나무서기 자세에 대한 표현이 나올 것을 기대했다면 실망할 수 있는 문제이다. 의외로 일반적인 내용인 실내에서 운동하는 부분이 문제의 포인트가 되었다.

lean against ~에 기대다 exercise 운동하다 indoors 실내에서 balance beam 평균대 lie face down 엎드리다

3 (A) One of the workers is making tracks on the road.
영M (B) Two passengers are getting off the train.
(C) The people are dressed identically.
(D) The people are engaged in maintenance work.
(A) 한 인부가 도로에 트랙을 만들고 있다.
(B) 두 명의 승객들이 기차에서 내리고 있다.
(C) 사람들이 옷을 똑같이 입었다.
(D) 사람들이 유지 보수 작업을 하고 있다.

기차 선로에서 두 명의 인부가 작업을 하고 있는데 옷은 서로 다르게 입었다.

track 트랙, 자국, 선로 get off 내리다 identically 꼭 같게 be engaged in ~하느라 바쁘다, ~에 종사하다 maintenance 유지 보수

4 (A) A painter is sketching at his desk.
미W (B) The man is shelving some books.
(C) The man has tools in both hands.
(D) The man is facing a machine.
(A) 화가가 책상에서 스케치를 하고 있다.
(B) 남자가 책을 선반에 얹고 있다.
(C) 남자가 양손에 도구를 들고 있다.
(D) 남자가 기계를 마주하고 있다.

남자가 조심스럽게 글씨를 쓰고 있는데 양손에 각기 다른 도구를 들고 있다.

sketch 스케치하다 shelve 선반에 얹다 face 마주하다, 직면하다

5 (A) Shelves are separated by dividers.
영W (B) Some crates are piled on the floor.
(C) A chair near the shelves is occupied.
(D) Every compartment requires bookends.
(A) 책장은 칸막이로 나눠져 있다.
(B) 나무 상자들이 바닥에 쌓여 있다.
(C) 책장 근처 의자에 누가 앉아 있다.
(D) 모든 칸은 북엔드가 필요하다.

책장은 칸막이로 나눠져 있고 책, 장식품 등 다양한 물품이 꽂혀 있다. 책꽂이 앞 의자는 비어 있는 상태이며 모든 칸은 칸막이가 있어서 북엔드가 필요한 것으로 단정 짓기 어렵다.

shelf 선반, 책장 separate 분리하다, 나누다 divider 칸막이 crate 대형 나무 상자 pile 쌓다 occupied 차지한, 점령된 compartment 물건 보관용 칸, 칸막이 있는 객실 bookend 책이 쓰러지지 않게 책 양쪽 끝에 받치는 것

6 (A) He is bowing to an audience.
미M (B) He is performing alone.
(C) He is adjusting the microphone.
(D) He is making a speech.
(A) 남자가 관객들에게 절하고 있다.
(B) 남자가 혼자 공연하고 있다.
(C) 남자가 마이크를 조절하고 있다.
(D) 남자가 연설을 하고 있다.

기타를 멘 남자가 마이크를 꼭 쥐고 노래를 하고 있다. 두 손에 마이크를 쥐고 있는 것이지 볼륨 등을 조절하는 것으로 보기는 어려우므로 (C)보다는 (B)가 더 적절한 설명이다.

bow 허리를 굽혀 절하다 audience 관객, 청중 perform 공연하다 alone 홀로 adjust 조절하다, 조정하다 make a speech 연설하다

PART 2

7 What time does the next train leave?
미M (A) Just 30 pounds.
미W (B) A round-trip ticket.
(C) At 2:45.

다음 기차는 몇 시에 떠납니까?
(A) 30파운드입니다.
(B) 왕복 티켓이요.
(C) 2시 45분에요.

의문사 what time 질문으로 시점에 대한 답이 나와야 하므로 정답은 (C)이다. (A)는 how much에 대한 답이고 (B)는 train을 들었을 때 연상되는 왕복 티켓을 이용한 함정이다.

pound 파운드(영국 화폐 단위) round-trip 왕복 여행

8 Who decorated the cookies?
영W (A) Sarah and I did.
영M (B) It's in the refrigerator.
(C) From the bakery.

누가 과자에 장식을 했나요?
(A) Sarah와 제가요.
(B) 그것은 냉장고 안에 있습니다.
(C) 빵집에서요.

의문사 who에 대한 정보를 주는 것은 'Sarah와 나'라고 답한 (A)뿐이다. (B)는 cookies를 들었을 때 연상되는 refrigerator(냉장고)를 이용한 오답이고, (C) 역시 연상어 bakery를 이용한 오답이다.

decorate 장식하다 refrigerator 냉장고

9 How did you learn about the sales job?
미W (A) Mary told me about it.
미M (B) No, it is too expensive.
(C) Spanish is my major.

판매직에 대해 어떻게 아셨나요?
(A) Mary가 말해줬어요.
(B) 아니오, 그것은 너무 비쌉니다.
(C) 스페인어는 제 전공입니다.

의문사 how 질문으로 learn about은 '~에 대해 알다'란 의미이다. 판매직에 대해 알게 된 경로를 묻는 것이 질문의 핵심이므로 제3자에게 들었다고 답한 (A)가 정답이다. 의문사 의문문에 Yes/No로 답하지 않으므로 (B)는 오답이고, (C)는 문맥에서 벗어난 답이다.

sales job 판매직 major 전공

10 Where are you taking the investor now?
영M (A) By ferry.
미W (B) To Monty's.
(C) All year around.

투자자를 지금 어디로 모시고 가나요?
(A) 페리를 타고요.
(B) Monty's로요.
(C) 일 년 내내요.

의문사 where 질문으로 투자자를 어디로 모시고 가는지를 묻고 있다. Monty's는 레스토랑 정도로 생각할 수 있으므로 정답은 (B)가 맞다. 'A를 B로 데려가다'라고 할 때 take A to B로 사용된다는 것도 추가적으로 암기해 두자. (A)는 의문사 how에 대한 답이고, (C)는 의문사 when에 대한 답이다.

take 데려가다 investor 투자자 ferry 연락선, 페리 all year around 일 년 내내(= all year round)

11 Did you drive to work or take the subway?
미M (A) I'll work overtime tonight.
영W (B) I came on foot.
(C) The cars are double-parked.

직장에 운전해서 왔나요 아니면 지하철을 탔나요?
(A) 오늘 밤에 야근할 겁니다.
(B) 걸어왔습니다.
(C) 차들이 이중 주차되어 있어요.

선택 의문문으로 선택 사항은 운전인지 지하철인지를 묻고 있다. 정답은 (B)로 주어진 선택 사항 대신에 제3의 수단을 답으로 주고 있다.

work overtime 야근하다 on foot 걸어서 double-park 이중 주차하다

12 When will the hotel renovation be completed?
미W (A) Within a week.
영M (B) Every Friday.
(C) To the lobby.

호텔 개조는 언제 완료될까요?
(A) 일주일 내로요.
(B) 매주 금요일에요.
(C) 로비로요.

의문사 when 질문으로 보수 공사가 끝나는 미래 시점을 묻고 있으므로 정답은 (A)이다. (B)는 언뜻 들었을 때는 요일을 말해주는 것 같지만 사실은 '매주 금요일마다'라는 의미이므로 의문사 how often에 대한 답이다.

renovation 개조, 보수공사 within ~내로

13 The summer sale lasts until Sunday, doesn't it?
미M (A) I'll see you then.
미W (B) You should buy the coat.
(C) It probably ends today.

여름 세일은 일요일까지 지속됩니다, 그렇지 않나요?
(A) 그때 뵐게요.
(B) 당신은 그 코트를 사는 게 좋겠어요.
(C) 오늘 끝날 겁니다.

Yes/No 여부를 묻는 질문으로 세일이 일요일에 끝나는지를 묻고 있으므로 오늘 끝난다고 답한 (C)가 정답이다. (A)는 문맥상 벗어난 답이고 (C)는 sale을 들었을 때 연상되는 buy, coat 등을 이용한 함정이다.

last 지속되다, 유지되다 end 끝나다

14 Could you lead a training session next week?
영M (A) Sure, I have time then.
영W (B) I forgot my password.
(C) I haven't read it yet.

다음 주에 있을 교육을 진행해 주실 수 있나요?
(A) **그럼요, 그때 시간이 됩니다.**
(B) 암호를 잊었어요.
(C) 아직 그것을 읽지 못했어요.

Yes/No 여부를 묻는 질문으로 Yes에 해당하는 Sure로 답하며 긍정적인 답을 하고 있는 (A)가 정답이다.

lead 진행하다, 이끌다 then 그때

15 How about meeting with Jim after his vacation?
영W (A) When exactly?
미M (B) He's an attorney.
(C) By noon tomorrow.

Jim의 휴가 후에 그를 만나보는 건 어떠세요?
(A) **정확하게 언제죠?**
(B) 그는 변호사입니다.
(C) 내일 정오까지요.

How about ~ ing?는 제안할 때 쓰는 표현으로 Jim을 휴가 후에 만나볼 것을 제안하고 있다. 정확하게 언제인지를 되묻고 있는 (A)가 정답이고 (B)와 (C)는 제안에 대한 답으로 볼 수 없다.

exactly 정확하게 attorney 변호사

16 Who will assist Ms. Park in scheduling the shifts?
미M (A) She's handling it by herself.
영W (B) All guests will be escorted.
(C) Between 5 P.M. and 7 P.M.

누가 Park 씨가 근무조 일정 짜는 걸 도울 건가요?
(A) **그녀 혼자서 그걸 처리할 것입니다.**
(B) 모든 손님들이 에스코트 받을 것입니다.
(C) 오후 5시에서 7시 사이에요.

의문사 who 질문으로 누가 Park 씨를 도울 것인지 묻고 있다. 정답은 Park 씨가 도움을 받지 않고 혼자 그 일을 할 것이라고 답한 (A)이다. 단, Ms. Park을 대명사 she, 재귀대명사 herself로 바꿔 표현된 것을 확인해두자. 질문 속에 등장하는 사람의 이름은 적어도 성별은 정확하게 파악해 두어야 하는 이유이다.

assist 돕다 handle 처리하다 by oneself 혼자서 be escorted 에스코트 받다

17 I'd like to reserve a room for a department meeting
미W this afternoon.
미M (A) Why don't you turn the volume up?
(B) They have met before.
(C) I'm afraid there are none available.

오늘 오후에 있을 부서 회의를 위해 방을 예약하고 싶습니다.
(A) 볼륨을 높여 주시겠어요?
(B) 그들은 전에 만난 적이 있어요.
(C) **유감스럽게도 이용 가능한 방이 없습니다.**

평서문 유형으로 I'd like to는 상대방에게 요청을 할 때 사용하는 표현이다. 방을 예약하고 싶다고 했으므로 정답은 이용할 수 있는 방이 없다고 답한 (C)가 된다.

reserve 예약하다 department meeting 부서 회의

18 Doesn't the furniture store accept credit cards?
영M (A) A table and two chairs.
미W (B) No, they only take cash.
(C) They don't deliver.

그 가구점은 신용 카드를 받지 않습니까?
(A) 테이블 한 개와 의자 두 개요.
(B) **아니오, 그들은 현금만 받습니다.**
(C) 그들은 배달하지 않습니다.

Yes/No 여부를 묻는 질문으로 상점에서 신용 카드를 받는지 물었으므로 받지 않는다고 답한 후, 현금만 받는다고 부연 설명한 (B)가 정답이다. 정답의 No는 질문의 동사 accept에 대해 답하는 것으로 반드시 해석하자.

accept 받다

19 Isn't it supposed to snow tomorrow?
미M (A) It arrives at six.
영W (B) Mike's supposed to do it.
(C) Yes, we should wear warm clothing.

내일 눈이 온다고 했나요?
(A) 그것은 6시에 도착합니다.
(B) Mike가 하기로 되어 있어요.
(C) **네, 옷을 따뜻하게 입어야겠어요.**

Yes/No 질문으로 내일 눈이 올지 여부를 묻고 있으므로 온다고 답하고 옷을 따뜻하게 입자고 한 (C)가 정답이 된다. be supposed to를 반복 사용하여 오답을 유도한 (B)는 오답이다.

be supposed to ~하기로 되어 있다 wear warm clothing 옷을 따뜻하게 입다

20 Can you repair the drainpipe under the sink or
영W should we call a plumber?
영M (A) You can leave me a message.
(B) I think I can fix it.
(C) Think it over until tomorrow.

싱크대 밑의 배수관을 고칠 수 있나요, 아니면 배관공에게 전화를 해 볼까요?
(A) 당신은 제게 메시지를 남기실 수 있어요.
(B) **제가 고칠 수 있을 것 같아요.**
(C) 내일까지 심사숙고하십시오.

선택 의문문으로 상대방이 직접 수리를 할 수 있는지 아니면 배관공을 부를지를 물었으므로 직접 고치겠다고 답한 (B)가 정답이 된다. 동사 repair는 fix로 바꿔 표현되었다.

drainpipe 배수관 plumber 배관공 think over 심사숙고하다

21 It looks like my job is done.
미W (A) You look good today.
영W (B) Can you assist Helen then?
(C) Around the bank.

제 일은 다 끝난 것 같네요.
(A) 오늘 좋아 보이시네요.
(B) **그럼 당신이 Helen을 도울 수 있나요?**
(C) 은행 주변에요.

평서문 유형으로 '나의 업무는 다 끝났다'고 말했으므로 가장 자연스러운 답변은 (B) 동료를 도와달라는 것이 된다. (A)는 look을 반복 사용한 오류이고, (C)는 where에 대한 답이다.

look like ~처럼 보이다 assist 돕다 then 그러면, 그렇다면

22 Why is Samantha flying back to Boston?
미M (A) It's been returned.
미W (B) She has a client to meet with.
(C) Let me tell you how.

Samantha는 왜 보스턴으로 돌아오나요?
(A) 그것은 반납되었습니다.
(B) 만나 볼 고객이 있거든요.
(C) 제가 방법을 말씀해 드릴게요.

의문사 why 질문으로 특정 지역에 오는 이유를 묻는 것이 요지가 된다. 그러므로 만날 사람이 있어서 온다고 답한 (B)가 정답이 된다. (A)는 질문의 back을 들었을 때 연상되는 return을 이용한 오답이고, (C)는 how에 대해 답하고 있으므로 오답 소거한다.

fly 비행기를 타고 가다 return 반납하다, 돌려주다

23 How do you know who is in charge of the hotel
영M construction project?
영W (A) He's the new hotel manager.
(B) No, this route is shorter.
(C) The work assignments were sent in an e-mail.

이 호텔 공사 프로젝트의 책임자가 누구인지 어떻게 아세요?
(A) 그는 새로운 호텔 매니저입니다.
(B) 아니오, 이 길이 더 짧습니다.
(C) 업무 배정표가 이메일로 왔거든요.

의문사 두 개를 모두 캐치하여 '누가 책임자인지 어떻게 아는지' 묻고 있음을 파악하자. (C)에서 work assignments(업무 배정)를 통해 알았다고 답한 것은 문맥상 가장 자연스러운 답변이다. (A)의 경우 주어인 he로 받을 수 있는 명사가 질문에 없었으므로 주어 오류가 된다. 또한 의문사 의문문에 대해 (B)처럼 No로 답할 수 없으므로 (B) 역시 오답이다.

in charge of ~의 책임인, 담당인 construction project 공사 프로젝트 route 노선, 길, 경로

24 Should I report to you or Kelly about the revisions?
미W (A) Let me review them first.
영M (B) Here are my suggestions.
(C) Yes, tomorrow please.

개정 사항에 대해 당신에게 보고해야 할까요 아니면 Kelly에게 해야 할까요?
(A) 제가 먼저 그것들을 검토할게요.
(B) 여기 제 제안 사항이 있습니다.
(C) 네, 내일로 부탁합니다.

선택 의문문으로 선택 사항만 간략하게 요약하면 '당신 or Kelly?'가 된다. 보고를 누구에게 해야 할지 물었으므로 '나에게'라고 답한 (A)가 정답이 된다. 선택 사항 두 개를 정확하게 캐치하는 것이 핵심이다.

report to ~에게 보고하다 revision 수정, 변경 review 검토하다 suggestion 제안

25 Why wasn't Molly at the computer training session?
미M (A) All the technicians were there.
영W (B) Because of a scheduling conflict.
(C) She prefers a different model.

Molly는 왜 컴퓨터 교육에 없었나요?
(A) 모든 기술자들은 거기에 있었어요.
(B) 일정이 겹쳤거든요.
(C) 그녀는 다른 모델을 선호합니다.

Molly가 교육에 안 온 이유를 물었으므로 다른 것과 일정이 겹쳤기 때문이라고 답한 (B)가 가장 자연스러운 답변이다. (A)는 computer에 대한 연상어 technician을 이용한 오답이고, (C)는 선호하는 모델을 말하고 있어 문맥상 벗어난 답이 된다.

technician 기술자 scheduling conflict 두 가지 이상의 일정이 겹치는 것 prefer 선호하다

26 Don't you think the board members should
미W reconsider their decision?
미M (A) It's too late to call.
(B) They really should.
(C) In the same direction.

이사회 위원들이 그들의 결정을 재고해야 한다고 생각하지 않으세요?
(A) 전화하기에 너무 늦었어요.
(B) 그들은 진짜 그래야 해요.
(C) 같은 방향에서요.

Yes/No 여부를 묻는 질문으로 don't you think와 같은 군더더기 표현은 해석상 제외시키고 핵심이 되는 board members, reconsider 등에 초점을 맞추자. (B)의 they는 board members를 가리키는 것이므로 해석상 Yes라고 답하고 있는 것이다. (A)와 (C)는 문맥상 완전히 벗어난 답이므로 오답으로 소거해야 한다.

reconsider재고하다 decision 결정 direction 방향

27 Did you order one or two boxes of photocopy
영M paper?
영W (A) I ordered three.
(B) Is it broken again?
(C) She's a talented photographer.

인쇄 용지 한 박스를 주문하셨나요 아니면 두 박스인가요?
(A) 3박스 주문했어요.
(B) 또 고장인가요?
(C) 그녀는 재능 있는 사진 작가입니다.

선택 의문문으로 선택 사항을 요약하면 '한 박스 혹은 두 박스?'가 된다. 그러므로 '세 박스'라고 답한 (A)가 정답이 된다. (B)와 (C)는 문맥상 맞지 않고 (C)는 주어 오류이기도 하다.

photocopy paper 인쇄 용지 broken 고장 난 talented 재능 있는 photographer 사진 작가

28 You already cancelled the job interview, didn't you?
미W (A) Yes, I'll take the offer.
영M (B) Oh no, it slipped my mind.
(C) Call the office.

이미 취업 면접을 취소하셨죠, 그렇지 않나요?
(A) 네, 저는 그 제안을 받아들이겠습니다.
(B) 오 어쩌죠, 깜빡 잊었네요.
(C) 사무실로 전화하세요.

Yes/No 질문으로 면접 일정을 취소했는지 여부를 물었으므로 깜빡 잊었다고 한 (B)가 결국 No라고 말하는 것이므로 정답이 된다. (A)는 상대방이 일자리를 제의할 경우에 이를 수락하겠다고 답하는 것이므로 연상어 오류 형태이다.

cancel 취소하다 job interview 취업 면접 offer 제안, (일자리) 제의 slip one's mind 깜빡 잊어 버리다

29 Isn't Ms. Chen out of town?
영W (A) From Berlin.
미M (B) No, she still has some.
(C) I heard her trip was cancelled.

Chen 씨는 도시에 안 계시나요?
(A) 베를린으로부터요.
(B) 아니오, 그녀는 아직도 조금 가지고 있습니다.
(C) 그녀의 출장이 취소되었다고 들었어요.

Yes/No 질문으로 Chen 씨가 도시에 있는지 여부를 물었고 (C)에서 그녀의 출장이 취소되었다는 것은 질문에 대해 No라고 답하는 것이 되므로 정답이다. 출장을 갔다는 표현은 out of town으로 종종 바꿔 표현되므로 출장이 취소되었으면 이에 대해 No라고 답하는 것으로 파악할 수 있다.

out of town 도시에 없는, 지방에 가 있는 (보통 출장 상황일 때 쓰임)

30 Refreshments can be delivered for tonight's office party, can't they?
영M 영W
(A) We'll go pick them up.
(B) Dinner for six.
(C) A last-minute change.

오늘 밤 사무실 파티를 위한 다과는 배달될 수 있어요, 그렇지 않나요?
(A) 우리가 가져올 것입니다.
(B) 6인분의 저녁입니다.
(C) 마지막 변경 사항이요.

Yes/No 질문으로 다과의 배달 여부를 묻고 있으므로 직접 가지러 가겠다고 답한 (A)가 정답이 되고 질문에 대해서는 No라는 답변이 성립된다.

refreshment 다과 office party 사무실에서 여는 파티 pick up 가지러 가다 last-minute 막판의, 마지막의

31 Your order for automobile parts has been filled.
미W 미M
(A) He faxed a cancellation form.
(B) Thanks. When can I expect them?
(C) Let me do the annual audit.

당신의 자동차 부품 주문 건이 처리되었습니다.
(A) 그는 취소 양식을 팩스로 보냈습니다.
(B) 감사합니다. 그것들이 언제쯤 올까요?
(C) 제가 연례 회계감사를 하겠습니다.

평서문 유형으로 상대방의 주문이 처리되었다고 정보를 주고 있으므로 감사하다고 답한 후 언제 배달이 올지를 묻고 있는 (B)가 정답이다. (A)는 order를 들었을 때 연상되는 cancellation을 이용한 오답이고 (C)는 문맥상 벗어난 답변이다.

part 부품, 부속품 fill an order 주문을 처리하다, 주문대로 물건을 만들다 expect (사람, 물건 등을) 기다리다, 언제 올지 예상하다 audit 회계 감사

PART 3

Questions 32-34 refer to the following conversation. 미W 영M

W Hi, Lawrence. Do you have a minute to talk?
M Sure. Please have a seat. What did you want to talk to me about?
W I was wondering if I could come to work by 9:30 instead of 9 o'clock as of March 2nd. I need to give my daughter a ride to school every morning when she starts school in March.
M I think there's no problem as long as you stay half an hour later in the evening.

여 안녕하세요, Lawrence. 잠깐 얘기할 시간 있으세요?
남 물론이지요. 앉으세요. 무슨 얘기를 하고 싶으세요?
여 3월 2일부터 9시 대신에 9시 30분까지 출근할 수 있는지 궁금해서요. 제 딸이 3월에 학기를 시작하는데 매일 아침 차로 데려다 줘야 하거든요.
남 당신이 저녁에 30분 더 일을 한다면 문제없을 것 같습니다.

come to work 출근하다 instead of ~대신에 as of + 시점 ~부터, ~부로

32 What does the woman want to do?
(A) Change her work schedule
(B) Carpool with her coworker
(C) Apply for a different position
(D) Volunteer at a school

여자는 무엇을 하고 싶어 하는가?
(A) 그녀의 업무 스케줄을 변경하고 싶어 한다.
(B) 그녀의 동료와 카풀을 하고 싶어 한다.
(C) 다른 직위에 지원하고 싶어 한다.
(D) 학교에서 자원봉사를 하고 싶어 한다.

여자가 원하는 일은 여자 대사에서 단서를 잡자. 여자 대사 I was wondering if I could come to work by 9:30 instead of 9 o'clock에서 출근 시간을 늦추고 싶어 한다는 것을 알 수 있고 정답은 work schedule의 변경을 원한다고 바꿔 표현되었다.

33 What does the woman say she needs to do every morning?
(A) Pick up some materials
(B) Take a class
(C) Drive her child to school
(D) Exercise at a gym

여자는 매일 아침에 무엇을 해야 한다고 말하는가?
(A) 물품 찾기
(B) 수업 듣기
(C) 아이 학교에 태워주기
(D) 체육관에서 운동하기

세부 사항 질문으로 every morning이 중요한 키워드가 되므로 여자 대사에서 every morning이 언급된 부분에 집중한다. 매일 아침 딸을 학교까지 데려다 줘야 한다고 했으므로 정답은 (C)가 된다.

34 What does the man tell the woman to do?
(A) Complete a time sheet every day
(B) Leave the office 30 minutes later
(C) Report to her supervisor
(D) Have another meeting with the man

남자는 여자에게 무엇을 하라고 말하는가?
(A) 매일 출퇴근 시간 기록지 완성하기
(B) 사무실에서 30분 늦게 퇴근하기
(C) 그녀의 상사에게 보고하기
(D) 남자와 한 번 더 회의하기

남자 대사에서 여자에게 요청하는 내용이 정답이 된다. 남자가 as long as you stay half an hour later in the evening(사무실에 30분 더 오래 있는 한 출근 시간을 늦춰도 된다)이라고 했으므로 정답은 이를 30분 늦게 퇴근하는 것으로 바꿔 표현한 (B)가 정답이 된다.

Questions 35-37 refer to the following conversation. (미M) (미W)

M Okay, I just replaced some loose wires and your oven is working fine now.
W Thank you for fixing it so quickly. All the tables in the restaurant are reserved for tonight and now we can start preparing food.
M That's great. If you need any further assistance, please contact me on my mobile phone. Here's my business card.

남 자, 지금 막 느슨한 전선을 교체했고 이제 당신의 오븐은 잘 작동합니다.
여 이렇게 빨리 고쳐주셔서 감사합니다. 레스토랑의 모든 테이블이 오늘 밤에 예약이 되었는데 이제 우리가 음식 준비를 시작할 수 있겠네요.
남 잘됐네요. 더 도움이 필요하신 경우에는 제 휴대 전화로 연락 주십시오. 명함이 여기 있습니다.

replace 교체하다 loose 느슨한 wire 전선 assistance 도움 mobile phone 휴대 전화 business card 명함

35 Who most likely is the man?
(A) A repair person
(B) A waiter
(C) A client
(D) A shop manager

남자는 누구일 것 같은가?
(A) 수리공
(B) 웨이터
(C) 고객
(D) 상점 매니저

남자의 직업을 유추하는 질문으로 도입부에 남자의 업무 내용을 듣고 유추할 수 있다. 느슨한 전선을 교체하여 오븐을 수리하는 업무를 하는 것에서 정답은 (A)로 선택한다. 장소가 restaurant으로 유추되므로 (B)와 (D) 같은 직업들이 함정으로 출제되었다.

36 Where most likely is the conversation taking place?
(A) At a restaurant
(B) At an auto repair shop
(C) In a hotel lobby
(D) At an electronics store

대화는 어디에서 일어날 것 같은가?
(A) 레스토랑
(B) 자동차 정비소
(C) 호텔 로비
(D) 전자제품 상점

대화 장소를 유추하는 질문으로 도입부에 오븐을 수리해서 잘 작동한다고 언급한 부분과 All the tables in the restaurant are reserved for tonight(레스토랑의 모든 테이블이 예약되었다)이라고 언급된 부분에서 (A)를 정답으로 처리한다. 수리와 관련된 장소인 (B)는 함정이 된다.

37 For what does the woman thank the man?
(A) Delivering some ingredients
(B) Finishing the work quickly
(C) Recommending a restaurant
(D) Changing dinner reservations

여자는 남자에게 무엇을 감사하는가?
(A) 재료를 배달해 준 것
(B) 일을 빨리 끝내준 것
(C) 레스토랑을 추천해준 것
(D) 저녁 식사 예약을 변경한 것

세부 사항 질문으로 여자 대사에서 감사하다는 언급이 되는 부분에 정답의 단서가 있다. Thank you for fixing it so quickly에서 수리를 빨리 해줘서 고맙다고 했으므로 정답은 (B)가 된다.

Questions 38-40 refer to the following conversation. (영M) (영W)

M Hi, Susan. I'm so glad that I bumped into you. I actually have a favor to ask of you. If you by any chance stay home on Tuesday afternoon, will you be able to sign for a package for me?
W I was going to do some gardening at home on Tuesday since the weather's supposed to be good. So I think I can receive a package for you. Just let me know when it should be delivered.
M Sure. It's supposed to be here by 3 o'clock. I'll ask the delivery service to deliver it next door to your house right now. I really appreciate your help, Susan.
W It's my pleasure.

남 안녕하세요, Susan. 당신과 마주치게 되어 정말 다행이네요. 실은 당신에게 부탁할 것이 있어요. 혹시라도 화요일 오후에 집에 계실 거라면, 제 소포를 대신 받고 서명을 해 주실 수 있을까요?
여 날씨가 좋을 거라고 해서 저는 화요일에는 집에서 정원 작업을 하려고 했어요. 그러니 소포를 대신 받아줄 수 있을 것 같네요. 그것이 언제쯤 배송될지 미리 알려 주세요.
남 물론이지요. 3시까지는 여기 도착하기로 되어 있습니다. 지금 배송 업체에 전화해서 옆집인 당신의 집으로 배송해 달라고 요청해야겠어요. 도와주셔서 정말 감사해요, Susan.
여 도움이 되어서 기뻐요.

bump into ~와 우연히 만나다 favor 부탁 by any chance 혹시라도 sign for 서명하다 gardening 정원 작업 next door 옆 집의 appreciate 고마워하다

38 What information does the woman request?
(A) A shipping cost
(B) A delivery time
(C) A street address
(D) An identification number
여자는 어떤 정보를 요청하는가?
(A) 운송 비용
(B) 배송 시간
(C) 거리 주소
(D) 식별 번호

세부 사항 문제로 여자 대사 요청 표현에서 정답을 찾는다. 여자가 Just let me know when it should be delivered(언제 배달되는지 알려 달라)라고 했으므로 정답은 (B)가 된다.

39 Who most likely are the speakers?
(A) Neighbors
(B) Coworkers
(C) Delivery people
(D) Gardeners
화자들은 누구일 것 같은가?
(A) 이웃
(B) 동료
(C) 배달원
(D) 정원사

화자 두 명의 관계를 묻는 질문으로 정답의 단서는 남자가 여자에게 소포를 대신 받아달라고 요청하는 부분과 여자는 집에서 정원 돌보기를 할 것이라는 점 등에서 이웃 관계임을 알 수 있다.

40 What does the man say he will do?
(A) Write a check list
(B) Purchase some tools
(C) Contact a company
(D) Change a delivery date
남자는 무엇을 할 것이라고 말하는가?
(A) 체크 리스트 작성하기
(B) 공구 구입하기
(C) 업체에 연락하기
(D) 배송 날짜 바꾸기

향후 행동을 묻는 질문으로 남자가 대화의 마지막 부분에 I'll ask the delivery service라고 말한 부분이 바로 정답이 된다. I'll이 들릴 때 반드시 정답을 캐치하자.

Questions 41-43 refer to the following conversation. (미W) (영M)

W Hi, Alex. I'm trying to finish a contract for our new client, Mr. Matt Taylor. Since you're in the editorial team, I thought it would be helpful if you could proofread it.
M Oh, I'd love to help but my director just gave me a new assignment which he said was quite urgent. Can it wait until tomorrow?
W No it cannot. I really need to finish it as soon as possible and send it over to Mr. Taylor by the end of the day.
M In that case, someone else in my team can help you out. Why don't you ask Ming to check your documents?

여 안녕하세요, Alex. 우리의 새 고객이신 Matt Taylor 씨를 위한 계약을 마무리하려고 하는데요. 당신이 편집부 소속이니, 이 계약서의 교정을 해 준다면 큰 도움이 될 것 같습니다.
남 아, 저도 도와 드리고 싶지만 저희 부장님이 저에게 꽤 급한 새로운 업무를 방금 배정해 주셨어요. 내일까지 기다릴 수 있는 일인가요?
여 아니요, 안 됩니다. 가능한 한 빨리 그걸 끝내서 오늘까지는 Taylor 씨에게 보내 드려야 하거든요.
남 그런 경우라면, 팀에서 다른 누군가가 도와줄 수 있을 거예요. Ming에게 당신의 문서를 검사해 달라고 부탁하면 어떨까요?

editorial 편집의 proofread (마지막 단계의) 교정 assignment 업무 urgent 급한 in that case 그런 경우라면

41 What does the woman ask the man to do?
(A) Read over some documents
(B) Submit a proposal
(C) Telephone a client
(D) Lead a training session
여자는 남자에게 무엇을 해 달라고 요청하는가?
(A) 문서 검토하기
(B) 제안서 제출하기
(C) 고객에게 전화하기
(D) 교육 진행하기

세부 사항 질문으로 여자 대사에서 남자에게 요청하는 내용에 집중한다. I thought it would be helpful if you could proofread it(서류의 교정을 해준다면 도움이 많이 되겠다)이라고 부탁하는 부분에서 정답을 (A)로 선택한다. it would be helpful if you could 표현은 상대방에게 정중하게 요청할 때 쓰이는 것으로 암기해 두자.

42 Why does the woman need to complete her work today?
(A) The office will be closed tomorrow.
(B) She has other tasks to take care of.
(C) She has to send it to a client.
(D) A director will visit in the morning.
여자는 왜 오늘 업무를 끝내야만 하는가?
(A) 사무실이 내일 문을 닫을 것이다.
(B) 그녀는 처리해야 할 다른 업무가 있다
(C) 그녀는 고객에게 업무를 보내야 한다.
(D) 부장님이 아침에 방문할 것이다.

세부 사항 질문으로 여자 대사에서 오늘 업무를 끝내야 한다는 내용을 노려 듣는다. 여자가 최대한 빨리 업무를 끝내야 한다고 언급하면서 오늘까지 고객에게 보내줘야 한다고 말했으므로 정답은 (C)이다.

43 What does the man suggest?
(A) Checking the documents herself
(B) Providing a list of references
(C) Negotiating the terms of a contract
(D) Asking another coworker

남자는 무엇을 제안하는가?
(A) 문서를 그녀 스스로 검토하는 것
(B) 참조 문헌의 목록을 제공하는 것
(C) 계약서의 조항을 협상하는 것
(D) 다른 동료에게 요청하는 것

남자의 제안 사항이므로 남자 대사에서 Why don't you가 들릴 때 정답의 단서를 잡는다. Ming에게 서류 검토를 요청하는 게 어떠냐고 제안했고, Ming을 another coworker로 바꿔 표현되었으므로 정답은 (D)가 된다.

Questions 44-46 refer to the following conversation. 미M 영W

M Hi, this is Dr. Roger Cooper calling from Shelton Dental Clinic. Some of my patients have asked me to recommend a toothpaste brand that effectively prevents gum pain. And I'd like to know more about the brand your company produces, Ultra Whitening.

W Thanks for your interest, Dr. Cooper. Ultra Whitening is actually our best-selling product. Perhaps, it would be best for one of our sales representatives to visit your clinic and explain it in detail.

M That's good. I'd like to know what ingredients are in it and how it performed during the clinical testing.

W Of course, Dr. Cooper. I'll send someone to your office next Monday if that's okay with you. He will demonstrate the product and give you all the information you need.

남 안녕하세요, Shelton Dental Clinic의 Roger Cooper 박사입니다. 제 환자들 중 몇 분이 저에게 잇몸의 통증을 효과적으로 예방해주는 치약 브랜드를 추천해 달라고 합니다. 그래서 귀사 회사 제품인 Ultra Whitening에 대해 더 알아보고자 합니다

여 관심을 가져주셔서 감사합니다 Cooper 박사님. Ultra Whitening은 사실 저희 베스트셀러 상품입니다. 아마도, 저희 영업 사원 중 한 명이 박사님의 병원을 방문해서 자세히 설명해 드리는 것이 가장 좋을 듯 합니다.

남 좋습니다. 안에 들어가는 성분에 대해 알고 싶고 임상 실험에서의 효능이 어땠는지 알고 싶습니다.

여 물론이죠, Cooper 박사님. 괜찮으시다면, 다음 주 월요일에 당신의 병원으로 사람을 보내겠습니다. 그가 제품을 시연하고 필요하신 정보를 모두 드릴 것입니다.

Dental clinic 치과 patient 환자 toothpaste 치약 prevent 예방하다 gum pain 잇몸 통증 sales representative 영업 사원 explain 설명하다 in detail 자세하게, 세부적으로 ingredient 성분, 재료 clinical testing 임상 실험 demonstrate 시연하다

44 Who most likely is the man?
(A) A sales representative
(B) A dentist
(C) A store clerk
(D) A research scientist

남자는 누구일 것 같은가?
(A) 영업 사원
(B) 치과 의사
(C) 가게 점원
(D) 연구 과학자

전화 대화에서 남자의 직업을 유추할 때는 남자가 본인을 소개하는 부분에서 정답을 처리하자. 도입부에서 남자가 this is Dr. Roger Cooper calling from Shelton Dental Clinic(치과에서 전화하는 Cooper 박사)이라고 본인을 소개했으므로 치과 의사임을 알 수 있다. 또한 Some of my patients에서도 의사 신분임을 파악할 수 있다.

45 Why is the man calling?
(A) To report a defective product
(B) To sign up for a course
(C) To request some information
(D) To place an order

남자는 왜 전화하는가?
(A) 결함 있는 상품을 보고하려고
(B) 강좌를 신청하려고
(C) 정보를 요청하려고
(D) 주문하려고

남자 대사에서 정답의 단서를 찾는다. I'd like to know more about the brand your company produces, Ultra Whitening에서 상품에 대해 더 알고 싶어서 전화했다고 파악할 수 있고 이를 To request some information으로 바꿔 표현한 (C)가 정답이다.

46 What does the woman offer to do?
(A) Contact another department
(B) Check the status of an order
(C) Send some brochures
(D) Arrange a meeting with a salesperson

여자는 무엇을 해 주겠다고 하는가?
(A) 다른 부서에게 연락하기
(B) 주문 상태 확인하기
(C) 안내 책자 보내기
(D) 영업 사원과 미팅 잡기

여자가 남자를 위해 제공하는 것을 묻는 세부 사항 질문으로, 여자 대사 I'll send someone to your office next Monday if that's okay with you에서 영업 사원을 치과로 보내 준다는 내용을 확인할 수 있고, 이것이 정답 (D)에서는 arrange a meeting with a salesperson으로 바꿔 표현되었다.

Questions 47-49 refer to the following conversation. (영M) (영W)

M Hi, I bought your Dynamic's 2000 software three days ago. I had no problem with the installation but when I tried to use it, I just got lost. It is very confusing and complicated to use. Do you provide any training courses?

W Have you tried the tutorial manual CD included in the package? It's designed to give users step-by-step instructions.

M Oh, I think I saw that CD actually. What should I do with it?

W Just insert the CD and type in the model number which you can find in your warranty book. You'll then get an access code to start the tutorial.

남 안녕하세요. 제가 3일 전에 Dynamic's 2000 소프트웨어를 구입했는데요. 설치에는 아무런 문제가 없었지만 이용하려고 하니, 아무것도 모르겠더군요. 이 제품은 사용하기가 매우 복잡하고 혼란스럽네요. 혹시 교육 과정을 제공하시나요?

여 포장에 들어있는 사용 지침 CD는 한 번 보셨나요? 그것은 사용자들에게 단계적인 설명을 제공하도록 만들어져 있어요.

남 아, 실은 그 CD를 본 것 같아요. 이것을 어떻게 해야 하나요?

여 CD를 넣고 품질보증서에서 찾을 수 있는 상품 번호를 입력해 주시면 됩니다. 그러면 사용 지침 프로그램을 시작할 수 있는 접근 코드를 받게 될 것입니다.

installation 설치 get lost 길을 잃다, 전혀 모르겠다 confusing 혼란스러운 complicated 복잡한 tutorial 사용 지침(프로그램) be designed to ~하도록 만들어졌다 instruction 설명, 지시 insert 삽입하다 warranty 품질 보증서 access code 접근 코드

47 What does the man say about his purchase?
(A) It comes with a tutorial.
(B) It is not user-friendly.
(C) It is hard to install.
(D) It is expensive.

남자는 그의 구입품에 관하여 무엇을 말하는가?
(A) 사용 지침 프로그램이 함께 나온다.
(B) 사용하기 쉽지 않다.
(C) 설치가 어렵다.
(D) 비싸다.

세부 사항 질문으로 반드시 남자 대사에서 그가 구입한 물건에 대한 언급을 할 때 일치하는 항목을 선택한다. 남자가 It is very confusing and complicated to use라고 했으므로 정답은 (B)가 맞고 not user-friendly라고 바꿔 표현된 부분을 암기해 두자. (A)는 여자가 말한 내용이므로 함정이고, (C)는 남자가 설치에는 문제가 없었다고 말했으므로 역시 오답이다.

48 What does the man ask about?
(A) A product exchange
(B) A training course
(C) A partial refund
(D) An extended warranty

남자는 무엇에 관해서 묻는가?
(A) 제품 교환
(B) 교육 과정
(C) 부분 환불
(D) 보증 기간 연장

남자 대사에서 질문 형태로 말하는 내용에 집중하자. 제품의 사용이 어렵다고 언급한 후 Do you provide any training courses?(훈련 과정을 제공하는지)라고 물었으므로 정답은 (B)이다.

49 What does the woman tell the man to do?
(A) Find a model code
(B) Visit a store
(C) Purchase a CD
(D) Request free service

여자는 남자에게 무엇을 하라고 말하는가?
(A) 상품 코드 찾기
(B) 상점 방문하기
(C) CD 구매하기
(D) 무료 서비스 요청하기

여자가 남자에게 하라는 내용 중 일치되는 정보를 정답으로 처리한다. 품질 보증서에서 상품 번호를 찾아 입력하라는 내용 중 일치하는 것은 (A)이다. CD는 삽입하라고 했으므로 (C)는 들리는 단어를 이용한 함정이 된다.

Questions 50-52 refer to the following conversation. (미M) (영W)

M Hello. This is Joshua Davis from JDB Marketing Agency. Last week, our facilities coordinator Mr. Dolan arranged for your company to transport some office equipment from our office to the PWA Center. We've just received the invoice and the total amount is greater than we anticipated. Could you please check it?

W Wait a second please. I'm looking at your information now. Is there any particular charge you wanted to ask about?

M Yes. I'm not quite sure about the $220 fee for storage. What is that for?

W Oh, let me explain it. According to the contract Mr. Dolan signed with us, we are supposed to pick up the equipment on Thursday and deliver it to the center the following morning. Because we keep it in our storage area overnight, the charge was included in the contract.

남 여보세요. JDB Marketing Agency의 Joshua Davis입니다. 지난주에, 저희 시설 책임자인 Dolan 씨가 저희 사무용 설비를 지금 사무실에서 PWA 센터로 옮기기 위해 그쪽 회사를 선정해 주셨습니다. 지금 막 청구서를 받았는데 총액이 예상보다 많이 나왔네요. 확인 좀 해주시겠습니까?

여 잠시만 기다리십시오. 지금 정보를 보고 있는데요. 특정 금액에 대해 궁금한 점이 있으신가요?

남 그렇습니다. 보관에 드는 220달러 수수료가 무엇인지 잘 모르겠습니다. 그것은 무엇에 드는 비용인가요?

여 아, 설명해 드리죠. Dolan 씨와 한 계약을 보면, 저희는 목요일에 장비를 가져오고 센터에 다음 날 아침에 배달하는 것으로 되어 있습니다. 하룻밤 동안 저희 창고에 보관해야 하기 때문에 그 비용이 계약서에 포함되어 있는 것입니다.

facilities coordinator 시설 책임자 arrange for 마련하다, 주선하다 transport 옮기다 invoice 청구서 anticipate 예상하다, 예측하다 particular 특정한 fee 요금 storage 저장, 보관 the following morning 다음 날 아침 overnight 하룻밤 동안

50 What type of business is the man contacting?
(A) An electronics firm
(B) A moving company
(C) An advertising agency
(D) An office furniture store

남자는 어떤 종류의 업체에 연락을 취하고 있는가?
(A) 전자제품 회사
(B) 이삿짐 회사
(C) 광고 대행사
(D) 사무용 가구 상점

남자가 연락을 취하는 업체이므로 여자의 직장을 묻는 질문으로 파악해 둔다. 사무용 설비를 옮기기 위해 이 업체를 이용하게 되었다고 하므로 이삿짐 회사임을 유추할 수 있다.

51 What problem is the man discussing?
(A) A center was closed for business.
(B) A mover delivered his package to the wrong location.
(C) An unexpected fee was charged to him.
(D) An event was delayed.

남자는 어떤 문제점에 대해 얘기하는가?
(A) 센터가 문을 닫았다.
(B) 이삿짐 센터 직원이 잘못된 장소로 물건을 배달했다.
(C) 예상치 못한 요금이 그에게 부과되었다.
(D) 행사가 연기되었다.

남자 대사를 집중해서 듣되, 부정적인 내용에 집중한다. 도입부에 청구서를 받았음을 언급하고 the total amount is greater than we anticipated(총액이 생각보다 더 많다)라고 했으므로 청구된 금액에 대한 문제임을 알 수 있다. 또한, storage에 대한 금액이 왜 부과됐는지 모르겠다고 했으므로 정답은 (C)가 된다.

52 What does the woman suggest about Mr. Dolan?
(A) He signed a contract.
(B) He organized an event.
(C) He will send a corrected bill.
(D) He will store some items.

여자는 Dolan 씨에 관하여 무엇을 암시하는가?
(A) 그가 계약서에 서명을 했다.
(B) 그가 행사를 주관했다.
(C) 그가 정정된 계산서를 보낼 것이다.
(D) 그가 일부 품목을 보관할 것이다.

여자가 Mr. Dolan을 언급하는 부분에 정답이 단서가 나온다. According to the contract Mr. Dolan signed with us에서 그가 계약서에 서명했다는 내용이 나오므로 정답은 (A)가 된다.

Questions 53-55 refer to the following conversation. 미M 미W

M Hey Sharon, aren't you going to the charity concert in Simon Park tonight?
W Yes. I just hope it is not cancelled because of the heavy rainfall we've been having lately. I heard they called off yesterday's show and there's more rain forecast this evening. I'm very worried that tonight's show will be cancelled too.
M Well, it is quite possible though. You know it's an outdoor event. So if it rains, they will have to cancel it. Would you like me to check the park's website to see whether the concert is still on?
W Why don't we just wait a bit longer? Last night's performance was cancelled only half an hour before the show was supposed to begin.

남 Sharon, 오늘 밤에 사이먼 공원에서 열리는 자선 연주회에 가지 않으시나요?
여 갑니다. 최근에 비가 많이 온 것 때문에 공연이 취소되지 않았으면 좋겠어요. 어제의 공연은 취소됐다고 들었고 오늘 저녁에 더 많은 비가 예보되어 있거든요. 오늘 공연도 취소될까봐 너무 걱정이 돼요.
남 음, 그럴 가능성이 꽤 있네요. 아시다시피 야외 행사니까요. 비가 온다면, 행사를 취소할 수 밖에는 없겠죠. 제가 공원 웹 사이트에서 콘서트가 여전히 진행되는지를 확인해 드릴까요?
여 우리 조금만 더 기다리는 게 어떨까요? 어젯밤의 공연도 쇼가 시작되기 30분 전에야 취소되었다고 해요.

charity concert 자선 콘서트 heavy rainfall 폭우 lately 최근에 call off 취소하다 forecast 예보하다, 예상하다 outdoor 야외의 performance 공연

53 What are the speakers discussing?
(A) A film screening
(B) A charity event
(C) An opening ceremony
(D) A sporting event

화자들은 무엇에 대해 이야기하는가?
(A) 영화 검열
(B) 자선 행사
(C) 개회식
(D) 스포츠 경기

대화의 주제를 묻는 질문으로 도입부 첫 문장에서 '오늘 밤 열리는 자선 콘서트에 가는지'를 물었을 때 정답은 (B)로 선택한다.

54 What does the man imply when he says "Well, it is quite possible though"?
(A) An outdoor event will be organized.
(B) Some equipment could be damaged.
(C) The concert is more likely to be cancelled.
(D) The weather will improve soon.

남자가 "음, 그럴 가능성이 꽤 있네요"라고 말한 의도는 무엇인가?
(A) 야외 행사가 조직될 것이다.
(B) 일부 장비가 손상될 수 있다.
(C) 콘서트가 취소될 것 같다.
(D) 날씨가 곧 좋아질 것이다.

화자의 의도를 파악하는 새로운 토익 유형으로 해당 표현의 앞뒤 문맥을 파악하는 것이 핵심이다. 비로 인해 행사가 취소될까 봐 걱정하는 여자에게 "그럴 가능성이 있다"고 말하며 야외 행사이기 때문이라고 부연 설명을 했으므로 정답은 (C)가 된다.

55 What does the man offer to do?
(A) Arrive half an hour early
(B) Call the park
(C) Go to the park
(D) Check for updates online
남자는 무엇을 해 주겠다고 하는가?
(A) 30분 일찍 도착하기
(B) 공원으로 전화하기
(C) 공원에 가기
(D) 갱신된 정보를 온라인으로 확인하기

남자의 대사에서 Would you like me to라는 제공 표현이 나왔을 때 정답을 처리하자. 웹 사이트에서 공연이 진행되는지를 확인해 줄지 물었으므로 정답은 (D)가 된다.

Questions 56-58 refer to the following conversation. 영M 영W

M Megan, could you help me with the library's budget for next year? I need some additional information to finish it. Could you check how much money was collected for late fees and lost item charges?
W I'd like to help, but I was about to leave for the day. I have a birthday party to attend tonight. Why don't I check it for you tomorrow morning?
M Well, actually, I really should finish this draft today since it's due by the end of tomorrow. Do you think I could look it up somewhere for myself?
W Oh yes. I've entered all the numbers you need into a spreadsheet on my laptop. If you open the budget file, you'll see the exact figures for the library fines income.

남 Megan, 내년 도서관 예산과 관련해서 좀 도와주시겠어요? 이걸 끝내려면, 추가 정보가 좀 더 필요합니다. 연체료와 분실 품목에 대한 벌금으로 얼마가 걷혔는지 확인해 주실 수 있으세요?
여 저도 돕고 싶습니다만, 지금 막 퇴근을 하려던 참이었어요. 오늘 밤에 참석해야 할 생일 파티가 있거든요. 내일 아침에 확인해 드리면 어떨까요?
남 실은, 내일까지 마감이기 때문에 오늘 초안을 완성해야만 합니다. 제가 혼자라도 어디서 찾아볼 수 있을까요?
여 아, 그럼요. 당신이 필요로 하는 모든 수치들을 제 휴대용 컴퓨터의 스프레드시트에 입력해 두었어요. 예산 파일을 열어보시면, 도서관 벌금 수입에 대한 정확한 수치를 보실 수 있을 거예요.

budget 예산 additional 추가의 last fee 연체료 lost item charge 분실물에 대한 벌금 be about to 막 ~하려고 하다 look up 찾아보다 numbers(= figures) 수치 fine 벌금

56 What is the man doing now?
(A) Collecting a fine
(B) Drafting a budget
(C) Preparing for a presentation
(D) Repairing a laptop computer
남자는 지금 무엇을 하고 있는가?
(A) 벌금 걷기
(B) 예산의 초안 작성
(C) 발표 준비
(D) 휴대용 컴퓨터 수리

세부 사항 질문으로 남자가 대화의 초반에 여자에게 내년도 예산안 작업을 도와달라는 부분에서 정답을 (B)로 선택한다.

57 Why is the woman not able to assist the man?
(A) She has to meet another deadline.
(B) She has a gathering to attend.
(C) She has to go to a bank.
(D) She cannot access the information.
여자는 왜 남자를 도와줄 수 없는가?
(A) 다른 마감을 맞춰야 한다.
(B) 참석할 모임이 있다.
(C) 은행에 가야만 한다.
(D) 정보에 접근할 수 없다.

세부 사항 why 질문을 통해 여자는 남자를 도울 수 없다는 정보를 미리 알아두자. 여자가 지금 퇴근을 해야 하는 이유로 생일 파티가 있다고 했고 이것을 gathering(모임)이 있다고 바꿔 표현한 (B)가 정답이다.

58 What will the man probably do next?
(A) Contact another coworker
(B) Check a book out of the library
(C) Calculate some figures
(D) Refer to a computer file
남자는 다음에 무엇을 할 것 같은가?
(A) 다른 동료에게 연락한다.
(B) 도서관에서 책을 대출한다.
(C) 수치를 계산한다.
(D) 컴퓨터 파일을 참고한다.

남자의 향후 행동을 묻는 질문으로 대화의 후반부 여자 대사에서 예산 파일을 열어 보면(If you open the budget file) 정확한 수치를 볼 수 있다고 했으므로 남자는 컴퓨터 파일을 열어 볼 것이라고 판단할 수 있다. 정답은 (D)이다.

Questions 59-61 refer to the following conversation. 영W 미M

W Hello Mr. Cohen. This is Sam Wilton. I'm getting back to you about the accounting position I applied for last week.

M Thanks for returning my call Ms. Wilton. I just wanted to make sure that you understand this is for a part-time job before we continue with the hiring process. You're well aware that it's not for full-time employment, right?

W **Actually I wasn't.** I was looking for a full-time position. But I think I'd be willing to consider a part-time position depending on what benefits are included and what my starting salary is. Could you give me more details about the job?

M We provide part-timers with health insurance as well as annual paid leave. You'll start around 800 dollars per month. How does that sound?

여 여보세요 Cohen 씨. Sam Wilton입니다. 지난주에 제가 지원했던 회계직과 관련해서 다시 전화드립니다.

남 답신해 주셔서 감사합니다, Wilton 씨. 우리가 고용 절차를 계속 진행하기에 앞서 당신이 이 직위는 시간제 고용직이라는 점을 알고 계신다는 것을 확실히 하고 싶습니다. 이 것은 전임 자리가 아니란 것을 잘 알고 계시죠?

여 **실은 저는 몰랐습니다.** 저는 전임 자리를 찾고 있었거든요. 그렇지만 어떤 복리후생이 포함되고 초봉이 어떤지에 따라 시간제 고용직도 고려해볼 의향이 있습니다. 저에게 이 업무에 관해서 더 상세히 설명해 주시겠습니까?

남 저희는 시간제 근무자들에게 건강 보험과 일 년에 한 번 유급 휴가를 제공합니다. 당신은 월 800달러에서 시작할 것입니다. 어떻습니까?

get back to ~에게 다시 전화하다 accounting position 회계직 continue with 계속 진행하다 hiring process 고용 절차 be aware that 알다 full-time 전임의 be willing to 기꺼이 하고자 하다 consider 고려하다 benefit 복리혜택 starting salary 초봉 health insurance 건강 보험 paid leave 유급 휴가

59 What are the speakers mainly discussing?
(A) Tax accounting
(B) A salary raise
(C) A job opening
(D) A reorganization of the company

화자들은 무엇에 대해 얘기하는가?
(A) 세무 회계
(B) 급여 인상
(C) 일자리
(D) 회사의 개편

대화의 주제를 찾는 문제로 도입부에 여자가 본인이 지원했던 회계직과 관련해서 다시 전화했다고 했으므로 정답은 (C)이다. 정답의 단서는 about the accounting position I applied for에서와 같이 about 뒤에 나오는 경우가 많다는 것을 기억하자.

60 What does the woman mean when she says "Actually I wasn't"?
(A) She thought the job she applied for was a full-time position.
(B) She thought she would work overseas.
(C) She thought the company pays well.
(D) She thought she was not qualified for the job.

여자가 "실은 저는 몰랐습니다"라고 말한 의미는 무엇인가?
(A) 지원한 직업이 정규직이라고 생각했다.
(B) 그녀가 해외에서 일할 것이라고 생각했다.
(C) 이 회사가 월급이 많다고 생각했다.
(D) 그녀가 이 직업에 대한 자격이 없다고 생각했다.

화자의 의도를 파악하기 위해서는 해당 표현의 앞뒤 문맥 파악이 중요하다. 남자가 여자에게 지원한 직업이 시간제 근무라는 사실을 아는지를 물었고 이에 대한 답으로서 여자가 Actually I wasn't(사실은 알지 못했다)라고 답하면서 본인은 정규직을 찾고 있다고 답했으므로 정답은 (A)가 된다.

61 What does the woman say she will consider?
(A) Offering benefits
(B) Applying for a different position
(C) Hiring more qualified workers
(D) Working as a part-timer

여자는 무엇을 고려하겠다고 말하는가?
(A) 혜택을 제공하는 것
(B) 다른 직위에 지원하는 것
(C) 자격이 더 나은 직원을 고용하는 것
(D) 시간제 근무자로 일하는 것

세부 정보를 묻는 질문으로 여자 대사에서 키워드인 consider가 언급될 때 정답을 캐치한다. I'll be willing to consider a part-time position에서 정답은 (D)가 된다. 단, 60번과 정답이 거의 동시에 주어지므로, 키워드인 consider를 들었을 때 61번에 대한 정답을 놓치지 않아야 한다.

Questions 62-64 refer to the following conversation with three speakers. (미W) (영W) (영M)

W1 Hello. My name is Isabelle Brooks and I'm here for my 2 o'clock appointment with Mr. William Gray.

W2 Hello Ms. Brooks. Wait a second please. I'll let him know that you're here. Hi Mr. Gray, this is Carrie from the reception desk. Ms. Isabelle Brooks is here to meet with you.

M Oh yes, she's a reporter from Riverdale News and she's supposed to come to interview me. But the thing is… it's only 1:35 and I wasn't expecting her this early. I was waiting for an important call.

W2 Should I ask her to wait then?

M Yes, please. Ask her to wait in the lobby and I'll be there in 20 minutes.

W2 All right Mr. Gray. Ms. Brooks, Mr. Gray says that he can see you in the lobby in 20 minutes. If you would like some coffee or tea while you're waiting, feel free to use the mini bar in the lobby.

W1 Oh, that'd be great. I think I'm going to have some coffee. Thanks for your help.

여1 안녕하세요. 저는 Isabelle Brooks이고 William Gray 씨와의 2시 약속 때문에 왔습니다.

여2 안녕하세요 Brooks 씨. 잠시만 기다리세요. 당신이 여기 왔다고 전해드릴게요. 안녕하세요 Gray 씨. 저는 안내 데스크의 Carrie 인데요. Isabelle Brooks 씨가 당신과 만나기 위해서 여기에 왔어요.

남 아 네. 그녀는 Riverdale 뉴스의 기자인데 저를 인터뷰하기 위해서 오기로 되어 있었어요. 그런데 문제는… 지금이 1시 35분밖에 안 되었고 이렇게 일찍 오실 줄 몰랐어요. 제가 중요한 전화를 기다리는 중이었거든요.

여2 그럼 기다리시라고 전할까요?

남 네 그렇게 해주세요. 로비에서 기다리라고 해주시면 제가 20분 후에 가겠습니다.

여2 알겠습니다 Gray 씨. Brooks 씨, Gray 씨께서 20분 후에 로비에서 만나실 수 있다고 합니다. 기다리시는 동안 커피나 차를 드시고 싶으시면, 로비에 있는 미니 바를 이용하셔도 됩니다.

여1 오, 잘됐네요. 커피를 좀 마셔야겠어요. 도와주셔서 감사합니다.

reporter 기자 feel free to 마음껏 하다

62 Who most likely is Isabelle Brooks?
(A) A receptionist
(B) A vice president
(C) A reporter
(D) A client

Isabelle Brooks는 누구일 것 같은가?
(A) 안내 접수원
(B) 부사장
(C) 기자
(D) 고객

3인 대화이므로 질문 속의 이름을 정확하게 파악하여 문제를 풀자. 대화를 시작하는 여자가 본인을 Ms. Isabelle Brooks라고 밝혔고 남자가 Oh yes, she's a reporter from Riverdale News에서 그녀는 기자라고 인터뷰를 하기 위해 왔다고 했으므로 정답은 (C)가 된다.

63 Why is the man unavailable for Ms. Brooks at the moment?
(A) She has arrived early for an appointment.
(B) He is in a meeting with an important client.
(C) A meeting room is being used by someone else.
(D) He has lost his mobile phone.

남자는 왜 지금 Brooks 씨를 만날 수 없는가?
(A) 여자가 약속보다 일찍 도착했다.
(B) 남자는 중요한 고객과 미팅 중이다.
(C) 회의실이 다른 사람에 의해 사용 중이다.
(D) 남자는 휴대 전화를 잃어버렸다.

남자가 But the thing is… it's only 1:35 and I wasn't expecting her this early. I was waiting for an important call이라고 말한 부분이 정답이 된다. 이렇게 일찍 올지 몰랐고 중요한 전화를 기다리고 있기 때문에 지금은 볼 수 없다고 해석되므로 정답은 (A)가 된다.

64 What will Ms. Brooks most likely do next?
(A) Return another day
(B) Make a copy
(C) Go to the lobby
(D) Read a newspaper

Brooks 씨는 다음에 무엇을 할 것 같은가?
(A) 다른 날 다시 오기
(B) 복사하기
(C) 로비에 가기
(D) 신문 읽기

Ms. Brooks의 향후 행동으로 대화의 후반부에서 단서를 찾자. 로비에 미니바가 있고 음료를 마실 수 있다고 들었을 때 Ms. Brooks가 I think I'm going to have some coffee라고 했으므로 로비에 가서 커피를 마실 것임을 알 수 있다. 정답은 (C)이다.

Questions 65-67 refer to the following conversation and list. (미M) (영W)

M Hello, Ms. Lopez. This is Dave calling from The EyeBuy Shop. We've received the online order for your new eyeglasses. You requested a Prism frame in black, which costs $40. But unfortunately that model is currently unavailable in black.

W Oh, that's too bad. When do you think it will be back in stock?

M We can order it today, but it won't be here until next Wednesday.

W I don't think I can wait that long. I'm going on a business trip on Monday and I want to take my new glasses with me. Do the Prism frames come in other colors?

M Yes, we currently have translucent ones in stock but they cost $50 each.

W I don't want to spend more than $40 on eyeglass frames. What other options do I have?

M Actually we have another model available in black right now and it costs just $40. Why don't you come in to the store and take a look, Ms. Lopez?

Eyeglass Frames in Stock		
MODEL	COLOR	PRICE
Prism	Translucent	$50
Emory	Leopard	$50
Vernon	Red	$80
Bristol	Black	$40

남 안녕하세요 Lopez 씨. 저는 EyeBuy Shop의 Dave입니다. 당신의 새 안경 주문서는 잘 받았습니다. 40달러 Prism 테를 검정색으로 주문하셨는데 안타깝게도 그 모델은 현재 검정으로는 주문 가능하지 않습니다.
여 오, 정말 안타깝네요. 언제쯤 재고가 다시 들어올 것 같으세요?
남 오늘 주문해 드릴 수 있지만, 다음 주 수요일이 되어야 올 것입니다.
여 그렇게 오래는 기다릴 수 없을 것 같아요. 저는 월요일에 출장을 가는데 새 안경을 꼭 가져가고 싶거든요. Prism 테가 다른 색상으로도 나오나요?
남 네, 지금 투명색 테로는 재고가 있습니다만 가격이 50달러입니다.
여 안경 테에 40달러 이상을 쓰고 싶지는 않아요. 다른 선택 사항은 어떤 게 있나요?
남 실은 다른 모델로는 검정이 지금 주문 가능하고요, 가격도 딱 40달러입니다. 한 번 매장에 오셔서 보시는 게 어떻겠어요, Lopez 씨?

안경 테 재고 리스트		
MODEL	COLOR	PRICE
Prism	투명	50달러
Emory	호피무늬	50달러
Vernon	빨강	80달러
Bristol	검정	40달러

frame (안경의) 테 unavailable 이용 불가능한, 재고가 없는 come in (색상, 사이즈가) ~로 나오다 translucent 투명의 take a look 살펴보다

65 What problem is being discussed?
(A) An item is out of stock.
(B) A manager is unavailable.
(C) A shipment has been delayed.
(D) Some lenses are damaged.

어떤 문제점이 이야기되고 있는가?
(A) 상품의 재고가 떨어졌다.
(B) 매니저가 시간이 없다.
(C) 배송이 지연되었다.
(D) 렌즈 일부가 파손되었다.

문제점을 찾을 때에는 부정어에 집중하자. unfortunately(안타깝게도)라고 언급하면서 물건이 특정 색상으로는 주문 가능하지 않다고 했으므로 정답은 (A)이다.

66 What does the woman mention about her new eyeglasses?
(A) She wants to try them on at the store.
(B) She wants to wear them on her trip.
(C) She has lost them on the subway.
(D) She purchased them at a reduced price.

여자는 그녀의 새 안경에 대해서 무엇을 언급하는가?
(A) 매장에서 안경을 착용해보길 원한다.
(B) 출장 중에 안경을 쓰길 원한다.
(C) 지하철에서 안경을 잃어버렸다.
(D) 할인 가격으로 안경을 구매하였다.

세부 사항 질문으로 반드시 여자의 대사에서 안경에 대한 언급을 찾아야 한다. 월요일에 출장에 간다고 했고 I wanted to take my new glasses with me(안경을 가지고 가고 싶다)라고 말했으므로 정답은 (B)가 된다.

67 Look at the graphic. Which model does the man recommend for the woman?
(A) Prism
(B) Emory
(C) Vernon
(D) Bristol

시각 정보를 보시오. 남자는 어떤 모델을 여자에게 추천하는가?
(A) Prism
(B) Emory
(C) Vernon
(D) Bristol

남자가 Actually we have another model available in black right now and it costs just $40(검정으로 다른 모델을 가지고 있는데 딱 40달러이다)라고 말한 부분이 정답이 된다. 재고 리스트에 검정으로 40달러인 모델명은 Bristol이므로 정답은 (D)이다.

Questions 68-70 refer to the following conversation and map.
영M 미W

M Hey Grace, I see you're reading today's newspaper. I've heard that the City Council has approved the plan to build a new subway station, which will be located very close to our company. Is there anything in the paper about it?
W Um... Let's see. Ah, here it is. It says that a new station will be added to the blue line between Roslyn and Tenth Avenue.
M Between Roslyn and Tenth Avenue? Oh, that's great news. You know I live in Hertford, near the Tenth Avenue Station. When the construction is completed, I can take the subway at Tenth Avenue and then get off at the next station to go to work.
W Wow, your commute will be even faster than now. The article says detailed information about the new station is available on the Transportation Department's website. You should check online.

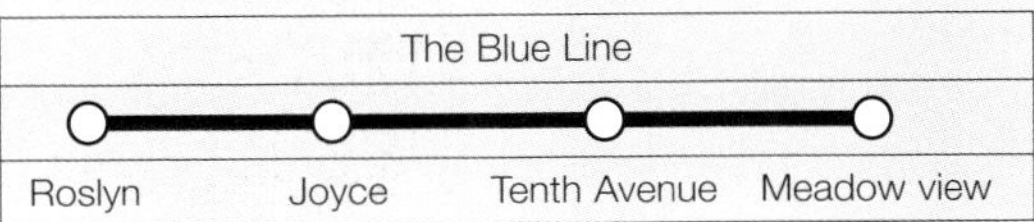

남 안녕 Grace, 오늘 신문을 읽고 있네요. 제가 듣기로는 시 의회에서 새로운 지하철역 짓는 것을 허가했는데 우리 회사와 매우 가까운 곳이 될 거라고 하던데요. 신문에 기사 나온 게 있나요?
여 음… 한 번 봅시다. 아, 여기 있네요. 블루 노선 Roslyn 역과 Tenth Avenue 역 사이에 새로운 역이 추가될 예정이라고 쓰여 있네요.
남 Roslyn과 Tenth Avenue 사이요? 정말 좋은 소식이네요. 아시다시피 제가 Tenth Avenue 역 근처 Hertford에 살잖아요. 공사가 마무리되면, 출근할 때 Tenth Avenue에서 지하철을 타서 그 다음 역에 내리면 되겠네요.
여 와, 출퇴근이 지금보다도 더 빨라지겠네요. 기사에 보면 새로운 역에 대한 자세한 정보가 교통부 웹 사이트에 가면 볼 수 있대요. 온라인으로 확인해 보시는 게 좋겠어요.

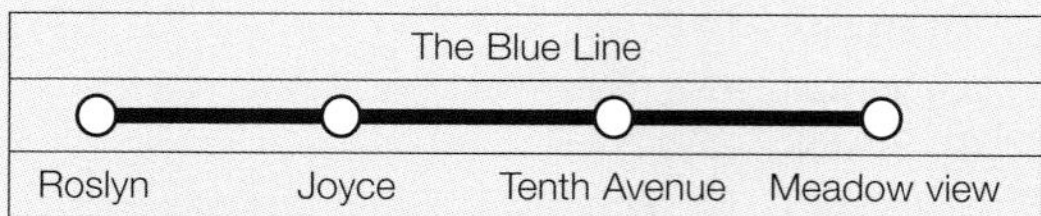

city council 시 의회 approve 승인하다 commute 통근 transportation department 교통부

68 What is the main topic of the conversation?
(A) The location of a new station
(B) The hours of operation
(C) The cost of a monthly pass
(D) The addition of a new subway line

대화의 주제는 무엇인가?
(A) 새 역의 위치
(B) 영업시간
(C) 월간 승차권의 가격
(D) 새 지하철 노선의 추가

주제를 묻는 질문으로 도입부의 I've heard that the city council has approved the plan to build a new subway station(시 의회가 새로운 지하철역을 짓는 계획을 승인했다)에서 정답을 (A)로 선택한다.

69 Look at the graphic. According to the speakers, what is the new station called?
(A) Roslyn
(B) Joyce
(C) Tenth Avenue
(D) Meadow view

시각 정보를 보시오. 화자들에 따르면, 새 역은 뭐라고 불리는가?
(A) Rosslyn
(B) Joyce
(C) Tenth Avenue
(D) Meadow view

시각 정보를 활용한 문제로 새 역의 이름을 찾는 질문이다. 새 역은 Roslyn과 Tenth Avenue 사이에 생긴다고 했으므로 정답은 (B)가 된다.

70 Why is the man pleased?
(A) He has found helpful information online.
(B) He will move to another city.
(C) His commute will be more convenient.
(D) His coworker has been promoted.

남자는 왜 기뻐하는가?
(A) 그는 유용한 정보를 온라인에서 찾았다.
(B) 그는 다른 도시로 이사할 것이다.
(C) 그의 통근이 더 편리해 질 것이다.
(D) 그의 동료가 승진했다.

남자가 Oh, that's great news(좋은 소식이네요)라고 말한 부분에 정답이 등장한다. 새 역이 생기면 출근할 때 지하철을 타고 다음 역에서 내리면 된다고 했으므로 통근이 더 편리해진다고 한 (C)가 정답이 된다.

PART 4

Questions 71-73 refer to the following talk. 영W

Good morning everyone, and welcome to your first day of the training course at Beacon Medical Center. My name is Claire Ross, the head laboratory researcher here. Today, I'll be showing you around the lab facilities and explaining some of our work. We're so proud of the fact that this research center is fully equipped with state-of-the-art equipment and often used by other lab technicians in the area to analyze samples. Okay now, let me go over the safety regulations first. In order to properly use the lab equipment, you must be aware of them at all times.

안녕하세요 여러분. Beacon Medical Center의 교육 과정 첫날에 오신 것을 환영합니다. 저는 Claire Ross이고, 이곳 실험실의 연구 팀장입니다. 오늘, 여러분에게 연구실 시설물을 보여 드리고 저희 업무에 대해 설명드릴 것입니다. 이 연구 센터는 최신 설비가 완비되어 있고, 이 지역의 다른 실험실 기술자들도 표본 분석을 위해 종종 사용한다는 사실이 우리는 자랑스럽습니다. 자 이제, 안전 규정에 대해서 먼저 설명해 드리도록 하죠. 제대로 실험실 장비를 사용하기 위해서, 여러분은 항상 그 규정을 인식하고 있어야 합니다.

head laboratory researcher 실험실 연구 팀장 show around 구경시켜 주다 be equipped with ~을 갖추고 있다 state-of-the-art 최신의, 최신식의 lab technician 실험실 기사[기술자] analyze 분석하다 go over 검토하다 safety regulations 안전 규정 be aware of 인지하다, 알다

71 Who most likely are the listeners of the talk?
(A) Visiting professors
(B) Laboratory trainees
(C) Medical insurance employees
(D) Safety inspectors

담화의 청자들은 누구일 것 같은가?
(A) 객원 교수
(B) 실험실 연수생
(C) 의료 보험 직원
(D) 안전 검사관

청자를 유추하는 질문으로 단서는 보통 도입부에 나온다. welcome to your first day of the training course at Beacon Medical Center에서 you에 해당하는 청자들은 교육을 받기 위해 온 사람들임을 알 수 있다.

72 What does the speaker say about the research center?
(A) It employs 32 technicians.
(B) It is up-to-date.
(C) It recently purchased a new device.
(D) It pays the researchers well.

화자는 연구소에 관하여 무엇을 말하는가?
(A) 32명의 기술자들을 고용하고 있다.
(B) 최신식이다.
(C) 최근에 새로운 장치를 구매했다.
(D) 연구원에게 대우를 잘해 준다.

세부 사항 질문으로 research center에 관한 언급 중에서 일치하는 정보를 정답으로 선택한다. this research center is fully equipped with state-of-the-art equipment에서 최신 설비를 갖추고 있다고 했으므로 정답은 (B)가 된다. equipment라는 단어 때문에 (C)를 선택한다면 함정이다.

73 What most likely will happen next?
(A) A group of people will go on a tour.
(B) Doctors will use the equipment.
(C) Technicians will begin a new project.
(D) Trainees will learn safety procedures.

다음에 무슨 일이 일어날 것 같은가?
(A) 사람들이 견학을 갈 것이다.
(B) 박사들이 장비를 사용할 것이다.
(C) 기술자들이 새로운 프로젝트를 시작할 것이다.
(D) 연수생들이 안전 절차를 배울 것이다.

담화 후에 일어날 일을 묻는 질문으로 Okay now, let me go over the safety regulations first가 정답의 단서이다. 먼저 안전 규정을 설명하겠다고 했으므로 정답은 (D)가 된다. 보통 향후 행동에 대한 힌트어로 now, first가 자주 쓰인다는 점을 꼭 기억해 두자.

Questions 74-76 refer to the following announcement. 미M

Attention shoppers. For today only, we're having a 30 percent sale on selected home furnishing accessories. The sale items include decorative mirrors, lighting fixtures and picture frames, which you can find in aisle 10. Please note that only the products in aisle 10 are part of this special promotion. In addition, if you are a member of our store, you can use your store credit to pay for your purchases. If you are not a current member yet, please visit the customer service desk to register now!

집중해 주세요 쇼핑객 여러분. 오늘 하루 동안만, 선정된 실내 장식용 소품에 대해 30퍼센트 세일을 실시합니다. 세일 상품에는 장식용 거울, 조명 및 액자가 포함되며 10번 통로에서 보실 수 있습니다. 10번 통로에 있는 상품들만이 이번 특별 행사의 대상이 된다는 점을 반드시 기억해 주세요. 그뿐만 아니라, 여러분이 저희 상점의 회원이라면, 구입 품목의 지불을 할 때 상점 포인트를 이용할 수 있습니다. 현재 회원이 아니라면, 지금 바로 고객 서비스 데스크로 방문하셔서 신청해 주세요!

selected 선택된, 선정된 home furnishing 실내 장식 decorative 장식이 된, 장식용의 lighting fixture 조명 기구 aisle 통로 note 주목[주의]하다 special promotion 특별 행사 store credit 상점 포인트 purchase 구입 품목

74 What merchandise is being promoted?
(A) Office furniture
(B) Sporting goods
(C) Home decorative accessories
(D) Construction supplies

어떤 상품이 홍보되고 있는가?
(A) 사무용 가구
(B) 스포츠 용품
(C) 실내 장식용 소품
(D) 건축 자재

행사의 대상이 되는 상품에 집중한다. 도입부에 30퍼센트 할인 혜택을 언급하며 on selected home furnishing accessories라고 했으므로 정답은 (C)가 된다.

75 According to the speaker, how can shoppers find sale items?
(A) By going to a designated area
(B) By receiving a brochure
(C) By calling customer service
(D) By looking for special signs

화자에 따르면, 쇼핑객들은 어떻게 세일 품목을 찾을 수 있는가?
(A) 지정된 구역에 가서
(B) 안내 책자를 받아서
(C) 고객 서비스부에 전화해서
(D) 특별한 표시를 찾아서

세부 사항 질문으로 세일 품목에 대한 정보를 집중해서 듣는다. 세일 품목이 10번 통로에 있음을 언급한 후, 10번 통로의 품목만 특별 행사에 포함된다고 했으므로 정답은 (A)가 된다. aisle 10(10번 통로)이 designated area로 바꿔 표현된 것을 기억해 두자.

76 Why should listeners visit the customer service desk?
(A) To return an item
(B) To report a defective product
(C) To sign up for a membership
(D) To pick up a discount coupon

청자들은 왜 고객 서비스 데스크를 방문할 것인가?
(A) 물건을 환불하려고
(B) 결함 있는 상품을 보고하려고
(C) 멤버십을 신청하려고
(D) 할인 쿠폰을 가져가려고

세부 사항 질문으로 키워드는 customer service desk이다. 현재 회원이 아닌 경우에는 신청을 위해 customer service desk를 방문해 달라고 했으므로 정답은 (C)이다.

Questions 77-79 refer to the following advertisement. (미W)

Do you want to give your garden a fresh new look cheaply and easily? Daisy's Landscaping Service can help you. We are a professional landscaping company offering unique garden designs and reliable maintenance services. This month only, if you sign up for one year of our routine garden maintenance, you can get a 20 percent discount on any of our services including design and installation. Act fast! Don't miss out on this great opportunity! Call 777-0182 now for more information.

저렴하고 쉽게 당신의 정원에 신선하고 새로운 모습을 선사하고 싶으신가요? Daisy's Landscaping Service가 도와 드리겠습니다. 저희는 전문적인 조경 회사로 특별한 정원 디자인과 신뢰할 수 있는 정원 관리 서비스를 제공합니다. 이번 달에만 1년짜리 정원 관리를 신청하시는 경우, 정원 디자인과 설치를 포함하는 저희의 모든 서비스에 대해서 20퍼센트 할인 혜택을 받으실 수 있습니다. 서두르세요! 이 엄청난 기회를 놓치지 마십시오! 더 많은 정보를 얻으시려면 777-0182로 지금 전화 주세요.

look 모습 cheaply 저렴하게 landscaping 조경 unique 독특한, 특별한 reliable 신뢰할 수 있는 sign up for 신청하다 garden maintenance 정원 관리 routine 일상적인, 반복적인 miss out on 놓치다

77 What type of company is being advertised?
(A) A home repair company
(B) A landscaping business
(C) A local supermarket
(D) A flower store

어떤 종류의 회사가 광고되고 있는가?
(A) 주택 수리 회사
(B) 조경 회사
(C) 지역 슈퍼마켓
(D) 꽃 가게

광고 유형에서 광고되는 업체에 대한 언급은 항상 도입부부터 등장한다. 정원을 새롭게 바꾸고 싶은지를 물으면서 호기심을 유발한 후 바로 Daisy's Landscaping Service can help you라고 언급했으므로 조경 회사가 광고되고 있음을 알 수 있다.

78 What should customers do to receive a discount?
(A) Sign a one-year contract
(B) Recommend a new client
(C) Get a membership
(D) Change a garden design

할인을 받기 위하여 고객은 무엇을 해야 하는가?
(A) 1년짜리 계약서에 서명하기
(B) 새로운 고객 추천하기
(C) 회원에 가입하기
(D) 정원 디자인 바꾸기

세부 사항 질문으로 키워드는 discount이다. 이번 달에만 one year of our routine garden maintenance에 가입한다면 할인을 받을 수 있다고 했으므로 정답은 (A)이고 a one-year contract로 바꿔 표현되었다.

79 Why does the speaker say, "Act fast"?
(A) To invite potential customers to the store
(B) To ask listeners to attend a special event
(C) To encourage listeners to purchase a service
(D) To offer additional discount to regular customers

왜 화자는 "서두르세요"라고 말하는가?
(A) 잠재 고객들을 상점으로 초대하려고
(B) 청자들에게 특별 행사에 참석하라고 요청하려고
(C) 청자들에게 서비스 구매를 권하려고
(D) 단골 고객들에게 추가 할인을 제공하려고

신토익 의도 파악 질문으로 화자가 "서두르세요"라고 말한 앞뒤 문맥에서 정답의 단서를 찾자. 1년짜리 정원 관리 서비스를 구매하면 할인을 받을 수 있다고 한 후 "서두르세요"라고 말한 것이므로 정답은 (C)가 된다.

Questions 80-82 refer to the following talk. (영W)

Thanks for coming to work early this morning. I have an important announcement about the new dress code for our airport VIP lounge. All staff members must wear the uniform and black dress shoes. Open-toe shoes or sandals are not permissible here in the lounge and you must remove any jewelry you may be wearing before your shift. If you are not sure about which items are allowed, you can consult the lounge manager Mr. Paul Pearson.

오늘 아침 일찍 출근해 주셔서 감사합니다. 우리 공항 VIP 라운지의 새로운 복장 규정에 대해 중요한 공지 사항이 있습니다. 전 직원들은 반드시 유니폼을 착용하고 검정색 정장 구두를 신어야 합니다. 앞 코가 트인 신발과 샌들은 이곳 라운지에서는 허용되지 않고 여러분은 반드시 교대 근무 전에 착용하고 있는 모든 장신구를 빼야 합니다. 어떤 품목이 허용되는지에 관하여 확실하지 않다면, 라운지 매니저인 Paul Pearson 씨에게 문의하면 됩니다.

dress code 복장 규정 dress shoes 정장용 구두 open-toe shoes 앞 코가 트인 신발 permissible 허용되는 remove 제거하다, 빼다

80 Who most likely are the listeners?
(A) Airport lounge staff
(B) Restaurant employees
(C) Office workers
(D) Flight attendants

청자들은 누구일 것 같은가?
(A) 공항 라운지 직원
(B) 레스토랑 직원
(C) 사무실 직원
(D) 항공 승무원

청자를 유추하는 문제로 도입부에서 유추를 통해 풀어낸다. 새로운 복장 규정에 대한 공지가 있다고 언급하며 for our airport VIP lounge '우리 공항 VIP 라운지를 위한'이라고 했으므로 이곳은 공항 라운지이고 청자들은 직원들임을 유추할 수 있다.

81 What is the talk mainly about?
(A) A customer satisfaction rating
(B) A promotional event
(C) Acceptable methods of payment
(D) A dress code at a workplace

담화는 무엇에 관한 것인가?
(A) 소비자 만족도 등급
(B) 판매 촉진 행사
(C) 수락 가능한 지불 수단
(D) **직장에서의 복장 규정**

주제를 묻는 질문으로, 특히 공지의 주제는 도입부에 등장하는 경우가 대부분이다. 공지가 about the new dress code(복장 규정에 관한)라고 언급한 부분에서 정답을 (D)로 선택한다. 이후의 문맥 역시 허용되는 복장과 허용되지 않는 복장이 나열되고 있다.

82 Why are listeners advised to consult a manager?
(A) To update a work schedule
(B) To address a complaint
(C) To inquire about a policy
(D) To make a suggestion

청자들은 왜 매니저와 상담하도록 권고 받는가?
(A) 업무 스케줄을 갱신하려고
(B) 불평에 대해 다루려고
(C) **정책에 관하여 문의하려고**
(D) 제안을 하려고

세부 사항 질문으로 키워드인 consult, manager에 집중한다. 담화의 마지막 부분에 어떤 품목이 허락되는지 확실치 않다면 lounge manager인 Paul Pearson에게 의논하라고 했으므로 정답은 (C)가 된다.

Questions 83-85 refer to the following telephone message. 영M

Hi, Steve! This is Hayashi. I'm calling because I have a favor to ask of you. Our department is planning a training workshop on the new spreadsheet program for all of our accounting staff on Tuesday. They need to learn how to build spreadsheets and charts using the software. Originally Karen was going to lead the session, but she is hospitalized with pleurisy now. So I'd really like you to take her place. I know it's on short notice, but you know the program better than anybody in our team. Please call me back and let me know if you can do it. In the meantime, I'll e-mail you a copy of the training agenda. So you have an idea as to which of the software's capabilities to focus on during the training. Thank you.

안녕하세요, Steve! Hayashi입니다. 부탁할 게 있어서 전화드립니다. 저희 부서는 화요일에 회계부서 직원들을 위해서 새로운 스프레드시트 프로그램에 관한 교육 워크숍을 진행하려고 합니다. 그들은 소프트웨어를 이용해서 스프레드시트와 도표 만드는 방법을 배워야 하거든요. 원래는, Karen이 세션을 진행하려고 했으나 그녀가 늑막염으로 병원에 입원을 했어요. 그래서 당신이 그녀의 자리를 대신해주길 바랍니다. 갑작스럽다는 것은 알지만, 당신이 우리 팀의 누구보다도 그 프로그램에 대해서 더 잘 알고 있어서요. 그렇게 하실 수 있는지 저에게 답신 전화를 주세요. 그동안 교육 목록을 이메일로 보내겠습니다. 교육 중에 어떤 소프트웨어 기능에 집중해야 할지 알 수 있을 것입니다. 감사합니다.

spreadsheet program (컴퓨터용)표 계산 프로그램 originally 원래 hospitalize 입원하다 pleurisy 늑막염 take one's place ~의 자리를 대신하다 short notice 촉박한 통보 in the meantime 그동안에 as to ~에 관해서 capability 기능

83 What is the topic of the training session?
(A) Online references
(B) Web design
(C) Computer software
(D) Home building

교육의 주제는 무엇인가?
(A) 온라인 참고 자료
(B) 웹 디자인
(C) **컴퓨터 소프트웨어**
(D) 주택 건설

세부 사항 질문으로 training session이 언급될 때 무엇에 관한 것인지 순발력 있게 캐치한다. a training workshop on the new spreadsheet program이 들리는 부분에서 바로 정답을 (C)로 선택할 수 있다. topic을 묻는 질문의 정답 앞에는 항상 전치사 on(~에 관한)이 나온다는 것을 기억해 두고 힌트로 활용하자.

84 What does the speaker mean when he says, "So I'd really like you to take her place"?
(A) There was a computer malfunction.
(B) Some equipment needs to be installed.
(C) He wants the listener to lead a workshop.
(D) The listener needs to meet a deadline.

화자가 "그래서 당신이 그녀의 자리를 대신해주길 바랍니다"라고 말한 의미는 무엇인가?
(A) 컴퓨터 오작동이 있다.
(B) 장비가 설치되어야 한다.
(C) **청자가 워크숍을 진행하기를 원한다.**
(D) 청자는 마감을 맞춰야 한다.

해당 표현 중 I'd like you to는 상대방에게 요청할 때 쓰이는데, 요청하는 내용이 take her place(그녀의 자리를 대신하다)이므로 여자가 하기로 했던 일을 대신 해달라는 의미가 된다. 앞서 원래 Karen이 워크숍을 하려고 했으나 아파서 병원에 입원했다는 언급을 했으므로 청자에게 대신 해 달라는 것은 워크숍 진행이 된다. 정답은 (C)이다.

85 What will the caller probably do next?
(A) Send an agenda
(B) Visit a hospital
(C) Plan an event
(D) Call tech support

전화를 건 사람은 다음에 무엇을 할 것 같은가?
(A) **목록 보내기**
(B) 병원 방문하기
(C) 행사 기획하기
(D) 기술 지원팀에 전화하기

I'll e-mail you a copy of the training agenda 부분에서 화자인 'I'가 하겠다는 내용이 '교육 목록을 이메일로 보내겠다'고 언급되므로 정답은 (A)가 된다.

Questions 86-88 refer to the following telephone message. (미W)

Hello, this is Cathy Ring from the Hester Theater. I'm calling about the auditorium you wanted to book for your dancing competition on Wednesday, March 11th. I'm very sorry to inform you that the theater has already been reserved for that day. However, it will be available the next day. I was wondering if you would consider putting off your event just for a day. If that's possible, we'd be happy to reduce the rental fee by 30%. Please get back to me as soon as possible, so we can discuss it in detail.

여보세요, Hester 극장의 Cathy Ring입니다. 수요일 댄스 대회를 위해 당신이 예약하고자 했던 공연장과 관련해서 전화드립니다. 그날은 이미 극장이 예약되었다는 것을 알려 드리게 되어 정말 유감입니다만, 다음 날에는 사용이 가능합니다. 그래서 당신이 하루만 행사를 연기하는 것을 고려해 주실 수 있는지 알고 싶습니다. 그게 가능하시다면, 저희가 기꺼이 임대료의 30퍼센트를 할인해 드리도록 하겠습니다. 좀 더 자세하게 이야기할 수 있도록 저에게 가능한 한 빨리 전화를 주시길 바랍니다.

auditorium 공연장 book 예약하다 dancing competition 댄스 경연 대회 put off 미루다 reduce 줄이다, 감소시키다 rental fee 임대료 in detail 상세히, 자세히

86 Where does the speaker work?
(A) At a hotel
(B) At a dance academy
(C) At a theater
(D) At a television station

화자는 어디에서 일하는가?
(A) 호텔
(B) 댄스 아카데미
(C) 극장
(D) 텔레비전 방송국

화자의 직장을 유추하는 질문으로 도입부에 화자가 자기소개를 하는 부분에서 단서를 잡는다. 이름과 함께 본인의 소속을 from the Hester Theater라고 밝혔으므로 이곳은 극장임을 알 수 있고 정답은 (C)이다.

87 What problem is mentioned by the speaker?
(A) They are understaffed.
(B) An auditorium is unavailable.
(C) Their rental fees have risen.
(D) Renovations are being carried out.

화자에 의해 어떤 문제가 언급되는가?
(A) 그들은 직원이 부족하다.
(B) 공연장을 이용할 수 없다.
(C) 그들의 임대료가 올랐다.
(D) 개조 공사가 시행되고 있다.

문제점을 찾는 질문으로 부정적인 표현들과 함께 정답이 등장하곤 한다. I'm very sorry to inform you that the theater has already been reserved for that day(극장이 그날은 이미 예약되었다)라고 했으니 정답은 (B)가 된다. theater는 auditorium으로 바꿔 표현되었다. I'm very sorry와 같은 부정적인 표현을 들으면 문제점이 언급될 것을 예상하자.

88 What does the speaker offer?
(A) A different location
(B) A dancing class
(C) A discounted rate
(D) A free stage effect

화자는 무엇을 제공하는가?
(A) 다른 장소
(B) 댄스 강습
(C) 가격 할인
(D) 무료 무대 효과

화자가 제공하는 것을 찾는 질문으로 we'd be happy to reduce the rental fee by 30%(기꺼이 30퍼센트를 깎아 주겠다)라고 했으므로 정답은 (C)가 된다.

Questions 89-91 refer to the following introduction. (영W)

Good evening ladies and gentlemen, welcome to our annual Biomass Association awards banquet. This year, we honor corporations and individuals who made contributions by donating and recycling used electronics. As you know, electronic products are made from valuable resources and materials. Donating or recycling them, therefore, conserves our natural resources and avoids air and water pollution. You'll find detailed information about the nominees on your table. I hope you enjoy the rest of your evening. This event is sponsored by Green Cross International.

안녕하세요 신사 숙녀 여러분, 연례 Biomass Association 시상식 만찬에 오신 것을 환영합니다. 올해는, 중고 전자제품을 재활용하거나 기부하는 방법으로 공헌을 해 주신 기업과 개인들에게 상을 수여합니다. 아시는 바와 같이, 전자제품은 귀중한 자원과 자재로 만들어집니다. 그러므로 그것들을 기부하고 재활용하는 것은 우리의 천연 자원을 보존하고 대기와 수질 오염을 막아줍니다. 여러분의 테이블 위에 후보자들에 관한 자세한 정보를 보실 수 있습니다. 남은 저녁 동안 즐거운 시간 보내시길 바랍니다. 이 행사는 Green Cross International 사가 후원합니다.

awards banquet 시상식 만찬 honor 상을 수여하다 make a contribution 공헌을 하다 be made from ~로 만들어지다 conserve (자원 등을) 보존하다, 아끼다 natural resources 천연 자원 avoid 피하다 pollution 오염 nominee 후보자 be sponsored 후원 받다

89 What will take place at the banquet?
(A) A demonstration will be given.
(B) Research results will be presented.
(C) Awards will be presented.
(D) A new president will be introduced.

연회에서는 무슨 일이 일어날 것인가?
(A) 시연회가 있을 것이다.
(B) 연구 결과가 발표될 것이다.
(C) 상이 수여될 것이다.
(D) 새로운 회장이 소개될 것이다.

행사의 목적과 관련된 질문으로 도입부에 awards banquet(시상식 만찬)에 오신 것을 환영한다고 했으므로 정답은 (C)가 된다. 또한 지문의 동사 honor는 '상을 수여하다'는 의미로도 사용된다는 것을 암기해 두자.

90 What information can be found on the table?
(A) A list of participants
(B) Changes to some rules
(C) Information on nominations
(D) Tips to conserve natural resources

테이블에서 어떤 정보를 찾을 수 있는가?
(A) 참석자 명단
(B) 규정에 대한 변경사항
(C) 후보자에 대한 정보
(D) 천연 자원을 아끼기 위한 방법

세부 사항 질문으로 키워드인 on the table에 집중한다. You'll find detailed information about the nominees on your table에서 후보자에 대한 세부 정보가 테이블에 놓여 있음을 알 수 있다. 정답은 (C)이다.

91 What is mentioned about Green Cross International?
(A) They are receiving an award.
(B) They are sponsoring the event.
(C) They donate used items every year.
(D) They are manufacturing electronic devices.

Green Cross International에 대해 무엇이 언급되었는가?
(A) 그들은 상을 받는다.
(B) 그들은 행사를 후원한다.
(C) 그들은 매해 중고 용품을 기부한다.
(D) 그들은 전자 기기를 생산한다.

세부 사항 질문으로 Green Cross International에 집중한다. 담화의 마지막 부분에 This event is sponsored by Green Cross International에서 행사의 후원을 해준다는 것을 알 수 있다. 정답은 (B)이다.

Questions 92-94 refer to the following recorded message. 미M

Thank you for calling Daniel's Dessert Factory. We produce the best-tasting desserts around and we also take your health very seriously. And we're very proud to be part of the Gluten-Free Certification Program. For those of you who want to take one of our factory tours, here's how you can do it! Family tours take place hourly on Saturdays and Sundays from 11 a.m. to 5 p.m. For the month of May only, we will provide all visitors with a special discount at our dessert shop after your tour. So come and see how our amazing gluten-free desserts are made. Please press 0 to speak to one of our employees about making reservations.

Daniel's Dessert Factory에 전화 주셔서 감사합니다. 저희는 최고로 맛있는 디저트를 생산하는 업체로 여러분의 건강 또한 진지하게 생각합니다. 그래서 저희는 글루텐 무첨가 인증 프로그램의 일원이라는 사실이 자랑스럽습니다. 공장 견학을 하길 원하시는 분들은, 어떻게 하면 되는지 알려 드리겠습니다! 가족 투어는 매주 토요일과 일요일마다 오전 11시부터 오후 5시까지 매 시간 진행합니다. 5월 한 달 동안은, 저희 디저트 가게에서 모든 방문객에게 특별 할인을 제공합니다. 그러니 오셔서 저희의 놀라운 글루텐 무첨가 디저트가 어떻게 만들어지는지 보십시오. 예약에 관련하여 저희 직원 중 한 명과 통화를 하시려면 0번을 눌러 주십시오.

best-tasting 최고로 맛있는 take seriously 진지하게 받아들이다 hourly 매 시간마다 provide A with B A에게 B를 제공하다 amazing 놀라운 gluten-free 글루텐 성분이 없는

92 What is special about the desserts?
(A) They don't contain gluten.
(B) They are popular with children.
(C) They are created by an award-winning pastry chef.
(D) They can be custom-made.

디저트는 무엇이 특별한가?
(A) 글루텐을 포함하지 않는다.
(B) 아이들에게 인기가 있다.
(C) 수상 경력이 있는 제빵사가 만든다.
(D) 주문 제작할 수 있다.

디저트에 대해 여러 번 강조된 내용은 도입부에 소개된 이 업체가 글루텐 무첨가 인증 프로그램 일원이라는 점과 공장 견학을 통해 gluten-free 디저트가 어떻게 만들어지는지 볼 수 있다는 점이다. 그러므로 정답은 (A)가 된다.

93 What does the speaker mean when he says, "here's how you can do it"?
(A) He will explain the history of the company.
(B) He will give listeners easy baking recipes.
(C) He will provide information about the factory tours.
(D) He will announce the winners of a competition.

남자가 "어떻게 하면 되는지 알려 드리겠습니다"라고 말한 의미는 무엇인가?
(A) 남자는 회사의 역사에 대해 설명할 것이다.
(B) 남자는 청자들에게 쉬운 베이킹 레시피를 줄 것이다.
(C) 남자는 공장 견학에 대한 정보를 제공할 것이다.
(D) 남자는 대회의 승자를 발표할 것이다.

해당 표현의 앞뒤 문맥을 통해 남자의 의도를 파악할 수 있다. 공장 견학을 원하는 사람들에게 Here's how you can do it(어떻게 하면 되는지 알려 주겠다)이라고 한 후 공장 견학에 대한 세부 정보를 주고 있으므로 정답은 (C)가 된다.

94 What is offered during the month of May?
(A) A catering service
(B) A complimentary breakfast
(C) A seasonal menu
(D) A store discount

5월 한 달 동안 무엇이 제공되는가?
(A) 출장 부페 서비스
(B) 무료 아침식사
(C) 계절 메뉴
(D) 상점 할인

세부 사항 질문으로 May가 키워드이다. 지문을 듣다가 For the month of May only가 언급되면 정답을 나올 것을 예상해야 하고, 방문객 모두에게 디저트 가게에서 특별 할인을 제공한다고 했으므로 정답은 (D)가 된다.

Questions 95-97 refer to the following excerpt from a meeting and event calendar. (영M)

Okay, before we start the meeting, I'd like to share with you the board's decision. Beginning May 1st, the museum will be required to make some changes due to budget cuts. Firstly, the number of lectures and events we're currently hosting will have to be reduced. We're going to keep the weekly events as they are, because the museum tours and storytelling sessions are the most popular among visitors. However, we will have to discontinue the monthly lecture series, which currently takes place on the second Thursday of each month. And starting next month, the museum will be closed on Mondays because of the budget reductions. So Maria, I'd like you to rearrange the work schedule for next month and update employees on the changes by the end of this week.

Lectures and Events @ Winston History Museum April 2018	
Lecture/Event	**Time**
Museum Highlights Tour	Every Tuesday
Storytelling for Kids	Every Friday
History Lecture Series	Thursday, April 13th
Genealogy Workshops	Saturday, April 22nd

자, 회의를 시작하기 전에, 이사회의 결정사항을 여러분께 알려 드리고 싶습니다. 5월 1일부터, 예산 삭감으로 인해 우리 박물관은 몇 가지 변화를 줄 것을 요구 받게 됩니다. 첫째로, 우리가 현재 개최하고 있는 강의와 행사의 숫자가 줄어야 합니다. 박물관 투어와 스토리텔링 수업은 방문객 사이에서 가장 인기가 많기 때문에 주간 행사들은 그대로 유지할 것입니다. 하지만, 지금 매달 둘째 목요일에 열리고 있는 월간 강의 시리즈는 중단해야 할 것입니다. 그리고 다음 달부터, 박물관은 예산 삭감 때문에 매주 월요일은 문을 닫게 됩니다. 그러니 Maria, 당신이 다음 달 근무 스케줄을 다시 짜서 직원들에게 이번 주 말까지 변경 사항을 알려 주시길 바랍니다.

윈스턴 역사 박물관의 강연과 행사들 2018년 4월	
강연/행사	**시간**
박물관 하이라이트 투어	매주 화요일
어린이 스토리텔링	매주 금요일
역사 강연 시리즈	4월 13일 목요일
족보학 워크숍	4월 22일 토요일

the board 이사회 budget cuts 예산 삭감 host 개최하다 discontinue 중단하다 take place 열리다, 발생하다 budget reductions 예산 삭감 rearrange (일정을) 재조정하다

95 Why is the museum required to make changes?
(A) A budget has decreased.
(B) More events are being held.
(C) A building is being renovated.
(D) Some exhibits have been canceled.

박물관은 왜 변화를 줄 것이 요구되는가?
(A) 예산이 줄었다.
(B) 더 많은 행사가 열린다.
(C) 빌딩이 수리되는 중이다.
(D) 일부 전시가 취소되었다.

질문을 미리 숙지하고 박물관이 변화를 줘야 하는 이유에 집중한다. the museum will be required to make some changes due to budget cuts를 통해 예산 삭감 때문에 변화가 필요한 상황임을 알 수 있다. 이유를 묻는 질문에서 due to는 정답을 알려 주는 힌트어가 된다.

96 Look at the graphic. Which event will not be held in May?
(A) Museum Highlights Tour
(B) Storytelling for Kids
(C) History Lecture Series
(D) Genealogy Workshops

시각 정보를 보시오. 5월에는 어떤 행사가 열리지 않을 것인가?
(A) 박물관 하이라이트 투어
(B) 어린이 스토리텔링
(C) 역사 강연 시리즈
(D) 족보학 워크숍

시각 정보를 참고하여 5월에 열리지 않는 행사를 찾는다. we will have to discontinue the monthly lecture series, which currently takes place on the second Thursday of each month에서 취소되는 행사는 시리즈 강연이며 현재는 목요일에 열리고 있다는 내용을 파악할 수 있다. 그러므로 정답은 (C)가 된다.

97 What is Maria asked to do?
(A) Work overtime
(B) Complete a survey
(C) Train new employees
(D) Revise a work schedule

Maria는 무엇을 할 것을 요청 받는가?
(A) 초과 근무를 할 것
(B) 설문조사를 끝낼 것
(C) 신입 사원을 교육할 것
(D) 근무 일정을 수정할 것

화자가 Maria를 언급하며 rearrange the work schedule(근무 일정을 재조정할 것)을 요청했으므로 정답은 (D)가 된다. 요청 표현으로 사용된 I'd like you to는 반드시 암기해 두자.

Questions 98-100 refer to the following announcement and list. 미M

Today I have an important announcement for all of you in sales. As you already know, we've recently replaced all the office equipment with more efficient models. I'd like you to understand the main features of each machine before you use it. So please take a look at the handout, which explains the features in detail. The new printer, the Linex 300, will be assigned to each sales team after the meeting. It has several useful capabilities, one of which is that it can print in color. And it can now print on both sides of a sheet of paper, which will save a lot of paper. But remember that this option is a little slow. If you want to make double-sided copies quickly, you should just print your original document from the printer, and then use the photocopier, the Linex 5X, to duplicate it. The new photocopiers we purchased are even faster than the old ones, and they have an energy-saving feature. You can find one on each floor. If you have any trouble connecting your computers with the new printers, please contact Michael in tech support.

Linex 300 Printer	Linex 5X Photocopier
· Print in color · Two-sided copies · Assigned to each team	· Slow · Two-sided copies · Energy-saving · Located on each floor

오늘은 세일즈 부서 여러분 모두에게 중요한 공지가 있습니다. 이미 아시다시피, 우리는 최근에 모든 사무기기를 보다 효율적인 모델로 교체했습니다. 여러분들이 각 기계를 사용하기 전에 주요 기능을 숙지하기를 바랍니다. 그러니 그 기능이 자세하게 설명되어 있는 유인물을 봐주세요. 새로운 프린터인 Linex 300는 회의 후에 각 판매팀에게 배정될 것입니다. 몇 가지 유용한 기능들이 있는데 그중 하나는 칼라 인쇄가 된다는 것입니다. 그리고 이제 양면으로 인쇄가 되어서 종이를 많이 아낄 수 있을 것입니다. 그러나 이 기능은 조금 느리다는 점을 기억해 두세요. 양면 복사를 빨리 하고 싶다면, 이 프린터로는 원본만 인쇄를 하는 게 좋고 그 후에 복사를 하려면 Linex 5X 복사기를 사용하세요. 우리가 구매한 이 새 복사기는 예전 것보다 훨씬 더 빠르고 절전 기능을 갖고 있습니다. 각 층에 1대가 있을 겁니다. 여러분의 컴퓨터와 새 프린터를 연결하는데 문제가 있다면, 기술 지원팀의 Michael에게 연락해 주세요.

Linex 300 Printer	Linex 5X Photocopier
· 칼라 복사 · 양면 복사 · 팀에 하나씩 배정	· 느림 · 양면 복사 · 절전 기능 · 각 층마다 위치

replace 교체하다 equipment 기계 efficient 효율적인 feature 기능 in detail 자세하게 assign 배정하다 capability 기능 in color 칼라로 double-sided 양면의 original 원본 duplicate 복사하다 energy-saving feature 절전 기능 have trouble -ing ~하는 데 어려움을 겪다 tech support 기술 지원부

98 Who is the speaker addressing?
(A) Marketing personnel
(B) Store attendants
(C) Factory workers
(D) Sales staff

화자는 누구에게 말하고 있는가?
(A) 마케팅 직원
(B) 상점 점원
(C) 공장 인부
(D) 판매 직원

담화의 도입부에 all of you in sales(판매부 전원)에게 중요한 공지가 있다고 했으므로 정답은 (D)임을 알 수 있다.

99 Look at the graphic. According to the speaker, which information about Linex 5X Photocopier is not correct?
(A) It is slow.
(B) It makes two-sided copies.
(C) It has an energy-saving feature.
(D) It is located on each floor.

시각 정보를 보시오. 화자에 따르면, Linex 5X 복사기에 대한 정보가 바르지 않은 것은 무엇인가?
(A) 느리다.
(B) 양면 복사를 한다
(C) 절전 기능이 있다.
(D) 각 층에 위치해 있다.

시각 정보와 비교하여 담화에 나온 복사기에 대한 내용이 잘못 설명된 부분을 고르자. 화자가 느리다는 말을 했지만 Linex 5X가 아니다. 오히려 예전 것보다 빠르다고 했으므로 바르지 않은 정보는 (A)가 된다.

100 What can Michael help employees to do?
(A) Repair a new printer
(B) Connect pieces of equipment
(C) Order office supplies
(D) Upgrade computer software

Michael이 직원들이 무엇을 하는 것을 도울 수 있는가?
(A) 새 프린터 고치기
(B) 기기들 연결하기
(C) 사무 용품 주문하기
(D) 컴퓨터 소프트웨어 업그레이드 하기

세부 사항 질문이므로 키워드인 Michael이 언급되는 부분을 잘 찾아 듣자. 컴퓨터와 프린터의 연결이 안 될 경우 Michael에게 연락하라고 했으므로 Michael은 기기 연결을 도와 줄 것임을 알 수 있다. 정답은 (B)가 된다.

Actual Test 8

PART 1

본책 p.96

1 (A)	2 (C)	3 (C)	4 (A)	5 (A)	6 (D)

PART 2

본책 p.100

7 (A)	8 (B)	9 (A)	10 (B)	11 (A)	12 (C)
13 (B)	14 (C)	15 (C)	16 (B)	17 (A)	18 (A)
19 (A)	20 (C)	21 (C)	22 (C)	23 (A)	24 (B)
25 (C)	26 (B)	27 (A)	28 (C)	29 (B)	30 (A)
31 (B)					

PART 3

본책 p.101

32 (B)	33 (B)	34 (C)	35 (D)	36 (C)	37 (A)
38 (A)	39 (D)	40 (C)	41 (C)	42 (A)	43 (D)
44 (B)	45 (C)	46 (A)	47 (B)	48 (C)	49 (C)
50 (A)	51 (C)	52 (D)	53 (D)	54 (B)	55 (A)
56 (C)	57 (C)	58 (A)	59 (C)	60 (A)	61 (B)
62 (C)	63 (A)	64 (C)	65 (B)	66 (C)	67 (D)
68 (D)	69 (A)	70 (C)			

PART 4

본책 p.105

71 (A)	72 (D)	73 (A)	74 (C)	75 (A)	76 (C)
77 (A)	78 (D)	79 (B)	80 (A)	81 (A)	82 (B)
83 (A)	84 (B)	85 (D)	86 (B)	87 (C)	88 (C)
89 (D)	90 (A)	91 (B)	92 (C)	93 (B)	94 (D)
95 (A)	96 (D)	97 (B)	98 (A)	99 (C)	100 (C)

PART 1

1 (A) The man is wearing something on his both hands.
영M (B) The man is passing an item to someone else.
(C) The man is carrying something for a friend.
(D) The man is greeting someone with a hug.

(A) 남자가 양손에 뭔가를 끼고 있다.
(B) 남자가 다른 이에게 물건을 건네주고 있다.
(C) 남자가 친구를 위해 뭔가를 들고 가는 중이다.
(D) 남자가 포옹으로 누군가를 맞이하고 있다.

고무장갑처럼 생긴 장갑을 낀 남자가 품에 어떤 도구를 갖고 있다. 박장대소하고 있는데 옆에 있는 사람의 웃는 얼굴도 보이나 둘이 어떤 관계인지는 알 수가 없다.

wear 입다, 끼다, 쓰다 pass 건네주다, 주다 greet 환영하다, 인사하다 hug 포옹

2 (A) A variety of clothing is on display.
미W (B) Some of the clothes need to be folded.
(C) The shelves are filled with items.
(D) Most ties require ironing.

(A) 여러 가지 옷이 진열되어 있다.
(B) 옷 몇 점은 접어야 한다.
(C) 선반들이 물건으로 가득하다.
(D) 대부분의 넥타이는 다림질을 해야 한다.

옷 가게로 보이는 곳에 셔츠가 접힌 채로 선반에 칸칸이 진열되어 있고 넥타이도 옆에 잘 진열되어 있다. 셔츠와 넥타이밖에 없으므로 (A)는 납득하기 어려우며 (D)는 넥타이가 모두 구겨진 상태라야 정답이 된다.

a variety of 다양한 clothing 옷, 의복 on display 진열 중인 fold 접다 shelves 선반, 책꽂이 tie 넥타이 ironing 다림질

3 (A) A man is getting off his motorcycle.
미M (B) A car is being towed away.
(C) Trees line at the side of the road.
(D) A motorcycle runs alongside a car.

(A) 남자가 오토바이에서 내리고 있다.
(B) 차가 견인되고 있다.
(C) 나무들이 도로 옆쪽에 늘어서 있다.
(D) 오토바이 한 대가 차와 나란히 달리고 있다.

오토바이 몇 대가 도로의 오르막을 오르고 있는데 이 도로의 한쪽에는 나무가, 맞은쪽에는 전봇대로 보이는 시설물들이 있다. 또한 오토바이 옆에 달리는 자동차는 보이지 않으므로 정답은 (C)이다.

get off 내리다 motorcycle 오토바이 tow away 끌다, 견인하다 alongside ~옆에, 나란히

4 (A) The boy is about to climb up something.
영W (B) The boy is balancing on a playground slide.
(C) The boy is strolling at a park.
(D) The boy is going down the slide.

(A) 남자 아이가 어딘가에 올라가려고 한다.
(B) 남자 아이가 놀이터 미끄럼틀에서 균형을 잡고 있다.
(C) 남자 아이가 공원에서 산책을 하고 있다.
(D) 남자 아이가 미끄럼틀에서 내려가고 있다.

남자 아이가 놀이터에서 사다리를 올라가고 있다. 따라서 정답은 (A)이다.

be about to 막 ~하려고 하다 climb up ~에 오르다 balance 균형을 잡다 playground 운동장, 놀이터 slide 미끄럼틀 stroll 산책하다 go down 내려가다

5 (A) The conical objects cover the entire tree.
미M (B) Some of the items are lying on mats.
(C) Long strings hang from tree to tree.
(D) Some of the pieces are on the benches.

(A) 원뿔 모양의 물건들이 나무 전체를 덮고 있다.
(B) 물건 일부가 매트에 놓여 있다.
(C) 긴 줄들이 나무에서 나무로 걸려 있다.
(D) 조각들이 벤치에 놓여 있다.

나뭇가지마다 선물로 추측되는 고깔 모양들이 주렁주렁 달려 있고 일부는 나무 아래 잔디 위에 깔린 천에 놓여 있다. 벤치에는 아무것도 없으므로 (A)만이 옳은 설명이다.

conical 원뿔 모양의 object 물건, 물체 entire 전체의 lie 놓다, 눕다 mat 깔개, 매트 string 줄, 현

6 (A) A computer has been set for a meeting.
미W (B) A man is glancing at a screen.
(C) A chair is being assembled.
(D) A desk is surrounded by dividers.

(A) 컴퓨터는 회의를 위해 준비되어 있다.
(B) 남자가 화면을 흘깃 보고 있다.
(C) 의자가 조립되고 있다.
(D) 책상이 칸막이로 둘러싸여 있다.

한 책상에 컴퓨터와 전화기가 놓여 있고 사람은 없다. 이 책상은 칸막이로 둘러싸여 있으므로 (D)는 옳은 설명이다. 컴퓨터가 준비되어 있긴 하지만 용도를 알 수 없으므로 (A)는 섣부른 추측이다.

glance 흘깃 보다 assemble 모이다, 모으다, 조립하다 be surrounded by ~로 둘러싸이다 divider 칸막이

PART 2

7 When does your passport expire?
미W (A) Next January.
미M (B) I finished it a long time ago.
(C) I'll fly from Madrid.

당신의 여권은 언제 만료됩니까?
(A) 내년 1월이요.
(B) 저는 그것을 오래전에 끝냈습니다.
(C) 저는 마드리드에서 비행기를 탈 것입니다.

의문사 when 질문으로 시점으로 답을 해준 (A)가 정답이다. (B) 역시 a long time ago란 시점이 언급되지만 finished it은 문맥상 맞지 않기 때문에 오답이다.

passport 여권 expire 만기가 되다 fly from ~로부터 비행기를 타다

8 What time do you leave for Sri Lanka?
영M (A) Some are left.
영W (B) My flight leaves at 9.
(C) For a medical convention.

몇 시에 스리랑카로 떠납니까?
(A) 일부는 남겨졌습니다.
(B) 제 비행기는 9시입니다.
(C) 의학 컨벤션 때문에요

의문사 what time 질문으로 비행기가 9시라고 답한 (B)가 정답이다. 시간을 언급할 때 반드시 o'clock, a.m., p.m. 등의 표현이 쓰이는 것은 아니다. 단순히 숫자만 언급되어 시간을 나타내는 경우도 많으므로 잘 기억해 두자.

leave for+장소 ~로 떠나다 flight 항공편

9 How can I get to the Alperton Tower?
미M (A) Take the first right.
미W (B) For 10 minutes.
(C) No problem.

어떻게 Alperton Tower로 갈 수 있나요?
(A) 첫 번째 모퉁이에서 오른쪽으로 가세요.
(B) 10분 동안이요.
(C) 문제없습니다.

의문사 how 질문으로 특히 'get to + 장소'가 함께 쓰이는 경우에는 그 장소에 가는 방법을 묻는 것이다. 보통 교통수단을 알려 주거나 길 안내를 하며 (A)는 길을 알려 주고 있으므로 정답이 된다.

get to+장소 ~로 가다

10 Who knocked on the door?
영W (A) It was not locked.
미M (B) Our new next door neighbor.
(C) In the barn.

누가 노크를 했나요?
(A) 그것은 잠기지 않았어요.
(B) 우리의 옆집 새 이웃이요.
(C) 헛간에서요.

의문사 who 질문으로 '옆집 이웃'이라고 사람을 언급한 (B)가 정답이 된다. (A)는 knocked와 발음이 유사한 locked를 이용한 함정이고 (C)는 의문사 where에 대한 답이다.

knock 노크하다 lock 잠그다 neighbor 이웃 barn 헛간, 축사

11 Could I help you with that suitcase?
미W (A) I'd appreciate that.
영M (B) How heavy is it?
(C) They are fragile.

제가 그 여행 가방을 좀 들어 드릴까요?
(A) 감사합니다.
(B) 그건 얼마나 무거운가요?
(C) 그것들은 깨지기 쉽습니다.

상대방에게 호의를 제공하는 제공 의문문으로, 호의에 대해 감사를 표한 (A)가 정답이다. (B)는 연상어 오류로 가방을 들고 있는 사람이 상대방에게 "그것은 얼마나 무거운가요?"라고 묻는 것은 문맥상 맞지 않으므로 오답이다.

suitcase 여행용 가방 appreciate 감사하다 fragile 깨지기 쉬운

12 Why is the art gallery closed to the public?
영M (A) We are sending out the invitations.
미W (B) Close it firmly.
(C) Because of a private exhibition.

화랑을 왜 일반 대중에게 공개하지 않나요?
(A) 우리는 초대장을 발송할 것입니다.
(B) 그것을 단단히 닫으세요.
(C) 개인 전시회 때문에요.

의문사 why 질문으로 화랑이 일반 대중에게는 문을 열지 않는 이유를 묻고 있다. 정답은 개인 전시회를 열기 때문이라고 답한 (C)이다. (A)는 gallery를 들었을 때 연상되는 invitations를 이용한 함정이고 (B)는 close가 사용된 유사 발음 함정이다.

the public 대중 firmly 단단히 private exhibition 개인 전시회

13 Where's the scientific journal you and Jeremy were talking about?
영W (A) He's not a scientist.
영M (B) In the staff lounge.
(C) That's near the library.

당신과 Jeremy가 이야기하던 과학 잡지는 어디에 있습니까?
(A) 그는 과학자가 아닙니다.
(B) 직원 휴게실에요.
(C) 그것은 도서관의 가까이에 있습니다.

의문사 where 질문으로 요지는 scientific journal(과학 잡지)이 어디 있는지를 묻는 것이다. 그러므로 휴게실에 있다고 답한 (B)가 정답이다. (C)는 journal을 들었을 때 연상되는 library를 이용한 함정으로, 책이 도서관 근처에 있다는 것은 매우 어색하므로 정답이 될 수 없다.

journal 잡지, 전문지 staff lounge 직원 휴게실

14 Will you stop by the bakery or the gift shop?
미W (A) I'd rather go.
영W (B) No, there is nothing left.
(C) Both actually.

빵집에 들를 건가요 아니면 선물 가게에 들를 건가요?
(A) 전 가는 게 낫겠어요.
(B) 아니오, 아무것도 남지 않았어요.
(C) 실은 두 곳 다요.

선택 의문문으로 선택 사항은 빵집 혹은 선물 가게로 압축된다. 정답은 두 곳 다 간다고 답한 (C)이다. either, neither, both, whichever 등은 선택 의문문에 대해 정답 표현으로 자주 쓰이므로 암기해 두자.

15 I'm having trouble with this fax machine.
미W (A) Where did you send it?
미M (B) Two copies.
(C) Why don't you call tech support?

이 팩스기가 말썽이네요.
(A) 그것을 어디로 보내셨나요?
(B) 2부요.
(C) 기술 지원부에 전화해보시면 어때요?

문제점에 대해 언급하는 평서문으로 팩스기가 잘 안 된다고 했으므로 기술 지원부에 연락해 보는 게 어떻겠냐고 해결책을 제시한 (C)가 정답이다. (A)와 (B)는 fax machine을 들었을 때 연상되는 단어를 이용한 오답이다.

have trouble with ~와 관련해 어려움을 겪다 tech support 기술 지원부

16 Who were the last people to use the meeting room?
영M (A) Yes, it is the last one.
영W (B) It was the sales team, I think.
(C) How to use the video equipment.

회의실을 마지막으로 이용했던 사람들은 누구였나요?
(A) 네, 이게 마지막 것입니다.
(B) 영업부였던 것 같아요.
(C) 비디오 장치를 사용하는 방법이요.

의문사 who 질문으로 사람 이름, 회사명, 부서명 등이 언급되어 정답이 되는 경우가 많다. 회의실을 이용했던 사람들을 물었으므로 영업부라고 답해 준 (B)가 정답이다.

how to ~하는 방법 equipment 기기, 장비

17 The grapes are growing beautifully this year.
미M (A) Yes, thanks to the nice weather.
미W (B) Because it looks expensive.
(C) The market is open today.

올해는 포도가 아주 잘 자라네요.
(A) 네, 좋은 날씨 덕분에요.
(B) 그것이 비싸 보이기 때문이죠.
(C) 시장은 오늘 열립니다.

평서문으로 요지는 올해 포도 농사가 잘되고 있다는 것이므로 이에 덧붙여 날씨가 좋기 때문이라고 답하는 (A)가 가장 어울리는 답변이 된다. (B)는 의문사 why에 대한 답이고, (C)는 grapes를 들었을 때 연상되는 market을 이용한 오답이다.

beautifully 아름답게, 아주 잘 thanks to ~덕분에

18 Would you rather have a pizza delivered or go out to
영W eat?
미M (A) I'd rather go to a Chinese restaurant.
(B) For the first time.
(C) A table for two, please.

피자를 배달시키고 싶으세요 아니면 외식을 하고 싶으세요?
(A) 중국 음식점에 가고 싶어요.
(B) 처음으로요.
(C) 2인용 테이블 주세요.

선택 의문문으로 선택 사항을 압축하여 '배달 혹은 외식?'으로 들을 수 있어야 한다. 중국 음식점에 가고 싶다고 외식을 바꿔 표현했으므로 정답은 (A)이다. (B)와 (C)는 문맥에서 벗어난 답으로, (C)의 경우 레스토랑에서 직원에게 테이블을 요청할 때 하는 말이다.

go out 외출하다 rather 오히려, 차라리

19 Which employees are being transferred to the
미W Singapore branch?
영M (A) Tim and Sara from the marketing team.
(B) They're still in transit.
(C) To make enough room.

어떤 직원이 싱가포르 지점으로 전근가나요?
(A) 마케팅 부서의 Tim과 Sara입니다.
(B) 그것들은 여전히 수송 중입니다.
(C) 충분한 공간을 만들려고요.

의문사 which 질문으로 바로 뒤에 등장하는 명사까지 함께 해석하는 것이 포인트이다. Which employees인지 물었으므로 결국 who 질문이 된다. 누가 전근되는지 물었으므로 정답은 사람의 이름으로 답한 (A)가 된다.

be transferred 전근되다 branch 지점 in transit 수송 중인, 운송 중인 make room 공간을 만들다

20 When will Michael assemble the table and chairs?
영M (A) The white ones look good.
미W (B) Put it against the wall.
(C) I thought he did it already.

Michael은 언제 테이블과 의자들을 조립할 건가요?
(A) 흰색이 좋아 보이네요.
(B) 그것을 벽에 기대어 두세요.
(C) 전 그가 이미 했다고 생각했어요.

의문사 when 질문으로 Michael이 언제 가구를 조립할 물었고 (C)는 간접적인 답변 형태지만 문맥상 어울리는 정답이다. 그에 반해 (A)는 특정 색상이 좋다고 답하고 있어 문맥상 벗어났고 (B)는 물건을 놓을 위치를 말해주므로 where에 대한 답이 된다.

assemble 조립하다 put 두다 against 기대어

21 I'm not familiar with the city.
영W (A) The tour begins at six.
영M (B) I wasn't there. Sorry.
(C) I'm sure you'll like it here.

전 이 도시에 익숙하지 않아요.
(A) 투어는 6시에 시작됩니다.
(B) 전 거기에 없었어요. 죄송합니다.
(C) 당신은 이곳을 분명히 좋아하게 될 거예요.

평서문으로 대화 상황은 처음 온 도시에 익숙하지 않다고 말하는 것이므로 앞으로 이곳을 좋아하게 될 것이라고 답한 (C)가 정답이다. (A)는 city를 들었을 때 연상되는 tour를 사용한 오답이고, (B)는 시제와 내용이 맞지 않는 어색한 답이다.

be familiar with ~에 익숙하다

22 What's the phone number for David's Catering?
미W (A) 15 Jackson Street.
영W (B) About our upcoming reception.
(C) I'll look it up in the directory.

David's Catering의 전화번호가 뭐죠?
(A) Jackson 가 15번지요.
(B) 곧 있을 연회에 관해서요.
(C) 전화번호부에서 찾아보겠습니다.

의문사 what 질문으로 키워드는 phone number이다. 전화번호가 무엇인지 물었으므로 직접 답변 형태는 전화번호를 알려 주는 것이 되겠지만, 여기서는 간접 답변으로 전화번호부에서 찾아보겠다고 했으므로 (C)가 정답이다. (C)와 같이 '모르지만 확인해 보겠다'는 의미의 답변은 정답으로 연결되는 경우가 매우 높은 답변이므로 암기해 두자.

upcoming 다가오는 reception 연회 look up 찾아보다 directory 전화번호부

23 You will be staying in the presidential suite, won't
미W you?
미M (A) No, I prefer a smaller room.
(B) The hotel looks new.
(C) No thanks, I'm not hungry.

특실에 투숙할 거죠 그렇지 않나요?
(A) 아니오, 전 더 작은 방을 선호합니다.
(B) 호텔이 새것처럼 보이네요.
(C) 감사합니다만 됐습니다. 전 배고프지 않아요.

Yes/No 여부를 묻는 질문으로 호텔의 특실에 머물 것인지 물었으므로 아니라고 언급한 후 특실보다 작은 방이 더 좋다고 답한 (A)가 정답이다. (B)는 연상어인 hotel을 이용한 오답이고, (C)는 음식 등을 먹겠냐고 제안한 경우 거절할 때 쓰는 표현이므로 답이 될 수 없다.

stay (호텔 등에) 머물다, 투숙하다 presidential suite 귀빈실, 특실 prefer 선호하다

24 We should explain to the tour guide why we're late.
영M (A) Because she can't cook.
영W (B) Okay, I'll call him right away.
(C) Until next Saturday.

왜 우리가 늦는지 투어 가이드에게 설명하는 게 좋겠어요.
(A) 그녀는 요리를 못하거든요.
(B) 좋습니다, 제가 당장 그에게 전화할게요.
(C) 다음 주 토요일까지요.

평서문으로 we should를 듣고 제안의 의도로 해석한다. 가이드에게 늦는 이유를 설명하자고 했으므로 제안을 받아들여 당장 가이드에게 전화하겠다고 답한 (B)가 정답이다.

explain to ~에게 설명하다 tour guide 투어 가이드 right away 당장, 즉시

25 When does Kyle take over as vice president?
미M (A) Just pull over near the curb.
미W (B) Congratulations!
(C) Did he get the position?

Kyle이 언제 부사장으로서 업무를 인계하나요?
(A) 연석 주변에 차를 세우세요.
(B) 축하합니다!
(C) 그가 그 직책을 맡았나요?

의문사 when 질문으로 Kyle이 언제 부사장으로서의 업무를 시작하는지 물었으므로, 보통 시점을 언급하는 직접적 답변이 일반적이다. 그러나 여기서는 그가 그 직위로 승진했는지를 되묻는 것이 정답이다. (A)의 curb는 도로와 인도 사이의 턱을 의미하여 문맥상 벗어난 답변이고, (B)는 승진과 관련된 어휘 congratulations를 이용한 오답이다.

take over (업무 등을) 인계하다 vice president 부사장 pull over 차를 세우다 curb 차도와 인도 사이의 턱, 연석 get a position 직위를 받다

26 Have you read Herald's new novel?
영W (A) I prefer a newer style.
미M (B) No, is it interesting?
(C) About the bank statement.

Herald의 신작 소설을 읽었나요?
(A) 전 새로운 스타일을 선호합니다.
(B) 아니오, 그 책 재미있나요?
(C) 입출금 내역서에 관해서요.

Yes/No 질문으로 신작 소설을 읽었는지 물었으므로 안 읽었다고 답한 후 그 책이 재미있는지를 되물은 (B)가 정답이 된다. (A)는 new와 발음이 유사한 newer를 이용한 오답이고, (C)는 세금 계산서에 대한 내용으로 문맥에서 벗어났다.

bank statement 입출금 내역서

27 Why don't we conduct the final interviews tomorrow
미W morning?
영M (A) Okay, let's make them around 10.
(B) The candidate was late.
(C) In the meeting room.

내일 아침에 최종 면접을 하면 어떨까요?
(A) 좋습니다, 10시쯤으로 잡으시죠.
(B) 그 후보자는 늦었습니다.
(C) 회의실에서요.

제안 의문문으로 최종 면접을 내일 하는 게 어떤지 물었으므로, 제안을 승낙한 후 10시쯤에 하자고 말한 (A)가 가장 자연스러운 답변이다. (B)는 interview에 대한 연상어 candidate를 이용한 오답으로 시제 오류 함정이기도 하다. (C)는 의문사 where에 대한 답이다.

conduct an interview 인터뷰를 하다 candidate 후보자

28 Which medical supplies company does Peter
영M represent?
미W (A) To get a medical checkup.
(B) Several sales representatives.
(C) He works for MDDI.

Peter는 어떤 의료 용품 회사를 대표하나요?
(A) 건강 검진을 받으려고요.
(B) 몇 명의 영업 사원들이요.
(C) 그는 MDDI에서 일합니다.

의문사 which 질문으로 which medical supplies company까지가 의문사에 연결되어 '어떤 의료 용품 회사'인지가 질문의 핵심이다. (C)는 회사의 이름을 언급하여 어떤 회사인지 답해 줬으므로 정답이 된다. (A)는 의문사 why 질문에 대한 답이고, (B)는 represent와 발음이 유사한 representative를 이용한 함정이다.

medical supplies company 의료 용품 회사 represent 대표하다 medical check-up 건강 진단 sales representative 영업 사원

29 Would you like to get a new cell phone or have your
영W old phone upgraded?
영M (A) It was a conference call.
(B) It depends on the cost.
(C) That seems to be a good deal.

새 휴대전화를 살 건가요 아니면 기존의 전화를 업그레이드 할 건가요?
(A) 그것은 전화 회의였습니다.
(B) 비용에 따라 달라요.
(C) 좋은 거래인 것 같네요.

선택 의문문으로 선택 사항은 '살 것인지 혹은 업그레이드 할 것인지'로 압축된다. (B)에서 가격에 따라 다르다고 답한 것이 정답이고, (A)는 phone을 들었을 때 연상되는 call을 이용한 오답이다. (C)는 물건의 가격이 싼 경우에 사용하는 표현으로 이 경우에는 문맥상 맞지 않다.

conference call 전화 회의 depend on ~에 달려 있다 deal 거래

30 Can I fax some documents from this hotel?
미W (A) Yes, if you're staying in our hotel.
영W (B) Did you check your e-mail?
(C) I'm sorry to hear that.

이 호텔에서 팩스로 서류를 좀 보낼 수 있을까요?
(A) 네, 당신이 우리 호텔에서 투숙하고 있다면요.
(B) 당신은 이메일을 확인하셨나요?
(C) 그걸 듣게 되어 유감입니다.

요청 의문문으로 팩스를 사용해도 되는지 허가를 요청하는 것이 질문의 핵심이다. (A)는 해당 호텔의 투숙객이라면 가능하다고 단서를 붙여 허가를 했으므로 정답이 맞다. (B)는 fax, documents를 들었을 때 연상되는 e-mail을 이용한 오답이고, (C)는 보통 고객의 불만 등에 대해 응대하는 표현으로 이 경우에는 어색한 답변이다.

stay in a hotel 호텔에 묵다

31 You ordered egg-fried noodles and a soda, right?
미W (A) I'd like a table for 4.
미M (B) That's Jimmy's order.
(C) Today's special looks good.

에그 프라이 누들과 탄산음료를 주문하셨죠, 맞죠?
(A) 4인석 테이블을 원합니다.
(B) 그것은 Jimmy의 주문입니다.
(C) 오늘의 특별 메뉴가 맛있어 보이네요.

Yes/No 질문으로 상대방이 주문한 항목이 맞는지 확인하는 것이 포인트이다. (B)는 다른 사람의 주문이라고 답하므로 질문에 대해 No라고 답하는 것으로 확인되어 정답이다.

today's special 오늘의 특별 메뉴

PART 3

Questions 32-34 refer to the following conversation. 미M 미W

M Excuse me, how long have you been waiting? The lines seem to be endless here.
W I've been waiting for 30 minutes now. My lunch break is almost over, but I really want to buy these boots. I can get them for half price, you know.
M Yeah, you can really save a lot of money with these low prices. I was going to buy some shirts too, but I have a meeting in 10 minutes. Maybe I'll come back after work.
W Well, that's a good idea. The store should be less crowded by then. I wish they had more cashiers working though.

남 실례지만 얼마나 오랫동안 기다리고 있는 중이세요? 여기 줄이 끝이 없어 보이네요.
여 이제 30분째 기다리고 있어요. 점심 시간이 거의 끝났는데, 이 부츠를 꼭 사고 싶어요. 아시다시피, 반값에 살 수 있거든요.
남 네, 이렇게 낮은 가격이면 돈을 아낄 수 있죠. 저는 셔츠를 몇 장 사려고 했었는데 10분 후에 미팅이 있어서요. 퇴근 후에 다시 와야 할 것 같아요.
여 음, 좋은 생각이네요. 그때쯤이면 가게도 덜 붐빌 거예요. 그래도 계산원이 더 있다면 좋을 텐데 말이죠.

endless 끝이 없는 half price 반값 after work 퇴근 후에 by then 그때쯤엔

32 What problem are the speakers discussing?
(A) A bank is closed.
(B) The wait is long.
(C) An event is delayed.
(D) The food is pricey.

화자들은 어떤 문제에 대해 이야기하는가?
(A) 은행이 문을 닫았다.
(B) 대기가 길다.
(C) 행사가 지연되었다.
(D) 음식이 비싸다.

대화의 시작부터 얼마나 오랫동안 기다리고 있는지에 대해서 물었고 여자는 30분째 기다리고 있다고 답했으므로 정답은 (B)가 된다.

33 Where is the conversation most likely taking place?
(A) In a gym
(B) In a store
(C) In a restaurant
(D) In an office

대화는 어디에서 일어나는 것 같은가?
(A) 체육관
(B) 상점
(C) 레스토랑
(D) 사무실

장소를 묻는 질문은 반드시 유추를 통해서 풀자. 여자가 I really want to buy these boots라고 했으므로 이곳은 부츠를 파는 상점이 된다. lunch라는 단어가 들린다고 해서 restaurant를 선택하는 일이 없도록 하자. 정답은 (B)이다.

34 What does the man say he will do?
(A) Reschedule an appointment
(B) Speak to a manager
(C) Return later
(D) Purchase an item

남자는 무엇을 하겠다고 하는가?
(A) 약속 일정 변경하기
(B) 매니저와 이야기하기
(C) 나중에 돌아오기
(D) 상품 구입하기

남자의 대사에서 정답을 찾는다. 10분 후에 미팅이 있다고 언급한 후 Maybe I'll come back after work(퇴근 후에 다시 와야 할 것 같다)라고 했으므로 정답은 (C)가 된다.

Questions 35-37 refer to the following conversation. 영M 영W

M The office is so cold today. Is the heater working?
W Let me check it for you. Hmm... It's plugged in all the way and I just pressed the reset button, but it's not running. I don't know what the problem is. Do you want me to call a technician?
M Not just yet. Sometimes the gas line valve goes off for some reason, and the heater stops working. Let me go check it first.
W Okay. In the meantime, why don't I make us some tea?
M Sounds great. It should help us stay warm a bit.

남 오늘 사무실이 무척 춥네요. 히터가 작동하고 있나요?
여 한 번 확인해 볼게요. 흠… 플러그는 완전히 꽂혀 있고 제가 방금 리셋 버튼을 눌렀는데도 작동을 안 하네요. 뭐가 문제인지 모르겠어요. 기술자에게 전화를 해 볼까요?
남 아직은 아니에요. 가끔씩 가스 밸브가 꺼질 때가 있는데 히터 작동이 중지되더라고요. 우선 그것부터 가서 확인해 볼게요.
여 좋아요. 그동안에 차를 좀 끓일까요?
남 좋죠. 차가 몸을 덥히는 데 도움이 되겠네요.

be plugged in 플러그가 꽂히다 run (기계 등이) 작동하다 technician 기술자 go off 꺼지다

35 Who most likely are the speakers?
(A) Store attendants
(B) Bank clerks
(C) Repair people
(D) Office workers

화자들은 누구일 것 같은가?
(A) 상점 점원
(B) 은행 직원
(C) 수리공
(D) 사무 직원

화자 직업을 유추하는 문제로 단서를 도입부에서 찾자. 남자가 사무실이 너무 춥다는 말로 대화를 시작하는 것에서 정답은 (D)임을 알 수 있다.

36 What does the man say he will do?
(A) Repair some equipment
(B) Read a safety manual
(C) Check the gas valve
(D) Call a professional

남자는 무엇을 할 것이라고 말하는가?
(A) 장비 고치기
(B) 안전 매뉴얼 읽어 보기
(C) 가스 밸브 확인하기
(D) 전문가에게 전화하기

남자 대사에 정답이 있으므로 남자 말에 집중한다. 가스 밸브가 꺼지면 히터가 작동을 멈추는 경우가 있다고 언급한 후 Let me go check it first(그것 먼저 확인해 보겠다)라고 했으므로 정답은 (C)가 된다.

37 What will the woman most likely do next?
(A) Make some tea
(B) Turn on a device
(C) Call a technician
(D) Go to a storage room

여자는 무엇을 할 것 같은가?
(A) 차 끓이기
(B) 기계 켜기
(C) 기술자에게 전화하기
(D) 창고에 가기

여자의 향후 행동이므로 여자가 대화의 후반부에 why don't I make us some tea?(제가 차를 좀 끓일까요?)라고 말했을 때 정답을 (A)로 선택한다.

Questions 38-40 refer to the following conversation. 미M 미W

M Hi Barbara, are you going to the company picnic this Saturday?
W Yes, I'm really looking forward to it. But I heard it's supposed to rain that day. I hope it is not called off because of bad weather.
M Don't worry. Even if it rains, we're still going to have it. Apparently there are some nice indoor recreational facilities we can use in the park.
W Oh, fantastic! I can't wait to see the jazz band play in the afternoon. The company hired Three Sounds Band this time.

남 안녕 Barbara, 이번 주 토요일에 회사 피크닉에 가실 건가요?
여 네, 정말 기대하고 있어요. 그런데 그날 비가 온다고 들었어요. 날씨가 나빠서 취소되지 않았으면 좋겠어요.
남 걱정 마세요. 비가 혹시 오더라도, 여전히 피크닉을 할 거예요. 공원 안에 우리가 이용할 수 있는 실내 레크리에이션 시설이 있거든요.
여 아, 잘됐네요! 오후에 재즈 밴드가 공연하는 걸 정말 보고 싶어요. 회사가 이번에는 Three Sounds Band를 고용했대요.

look forward to 기대하다 call off 취소하다 indoor 실내의 can't wait to ~를 매우 하고 싶다

38 What are the speakers mainly discussing?
(A) A company outing
(B) A charity banquet
(C) An awards ceremony
(D) A community park

화자들은 무엇에 대해 이야기하고 있는가?
(A) **회사 야유회**
(B) 자선 연회
(C) 시상식
(D) 지역 공원

주제를 찾는 질문으로 단서는 도입부에 나온다. 남자가 회사 피크닉에 갈 것인지 물으며 대화를 시작하는 것으로 보아 정답은 (A)가 된다. picnic은 outing으로 패러프레이징되었다.

39 Why is the woman concerned?
(A) She cannot make it to a party.
(B) She does not have an umbrella.
(C) A performer is off sick.
(D) An event might be cancelled.

여자는 왜 염려하는가?
(A) 여자는 파티에 갈 수가 없다.
(B) 여자는 우산이 없다.
(C) 공연자가 아프다.
(D) **행사가 취소될 수도 있다.**

여자의 대사에서 언급되는 문제점에 주목하자. 회사 야유회에 대해 이야기하면서 I hope it is not called off because of bad weather(날씨가 안 좋아서 취소되지 않았으면 좋겠다)라고 했으므로 정답은 (D)가 된다. call off는 '취소하다' 의미로 암기해 두자.

40 According to the woman, what will take place on Saturday afternoon?
(A) A barbecue dinner
(B) A used book sale
(C) A musical performance
(D) An office party

여자에 따르면, 토요일 오후에 어떤 일이 있을 것인가?
(A) 바비큐 저녁 식사
(B) 중고 서적 판매
(C) **음악 공연**
(D) 사무실 파티

Saturday afternoon 시점이 언급되는 부분에 정답이 함께 등장하므로 시점에 집중한다. 여자가 I can't wait to see the jazz band play in the afternoon(오후에 있을 재즈 공연을 빨리 보고 싶다)이라고 했으므로 정답은 (C)가 된다.

Questions 41-43 refer to the following conversation. (영W) (미M)

W Excuse me. One of the vending machines near the main entrance isn't working properly. I put my money in but it won't take it. The bill acceptor may be broken, I think. I was told to come to the reception desk if there's any problem with the vending machines.

M We're sorry for the inconvenience. Could you tell me which machine it is? I'd better put up an 'out of order' sign on it right now, so no one else tries to use it.

W It's the yellow soda machine. And I'd like to know where I can find another machine around here.

M Of course. There's one in the lounge on the second floor. You can take the stairs over there.

여 실례합니다. 정문 근처의 자판기 중 하나가 제대로 작동이 안되네요. 제가 돈을 넣어도 들어가지를 않아요. 제 생각에는 지폐 들어가는 부분이 고장인 것 같아요. 자판기에 문제가 있는 경우에는 접수 데스크로 가라고 듣고 왔습니다.

남 불편을 드려서 죄송합니다. 저에게 어느 기계인지 말해줄 수 있을까요? 사람들이 사용하지 않도록 지금 바로 고장 표지판을 붙이는 게 좋겠네요.

여 노란색 탄산 음료수 기계입니다. 그리고 이 근처 어디에서 다른 자판기를 찾을 수 있는지 알고 싶은데요.

남 물론입니다. 2층 라운지에 하나가 있습니다. 저쪽에 있는 계단을 이용하시면 됩니다.

vending machine 자판기 work 작동하다 properly 적절하게 bill acceptor 지폐 넣는 곳 inconvenience 불편 out of order 고장 take the stairs 계단을 이용하다

41 What problem are the speakers discussing?
(A) A worker is not available.
(B) A sign is damaged.
(C) A machine is out of order.
(D) A fee is incorrect.

화자들은 어떤 문제에 대해 이야기하는가?
(A) 직원이 자리에 없다.
(B) 간판이 손상되었다.
(C) **기계가 고장이다.**
(D) 요금이 부정확하다.

문제점을 찾는 질문은 보통 주제와 관련되어 도입부에 언급되는 경우가 많다. 여자가 대화를 시작하면서 자판기 중 하나가 제대로 작동되지 않는다고 언급했을 때 정답을 (C)로 선택한다. (B)는 대화 중 언급된 sign(표지판)을 이용한 들리는 단어 함정에 해당하는 오답이다.

42 What does the man say he will do next?
(A) Hang a sign
(B) Notify his supervisor
(C) Repair the machine
(D) Print out a document

남자는 다음에 무엇을 하겠다고 하는가?
(A) **표지판 걸기**
(B) 상사에게 알리기
(C) 기계 고치기
(D) 문서 인쇄하기

남자가 대화를 마치고 할 일이므로 보통은 후반부에 단서가 나오지만, 이 대화에서는 중반부 남자가 I'd better put up an 'out of order' sign on it right now라고 말할 때 정답을 (A)로 선택해야 한다. 향후 행동에 대한 힌트어로 I'd better가 쓰였다는 점을 반드시 암기해 두자.

43 Where most likely will the woman go next?
(A) To the elevator
(B) To the reception desk
(C) To the parking lot
(D) To the lounge

여자는 다음에 어디로 갈 것 같은가?
(A) 엘리베이터
(B) 접수 데스크
(C) 주차장
(D) **라운지**

여자의 향후 행동을 묻는 질문으로 키워드는 go(갈 장소)가 된다. 여자가 다른 자판기를 어디서 찾을 수 있는지 물었고, 남자가 라운지에서 찾을 수 있다고 했으므로 정답은 (D)가 된다.

Questions 44-46 refer to the following conversation. (영M) (미W)

M Hello, Ms. Jones. This is Greg calling from the Merton Library. According to our records, you currently have a book which should have been returned 5 days ago. The title of the book is *How To Become An Effective Speaker*.

W Oh, I'm sorry. I didn't realize that it's overdue. Is there any way I can renew it? I haven't finished reading it yet.

M I'm afraid it can't be renewed since it's already been reserved by someone else. Also, you need to pay a fine of 2 dollars and 50 cents.

W I see. I guess I'll drop by the library after work to return the book and pay the fine.

남 여보세요, Jones 씨. Merton 도서관에서 전화드리는 Greg입니다. 저희 기록에 따르면, 당신은 지금 5일 전에 반납하셨어야 할 책을 갖고 있습니다. 책의 제목은 〈효과적인 연사가 되는 방법〉입니다.

여 오, 미안합니다. 그 책이 기한이 지났는지 몰랐어요. 갱신할 수 있는 방법이 있을까요? 아직 다 못 읽었거든요.

남 안타깝게도 이미 다른 사람에 의해 예약이 되었기 때문에 갱신이 불가능합니다. 또한, 당신은 2달러 50센트의 벌금을 지불해야 합니다.

여 알겠습니다. 퇴근 후에 도서관에 들러서 책을 반납하고 벌금을 내겠습니다.

according to ~에 따르면 records 기록 return 반납하다 realize 알다, 알아채다 renew 갱신하다 fine 벌금 drop by 들르다

44 Why is the man calling?
(A) To place an order
(B) To discuss an overdue book
(C) To renew a membership
(D) To inquire about a lost item

남자는 왜 전화하는가?
(A) 주문하려고
(B) 기한 초과된 책에 대해 이야기하려고
(C) 멤버십을 갱신하려고
(D) 분실된 품목에 관하여 문의하려고

도입부 남자 대사에서 전화 목적에 집중한다. 도서관 직원이라고 밝힌 후 여자가 5일 전에 반납했어야 할 책을 갖고 있다고 했으므로 정답은 (B)가 된다.

45 What does the woman ask about?
(A) Renting a facility
(B) Finding a new job
(C) Renewing a book
(D) Teaching a class

여자는 무엇에 대해 묻는가?
(A) 시설물을 임대하는 것
(B) 새로운 직업을 찾는 것
(C) 책을 갱신하는 것
(D) 수업을 가르치는 것

여자 대사에서 질문 형태로 언급되는 내용에 집중한다. 기간이 초과된 책에 대해서 Is there any way I can renew it?라고 질문했으므로 정답은 책을 갱신하는 것이 된다.

46 What is the woman planning to do today?
(A) Return an item
(B) Buy a present
(C) Visit a museum
(D) Take some time off

여자는 오늘 무엇을 하려고 하는가?
(A) 물건 반납하기
(B) 선물 사기
(C) 박물관 방문하기
(D) 휴식 취하기

세부 사항 질문으로 키워드는 woman, do, today이다. 대화의 후반부에 여자가 I'll drop by the library after work to return the book(도서관에 들러 책을 반납하겠다)이라고 했으므로 정답은 (A)가 된다. 질문의 키워드 today는 after work(퇴근 후에)라는 말로 바꿔 표현되었다.

Questions 47-49 refer to the following conversation. (미W) (영M)

W Hi Jerry. This is Miranda Jung calling from Oakville Ad Agency. I'd like to thank you for giving our staff the training session on Tuesday on the new image editing software at our office.

M You're welcome. I had a good time too. The software requires certain techniques that are not easy to learn, but your employees were all very enthusiastic.

W Thanks. They said that they learned a lot from your workshop. However, some of the employees couldn't participate in it. I was wondering if you could visit our office again and offer the same session for those who missed the first one.

M I'd be glad to. Why don't we set it up for next week? I'll be on a business trip all this week.

여 안녕하세요 Jerry. Oakville 광고 회사에서 전화드리는 Miranda Jung입니다. 화요일에 저희 사무실에서 직원들에게 이미지 편집 소프트웨어에 대한 교육을 진행해 주셔서 감사합니다.

남 천만에요. 저 역시 좋은 시간을 보냈습니다. 그 소프트웨어는 배우기 쉽지 않은 기술들을 요구하는데, 당신의 직원들은 모두 굉장히 열성적이었어요.

여 감사합니다. 그들은 당신의 워크숍으로부터 많이 배웠다고 말하더군요. 그런데, 일부 직원은 참가할 수가 없었습니다. 사무실에 다시 방문하셔서 첫 번째 교육을 놓친 사람들에게 같은 과정을 가르쳐 주실 수 있는지 궁금합니다.

남 기꺼이 그렇게 하겠습니다. 다음 주로 그 일정을 잡으면 어떨까요? 전 이번 주 내내 출장에 가 있을 겁니다.

training session 교육 과정 image editing software 이미지 편집 소프트웨어 certain 특정한 enthusiastic 열성적인, 열정적인 participate in 참여하다 set up 일정을 잡다 on a business trip 출장 중인

47 What did the man do on Tuesday?
(A) He mastered some techniques.
(B) He led a workshop.
(C) He moved to another city.
(D) He wrote a manual

남자는 화요일에 무엇을 했는가?
(A) 그는 일부 기술을 습득했다.
(B) 그는 워크숍을 진행했다.
(C) 그는 다른 도시로 이사했다.
(D) 그는 매뉴얼을 썼다.

세부 사항 질문으로 Tuesday에 남자가 한 일에 집중한다. 화요일에 직원들에게 교육을 진행해줘서 고맙다고 했으므로 정답은 (B)가 된다. 가장 중요한 키워드인 Tuesday가 언급될 때 정답을 순발력 있게 처리하는 것이 포인트이다.

48 What does the woman ask the man to do?
(A) Develop some software
(B) Make a change in travel plans
(C) Repeat a class
(D) Evaluate some workers

여자는 남자에게 무엇을 해달라고 요청하는가?
(A) 소프트웨어 개발하기
(B) 여행 계획 수정하기
(C) 수업 반복하기
(D) 직원들 평가하기

여자 대사에서 남자에게 부탁하는 내용을 노려 듣는다. 첫 교육을 놓친 사람들을 위해서 same session을 제공해 달라고 했으므로 정답은 (C)가 된다. 여자 대사에서 요청 표현인 I was wondering if you could를 들었을 때 정답이 나올 것을 예상할 수 있어야 한다.

49 What does the man suggest?
(A) Reviewing some specifications
(B) Learning from another instructor
(C) Arranging an appointment for next week
(D) Removing outdated computers

남자는 무엇을 제안하는가?
(A) 설명서를 검토하는 것
(B) 다른 강사로부터 배우는 것
(C) 다음 주로 약속을 잡는 것
(D) 구식 컴퓨터를 제거하는 것

남자 대사에서 제안 표현인 why don't we를 들으면서 집중한다. 다음 주로 교육 일정을 잡자고 했으므로 정답은 (C)가 된다. 대화 속의 set it up(일정을 잡다)은 표현은 정답에서는 arrange로 바꿔 표현되었다.

Questions 50-52 refer to the following conversation. (영M) (영W)

M Hi. I stopped by the bank yesterday to open an account and I was very impressed with the excellent service your business offered. The clerk who helped me was especially kind and knowledgeable.
W Oh, I'm so happy to hear that. Do you happen to remember the name of the employee?
M Well, I can't remember her full name but Jocelyn was her first name.
W Oh, that's Jocelyn Brown. She's not in at the moment. But when she gets in, I'll be sure to pass on the compliment.

남 안녕하세요. 제가 어제 계좌를 개설하기 위해 은행에 들렀다가 그 은행이 제공하는 훌륭한 서비스에 감동을 받았습니다. 저를 도왔던 직원이 특히나 친절하고 지식이 풍부했어요.
여 오, 그 얘기를 들으니 정말 기쁘네요. 혹시라도 그 직원의 이름을 기억하시나요?
남 음, 성까지 기억나지는 않지만 Jocelyn이 그녀의 이름이었어요.
여 Jocelyn Brown말이군요. 그녀는 지금 자리에 없습니다. 그러나 그녀가 들어오면, 꼭 칭찬을 전달하겠습니다.

stop by 들르다, 방문하다 open an account 계좌를 개설하다 be impressed with ~에 감명을 받다 offer 제공하다 especially 특히나 knowledgeable 지식이 많은 full name 성을 포함한 이름 전체 first name 성을 제외한 이름 at the moment 바로 지금 pass on 전달하다 compliment 칭찬

50 Why is the man calling?
(A) To praise an employee
(B) To inquire about opening an account
(C) To offer a suggestion
(D) To request a statement

남자는 왜 전화를 하는가?
(A) 직원을 칭찬하려고
(B) 계좌 개설하는 것에 대해 문의하려고
(C) 제안을 하려고
(D) 입출금 내역서를 요청하려고

전화 대화에서의 목적을 묻는 질문으로 도입부 남자 대사에서 정답을 처리한다. 남자가 어제 은행을 방문했고 직원의 서비스에 감동했다고 설명한 도입부를 정확하게 바꿔 표현한 것은 (A)이다. (B)는 opening an account처럼 대화 중에 들리는 단어를 이용한 오답 함정이다.

51 What does the woman ask about?
(A) The address of a customer
(B) The cost of a service
(C) The name of an associate
(D) The location of an event

여자는 무엇에 관해 질문하는가?
(A) 고객의 주소
(B) 서비스의 비용
(C) 동료의 이름
(D) 행사의 위치

세부 사항 질문으로 여자가 질문 형태로 언급하는 내용에 집중한다. Do you happen to remember the name of the employee?에서 여자가 직원의 이름을 기억하는지 물었으므로 정답은 (C)가 된다. employee(직원)가 associate(동료)로 바꿔 표현된 것을 주목하자.

52 What does the woman say she will do?
(A) Telephone a supplier
(B) Call a special meeting
(C) Check in a directory
(D) Speak to a colleague

여자는 무엇을 할 것이라고 말하는가?
(A) 공급자에게 전화하기
(B) 특별 미팅 소집하기
(C) 전화번호부 확인하기
(D) 동료에게 이야기하기

여자의 향후 행동을 묻는 질문으로 대화의 후반부에 when she gets in, I'll be sure to pass on the compliment(동료가 들어오면 칭찬을 전달해 주겠다)라고 했으므로 정답은 (D)가 된다. 대화 속의 pass on the compliment란 표현은 speak to a colleague로 바꿔 표현되었다.

Questions 53-55 refer to the following conversation. (미M) (영W)

M Ms. Wagner, I have one final question before we finish the interview. What makes you think that you are the strongest candidate for our international sales division?

W Well, I have 5 years of field experience in sales and I enjoy working with other people. In addition, I am fluent in Japanese and Cantonese, which I believe will be an asset to your department.

M Great. I was looking for someone who can work in our Hong Kong office. Do you mind working overseas?

W Not at all. In fact, I lived in Hong Kong before and I loved it there.

남 Wagner 씨, 면접을 끝내기 전에 마지막 질문이 하나 있습니다. 당신이 우리 해외영업부를 위한 가장 강력한 후보자라고 생각할 수 있는 점은 무엇인가요?

여 음, 저는 영업 분야에서 5년간의 경력이 있고 다른 사람들과 함께 일하는 것을 즐깁니다. 그뿐만 아니라, 제가 일본어와 중국어에 유창하다는 점은 당신의 부서에 자산이 될 것이라고 믿습니다.

남 좋습니다. 우리 홍콩 사무실에서 일할 수 있는 누군가를 찾고 있었어요. 당신은 해외에서 일하는 것은 꺼리십니까?

여 천만에요. 실은, 전에 홍콩에서 살았었고 그곳을 좋아했었습니다.

final question 최종 질문 candidate 후보자 field experience 현장 경험, 경력 in addition 게다가, 그뿐만 아니라 fluent 유창한 asset 자산, 재산 mind 꺼리다, 싫어하다 work overseas 해외에서 일하다

53 What are the speakers mainly discussing?
(A) A company logo
(B) A foreign country
(C) A sales strategy
(D) A job opportunity

화자들은 주로 무엇에 대해 이야기하는가?
(A) 회사 로고
(B) 다른 나라
(C) 영업 전략
(D) 취업 기회

주제를 묻는 질문으로 도입부의 내용을 잘 노려 듣고 정답을 찾는다. 남자가 면접을 끝내기 전에 최종 질문이 있다고 말한 부분에서 지금은 취업 면접을 하는 상황임을 알 수 있고 정답은 (D)가 된다.

54 Who most likely is the woman?
(A) A department head
(B) A potential employee
(C) A language instructor
(D) A travel agent

여자는 누구일 것 같은가?
(A) 부서장
(B) 잠재 직원
(C) 어학 강사
(D) 여행사 직원

여자의 직업을 유추하는 질문으로 보통 도입부에 단서가 등장한다. 남자가 여자에게 왜 당신이 가장 강력한 후보인지를 물었으므로, 여자는 면접을 보고 있는 구직자임을 알 수 있고 정답은 potential employee(잠재적인 직원)로 바꿔 표현되었다.

55 What does the woman imply when she says, "Not at all"?
(A) She is willing to work abroad.
(B) She wants to attend a sales meeting.
(C) She does not speak a foreign language.
(D) She has not signed the contract.

여자가 "천만에요"라고 말한 의도는 무엇인가?
(A) 그녀는 해외에서 일하고 싶어 한다.
(B) 그녀는 세일즈 미팅에 참석하기 원한다.
(C) 그녀는 외국어를 하지 못한다.
(D) 그녀는 계약서에 서명하지 않았다.

해당 표현의 앞뒤 문맥을 통해 의도를 파악하는 질문이다. 남자가 해외에서 일하는 것을 꺼리는지 물었고 여자는 Not at all(전혀 아니다)이라고 답하며 홍콩에서 살았던 경험이 즐거웠다고 했으므로 정답은 (A)가 된다. Do you mind는 어떤 것을 꺼리는지 묻는 질문으로 Not at all이라고 답할 경우 오히려 꺼리지 않는다는 뜻, 즉 긍정의 답이 된다.

Questions 56-58 refer to the following conversation. (미W) (미M)

W Hi, Mr. Winters. This is Janet Robinson from Dolphin Books. I called you earlier to inform you that we've reviewed the latest version of your manuscript. And everyone in our department said that you did a wonderful job in vitalizing the main characters in your story. I think your book will sell well.

M Thank you for the positive feedback, Ms. Robinson. And now what's the next step?

W Well, our visual artists will design the cover for your book, which will take a couple of weeks. After that, we're going to have a meeting.

M Oh, I'm looking forward to it. Just let me know when and where we will meet.

여 안녕하세요, Winters 씨. Dolphin Books의 Janet Robinson입니다. 당신의 원고 최종본을 모두 검토했다는 것을 알려 드리려고 아까 전화했었습니다. 우리 부서 직원들 모두 당신이 이야기 속 주인공들을 잘 살렸다고 하더군요. 당신의 책이 잘 팔릴 것이라고 생각합니다.

남 긍정적으로 평가해주셔서 감사합니다, Robinson 씨. 그러면 다음 단계는 무엇인가요?

여 음, 저희 시각 디자이너들이 책 표지를 만들 건데, 두어 주 정도가 소요될 겁니다. 그 후에 저희는 미팅을 가지려고 합니다.

남 오, 기대가 되는군요. 언제 어디서 만날지 알려 주세요.

earlier 아까, 일찍 manuscript 원고 do a wonderful job 훌륭히 하다 vitalize 생기를 불어넣다 main character 주인공 positive 긍정적인 visual artist 시각 디자이너

56 What are the speakers mainly discussing?
(A) A business contract
(B) An art exhibit
(C) A new publication
(D) Company handbooks

화자들은 주로 무엇에 대해 이야기하는가?
(A) 사업 계약
(B) 예술 전시회
(C) 신작 출판물
(D) 회사 안내서

대화의 주제를 찾는 질문으로 도입부의 내용을 잘 듣는다. 상대방이 쓴 원고의 최종본을 검토하고 전화했다고 했으므로 정답은 한마디로 요약하여 a new publication이 된다. (D)의 경우 handbook(안내서, 편람)이라는 어휘를 통해 함정을 주고 있다.

57 What does the woman like about the book?
(A) The plot is interesting.
(B) It has been a best-seller.
(C) The characters are well developed.
(D) It has been written for children.

여자는 책에 대해 어떤 점을 좋아하는가?
(A) 줄거리가 재미있다.
(B) 그동안 베스트셀러였다.
(C) 등장인물이 잘 전개되었다.
(D) 아이들을 위해 쓰여졌다.

세부 사항 질문으로 여자 대사에 정답의 단서가 있다. 남자의 책에 대해서 칭찬한 부분은 you did a wonderful job in vitalizing the main characters in your story이므로 등장인물에 대한 것을 좋아한다고 볼 수 있다. 정답은 (C)이다.

58 What does the woman say will happen next?
(A) A design will be created.
(B) A book signing will be held.
(C) A contract will be finalized.
(D) The story will be edited.

여자는 다음에 무슨 일이 있을 거라고 말하는가?
(A) 디자인이 만들어 질 것이다.
(B) 사인회가 열릴 것이다.
(C) 계약이 마무리될 것이다.
(D) 이야기가 편집될 것이다.

여자 대사에서 앞으로 있을 일에 대한 내용을 집중해서 듣는다. 우선 남자가 next step이 무엇인지 물어 힌트를 주었고, 여자가 책 표지를 디자인할 것이라고 답했으므로 다음 단계는 디자인 작업이 된다. 그러므로 정답은 (A)이다.

Questions 59-61 refer to the following conversation. (미W) (영M)

W Hi, I'm here to get some home gardening tips. I've recently moved to a new house with a yard. And I'm interested in starting a flower garden. Could you recommend some flowers that grow well in this region?

M I could, but it would be best to take one of our store's classes if you have no prior experience in gardening. A two-week course for beginners starts next Monday.

W Oh, that's exactly what I need. Could you give me some more details about the class?

M Well, it's held every Monday and Thursday nights, right here in the shop. Here's a list of items you should prepare for class. Would you like to get what you need now?

여 안녕하세요, 집 정원 가꾸는 것에 대한 조언을 얻기 위해서 왔습니다. 제가 정원이 있는 집으로 최근에 이사를 왔는데요, 화원을 시작해 보려고 해요. 이 지역에서 잘 자라는 꽃들을 추천해 주실 수 있나요?

남 그럼요, 그러나 예전에 정원을 가꿔 본 경험이 없으시다면, 우리 가게에서 수업을 들으시는 것이 가장 좋을 것 같습니다. 초보자를 위한 2주 과정이 다음 주 월요일에 시작되거든요.

여 아, 그게 저에게 딱 필요한 것이네요. 수업에 대해서 좀 더 자세한 정보를 주시겠어요?

남 음, 매주 월요일과 목요일 저녁에 바로 이곳 상점 안에서 수업이 진행됩니다. 수업에 준비해 오셔야 할 물건 리스트가 여기 있어요. 지금 필요한 물건을 구입하시겠어요?

home gardening 가정 원예 yard 뜰, 정원 recommend 추천하다 region 지역 prior 사전의, 이전의 beginner 초보자 exactly 정확하게

59 What is the woman interested in doing?
(A) Buying gardening equipment
(B) Moving into a new house

(C) Growing some flowers
(D) Hiring a landscaping company

여자는 무엇을 하는 데 관심 있는가?
(A) 정원 장비를 구입하는 것
(B) 새 집으로 이사 가는 것
(C) 꽃을 기르는 것
(D) 조경 회사를 고용하는 것

여자 대사에서 정답을 선택하되 키워드 interested in(하고 싶은)에 집중한다. I'm interested in starting a flower garden(화원을 시작하는 것에 관심이 있다)이라고 했으므로 정답은 (C)가 된다.

60 What does the woman mean when she says, "Oh, that's exactly what I need"?
(A) She would like to learn from an expert.
(B) She would like to subscribe to a magazine.
(C) She would like to create a new website.
(D) She would like to go to another shop.

여자가 "아, 그게 저에게 딱 필요한 것이네요"라고 말한 의미는 무엇인가?
(A) 전문가로부터 배우고 싶어 한다.
(B) 잡지를 구독하고 싶어 한다.
(C) 웹 사이트를 만들고 싶어 한다.
(D) 다른 상점에 가고 싶어 한다.

해당 표현의 앞뒤 문맥을 통해 의도를 파악하는 질문이다. 남자가 2주짜리 수업에 대해 언급했을 때 여자가 Oh, that's exactly what I need(아, 그게 저에게 딱 필요한 것이네요)라고 답하며 수업에 대한 더 많은 정보를 달라고 했으므로 정답은 (A)가 된다.

61 What does the man give the woman?
(A) A free trial membership
(B) A list of necessary supplies
(C) A reduced price
(D) A newsletter

남자는 여자에게 무엇을 주는가?
(A) 무료 체험 멤버십
(B) 필요한 물품의 리스트
(C) 가격 할인
(D) 소식지

세부 사항 질문으로 상대방에게 뭔가를 주면서 하는 표현인 Here's가 들릴 때 정답을 캐치하는 것이 중요하다. a list of items you should prepare for class(수업에 준비해야 할 물건 리스트)라고 했으므로 정답은 (B)가 된다.

Questions 62-64 refer to the following conversation with three speakers. 영W 영M 미M

W Carl, the store displays look great! I really like the way you arranged the dining tables. So is everything set for tomorrow's sale?
M1 I'm almost done with the displays. Hey Daniel, have you sent our advertisement to the newspaper yet?
M2 Yes, I sent it with the photographs of our furniture this morning. But I'm not sure how large the advertisement should be. Do we want to run a full or half-page ad?
W Well, it depends. What's the difference in cost?
M2 I'll call the newspaper right away to find out.
M1 I remember that we had a half-page ad last year and things worked out just fine.

여 Carl, 상점의 진열이 멋지네요. 식탁을 나열해 놓은 것이 정말 보기 좋아요. 그럼, 내일 세일 준비는 다 된 건가요?
남1 진열은 거의 끝났습니다. 저기 Daniel, 저희 광고는 신문사로 보내셨나요?
남2 네, 오늘 아침에 가구 사진들과 함께 보냈습니다. 그런데 광고가 얼마나 커야 할지 잘 모르겠어요. 반 페이지 광고와 전면 광고 중에서 어떤 것이 좋을까요?
여 글쎄요, 경우에 따라 다르죠. 가격 차이가 얼마인가요?
남2 지금 바로 신문사에 전화해서 알아보겠습니다.
남1 제 기억으로는 작년에 반 페이지 광고를 냈었는데 꽤 효과가 좋았던 것 같아요.

arrange 정돈하다 dining table 식탁 run an ad 광고를 내다 find out 알아보다

62 What does the woman say she likes?
(A) Some pictures of the store
(B) The price of an item
(C) The appearance of some displays
(D) A newspaper article

여자는 무엇이 좋다고 말하는가?
(A) 상점의 사진
(B) 물건의 가격
(C) 진열품의 모양
(D) 신문 기사

도입부 여자의 대사에서 좋다고 언급된 것은 the store displays이며 식탁을 정돈해 놓은 방식이 마음에 든다고 했으므로 정답은 (C)가 된다.

63 What will happen tomorrow?
(A) A sale will be held.
(B) A reporter will visit the store.
(C) A television show will premiere.
(D) A new store will open.

내일 무슨 일이 있는가?
(A) 세일이 있을 것이다.
(B) 리포터가 상점을 방문할 것이다.
(C) 텔레비전 쇼가 시작될 것이다.
(D) 상점이 문을 열 것이다.

키워드인 tomorrow가 들리는 부분에서 정답을 순발력 있게 처리한다. tomorrow's sale 준비가 다 끝났는지 묻는 부분에서 정답을 (A)로 선택할 수 있어야 한다.

64 What does Daniel ask about the advertisement?
(A) Where it should be placed
(B) How much he should spend on it
(C) How large it should be
(D) How many days it should appear

Daniel은 광고에 대해서 무엇을 물어보는가?
(A) 어디에 위치하는 것이 좋을지
(B) 얼마 정도 돈을 들여야 할지
(C) 얼마나 커야 할지
(D) 며칠 동안 광고하는 것이 좋을지

3인 대화에서 이름은 중요한 단서이자 키워드가 된다. Carl이 Daniel에게 광고를 신문사에 보냈는지 물었고 Daniel이 I'm not sure how large the advertisement should be(광고가 얼마나 커야할지 모르겠다고)라고 했으므로 정답은 (C)가 된다.

Questions 65-67 refer to the following conversation and schedule. (미W) (미M)

W Hi, Chris. How are your preparations coming for the new employee training next week? I thought you might have some questions since this is your first time leading a session.
M Thanks for asking. I just received the schedule and I was wondering if I can do my presentation after lunch. I have to meet with a client in the morning that day, so the afternoon works better for me.
W Oh, okay. Let's see… Ms. Rodriguez personally asked me to put her at 1 p.m. in the schedule. How about you switch times with Mr. Tomlin? He wouldn't mind conducting his session in the morning.
M That sounds great.
W All right then. I'll let the other presenters know about the change.

Schedule	
Presenter	**Time**
Evelyn Whitney	10:00 ~ 10:50
Chris Hunter	11:00 ~ 11:50
Lunch	12:00 ~ 12:50
Jane Lopez	13:00 ~ 13:50
Chuck Tomlin	14:00 ~ 14:50

여 안녕하세요, Chris. 다음 주에 있을 신입사원 교육 준비는 어떻게 되어 가나요? 이번이 교육을 진행하는 건 처음이라 질문이 있을 수 있겠다고 생각했어요.
남 물어봐 주셔서 고맙습니다. 지금 막 일정표를 받았는데 제가 발표를 점심 후에 할 수 있는지 궁금해서요. 아침에는 고객을 만나야 해서 오후 시간이 저는 더 좋습니다.
여 오, 알겠어요. 봅시다… Rodriguez 씨는 본인을 1시에 넣어달라고 특별히 요청을 했었어요. Tomlin 씨와 시간을 바꾸면 어떠세요? 그는 오전에 교육을 진행하는 걸 싫어하지 않을 겁니다.
남 저는 좋습니다.
여 알겠습니다. 제가 다른 발표자들에게도 변경 사항을 알릴게요.

일정표	
발표자	**시간**
Evelyn Whitney	10:00 ~ 10:50
Chris Hunter	11:00 ~ 11:50
점심	12:00 ~ 12:50
Jane Lopez	13:00 ~ 13:50
Chuck Tomlin	14:00 ~ 14:50

work (일정, 시간 등이)맞다, 되다 conduct a session (수업, 훈련 등) 세션을 진행하다

65 What is the man preparing to do?
(A) Conduct a job interview
(B) Lead a training session
(C) Write a company handbook
(D) Post some information online

남자는 무엇을 할 것을 준비 중인가?
(A) 채용 면접을 보는 것
(B) 교육을 진행하는 것
(C) 회사 안내서를 쓰는 것
(D) 온라인에 정보를 게시하는 것

대화의 첫 시작 부분에서 여자가 남자에게 신입 사원 교육 준비는 잘 되고 있는지를 물었으므로 정답은 (B)가 된다.

66 Why does the man request a change to the schedule?
(A) His presentation notes are incomplete.
(B) His computer is out of order.
(C) He has a scheduling conflict.
(D) He is not feeling well.

남자는 왜 스케줄의 변경을 요청하는가?
(A) 그의 발표 노트가 완성되지 않았다.
(B) 그의 컴퓨터가 고장 났다.
(C) 그의 일정이 겹친다.
(D) 그는 몸이 좋지 않다.

남자가 스케줄 변경을 요청한다는 사실을 미리 알고 대화의 내용을 듣는 것이 중요하다. 남자가 오전에서 오후로 스케줄을 바꾸고 싶다고 언급한 후 그 이유로 오전에는 고객을 만나야 한다고 했으므로 정답은 (C)가 된다. 같은 시간대에 하나 이상의 일정이 겹치는 경우를 a scheduling conflict라고 한다.

67 Look at the graphic. What time will the man begin his presentation now?
(A) At 10 a.m.
(B) At 11 a.m.
(C) At 1 p.m.
(D) At 2 p.m.

시각 정보를 보시오. 남자는 이제 발표를 언제 시작할 것인가?
(A) 오전 10시
(B) 오전 11시
(C) 오후 1시
(D) 오후 2시

시각 정보를 함께 활용하여 푸는 신토익 유형으로 기존 스케줄에서 변경된 부분을 잘 듣는다. 남자(Chris)는 오후 시간으로 변경을 원했고, 이에 여자가 How about you switch the times with Mr. Tomlin?(Tomlin 씨와 시간을 바꾸면 어떠세요?)이라고 했으므로 기존 스케줄 상에서 Mr. Tomlin의 발표 시간이 정답이 된다. 정답은 (D)이다.

Questions 68-70 refer to the following conversation and account. 미W 영M

W Welcome to ACE Car Rental. Can I help you?
M Hello, my name is Joshua Park and I'm here to pick up the car I reserved.
W Sure, Mr. Park. Please have a seat while I check your account. Yes, here it is. You've booked a compact car for four days and you're going to drop the car off here at the San Francisco Airport on Friday. How would you like to pay for it, cash or credit card?
M By credit card, please. Oh, I almost forgot! Actually I'm planning to drive to Seattle after I spend two days here in San Francisco. So I'd like to change my drop-off location to the Seattle Airport. Could you help me with that?
W Of course Mr. Park. According to our policy, you may change your drop-off location before you pick up your car. However, we do charge an 80 dollar fee for returning the vehicle to a different location.
M Oh, that's no problem. I'll pay the full amount by credit card now.

ACE Car Rental	
Pick Up Location:	San Francisco Airport
Pick Up Date/Time:	Tue, 26 Jan 2017 12:00 P.M.
Drop Off Location:	San Francisco Airport
Drop Off Date/Time:	Fri, 29 Jan 2017 5:00 P.M.
Total Estimate of Charges:	$600.00

여 ACE 렌터카에 오신 것을 환영합니다. 제가 도와 드릴까요?
남 안녕하세요, 저는 Joshua Park이고요 예약한 차를 가지러 왔습니다.
여 네, Park 씨. 계정을 확인하는 동안 앉아 계세요. 여기 있네요. 소형차 한 대를 4일 동안 예약하셨고 금요일에 이곳 샌프란시스코 공항에 반납하시기로 했네요. 지불은 어떻게 하시겠어요, 현금인가요 아니면 신용 카드인가요?
남 신용 카드로 해주세요. 오, 깜빡할 뻔했네요. 실은, 제가 샌프란시스코에서 2일을 지내고 시애틀로 운전을 해서 갈 예정입니다. 그래서 반납 장소를 시애틀 공항으로 변경하고 싶습니다. 그렇게 해주실 수 있나요?
여 그럼요, Park 씨. 저희 정책에 따르면, 차를 가져가기 전에는 반납 장소를 변경할 수 있습니다. 그러나, 다른 곳에 차량을 반납하는 것에 대해 80달러의 수수료를 부과합니다.
남 오, 문제없습니다. 지금 전액을 신용 카드로 지불할게요.

ACE Car Rental	
픽업 장소:	샌프란시스코 공항
픽업 날짜 시간:	2017년 1월 26일 화요일 오후 12시
반납 장소:	샌프란시스코 공항
반납 날짜 시간:	2017년 1월 29일 금요일 오후 5시
총 견적 금액:	600.00달러

account 계정 book 예약하다 drop-off location 반납 장소 policy 정책 charge 부과하다

68 Where does the woman most likely work?
(A) At a hotel
(B) At a travel agency
(C) At an airline ticketing desk
(D) At a car rental agency

여자는 어디서 일할 것 같은가?
(A) 호텔
(B) 여행사
(C) 항공사 티켓 창구
(D) 렌터카 업체

여자의 직장을 유추하는 질문으로 단서는 도입부에서 찾을 수 있다. 여자가 고객에게 Welcome to ACE Car Rental이라고 한 부분에서 바로 정답을 (D)으로 선택한다.

69 What does the man want to do?
(A) Return a vehicle to a different location
(B) Travel back home by car
(C) Rent a larger meeting space
(D) Take an early flight

남자는 무엇을 하기 원하는가?
(A) 다른 장소에 차량을 반납하는 것
(B) 차로 집까지 돌아가는 것
(C) 더 넓은 미팅 장소를 빌리는 것
(D) 이른 항공편을 타는 것

남자가 하고자 하는 일은 남자 대사에서 언급된다. 남자가 I'd like to change my drop-off location to the Seattle Airport(반납 장소를 시애틀 공항으로 변경하고 싶다)라고 말했을 때 정답을 (A)로 선택한다. 특히 I'd like to라는 표현은 '~을 하고 싶다'는 의미이기 때문에 이 질문에 대한 직접적인 힌트 표현이 된다. 반드시 암기해 두자.

70 Look at the graphic. How much will the man pay now?
(A) $80
(B) $600
(C) $680
(D) $1800

시각 정보를 보시오. 남자는 이제 얼마를 지불할 것인가?
(A) 80달러
(B) 600달러
(C) 680달러
(D) 1800달러

주어진 시각 정보를 함께 활용하여 문제를 풀자. 여자가 고객의 계정을 보며 How would you like to pay for it, cash or credit card라고 물었으므로 시각 자료상의 총액인 600달러는 미납 상태임을 알 수 있다. 이후 반납 장소를 변경하는 것에 80달러 수수료가 더해졌으므로 남자가 마지막에 I'll pay the full amount by credit card now라고 말한 후 결제할 금액은 680달러가 된다.

PART 4

Questions 71-73 refer to the following announcement. 미M

Attention, members of Good Life Fitness Center! We're very happy to announce that a new class has been added to this month's schedule. Heidi Grey, one of the most inspiring yoga teachers, will be teaching a yoga healing class for beginners on Friday evenings. She is passionate about sharing her love of yoga with others and you'll definitely find her classes easy and fun. Please pick up this month's newsletter on your way out for more information about the class.

Good Life Fitness Center의 회원 여러분, 주목해 주세요! 이번 달 스케줄에 수업이 추가되었음을 기쁘게 알려 드립니다. 가장 영감을 주는 요가 강사 중 한 분인 Heidi Grey 선생님께서 매주 금요일 저녁에 초보자를 위한 치유 요가 수업을 하실 것입니다. 그녀는 요가에 대한 애정을 사람들과 나누는 것에 열정적이고 여러분 모두 그녀의 수업을 쉽고 재미있다고 생각할 겁니다. 이 수업에 대해 더 많은 정보를 얻으시려면 나가는 길에 이번 달 소식지를 가져가시기 바랍니다.

add 추가하다 inspiring 의욕을 고취시키는, 영감을 주는 beginner 초보자 be passionate about ~에 열정적이다 share 나누다 definitely 반드시, 틀림없이

71 What is the announcement about?
(A) An additional class
(B) Extended hours of operation
(C) A new facility
(D) Benefits for the members

공지는 무엇에 관한 것인가?
(A) 추가 수업
(B) 연장된 영업시간
(C) 새로운 시설
(D) 회원을 위한 혜택

공지의 주제를 묻는 질문으로 도입부에서 정답의 단서를 찾는다. We're very happy to announce that a new class has been added to this month's schedule에서 새로운 수업이 추가된 것을 알린다고 했으므로 정답은 (A)이다.

72 Who is Heidi Grey?
(A) A receptionist
(B) A prospective member
(C) A center manager
(D) A yoga instructor

Heidi Grey는 누구인가?
(A) 접수원
(B) 잠재 회원
(C) 센터 매니저
(D) 요가 강사

세부 사항 질문으로 키워드는 Heidi Grey라는 이름이다. 이름이 언급되고 바로 one of the most inspiring yoga teachers라고 직업을 언급해 주었으므로 정답은 (D)가 된다.

73 How can listeners learn more about the class?
(A) From a newsletter
(B) From an employee
(C) From a review
(D) From a magazine

청자들은 수업에 대하여 어떻게 더 알 수 있는가?
(A) 소식지로부터
(B) 직원으로부터
(C) 후기로부터
(D) 잡지로부터

세부 사항 질문으로 수업에 대한 정보를 얻을 수 있는 방법에 집중한다. 후반부에 이번 달의 newsletter를 가져가라고 언급한 후 for more information about the class(수업에 대한 더 많은 정보를 위해서)라고 했으므로 정답은 (A)가 된다.

Questions 74-76 refer to the following talk. 영M

It is my privilege to introduce tonight's lecturer, Dr. Marilyn Chan. Dr. Chan has been the head of the state Division of Forestry for a decade, and the professor of the Houston School of Forestry Preservation for 3 years. Most of you here have read her latest book, *Appropriate Pruning Methods*, which offers new and different approaches to caring for trees. In just a minute, she will be sharing with us some effective techniques for checking tree health. Now, please give a warm welcome to Dr. Chan.

오늘 밤의 강연자인 Marilyn Chan 박사를 소개하게 되어 큰 영광입니다. Chan 박사는 10년간 주립 산림청의 수장을 맡아 오셨고, 3년간 Houston School의 산림 보존학과 교수로 재직해 왔습니다. 여기 계신 여러분 대부분은 나무를 돌보는 새롭고 색다른 접근 방법을 제시하는 그녀의 최근 서적 〈적절한 전지작업 방법〉을 읽어 보셨을 겁니다. 잠시 후, 그녀는 나무의 건강 상태를 확인할 수 있는 효율적인 테크닉을 우리에게 알려줄 것입니다. 이제, Chan 박사를 따뜻한 박수로 환영해 주십시오.

privilege 특권 lecturer 강연자 head 수장, 책임자 forestry preservation 산림 보존 pruning method 가지치기 방법, 전지 방법 approach 접근법 care for 돌보다 effective 효과적인 technique 기술, 테크닉 give a warm welcome ~을 환대하다

74 What is the purpose of the talk?
(A) To announce the opening of an event
(B) To deliver a lecture
(C) To introduce a speaker
(D) To present an award
담화의 목적은 무엇인가?
(A) 행사의 시작을 알리려고
(B) 강의를 전달하려고
(C) 화자를 소개하려고
(D) 상을 수여하려고

행사의 목적은 대부분 도입부에 정답이 언급된다. 첫 문장에서 lecturer(강연자)를 소개하게 되어 영광이라고 했으므로 정답은 (C)가 된다.

75 According to the speaker, what has Dr. Chan recently done?
(A) Wrote a book
(B) Started to teach at a school
(C) Planted various trees
(D) Resigned from a job
화자에 따르면, Chan 박사는 최근에 무엇을 했는가?
(A) 책을 썼다.
(B) 학교에서 가르치는 것을 시작했다.
(C) 각종 나무를 심었다.
(D) 일에서 물러났다.

세부 사항 질문으로 키워드인 recently에 집중하여 듣는다. Most of you here have read her latest book에서 '그녀의 가장 최근 책'을 듣고 최근에 책을 썼다는 것을 캐치할 수 있어야 한다. 선택지를 먼저 파악해 놓고 일치하는 내용이 언급될 때 빠르게 정답을 처리하는 것이 이와 같은 세부 사항 문제를 잘 풀 수 있는 포인트이다.

76 What will Dr. Chan discuss?
(A) Developing people skills
(B) Community volunteering
(C) Techniques for caring for trees
(D) A divisional budget
Chan 박사는 무엇에 대해 이야기할 것인가?
(A) 사람을 대하는 기술을 발전시키는 것
(B) 지역 봉사 활동
(C) 나무를 돌보는 기술
(D) 부서의 예산

강연의 주제를 묻는 질문으로 보통 discuss, share 동사가 키워드로 언급된다. 이 지문에서도 she will be sharing with us some effective techniques for checking tree health 부분이 정답이 된다. 나무 건강 상태를 확인하는 기술에 대해 알려 줄 것이라고 했으므로 정답은 (C)가 된다.

Questions 77-79 refer to the following radio advertisement. 영W

Don't miss out on the grand summer sale at Troy's. Today through Sunday, all men's, women's, and children's summer clothing is half price. That's right. Swimming suits, shorts, sandals, and a variety of accessories are all 50% off. We have a new shipment of fall fashion arriving on Monday so we have to make room. Now is the time for you to get the styles you love at a special price. Hurry up and visit us today for the best selection!

Troy's의 엄청난 여름 세일을 놓치지 마십시오. 오늘부터 일요일까지, 모든 남자, 여자 및 아이들의 여름 의류가 절반 가격으로 판매됩니다. 그렇습니다. 수영복, 반바지, 샌들 및 다양한 액세서리들이 모두 50퍼센트 할인됩니다. 저희는 월요일에 가을 패션 상품의 배송을 받기 때문에 공간이 필요합니다. 바로 지금이 여러분이 원하는 스타일을 특가로 얻을 수 있는 기회입니다. 최고의 상품 구성을 원하시면 서둘러서 오늘 방문해 주세요!

miss out on ~을 놓치다 half price 절반 가격 swimming suit 수영복 shorts 반바지 shipment 선적 make room 공간을 만들다 selection 상품 구성

77 What kind of products does Troy's sell?
(A) Apparel
(B) Sporting goods
(C) Home decorations
(D) Household appliances
Troy's는 어떤 종류의 제품을 판매하는가?
(A) 의복
(B) 스포츠 용품
(C) 가정용 장식용품
(D) 가정용 전자 제품

세부 사항 질문으로 Troy's라는 특정 업체가 판매하는 제품군에 집중한다. 도입부에 세일을 안내하면서 all men's, women's, and children's summer clothing을 할인한다고 했으므로 정답은 (A)가 된다.

78 When does the special offer end?
(A) On Monday
(B) On Tuesday
(C) On Friday
(D) On Sunday
특별 할인은 언제 끝나는가?
(A) 월요일
(B) 화요일
(C) 금요일
(D) 일요일

세부 사항 질문으로 행사의 시작과 끝을 정확하게 파악해서 듣는다. 순서가 변경되는 형태로 세일이 있을 것임을 언급한 후, Today through Sunday라고 세일 기간을 말해줄 때 정답을 (D)로 선택한다. through라는 전치사가 '~까지'라는 의미이므로 세일은 Sunday까지라고 해석된다.

79 Why is the store having a half-off sale?
(A) It is undergoing renovation.
(B) It is making room for new arrivals.

(C) It is opening a new branch.
(D) It is celebrating its 10th anniversary.

상점은 왜 절반 가격의 할인을 하는가?
(A) 개조 공사를 할 것이다.
(B) 신상품을 위한 공간을 만들 것이다.
(C) 새로운 지점을 열 것이다.
(D) 10주년 기념일을 축하할 것이다.

세부 사항 질문으로 미리 절반 가격 할인이 언급될 것을 파악해두자. 지문 속에서는 half-off sale이 50% off로 바꿔 표현되었고 가을 패션 상품이 도착하는데 공간을 만들어야 한다고 언급했으므로 정답은 (B)가 된다.

Questions 80-82 refer to the following demonstration. 미M

Don't you love the aroma of freshly brewed coffee in the morning? Now you can enjoy the perfect cup of coffee at home with this new compact espresso machine. Some customers choose this home appliance because of its beautiful design. However, the real value of this product is that its pressurized brewing process creates a delicious coffee topped with a layer of creamy foam. At the end of today's demonstration, you will all receive a coffee recipe book for free. Now, I'm going to show you how to make the 10 most popular coffee drinks out there.

아침에 맡는 신선한 커피 향을 좋아하지 않으세요? 이제 이 새로운 소형 에스프레소 기계만 있으면 여러분도 집에서 완벽한 커피 한잔을 즐기실 수 있습니다. 일부 고객은 아름다운 디자인 때문에 이 제품을 선택하곤 합니다. 그러나, 이 제품의 진짜 가치는 위에 크레마가 형성되는 맛있는 커피를 만들어주는 압력 제조 과정입니다. 오늘 시연이 끝날 때, 여러분은 모두 공짜로 커피 레시피 책을 받게 될 것입니다. 이제, 제가 10가지 가장 인기 있는 커피 음료를 만드는 방법을 여러분에게 보여 드리겠습니다.

aroma 향 freshly 신선하게 brew (커피, 차 등을) 끓이다, 만들다 compact 소형의 home appliance 가전제품 value 가치 pressurized 압력이 가해진 layer 층 foam 거품 demonstration 시연 drink 음료

80 What type of merchandise is being demonstrated?
(A) A kitchen appliance
(B) A vacuum cleaner
(C) A lawn mower
(D) A car repair tool

어떤 종류의 상품이 시연되고 있는가?
(A) 주방용 가전제품
(B) 진공 청소기
(C) 잔디 깎는 기계
(D) 차 수선 공구

도입부에 상품에 대한 정보가 this new compact espresso machine으로 주어졌으므로, 커피 머신은 kitchen appliance(주방용 가전제품)로 표현하는 것이 적절하다. 정답은 (A)이다.

81 What is the most important aspect of the product?
(A) Its quality
(B) Its size
(C) Its durability
(D) Its color

제품의 가장 중요한 면은 무엇입니까?
(A) 질
(B) 크기
(C) 내구성
(D) 색깔

세부 사항 질문으로 키워드는 the most important aspect이다. 지문 속에서 the real value of this product라고 말한 부분이 '상품의 가장 중요한 면'을 대신하므로 정답은 맛있는 커피를 만들어주는 제조 과정임을 알 수 있다. 이를 한 마디로 줄여서 quality(질)로 표현한 (A)가 정답이다.

82 What will happen at the end of the event?
(A) Some refreshments will be served.
(B) Some books will be handed out.
(C) Participants will receive a certificate.
(D) An expert will give a lecture.

행사의 끝에 무슨 일이 있을 것인가?
(A) 다과가 대접될 것이다.
(B) 책이 배부될 것이다.
(C) 참가자가 증명서를 받을 것이다.
(D) 전문가가 강의를 할 것이다.

세부 사항 질문으로 키워드는 at the end of the event이다. 지문 속에서 At the end of today's demonstration이 언급되었을 때 집중하여 커피 레시피 책을 받게 될 것이라는 부분을 정답으로 연결한다. 레시피 책 역시 book으로 볼 수 있으므로 정답은 (B)가 된다.

Questions 83-85 refer to the following announcement. 미W

Ladies and gentlemen, my name is Alisa Gerrard and I'm your chief flight attendant. On behalf of Captain Lance and the entire crew, welcome aboard Flight 728 with non-stop service from Boston to Paris. As you can see, tonight's flight is not fully booked. So you are allowed to move to a more comfortable seat, if you'd like. But please wait until the seat belt sign is turned off to do so. Also, if you would like a set of headphones for tonight's in-flight movie, please notify one of the flight attendants. The estimated arrival time in Paris is 5 a.m. local time. Now sit back, relax, and enjoy the flight. Thank you.

신사 숙녀 여러분, 저는 Alisa Gerrard로 여러분의 수석 승무원입니다. Lance 기장님과 전체 승무원을 대신하여, 보스톤에서 파리로 가는 직행 항공편 728에 탑승하신 것을 환영합니다. 보시는 바와 같이, 오늘 밤의 항공편은 예약이 완전히 차지 않았습니다. 그래서 원하실 경우, 여러분은 더 안락한 좌석으로 이동하는 것이 허용됩니다. 그러나 그러기 위해서는 안전벨트 사인이 꺼질 때까지 기다려 주십시오. 오늘 밤의 기내 영화를 보기 위해 헤드폰을 원하신다면, 저희 승무원 중 한 명에게 알려 주십시오. 파리에 도착하는 예상 시각은 현지 시간으로 오전 5시입니다. 이제 기대어 앉아서, 긴장을 푸시고, 비행을 즐기십시오. 감사합니다.

chief flight attendant 수석 승무원 on behalf of ~을 대신해서 crew 승무원 welcome aboard 승선[탑승]을 환영합니다 non-stop 직행의 book 예약하다 comfortable 편안한 in-flight movie 기내 영화 notify 알리다 estimated 예정된 arrival time 도착 시간 local time 현지 시간

83 What is the destination of the flight?
(A) Paris
(B) Madrid
(C) Boston
(D) Mexico City

항공편의 목적지는 어디인가?
(A) 파리
(B) 마드리드
(C) 보스톤
(D) 멕시코 시티

세부 사항 질문으로 반드시 출발지와 목적지를 구별해서 듣는 것이 필요하다. from Boston to Paris라고 했으므로 정답은 (A)가 맞다.

84 According to the speaker, what are passengers allowed to do?
(A) Use a mobile phone
(B) Move to a different seat
(C) Wear a life vest
(D) Order a drink

화자에 따르면, 승객들은 무엇을 하는 것이 허용되는가?
(A) 휴대 전화 사용하기
(B) 다른 좌석으로 옮기기
(C) 구명 조끼 착용하기
(D) 음료 주문하기

세부 사항 질문으로 키워드는 allowed(허용되는) 것이다. 지문 속에 you are allowed가 들리면 바로 정답을 캐치할 준비를 해야 하고 더 편안한 좌석으로 옮기는 것이 허용된다고 했으므로 정답은 (B)가 된다.

85 Why are passengers instructed to speak to a flight attendant?
(A) To receive a gift
(B) To purchase duty-free items
(C) To inquire about flight information
(D) To request a headset

왜 승객들은 승무원에게 이야기하라는 말을 듣는가?
(A) 선물을 받으려고
(B) 면세 품목을 구매하려고
(C) 비행 정보에 관하여 문의하려고
(D) 헤드폰을 요청하려고

질문을 통해 키워드를 '승무원에게 얘기를 하는 이유'로 미리 파악해 두고, 만약 기내 영화를 보기 위해 a set of headphones를 원한다면 승무원에게 알리라는 부분에서 정답을 (D)로 선택한다.

Questions 86-88 refer to the following telephone message. 영M

Hi. This is Walter Rice. About three weeks ago, I hired your roofing company to replace my roof. It was fine at first, but ever since it rained really hard two days ago, it has been leaking. It really worries me because the rain water is still dripping through a crack in the ceiling. And even more rain is forecast for the weekend. I've already covered my TV and other electrical appliances with plastic sheets, but I'd like to get it fixed as soon as possible. Please return my call about when you can visit my house for repairs. My number is 555-3231. Thanks.

안녕하세요. 저는 Walter Rice입니다. 약 3주 전에 귀하의 지붕 수리 회사를 고용해서 지붕을 교체했습니다. 처음에는 괜찮았었지만, 이틀 전에 비가 많이 온 이후로 물이 새고 있습니다. 빗물이 천장의 틈을 통해 아직도 뚝뚝 떨어지고 있어서 정말 걱정이 됩니다. 그리고 심지어 더 많은 비가 주말에 예보되어 있어요. 제가 이미 TV와 다른 전자 제품은 비닐 천으로 덮어 두었습니다만, 가능한 한 빨리 이걸 고치고 싶습니다. 언제 수리를 위해 저희 집을 방문할 수 있을지 답신 전화해 주세요. 제 번호는 555-3231입니다. 감사합니다.

roofing company 지붕 수리 업체 replace 교체하다 at first 처음에는 leak (물 등이) 새다 drip 뚝뚝 떨어지다 crack (갈라진) 틈 ceiling 천장 electrical appliance 전자 제품 plastic sheet 비닐 천 return one's call ~에게 답신 전화하다

86 What type of business is the speaker calling?
(A) A gardening company
(B) A roofing company
(C) An auto repair shop
(D) A home-improvement store

화자는 어떤 종류의 업체에 전화하고 있는가?
(A) 정원 관리 회사
(B) 지붕 수리 업체
(C) 차량 정비 업체
(D) 주거 개선용품 상점

화자가 전화하는 상대방 업체를 묻는 질문으로 I hired your roofing company를 듣고 지붕 수리 업체에 전화하고 있음을 알 수 있다.

87 What does the speaker mean when he says, "And even more rain is forecast for the weekend"?
(A) A repair person will be late.
(B) He cannot keep windows open.
(C) A problem will get worse.
(D) He will have to change his schedule.

화자가 "그리고 심지어 더 많은 비가 주말에 예보되어 있어요"라고 말한 의미는 무엇인가?
(A) 수리공이 늦을 것이다.
(B) 남자는 창문을 열어 둘 수 없다.
(C) 문제가 더 심각해질 것이다.
(D) 남자는 일정을 바꿔야만 할 것이다.

해당 표현의 앞뒤 문맥을 통해 화자의 의도를 파악한다. 비가 온 후 지붕이 새고 있다고 문제점을 언급한 후 And even more rain is forecast for the weekend라고 말했으므로 문제가 더 심각해질 거라는 의미가 된다. 정답은 (C)이다.

88 What does the speaker ask the listener to do?
(A) Visit his office
(B) Deliver some items to his home
(C) Call him back
(D) Give him a discount

화자는 청자에게 무엇을 해달하고 요청하는가?
(A) 그의 사무실 방문하기
(B) 그의 집으로 물품 배달하기
(C) 그에게 답신 전화하기
(D) 그에게 할인해 주기

화자가 요청 표현으로 Please를 언급하는 부분에서 정답을 캐치한다. 수리 일정과 관련해 답신 전화를 해달라고 했으므로 정답은 (C)가 된다. return one's call이 call back으로 바꿔 표현되었다.

Questions 89-91 refer to the following telephone message. (영W)

Hello, Ms. Peterson? This is Audrey from maintenance. We received your message about the Internet connection not working properly in your office. Other people on the eleventh floor also complained about it earlier today. We think there must be a problem with the Internet router. I heard that there are lots of orders you need to process online this week. I'm very sorry for the inconvenience. I've already put in a service request but unfortunately a technician won't be able to visit your office until this evening. But don't worry. By the time you come to work tomorrow, the Internet will be working fine.

여보세요, Peterson 씨? 관리부의 Audrey입니다. 당신의 사무실에 인터넷 연결이 제대로 작동하지 않는다는 메시지를 받았습니다. 오늘 일찍 11층에 있는 다른 사람들도 같은 내용의 불평을 했고요. 저희는 인터넷 라우터에 문제가 생긴 게 틀림없다고 생각합니다. 이번 주에 온라인으로 처리해야 할 주문 건이 많다는 얘기를 들었습니다. 불편을 드려서 대단히 죄송합니다. 제가 이미 서비스 요청은 해 두었지만 안타깝게도 기술자가 오늘 저녁이 되어야 당신의 사무실을 방문할 수 있을 것 같습니다. 그러나 걱정하지 마세요. 내일 당신이 출근할 때쯤에는 인터넷이 잘 작동될 것입니다.

maintenance (department) 관리부 work 작동하다 properly 제대로, 적절하게 Internet router 인터넷 라우터(중계 장치) process 처리하다 inconvenience 불편 put in a service request 서비스 요청서를 넣다

89 What is the purpose of the call?
(A) To ask for directions to an office
(B) To provide some product information
(C) To place an order online
(D) To respond to a complaint

전화의 목적은 무엇인가?
(A) 사무실로 가는 길 안내를 요청하려고
(B) 상품 정보를 제공하려고
(C) 온라인으로 주문하려고
(D) 불평에 응대하려고

전화 메시지의 목적은 도입부에 보통 언급된다. 인터넷 작동에 문제가 있다는 메시지를 이미 받았고 이와 관련해서 답신 메시지를 남기는 상황이므로, 불평에 응대하기 위해 전화한다고 파악할 수 있다. 정답은 (D)이다.

90 What needs to be repaired?
(A) An Internet device
(B) A photocopier
(C) An air conditioning system
(D) A light switch

무엇이 수리되어야 하는가?
(A) 인터넷 장치
(B) 복사기
(C) 냉방 장치
(D) 전등 스위치

인터넷 작동 문제가 도입부에서 언급되었고, 직후 there must be a problem with the Internet router라고 인터넷 기기에 문제가 있음을 또 한 번 언급하고 있으므로 정답은 (A)이다.

91 According to the speaker, when will the technical problem be solved?
(A) This morning
(B) This evening
(C) Tomorrow evening
(D) This weekend

화자에 따르면, 기술 문제는 언제 해결될 것인가?
(A) 오늘 아침
(B) 오늘 저녁
(C) 내일 저녁
(D) 이번 주말

세부 사항 질문으로 문제가 해결되는 시점은 기계가 고쳐지는 시점을 뜻한다. a technician won't be able to visit your office until this evening이라고 기술자는 오늘 저녁에 사무실을 방문한다고 했으므로 기계가 고쳐지는 시점은 오늘 저녁이 된다. 'not~until+(시점)'은 '(시점)이 되어야 ~하다'라고 해석할 수 있어야 한다.

Questions 92-94 refer to the following advertisement. 미M

If you're looking for a fun night out in the city, come to Claret Tours. We offer a thrilling night out including a cruise that travels past the city's world renowned skyscrapers. **And that's not all.** You can enjoy a gourmet seafood dinner at a riverside restaurant as well. Finally you will conclude a memorable evening by going to the Red Hill Observatory for magnificent views of the city's skyline. Tours begin at 5 and 6 o'clock every night and last about 3 hours. Seats are limited, so act quickly! Call now to make a reservation at 555-8219.

이 도시에서 즐거운 저녁 외출을 하고 싶다면, Claret Tours로 오십시오. 저희는 세계적으로 유명한 마천루들을 지나는 유람선 관람을 포함한 황홀한 저녁 외출을 선사해 드립니다. **그게 다가 아니죠.** 강변 레스토랑에서 고급 해산물 저녁 식사도 즐길 수 있습니다. 그리고 마지막으로 Red Hill 천문대에서 이 도시의 스카이라인이 한 눈에 펼쳐지는 장관을 감상하면서 여러분의 잊지 못할 저녁을 마무리하게 됩니다. 투어는 매일 밤 5시와 6시에 시작되고 3시간 동안 지속됩니다. 좌석이 제한되어 있으니 서두르세요. 555-8219로 지금 전화해서 예약해 주세요.

thrilling 황홀한, 아주 신 나는 renowned 유명한 skyscraper 고층건물, 마천루 gourmet 고급의 riverside 강가의 conclude 끝내다, 마치다 memorable 잊지 못할, 기억에 남을 magnificent 웅장한, 장엄한, 매우 아름다운 limited 제한적인

92 What is being advertised?
(A) A famous restaurant
(B) Boat rentals
(C) A city tour
(D) An online reservation

무엇이 광고되고 있는가?
(A) 유명한 레스토랑
(B) 보트 대여
(C) 도시 투어
(D) 온라인 예약

광고 대상을 도입부에서 단서를 찾는다. 이 도시에서 즐거운 저녁 외출을 원한다면 Claret Tours로 오라는 부분을 듣고 정답을 (C)로 선택한다. 여행업체가 야간 도시 투어 상품을 광고하고 있는 것으로 파악할 수 있어야 한다. 유람선 관람을 포함한다는 정보가 있었으나 보트 대여를 광고하는 것은 아니었으므로 (B)는 함정이 된다.

93 What does the speaker imply when he says, "And that's not all"?
(A) He will give directions to the tourist center.
(B) He will introduce an additional feature of the tour.
(C) He will offer a discount on some products.
(D) He will go to a restaurant for dinner.

화자가 "그게 다가 아니죠"라고 말한 의도는 무엇인가?
(A) 남자는 여행자 센터에 가는 방법을 알려줄 것이다.
(B) 남자는 여행의 또 다른 특징을 소개할 것이다.
(C) 남자는 일부 상품에 대한 할인을 제공할 것이다.
(D) 남자는 저녁을 먹으러 레스토랑에 갈 것이다.

해당 표현의 앞뒤에서 문맥을 파악하여 정답을 고르자. 도시 투어 상품에 유람선 관람이 있다고 언급한 후, And that's not all(그것이 다가 아니다)라고 말하며 레스토랑 씨푸드 저녁 식사도 포함된다고 했으므로 정답은 (B)가 된다.

94 What should listeners do to make a reservation?
(A) Visit a website
(B) Talk to a representative in person
(C) Fill out a form
(D) Contact the business

예약하기 위하여 청자들은 무엇을 해야 하는가?
(A) 웹 사이트 방문하기
(B) 직원에게 직접 얘기하기
(C) 양식 작성하기
(D) 업체에 연락하기

세부 사항 질문으로 키워드는 reservation이다. 광고의 마지막 부분에 call us to make a reservation을 듣고 call us를 contact the business로 바꿔 표현한 (D)를 정답으로 처리한다.

Questions 95-97 refer to the following announcement and chart. 미W

Before I end today's sales seminar, I'd like to give you one last tip. Many new sales representatives just assume that our customers are more interested in low prices than quality. But that is not true. The market research group conducted a survey of 10 thousand customers who have purchased our home appliances and this is what they found. Take a look at the chart and see what the most important factor in their buying decision was. When people make major purchases that will last for many years, they want to get the best product for their money. So from now on, you should tell customers how long our washing machines last and how durable our vacuum cleaners are.

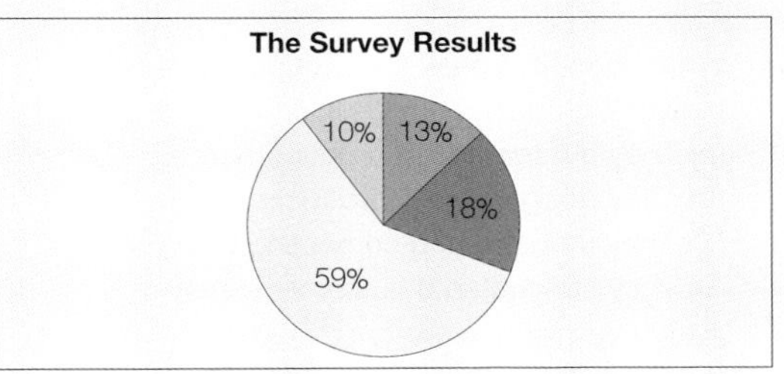

오늘의 영업 세미나를 끝내기 전에, 여러분에게 마지막 조언을 해주고 싶습니다. 많은 신입 영업 사원들은 고객이 질보다 낮은 가격에 더 관심이 있을 거라고 추측합니다. 그러나 그것은 사실이 아니죠. 시장 조사팀이 우리 가전제품을 구매한 경험이 있는 만 명의 고객들에게 설문 조사를 하였고 다음 사실을 알게 되었습니다. 차트에서 그들의 구매 결정에서 가장 중요한 요인이 무엇이었는지 보세요. 사람들은 오래 쓰는 물건을 구매할 때에는 돈의 가치를 하는 상품을 사고 싶어 하죠. 그러니 이제부터는 고객들에게 우리 세탁기가 얼마나 오래가는지 우리 진공 청소기가 얼마나 내구성이 좋은지 알리도록 하십시오.

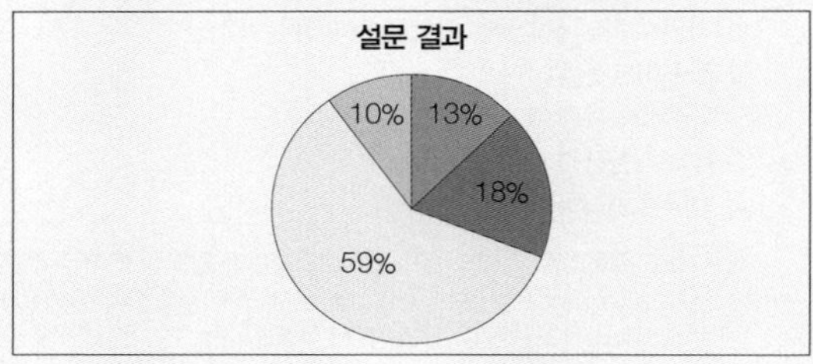

assume 추정하다, 예측하다　market research 시장 조사　conduct a survey 설문 조사하다　home appliances 가전제품　factor 요인　buying decision 구매 결정　durable 내구성이 좋은

95 What merchandise does the speaker's company sell?
(A) Home appliances
(B) Office equipment
(C) Motor vehicles
(D) Cleaning products

화자의 회사는 어떤 상품을 파는가?
(A) 가전제품
(B) 사무기기
(C) 자동차
(D) 청소용품

화자가 our home appliances라고 칭한 부분에서 화자의 회사가 판매하는 제품은 (A)임을 알 수 있다. my, our, your, their 등의 소유격에서 유추의 단서가 많이 나오므로 놓치지 않도록 듣기 훈련을 하자.

96 What does the speaker say about the market research group?
(A) They put together a product manual.
(B) They designed new products.
(C) They researched a competing brand.
(D) They conducted a customer survey.

화자는 시장 조사팀에 대해서 뭐라고 하는가?
(A) 상품 매뉴얼을 만들었다.
(B) 신상품을 개발했다.
(C) 경쟁 상품을 조사했다.
(D) 고객 설문 조사를 진행했다.

질문의 키워드 market research group에 집중하여 듣는 것이 포인트이다. The market research group conducted a survey of 10 thousand customers라고 언급된 부분에서 정답은 (D)임을 알 수 있다.

97 Look at the graphic. Which survey item accounts for 59 percent?
(A) Competitive prices
(B) Product quality
(C) Free shipping
(D) Customer reviews

시각 정보를 보시오. 어떤 조사 항목이 59퍼센트를 차지하는가?
(A) 경쟁력 있는 가격
(B) 상품 품질
(C) 무료 배송
(D) 고객 후기

설문 조사 결과에서 고객이 제품 구매 시 가장 중요하게 여기는 요인이 무엇인지 보라고(see what the most important factor in their buying decision was) 했으며, 사람들은 오래 쓰는 물건을 구매할 때 돈의 가치를 하는 물건을 사고 싶어 한다고 했다. 따라서 도표에서 가장 높은 59%를 차지한 항목은 (B) 상품 품질이다.

Questions 98-100 refer to the following talk and directory. (영W)

Hello, Larry. This is Martha Chang calling from the payroll department. I've read your e-mail concerning travel reimbursement. You wanted to know when you're going to get reimbursed for your travel expenses. In order for me to process a reimbursement payment, I need approval from Debra Avery in accounting. She usually takes care of expense reports and approves the payment as long as there are no problems. So I suggest that you contact Ms. Avery to see if there are any discrepancies between your expense report and the receipts you submitted. I think she will give you a better explanation than I can provide. You can find her extension number in the employee directory.

Employee Directory	
Name	Extension
Martha Chang	05
Lawrence Hwang	13
Debra Avery	22
Gwen McCoy	56

안녕하세요 Larry, 저는 급여 정산 부서의 Martha Chang입니다. 출장비 환급과 관련한 당신의 이메일을 읽었어요. 출장비 환급을 언제 받게 되는지 알고 싶어 하셨죠. 제가 환급금을 처리해 드리기 위해서는 회계부서의 Debra Avery 씨로부터의 승인이 필요합니다. 그녀가 비용 보고서 업무를 담당하고 문제가 없는 한 지불을 승인해 줍니다. 그러니 당신이 제출한 비용 보고서와 영수증 사이에 불일치하는 것이 있는지 Avery 씨에게 연락해 보실 것을 권고드립니다. 그녀가 저보다는 더 자세한 설명을 해 줄 겁니다. 직원 전화번호부에서 그녀의 내선번호를 찾을 수 있을 겁니다.

직원 전화번호부	
이름	내선 번호
Martha Chang	05
Lawrence Hwang	13
Debra Avery	22
Gwen McCoy	56

payroll department 급여 정산 부서 get reimbursed 환급을 받다 travel expenses 출장 경비 approval 승인 discrepancy 불일치 receipt 영수증 extension 내선 번호

98 What is the main purpose of the message?
(A) To respond to an inquiry
(B) To request a document
(C) To provide contact information
(D) To explain a new policy

메시지의 주된 목적은 무엇인가?
(A) 문의에 답하려고
(B) 서류를 요청하려고
(C) 연락처를 제공하려고
(D) 새로운 정책을 설명하려고

메시지의 도입부에 본인을 밝히면서 출장비 환급에 대한 이메일을 읽고 답신 전화를 한다고 했으니 정답은 (A) 상대방이 문의한 것에 답하기 위해서 메시지를 남기는 것이 된다.

99 What is mentioned about Debra Avery?
(A) She is on a business trip.
(B) She works in the payroll department.
(C) She reviews expense reports.
(D) She runs her own business.

Debra Avery에 대해서 언급된 것은 무엇인가?
(A) 출장 중이다.
(B) 급여 정산 부서에서 일한다.
(C) 비용 보고서를 검토한다.
(D) 본인의 사업체를 이끈다.

질문의 키워드인 Debra Avery가 언급되는 부분을 놓치지 말자. Debra Avery로부터 승인이 필요하다는 말과 함께 She usually takes care of expense reports(그녀가 비용 보고서를 담당한다)라고 했으므로 Debra Avery가 하는 일이 비용 보고서를 결제하는 일임을 알 수 있다.

100 Look at the graphic. Which extension will the listener probably dial?
(A) 05
(B) 13
(C) 22
(D) 56

시각 정보를 보시오. 청자는 어떤 내선번호로 전화할 것인가?
(A) 05
(B) 13
(C) 22
(D) 56

전화를 해야 할 사람이 Debra Avery이므로 직원 전화번호부와 대조하여 22번임을 바로 알 수 있다.

Actual Test 9

PART 1

본책 p.108

1 (C)	2 (D)	3 (A)	4 (A)	5 (B)	6 (C)

PART 2

본책 p.112

7 (A)	8 (B)	9 (B)	10 (B)	11 (B)	12 (C)
13 (A)	14 (B)	15 (C)	16 (C)	17 (C)	18 (C)
19 (A)	20 (C)	21 (A)	22 (C)	23 (B)	24 (A)
25 (C)	26 (C)	27 (A)	28 (B)	29 (C)	30 (C)
31 (A)					

PART 3

본책 p.113

32 (A)	33 (B)	34 (D)	35 (D)	36 (B)	37 (C)
38 (B)	39 (C)	40 (A)	41 (C)	42 (A)	43 (C)
44 (B)	45 (A)	46 (D)	47 (B)	48 (C)	49 (A)
50 (B)	51 (C)	52 (D)	53 (A)	54 (B)	55 (C)
56 (D)	57 (A)	58 (D)	59 (A)	60 (B)	61 (C)
62 (A)	63 (C)	64 (D)	65 (A)	66 (D)	67 (D)
68 (B)	69 (A)	70 (C)			

PART 4

본책 p.117

71 (B)	72 (D)	73 (C)	74 (C)	75 (B)	76 (A)
77 (D)	78 (B)	79 (B)	80 (B)	81 (A)	82 (C)
83 (C)	84 (B)	85 (A)	86 (A)	87 (D)	88 (C)
89 (C)	90 (A)	91 (A)	92 (C)	93 (C)	94 (A)
95 (D)	96 (A)	97 (B)	98 (C)	99 (B)	100 (A)

PART 1

1 (A) A man is heating up some chemical solution.
영M (B) A man is wearing gloves in handling a liquid.
(C) A man is concentrating on a delicate task.
(D) A man is looking closely into a microscope.

(A) 남자가 화학 용액을 가열하고 있다.
(B) 남자가 액체를 취급하는 데 장갑을 끼고 있다.
(C) 남자가 세심한 주의가 필요한 일에 집중하고 있다.
(D) 남자가 현미경을 자세히 들여다보고 있다.

남자가 도구를 들고 실험하는 데 집중하고 있다. (A), (B)는 가열하거나 데우는 행위가 없고 장갑을 끼지 않고 있으므로 모두 오답이다.

heat up 뜨겁게 만들다, 데우다 chemical solution 화학 용액 handle 다루다, 취급하다 liquid 액체 concentrate on ~에 집중하다 delicate task 섬세한 일, 세심한 주의가 필요한 일 look into 조사하다, 속을 들여다보다 closely 접근하여, 바싹 microscope 현미경

2 (A) Traffic signs are being repaired by a crew.
미W (B) Some trucks are parked along the street.
(C) The road is packed with cars in both directions.
(D) A vehicle is passing over a crosswalk.

(A) 교통 표지판이 팀에 의해 수리되고 있다.
(B) 트럭 몇 대가 길을 따라 주차되어 있다.
(C) 도로는 양쪽 방향에 차로 가득 차 있다.
(D) 차가 횡단보도 위를 지나가고 있다.

밤에 도로를 차 몇 대가 달리고 있는데 가장 앞쪽에 있는 자동차가 횡단보도 위를 막 지나고 있다.

traffic sign 교통 표지판 crew 팀, 반, 조 be packed with ~로 가득 차다 direction 방향 crosswalk 횡단보도

3 (A) The building overlooks the park.
미M (B) The crane is currently in operation.
(C) The sculpture's exterior is highly reflective.
(D) People are gathered to look at the sculpture.

(A) 건물은 공원을 내려다보고 있다.
(B) 기중기가 지금 작동 중이다.
(C) 조각상의 외관이 매우 반사된다.
(D) 사람들이 조각상을 보려고 모였다.

둥근 조각품이 공원에 있고 뒤에 높은 건물이 있는데 (B), (C)는 이 사진만으로 판단하기 어렵다.

overlook 내려다보다, 간과하다 crane 기중기, 크레인 currently 현재 in operation 작동 중인, 운영 중인 sculpture 조각, 조각품 exterior 외부 highly 매우 reflective 반사하는, 반영하는, 사색적인 gather 모으다

4 (A) The man is likely selling some merchandise.
미W (B) The man has many umbrellas in a bag.
(C) There are no pedestrians on the street.
(D) The man is closing an umbrella.

(A) 남자는 상품을 팔고 있는 것 같다.
(B) 남자는 가방에 우산이 많이 있다.
(C) 길에 보행자들이 없다.
(D) 남자는 우산을 접고 있다.

새 우산을 여러 개 쥐고 있는 것으로 보아 이 사람이 현재 우산을 팔고 있는 것으로 짐작할 수 있다.

be likely -ing ~할 것 같다 merchandise 상품, 물품 pedestrian 보행자 close an umbrella 우산을 접다

5 (A) The man is trimming tree branches.
영M (B) The man is straddling a ladder.
(C) The man is taking a photograph.
(D) The ladder is leaning on the shrub.

(A) 남자가 나뭇가지를 다듬고 있다.
(B) 남자가 사다리 양쪽으로 다리를 벌리고 서 있다.
(C) 남자가 사진을 찍고 있다.
(D) 사다리가 관목에 기대어 있다.

수풀 앞에 사다리를 세워 두고 그 위에 양쪽 다리를 벌린 채 서 있는데 뒷모습이지만 (C)라고 단정할 수는 없는 상황이다.

trim 다듬다, 손질하다 straddle 양쪽으로 다리를 벌리고 서거나 앉다 ladder 사다리 take a photograph 사진을 찍다 lean on ~에 기대다 shrub 관목

6 (A) Protesters are demonstrating in a park.
영W (B) Marchers are disrupting a political speech.
(C) A woman is speaking in front of a camera.
(D) Some people are attending a presentation.

(A) 시위자들이 공원에서 시위에 참여하고 있다.
(B) 가두 행진 참가자들이 정치 연설을 방해하고 있다.
(C) 여자가 카메라 앞에서 말하고 있다.
(D) 일부 사람들이 발표에 참석하고 있다.

잔디밭에서 방송사 기자가 뉴스나 소식을 전달하는 분위기이다. 이들의 직업을 정확히 알 수는 없지만 분명한 건 여자가 카메라 앞에서 말하고 있다는 점이다.

protester 시위자 demonstrate 시위에 참여하다, 시연하다, 설명하다 marcher 가두 행진 참가자 disrupt 방해하다, 지장을 주다 political speech 정치적인 연설 in front of ~ 앞에

PART 2

7 Where are you meeting the accountants?
미W (A) In their office.
미M (B) Online applications.
(C) Friday of last week.

당신은 어디에서 회계사들을 만납니까?
(A) 그들의 사무실에서요.
(B) 온라인 신청서요.
(C) 지난주 금요일이요.

의문사 where 질문으로 미팅 장소를 묻고 있으므로 정답은 (A)가 된다. (B)는 accountants와 발음이 유사한 applications를 이용한 함정이고, (C)는 의문사 when에 대한 정보를 주고 있으므로 오답이다.

accountant 회계사 application 지원서, 신청서

8 What do you do professionally?
미W (A) There's a missing document.
영W (B) I'm an accountant.
(C) Shannon and her team.

직업이 무엇입니까?
(A) 없어진 서류가 있습니다.
(B) 회계사입니다.
(C) Shannon과 그녀의 팀이요.

의문사 what 질문으로 상대방의 직업을 묻는 것으로 암기해두자. What do you do for a living? 역시 직업을 묻는 대표적인 질문에 해당하고 답은 직업을 말한 (B)가 정답이다.

professionally 전문적으로 missing 없어진 accountant 회계사

9 Should I send the letter by express or regular mail?
미M (A) I can write it down for you.
미W (B) Regular mail costs less.
(C) By tomorrow.

그 편지를 빠른 우편으로 보낼까요 아니면 일반 우편으로 보내야 할까요?
(A) 제가 그걸 적어 드릴 수 있어요.
(B) 일반 우편이 비용이 덜 듭니다.
(C) 내일까지요.

선택 의문문으로 선택 사항만 간략하게 압축하면 '빠른 혹은 일반'이다. 그러므로 일반 우편이 비용이 덜 든다고 답한 (B)는 일반 우편을 선택한 것이므로 정답이 된다. (A)는 letter를 들었을 때 연상되는 write down을 이용한 오답이고, (C)는 when에 대한 답이다.

express 급행, 고속 regular 일반, 보통 cost 비용이 들다

10 Which company did you hire?
영W (A) The office has a nice view.
미M (B) I can't recall its name.
(C) Computers and printers.

어떤 회사를 고용했나요?
(A) 그 사무실은 전망이 좋습니다.
(B) 회사 이름이 기억이 안 나네요.
(C) 컴퓨터와 프린터요.

의문사 which 질문으로 핵심은 '어떤 회사'인지는 묻는 것이다. 회사의 이름 등으로 답을 주는 형태가 일반적이지만, 이 경우는 간접 답변 형태로 회사 이름이 기억나지 않는다는 (B)가 정답이다.

nice view 좋은 전망 recall 떠올리다, 기억하다

11 How many applications have you received?
미W (A) She's a promising candidate.
영M (B) Just two so far.
(C) No, not today.

얼마나 많은 신청서를 받으셨나요?
(A) 그녀는 유망한 후보자입니다.
(B) 지금까지 단 두 개요.
(C) 아니오, 오늘은 아닙니다.

의문사 how many 질문으로 받은 신청서 숫자를 물었기 때문에 두 개라고 답한 (B)가 정답이다. (A)는 applications를 들었을 때 연상되는 candidate을 이용한 오답 함정이고, (C)는 의문사 의문문에 No라고 답했으므로 아예 정답의 가능성이 없음을 기억해 두자.

promising 유망한 so far 현재까지

12 Who will be on duty at the security desk tonight?
영M (A) A photo ID badge.
미W (B) Go straight down the hall.
(C) Jim and Susie will.

누가 오늘 밤에 보안 데스크에서 근무합니까?
(A) 사진이 부착된 신분증 배지요.
(B) 복도 끝으로 쭉 직진하세요.
(C) Jim과 Susie가 할 겁니다.

의문사 who 질문으로 누가 근무할지를 물었으므로 근무자의 이름으로 답한 (C)가 정답이다. (A)는 security 관련 어휘인 photo ID badge를 이용한 연상어 함정이고, (B)는 길을 안내하고 있으므로 문맥상 벗어난 답이다.

on duty 근무 중인, 당번인 security desk 경비 데스크, 보안 데스크 go straight 직진하다

13 Why were you late this morning?
영W (A) I was in a meeting on the second floor.
영M (B) No, Tom didn't want to go.
(C) He always takes the bus.

왜 오늘 아침에 지각했나요?
(A) 2층에서 회의 중이었습니다.
(B) 아니오, Tom은 가고 싶지 않아 했어요.
(C) 그는 항상 버스를 탑니다.

의문사 why 질문으로 아침에 지각한 이유를 물었으므로, 지각이 아니라 2층에서 미팅을 하고 있었다고 답한 (A)가 정답이다.

in a meeting 미팅 중인

14 When will the next tenant move in?
미W (A) Two of each.
영W (B) Probably on July 22.
(C) The old warehouse.

다음 세입자는 언제 이사 오나요?
(A) 각각 두 개씩이요.
(B) 아마도 7월 22일이요.
(C) 오래된 창고예요.

의문사 when 질문으로 시점을 날짜로 언급해 준 (B)가 가장 어울리는 정답이다. (A)는 how many에 대한 답이고, (C) 역시 where에 대한 답이라고 볼 수 있다.

tenant 세입자 move in 이사 오다 warehouse 창고

15 How much is the ticket to the concert?
미W (A) We enjoyed it.
미M (B) By taxi.
(C) 34 dollars.

콘서트 표는 얼마입니까?
(A) 우리는 그것을 즐겼습니다.
(B) 택시로요.
(C) 34달러예요.

의문사 how much로 금액을 묻는 질문이므로 (C)가 정답이 된다. (A)는 concert를 들었을 때 연상되는 enjoy를 이용한 오류이다.

16 What did you think about the detective novel?
영M (A) At the nearest bookstore.
영W (B) Yes, I'm full.
(C) It was excellent.

그 추리 소설에 대해서 어떻게 생각하셨어요?
(A) 가장 가까운 책방에서요.
(B) 네, 전 배가 불러요.
(C) 그것은 훌륭했습니다.

상대방의 의견, 견해를 묻는 관용 표현으로 what do you think about과 how do you like를 암기해 두자. 이 질문에서는 소설에 대한 의견, 견해를 물었으므로 훌륭했다고 답한 (C)가 정답이 된다.

detective novel 탐정[추리] 소설 full 배부른, 꽉 찬

17 Who's the marketing head?
미M (A) We're ahead of schedule.
미W (B) Put it there.
(C) The man in a black suit.

마케팅 부서장은 누구입니까?
(A) 우리는 일정보다 앞서 있어요.
(B) 그것을 거기에 두세요.
(C) 검은 양복을 입은 저 남자요.

의문사 who 질문으로 '누구'에 대한 정보를 준 답은 (C)이므로 정답이다. (A)는 일정이 앞서 있다는 내용이므로 문맥상 벗어난 답이고, (B) 역시 물건을 저쪽에 두라고 말하고 있어 문맥상 맞지 않다.

head (부서, 조직을 이끄는) 장 ahead of schedule 일정보다 앞선 suit 양복

18 When are the product designs due?
영W (A) A new line of shoes.
미M (B) For research and development.
(C) No later than 3.

상품 디자인은 언제 마감인가요?
(A) 새로운 모델의 신발이에요.
(B) 연구 개발부를 위해서요.
(C) 늦어도 3시까지요.

의문사 when 질문으로 마감 시점을 묻고 있으므로 정답은 (C)이다. '까지'라는 표현으로 by, not until, no later than 등을 암기해 두자.

a new line of 새로운 모델의, 신상품의 research and development 연구개발부서(=R&D) no later than 늦어도 ~까지

19 Isn't everything in this shop on sale?
미W (A) No, the sale ended yesterday.
영M (B) Linda is the manager.
(C) We close at 7:30.

이 상점의 모든 상품은 할인되지 않나요?
(A) 아니오, 세일은 어제 끝났습니다.
(B) Linda가 매니저입니다.
(C) 우리는 7시 30분에 닫습니다.

Yes/No 여부를 묻는 질문으로 상품이 모두 할인되는지를 물었으므로 아니라고 답한 후 세일은 어제 끝났다고 덧붙여 준 (A)가 정답이다. (C)는 의문사 what time에 대한 답으로 영업 종료 시간을 말하고 있으므로 오답이다.

on sale 세일 중인, 할인되는

20 I'm planning to stay in Berlin for the weekend.
영M (A) They flew in from Munich.
미W (B) I think it will.
(C) You should visit the East Side Gallery.

저는 주말 동안 베를린에서 머물 계획입니다.
(A) 그들은 뮌헨에서 비행기를 타고 왔습니다.
(B) 그럴 거예요.
(C) East Side Gallery를 방문해 보세요.

평서문 유형으로 주말 동안 특정 장소에서 여행을 할 것이라고 말했으므로, 그곳에서 가 볼 곳을 추천해 주고 있는 (C)가 가장 자연스러운 답변이다. (A)는 Berlin을 들었을 때 연상되는 다른 도시 이름인 Munich를 이용해 함정을 준 것이고, (B)는 주어 it이 무엇을 가리키는지 파악할 수 없는 주어 오류 형태이다.

stay 머물다 flew (fly의 과거형) 비행기를 타다

21 Why didn't Theresa show up to the party?
영W (A) She was out of town actually.
영M (B) A lot of food and beverages.
(C) It is too late.

Theresa는 왜 파티에 나타나지 않았나요?
(A) 그녀는 실은 다른 지역에 있었어요.
(B) 많은 음식과 음료요.
(C) 너무 늦습니다.

의문사 why 질문으로 Theresa가 파티에 참석하지 않은 이유를 찾아야 하므로, 다른 지역에 있었기 때문이라고 답한 (A)가 정답이다. (B)는 party를 듣고 연상할 수 있는 food, beverages를 이용한 오답 함정이고, (C) 역시 not show up(나타나지 않다)을 듣고 떠올릴 수 있는 too late를 이용한 연상어 오류이다.

show up to ~에 나타나다 out of town 도시를 떠나, 타 지역으로 간 beverage 음료

22 Have you been waiting in this line long?
미W (A) In the evening, please.
영W (B) We're short-staffed.
(C) Longer than I thought.

이 줄에서 오래 기다리고 있는 중인가요?
(A) 저녁에 해 주세요.
(B) 우리는 인력이 부족합니다.
(C) 생각했던 것보다 더 오래요.

Yes/No 여부를 묻는 질문으로 줄 서서 오래 기다리고 있는지를 물었으므로 (C)가 정답이다. 생각보다 더 오래 기다렸다는 것은 결국 질문에 대해 Yes라고 답하는 것이 된다. (A)는 when에 대한 답이고 (B)는 질문의 long을 듣고 연상되는 short를 이용해 함정을 준 것이다.

line (대기) 줄 short-staffed 일손이 부족한

23 Do you happen to know anyone who works in finance?
미W (A) Just 50 dollars.
미M (B) My husband does.
(C) No, I remembered to visit the bank this morning.

혹시 금융 분야에서 일하는 사람을 누구든 알고 있나요?
(A) 단지 50달러요.
(B) 제 남편이 일해요.
(C) 아니오, 오늘 아침에 잊지 않고 은행을 방문했어요.

Yes/No 여부를 묻는 질문이지만 관계대명사 who에 대해 묻는 것이 요지가 된다. 특정 분야에서 일하는 사람을 아는지 물었기 때문에 (B)처럼 who에 대한 정보를 주는 것이 정답이다. 남편이 그 분야에서 일한다고 답했으므로 전체 질문에 대해서도 Yes라고 답한 것이 된다. (A)는 finance를 들었을 때 연상되는 dollars를 이용한 함정이고, (C)는 문맥상 어긋난 답변이다.

happen to 혹시 ~하다 finance 금융 (분야) remember to ~할 것을 기억하다, 잊지 않고 ~하다

24 Jason will show us around the city.
영M (A) Great. I like sightseeing.
영W (B) It is expensive.
(C) A couple of times.

Jason이 우리에게 도시 구경을 시켜줄 겁니다.
(A) 잘됐네요. 전 관광하는 걸 좋아해요.
(B) 그것은 비쌉니다.
(C) 두 번 정도요.

평서문 유형으로 Jason이 도시를 구경시켜 줄 것임을 알리고 있으므로, 관광하는 것을 좋아한다고 답한 (A)가 가장 자연스러운 답이다. (B)의 경우 주어 it이 무엇을 가리키는지 알 수 없는 주어 오류 형태이고, (C)는 두 번이라고 답하고 있어 문맥상 어색한 답이다.

show around ~를 구경시켜 주다 sightsee 관광하다

25 You have finished preparations for the fundraiser,
미M haven't you?
미W (A) It's a larger ballroom.
(B) The children had a fun time.
(C) We're not done yet.

당신은 기금모금 행사를 위한 준비를 모두 마쳤어요, 그렇지 않나요?
(A) 이건 더 큰 무도회장입니다.
(B) 아이들은 즐거운 시간을 보냈어요.
(C) 우리는 아직 끝내지 못했어요.

Yes/No 질문으로 업무를 다 끝냈는지 여부를 현재완료형으로 묻고 있다. 아직 끝내지 못했다고 답한 (C)는 질문에 대해 No라고 답하는 것이 성립되므로 정답이다. (A)는 무도회장의 크기에 대해 말하고, (B)는 주어 children만으로도 문맥상 벗어난 답이란 것을 알 수 있다.

preparation 준비 사항 fundraiser 기금모금 행사 ballroom 무도회장 have a fun time 즐거운 시간을 보내다

26 Would you like to go to the movies or a concert?
영W (A) Usually after dinner.
미M (B) She moved to Sydney.
(C) How about going shopping?

영화를 보러 가고 싶으세요 아니면 콘서트에 가고 싶으세요?
(A) 보통 저녁식사 후에요.
(B) 그녀는 시드니로 이사 갔어요.
(C) 쇼핑을 가는 건 어때요?

선택 의문문으로 선택 사항만 압축하면 '영화 혹은 콘서트'이다. 정답으로는 둘 중 하나를 선택할 수도 있지만 (C)처럼 다른 선택 사항을 제시할 수 있다. 이때 중요한 것은 선택 사항 A, B와 C가 같은 맥락에 있어야만 한다. 다시 말해, '피자가 좋은지 파스타가 좋은지' 물었는데 '1시가 좋다'고 답하는 게 정답이 될 수는 없다.

usually 보통, 대개 how about -ing? ~하는 게 어때요?

27 Where is the cheapest place to rent a motorbike?
미W (A) Across the street from your apartment building.
영M (B) I always ride it.
(C) He put it in the rear seat.

오토바이를 빌릴 수 있는 가장 저렴한 곳은 어디인가요?
(A) 당신의 아파트 건물 길 건너편이요.
(B) 전 항상 그것을 탑니다.
(C) 그는 뒷좌석에 그것을 두었어요.

의문사 where 질문으로 장소에 대한 답을 주는 (A)가 맞다. (B)는 motorbike를 들었을 때 연상되는 ride를 이용해서 함정을 준 것이고 (C)는 주어인 he부터 오류이므로 정답이 될 수 없다.

cheapest 가장 저렴한 rent 빌리다, 대여하다 motorbike 오토바이 ride 타다 rear seat (차량 등의) 뒷좌석

28 How should I summarize the survey results?
영M (A) The next meeting is in three days.
미W (B) By analyzing the response rate.
(C) No, you shouldn't.

제가 어떻게 설문 결과를 요약하는 게 좋을까요?
(A) 다음 회의는 3일 후입니다.
(B) 회답률을 분석해서요.
(C) 아니오, 그러지 않는 게 좋겠어요.

의문사 how 질문으로 키워드인 summarize를 연결해서 '요약하는 방법'을 묻고 있다고 파악한다. 정답은 (B)로 by -ing 자체가 방법을 알려 줄 때 쓰는 표현으로 '~함으로써'라고 해석된다. 설문 조사에서의 회답률을 response rate이라고 하므로 문맥상으로도 가장 적절한 답이다. (A)는 시점에 대해 알려 주고 있고, (C)는 의문사 의문문에 No라고 답하고 있으므로 오답이 된다.

summarize 요약하다 survey result 설문조사 결과 analyze 분석하다 response rate (시장 조사에서의) 회답률

29 Where can I get a copy of the convention schedule?
영W (A) That's what I thought.
영M (B) At Kennedy Park every year.
(C) I'll give you one.

어디에서 컨벤션 일정표를 한 부 얻을 수 있을까요?
(A) 그것이 제가 생각한 바입니다.
(B) 매년 Kennedy 공원에서요.
(C) 하나 드릴게요.

의문사 where 질문으로 일정표를 어디서 구할 수 있는지 물었으므로, 내가 주겠다고 답한 (C)는 충분히 정답이 되지만, (B)는 매년 공원에서라고 답했으므로 어색하다. 질문에 대한 해석이 부정확하면 (B)와 같은 함정에 빠지게 된다.

convention 대규모 회의 schedule 일정표

30 Did Neil notify the client of the changes?
미W (A) By next Wednesday.
영W (B) I suggested some revisions.
(C) Yes, right before the meeting.

Neil이 변경 사항에 대해 고객에게 알렸나요?
(A) 다음 주 수요일까지요.
(B) 저는 몇 가지 수정을 제안했어요.
(C) 네, 회의 바로 전에요.

Yes/No 여부를 묻는 질문으로 Neil이 고객에게 변경을 알렸는지 여부에 대한 답을 찾아야 하므로 정답은 회의 직전에 알렸다고 답한 (C)이다. (A)는 마감 시점을 언급하며 when에 대한 정보를 주었고, (B)는 changes를 들었을 때 연상되는 revisions를 이용한 오답 함정이다.

notify A of B A에게 B를 알리다 change 변경 revision 수정

31 Why won't the speakers turn on?
미W (A) Did you check the batteries?
미M (B) He took a day off.
(C) It's too loud.

스피커가 왜 안 켜지죠?
(A) 건전지는 확인하셨나요?
(B) 그는 하루를 쉬었습니다.
(C) 그것은 너무 시끄럽습니다.

의문사 why 질문으로 스피커가 왜 안 켜지는지 물었으므로, 건전지를 확인했는지 되묻는 (A)가 가장 자연스러운 답이 된다. (B)는 주어 he가 가리키는 사람이 누군지 파악할 수 없는 주어 오류이고, (C)는 speakers에서 연상되는 too loud라는 어휘를 이용한 함정이다.

turn on 켜다, 켜지다 take a day off (직장으로부터) 하루 쉬다 loud 시끄러운

PART 3

Questions 32-34 refer to the following conversation. 미M 미W

M Ariana, I'm looking for the folder where we keep all the applications. Have you seen it?
W I saw Jacob with the folder this morning. Have you checked with him?
M No, he's at lunch now. I'm supposed to conduct an interview at 1 so I was going to review the applicant's résumé.
W Oh, I think I still have job applicants' résumés in my e-mail box since they send their résumés by e-mail too. I'll look it up for you. What is the applicant's name?

남 Ariana, 지원서들을 다 모아 두는 폴더를 찾고 있는 중인데요, 혹시 보신 적 있나요?
여 오늘 아침에 Jacob이 가지고 있는 걸 봤어요. 그에게 확인해 보셨나요?
남 아니요, 그는 지금 점심 중이에요. 1시에 면접을 보기로 되어 있어서 지원자의 이력서를 살펴보려고 했거든요.
여 오, 지원자들이 이메일로도 이력서를 보내니까 제 이메일함에 이력서들이 아직 있을 거예요. 찾아봐 드릴게요. 지원자의 이름이 어떻게 되죠?

application 지원서 conduct an interview 면접을 보다 look up ~을 찾다 applicant 지원자

32 What is the man trying to locate?
(A) A folder
(B) A telephone number
(C) A manual
(D) A photocopier

남자는 무엇을 찾고 있는가?
(A) 폴더
(B) 전화번호
(C) 사용 설명서
(D) 복사기

남자가 대화의 시작 부분에서 I'm looking for the folder(폴더를 찾는 중이다)라고 말했을 때 정답을 바로 (A)로 선택한다. look for와 locate는 '~을 찾다'는 뜻의 동의어이다.

33 What is the man scheduled to do this afternoon?
(A) Introduce a new employee
(B) Interview a job candidate
(C) Meet with a client
(D) Speak to a manager

남자는 오늘 오후에 무엇을 하기로 되어 있는가?
(A) 신입 사원 소개하기
(B) 지원자 면접보기
(C) 고객 만나기
(D) 매니저와 이야기하기

질문의 this afternoon은 대화문의 at 1(한 시에)의 다른 표현이다. 남자는 지원자를 인터뷰하기로 되어 있다고 했으므로 정답은 (B)가 된다.

34 What does the woman offer to do?
(A) Ask a coworker
(B) E-mail a résumé
(C) Reschedule an interview
(D) Find a document

여자는 무엇을 해 주겠다고 하는가?
(A) 동료에게 요청하기
(B) 이력서를 이메일로 보내기
(C) 면접의 일정을 바꾸기
(D) 서류 찾기

여자가 해주겠다고 언급하는 것이 정답이 된다. 지원자의 이력서를 이메일함에 보관하고 있다고 하며 I'll look it up for you(제가 찾아봐 드릴게요)라고 했으므로 지원자의 이력서를 찾아봐 주겠다는 의미가 된다. 이력서는 a document로 바꿔 표현되었으며 정답은 (D)가 된다.

Questions 35-37 refer to the following conversation. 영M 영W

M Have you tried the new coffee shop in the lobby? I've already become a big fan of their coffee.
W Really? Do they offer fast service too? I always wanted a coffee place in the building, but I don't want to wait in a long line to get a cup of coffee every morning.
M You'll love that place then. The service is fast and they'll start offering a selection of quick breakfast menu items next week.

남 로비에 새로 생긴 커피숍에 가보셨나요? 전 이미 그들의 커피에 열혈 팬이 되어 버렸어요.
여 진짜요? 서비스도 빠른가요? 항상 건물 내에 커피숍이 있었으면 좋겠다고 생각했지만, 매일 아침마다 커피 한 잔을 사려고 길게 줄을 서서 기다리고 싶지는 않거든요.
남 그렇다면 그곳을 좋아할 겁니다. 서비스도 빠르고 빠른 아침 메뉴도 제공하기 시작할 거예요.

big fan 열혈 팬 in a long line 길게 줄 서서

35 What are the speakers mainly discussing?
(A) A company policy
(B) A coffee machine
(C) A recipe for cooking
(D) A new business

화자는 무엇에 대해 주로 얘기하는가?
(A) 회사 정책
(B) 커피 기계
(C) 요리 조리법
(D) 새로운 업체

대화의 주제를 찾는 질문으로 도입부에서 단서를 찾는다. 남자가 대화를 시작하면서 로비에 새로 생긴 커피숍에 가 봤는지 물었고, 새로운 커피숍은 a new business로 바꿔 표현될 수 있으므로 (D)가 정답이다.

36 What does the woman not want to do?
(A) Work overtime
(B) Wait in line
(C) Work out regularly
(D) Take the subway in the morning

여자는 무엇을 하고 싶지 않은가?
(A) 시간외 근무하기
(B) 줄 서서 기다리기
(C) 규칙적으로 운동하기
(D) 아침에 지하철 타기

여자가 원하지 않는 일을 물었으므로 여자 대사에서 부정적인 내용에 집중해야 한다. 여자가 I don't want to wait in a long line이라고 언급한 부분이 그대로 정답 (B)가 된다. 질문의 키워드가 들리는 부분을 정확하게 캐치해서 정답으로 연결하자.

37 What will start next week?
(A) A coffee-brewing class
(B) A construction project
(C) The sale of breakfast menu items
(D) A series of professional workshops

다음 주에 무엇이 시작될 것인가?
(A) 커피 만들기 수업
(B) 공사 프로젝트
(C) 아침 메뉴의 판매
(D) 일련의 업무 관련 워크숍

세부 사항 질문으로 키워드는 next week이다. 새로 개업한 커피숍에 대한 정보를 주면서 they'll start offering a selection of quick breakfast menu items next week라고 했으므로 다음 주에 시작될 것은 아침 메뉴 판매가 된다.

Questions 38-40 refer to the following conversation. 미W 미M

W I heard you're attending the regional marketing meeting in San Francisco on Monday too. How about we share a ride?
M Actually, I'm not driving this time. I've decided to take the train because I won't have to deal with the morning traffic that way. Why don't you come with me?
W That's a great idea. In fact I can go over my presentation notes on the train as well.
M Perfect! I'll book two train tickets online then.

여 당신도 월요일에 샌프란시스코에서 열리는 지역 마케팅 회의에 참석하신다고 들었어요. 차를 함께 타고 가면 어떨까요?
남 실은 이번에는 제가 운전을 안 하려고요. 기차를 타고 가기로 했어요. 그렇게 하면 아침 교통 체증을 피할 수 있으니까요. 저랑 같이 가시면 어때요?
여 좋은 생각이에요. 저도 기차에서 발표 노트를 검토할 수 있겠네요.
남 잘됐네요! 그럼 온라인으로 티켓 두 장을 예매할게요.

share a ride 차를 함께 타다 deal with 처리하다 book 예약하다

38 What will the speakers probably do on Monday?
(A) Share a taxi
(B) Attend a meeting
(C) Finish a report
(D) Check a schedule

화자들은 월요일에 무엇을 할 것 같은가?
(A) 택시 함께 타기
(B) 회의에 참석하기

(C) 보고서 끝내기
(D) 스케줄 확인하기

Monday라는 시점 힌트에 집중하여 듣는다. 월요일에 regional marketing meeting에 참석한다는 언급을 했으므로 정답은 (B)가 된다.

39 Why does the man want to take the train?
(A) His car is being repaired.
(B) Train fares are not expensive.
(C) He will not be stuck in traffic.
(D) It is more comfortable than the bus.

남자는 왜 기차를 타고 싶어 하는가?
(A) 그의 차가 수리 중이어서
(B) 기차 운임이 비싸지 않아서
(C) 교통 체증에 갇히지 않을 것이라서
(D) 버스보다 더 편안해서

남자가 기차를 탈 것이란 정보를 미리 염두에 두고 대화를 듣자. 남자가 because I won't have to deal with the morning traffic(아침 교통 체증을 피할 수 있다)이라고 했으므로 정답은 (C)가 된다. 이유를 묻는 질문이므로 because와 같은 키워드를 놓치지 말자.

40 What will the man probably do next?
(A) Reserve tickets
(B) Go to the station
(C) Review some notes
(D) Call a travel agency

남자는 다음에 무엇을 할 것 같은가?
(A) 티켓 예매하기
(B) 역으로 가기
(C) 노트 검토하기
(D) 여행사에 전화하기

대화의 후반부에 남자가 I'll book two train tickets online then이라고 말한 부분이 바로 정답이 된다. 동사 book과 reserve는 '예약하다'는 뜻의 동의어이다.

Questions 41-43 refer to the following conversation. (미M) (영W)

M Stephanie, do you see that large crowd of people around the theater? The play doesn't start for two hours and there is already a huge line.
W Wow, I'm so excited. I've really wanted to see the play since I read a review about it in the daily news last week.
M Oh, yes. I read the same review. I think the publicity from that article has paid off. By the way, I don't see any parking spaces around here.
W Actually there's a parking lot in the next block over. You see that multi-level parking garage? Why don't we try parking there?
M Okay. It is just a short walk to the theater from there.

남 Stephanie, 극장 주변에 저 인파가 보이세요? 연극은 두 시간 후에 시작하는데 벌써 사람들이 많이 있네요.
여 와, 너무 신 나요. 지난주에 일간지에서 이 연극에 대한 평론을 본 이후로 무척 보고 싶었거든요.
남 아 네. 저도 같은 평론을 봤어요. 그 기사의 홍보가 효과가 있었던 것 같네요. 그나저나 이 근처에 주차할 곳이 안 보이네요.
여 실은 다음 블록에 주차장이 있어요. 저기 저 주차 건물 보이죠? 저 곳에 주차하면 어떨까요?
남 좋아요. 거기에서 극장까지 조금만 걸어오면 되겠네요.

crowd 인파 review 평론 publicity 홍보 pay off 효과를 내다 multi-level 여러 층의

41 What event are the speakers planning to attend?
(A) An art exhibit
(B) A music concert
(C) A theater performance
(D) A corporate function

화자들은 어떤 행사에 참석하려고 하는가?
(A) 미술 전시회
(B) 음악 공연
(C) 무대 공연
(D) 기업 행사

대화의 도입부에 theater(극장) 주변에 인파가 많다고 하며 연극이 2시간 후에 시작한다고 했으므로 정답은 (C)가 된다.

42 How did the woman learn about the event?
(A) From an article
(B) From a colleague
(C) From a brochure
(D) From a close friend

여자는 행사에 대해 어떻게 알았는가?
(A) 기사를 통해
(B) 동료를 통해
(C) 안내 책자를 통해
(D) 친한 친구를 통해

여자가 신문에 난 review(평론)를 읽고 연극을 보고 싶었다고 했으므로 정답은 (A)가 된다.

43 What does the woman suggest?
(A) Watching a different show
(B) Going for a walk
(C) Parking in a garage
(D) Reading a newspaper

여자는 무엇을 제안하는가?
(A) 다른 공연을 볼 것
(B) 산책을 갈 것
(C) 주차장에 주차할 것
(D) 신문을 읽을 것

여자 대사의 제안 표현을 잘 듣자. 주차 건물이 있다고 말하며 Why don't we try parking there?라고 제안했으므로 정답은 (C)가 된다.

Questions 44-46 refer to the following conversation. 영M 미W

M Hi Alice. Earlier today, James came up with an idea that we start a tennis team as a way of getting exercise after work. 5 of us in the office have decided to join it. So would you like to go along with us?

W Oh, I could absolutely use more exercise and I just love playing tennis. But I don't think I have time because I volunteer at the community center after work.

M In that case, we could possibly meet over the weekend. Can you participate if we play tennis on Sundays?

W Definitely. Just let me know the time and place, and I'll be there.

남 안녕하세요 Alice. 아까 James가 퇴근 후에 운동을 하기 위한 방법으로 테니스 팀을 시작하자는 아이디어를 냈어요. 사무실 중 다섯 명은 같이 하기로 했는데요. 함께 하시겠어요?

여 오, 정말 운동을 더 해야 하고 테니스 치는 것도 아주 좋아해요. 그러나 퇴근 후에는 지역 회관에서 자원봉사를 하기 때문에 시간이 없을 것 같아요.

남 그런 경우라면, 주말 동안에 만나는 것도 가능할 거예요. 일요일에 테니스를 친다면 참여할 수 있으세요?

여 그럼요. 저한테 시간과 장소만 알려 주시면, 꼭 가겠습니다.

come up with 생각해내다, 떠올리다 as a way of -ing ~하는 방법으로 go along with ~와 함께 가다, ~에 찬성하다 could use 필요하다 volunteer 자원 봉사하다 participate 참여하다

44 What are the speakers discussing?
(A) Purchasing some sporting goods
(B) Putting together an athletic team
(C) Changing the work hours
(D) Reserving some concert tickets

화자는 무엇에 대해 토론하고 있는가?
(A) 스포츠 용품을 구매하는 것
(B) 스포츠 팀을 구성하는 것
(C) 업무 시간을 변경하는 것
(D) 콘서트 티켓을 예매하는 것

주제를 묻는 질문으로 남자가 도입부에 James came up with an idea that we start a tennis team이라고 말하는 부분을 정답으로 연결한다. start a tennis team이 putting together an athletic team으로 바꿔 표현되었다. 동사 put together는 '~을 구성하여 만들다'는 뜻으로 암기해 두자.

45 What does the woman usually do after work?
(A) Volunteer in the community
(B) Work out at the gym
(C) Take a course
(D) Do household chores

여자는 보통 퇴근 후에 무엇을 하는가?
(A) 지역 사회에서 자원 봉사하기
(B) 체육관에 운동하기
(C) 수업 듣기
(D) 집안일 하기

여자가 평소 퇴근 후에 하는 일을 묻는 세부 사항 질문으로 키워드 after work에 집중한다. I volunteer at the community center after work를 듣고 정답을 (A)로 선택한다.

46 What does the man suggest?
(A) Sharing a ride to work
(B) Searching for another place
(C) Taking the woman out for dinner
(D) Meeting on a different day

남자는 무엇을 제안하는가?
(A) 직장까지 차를 함께 타는 것
(B) 다른 장소를 찾는 것
(C) 여자에게 저녁 식사를 대접하는 것
(D) 다른 요일에 만나는 것

남자의 대사 Can you participate if we play tennis on Sundays?를 듣고 '퇴근 후' 대신 '일요일마다' 만날 것을 제안함을 알 수 있다. 정답은 meeting on a different day로 바꿔 표현되었다.

Questions 47-49 refer to the following conversation. 영M 미W

M Hi, Ms. Kang. This is Martin Smith from IPS Financial Services Inc. Thank you for your interest in the position of advertising director. I've reviewed your résumé and references and I'd like you to come in for an interview. How about Thursday morning?

W Um... I'll be in Chicago on business on Thursday. I have to attend a conference in the morning, but I can be there by 3 in the afternoon since your company is close to the city.

M Very good. I'll see you then. And I'd like to see some of your most recent work. Could you please bring your portfolio?

남 안녕하세요, Kang 씨. 저는 IPS Financial Services 사의 Martin Smith입니다. 광고 부서장 직에 관심을 가져 주셔서 감사합니다. 당신의 이력서와 추천서는 살펴보았고요, 면접을 위해 한 번 와주셨으면 합니다. 목요일 아침은 어떠세요?

여 전 목요일에 업무상 시카고에 있을 것입니다. 아침에 회의에 참석해야 하지만, 당신의 회사가 그 도시에서 가깝기 때문에 오후 3까지는 그쪽으로 갈 수 있습니다.

남 아주 좋습니다. 그때 뵙겠습니다. 그리고 당신의 가장 최근 업무를 보고 싶은데요. 포트폴리오를 가져 오실 수 있을까요?

interest in ~에 대한 관심 position 직위 references 추천서 most recent 가장 최근의 portfolio (업무 관련)작품집

47 Where most likely does the man work?
(A) At a recruiting agency
(B) At a financial company
(C) At a convention center
(D) At an interior design company

남자는 어디에서 일할 것 같은가?
(A) 고용 대행사
(B) 금융 회사
(C) 컨벤션 센터
(D) 실내 디자인 회사

남자의 직장을 유추하는 문제로 도입부에 남자가 본인을 소개하는 This is Martin Smith from IPS Financial Services Inc에서 남자가 소속된 직장이 금융 회사임을 유추한다. 소속을 말할 때는 보통 전치사 from이 쓰이므로 from 뒤에 언급되는 회사명에서 빠르게 유추할 수 있는 형태이다.

48 When will the speakers meet for an interview?
(A) Tuesday
(B) Wednesday
(C) Thursday
(D) Friday

화자들은 언제 면접을 위해 만날 것인가?
(A) 화요일
(B) 수요일
(C) 목요일
(D) 금요일

최종 면접 일자를 묻는 질문으로 남자가 목요일을 제시했고, 여자는 목요일에 다른 일정이 있으나 오후에는 갈 수 있다고 답했으므로 면접 일자는 변경 없이 목요일이 된다. 정답은 (C)이다.

49 What does the man ask the woman to do?
(A) Bring some work samples
(B) Contact a colleague
(C) Return a call
(D) Submit an application

남자는 여자에게 무엇을 하도록 요청하는가?
(A) 업무 샘플 가져오기
(B) 동료에게 연락하기
(C) 전화 다시 하기
(D) 지원서 제출하기

세부 사항 질문으로 남자 대사에서 요청 표현과 함께 언급되는 내용에 집중한다. Could you please는 상대방에게 요청할 때 쓰는 대표적인 표현으로, portfolio를 가져오라고 한 것을 work samples로 바꿔 표현한 (A)가 정답이다.

Questions 50-52 refer to the following conversation. 영W 영M

W Hey Travis. Have you completed the equipment budget for next year? It's due tomorrow.
M No, I haven't finished it yet. I'm still waiting for Janice to give me a list of new equipment for her department and the cost estimates. I can't finish the report without that information.
W I'm actually heading over to the sales department right now. Do you want me to remind Janice to give that information to you by the end of the day?
M Oh, that'd be great. I really want to get it over with before I leave for the day.

여 Travis, 내년 장비 예산 보고서는 다 완성했나요? 그건 내일까지 마감이에요.
남 아니요, 아직 끝내지 못했어요. 아직 Janice가 그녀의 부서에서 사용할 장비 리스트와 가격 견적서를 주길 기다리고 있습니다. 그 정보 없이는 이 보고서를 끝낼 수가 없거든요.
여 실은 제가 지금 영업 부서로 가는 길이었어요. Janice에게 그 정보를 오늘까지 당신에게 주라고 다시 상기시켜 줄까요?
남 그러면 좋겠네요. 퇴근하기 전에 이걸 꼭 끝내고 싶거든요.

complete 끝내다 equipment budget 장비 예산(안) due 마감인, 만기인 cost estimate 가격 견적서 head over to ~로 가다 remind 상기시키다 get it over with ~을 끝내다 leave for the day 퇴근하다

50 What is the conversation mainly about?
(A) An installation manual
(B) An annual budget
(C) A missed deadline
(D) A meeting schedule

대화는 주로 무엇에 관한 것인가?
(A) 설치 매뉴얼
(B) 연간 예산안
(C) 놓친 마감
(D) 회의 일정

대화의 주제는 도입부에서 단서를 찾는다. 여자가 Have you completed the equipment budget for next year?에서 budget(예산안)을 끝냈는지 물었으므로 정답을 (B)로 선택한다. 마감에 대한 언급이 있었지만 마감은 내일이라고 했기 때문에 (C)는 오답이 된다.

51 According to the man, why has he not finished his report?
(A) He has another assignment to complete.
(B) A purchase hasn't been approved.
(C) Some information hasn't been received.
(D) His coworker has been off sick.

남자에 따르면, 그는 왜 보고서를 완료할 수 없는가?
(A) 그는 끝내야 할 다른 업무가 있다.
(B) 구매가 승인이 되지 않았다.
(C) 일부 정보를 받지 못했다.
(D) 그의 동료가 병가 중이다.

남자 대사에서 정답을 노리고 why 질문의 경우 미리 들을 내용을 파악해 두는 것이 필수적이다. 남자가 보고서를 끝내지 못하는 상황이란 점을 미리 알고, 이 부분을 집중해서 듣자. 동료가 장비 리스트와 가격 견적을 주기를 기다리고 있다고 했고, I can't finish the report without that information(그 정보 없이는 보고서를 끝낼 수 없다)이라고 했으므로 정답은 (C)이다.

52 What does the woman offer to do?
(A) Calculate some prices
(B) Extend a deadline
(C) Deliver a document
(D) Speak to a colleague

여자는 무엇을 해 주겠다고 하는가?
(A) 가격 계산하기
(B) 마감 연장하기
(C) 문서 전달하기
(D) 동료에게 이야기하기

여자 대사에서 남자를 위해 해 주겠다는 내용을 노려 듣는다. 보통 would you like me to, do you want me to는 이런 제공 표현에 대한 힌트어가 되므로 암기해 두자. 여자가 Do you want me to remind Janice라고 말한 부분이 정답이 되고 Janice는 a colleague(동료)로 바꿔 표현되었다.

Questions 53-55 refer to the following conversation. 영W 미M

W Hello. I saw your ad for the two-bedroom apartment on First Avenue for rent in today's newspaper. Is it still vacant?

M Yes. We're currently looking for a renter who can move in before September 1st. The apartment is in great condition and it actually has the only bedroom in the entire building that faces the river. So the view is fantastic. If you would like to come see it, I can arrange a time for you.

W I'd love that. I'll be free after 3 P.M. tomorrow.

M Why don't you visit my office on Royce Street first at 4 tomorrow? I'll show you some photos of other available places as well.

여 여보세요. 제가 오늘 신문에서 임대용으로 나온 First Avenue에 있는 방 2개짜리 아파트 광고를 보았습니다. 그건 아직 비어 있나요?

남 네. 9월 1일전에 이사올 수 있는 세입자를 지금 찾고 있는 중입니다. 아파트는 매우 좋은 상태이고 전체 건물에서 강 쪽을 향하는 침실을 유일하게 가지고 있습니다. 그래서 경치가 환상적이죠. 오셔서 보고 싶으시면, 제가 시간을 잡아 드리겠습니다.

여 좋습니다. 내일 오후 3시 이후에 시간이 됩니다.

남 Royce 가에 있는 제 사무실로 내일 4시에 먼저 오시는 건 어떠세요? 다른 이용 가능한 곳들의 사진도 보여 드릴게요.

ad 광고 for rent 임대용의 vacant 비어 있는 currently 현재, 지금 renter 세입자 in great condition 좋은 상태인 face 바라보다, 향하다 arrange a time 시간을 잡다, 스케줄을 정하다

53 Who is the woman talking to?
(A) A real estate agent
(B) A park ranger
(C) An apartment janitor
(D) A photographer

여자는 누구에게 이야기하고 있는가?
(A) 부동산 중개인
(B) 공원 관리원
(C) 아파트 수위
(D) 사진사

질문은 여자가 이야기하는 상대방, 즉 남자가 누구인지를 유추하는 문제이다. 도입부에 여자가 남자에게 아파트 임대 광고를 봤다고 말하며 아직 비어 있는지 물었을 때, 남자는 부동산 중개인임을 알 수 있다.

54 What does the man say about the apartment?
(A) It is located on Royce Street.
(B) It has a nice view.
(C) It is fully furnished.
(D) It needs repairing.

남자는 아파트에 관하여 무엇을 말하는가?
(A) Royce 가에 있다.
(B) 전망이 좋다.
(C) 가구가 비치되어 있다.
(D) 고칠 필요가 있다.

세부 사항 질문으로 남자 대사에서 아파트에 관해 언급된 것이 정답이 된다. it actually has the only bedroom in the entire building that faces the river(건물 전체에서 강을 바라보는 침실을 가지고 있는 유일한 아파트)라고 했으므로, 이를 a nice view가 있다고 바꿔 표현한 (B)가 정답이다. (A)는 남자의 사무실이 Royce 가에 있다고 했으므로 오답이고, 나머지 (C)와 (D)는 언급되지 않았다.

55 What does the woman mean when she says, "I'd love that"?
(A) She would like to sign a contract.
(B) She would like to move into a new apartment.
(C) She would like to look at the property.
(D) She would like to leave the office early.

여자가 "좋습니다"라고 말한 의미는 무엇인가?
(A) 그녀는 계약서에 서명을 하고 싶다.
(B) 그녀는 새 아파트로 이사 가고 싶다.
(C) 그녀는 부동산을 보고 싶다.
(D) 그녀는 일찍 퇴근하고 싶다.

여자가 해당 표현을 언급한 앞뒤 문맥에서 정답의 단서를 찾자. 아파트를 보고 싶다면 시간을 잡아 주겠다는 남자의 제안에 대해 I'd love that(좋습니다)라고 말하며 3시 이후에 시간이 된다고 했으므로 정답은 (C)가 된다.

Questions 56-58 refer to the following conversation. 영M 영W

M Hello, I'm calling to get some information about your intercity high-speed trains. Is it possible for me to take my bicycle on the train? And are there any other regulations I should know about?

W Well, you're allowed to take your bicycle on the train. But you should avoid traveling during the rush hour and on weekends since it gets really crowded. It's generally less crowded between 11 a.m. to 5 p.m. on weekdays.

M Oh, I see. Is it necessary to reserve a space for the bike in advance?

W No, you can use any bicycle rack available on the train. However, if there's no space available, you'll have to wait 10 more minutes for the next train to come.

남 여보세요, 도시간 고속 열차에 관하여 정보를 얻기 위해 전화드립니다. 기차에 자전거를 가지고 타는 것이 가능할까요? 그리고 제가 알아야 하는 어떤 다른 규정이 있나요?

여 음, 기차에 자전거를 가지고 타는 것은 허용됩니다. 그러나 주말이나 러시아워 중에는 많이 붐비기 때문에 그때 여행하는 건 피하시는 게 좋습니다. 일반적으로 주중 오전 11시부터 오후 5시까지가 덜 혼잡합니다.

남 아, 알겠습니다. 자전거를 위한 공간을 미리 예약하는 것이 필요할까요?

여 아닙니다. 기차에 비어 있는 자전거 거치대를 아무거나 사용하면 됩니다. 그러나 빈 공간이 없는 경우에는 다음 기차가 올 때까지 10분을 더 기다려야 합니다.

intercity 도시간 high-speed train 고속 열차 regulations 규정 avoid 피하다 crowded 붐비는 generally 보통, 일반적으로 weekday 주중(월요일부터 금요일까지) bicycle rack 자전거 거치대

56 What is the man interested in doing?
(A) Purchasing a special carrier
(B) Taking a highway
(C) Reserving a ticket
(D) Transporting a bicycle

남자는 무엇을 하고 싶어 하는가?
(A) 특별 운반대를 구입하는 것
(B) 고속 도로를 타는 것
(C) 표를 예매하는 것
(D) 자전거를 옮기는 것

남자 대사에서 남자가 하고 싶어 하는 일을 노려 듣는다. 대화의 도입부에 Is it possible for me to take my bicycle on the train?이라고 물었으므로 남자가 하고자 하는 일은 자전거를 기차로 옮기는 일이다. take my bicycle on the train이 transporting a bicycle로 바꿔 표현되었다.

57 What does the woman suggest the man do?
(A) Avoid a specific time
(B) Receive a group discount
(C) Pay in cash
(D) Travel with a pet

여자는 남자에게 무엇을 하라고 제안하는가?
(A) 특정 시간 피하기
(B) 그룹 할인 받기
(C) 현금으로 지불하기
(D) 애완 동물과 함께 여행하기

여자 대사에서 남자에게 하라고 권고하는 내용에 집중한다. you should avoid traveling during the rush hour and on weekends에서 러시아워와 주말을 피하라고 했으므로 이를 specific time으로 바꿔 표현한 (A)가 정답이다. 상대방에게 권고할 때 쓰는 표현인 you should를 들었을 때 정답이 나올 것을 예상할 수 있으므로 이런 표현은 암기 해두자.

58 What does the woman suggest about the bicycle racks?
(A) They can be reserved online.
(B) They were installed last year.
(C) They are provided only for the handicapped.
(D) They are available on a first come first served basis.

여자는 자전거 거치대에 관해서 무엇을 암시하는가?
(A) 온라인으로 예약될 수 있다.
(B) 작년에 설치되었다.
(C) 신체 장애자에게만 제공된다.
(D) 선착순으로 이용 가능하다.

세부 사항 질문으로 여자 대사에서 정답을 처리하되, bicycle racks에 대한 정보를 노려 듣는다. you can use any bicycle rack available on the train(기차에 비어 있는 자전거 거치대를 아무거나 이용할 수 있다)이라고 했고, 이어 빈 것이 없으면 다음 기차를 기다려야 한다고 했으므로 선착순으로 이용할 수 있다고 바꿔 표현한 (D)가 정답이 된다. on a first come first served basis는 '선착순 제도에 기반하여'라는 의미로 암기해 두자. (C)의 the handicapped는 '장애가 있는 사람들'이란 의미로 대화에서 언급되지 않았으므로 정답이 될 수 없다.

Questions 59-61 refer to the following conversation. 미W 미M

W Mr. Morris, our apologies for keeping you waiting for so long. I understand you're here to pick up your medication, right?

M Yes, my doctor ordered a medication for me by phone earlier today. It's called Zyflo and it's for my spring allergies. Is it ready yet? Oh, and I have one more question. I was thinking of taking some additional medicine to deal with my constant sneezing. But I'm not sure if it's a good idea.

W Well, most allergy medications are only available with a doctor's prescription. So if you keep experiencing discomfort after taking this medication, I recommend that you see your doctor to discuss an alternative solution.

여 Morris 씨, 오랫동안 기다리게 해서 죄송합니다. 약을 가지러 오신 것이 맞죠?

남 그렇습니다. 아까 오전에 제 담당 의사가 전화로 제 약을 주문했습니다. Zyflo라는 이름의 약이고 봄 알레르기를 위해 것입니다. 준비가 다 되었나요? 아, 그리고 질문이 하나 더 있는데요. 재채기가 계속 나와서 그걸 치료하기 위해 추가로 약을 복용해 보려고 합니다. 그런데 그게 좋은 생각인지 잘 모르겠어요.

여 음, 대부분의 알레르기 약은 의사의 처방전이 있어야 살 수 있습니다. 따라서 당신이 이 약을 복용한 후에도 계속 불편을 경험하는 경우에는, 의사를 만나서 대안에 대해 의논하는 것을 추천합니다.

apology 사과 pick up (주문한 것을) 가져가다 medication 약 spring allergy 봄 알레르기 think about -ing ~하려고 하다 additional 추가의 deal with (문제 등을) 처리하다, 다루다 constant 끊임없는, 계속되는 sneeze 재채기하다 prescription 처방전 discomfort 불편함 alternative solution 대안책

59 Why is the man at the pharmacy?
(A) To pick up some medication
(B) To apply for a position
(C) To get some directions
(D) To place an order

남자는 왜 약국에 있는가?
(A) 약을 가져가려고
(B) 일자리에 지원하려고
(C) 길 안내를 받으려고
(D) 주문을 하려고

질문으로부터 남자는 현재 약국에 있다는 정보를 미리 파악해 두고 대화를 듣자. 대화의 도입부에 여자가 I understand you're here to pick up your medication, right?(약을 가지러 오셨죠?)라고 물었고 남자가 그렇다고 답했으므로 정답은 (A)가 된다. 주문은 남자의 의사가 이미 전화로 했다고 언급했으므로 (D)는 함정이 된다.

60 What does the man imply when he says, "But I'm not sure if it's a good idea"?
(A) He thinks that the quality of a service is poor.
(B) He is unsure of the effect of additional medicine.
(C) He cannot remember the name of a nurse.
(D) He does not know the dosage of a medication.

남자가 "그런데 그게 좋은 생각인지 잘 모르겠어요"라고 말한 의도는 무엇인가?

(A) 남자는 서비스의 질이 나쁘다고 생각한다.
(B) 남자는 추가 약의 효과에 대해 확실치 않다.
(C) 남자는 간호사의 이름을 기억할 수 없다.
(D) 남자는 약물의 복용량을 모른다.

남자 대사에서 해당 표현 앞뒤의 문맥을 잘 파악하는 것이 중요하다. 남자는 재채기 때문에 추가로 약을 복용해 보려고 한다는 언급을 한 후 바로 But I'm not sure if it's a good idea(그런데 그게 좋은 생각인지 모르겠다)로 했으므로 정답은 (B)가 된다.

61 What does the woman suggest?
(A) Coming back later
(B) Using a different product
(C) Seeing a doctor
(D) Ordering online

여자는 무엇을 제안하는가?
(A) 나중에 다시 오는 것
(B) 다른 제품을 사용하는 것
(C) 의사를 만나는 것
(D) 온라인으로 주문하는 것

세부 사항 질문으로 여자가 I recommend라고 제안 표현을 말했을 때 집중한다. 의사를 만나 보는 것을 추천한다고 했으므로 정답은 (C)가 된다.

Questions 62-64 refer to the following conversation with three speakers. 미W 미M 영W

W1 Have you two finished the proposal for the Chelsea Hotel renovation?
M Yeah, I've just completed the floor plans with 3D images. How's your paperwork coming along, Luisa?
W2 I still need to go over the wording of the proposal. But it's not due until April 19th, is it?
W1 No. Didn't you get my e-mail? The clients want to meet with us at 10 tomorrow morning.
W2 **What? Tomorrow morning?** But it's already 6 o'clock now.
M I didn't know the meeting was moved up either. Is there anything I can help you with, Luisa?
W2 Thanks, but I can manage it by myself. I think I'm going to be here pretty late tonight. But don't worry. I'll make sure to complete my work before we meet the client tomorrow morning.

여1 Chelsea 호텔의 레노베이션 제안서를 다 끝내셨나요?
남 네, 지금 막 3D 이미지를 포함한 평면도를 완성했습니다. 당신의 서류작업은 어떻게 진행되고 있나요, Luisa?
여2 저는 아직 제안서의 문구를 검토해 야 해요. 하지만 마감은 4월 19일이잖아요, 그렇지 않나요?
여1 아니에요, 제 이메일을 못 받으셨나요? 고객들은 내일 아침 10시에 우리와 미팅을 하고 싶어 해요.
여2 **뭐라고요? 내일 아침이라고요?** 그렇지만 지금 벌써 6시인걸요.
남 저도 미팅이 앞당겨졌는지 몰랐어요. 제가 도와 드릴 게 있을까요, Luisa?
여2 고맙지만 혼자 할 수 있어요. 오늘 밤 늦게까지 여기 있어야겠네요. 그렇지만 걱정 마세요. 내일 아침 고객 미팅 전까지는 제 업무를 반드시 끝낼게요.

floor plan 평면도 paperwork 서류 작업 get along (진척 사항을 물을 때) 되어가다 move up (일정을) 앞당기다

62 Where do the speakers probably work?
(A) At an architectural firm
(B) At a hotel
(C) At a publishing company
(D) At a photo studio

화자들은 어디에서 일할 것 같은가?
(A) 건축회사
(B) 호텔
(C) 출판사
(D) 사진관

화자들의 업무 내용으로부터 직장을 유추하는 문제이다. 도입부에 여자가 호텔 레노베이션에 대한 제안서를 다 끝냈는지 묻는 것을 통해 화자들은 (A)건축회사에서 일한다는 것을 유추할 수 있다. 첫 문장 Have you two finished the proposal for the Chelsea Hotel renovation?에서 이미 정답의 단서가 등장하므로 도입부에 대한 집중력을 높여 듣는 훈련을 하자.

63 Why does Luisa say, "What? Tomorrow morning"?
(A) She has missed a client meeting.
(B) She plans to take the day off tomorrow.
(C) She was not aware of a change in the schedule.
(D) She disagrees with her coworkers.

Luisa는 왜 "뭐라고요? 내일 아침이라고요"라고 말하는가?
(A) 그녀는 고객 미팅을 놓쳤다.
(B) 그녀는 내일 휴가를 가질 계획이다.
(C) 그녀는 스케줄 변경에 대해 몰랐다.
(D) 그녀는 동료들에게 동의하지 않는다.

특정 표현에 대한 화자의 의도를 묻는 신토익 유형이다. 여성 화자가 두 명 등장하므로 Luisa라는 이름이 누구인지 파악해두자. 고객 미팅이 내일로 바뀌었음을 말했을 때 "What? Tomorrow morning?"이라고 깜짝 놀라며 반문하는 것을 통해 여자는 미팅이 앞당겨졌음을 모르고 있었다고 추론할 수 있다. 그러므로 정답은 (C)가 된다.

64 What will Luisa probably do tonight?
(A) Start a renovation
(B) Schedule a meeting
(C) Write a new contract
(D) Work overtime

Luisa는 오늘 밤에 무엇을 할 것 같은가?
(A) 공사 시작하기
(B) 미팅의 일정 잡기
(C) 새 계약서 쓰기
(D) 야근하기

3인 대화 상황을 다룬 신토익 유형으로 여성 화자가 두 명 등장하므로 Luisa라는 이름이 누구인지 파악해 두고 질문의 키워드인 tonight에 집중해서 정답의 단서를 찾는다. Luisa는 오늘 밤 사무실에 늦게까지 있어야겠다고 말하며 업무를 끝내 놓겠다고 했으므로 정답은 (D) 야근을 하는 것이 된다.

Questions 65-67 refer to the following conversation and list. 영M 영W

M Hey Alyssa, how many people are attending tomorrow's lunch meeting?
W Including our manager, Mr. Phillips, there will be 20 of us.
M Oh, that's more than we expected. Do we have enough seats for everyone?
W Yes, I already put some extra chairs in the main meeting room to accommodate everyone.
M That's good. And did you order catering too?
W Oh, yes. I ordered food from the same catering company we used last month, Wally's Fresh Catering. Here's the list of dishes I ordered.
M Hmm... people said that the sandwiches were really good last time. Why don't we order some more of the sandwich platters? And I think it is okay to skip on desserts.
W All right. I'll call the caterer to add two more sandwich platters and remove the last item on our order.

Wally's Fresh Catering	
Customer: Alyssa Kim	Order Number: N00013
Item	Quantity
Mixed Sandwich Platter	5 platters
Cheese & Olive Tray	3 trays
Lemonade	20 glasses
Dark Chocolate Cake	12 pieces

남 Alyssa, 내일 점심 미팅에는 몇 명이 참석하나요?
여 저희 매니저인 Phillips 씨를 포함해서 20명이 될 겁니다.
남 오, 우리 예상보다 더 많군요. 좌석이 충분히 있나요?
여 네, 모두 앉을 수 있도록 이미 대회의실에 의자를 추가로 갖다 놓았습니다.
남 잘됐네요. 그리고 출장 음식도 주문하셨나요?
여 아, 네. 지난달에 우리가 이용했던 출장 요리 업체인 Wally's Fresh Catering에서 주문했습니다. 여기 주문한 음식 목록이에요.
남 흠… 사람들이 지난번에 샌드위치가 맛있다고 했었죠. 샌드위치 플래터를 더 주문하는 게 어때요? 그리고 디저트는 없어도 괜찮을 것 같네요.
여 알겠습니다. 제가 업체에 전화해서 샌드위치 플래터를 2개 더 주문하고 주문서의 마지막 품목을 빼도록 하겠습니다.

Wally's Fresh Catering	
고객명: Alyssa Kim	주문 번호: N00013
품목	양
혼합 샌드위치 플래터	5접시
치즈와 올리브 트레이	3접시
레모네이드	20잔
진한 초콜릿 케이크	12조각

sandwich platter (다양한 종류의) 샌드위치 skip 지나치다 remove 없애다, 제거하다

65 What are the speakers discussing?
(A) The details of a meeting
(B) The location of an office
(C) The price of an item
(D) The business hours of a restaurant

화자들은 무엇에 대해 논의 중인가?
(A) 미팅의 세부 사항
(B) 사무실의 위치
(C) 상품의 가격
(D) 레스토랑의 영업 시간

대화의 도입부에서 남자가 내일 점심 미팅에 몇 명이 참석하는지를 묻고 좌석이 충분한지 등을 파악하는 것에서 정답을 (A)로 선택한다.

66 What does the woman mention about Wally's Fresh Catering?
(A) It offers a wide range of menu options.
(B) Its prices are reasonable.
(C) Many people are happy with its service.
(D) She has used the company before.

여자는 Wally's Fresh Catering에 대해서 무엇을 언급하는가?
(A) 다양한 메뉴를 제공한다.
(B) 가격이 합리적이다.
(C) 많은 사람들이 서비스에 만족한다.
(D) 여자는 전에 이 회사를 이용한 적이 있다.

여자 대사에서 Wally's Fresh Catering이라는 업체가 언급되는 부분을 놓치지 않고 파악하자. I ordered food from the same catering company we used last month, Wally's Fresh Catering 부분에서 여자는 지난달에도 이 업체에 주문했었음을 알 수 있다. 정답은 (D)가 된다.

67 Look at the graphic. Which item will be eliminated from the order form?
(A) Mixed Sandwich Platter
(B) Cheese & Olive Tray
(C) Lemonade
(D) Dark Chocolate Cake

시각 정보를 보시오. 어떤 품목이 주문서에서 빠지게 될 것인가?
(A) 혼합 샌드위치 플래터
(B) 치즈와 올리브 트레이
(C) 레모네이드
(D) 진한 초콜릿 케이크

기존의 주문서를 보면서 변경하는 내용에 정답이 있다. 샌드위치를 더 주문하고 it is okay to skip on desserts(디저트는 없어도 괜찮다)라고 말했으므로 디저트에 해당하는 초콜릿 케이크가 빠지게 될 것임을 알 수 있다. 정답은 (D)이다.

Questions 68-70 refer to the following conversation and chart.
미M 미W

M Ms. Tanaka, as you can see from the chart, our annual car sales decreased a lot last year.

W You're right. It doesn't look good. Although our compact models continued to be in high demand, our large automobiles did not sell well.

M Yes. In fact, the sales of our C-1 and G-1 models have been pretty weak in Europe as well.

W One thing that interests me, though, is that the G-2 and X-5 are both compact models, yet one sold much better than the other.

M Oh, that model is actually our best seller in Europe as well.

W Could you look into why this model is the most popular both here and overseas? I'd like to talk more about it at the next department meeting.

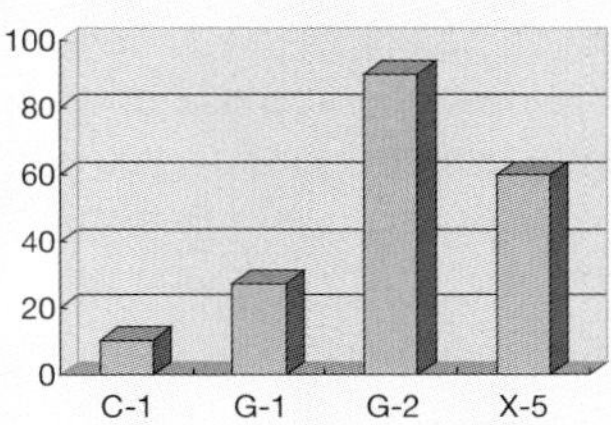

남 Tanaka 씨, 차트에서 보시는 것과 같이 우리 연간 자동차 판매가 작년에 매우 줄었습니다.

여 그렇군요. 좋지 않아 보이네요. 소형차 모델들은 계속해서 수요가 많았지만, 큰 차량들은 잘 팔리지 않았군요.

남 네, 사실 C-1과 G-1의 판매는 유럽에서도 매우 약했어요.

여 그런데 한가지 흥미로운 점은 G-2와 X-5는 둘 다 소형차인데도 한 모델이 다른 것보다 훨씬 잘 팔렸다는 거예요.

남 아, 그 모델은 유럽에서도 베스트셀러예요.

여 왜 이 모델이 국내와 해외에서 가장 인기가 많은지 조사를 해주시겠어요? 다음 부서 회의 때 이것에 대해 더 이야기를 나누고 싶네요.

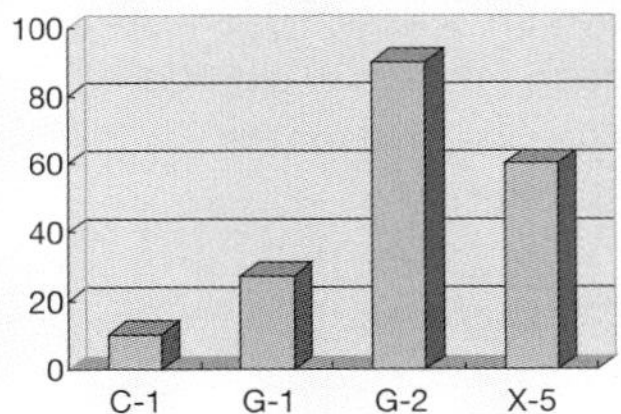

decrease 감소하다 in high demand 수요가 높은 particular 특정한, 특별한 overseas 해외에서

68 What are the speakers mainly discussing?
(A) Import and export regulations
(B) Concerns about the company's sales
(C) The launch of a new luxury sedan
(D) Safety regulations for automobiles

화자들은 무엇에 대해 주로 이야기하는가?
(A) 수출입 규정
(B) 회사 판매에 대한 염려
(C) 새로운 고급 세단의 출시
(D) 자동차에 대한 안전 규정

주제를 찾는 문제는 대화의 도입부에서 해결하자. 작년 자동차 판매 수치가 많이 줄었다는 이야기로 대화를 시작했으므로 정답은 (B)가 된다.

69 What problem is being discussed?
(A) Sales of bigger vehicles have decreased.
(B) The supply cannot meet the demand.
(C) The workers are on strike.
(D) Compact cars did not appeal to European customers.

어떤 문제점이 논의되고 있는가?
(A) 큰 차량의 판매가 감소했다.
(B) 공급이 수요를 따라가지 못한다.
(C) 직원들이 파업하였다.
(D) 소형차들이 유럽 고객들의 관심을 끌지 못했다.

회사의 연간 판매가 감소한 이유로서 Although our compct models continued to be in high demand, our large automobiles did not sell well(소형차는 여전히 수요가 높았지만 큰 차량들은 잘 팔리지 않았다)이라고 언급했으므로 정답은 (A)가 된다.

70 Look at the graphic. Which car model does the woman ask the man to investigate?
(A) C-1
(B) G-1
(C) G-2
(D) X-5

시각 정보를 보시오. 여자는 남자에게 어떤 차 모델을 조사해달라고 하는가?
(A) C-1
(B) G-1
(C) G-2
(D) X-5

시각 정보를 활용해서 정답을 구하는 신토익 유형이다. 여자는 남자에게 G-2와 X-5모델 중 한 모델이 특히 더 잘 팔렸으니 조사해 달라고 요청을 한다. 차트상 두 모델 중 판매 수치가 높은 것은 G-2이므로 정답은 (C)가 된다.

PART 4

Questions 71-73 refer to the following talk. (미W)

Thank you for all coming in today for training. My name is Sophia Wilson, the manager here at Ballistic Shrimp. You've been hired to serve diners during the tourist season, which begins tomorrow. We have a lot to cover today, but first I'd like each of you to change into a uniform. After that, we're going to review our menu items along with the wine list.

오늘 교육을 위해 모두 와 주셔서 감사합니다. 저는 Sophia Wilson으로, 이곳 Ballistic Shrimp의 매니저입니다. 여러분은 내일부터 시작되는 관광 시즌 동안 서빙을 하기 위하여 고용되었습니다. 우리는 오늘 다룰 내용이 많습니다. 그러나 먼저 여러분이 유니폼으로 갈아입었으면 좋겠습니다. 그 후에 와인 메뉴와 함께 식사 메뉴들을 검토해 볼 것입니다.

diner 식사하러 온 손님 tourist season 관광 시즌 change into ~로 갈아 입다 wine list 와인 메뉴

71 Who most likely is the speaker?
(A) A new waitress
(B) A restaurant manager
(C) A regular customer
(D) A food critic

화자는 누구일 것 같은가?
(A) 새로운 웨이트리스
(B) 레스토랑 매니저
(C) 단골 손님
(D) 음식 비평가

화자의 직업을 유추하는 문제로 도입부에 본인을 소개할 때 My name is Sophia Wilson, the manager here at Ballistic Shrimp라고 이름과 함께 직위를 매니저로 밝혔으므로 정답은 (B)이다.

72 What does the speaker say will happen tomorrow?
(A) A free beverage will be served.
(B) A jazz band will play.
(C) A restaurant will be inspected.
(D) A busy season will begin.

화자는 내일 무엇이 일어날 거라고 말하는가?
(A) 무료 음료가 대접될 것이다.
(B) 재즈 밴드가 공연할 것이다.
(C) 레스토랑이 검사 받을 것이다.
(D) 바쁜 시즌이 시작될 것이다.

세부 사항 질문으로 키워드는 tomorrow이다. the tourist season, which begins tomorrow에서 내일 관광 시즌이 시작된다고 했으므로 tourist season을 busy season으로 바꿔 표현한 (D)가 정답이다.

73 What will listeners most likely do next?
(A) Memorize menu items
(B) Prepare food
(C) Put on a uniform
(D) Sign a contract

청자들은 다음에 무엇을 할 것 같은가?
(A) 메뉴 항목 암기하기
(B) 음식 준비하기
(C) 유니폼 입기
(D) 계약서에 서명하기

향후 행동 질문은 담화가 끝난 후 바로 할 행동을 묻는 것으로 내용상 do first에 해당하는 것이 정답이 된다. 교육 일정을 알려 주면서 first I'd like each of you to change into a uniform(먼저 유니폼으로 갈아입으세요)이라고 요청했으므로 담화가 끝난 후 청자들이 할 일은 (C)가 된다. 그 후에 메뉴를 살펴보겠다고 했으므로 (A)는 함정으로 쓰인 것이다.

Questions 74-76 refer to the following radio broadcast. (영M)

Don't forget that all public schools, banks and government offices will be closed tomorrow in observance of the national holiday. There will be a number of events and activities, such as traditional dancing, music and feasts, to celebrate and share in the culture of the Aboriginal people. If you're planning to attend one of the events in your region, you should leave early to ensure yourself a good spot. And, if you're going to take the subway, you will be pleased to know that you can ride free on the subway all day tomorrow. Now, here's Joseph with the weather report.

내일 모든 공립학교, 은행과 정부 기관들이 국경일을 준수하기 위하여 문을 닫는다는 것을 잊지 마십시오. 원주민 문화를 나누고 기념하기 위해서 전통 댄스와 음악, 연회와 같은 다양한 행사와 활동이 열릴 것입니다. 여러분의 지역에서 열리는 행사 중 하나에 참석하려고 한다면, 좋은 자리를 확보하기 위해서 일찍 출발하는 것이 좋겠습니다. 그리고, 지하철을 타는 경우에는, 내일 하루 종일 지하철을 무료로 탈 수 있습니다. 다음은 일기 예보의 Joseph입니다.

in observance of ~을 준수하여 a number of 많은, 다양한 feast 연회, 만찬 share in ~을 서로 나누다 region 지역 ensure 확보하다, 확실히 하다 good spot 좋은 자리

74 What is the purpose of the broadcast?
(A) To interview a famous author
(B) To advertise a local music festival
(C) To inform listeners of a holiday
(D) To announce road repairs

방송의 목적은 무엇인가?
(A) 유명한 작가를 인터뷰하려고
(B) 지역 음악 축제를 광고하려고
(C) 청자에게 휴일에 대해 알리려고
(D) 도로 수리를 발표하려고

도입부의 내용에 집중하여 목적을 파악한다. 모든 학교와 정부 기관 등이 휴일을 준수하여 문을 닫는다고 했으므로 정답은 (C)가 된다. 그 이후에도 휴일 관련 행사와 혜택에 대한 정보가 주어짐을 파악하자.

75 What does the speaker recommend listeners should do?
(A) Purchase tickets online
(B) Leave early for an event

(C) Listen to a radio show
(D) Use a different road

화자는 청취자들이 무엇을 하라고 권고하는가?
(A) 온라인으로 표 구입하기
(B) 행사를 위해 일찍 떠나기
(C) 라디오 쇼를 경청하기
(D) 다른 도로 이용하기

화자가 권고 표현과 함께 말해주는 내용에 집중하자. 행사에 참석한다면, you should leave early to ensure yourself a good spot이라고 했으므로 일찍 출발할 것을 권고한다고 알 수 있다. 정답은 (B)이다.

76 What does the speaker mention about the subway?
(A) Service will be provided free of charge.
(B) An extra route will be added.
(C) The timetable has been revised.
(D) More frequent services have been demanded.

화자는 지하철에 관하여 무엇을 언급하는가?
(A) 서비스가 무료로 제공될 것이다.
(B) 노선이 하나 더 추가될 것이다.
(C) 스케줄 표가 수정되었다.
(D) 더 빈번한 서비스가 요구되었다.

키워드인 subway에 집중하고 선택지와 일치하는 정보가 나올 때 정답으로 처리한다. if you're going to take the subway 부분에서 하루 종일 무료로 탈 수 있다고 언급된 내용이 정답이다. ride free on the subway를 service will be provided free of charge로 바꿔 표현하였다.

Questions 77-79 refer to the following radio report. (영W)

This is Alicia Chung with today's business news. Macy's, the biggest shopping mall chain in North America, announced the completion of its new shopping complex today. Due to the severe snowstorms over the winter, the grand opening of the new facility has been postponed several times. However, this modern, high-tech complex, located in the heart of the city, is expected to create at least 600 new jobs and boost the local economy. The spokesperson for Macy's announced today that the shopping center will offer a variety of promotional events during the first month of business. Today through the weekend, all visitors to the shopping center will receive a 10 percent discount on all their purchases.

오늘의 비즈니스 뉴스의 Alicia Chung입니다. 북아메리카에 있는 가장 큰 쇼핑몰 체인, Macy's가 새 복합 쇼핑몰의 완공을 오늘 발표했습니다. 겨울 내내 혹독한 눈보라 때문에 새 시설의 개관식은 몇 차례 연기되었습니다. 그러나, 도시의 한복판에 위치한 이 현대적인 최신식 시설물은 적어도 600개의 새로운 일자리를 창출하고 지역 경제를 신장시켜 줄 것으로 예상됩니다. Macy's의 대변인은 쇼핑센터가 영업 첫 달에 다양한 판촉 행사들을 제공할 것이라고 밝혔습니다. 오늘부터 주말까지 쇼핑센터의 모든 방문자는 그들의 구입 품목 전체의 10퍼센트를 할인 받을 수 있습니다.

completion 완성, 완공 complex 복합 시설물 severe 혹독한 postpone 연기하다 high-tech 최신식의 in the heart of ~의 중심부에 boost 신장시키다 promotional 판매 촉진의 purchase 구입 품목

77 What is the report about?
(A) A construction company
(B) A marketing company
(C) A conference center
(D) A shopping mall

보도는 무엇에 관한 것인가?
(A) 건축 회사
(B) 마케팅 회사
(C) 컨퍼런스 센터
(D) 쇼핑몰

보도의 주제를 묻는 질문으로 도입부에 쇼핑몰 체인인 Macy's가 새 복합 쇼핑몰을 완공했다고 알렸으므로 정답은 (D)가 된다.

78 Why was the construction delayed?
(A) Equipment malfunction
(B) Poor weather conditions
(C) A series of strikes
(D) A lack of construction materials

건설은 왜 연기되었는가?
(A) 장비 오작동
(B) 안 좋은 날씨 상태
(C) 일련의 파업
(D) 건축 자재의 부족

세부 사항 질문으로 미리 건설이 연기되었음을 파악해 두고 이유에 집중한다. due to가 들리면 이유에 대해 언급하는 것이므로 집중한다. severe snowstorms 때문이라고 했으므로 정답은 (B)가 된다.

79 What will the business provide for the first month?
(A) Gift certificates
(B) Reduced prices
(C) Shuttle services
(D) Meal vouchers

업체는 첫 한 달 동안 무엇을 제공할 것인가?
(A) 상품권
(B) 가격 할인
(C) 셔틀 서비스
(D) 식사 쿠폰

세부 사항 질문으로 first month 동안의 혜택에 주목한다. 모든 쇼핑객들이 10퍼센트의 할인을 받을 수 있다고 했으므로 정답은 (B)가 된다.

Questions 80-82 refer to the following recorded message. (미M)

Hi, you've reached Rico Restaurant. We're open from 11 a.m. to 10 p.m. from Monday to Friday and from 9 a.m. to 10 p.m. on the weekends. But today, we'll be closed in the afternoon for a private luncheon and reopen for dinner at 5 p.m. We also have an important update for all customers! This Saturday, we're having the grand opening of our second location at 24th Street and Jackson, across from City Lake. You can enjoy the same, delicious food. And only at our new location, we're offering free in-store cooking classes every Wednesday at 9 a.m. For more information about the classes, please leave a message with your name and number. Joanna, our restaurant manager, will return your call as soon as possible.

안녕하세요, Rico Restaurant입니다. 저희는 월요일부터 금요일까지는 오전 11시에서 저녁 10시까지, 주말에는 오전 9시에서 저녁 10시까지 문을 엽니다. 그러나 오늘은 사적인 오찬으로 인해 오후에 문을 닫고 저녁 5시에 다시 문을 엽니다. 모든 고객들께 다른 중요한 공지가 있습니다! 이번 주 토요일, 우리는 City Lake 건너편에 있는 24번가와 Jackson 가에 두 번째 지점을 오픈하고 그곳에서도 똑같이 맛있는 음식을 즐기실 수 있습니다. 그리고 오직 새 지점에서만, 매주 수요일 오전 9시에 매장 안에서 무료로 요리 수업을 제공합니다. 수업에 관해 더 많은 정보를 원하시면 이름과 전화번호를 메시지로 남겨 주세요. 저희 레스토랑 매니저인 Joanna가 최대한 빨리 응답전화를 드릴 것입니다.

private luncheon 비공개의 사적인 오찬 update 새로운 소식 location 지점 in-store 매장내의

80 Why will the restaurant be closed until 5 P.M.?
(A) To celebrate the opening of the new building
(B) To host a private function
(C) To restock ingredients
(D) To train some employees

레스토랑은 왜 오후 5시까지 문을 닫는가?
(A) 새 건물의 개관을 축하하려고
(B) 개인적인 행사를 열려고
(C) 재료의 재고를 보충하려고
(D) 직원을 교육하려고

세부 사항 질문으로 오후 5시까지는 레스토랑이 문을 닫는다는 정보를 미리 파악해 두자. 해당 내용이 언급될 때 for a private luncheon(사적인 오찬)이라고 했으므로 정답은 (B)가 된다. function은 event와 같이 '행사'라는 뜻이 있다.

81 What news does the speaker mention about the restaurant?
(A) It is adding a new location.
(B) It is moving to a different city
(C) It is serving some exotic dishes.
(D) It is hiring a renowned chef.

화자는 레스토랑에 관하여 어떤 뉴스를 언급하는가?
(A) 새로운 지점을 추가한다.
(B) 다른 도시로 이전한다.
(C) 이국적인 요리를 제공한다.
(D) 유명한 요리사를 고용한다.

레스토랑에 관한 내용 중 important update가 있다고 말하며 we're having the grand opening of our second location이라고 했으므로 두 번째 지점을 열 것임을 알 수 있다. 정답은 (A)가 된다.

82 What is offered at the new restaurant for free?
(A) Meal vouchers
(B) Wine tasting events
(C) Cooking classes
(D) Homemade cakes

레스토랑에서 공짜로 제공되는 것은 무엇인가?
(A) 식사 쿠폰
(B) 와인 시음 행사
(C) 요리 수업
(D) 홈메이드 케이크

세부 사항 질문으로 for free(공짜)에 집중한다. 새로운 지점에서만 무료 요리 수업을 제공한다고 했으므로 정답은 (C)이다.

Questions 83-85 refer to the following excerpt from a meeting. (영M)

First, I'd like to talk about the new recycling procedures. We've recently changed recycling companies to Blue Planet Recycling Inc. With the previous company we had to use 4 different bins, and many of you did not appreciate the fact that those bins were taking up a lot of office space. **But it's going to be different with the new company.** Now, you can put all the recyclable materials into one container. But please make sure you put only recyclable materials into the bin. If you're not sure whether or not a material can be recycled, please check the list of recyclable materials, which is posted near the container.

첫 번째로 저는 새로운 재활용 절차에 대해서 이야기하고 싶습니다. 우리는 최근에 재활용 업체를 Blue Planet Recycling으로 바꾸었습니다. 이전 회사와는 4개의 다른 재활용 용기를 이용해야 했었고, 여러분 중 다수가 그 용기들이 사무실 공간을 많이 차지한다는 점에 대해서 좋아하지 않았습니다. **그러나 새 회사에서는 다를 것입니다.** 이제 한 개의 통에 모든 재활용이 가능한 물건을 넣을 수 있게 되었습니다. 반드시 재활용이 가능한 물건만 용기 안에 넣어 주세요. 어떤 물건이 재활용 가능한 것인지 확실하지 않은 경우, 용기 근처에 붙어 있는 공지에서 재활용 가능 물품의 명단을 확인해 주십시오.

recycling procedures 재활용 절차 previous 이전의 bin 용기, 통 take up (공간을) 차지하다 container 용기, 통 material 물질, 재질, 물건 recyclable 재활용 할 수 있는 notice 공지

83 What change has the company recently made?
(A) It has adopted a strict recycling policy.
(B) It has moved to a more spacious office.
(C) It has replaced a service provider.
(D) It has hired additional employees.

회사는 최근에 무엇을 변경했는가?
(A) 엄격한 재활용 정책을 채택했다.
(B) 더 넓은 사무실로 이전했다.
(C) 서비스 제공 업체를 교체했다.
(D) 추가 직원을 고용했다.

회사가 변경한 내용을 묻는 세부 사항 질문으로 We've recently changed recycling companies to Blue Planet Recycling Inc.에서 재활용 업체를 바꿨다고 말하며 새로운 회사의 이름을 말해주고 있으므로 정답을 (C)로 선택한다. recycling company를 service provider로 바꿔 표현하고 있다.

84 What does the speaker mean when he says, "But it's going to be different with the new company"?
(A) Uncomfortable office furniture will be replaced soon.
(B) Problems regarding insufficient office space will be resolved.
(C) The company will purchase new office equipment.
(D) Employees will not need to do unnecessary paperwork.

화자가 "그러나 새 회사에서는 다를 것입니다"라고 말한 의미는 무엇인가?
(A) 불편한 사무 가구가 곧 교체될 것이다.
(B) 부족한 사무실 공간에 관한 문제점이 해결될 것이다.
(C) 회사는 새 사무 기기를 구매할 것이다.
(D) 직원들은 불필요한 문서 업무를 할 필요가 없을 것이다.

해당 표현의 앞뒤 문맥을 통해 의미를 유추하는 것이 중요하다. 기존 회사는 4개의 재활용 용기를 써서 사무실 공간 부족에 대한 불평이 많았다는 점을 언급한 후 But it's going to be different with the new company(새 회사에서는 다를 것이다)라고 말했으므로 사무 공간 부족이 해결될 것이란 의미가 된다. 새로운 회사는 1개의 용기만을 사용할 것이라고 덧붙여 설명한 것이 이를 뒷받침한다. 정답은 (B)가 된다.

85 What are listeners encouraged to do?
(A) Read a list
(B) E-mail a supplier
(C) Conserve paper
(D) Work overtime

청자들은 무엇을 하라고 권고되는가?
(A) 목록 읽기
(B) 공급자에게 이메일 보내기
(C) 종이 아껴 쓰기
(D) 시간 외 근무하기

화자가 요청/권고하는 표현과 함께 언급한 내용을 찾는다. please check the notice에서 공지를 확인하라고 했고, 공지에서 재활용 가능한 물품 명단을 볼 수 있다고 했으므로 정답은 (A)이다.

Questions 86-88 refer to the following excerpt from a meeting. 영W

Attention everyone. Let me begin today's staff meeting by explaining the company policy on handling customer data. Many customers have recently asked questions about the type and amount of personal information we collect and how we protect it from misuse. It is clearly stated in the policy that you're allowed to access the transaction history of your customers in the system in order to serve them better. However, you must not replicate any customer data or store it on other storage devices. Once again, please be extra cautious about handling customer information.

모두 집중해 주세요. 오늘 직원 회의는 고객 자료를 취급하는 것에 대한 회사 정책을 설명하면서 시작하겠습니다. 최근 들어 많은 고객이 우리가 모으는 인적 사항의 유형과 양 그리고 그것이 잘못 사용되지 않도록 보호하는 방법에 관해서 질문을 하고 있습니다. 회사의 정책에 명확하게 명시되어 있는 대로 여러분은 고객을 더 잘 모시기 위해서 고객의 계약 내역에 접근하는 것이 허락됩니다. 그러나 여러분은 어떤 고객 자료든지 복제하거나 다른 저장 장치에 저장해서는 안 됩니다. 다시 한 번, 고객 정보 취급에 관하여 주의를 더욱 기울여 주십시오.

company policy 회사 정책 handle 처리하다, 다루다 collect 수집하다 misuse 오용, 잘못된 사용 transaction history 과거 계약 내역 replicate 복제하다 storage device 저장 장치 be extra cautious 더욱 주의를 기울이다

86 What is the talk mainly about?
(A) Handling certain data
(B) Responding to complaints
(C) Training new employees
(D) Installing some software

담화는 주로 무엇에 관한 것인가?
(A) 특정 자료를 취급하는 것
(B) 불만에 응대하는 것
(C) 신입 직원을 교육하는 것
(D) 소프트웨어를 설치하는 것

주제를 묻는 질문으로 도입부의 the company policy on handling customer data를 듣고 정답을 (A)로 선택한다. customer data는 certain data로 바꿔 표현되었다.

87 What have some customers asked questions about?
(A) Who to speak to about technical difficulties
(B) When a scheduled update takes place
(C) Where to get a certificate issued
(D) How their information is protected

고객은 무엇에 관하여 질문했는가?
(A) 기술적인 문제에 대해 누구와 얘기할지
(B) 예정된 업데이트가 언제 발생하는지
(C) 증명서를 어디에서 발급받는지
(D) 그들의 정보가 어떻게 보호되는지

세부 사항 질문으로 키워드인 customers, asked questions가 언급되는 주변에 답이 있다. 고객들이 질문을 하는 내용으로 언급된 것은 the type and amount of personal information we collect and how we protect it from misuse인데 그중 선택지와 일치하는 정보는 how we protect it from misuse(고객 정보가 오용되지 않도록 어떻게 보호하는지)이다. 정답은 (D)가 된다.

88 What are employees asked to refrain from?
(A) Viewing business contracts
(B) Reporting technical problems
(C) Copying restricted information
(D) Purchasing extra office supplies

직원은 무엇을 하지 않도록 요청 받는가?
(A) 사업 계약서를 보는 것
(B) 기술 문제를 보고하는 것
(C) 제한된 정보를 복제하는 것
(D) 여분의 사무용품을 구입하는 것

세부 사항 질문으로 직원들이 하지 말아야 할 일을 선택하는 것이 포인트이다. 고객 정보를 취급하는 정책으로 you must not replicate any customer data or store it on other storage devices라고 했으므로 정답은 (C)가 된다. customer data가 restricted information으로 바꿔 표현되었다.

Questions 89-91 refer to the following talk. 미W

Welcome everyone to Springfield State Park. My name is Jessica Holmes and I'll be your guide tonight. As you may know, this is one of the best places in the region to see stars in the sky. In order for you to enjoy your stargazing experience tonight, you should first listen to the explanation about naked-eye observations, which will take place right here in the visitor's center. You'll learn how to read a sky map and how to recognize the main stars. And if you're serious about stargazing, you can visit our website for monthly sky-watching information. All right everyone, let's get started.

Springfield 주립 공원에 오신 모든 분들을 환영합니다. 저는 Jessica Homes이고 오늘 밤 여러분의 가이드가 될 것입니다. 아시겠지만, 이 곳은 이 지역에서 하늘의 별을 가장 잘 볼 수 있는 최고의 장소 중 하나입니다. 여러분이 오늘 밤 별 관측 경험을 즐길 수 있도록, 이곳 방문자 센터에서 육안 관측에 관한 설명을 잘 들어 주십시오. 여러분은 별자리를 보는 방법과 중요한 별들을 알아보는 방법을 배우게 될 것입니다. 그리고 만약 여러분이 별 관측을 진지하게 생각한다면, 저희 웹 사이트에 방문하셔서 매달 진행되는 천체 관측에 대한 정보를 더 보실 수 있습니다. 좋습니다 여러분. 이제 시작합시다.

stargazing 별 관측 explanation 설명 naked-eye observation (기기를 사용하지 않는) 육안 관측 sky map 별자리 지도 recognize 알아보다 be serious about ~에 대하여 진지하다 sky-watching 천체 관측

89 Where is the talk most likely taking place?
(A) In a laboratory
(B) In a theater
(C) At a visitor's center
(D) At a festival

담화는 어디에서 일어나는 것 같은가?
(A) 실험실
(B) 극장
(C) 방문자 센터
(D) 축제

장소를 유추하는 질문으로 도입부 Welcome everyone to Springfield State Park에서 이곳은 주립 공원임을 알 수 있고, right here in the visitor's center를 통해 지금 있는 곳은 방문자 센터임을 알 수 있다. 장소를 알려 주는 힌트어는 welcome to, here at/in 등이 대표적이므로 반드시 암기해 두자.

90 According to the speaker, what will listeners learn?
(A) How to read a sky map
(B) Where to sign up for a lecture
(C) How to use a telescope
(D) Where to find photos of the stars

화자에 따르면, 청자들은 무엇을 배울 것인가?
(A) 별자리 지도를 보는 방법
(B) 강의를 신청하는 장소
(C) 망원경을 사용하는 방법
(D) 별의 사진을 찾을 수 있는 장소

세부 사항 질문으로 청자들이 배울 내용에 집중한다. You'll learn how to read a sky map를 듣고 별자리 지도 읽는 방법을 배울 것이라고 파악한다. 정답은 (A)이다. (D)은 stars가 언급되었지만 별의 사진에 대한 내용이므로 함정이다.

91 For which information should listeners visit a website?
(A) Monthly stargazing information
(B) Some astronomical photographs
(C) Directions to the center
(D) Some research studies

청자들은 무슨 정보를 위해 웹 사이트를 방문해야 하는가?
(A) 매달 있는 별 관측 정보
(B) 천문학적인 사진
(C) 센터로 가는 길 안내
(D) 학문 연구

세부 사항 질문으로 키워드는 website이다. you can visit our website for monthly sky-watching information이라는 언급을 통해 웹 사이트에서 매달 있는 천체 관측에 대한 정보를 얻을 수 있음을 확인한다. sky-watching은 stargazing으로 바꿔 표현되었다.

Questions 92-94 refer to the following telephone message. 영M

Hi. This is Elliot Morley in unit 303. I called you earlier to report a leak in the ceiling of my apartment. And it looks even worse now. I was wondering if someone from your maintenance office can come take a look at it as soon as possible. I really want to get it repaired by tonight. If you're coming tomorrow though, I usually get home after 5 p.m. The water hasn't come into my living room yet, but if it does, it will damage all the expensive electrical equipment that I have, including my stereo system. I'm going to cover my stuff with plastic sheets for the time being so nothing gets wet. But I'd really like you to come and fix it as soon as you can. Thank you.

안녕하세요. 303호의 Elliot Morley입니다. 제가 아까 제 아파트 천장이 새는 것을 보고하기 위해 전화했었는데요. 지금은 더 안 좋아 보입니다. 관리 사무실에서 누가 최대한 빨리 와서 봐주실 수 있을까요? 오늘 밤까지 수리를 받고 싶지만 만약 내일 오신다면 저는 오후 5시 이후에 보통 집에 옵니다. 물이 아직 거실까지 들어오지는 않았지만 거실까지 들어온다면, 오디오를 포함하여 제가 가지고 있는 값비싼 가전제품들이 모두 손상될 것입니다. 당장은 아무것도 젖지 않도록 제가 비닐로 그것들을 덮어두겠지만 최대한 빨리 이것을 고쳐주시길 바랍니다. 감사합니다.

unit (아파트의) 호 leak 누수 get worse 더 악화되다 damage 손상시키다 plastic 비닐 electrical device 가전제품 get wet 젖다

92 What does the speaker mean when he says, "And it seems even worse now"?
(A) The maintenance office is closed.
(B) Heavy rains have caused a flood.
(C) A leak has gotten more serious.
(D) A burglar broke into his apartment.

남자가 "지금은 더 안 좋아 보입니다"라고 말한 의미는 무엇인가?
(A) 관리 사무실이 문을 닫았다.
(B) 폭우가 홍수를 야기시켰다.
(C) 누수가 더욱 심각해졌다.
(D) 도둑이 그의 아파트에 침입했다.

해당 표현 전에 천정의 누수(leak)에 대해 언급을 하였고 이것이 더 안 좋아 보인다고 말했으므로 정답은 (C)가 된다.

93 What is the purpose of the message?
(A) To estimate the costs
(B) To inform of a procedure
(C) To schedule a repair
(D) To request advice

메시지의 목적은 무엇인가?
(A) 비용을 예측하려고
(B) 절차에 대해 알리려고
(C) 수리 일정을 잡으려고
(D) 조언을 구하려고

전화 메시지에서 목적은 도입부에 대부분 힌트가 나온다. 처음부터 천장의 leak(누수)에 대해 언급했고 관리 사무실에서 누가 와서 고쳐주길 바란다고 했으므로 정답은 (C)가 된다.

94 What is the speaker going to do?
(A) Protect some equipment
(B) Return a call
(C) Listen to a weather forecast
(D) Remove some furniture

화자는 무엇을 할 것인가?
(A) 일부 기기를 보호한다.
(B) 답신 전화를 한다.
(C) 일기 예보를 듣는다.
(D) 가구를 치운다.

화자가 할 일이므로 'I'라는 주어가 중요하다. I'm going to cover my stuff with plastic sheets for the time being so nothing gets wet이라고 했으니 기기를 보호한다고 바꿔 표현된 (A)가 정답이 된다. (B)의 답신 전화는 상대방에게 하라고 했으니 오답이고 나머지 역시 연상되는 단어들을 이용한 오답이 된다.

Questions 95-97 refer to the following message and schedule. 미W

Hi, it is Liz Sacco. Congratulations on your promotion, Luke. We're really looking forward to having you on our production development team. You've probably had a chance to look at the meeting schedule I sent to you by now. But there have been some changes made to it. Originally, Karen Park's presentation was scheduled for 10 in the morning and Santiago's presentation for 11 a.m. However, they've both agreed to push back their presentations to the afternoon so that I can give you an update on the products we're currently developing in the morning first. After that, I'll introduce you to the team and you can say a few words before lunch. After the lunch break, Karen will present our next product launch at 1 o'clock. And Santiago's presentation will follow after that. If you have any questions, please call me at any time. I'll see you on Monday.

Meeting Schedule	
Karen Park	10:00 a.m.
Santiago Juarez	11:00 a.m.
Lunch	12:00 p.m.
Liz Sacco	1:00 p.m.
Luke Smith	2:00 p.m.

안녕하세요, 저는 Liz Sacco입니다. 승진을 축하합니다, Luke. 저희 상품 개발팀에 합류하게 되어서 정말 기대가 됩니다. 지금쯤이면 제가 보내드린 미팅 스케줄을 보셨을 것 같습니다. 그런데 몇 가지 변경 사항이 생겼습니다. 원래는 Karen Park의 발표가 오전 10시에 잡혀 있었고 Santiago의 발표가 11시였습니다. 그러나, 그들 둘 다 오후로 발표를 미뤄주기로 합의를 했어요. 제가 아침에 먼저 우리가 작업 중인 상품들에 대해 보고를 해드릴 수 있도록요. 그 이후에, 제가 당신을 팀원들에게 소개할 것이고 점심 전에 짧게 한 말씀 해주시면 됩니다. 점심 시간 후에, Karen이 1시에 다음 상품 출시에 대해 발표를 할 것이고 Santiago의 발표가 그 뒤를 따를 것입니다. 질문이 있으시면, 저에게 언제든 전화 주세요. 월요일에 뵙겠습니다.

회의 일정	
Karen Park	오전 10시
Santiago Juarez	오전 11시
점심	오후 12시
Liz Sacco	오후 1시
Luke Smith	오후 2시

congratulations on ~을 축하하다 look forward to ~을 기대하다 have a chance to ~할 기회를 갖다 originally 원래는 push back ~을 미루다 product launch 상품 출시

95 Why is the speaker congratulating Luke?
(A) He has won an award.
(B) He has met a deadline.
(C) He has developed a new product.
(D) He has been promoted at work.

화자는 왜 Luke에게 축하하는가?
(A) 그는 상을 받았다.
(B) 그는 마감을 맞췄다.
(C) 그는 신상품을 개발했다.
(D) 그는 직장에서 승진되었다.

Congratulate란 키워드가 들리는 부분에서 이유까지 함께 캐치하는 것이 포인트이다. Congratulations on your promotion, Luke에서 승진 때문에 축하한다는 것을 알 수 있다. 정답은 (D)이다.

96 Look at the graphic. According to the revised schedule, who will give a presentation at 1 p.m. on Monday?
(A) Karen Park
(B) Santiago Juarez
(C) Liz Sacco
(D) Luke Smith

시각 정보를 보시오. 바뀐 스케줄에 따르면 누가 월요일 오후 1시에 발표를 할 것인가?
(A) Karen Park
(B) Santiago Juarez
(C) Liz Sacco
(D) Luke Smith

주어진 시각 정보에서 회의 일정이 변경된 부분을 잘 듣고 판단한다. 오전 발표자들이 오후로 시간 변경을 해주기로 했다고 말했고 Karen이 1시에 상품 출시에 대한 발표를 한다고 했으므로 정답은 (A)가 된다.

97 What is the topic of Karen's presentation?
(A) A marketing strategy
(B) A product launch
(C) A new advertisement
(D) A product budget

Karen의 발표 주제는 무엇인가?
(A) 마케팅 전략
(B) 상품 출시
(C) 새 광고
(D) 상품 예산

Karen will present our next product launch at 1 o'clock에서 상품 출시가 발표 주제임을 알 수 있다.

Questions 98-100 refer to the following message and list. 영M

Hello, Reina. This is Jonathan Song calling from the Purchasing department. I've received the list of items your department needs to purchase. I was going to order them for you today but I just heard that Aden Electronics is having a spring sale starting next week. I asked them to fax me a list of products that are going to be on sale, and I have good news! Every item on your 'to-buy' list will be on sale except for the laptop computers. All computer accessories including monitors and keyboards are 20% off, and desktop PCs are 30% off the regular price. So I'm going to wait until next Monday to place an order if that's okay with you. If you need those items immediately, please call me at extension 2920 to let me know.

Item	Price	Quantity
Desktop PC	$450	3
Laptop Computer	$550	1
Monitor	$140	3
Keyboard	$15	3

안녕하세요 Reina. 구매 부서의 Jonathan Song입니다. 당신의 부서에서 구매하고자 하는 품목의 리스트를 받았습니다. 오늘 주문을 하려고 했으나 방금 Aden Electronics가 다음 주에 봄 세일을 연다는 소식을 들었어요. 그들에게 세일하는 물건 리스트를 팩스로 보내 달라고 했는데 좋은 소식이 있네요. 노트북 컴퓨터를 제외하고는 당신의 '구매 품목' 리스트에 있는 전 제품이 세일할 것이라고 합니다. 모니터와 키보드를 포함한 모든 컴퓨터 액세서리가 20퍼센트 할인되고 데스크톱 컴퓨터는 정가에서 30퍼센트 할인됩니다. 그래서 괜찮으시다면 저는 다음 주 월요일까지 기다렸다가 주문을 하려고 합니다. 만약 이 물건들이 당장 필요하시다면, 제 내선번호 2920으로 전화하셔서 제게 알려주세요.

품목	가격	양
데스크톱 PC	450달러	3
노트북 컴퓨터	550달러	1
모니터	140달러	3
키보드	15달러	3

purchasing department 구매 부서 except for ~을 제외하고 regular price 정가 extension 내선 번호

98 In what department does the speaker work?
(A) Sales
(B) Shipping
(C) Purchasing
(D) Advertising

어떤 부서에서 화자는 일하는가?
(A) 영업
(B) 배송
(C) 구매
(D) 광고

메시지의 도입부에 화자가 본인의 신분을 밝히는 부분에서 정답을 선택한다. This is Jonathan Song calling from the purchasing department를 통해 정답이 (C)임을 알 수 있다. 소속을 말할 때 전치사 from이 사용됨을 기억해 두자.

99 Look at the graphic. According to the speaker, what price will stay the same?
(A) $450
(B) $550
(C) $140
(D) $15

시각 정보를 보시오. 화자에 따르면, 어떤 가격은 똑같이 유지될 것인가?
(A) 450달러
(B) 550달러
(C) 140달러
(D) 15달러

할인이 되는 품목과 안 되는 품목을 잘 구별하며 듣는 것이 포인트이다. Every item on your 'to-buy' list will be on sale except for the laptop computers(노트북 컴퓨터만 빼고 리스트 상의 전 품목이 할인된다)라고 했으므로 노트북 컴퓨터만 가격 변동이 없을 것임을 알 수 있다. 그러므로 정답은 (B)가 된다.

100 What will the speaker do on Monday?
(A) He will order some items.
(B) He will contact a store.
(C) He will install some equipment.
(D) He will revise a report.

화자는 월요일에 무엇을 할 것인가?
(A) 물건을 주문할 것이다.
(B) 상점에 전화를 할 것이다.
(C) 기계를 설치할 것이다.
(D) 보고서를 수정할 것이다.

Monday라는 키워드가 언급될 때 정답이 함께 나오므로 So I'm going to wait until next Monday to place an order 부분을 놓치지 말고 정답을 캐치한다. 월요일까지 기다렸다가 주문을 할 것이라고 했으므로 정답은 (A)가 된다.

Actual Test 10

PART 1

본책 p.120

1 (B)	2 (D)	3 (C)	4 (C)	5 (A)	6 (B)

PART 2

본책 p.124

7 (A)	8 (A)	9 (C)	10 (A)	11 (A)	12 (B)
13 (B)	14 (C)	15 (C)	16 (B)	17 (C)	18 (C)
19 (C)	20 (B)	21 (A)	22 (A)	23 (C)	24 (B)
25 (A)	26 (A)	27 (B)	28 (C)	29 (B)	30 (C)
31 (A)					

PART 3

본책 p.125

32 (B)	33 (A)	34 (B)	35 (D)	36 (A)	37 (C)
38 (C)	39 (A)	40 (C)	41 (A)	42 (B)	43 (D)
44 (A)	45 (C)	46 (B)	47 (D)	48 (C)	49 (B)
50 (B)	51 (D)	52 (B)	53 (D)	54 (C)	55 (B)
56 (C)	57 (A)	58 (D)	59 (A)	60 (B)	61 (C)
62 (B)	63 (C)	64 (C)	65 (C)	66 (B)	67 (A)
68 (B)	69 (D)	70 (A)			

PART 4

본책 p.129

71 (A)	72 (C)	73 (B)	74 (C)	75 (A)	76 (D)
77 (D)	78 (B)	79 (C)	80 (B)	81 (C)	82 (A)
83 (B)	84 (A)	85 (D)	86 (C)	87 (C)	88 (A)
89 (C)	90 (D)	91 (A)	92 (A)	93 (D)	94 (B)
95 (A)	96 (C)	97 (D)	98 (B)	99 (D)	100 (A)

PART 1

1 (A) The mop is being washed.
미W (B) She is bending over the bucket.
(C) She is wiping the floor.
(D) She is filling the basket with linen.

(A) 대걸레를 빨고 있다.
(B) 여자가 양동이 위로 몸을 굽히고 있다.
(C) 여자가 바닥을 닦고 있다.
(D) 여자가 바구니에 리넨 제품을 채우고 있다.

건물의 복도에서 여자가 양동이 위로 몸을 굽히고 있다. 청소를 하는 중인지 끝낸 상황인지 알 수 없고 옆에 대걸레가 있지만 빨거나 닦고 있는 중은 아니므로 정답은 (B)이다. 배경 지식에 의한 추측보다는 지금 이 순간의 동작에만 초점을 맞추도록 한다.

mop 대걸레, 자루걸레 bend over ~위로 몸을 굽히다 bucket 양동이 wipe 닦다, 훔치다 fill 채우다 linen 침대 시트, 식탁보 등의 리넨 제품

2 (A) A plane has just landed.
영M (B) Some people are exiting the craft.
(C) An airplane is taking off from a runway.
(D) A road runs through the field.

(A) 비행기 한 대가 막 착륙했다.
(B) 사람들이 비행기에서 내리고 있다.
(C) 비행기 한 대가 활주로를 이륙하고 있다.
(D) 길은 들판을 가로지른다.

들판 가운데 길이 있고 비행기 한 대가 있다. 사진만으로는 막 도착한 것인지 이륙 준비를 하는 것인지 분명하지 않다. 사람도 보이지 않으므로 정답은 (D)이다. 들판이나 강 가운데 길이 나 있는 경우 run through라는 표현이 자주 등장하므로 주의하자.

land 착륙하다 exit 나가다, 떠나다 craft 항공기, 우주선 take off 이륙하다 runway 활주로 run through 가로지르다

3 (A) They are playing stringed instruments.
미M (B) They are going up the stage.
(C) They are performing on the move.
(D) They are ascending the steps.

(A) 사람들이 현악기를 연주하고 있다.
(B) 사람들이 무대에 오르고 있다.
(C) 사람들이 이동하면서 공연하고 있다.
(D) 사람들이 계단을 오르고 있다.

여러 사람들이 길을 걸으며 악기를 연주하고 있다. 모두 금관 악기이며 바이올린이나 첼로 등의 현악기는 아니고, 무대나 계단을 올라가고 있는 모습도 아니므로 정답은 (C)이다. 걷는다는 표현을 직접적으로 쓰지 않고 '이동 중'이라는 on the move라는 말로 달리 표현했다.

stringed instrument 현악기 go up 올라가다 stage 무대 on the move 이동 중인 ascend 오르다 step 계단

4 (A) People are climbing into a boat.
미W (B) A man is walking his dog along the riverbank.
(C) Some boats are parked at the shore.
(D) A leaf has fallen on the beach.

(A) 사람들이 보트 안에 오르고 있다.
(B) 남자가 해변을 따라 개를 산책시키고 있다.
(C) 보트는 해안가에 있다.
(D) 나뭇잎 하나가 해변에 떨어져 있다.

사람은 전혀 보이지 않고 바닷가 모래사장에 그물 같은 낚시 도구와 배가 묶여 있는 모습이다. 따라서 사람을 등장시킨 (A), (B)는 오답이며, (D)도 이 사진만으로는 정확히 나뭇잎이 떨어져 있는지 알아보기 어려우므로 정답과 거리가 멀다. 해안이나 강가를 나타내는 beach, shore, riverbank 외에 waterfront, pier, harbor 등도 같이 알아 두자.

walk one's dog 개를 산책시키다 riverbank 강둑 shore 해안 fall onto ~위에 떨어지다

5 (A) The man is concentrating on something.
영M (B) The man is passing through the doorway.
(C) Some crops are being planted.
(D) The trees have lost their leaves.

(A) 남자가 뭔가에 집중하고 있다.
(B) 남자가 출입구를 지나가고 있다.
(C) 농작물을 심고 있다.
(D) 나무들은 잎이 없다.

남자가 골프장에서 혼자 골프를 치는 모습이다. 하고 있는 일을 구체적으로 언급할 수도 있지만 일반적으로 설명할 수도 있는데 정답 (A)에서는 골프를 something으로 묘사했다.

concentrate 집중하다 pass through 거쳐 가다, 지나가다 crop 농작물 plant 심다

6 (A) Some vehicles are crossing a bridge.
미W (B) A building is being torn down.
(C) Workers are carrying the bricks side by side.
(D) Some equipment is being removed from the house.

(A) 차 몇 대가 다리를 건너고 있다.
(B) 건물이 허물어지고 있다.
(C) 인부들이 나란히 벽돌을 들고 가고 있다.
(D) 장비가 집에서 치워지고 있다.

중장비로 건물을 부수고 있는 모습이다. Part 1에서는 건물이 철거되거나 부서지는 모습이 종종 등장하는데 이때 자주 나오는 표현인 tear down을 꼭 기억하도록 한다.

vehicle 차량 cross 건너다 tear down 허물다, 해체하다 side by side 나란히 equipment 장비 remove 제거하다, 없애다

PART 2

7 Where was last year's fundraiser held?
미W (A) At the public library.
미M (B) That sounds like fun.
(C) To help children.

작년의 기금 모금행사는 어디에서 열렸었나요?
(A) 공립 도서관에서요.
(B) 재미있을 것 같네요.
(C) 아이들을 도우려고요.

의문사 where 질문으로 장소를 직접 언급한 (A)가 정답이다. (B)는 문맥상 어긋나는 답변으로 작년의 행사 장소를 물었는데 '재미있을 것 같다'고 엉뚱하게 답하고 있다. (C)는 의문사 why에 대한 답이므로 오답이다.

fundraiser 기금 모금 행사 be held (행사 등이) 열리다

8 When will I be served?
영M (A) Very shortly.
영W (B) At the table outside.
(C) He'll arrive later.

언제 음식이 나올까요?
(A) 금방이요.
(B) 야외 테이블에서요.
(C) 그는 나중에 도착할 거예요.

의문사 when 질문으로 서빙을 받게 될 시점을 물었으므로 금방이라고 답한 (A)가 정답이다. (B)는 연상어인 table을 이용한 오답이며, (C)는 주어 자체가 잘못 쓰인 주어 오류이다.

serve (음식을) 제공하다 outside 야외의

9 What was your presentation about?
미M (A) To better serve customers.
미W (B) In ten days.
(C) How to promote communication skills.

당신의 발표는 무엇에 관한 것이었습니까?
(A) 고객을 더 잘 모시기 위해서요.
(B) 10일 후에요.
(C) 커뮤니케이션 기술을 향상시키는 방법이요.

의문사 what 질문으로 발표의 주제가 무엇인지 물었으므로 주제를 그대로 말해 준 (C)가 정답이다. (A)는 의문사 why에 대해 to부정사로 답하는 경우이고 (B)는 의문사 when에 대한 답이다.

serve (고객 등에게) 제공하다, 시중을 들다 promote 향상시키다

10 Are you using the copier or can I use it?
영W (A) It's all yours.
미M (B) It is very useful.
(C) She'll be here soon.

지금 복사기를 사용 중인가요 아니면 제가 사용해도 될까요?
(A) 얼마든지 쓰세요.
(B) 이것은 아주 유용합니다.
(C) 그녀는 곧 여기로 올 것입니다.

선택 의문문으로 선택 사항을 압축하면 '복사기 사용 중인지 아닌지'이다. 상대방에게 물건 등을 얼마든지 쓰라고 말할 때 'It's all yours'라는 표현을 사용할 수 있으니 알아두자. 사용해도 된다고 했으므로 (A)가 정답이 된다.

copier 복사기 useful 유용한

11 Who is using the photocopier now?
미W (A) Sandra's assistant.
영M (B) He e-mailed me instead.
(C) It seems quite fast.

누가 지금 복사기를 사용하고 있습니까?
(A) Sandra의 조수요.
(B) 그는 대신 저에게 이메일을 보냈어요.
(C) 그것은 꽤 빨라 보이네요.

질문의 요지는 기계를 사용 중인 사람이 누구인지 묻는 것으로 Sandra의 조수라고 답한 (A)가 정답이다. (B)는 주어로 쓰인 he가 누구인지 파악이 안되므로 who 질문에 대해 답이 될 수 없다.

assistant 조수, 보조 instead 대신에 quite 꽤

12 Which coat suits me better, the black or the red?
영M (A) You haven't met them yet.
미W (B) How about this gray one?
(C) Yes, try on the coat.

어떤 코트가 제게 더 잘 어울리나요, 검은색이요 아니면 빨간색이요?
(A) 당신은 그들을 아직 만나보지 못했어요.
(B) 이 회색은 어떠세요?
(C) 네, 코트를 입어보세요.

선택 의문문으로 선택 사항만 압축하면 '검정 혹은 빨강'이다. 정답으로는 둘 중 하나를 선택할 수도 있지만 (B) 회색은 어때요?처럼 다른 선택 사항을 제시할 수 있다. 이때 중요한 것은 선택 사항 A, B와 C가 같은 맥락에 있어야만 한다. 즉, '커피를 마실지 차를 마실지' 물었는데 '쇼핑이 좋다'고 답하는 게 정답이 될 수는 없다. (C)는 Yes라고 답하는 부분 때문에 오답이 된다. 선택 의문문에서는 Yes/No로 답하지 않는다.

suit 맞다, 어울리다 try on ~을 입어보다

13 Is it alright if I take the day off tomorrow?
영W (A) I'll arrive next week.
영M (B) Yes, if you're finished with your report.
(C) At 3:30, I guess.

제가 내일 휴가를 내도 괜찮을까요?
(A) 전 다음 주에 도착할 것입니다.

(B) 네, 보고서를 끝냈다면요.
(C) 3시 30분일 거예요.

요청 의문문으로 내일 월차를 내는 것에 대한 허가를 요청하고 있으므로 업무를 끝냈다면 좋다고 답한 (B)가 정답이다. if절로 단서를 붙여 Yes/No 여부를 답하는 형태는 빈출 유형이자 고난도에 속하니 잘 정리해두자.

is it alright if ~한다면 괜찮을까요?(요청) be finished with ~을 끝내다

14 Why don't we double-check the figures?
미W (A) They probably are.
영W (B) The power is out.
(C) That sounds great.

그 수치들을 한 번 더 확인하면 어떨까요?
(A) 아마 그들은 그럴 겁니다.
(B) 전기가 나갔어요.
(C) **좋습니다.**

제안 의문문 유형으로 제안에 승낙하는 표현들, that's a good idea, that sounds good 등은 반드시 암기해두자. 정답은 (C)로 어떤 제안 의문문에도 정답이 될 수 있는 승낙 표현이다.

double-check 한 번 더 확인하다 figure 수치 power 전력, 전기

15 So, that is the new restaurant logo.
미W (A) Yes, you do.
미M (B) About 30 dollars.
(C) It stands out.

그러니까, 저것이 레스토랑의 새 로고입니다.
(A) 네, 당신은 그래요.
(B) 30달러 정도입니다.
(C) **눈에 잘 띄네요.**

평서문 유형으로 대화의 상황은 상대방에게 새 로고를 보여 주는 것이다. 로고가 눈에 잘 띈다고 답한 (C)가 가장 자연스러운 답변이 된다. (A)의 경우 로고에 대한 내용이 아니므로 문맥에서 벗어나 오답이고, (B)는 의문사 how much에 대한 답이다.

logo 로고 stand out 눈에 잘 띄다, 두드러지다, 빼어나다

16 You didn't send the seating arrangements to
영M Jonathan yet, did you?
영W (A) I liked the gray one better.
(B) Yes, just 10 minutes ago.
(C) 2 extra chairs.

Jonathan에게 좌석 배치도를 아직 보내지 않으셨죠, 그렇죠?
(A) 전 회색이 더 좋았습니다.
(B) **보냈어요, 10분 전에요.**
(C) 여분의 의자 2개요.

Yes/No 여부를 묻는 질문으로 포인트는 좌석 배치도를 Jonathan에게 보냈는지에 대한 사실 여부 파악이다. 이때 Yes/No 질문 속의 부정어 not은 해석상 제외시키는 것이 필수 스킬이다. 정답의 Yes는 동사 send에 대한 답이므로 '보냈다'는 의미가 되고 10분 전에 보냈다는 세부 정보가 자연스럽게 연결된다.

seating attrangements 좌석 배치도

17 Would you prefer to work the morning or the night shift?
미M (A) A 10 minute break.
미W (B) I am leaving after work.
(C) Morning would be better.

아침에 일하는 것을 선호하세요 아니면 야간 근무조를 선호하세요?
(A) 10분간의 휴식이요.
(B) 저는 퇴근 후에 떠날 겁니다.
(C) **아침이 더 좋습니다.**

선택 의문문으로 or를 놓치지 않고 듣되, 선택 사항 A와 B를 순발력 있게 파악한다. 아침 근무 혹은 저녁 근무를 선호하는지 물었으므로 아침을 선택한 (C)가 정답이다. (A)는 일과 관련된 어휘 break를 사용한 함정이고, (B)는 work를 반복 사용한 함정이 된다.

prefer 선호하다 shift 근무조, 교대조

18 Do you know why our utility costs are so high this month?
영W (A) No, higher than that.
미M (B) By utilizing natural resources.
(C) Energy is more expensive now.

이번 달 우리 관리비가 왜 이렇게 비싼지 아세요?
(A) 아니요, 그것보다 높아요.
(B) 천연 자원을 이용해서요.
(C) **연료가 요즘 더 비쌉니다.**

질문의 핵심은 의문사 why가 된다. 관리비가 비싸게 나온 이유를 물었으므로 정답은 (C)이다. 특히 의문사가 질문의 중간에 위치하는 경우 놓치기 쉬우므로 듣기 훈련을 반복하는 것이 중요하다.

utility costs (시설물, 아파트 등의) 관리비 utilize 이용하다 natural resources 천연 자원

19 How long did Sonia stay in Thailand?
미W (A) It is a major city.
영M (B) Three weeks ago.
(C) About a month.

Sonia는 태국에 얼마나 오래 머물렀나요?
(A) 대도시입니다.
(B) 3주일 전에요.
(C) **약 한 달이요.**

의문사 how long은 기간을 묻는 질문이므로 한 달이라고 답한 (C)가 정답이다.

20 Is there any more paper in the supply room?
영M (A) I didn't read the news today.
미W (B) Yes, I just got back from there.
(C) In the banquet room.

창고에 종이가 더 있나요?
(A) 오늘 뉴스를 읽지 않았어요.
(B) **네, 지금 막 거기에 갔다 왔어요.**
(C) 연회장에서요.

'Is there + 명사'는 '명사가 있나요?'라고 물어보는 Yes/No 질문으로 빈출 유형에 해당하니 반드시 암기하자. 창고에 종이가 더 있는지에 대한 답은 (B)뿐이고, 막 그곳에 갔다 왔다고 말한 부연 설명도 문맥상 흐름이 매끄럽다.

banquet room 연회장

21 Would you like some coffee while you are waiting?
영W (A) Thank you. That's very generous of you.
영M (B) The copier is broken.

(C) I made it this morning.

기다리시는 동안 커피를 드릴까요?

(A) 감사합니다. 매우 친절하시군요.

(B) 복사기는 고장입니다.

(C) 오늘 아침에 그것을 만들었어요.

상대방에게 커피를 드릴까요라고 물었으므로 정답은 (A)가 가장 알맞다. coffee와 발음이 비슷한 copier를 사용한 (B)와 같은 함정에 유의하자.

generous 친절한, 관대한 broken 고장 난

22 Isn't that the key to your office?
미W (A) Yes, I've been looking for it all day.
영W (B) She will make an official announcement.
(C) At the repair shop.

저것이 당신 사무실 열쇠 아닌가요?

(A) 맞아요, 하루 종일 찾았어요.

(B) 그녀는 공식 발표를 할 겁니다.

(C) 수리점에서요.

Yes/No 여부를 묻는 질문으로 that(주어)이 the key(주격 보어)인지/아닌지 여부에 대한 답은 (A)뿐이다. 위의 질문과 같은 2형식(주어+be동사+주격 보어)은 어려운 구조이므로 잘 복습해두자.

official 공식적인 repair shop 수리점

23 Isn't Steve going to paint the table and chairs?
미W (A) When did you go?
미M (B) Not all merchandise is on sale.
(C) They are not ready for painting yet.

Steve가 테이블과 의자를 페인트 칠할 것 아닌가요?

(A) 언제 갔었어요?

(B) 모든 상품이 할인되지는 않아요.

(C) 그것들은 아직 페인트 칠할 준비가 안 됐어요.

질문의 tables and chairs는 정답 (C)의 they로 받고 있다. 테이블과 의자가 아직 페인트 칠할 준비가 안 되어서 Steve가 페인트 칠을 안 하는 것이라는 No 답변이 성립된다.

merchandise 상품 on sale 할인되는

24 Why do you keep the window open?
영M (A) Because your office is closer.
영W (B) It is very hot in here.
(C) At 7 p.m.

왜 창문을 열어 두시나요?

(A) 당신의 사무실이 더 가깝기 때문입니다.

(B) 안이 매우 더워서요.

(C) 저녁 7시에요.

창문을 열어두는 이유를 물었으므로 더워서라고 답한 (B)가 정답이고 (A)는 because라는 단어만을 이용한 함정이 된다. 실제로 토익 시험에서 why 의문문에 대한 정답으로는 because로 시작되는 정답이 많이 출제되었지만, because로 시작되는 함정도 여러 차례 등장했다.

25 The plumbers left their tools in the bathroom, didn't
미M they?
미W (A) Those pipe cutters are ours.
(B) From an interior design company.
(C) They are not expensive.

배관공이 욕실에 그들의 연장을 놓고 갔네요, 그렇지 않나요?

(A) 그 파이프 절단기는 우리 것입니다.

(B) 실내 디자인 회사로부터요.

(C) 그것들은 비싸지 않습니다.

Yes/No 여부를 묻는 부가 의문문이다. 주어는 the plumbers로 연장을 놓고 갔는지 여부를 물었으므로 그 연장들은 우리 것이라고 답한 (A)가 정답이다. 간접적이지만 질문에 대해 No의 의미가 성립되기 때문이다.

plumber 배관공 leave 남겨두다, 놓다 tool 연장, 도구 pipe cutter 파이프 절단기

26 I have to leave early tomorrow for a doctor's
영W appointment.
미M (A) Okay, I'll let the team know.
(B) Actually I'm going to Mexico.
(C) The clinic is on Main Street.

저는 내일 진료 예약 때문에 일찍 퇴근해야 합니다.

(A) 알겠어요. 제가 팀에 알릴게요.

(B) 실은 저는 멕시코에 갑니다.

(C) 병원은 Main 가에 있어요.

평서문으로 내일 퇴근을 일찍 해야 한다는 요지이므로 그 사실을 팀원들에게 알려 주겠다고 답한 (A)가 정답이 된다.

let ~ know ~에게 알리다

27 Doesn't this expense report include the purchases
미W we made yesterday?
영M (A) That model is not expensive.
(B) No, it needs to be updated.
(C) Yes, I'll pay in cash.

이 비용 보고서는 어제 우리가 구매한 것을 포함하고 있나요?

(A) 그 모델은 비싸지 않아요.

(B) 아니요, 최신 정보로 바꿔야 합니다.

(C) 네, 현금으로 낼게요.

Yes/No 여부로 묻고 있는 것이 비용 보고서에 어제의 구매 사항도 포함 되었는지 여부이므로 정답은 (B)가 된다. update라는 동사는 새로운 사항이 포함되도록 고친다는 의미이다.

expense report 비용 보고서 purchase 구매품, 구매 in cash 현금으로

28 The technicians just finished updating our
영M computer's operating system.
미W (A) I'd be glad to.
(B) Only for a while.
(C) Oh, did they?

기술자들이 막 우리 컴퓨터 운영 체제의 업데이트를 마쳤습니다.

(A) 기꺼이 하겠습니다.

(B) 잠시 동안만요.

(C) 오, 그들이 다 했나요?

정보를 주는 평서문으로 기술자들이 업무를 다 마쳤다고 했으므로 이를 재확인하는 (C)가 가장 자연스러운 답변이다. (A)는 상대방에게 요청을 받았을 때 '기꺼이 하겠다'고 답하는 것이므로 이 경우에는 어색하다.

technician 기술자 operating system 운영 체계

29 Carmen Santos did a good job delivering a speech
영W at the awards ceremony, didn't she?
영M (A) No, it didn't arrive on time.
(B) Yes, she impressed everyone.
(C) An award for good citizenship.

Carmen Santos는 시상식에서 연설을 잘 했어요, 그렇지 않나요?
(A) 아니요, 그것은 제때에 도착하지 않았어요.
(B) 네, 그녀는 모든 이들에게 감동을 주었어요.
(C) 훌륭한 시민상입니다.

질문의 핵심은 do a good job delivering a speech를 정확하게 해석하는 것이다. do a good job -ing는 '~을 잘하다'라는 뜻이므로 연설을 잘했는지 여부가 요지이다. 정답은 (B)가 된다.

do a good job -ing ~을 잘하다 deliver a speech 연설을 하다 awards ceremony 시상식 impress 감동시키다 good citizenship 훌륭한 시민

30 Who organized the charity bazaar last year?
미W (A) It will be held at the central square.
영W (B) I didn't get a ticket.
(C) I don't think there was one.

누가 작년의 자선 바자회를 조직했나요?
(A) 그것은 중앙 광장에서 열릴 것입니다.
(B) 저는 표를 못 샀어요.
(C) 없었던 것으로 아는데요.

who 의문문으로 작년 행사를 준비한 사람이 누구인지 물었으나 행사 자체가 없었다고 답한 (C)가 정답이 된다. 특히 이러한 간접 답변 유형들은 part2의 고난도 질문에 해당하므로 잘 복습해두자.

charity bazaar 자선 바자 행사 square 광장

31 Why aren't my documents printing?
미W (A) Paper must've gotten stuck inside.
미M (B) It will arrive tomorrow.
(C) Online ads are better.

제 서류가 왜 인쇄가 안 되는 거죠?
(A) 안에 종이가 끼인 것이 분명합니다.
(B) 그것은 내일 도착할 것입니다.
(C) 온라인 광고가 더 낫습니다.

서류가 인쇄되지 않는 이유를 묻는 why 의문문이므로 종이가 끼어서라고 답한 (A)가 가장 어울리는 정답이 된다.

print 인쇄하다 get stuck 꼼짝하지 못하게 되다, 막히다, 갇히다 inside 내부에 online ad 온라인 광고

PART 3

Questions 32-34 refer to the following conversation. 미W 미M

W Have you met the new graphic designer yet? I thought he was starting this week.
M Actually he is in a training program right now. Every new employee has to finish staff training at the headquarters first.
W Oh, I didn't know that. So, when does he start working in our office?
M Well, from what I heard, he will be introduced to everyone at our staff meeting on Monday.

여 새로 온 그래픽 디자이너 보셨나요? 전 그가 이번 주에 시작하는 줄만 알았어요.
남 실은 지금 교육을 받고 있어요. 모든 신입 직원들은 본사에서 우선 교육을 마쳐야만 하거든요
여 아, 그걸 몰랐네요. 그래서 언제 우리 사무실에서 일을 시작하나요?
남 음, 제가 들은 바로는, 월요일 직원 회의 때 그가 소개될 거라고 합니다.

headquarters 본사

32 What are the speakers mainly discussing?
(A) A meeting agenda
(B) A new employee
(C) The relocation of a company
(D) A new software program

화자들은 무엇에 대해 주로 이야기하는가?
(A) 미팅 안건
(B) 신입 사원
(C) 회사의 이전
(D) 새 소프트웨어 프로그램

주제를 묻는 질문의 정답은 도입부에 주로 등장한다. 여자가 새 그래픽 디자이너를 만나 보았는지 물었을 때 바로 신입 직원에 대한 대화임을 파악할 수 있다.

33 What are new employees required to do?
(A) Receive training
(B) Write sales reports
(C) Sign an agreement
(D) Finish a budget analysis

신입 사원들은 무엇을 하도록 요구되는가?
(A) 교육 받기
(B) 영업 보고서 쓰기
(C) 계약서에 서명하기
(D) 예산 분석표 끝내기

신입 직원에 대한 언급은 남자가 Every new employee has to finish staff training at the headquarters first라고 말한 부분이다. 본사에서 교육을 먼저 마쳐야만 한다고 했으므로 정답은 (A)가 된다.

34 According to the man, what will happen on Monday?
(A) A meeting will be cancelled.
(B) A new colleague will be introduced.
(C) An office will be renovated.
(D) A training program will begin.

남자에 따르면, 월요일에는 무슨 일이 있을 것인가?
(A) 미팅이 취소될 것이다.
(B) 새 동료가 소개될 것이다.
(C) 사무실이 개조될 것이다.
(D) 교육 프로그램이 시작될 것이다.

질문의 키워드인 on Monday가 언급되는 부분에서 정답을 파악하자. he will be introduced to everyone at our staff meeting on Monday에서 월요일 미팅 때 그가 소개될 것이라고 하였고 he는 a new graphic designer를 가리키므로 정답은 (B)가 된다.

Questions 35-37 refer to the following conversation. 영W 영M

W Did you watch the tennis match between Rebecca Green and Cynthia Peterson on television last night? It was so exciting.
M I was really looking forward to the match but I had to work extra hours. I got home around 10 last night. Rebecca Green is my favorite player.
W Guess what? You can actually watch it tonight. They are replaying the match at 8 on Channel 9.
M Really? That's great. I'd better make a note of that so I don't forget.

여 어젯밤 텔레비전에서 Rebecca Green과 Cynthia Peterson의 테니스 경기 보셨나요? 정말 흥미진진했어요.
남 그 경기를 정말 기대하고 있었는데 야근을 해야만 했어요. 어젯밤에 집에 10시쯤 들어갔죠. Rebecca Green은 제가 제일 좋아하는 선수예요.
여 그거 아세요? 실은 오늘 밤에 경기를 볼 수 있어요. 채널 9에서 8시에 그 경기를 재방송하거든요.
남 진짜요? 잘됐네요. 잊어버리지 않도록 메모를 해야겠어요.

tennis match 테니스 경기 work extra hours 추가 근무하다

35 What is the conversation mainly about?
(A) A new play
(B) A charity concert
(C) A television show
(D) A tennis match

대화는 무엇에 관한 것인가?
(A) 새로운 연극
(B) 자선 콘서트
(C) 텔레비전 쇼
(D) 테니스 경기

주제는 도입부에 등장하므로 집중력을 발휘하자. Did you watch the tennis match를 듣는 순간 정답을 (D)로 처리하는 순발력이 요구된다.

36 Who is Rebecca Green?
(A) A tennis player
(B) A TV show host
(C) An entertainer
(D) A business owner

Rebecca Green은 누구인가?
(A) 테니스 선수
(B) TV 쇼 진행자
(C) 연예인
(D) 사업가

Rebecca Green이라는 이름을 놓치지 않는 것이 중요하다. 테니스 경기가 Rebecca Green 과Cynthia Peterson의 경기라고 했고, 남자는 가장 좋아하는 선수라고 했으므로 정답은 (A)가 된다.

37 What will the man probably do tonight?
(A) Purchase a ticket online
(B) Make dinner at home
(C) Watch a match on television
(D) Go to the movies

남자는 오늘 밤에 무엇을 할 것 같은가?
(A) 온라인에서 티켓 구입하기
(B) 집에서 저녁 만들기
(C) 텔레비전에서 경기 보기
(D) 영화 보러 가기

대화의 후반부에 정답의 단서가 등장하지만 문맥을 유지하며 듣는 것이 필요하다. tonight에 관하여 여자가 테니스 경기 재방송이 있을 것이라고 말했고 이에 대해 남자가 I'd better make a note of that so I don't forget이라고 했으므로 정답은 (C)임을 알 수 있다.

Questions 38-40 refer to the following conversation. 미M 미W

M Check this out, Cindy. We got a great review in the local restaurant section of the paper.
W Really? That's wonderful. What does the article mention about our dishes?
M Uh, it says that the critic enjoyed everything on our menu, but she especially liked the grilled salmon steak with sautéed vegetables.
W Wow, I really want to go get some more copies of the paper but the lunch crowd will start to arrive in a few minutes.
M You're right. Are the tables all set? I'm sure the review will attract even more customers.

남 이것 좀 봐요, Cindy. 우리가 신문의 지역 레스토랑 면에서 좋은 평을 받았어요.
여 진짜요? 훌륭하네요. 우리 음식에 대해서 기사에서 뭐라고 하던가요?
남 어, 평론가가 우리 메뉴의 모든 음식을 좋아했다고 쓰여 있고요, 특히 볶은 채소를 곁들인 연어 스테이크를 좋아했다고 해요.
여 와, 그 신문을 몇 부 사러 나가고 싶지만 잠시 후면 점심 손님들이 오기 시작하겠네요.
남 맞아요. 테이블은 다 준비됐나요? 그 평론 때문에 손님이 더 많이 몰릴 거예요.

grilled 그릴에 구운 sautéed 볶은 lunch crowd 점심 손님들

38 What type of business do the speakers work for?
(A) A supermarket
(B) A newspaper
(C) A restaurant
(D) A movie theater

화자들은 어떤 업체에서 일하는가?
(A) 슈퍼마켓
(B) 신문사
(C) 레스토랑
(D) 영화관

화자들의 직장을 유추할 때는 We got a great review in the local restaurant section of the paper의 we(우리)가 어떤 업무를 하는지가 중요한 유추 포인트가 된다. 신문의 지역 레스토랑 면에서 좋은 평을 받았다고 했으므로 둘 다 레스토랑 직원들이다.

39 What are the speakers mainly discussing?
(A) A critic's review
(B) An interview with an author
(C) A new menu selection
(D) A local food festival

화자들은 주로 무엇에 대한 이야기를 하는가?
(A) 비평가의 평론
(B) 작가와의 인터뷰
(C) 새로운 메뉴
(D) 지역 음식 축제

주제 역시 도입부의 We got a great review in the local restaurant section of the paper 부분에서 정답을 찾을 수 있다. 신문에 실린 평론에 대한 이야기이다.

40 What does the man expect to happen?
(A) They will hire more employees.
(B) A popular dish will sell out.
(C) The restaurant will be busier.
(D) They will raise their prices.

남자는 무슨 일이 있을 것으로 예상하는가?
(A) 더 많은 직원들을 고용할 것이다.
(B) 인기 있는 음식이 다 떨어질 것이다.
(C) 레스토랑이 더 바빠질 것이다.
(D) 그들은 가격을 올릴 것이다.

남자 대사의 I'm sure the review will attract even more customers(이용 후기가 손님들을 더 끌어 모을 것이다)라고 말한 부분이 레스토랑이 더 바빠질 것이라는 표현으로 패러프레이징되었다.

Questions 41-43 refer to the following conversation. (영W) (미M)

W Hello. My name is Valerie Chang and I'm calling about the sales position posted on your company's web site. Is it still available?
M Yes, it is. We're currently looking for someone with experience selling household appliances. Do you have experience in sales?
W I have sold electrical appliances at Creatron Company for 5 years. And I received the Salesperson of the Year Award last year.
M Sounds like you will fit in well here. Why don't you send us your résumé?

여 안녕하세요 Valerie Chang인데요. 회사 웹 사이트에 올려진 영업직 구인에 관해서 전화합니다. 아직 지원이 가능한가요?
남 네 그렇습니다. 저희는 현재 가전제품 영업 경력이 있는 사람을 찾고 있어요. 영업 경력이 있으신가요?
여 전 Creatron Company에서 5년 동안 전자제품을 판매했습니다. 그리고 작년에는 올해의 판매왕 상도 받았습니다.
남 저희 회사에 딱 맞을 것 같네요. 지원서를 보내 주시겠어요?

available 이용 가능한 household appliances 가전제품

41 Who most likely is the woman?
(A) A job applicant
(B) A graphic designer
(C) An engineer
(D) A department head

여자는 누구일 것 같은가?
(A) 지원자
(B) 그래픽 디자이너
(C) 기술자
(D) 부서장

도입부에서 여자가 누구인지 유추하자. 구인 광고를 보고 전화한다고 말했으므로 정답은 (A)이다. 영업직에 관심이 있다고 했으므로 다른 보기들은 모두 오답이 된다.

42 What requirement of the job does the man mention?
(A) A college degree
(B) Relevant experience
(C) In-depth knowledge
(D) Good people skills

남자는 직업의 어떤 지원 요건을 언급하는가?
(A) 대학 학위
(B) 관련 경력
(C) 깊은 지식
(D) 좋은 유대관계

회사는 현재 someone with experience selling household appliances(가전제품을 판매한 경력이 있는 사람)를 구하고 있다고 했으므로 정답은 (B)가 된다.

43 What does the man suggest the woman do?
(A) Attend an awards ceremony
(B) Contact a hiring manager
(C) Sign a contract
(D) Submit a document

남자는 여자에게 무엇을 하라고 제안하는가?
(A) 시상식에 참석하기
(B) 인사 부장에게 연락하기
(C) 계약서에 서명하기
(D) 서류 제출하기

남자의 대사에서 Why don't you send us your résumé?라고 말하며 이력서를 보내 달라고 제안했으므로 정답은 (D)가 된다.

Questions 44-46 refer to the following conversation. (미W) (영M)

W Hello. I'm here to get this prescription filled.
M Okay. Have you ever filled a prescription at our pharmacy before?
W No. I just moved to this neighborhood a few days ago. So this is my first time here.
M All right. Could you tell me your name and telephone number so I can enter your information in our computer system?
W Sure. My name is Emily Chang and my number is 555-0901.
M Thanks. Now, it's going to take some time for us to complete your order so I suggest you come back in an hour to pick it up.

여 안녕하세요. 이 처방전으로 약을 짓기 위해서 왔습니다.
남 좋습니다. 저희 약국에서 약을 지어본 적이 있으세요?
여 아니요. 전 며칠 전에 이 동네로 이사를 와서요. 이번이 처음입니다.
남 알겠습니다. 저희 컴퓨터 시스템에 정보를 입력하도록 이름과 전화 번호를 말해주시겠어요?
여 네. 저는 Emily Chang이고 제 번호는 555-0901입니다.
남 고맙습니다. 이제 주문을 처리하는 데 시간이 좀 걸릴 거라서 한 시간 후에 가지러 오시는 게 좋을 것 같아요.

get a prescription filled 처방전대로 약을 짓다 pharmacy 약국

44 What does the woman want to do?
(A) Place an order
(B) Get directions to a store
(C) Examine some items
(D) Sign up for a subscription

여자는 무엇을 하고 싶어 하는가?
(A) 주문하기
(B) 가게에 가는 길 안내를 받기
(C) 상품 살펴보기
(D) 구독 신청하기

도입부에 여자가 I'm here to(~을 하기 위해 여기에 왔다)라고 말하는 부분에서 원하는 것을 파악하자. 처방전대로 약을 짓고 싶다고 했으므로 정답은 (A)가 된다.

45 Where most likely are the speakers?
(A) At a doctor's office
(B) At a café
(C) At a pharmacy
(D) At a community center

화자들은 어디에 있을 것 같은가?
(A) 병원
(B) 카페
(C) 약국
(D) 커뮤니티 센터

장소를 유추하는 질문으로 도입부의 상황에서 유추를 끝내도록 하자. 약을 짓고 싶다는 여자에게 남자가 우리 pharmacy에 와 본 적이 있는지 물었으므로 정답은 (C)이다.

46 What does the man suggest?
(A) Completing a form
(B) Returning later
(C) Staying in the waiting room
(D) Seeing a doctor

남자는 무엇을 제안하는가?
(A) 양식을 작성할 것
(B) 나중에 다시 올 것
(C) 대기실에서 기다릴 것
(D) 의사를 만날 것

남자가 제안의 표현을 사용한 부분은 I suggest you come back in an hour to pick it up이다. 한 시간 후에 가지러 오라는 것을 return later로 바꿔 표현한 (B)가 정답이다.

Questions 47-49 refer to the following conversation. 미M 영W

M Bazara Asian Cuisine. This is Stanley Jones. How may I help you?
W Mr. Jones, I found a wallet in the subway and there was your business card in it. Is it yours?
M **Yes! What a relief!** I thought I left it at the dentist's office where I had a check-up this morning. I never thought about the subway.
W Well, that's where it was. I see from your card that your restaurant is on Andrew Street. I actually work at a camera shop right on Yonge Street, which is just a block away from your restaurant. So you can come over to my store any time to pick up your wallet.

남 Bazara Asian Cuisine입니다. 저는 Stanley Jones입니다. 어떻게 도와 드릴까요?
여 Jones 씨, 제가 지하철에서 지갑을 발견했는데 안에 당신의 명함이 있었어요. 이 지갑이 당신 것인가요?
남 **네! 다행이네요!** 아침에 제가 검진 받았던 치과에 두고 온 줄 알았어요. 지하철일 줄은 몰랐네요.
여 지하철에 있었답니다. 명함에 보니까 당신의 레스토랑이 Andrew 가에 있네요. 저는 바로 Yonge 가에 있는 카메라 상점에서 일하는데 그 레스토랑에서 한 블록 떨어진 곳이에요. 언제든 여기로 오셔서 지갑을 가져가도록 하세요.

relief 안도, 안심 check-up 검진

47 What does the man imply when he says, "Yes! What a relief"?
(A) He can make a reservation for dinner tonight.
(B) A new subway line will start operating.
(C) He can make it to the dental clinic on time.
(D) He is glad to hear that his wallet has been found.

남자가 "네! 다행이네요"라고 말한 의미는 무엇인가?
(A) 그는 오늘 저녁 예약을 할 수 있다.
(B) 새 전철 노선이 운행을 시작할 것이다.
(C) 그는 치과에 늦지 않게 갈 수 있다.
(D) 그의 지갑이 발견되었다는 것을 듣고 기쁘다.

신토익 유형으로 해당 표현을 언급한 앞뒤 문맥에서 답을 찾자. 여자가 남자의 지갑을 전철에서 발견했다는 것에 대해 What a relief(다행이네요)라고 했으므로 정답은 (D)가 가장 적절하다.

48 What does the man mention about the dentist's office?
(A) He works there.
(B) He found his wallet there.
(C) He had a check-up there today.
(D) It is located on Andrew Street.

남자는 치과에 대해서 무엇을 언급하는가?
(A) 그곳에서 일한다.
(B) 지갑을 그곳에서 찾았다.
(C) 오늘 그곳에서 검진을 받았다.
(D) 그것은 Andrew 가에 있다.

질문의 키워드인 dentist's office가 언급된 부분에 정답이 있다. the dentist's office where I had a check-up this morning(오전에 검진을 받은 치과)이라고 했으므로 정답은 (C)가 된다.

49 What does the woman suggest the man do?
(A) Contact a restaurant
(B) Visit the woman's workplace
(C) Purchase a new wallet
(D) Order more business cards

여자는 남자에게 무엇을 할 것을 제안하는가?
(A) 레스토랑에 연락하기
(B) 여자의 근무지에 방문하기
(C) 새 지갑 구입하기
(D) 명함 더 주문하기

대화의 후반부에 여자의 가게가 남자의 레스토랑 근처에 있다고 언급한 후 지갑을 가지러 언제든 가게에 와도 된다고 했으므로 정답은 (B)가 된다.

Questions 50-52 refer to the following conversation. 미W 영M

W Hi, Robert. This is Camilla calling from Forest of Flowers Headquarters. How was the grand opening sale at your Rockport store?
M It was excellent. The weather was perfect so there were a great many people enjoying the day at Douglas Park. Since our shop is right next to the park, many of them stopped by our outdoor displays of floral arrangements and bouquets.
W Wow, sounds like it was a big success. Do you have the exact sales figures for the day?
M I'm working on them now. But my guess is that we exceeded our sales projections. I'll send you the exact numbers by e-mail very shortly.

여 안녕하세요, Robert, Forest of Flowers 본사에서 전화드리는 Camilla입니다. Rockport 지점의 오프닝 세일은 어떠셨나요?
남 매우 훌륭했습니다. 날씨가 매우 좋아서 Douglas Park에서 즐겁게 시간을 보내는 사람들이 많이 있었어요. 우리 상점이 공원 바로 옆이었기 때문에, 많은 사람들이 야외에 전시해 놓은 꽃다발과 꽃 장식을 구경하러 들렀습니다.
여 와, 매우 성공적이었던 것 같네요. 그날의 정확한 판매 수치가 나왔나요?
남 지금 계산을 하고 있었습니다만 판매 예상치를 넘었다고 예상합니다. 곧 이메일로 정확한 수치를 보내 드릴게요.

stop by 들르다 outdoor display 야외 전시대 exact 정확한 figure 수치 exceed 넘다 shortly 곧

50 What type of business do the speakers work for?
(A) A book store
(B) A florist shop
(C) A supermarket
(D) A restaurant

어떤 종류의 업체에서 화자들은 일하는가?
(A) 서점
(B) 꽃 가게
(C) 슈퍼마켓
(D) 레스토랑

화자들의 직장을 유추하는 질문으로 도입부에 보통 단서가 있다. 처음에 여자가 본인을 소개할 때 from Forest of Flowers Headquarters라고 소속을 밝혔으므로 꽃 가게의 본사임을 알 수 있고, 특정 지점의 개점 행사가 어땠는지 물어보는 것에서도 다시 한 번 확인할 수 있다.

51 What does the man say helped sales?
(A) A local festival
(B) Good reviews from experts
(C) A special sale
(D) The nice weather

남자는 무엇이 판매를 도왔다고 말하는가?
(A) 지역 페스티벌
(B) 전문가로부터의 좋은 후기
(C) 특별 세일
(D) 좋은 날씨

세부 사항 질문으로 남자 대사에서 정답을 찾아야 한다. 남자가 판매가 매우 좋았음을 언급하면서 날씨가 좋아서 많은 사람들이 공원을 찾았고, 공원 옆에 위치한 본인의 가게에도 많이 들렸다고 언급했으므로 정답은 (D)가 된다.

52 What will the man send the woman electronically?
(A) A copy of a license
(B) Some sales figures
(C) An updated brochure
(D) Pictures of a store

남자는 여자에게 무엇을 전자우편으로 보낼 것인가?
(A) 허가증 사본
(B) 판매 수치
(C) 개정된 안내 책자
(D) 상점의 사진

세부 사항 질문으로 질문의 키워드 send, electronically에 집중한다. 남자가 I'll send you the exact numbers by e-mail이라고 말한 부분에서 판매 수치를 보낼 것임을 알 수 있다. electronically는 by e-mail로 바꿔 표현되었다.

Questions 53-55 refer to the following conversation. 미W 영M

W Sean, have you finished with next month's fitness schedule yet? I'd like to post it on the center's website today.
M It hasn't been completed yet. I have confirmed the schedule with all the instructors except for one. I'm still waiting to hear from Janice, the yoga instructor.
W I see. Could you speak with her as soon as she gets in and finalize the schedule by noon today? Next month's schedule should be posted on the website by the end of the day and copies mailed to all the club members.
M Okay. I'll be sure to finish it by then.

여 Sean, 다음 달 피트니스 스케줄은 마무리했나요? 오늘 우리 센터 웹 사이트에 올리고 싶은데요.
남 아직 끝내지 못했습니다. 한 명만 빼고 모든 강사들과 스케줄을 확인했고요, 아직 요가 강사인 Janice로부터 확인을 기다리고 있습니다.
여 그렇군요. 그녀가 출근하자마자 얘기를 해 보시고 오늘 정오까지는 스케줄을 끝내주시겠어요? 다음 달 스케줄은 오늘까지는 웹 사이트에 게시되어야 하고 회원들에게도 우편으로 보내야 하거든요.
남 알겠습니다. 그때까지 반드시 끝내겠습니다.

post (정보 등을) 게시하다 except for ~을 제외하고 finalize 마무리하다

53 What type of business do the speakers probably work for?
(A) A manufacturing plant
(B) A community park
(C) A high school
(D) A fitness center

화자들은 어떤 종류의 업체에서 일하는가?
(A) 생산 공장
(B) 지역 공원
(C) 고등학교
(D) 피트니스 센터

도입부 대화의 내용이 fitness schedule을 작성하는 것이므로 정답은 (D)가 된다.

54 What is the man waiting for?
(A) Some fitness equipment
(B) A package from his family
(C) Confirmation from an instructor
(D) A list of mailing addresses

남자는 무엇을 기다리고 있는가?
(A) 운동 장비
(B) 가족으로부터 온 소포
(C) 강사로부터의 확인
(D) 우편 주소의 리스트

남자가 스케줄 확인을 한 명의 강사 빼고는 다 했다고 언급했고 바로 I'm still waiting to hear from Janice, the yoga instructor라고 했으므로 정답은 (C)가 된다.

55 What does the woman ask the man to do?
(A) Send an e-mail
(B) Complete a schedule
(C) Go to the post office
(D) Finalize a contract

여자는 남자에게 무엇을 할 것을 요청하는가?
(A) 이메일 보내기
(B) 스케줄 마무리하기
(C) 우체국으로 가기
(D) 계약 마무리하기

여자가 남자에게 요청하는 부분은 Could you라는 요청 표현과 함께 나온다. 정오까지 finalize the schedule 할 것을 요청했으므로 정답은 (B)이고 finalize와 complete은 동의어이다.

Questions 56-58 refer to the following conversation. (영M) (영W)

M Hi, Jessica. Are you available to lead a training session next Tuesday? I'd like you to teach new employees how to use our company's intranet system.
W Sure, Marcus. I'd be glad to. But you usually do the computer training, don't you?
M Yes, but we're going to need one more session this time because more than 50 people are expected to attend. I'll teach the first group in meeting room A and you can work with the other group in meeting room B.
W Sounds great. Please let me know what you'd like me to cover during the session. Why don't we meet after lunch to talk more about it?

남 안녕하세요, Jessica. 다음 주 화요일에 교육을 지도할 시간이 되나요? 사내 통신망을 사용하는 방법을 신입 직원들에게 가르쳐 주셨으면 합니다.
여 그럼요, Marcus. 기꺼이 하겠습니다. 그런데 보통은 당신이 컴퓨터 교육을 하잖아요, 그렇지 않나요?
남 네, 그런데 이번에는 50명 이상의 참가자가 올 것으로 예상되어서 수업이 하나 더 필요할 것입니다. 제가 회의실 A에서 첫 번째 그룹을 가르치고, 당신은 회의실 B에서 다른 그룹을 가르치면 됩니다.
여 좋습니다. 제가 교육 중에 어떤 것을 다루길 원하시는지 알려 주세요. 점심 후에 만나서 더 얘기를 하는 건 어떨까요?

lead a session 교육을 이끌다 intranet 사내 통신망 cover (주제 등을) 다루다, 가르치다

56 What does the man ask the woman to do?
(A) Test a system
(B) Attend a meeting
(C) Lead a session
(D) Order a computer

남자는 여자에게 무엇을 하도록 부탁하는가?
(A) 시스템 시험하기
(B) 회의에 참석하기
(C) 교육 지도하기
(D) 컴퓨터 주문하기

남자가 여자에게 요청하는 것으로 남자 대사에서 Are you available to lead a training session이 언급되었을 때 여자에게 요청하는 것은 교육을 지도해 달라는 것으로 알 수 있다. 정답은 (C)가 된다.

57 Why does the man need assistance?
(A) An extra session has been added.
(B) A deadline has to be met.
(C) A room has to be cleaned.
(D) A speaker will be unavailable.

남자는 왜 도움을 필요로 하는가?
(A) 교육이 하나 더 추가되었다.
(B) 마감이 지켜져야만 한다.
(C) 방은 청소되어야 한다.
(D) 연사가 시간이 되지 않는다.

세부 사항 why 질문으로 남자가 도움을 필요로 한다는 사실을 미리 알려주었으므로, 대화를 들을 때 해당 내용에 집중하여 정답을 찾는다. 남자가 여자에게 교육을 지도할 것을 부탁했고 그 이유로 because more than 50 people are expected to attend(50명 이상의 참석자가 예상되기 때문에)라고 언급했다. 또한 미팅 룸 A, B 두 곳에서 열릴 것이라고 말해준 것에서 정답을 (A)로 선택한다.

58 What does the woman suggest?
(A) Having lunch together
(B) Registering for the session
(C) Contacting the manager
(D) Meeting to discuss plans

여자는 무엇을 제안하는가?
(A) 점심을 함께 먹는 것
(B) 교육에 등록하는 것
(C) 매니저에게 연락하는 것
(D) 만나서 계획에 대해 논의하는 것

세부 사항 질문으로 여자가 Why don't we meet after lunch to talk more about it?이라고 제안한 부분에서 정답을 찾을 수 있다. 점심 후에 만나서 더 얘기 나누자고 했으므로 정답은 (D)이다.

Questions 59-61 refer to the following conversation. 영M 미W

M Margot, did you apply for the position I e-mailed you about?
W No. Actually I haven't had a chance to take a good look at the job description yet. Could you tell me what the position is again?
M Well, it's for an advertising copywriter, which is basically the same job you have now. However, this firm is larger than the agency you currently work for. And they offer a better salary and benefits too. You really should apply for it.
W There's no such thing as a free lunch. A high salary may look good initially but I may have to work really long hours. I think I should find out more about the company before I apply.

남 Margot, 제가 이메일로 보내 준 일자리 지원해 보셨나요?
여 아니요, 실은 업무 내용도 제대로 볼 기회가 없었어요. 어떤 일이었는지 다시 알려 주실래요?
남 음, 현재 당신의 직업과 동일한 광고 카피라이터 직이에요. 그렇지만 이 회사가 당신이 현재 일하고 있는 회사보다 크죠. 그래서 더 좋은 봉급과 복리 혜택을 제공하는 것이고요. 지원 한 번 해보시는 게 좋겠어요.
여 세상에 공짜는 없는 법이죠. 처음에는 높은 봉급이 좋아 보이지만 일을 그만큼 많이 해야 할 수도 있어요. 지원하기 전에 그 회사에 대해 더 알아보는 게 좋겠어요.

have a chance to ~할 기회를 갖다 benefit 복리 혜택 initially 처음에는

59 What are the speakers mainly discussing?
(A) An employment opportunity
(B) A new advertising campaign
(C) A colleague's salary
(D) A retirement plan

화자들은 무엇에 관하여 이야기하는가?
(A) 취업 기회
(B) 새로운 광고
(C) 동료의 봉급
(D) 은퇴 계획

대화의 도입부에서 남자가 여자에게 일자리에 지원은 해 봤는지 물었으므로 취업 기회에 대한 대화임을 알 수 있다.

60 What type of company does the woman work for?
(A) A staffing agency
(B) An advertising firm
(C) An insurance company
(D) A catering company

여자는 어떤 종류의 업체에서 일하는가?
(A) 채용 업체
(B) 광고 회사
(C) 보험 회사
(D) 출장 뷔페 회사

여자의 직장을 알 수 있는 부분은 it's for an advertising copywriter, which is basically the same job you have now이다. 현재의 직업과 동일한 광고 카피라이터 직이라고 했으므로 여자는 광고 회사에 다님을 알 수 있다.

61 What does the woman imply when she says, "There is no such thing as a free lunch"?
(A) She is willing to apply for the job.
(B) The position requires many years of experience.
(C) The job may pay well because it is demanding.
(D) She will review the job description.

여자가 "세상에 공짜는 없는 법이죠"라고 말한 의도는 무엇인가?
(A) 여자는 그 직위에 지원하고자 한다.
(B) 그 직위는 수년의 경력을 요구한다.
(C) 일이 힘들기 때문에 급여가 높을지도 모른다.
(D) 업무 내용을 확인해 볼 것이다.

신토익 유형으로 우선은 여자가 언급한 표현의 의미를 알아두자. 세상에 공짜는 없다는 의미임으로 이 일자리가 급여가 높은 대신 그만큼의 어려움이 있을 것이라는 뜻이 된다. 해당 표현 직후에 I may have to work really long hours(일을 많이 해야만 할 수도 있다)라고 말했으므로 정답은 (C)가 맞다. 경력에 대한 언급은 없었으므로 (B)는 오답이 된다.

Questions 62-64 refer to the following conversation with three speakers. 미W 미M 영W

W1 Roy, what did you think about Mr. Michael Carlson, the candidate we met this afternoon?

M I think he is one of the strongest candidates so far but he may be overqualified for this position. You know, he managed more than a hundred employees in his last position.

W2 You make a good point, Roy. Speaking of which, why don't we recommend him for the managerial position in Hong Kong? He wouldn't be overqualified for that, right?

W1 Oh, you're right Sophia. Plus, the Hong Kong office wants to fill the position right away because the construction of our new shopping center will begin in two weeks.

M I just wonder if he is willing to relocate to another country immediately.

W2 Why don't I call him to discuss the position? If he is interested, I'll arrange a phone interview with the Hong Kong office.

여1 Roy, 오늘 오후에 면접 본 Michael Carlson 씨에 대해 어떻게 생각했나요?

남 현재까지 가장 강력한 지원자 중 한 명이라고 생각하지만 이 직위에는 지나치게 경력이 좋은 것 같아요. 아시다시피 그는 마지막 직장에서 수백 명의 직원들을 관리했잖아요.

여2 좋은 지적이에요, Roy. 얘기가 나와서 말인데, 그를 홍콩의 매니저 직에 추천하는 것은 어떨까요? 그 직위에는 경력이 지나치지 않을 거예요, 그렇죠?

여1 오, 당신 말이 맞아요, Sophia. 게다가 새로운 쇼핑센터의 공사가 2주일 후면 시작되기 때문에 홍콩 사무실은 그 공석을 빨리 채우고 싶어해요.

남 전 다만 그가 해외로 당장 전근하기를 원할지 모르겠어요.

여2 제가 그것에 대해서 그와 상의를 해 볼까요? 관심 있어 하면, 홍콩 사무실과 전화 인터뷰를 마련해 볼게요.

overqualified 필요 이상의 자격을 갖춘 fill a position 공석을 채우다

62 What does the man say about Michael Carlson?
(A) He has lived in a foreign country.
(B) He has more experience than required.
(C) He does not want to travel often.
(D) He applied for several positions.

Michael Carlson에 대해서 남자는 뭐라고 말하는가?
(A) 그는 해외에 살아본 적이 있다.
(B) 그는 요구한 것보다 더 경력이 많다.
(C) 그는 자주 출장 가기를 원치 않는다.
(D) 그는 여러 직위에 지원하였다.

Michael Carlson은 대화의 도입부에 언급된 지원자의 이름으로 남자는 그가 overqualified(경력이 요구보다 초과된다)라고 하였으므로 정답은 (B)가 된다.

63 What does Sophia suggest doing?
(A) Building a new shopping center overseas
(B) Relocating the company's headquarters
(C) Recommending a candidate for another position
(D) Advertising job openings in a newspaper

Sophia는 무엇을 할 것을 제안하는가?
(A) 해외에 새로운 쇼핑센터를 짓는 것
(B) 회사의 본사를 이전하는 것
(C) 다른 직위에 지원자를 추천하는 것
(D) 신문에 일자리 광고를 내는 것

3인 대화이므로 대화자의 이름을 잘 파악하는 것이 중요하다. Sophia가 why don't we recommend him for the managerial position in Hong Kong?(홍콩의 매니저직에 추천하는 게 어때요?)이라고 했으므로 정답은 (C)가 된다.

64 What will happen in Hong Kong in two weeks?
(A) A phone interview will be conducted.
(B) A computer system will be upgraded.
(C) A construction project will begin.
(D) An annual event will be held.

이주일 후에 홍콩에서 무슨 일을 있을 것인가?
(A) 전화 인터뷰가 진행될 것이다.
(B) 컴퓨터 시스템이 업그레이드될 것이다.
(C) 공사 프로젝트가 시작될 것이다.
(D) 연례 행사가 열릴 것이다.

키워드는 Hong Kong, in two weeks로 이 단어들이 들리는 부분에서 정답을 처리하는 것이 중요하다. the construction of our new shopping center will begin in two weeks 부분에서 정답을 (C)로 선택한다.

Questions 65-67 refer to the following conversation and list.
미W 영M

W Thank you for coming, Mac. Did you bring the chart of last month's sales?

M Yes, here's a copy. As you can see, hardwood flooring is the best-selling material in our store. So I think we should start selling other types of wood flooring, such as bamboo.

W Bamboo flooring? I don't know much about it. Do you think our customers will like it?

M Definitely. It is much like hardwood flooring, which has proved to be popular, and it is an eco-friendly option. So I think many people will buy it.

W Okay, Let's try selling bamboo flooring. By the way, this material has been a bad seller for the last 3 months. What do you think is the problem?

M Well, I'm not sure. I just assume that many people are looking for something new for their homes these days.

W Hmm... Could you conduct a survey to find out why this material is not selling well?

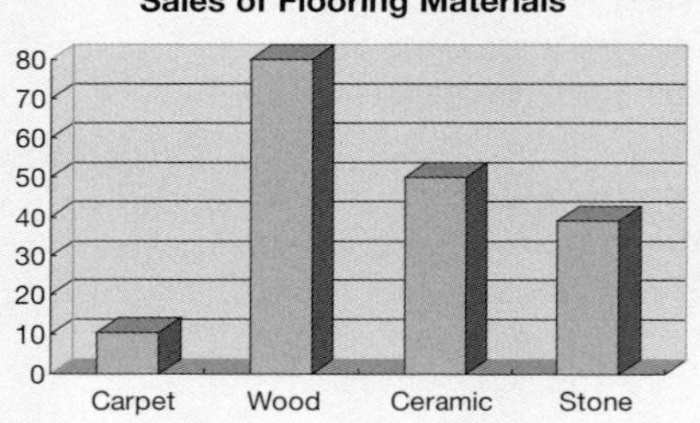

여 와 주셔서 감사합니다, Mac. 지난달 판매 차트는 가져 오셨나요?

남 네, 여기 한 부 있습니다. 보시다시피, 우리 가게에서 제일 잘 팔리는 재질은 강화 나무 바닥입니다. 그래서 대나무와 같은 다른 종류의 나무 바닥재의 판매를 시작하는 게 좋을 것 같아요

여 대나무 바닥재요? 전 그것에 대해서는 잘 몰라서요. 우리 고객들이 좋아할까요?

남 당연합니다. 이미 인기가 증명된 강화 나무 바닥재와 비슷하면서 친환경적 제품입니다. 그래서 많은 사람들이 구매할 것 같습니다.

여 좋아요. 대나무 바닥재를 팔아 보도록 하죠. 그나저나 이 재질은 지난 3개월 동안 판매가 저조하군요. 뭐가 문제인가요?

남 음, 잘 모르겠습니다. 제 추측으로는 많은 사람들이 최근에는 집에 놓을 뭔가 새로운 것을 원하는 것 같습니다.

여 흠… 이 제품이 왜 잘 안 팔리는지 고객 설문 조사를 진행해 주시겠어요?

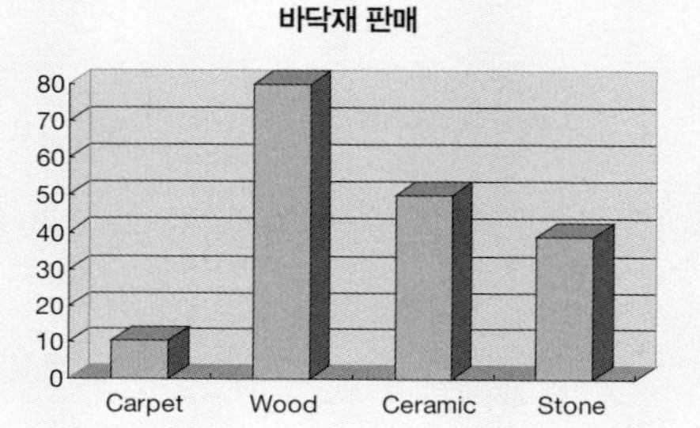

hardwood flooring 강화 나무 바닥재 bamboo 대나무 eco-friendly 친환경적인 a bad seller 잘 안 팔리는 제품 conduct a survey 설문 조사를 하다

65 Which material is the best seller in the store?
(A) Bamboo
(B) Carpet
(C) Hardwood
(D) Ceramic

어떤 재질이 이 가게에서 가장 잘 팔리는가?
(A) 대나무
(B) 카페트
(C) 강화 나무
(D) 세라믹

질문의 키워드인 the best seller에 집중하자. 도입부에 hardwood flooring이 가장 잘 팔린다고 했으므로 정답은 (C)이다.

66 What does the man mention about bamboo flooring?
(A) It is easy to clean.
(B) It is environmentally friendly.
(C) It is affordable.
(D) It is durable.

대나무 바닥재에 대해서 남자는 무엇을 언급하는가?
(A) 청소가 쉽다.
(B) 친환경적이다.
(C) 가격이 적절하다.
(D) 내구성이 좋다.

남자 대사에 정답이 있으므로 집중하자. 대나무 바닥재에 대하여 언급된 것은 hardwood flooring과 비슷하면서 eco-friendly option이라고 했으므로 정답은 (B)가 된다. environmentally friendly와 eco-friendly는 동의어이다.

67 Look at the graphic. Which material will the man investigate?
(A) Carpet
(B) Wood
(C) Ceramic
(D) Stone

시각 정보를 보시오. 남자는 어떤 재질을 조사할 것인가?
(A) 카펫
(B) 나무
(C) 세라믹
(D) 돌

대화의 내용상 a bad seller(잘 안 팔리는 제품)에 대하여 왜 안 팔리는지 고객 설문을 진행하라고 했으므로 정답은 (A)가 된다. 차트에서 판매가 저조한 항목은 carpet뿐이다.

Questions 68-70 refer to the following conversation and chart. (영M) (영W)

M So, how are the preparations for the office party going? It's in two days from now.

W Well, everything is set except for the catering order. I e-mailed everybody in our department, requesting RSVP by the 21st, which was yesterday. However, only half of them have replied so far. 20 people have confirmed they will be attending so I just placed a catering order for one tray of Spanish salad and one tray of chicken wings, which will cost us $300 in total.

M Oh, but I'm sure there will be more than 40 of us at the party. Why don't you order another tray of chicken wings?

W Okay. We can actually get a discount on the second tray. I'll call the caterer to add the item to our order and ask for a revised price estimate.

Anne's Catering MENU		
Item	Tray for 20	Each Additional Tray
Spanish Salad	$100	$90
Chicken wings	$200	$180

남 그래서 사무실 파티 준비는 어떻게 진행이 되고 있나요? 이제 이틀 밖에 남지 않았어요.

여 음, 출장 뷔페 주문 외에는 모두 준비가 되었습니다. 부서 사람들 모두에게 어제인 21일까지 참석 여부를 알려 달라는 이메일을 보냈습니다. 그렇지만 현재까지 절반만 답장을 주었어요. 20명이 참석을 확인해 주었기 때문에 스페인식 샐러드 트레이 하나와 치킨 윙 트레이 하나를 주문하였고 총 300달러가 들 예정입니다

남 아, 그런데 파티에는 40명 이상은 확실히 올 거예요. 치킨 윙 트레이를 하나 더 주문하는 게 어떨까요?

여 알겠습니다. 실은 두 번째 트레이는 할인을 받을 수 있어요. 지금 업체에 전화해서 그 품목을 추가하고 수정된 가격 견적서를 요청하겠습니다.

Anne's 출장 뷔페 메뉴		
품목	20인분 트레이	추가 트레이
Spanish Salad	100달러	90달러
Chicken wings	200달러	180달러

RSVP répondez s'il vous plait (please reply)를 줄인 말 reply 답장하다 tray 쟁반 revised 수정된

68 What problem does the woman mention?
(A) A rain shower is forecast.
(B) Not many people have replied.
(C) A supplier has raised its prices.
(D) A restaurant does not accept reservations.

여자는 어떤 문제점을 언급하는가?
(A) 소나기가 예보되었다.
(B) 많은 사람들이 답을 하지 않았다.
(C) 공급업체가 가격을 올렸다.
(D) 레스토랑이 예약을 받지 않는다.

여자 대사에 집중하여 문제점을 파악하자. 부서 사람들에게 참석 여부를 알려 달라고 이메일을 보냈다고 하며 only half of them have replied so far(절반만 답을 보냈다)라고 했으므로 정답은 (B)가 된다.

69 Look at the graphic. How much is it for the entire catering order?
(A) $100
(B) $200
(C) $300
(D) $480

시각 정보를 보시오. 전체 출장 뷔페 주문은 얼마인가?
(A) 100달러
(B) 200달러
(C) 300달러
(D) 480달러

메뉴에서 주문된 음식의 가격을 합한 것이 정답이 된다. 치킨윙이 2 트레이 주문되나 추가 트레이는 할인이 되고, 스페인식 샐러드 1 트레이므로 총액은 480달러가 된다.

70 What will the woman probably do next?
(A) Contact a catering company
(B) Pay a bill
(C) Call a party planner
(D) Cancel an event

여자는 다음에 무엇을 할 것 같은가?
(A) 출장 뷔페 업체에 연락하기
(B) 청구서의 돈을 지불하기
(C) 파티 플래너에게 전화하기
(D) 이벤트 취소하기

대화의 후반부에서 단서를 찾는다. 주문 변경에 대해서 I'll call the caterer(업체에 전화하겠다)라고 했으므로 정답은 (A)가 된다.

PART 4

Questions 71-73 refer to the following advertisement. 영M

Are you looking for a used car or truck? Come to Best Dealership this weekend for the biggest sale of the year. Every vehicle in our showroom will be at least half off the regular price. This weekend only, you'll find a two-day sale like no other. Plus, every vehicle will be covered by our three-year platinum warranty. So come to Best Dealership located at 325 Front Street this Saturday and Sunday.

중고차나 트럭을 찾고 계십니까? 이번 주말에 Best Dealership로 오시면 일 년 중 가장 큰 할인을 합니다. 저희 전시장의 모든 차량이 소비자 가격에서 50퍼센트 이상 할인됩니다. 이번 주말에만 여러분은 한 번도 볼 수 없었던 이틀 간의 할인을 볼 수 있을 겁니다. 게다가, 전 차량은 3년간의 무상 수리 혜택을 받을 수 있습니다. 그러니 이번 주 토요일과 일요일에 Front Street 325번지에 있는 Best Dealership으로 오십시오.

be covered 보장되다 warranty 무상 수리 기간

71 What kind of company is being advertised?
(A) A car dealership
(B) A clothing shop
(C) A new restaurant
(D) A furniture store
어떤 종류의 업체가 광고되고 있는가?
(A) 자동차 판매업체
(B) 의류 상점
(C) 새로운 레스토랑
(D) 가구점

광고의 도입부에서 광고되는 업체를 파악하자. Are you looking for a used car or truck?에서부터 자동차 판매점이라는 것을 알 수 있다.

72 What is the purpose of the advertisement?
(A) To introduce a new car
(B) To announce a new location
(C) To promote a special sale
(D) To provide a free service
광고의 목적이 무엇인가?
(A) 신차를 소개하려고
(B) 새로운 지점을 발표하려고
(C) 특별 세일을 홍보하려고
(D) 무료 서비스를 제공하려고

광고의 목적 역시 도입부에 언급이 된다. 업체에서 여는 행사가 for the biggest sale of the year(일 년 중 가장 큰 할인 행사)라고 했으므로 정답은 (C)가 된다.

73 What does the speaker say about Best Dealership?
(A) It specializes in cars for families.
(B) It provides warranty service.
(C) It has opened another showroom.
(D) It opens only on weekends.
화자는 Best Dealership에 대해서 뭐라고 하는가?
(A) 가족을 위한 차를 전문으로 한다.
(B) 무상수리 서비스를 제공한다.
(C) 다른 전시장을 오픈하였다.
(D) 주말에만 문을 연다.

업체에 대해 언급된 내용 중 일치하는 것은 every vehicle will be covered by our three-year platinum warranty(3년 동안 무상 수리를 받을 수 있다)라는 것이므로 정답은 (B)이다.

Questions 74-76 refer to the following message. 영W

Hello, Ms. Miller. This is Joanna from Patina Antique Furniture. You ordered a vintage teak coffee table on our Web site this morning and I wanted to follow up on your order. I'm sorry to inform you that the coffee table you wanted was out of stock when you placed the order because our online ordering system was not properly updated. We're very sorry about the mistake and we would like to offer you a 20 percent discount on your next purchase. And if you can stop by our showroom, I'll show you some other coffee tables in a similar style.

안녕하세요, Miller 씨. 저는 Patina Antique Furniture의 Joanna입니다. 오늘 아침 저희 웹 사이트를 통해 티크로 된 커피 테이블을 주문하셨고 그 주문 건에 관련하여 전화합니다. 죄송하게도 저희 온라인 주문 시스템이 제대로 업데이트가 되지 않았기 때문에 주문하실 당시에 원하셨던 그 커피 테이블은 재고가 없는 상태였습니다. 실수에 대해 사과 드리고 다음 구매 시에 20퍼센트 할인을 해 드리고 싶습니다. 그리고 만약 저희 매장에 들르실 수 있다면, 제가 비슷한 스타일의 커피 테이블들을 보여 드리도록 하겠습니다.

teak 티크 나무 out of stock 재고가 없는

74 What did the listener recently order?
(A) A mini dress
(B) A computer
(C) A coffee table
(D) A refrigerator
청자는 최근에 무엇을 주문했는가?
(A) 짧은 원피스
(B) 컴퓨터
(C) 커피 테이블
(D) 냉장고

메시지의 도입부에 화자가 You ordered a vintage teak coffee table이라고 했으므로 청자가 주문한 물건은 커피 테이블이 된다.

75 What is the problem?
(A) An item is unavailable.
(B) A delivery is delayed.
(C) Some equipment is outdated.
(D) There is a mistake on the bill.
문제가 무엇인가?
(A) 상품이 이용 가능하지 않다.
(B) 배송이 지연된다.
(C) 기계가 오래됐다.
(D) 청구서에 실수가 있다.

메시지를 남기는 이유가 the coffee table you wanted was out of stock(당신이 원했던 커피 테이블은 재고가 없다)이라고 했으므로 정답은 (A)가 된다. out of stock과 unavailable은 토익에 자주 등장하는 동의어이다.

76 What does the speaker offer to do?
(A) Cancel an order
(B) Rent some tables
(C) Reserve some items
(D) Provide a discount

화자는 무엇을 해 주겠다고 하는가?
(A) 주문 취소하기
(B) 테이블 빌리기
(C) 상품 예약하기
(D) 할인 제공하기

컴퓨터 주문 시스템에 업데이트가 잘 안되었던 점을 사과하면서 다음 구매에 쓸 수 있도록 we would like to offer you a 20 percent discount(20퍼센트 할인을 제공하겠다)라고 했으므로 정답은 (D)가 된다.

Questions 77-79 refer to the following broadcast. 미M

This is Matt Wood with your local traffic report. It is three o'clock on Friday afternoon and today's weather is picture perfect! Well, everybody seems to be leaving work early today to enjoy the sun. The highways leading out of the city are already jam-packed with cars. Tomorrow is the start of the Annual Summer Music Festival, which is being held all weekend at the Clapton Hall and surrounding beaches. So you should avoid that area. Try taking Route 16 instead. Have a nice weekend, and stay tuned for the local news report.

교통 정보를 알려 드리는 Matt Wood입니다. 지금은 금요일 오후 3시 정각이고 날씨는 완벽합니다! 모든 사람들이 햇볕을 즐기기 위해서 오늘은 일찍 퇴근을 하는 것 같습니다. 도시를 빠져나가는 고속 도로가 이미 차들로 꽉 차 있습니다. 내일은 연례 여름 음악 축제의 첫날로, 주말 내내 Clapton Hall과 주변 해변가에서 열리게 됩니다. 그러니 그 지역은 피하시는 게 좋겠습니다. 대신 Route 16을 이용해 주세요. 좋은 주말 보내시고 지역 뉴스를 듣기 위해 주파수를 고정해 주세요.

picture perfect 완벽한 leading out of ~을 빠져 나가는 jam-packed 꽉 차 있는

77 What is the main topic of the report?
(A) Music
(B) Weather
(C) Finance
(D) Traffic

보도의 주제는 무엇인가?
(A) 음악
(B) 날씨
(C) 금융
(D) 교통

방송의 도입부에 화자가 본인을 소개할 때 This is Matt Wood with your local traffic report라고 말한 부분에서 교통 방송임을 알 수 있다.

78 Why is everybody leaving work early today?
(A) To attend a local festival
(B) To enjoy the good weather
(C) To avoid traffic jams
(D) To go on summer vacation

왜 모든 사람들이 오늘 일찍 퇴근하는가?
(A) 지역 페스티벌에 참석하려고
(B) 좋은 날씨를 즐기려고
(C) 교통 체증을 피하려고
(D) 여름 휴가를 가려고

사람들이 오늘 일찍 퇴근한다는 이유는 everybody seems to be leaving work early today to enjoy the sun에서 언급된 것처럼 햇볕을 즐기기 위해서라고 했으므로 정답은 (B)가 된다.

79 What event will begin tomorrow?
(A) A sporting event
(B) A ballet performance
(C) An annual festival
(D) A singing competition

내일 어떤 행사가 시작되는가?
(A) 스포츠 행사
(B) 발레 공연
(C) 연례 페스티벌
(D) 노래 경연

Tomorrow is the start of the Annual Summer Music Festival에서 내일 시작될 행사는 매년 열리는 음악 페스티벌임을 알 수 있다. 정답은 (C)이다.

Questions 80-82 refer to the following excerpt from a meeting. 미W

Welcome to the 10th monthly meeting of the Thornhill Community Association. I'm Stephanie Green, the chairperson of the group for this year. First I'd like to welcome new residents and we'll get to introductions shortly. As you already know, we get together every month to talk about things we can do in order to make our town a better place to live. The first item on our agenda today is the proposed sports arena on Henderson Boulevard. The good news is that several local businesses have agreed to fund the project. Construction will begin soon and the sports arena should be ready by spring next year.

제10회 Thornhill Community Association 월례 회의에 오신 것을 환영합니다. 저는 올해의 회장인 Stephanie Green입니다. 우선 신규 거주민들을 환영하며 곧 소개를 드리도록 하겠습니다. 이미 아시는 것처럼, 저희는 매달 모여서 우리 마을을 더 살기 좋은 곳으로 만들기 위해 할 수 있는 일들에 대해 논의합니다. 오늘 안건의 첫 번째 항목은 Henderson Boulevard에 스포츠 경기장을 세우자는 제안입니다. 좋은 소식은 몇 개의 지역 사업체들이 이 프로젝트를 후원해 주기로 결정했다는 것입니다. 공사는 곧 시작될 것이고 경기장은 내년 봄까지 준비될 것입니다.

chairperson 회장 resident 거주민 proposed 제안된 sports arena 경기장 fund 재정적으로 후원하다

80 Who is the intended audience of the talk?
(A) Business owners
(B) Local residents
(C) Soccer players
(D) Real estate agents
담화의 의도된 청중은 누구인가?
(A) 사업가
(B) 지역 주민
(C) 축구 선수
(D) 부동산 중개인

도입부에 청자를 유추할 수 있는 부분은 Thornhill Community Association 월례 회의라는 점과 새로운 주민을 환영하는 부분 등이다. 정답은 (B)가 된다.

81 According to the speaker, what will be constructed?
(A) A hospital
(B) A community center
(C) A sports stadium
(D) A subway station
화자에 따르면, 무엇이 건설될 것인가?
(A) 병원
(B) 커뮤니티 센터
(C) 스포츠 경기장
(D) 지하철역

회의의 첫 안건이 the proposed sports arena(제안된 스포츠 경기장 → 스포츠 경기장을 짓자는 제안)로 공사가 바로 시작될 것이라고 했으므로 정답은 (C)가 된다.

82 What does the speaker mention about some local businesses?
(A) They will provide financial support.
(B) They will host a charity banquet.
(C) They will attract more tourists.
(D) They have signed an agreement.
화자는 일부 지역 사업체들에 대해서 무엇을 언급하는가?
(A) 재정 지원을 제공할 것이다.
(B) 자선 연회를 개최할 것이다.
(C) 더 많은 관광객을 유치할 것이다.
(D) 계약서에 서명하였다.

지역 사업체가 언급된 several local businesses have agreed to fund the project에서 업체들이 프로젝트를 후원해 주기로 합의하였다고 했으므로 정답은 (A)가 된다.

Questions 83-85 refer to the following excerpt from a meeting. (영W)

Okay everyone. As you already know, PA Accounting Firm is having a private dinner party in the main dining hall. Therefore, the restaurant will be closed to the public this evening. PA Accounting always chooses our restaurant to hold their special events because they know they can get the best food and outstanding service here at Aberdeen's Dining. So, let's make sure that's what they receive. There will be 300 guests to serve at the same time, and some of them have specially requested vegetarian dishes. So you'll need to pay special attention. Please take a good look at your work assignments and let's get started.

좋습니다 여러분. 아시다시피, PA Accounting Firm이 메인 홀을 빌려 저녁 파티를 합니다. 그러므로 레스토랑은 오늘 저녁 일반 손님들에게는 문을 닫습니다. PA Accounting은 항상 특별 행사를 할 때 저희 레스토랑을 선택하는데 Aberdeen's Dining에서는 최고의 음식과 훌륭한 서비스를 받을 수 있다는 것을 알기 때문입니다. 그러니 그들이 그것을 받을 수 있도록 합시다. 동시에 300명의 손님이 있을 것이고 일부는 특별히 채식 요리을 요청하였습니다. 그러니 각별히 주의를 기울여야 할 것입니다. 본인의 업무 내용을 잘 살펴보시고 일을 시작합시다.

the public 일반 대중 outstanding 뛰어난 vegetarian dishes 베지테리언 메뉴

83 Where does the speaker most likely work?
(A) At an accounting firm
(B) At a restaurant
(C) At a convention center
(D) At a radio station
화자는 어디서 일할 것 같은가?
(A) 회계 사무소
(B) 레스토랑
(C) 컨벤션 센터
(D) 라디오 방송국

화자의 업무 내용을 통해 일하는 곳을 유추할 수 있다. 회계 사무소가 저녁 파티를 열 것이고 그래서 the restaurant will be closed to the public(레스토랑이 일반 손님에게는 문을 닫는다)이라고 했으므로 이곳은 레스토랑이 맞다.

84 Why does the speaker say, "So, let's make sure that's what they receive"?
(A) To encourage employees to provide excellent food and service
(B) To provide PA Accounting staff with a promotional gift
(C) To invite as many people as possible to an event
(D) To announce that the restaurant will receive an award

왜 화자는 "그러니 그들이 그것을 받을 수 있도록 합시다"라고 말하는가?

(A) 직원들이 훌륭한 음식과 서비스를 제공하도록 하려고
(B) PA Accounting직원들에게 홍보용 선물을 제공하려고
(C) 행사에 최대한 많은 사람들을 초대하려고
(D) 레스토랑이 상을 받는다는 걸 알리려고

해당 표현 직전에 그 회사가 항상 이 레스토랑을 선택하는 이유가 좋은 음식과 훌륭한 서비스 때문이라고 했고 그 후에 So, let's make sure that's what they receive(그러니 그들이 그것을 받을 수 있도록 합시다)라고 말했으므로 정답은 (A)가 된다.

85 What will the listeners probably do next?
(A) Clean a dining room
(B) Start serving dinner
(C) Contact an accounting firm
(D) Check their work assignments

청자들은 다음에 무엇을 할 것 같은가?
(A) 식당 청소하기
(B) 저녁 서빙 시작하기
(C) 회계 사무소에 연락하기
(D) 업무 내용 확인하기

향후 행동의 단서는 후반부에 있다. 직원들에게 업무 내용을 살펴본 후 일을 시작하자고 했으므로 정답은 (D)가 된다.

Questions 86-88 refer to the following telephone message. (미M)

Hi, Adele, this is Jose Johnson in Human Resources. I apologize for missing today's meeting. Unfortunately, my car got a flat tire on my way to work this morning. I know that one of the accountants in your department resigned last month and you would like to fill the opening as soon as possible. So I'm planning to post an advertisement on the company website by tomorrow morning. To make the process faster, I need you to e-mail me a draft of the job description and qualifications by 5. I'll be working late tonight, reviewing the wording of the announcement.

안녕하세요 Adele. 인사부서의 Jose Johnson입니다. 오늘 회의에 참석하지 못해서 사과드립니다. 불행히도, 아침에 제 차의 타이어에 펑크가 났습니다. 당신 부서의 회계사 중 한 명이 퇴직해서 빨리 공석을 채우고 싶어 하신다는 것을 알고 있습니다. 그래서 저는 내일 아침까지는 회사 웹 사이트에 구인 광고를 낼 예정입니다. 더 빠른 진행을 위해서, 당신이 업무 소개와 자격 요건에 대한 초안을 5시까지 저에게 이메일로 보내 주셨으면 합니다. 저는 공지에 쓰인 표현을 검토하면서 오늘 밤 늦게까지 일할 것입니다.

human resources 인사부 apologize for ~에 대해 사과하다 flat tire (자동차의) 펑크 post an advertisement 광고를 게시하다 drift 초안 job description 업무 설명 qualification 자격 요건 wording (글의) 표현, 어투

86 In what department does Adele most likely work?
(A) Human Resources
(B) Advertising
(C) Accounting
(D) Engineering

Adele은 어떤 부서에서 일하는가?
(A) 인사부
(B) 광고
(C) 회계
(D) 엔지니어링

담화에 언급된 부서는 2개이므로 질문의 키워드인 Adele의 부서를 정확히 확인한다. Adele은 메시지를 받는 사람이므로 대명사 you로 받는 점에 주목하자. one of the accountants in your department resigned(부서에서 회계사 중 한 명이 퇴직했다) 부분에서 정답은 (C)임을 알 수 있다.

87 Why does the speaker apologize?
(A) His report was overdue.
(B) His client complained about his work.
(C) He did not attend the meeting.
(D) He was late for the company event.

화자는 왜 사과하는가?
(A) 그의 보고서가 기한이 초과되었다.
(B) 그의 고객이 그의 업무에 대해 불평했다.
(C) 그는 회의에 참석하지 못했다.
(D) 그는 회사 행사에 늦었다.

화자가 사과하는 표현을 말할 때 이유가 함께 언급된다. I apologize for를 언급하고 오늘의 회의를 놓쳤다고 했으므로 정답은 (C)가 된다.

88 What does the speaker say he will do tonight?
(A) Examine a document
(B) Calculate sales figures
(C) Write up an agenda
(D) Speak with a client

화자는 오늘 밤에 무엇을 하겠다고 하는가?
(A) 서류 검토하기
(B) 판매 수치 계산하기
(C) 안건 작성하기
(D) 고객과 이야기하기

세부 사항 질문으로 tonight이 가장 중요한 키워드이다. 화자가 working late tonight을 언급하고 공지에 쓰인 문구를 검토할 것이라고 했으므로 정답은 (A)가 된다.

Questions 89-91 refer to the following talk. (미W)

I'm very happy to announce that Dr. Jack Irwin will start working at our healthcare laboratory as a visiting consultant beginning tomorrow. So I'd like to tell you what is planned for tomorrow. First, I will give him a tour of our facilities in the morning. Then at 1 p.m. there will be a welcome party in the main meeting room and you're all invited to attend. This is a great opportunity to meet Dr. Irwin in person. So, please make every effort to be there. As you know, Dr. Irwin is a world leading expert in the field of healthcare, and collaborating with him will be very beneficial to our company.

내일부터 Jack Irwin 박사님이 초청 컨설턴트로서 우리 의료 연구실에서 일하게 되었다는 사실을 알리게 되어 기쁩니다. 자 내일의 일정을 알려 드리도록 하겠습니다. 우선, 제가 오전에 우리 시설물을 구경시켜 드릴 것입니다. 그리고 오후 1시에 대회의실에서 환영 파티가 있을 것이고 여러분 모두 초대되었습니다. Irwin 박사님을 직접 만날 수 있는 굉장한 기회이지요. 그러니 반드시 그곳에 올 수 있도록 해주세요. 아시다시피 Irwin 박사님은 의료 업계에서 가장 선두적인 전문가이고 그와 공동으로 일을 진행하는 것은 우리 회사에도 굉장히 이득이 될 것입니다.

visiting consultant 초청 컨설턴트 give a tour ~를 구경시켜주다 make every effort to ~하기 위해 최선을 다하다 collaborate with ~와 협동하다, 공동으로 일을 진행하다 beneficial 이득이 되는

89 Who is Dr. Jack Irwin?
(A) The CEO of the company
(B) A famous athlete
(C) A visiting consultant
(D) A heart surgeon

Jack Irwin 박사는 누구인가?
(A) 회사의 대표
(B) 유명한 운동선수
(C) 초청 컨설턴트
(D) 심장 전문 의사

질문의 키워드인 Jack Irwin 박사 주변에 정답이 있다. Dr. Jack Irwin will start working at our healthcare laboratory as a visiting consultant를 통해 Jack Irwin은 초청 컨설턴트라는 것을 알 수 있다.

90 What is Dr. Jack Irwin's area of expertise?
(A) Chemistry
(B) Marketing
(C) Technology
(D) Healthcare

Jack Irwin 박사의 전문 분야는 무엇인가?
(A) 화학
(B) 마케팅
(C) 기술
(D) 의료

Jack Irwin 박사는 초청 컨설턴트로서 일할 업체가 our healthcare laboratory(의료 연구실)이므로 전문 분야는 의료 분야가 된다.

91 What does the woman imply when she says "So, please make every effort to be there"?
(A) Employees should be present at the party.
(B) Employees should be determined to reach a goal.
(C) Employees should work as a team.
(D) Employees should not be late for work.

화자가 "그러니 반드시 그곳에 올 수 있도록 해주세요"라고 말한 의미는 무엇인가?
(A) 직원들은 파티에 참석해야 한다.
(B) 직원들은 목표를 이루기 위해 노력해야 한다.
(C) 직원들은 팀으로서 일해야 한다.
(D) 직원들은 직장에 늦지 않아야 한다.

의도 파악 문제를 풀 때는 해당 표현의 앞뒤 문맥을 이용하는 것이 중요하다. 점심에 환영파티가 있을 것이고 Irwin 박사를 직접 만날 수 있는 좋은 기회라고 언급한 후에 "그러니 반드시 그곳에 올 수 있도록 해주세요"라고 했으므로 정답은 (A)가 된다.

Questions 92-94 refer to the following excerpt from a meeting. (영W)

Good morning, everyone. I've called this meeting to discuss our new line of athletic wear here at Keylime Sports Wear. As you may already know, this new line has been developed specifically for a younger generation who enjoy outdoor activities on a regular basis. In order to boost sales in the under-30 market, we need to create a new, exciting image for the line. Therefore, I'm suggesting that we hire another ad agency this time, Upstream Advertising. They have produced brilliant marketing campaigns in the under-30 market and I believe that they would be a perfect fit for us.

안녕하세요, 여러분. 우리 Keylime Sports Wear의 신상품 운동복에 관해 얘기하려고 이 회의를 소집했습니다. 이미 아시다시피, 이 새로운 라인은 야외 활동을 주기적으로 즐기는 젊은 세대를 위해 특별히 개발되었습니다. 30세 미만 시장에서의 판매를 증가시키기 위해서 우리는 새롭고, 신 나는 이미지를 만들 필요가 있습니다. 그러므로, 저는 이번에 Upstream Advertising이라는 새로운 광고 대행사를 고용할 것을 제안합니다. 그들은 30세 미만 시장을 겨냥해 매우 성공적인 마케팅 캠페인을 만들어왔고 우리와 완벽한 파트너가 될 수 있으리라 생각합니다.

new line 신상품 라인 athletic 운동의, 스포츠의 generation 세대 outdoor activities 야외 활동 on a regular basis 주기적으로, 정기적으로 boost 높이다, 증가시키다 brilliant 멋진, 성공적인, 뛰어난 fit 어울림, 조화

92 Where does the speaker most likely work?
(A) At a clothing manufacturer
(B) At a fashion magazine
(C) At a shoe store
(D) At an advertising firm

화자는 어디에서 일할 것 같은가?
(A) 의류 제조 업체
(B) 패션 잡지사
(C) 구두 가게
(D) 광고 대행사

화자의 직장을 유추하는 질문으로 도입부의 our new line of athletic wear here at Keylime Sports Wear에서 화자가 우리의 운동복 신상품이라고 말한 점, 회사의 이름에 Sports Wear가 들어가는 점을 통해 의류 제조업체임을 유추한다.

93 What is special about the new merchandise?
(A) It has come down in price.
(B) It is popular in many countries
(C) It can be custom-made.
(D) It targets a specific age group.

신상품에 관하여 무엇이 특별한가?
(A) 가격이 내렸다.
(B) 많은 국가에서 인기이다.
(C) 주문제작할 수 있다.
(D) 특정한 연령 집단을 타깃으로 한다.

신상품에 대해서 언급된 내용을 묻는 세부 사항 질문으로, 정답을 신속하게 처리하기 위해서는 반드시 미리 질문 해석이 되어 있어야 한다. 지문에서는 a younger generation(젊은 세대)을 위해 개발되었다는 것이 선택지에서는 a specific age group(특정 연령 집단)으로 바꿔 표현되었으므로 정답은 (D)이다.

94 What does the speaker suggest doing?
(A) Conducting a survey
(B) Changing advertising agencies
(C) Merging with a competitor
(D) Analyzing consumer preferences

화자는 무엇을 할 것을 제안하는가?
(A) 설문조사를 하는 것
(B) 광고 대행사를 바꾸는 것
(C) 경쟁사와 합병하는 것
(D) 소비자 선호도를 분석하는 것

화자가 제안하는 내용을 묻는 질문으로 I'm suggesting that이란 제안 표현을 들었을 때 정답을 처리한다. 다른 광고 대행사를 고용할 것을 언급했고 정답 (B)에서는 광고 대행사를 바꾼다고 다른 표현으로 쓰여 있다.

Questions 95-97 refer to the following message and schedule. 영M

Hello, Ms. Kelly Hill. This is Ben Clark from Theodore Design Store. I just received your online order form and found an error that needs to be rectified before we process your order. You selected one of our cotton polo shirts and paid $27 with your credit card because you received a 10% discount. But the problem is that the shirt you selected comes only in gray. So I'm asking that you visit our website to check if you placed the order correctly. You may have confused it with another item. If the shirt is what you're looking for, please let me know as soon as possible so we can ship it today. My phone number here at the store is 555-2309.

Order Form

Name: Kelly Hill
Address: 511 King Street
Telephone: 555–0078

Item	Unit Price	Quantity	Color
Cotton Polo Shirt	$30	1	Green
		Discount coupon:	10% off
		Grand Total:	$27

안녕하세요, Kelly Hill 씨. 저는 Theodore Design Store의 Ben Clark입니다. 당신의 온라인 주문서를 막 받아 보았는데요 주문을 처리하기에 앞서 고쳐야 할 문제를 발견했습니다. 저희 면 폴로 셔츠 하나를 선택하셨고 10퍼센트 할인을 받아서 신용 카드로 27달러를 지불하셨습니다. 그러나 문제는 선택하신 셔츠는 회색으로만 나옵니다. 그러니 저희 웹 사이트에 다시 방문하셔서 주문을 정확하게 하셨는지 확인을 해 주셨으면 합니다. 다른 상품과 혼동했을 수도 있거든요. 이 셔츠가 찾고 있는 상품이 맞으면, 오늘 발송할 수 있도록 최대한 빨리 저에게 알려 주세요. 상점 내 저의 전화번호는 555–2309입니다.

주문 양식

이름: Kelly Hill
주소: 511번지 King Street
전화번호: 555–0078

상품	가격	수량	색상
Cotton Polo Shirt	30달러	1	Green
		할인 쿠폰:	10퍼센트 할인
		총 금액:	27달러

rectify 바로잡다 process 처리하다 select 선택하다 confuse 혼동하다

95 What does the speaker say about Ms. Hill's order?
(A) A discount was applied to it.
(B) It has already been processed.
(C) She paid more than she owed.
(D) It does not include shipping costs.

Hill 씨의 주문에 관해서 화자는 뭐라고 하는가?
(A) **할인이 적용되었다.**
(B) 이미 처리가 완료되었다.
(C) 그녀는 내야 할 금액보다 많이 지불하였다.
(D) 배송료를 포함하지 않는다.

화자가 Hill 씨의 주문 내역에 대해 언급한 부분 중 일치하는 내용은 paid $27 with your credit card because you received a 10% discount(10퍼센트 할인이 되어 27달러를 신용 카드로 결제했다)라는 부분이다. 정답은 (A)가 된다.

96 Look at the graphic. According to the speaker, what information needs to be corrected?
(A) Item
(B) Quantity
(C) Color
(D) Discount rate

시각 정보를 보시오. 화자에 따르면, 어떤 정보가 부정확한가?
(A) 품목
(B) 수량
(C) **색상**
(D) 할인율

화자가 주문과 관련해 언급한 문제점이 정답의 단서이다. 청자가 선택한 상품이 gray 색상으로만 나온다고 했으므로 주문 양식에서 부정확한 정보는 색상이 된다.

97 What is the listener asked to do?
(A) Select another item
(B) Visit a retail shop
(C) Check the inventory
(D) Confirm an order

청자는 무엇을 할 것을 요청 받는가?
(A) 다른 상품 고르기
(B) 소매 상점 방문하기
(C) 재고 확인하기
(D) **주문 확인하기**

주문서의 error에 대해 언급한 후 웹 사이트에 방문하여 check if you placed the order correctly(주문이 정확한지 확인하라)라고 했으므로 정답은 (D)이다.

Questions 98-100 refer to the following message and list. (미M)

The first thing I'd like to discuss is the upcoming inspection of our restaurant. An inspection team from the main office will be visiting us sometime next week. Applebee's Restaurant Chain performs an inspection every year to maintain customer satisfaction and produce consistent food products and service. Our restaurant has done very well on the inspections before and I expect that once again we will earn a certificate with the company's highest rating. In order to prepare for the upcoming inspection, I examined our restaurant using this checklist. Although you all did a pretty good job overall, there was one area where we definitely need to improve. Kitchen staff did a great job so I gave them a passing grade on three of the criteria. But there was an issue with cleanliness. The wait staff really need to take extra care to keep every section of the restaurant clean and tidy at all times so that we can pass the upcoming inspection next week.

Restaurant Inspection Checklist				
	Criteria	Grading		
		3	2	1
1	Toilet cleanliness			
2	Condition of kitchen equipment			
3	Condition of prepared foods			
4	Left-over food management			

첫 번째로 이야기할 내용은 다가오는 레스토랑 검사입니다. 본사의 검사팀이 다음 주에 우리를 방문할 것입니다. Applebee's Restaurant Chain은 고객 만족과 한결 같은 음식과 서비스를 유지하기 위해서 매년 검사를 실시합니다. 우리 레스토랑은 앞서 있었던 검사에서 매우 잘해 왔고 이번에도 회사의 최고 등급으로 검사 통과서를 받기 바랍니다. 다가오는 검사에 대비하기 위해서 제가 이 체크리스트를 이용하여 레스토랑을 점검해 봤습니다. 전반적으로 여러분은 잘해 주었지만 우리가 더 향상시켜야 할 부분이 하나 있었습니다. 주방 직원들은 훌륭하게 일을 해주셔서 3가지 항목 모두 합격 점수를 드렸습니다. 그러나 청결과 관련해서 문제가 하나 있었습니다. 서빙 직원들은 레스토랑의 모든 공간이 항상 깨끗하고 정돈되어 있도록 좀 더 신경을 써서 다음 주에 있을 검사를 통과할 수 있도록 해주셔야 합니다.

레스토랑 검사 체크리스트				
	검사 요건	등급		
		3	2	1
1	화장실 청결			
2	주방 기기 상태			
3	준비된 음식 상태			
4	남은 음식 처리			

upcoming 다가오는 inspection 검사 customer satisfaction 고객 만족 consistent 일정한, 한결 같은 a passing grade 합격 점수 criteria 요건 take extra care 더 신경을 쓰다

98 Who most likely is the speaker?
(A) A chef
(B) A restaurant manager
(C) A marketing consultant
(D) An inspector

누가 화자일 것 같은가?
(A) 요리사
(B) 레스토랑 매니저
(C) 마케팅 컨설턴트
(D) 검사관

화자를 유추하는 질문으로 도입부에 단서가 있다. 레스토랑의 검사가 있을 것이라고 언급한 부분에서 말하는 이는 레스토랑의 매니저임을 알 수 있다.

99 What did the speaker do to prepare for an inspection?
(A) Approved a budget
(B) Rearranged a dining room
(C) Conducted a customer survey
(D) Examined the dining facilities

검사에 대비하기 위해서 화자는 무엇을 했는가?
(A) 예산을 승인했다.
(B) 식당을 다시 정리하였다.
(C) 고객 설문 조사를 하였다.
(D) 식당을 점검하였다.

화자가 검사 준비를 위해 이미 한 일에 집중하여 듣자. I examined our restaurant using this checklist(체크리스트를 이용해서 레스토랑을 점검했다)라고 한 부분이 정답이다.

100 Look at the graphic. What criterion should the wait staff try to improve on?
(A) Toilet cleanliness
(B) Condition of kitchen equipment
(C) Condition of prepared foods
(D) Left-over food management

시각 정보를 보시오. 어떤 요건을 서빙 직원들은 향상시켜야 하는가?
(A) 화장실 청결
(B) 주방 기기 상태
(C) 준비된 음식 상태
(D) 남은 음식 처리

시각 정보의 검사요건 중에서 부족하다고 언급된 부분은 But there was an issue with cleanliness에서 알 수 있듯이 청결과 관련된 문제라고 했고 서빙 직원들에게 청소와 정돈을 부탁했으므로 정답은 (A)이다.

Actual Test 11

PART 1

본책 p.132

1 (C)	2 (A)	3 (C)	4 (B)	5 (D)	6 (B)

PART 2

본책 p.136

7 (B)	8 (B)	9 (C)	10 (C)	11 (B)	12 (A)
13 (A)	14 (B)	15 (B)	16 (C)	17 (B)	18 (A)
19 (A)	20 (B)	21 (B)	22 (C)	23 (A)	24 (A)
25 (B)	26 (C)	27 (B)	28 (B)	29 (A)	30 (C)
31 (A)					

PART 3

본책 p.137

32 (B)	33 (D)	34 (A)	35 (A)	36 (C)	37 (A)
38 (B)	39 (D)	40 (D)	41 (C)	42 (B)	43 (A)
44 (A)	45 (C)	46 (D)	47 (B)	48 (D)	49 (A)
50 (C)	51 (A)	52 (B)	53 (C)	54 (A)	55 (D)
56 (A)	57 (D)	58 (C)	59 (A)	60 (D)	61 (A)
62 (C)	63 (A)	64 (B)	65 (D)	66 (D)	67 (D)
68 (A)	69 (C)	70 (D)			

PART 4

본책 p.141

71 (C)	72 (C)	73 (B)	74 (B)	75 (D)	76 (C)
77 (B)	78 (D)	79 (C)	80 (A)	81 (C)	82 (D)
83 (A)	84 (B)	85 (D)	86 (C)	87 (A)	88 (D)
89 (A)	90 (C)	91 (D)	92 (B)	93 (C)	94 (A)
95 (D)	96 (C)	97 (A)	98 (A)	99 (C)	100 (D)

PART 1

1 (A) He is fixing his laptop.
영M (B) He is turning on the computer.
(C) He is typing on a keyboard.
(D) He is sorting through some papers.

(A) 남자가 노트북을 수리하고 있다.
(B) 남자가 컴퓨터를 켜고 있다.
(C) 남자가 키보드를 두드리고 있다.
(D) 남자가 문서를 자세히 살펴보고 있다.

컴퓨터 앞에 앉은 남자가 키보드를 두드리는 중이다.

fix 고치다, 해결하다 sort through 자세히 살펴보다

2 (A) The vehicles are lined up in a row.
미W (B) People are inspecting the cars.
(C) People are making deals for the vehicles.
(D) The tractors have just arrived in a harbor.

(A) 차량들이 한 줄로 늘어서 있다.
(B) 사람들이 차들을 살펴보고 있다.
(C) 사람들이 자동차 거래를 하고 있다.
(D) 트랙터들이 항구에 막 도착했다.

트랙터들이 한 줄로 세워져 있지만 사람들이 살펴보고 있거나 거래하고 있다고 단정하기는 어렵다.

in a row 한 줄로 inspect 조사하다, 점검하다 make a deal 거래를 하다 harbor 항구

3 (A) Cartons are being moved from a warehouse.
미M (B) A step ladder goes up into the vehicle.
(C) The back of the car is open.
(D) Items are being loaded onto a truck.

(A) 곽들이 창고에서 치워지고 있다.
(B) 발판 사다리가 자동차로 이어져 있다.
(C) 차의 뒤쪽이 열려 있다.
(D) 물건들이 트럭에 실리는 중이다.

트럭 뒷부분이 열려 있지만 짐을 싣고 있지는 않다. (B)가 정답이 되려면 계단식으로 된 사다리가 차 뒤쪽에 연결되어 있어야 한다.

carton 곽, 통, 상자 warehouse 창고 step ladder 발판 사다리 load 싣다

4 (A) The horse is chasing a man.
미M (B) The man is holding his reins.
(C) The horse is following a road.
(D) A man is riding a saddle.

(A) 말이 남자의 뒤를 쫓아가고 있다.
(B) 남자가 고삐를 쥐고 있다.
(C) 말이 길을 따라가고 있다.
(D) 남자는 말의 안장에 타고 있다.

남자가 말의 고삐를 잡고 있고 말은 달리는 중이다. 이때 남자는 말 위의 안장이 아니라 말이 끄는 마차류에 앉아 있다.

chase 뒤쫓다 reins 고삐 follow 따라가다 saddle 말에 얹는 안장

5 (A) There is a lot of debris on the street.
미W (B) Cars are moving carefully around the man.
(C) Pedestrians are walking past without glancing.
(D) The road is being swept with a broomstick.

(A) 거리에 쓰레기가 많이 있다.
(B) 자동차들이 남자 주변에서 조심스럽게 움직이고 있다.
(C) 보행자들이 눈길을 주지 않고 걸어서 지나가고 있다.
(D) 도로는 빗자루로 청소되고 있다.

남자가 긴 빗자루로 거리를 쓸고 있는데 쓰레기는 떨어져 있지 않다. 지나가는 사람들은 보이지 않으며 자동차 한 대의 일부만 보인다.

debris 잔해, 쓰레기 walk past 걸어서 지나가다, 지나쳐 가다 glance 흘깃 보다 sweep 쓸다, 청소하다 broomstick 대가 긴 빗자루

6 (A) Chickens are walking around the house.
영W (B) Pieces of wood are in a pile.
(C) Paint is being applied to a wall.
(D) The owner is working on a farm.

(A) 닭들이 집 주위를 돌아다니고 있다.
(B) 나무 조각들이 쌓여 있다.
(C) 페인트가 벽에 발리고 있다.
(D) 주인이 농장에서 일하고 있다.

나무로 만든 집 밖에 작게 잘라 놓은 나무가 가지런히 쌓여 있다.

walk around 돌아다니다 pile 더미, 쌓아 놓은 것 apply 바르다, 적용하다 owner 주인

PART 2

7 Where is that cruise going?
영M (A) Next Saturday.
미W (B) On a round-the-world trip.
(C) Walking to work.

저 크루즈는 어디로 갑니까?
(A) 다음 주 토요일이요.
(B) 세계를 여행합니다.
(C) 걸어서 출근하는 거요.

의문사 where 질문으로 크루즈가 어디로 가는지 물었으므로 세계 일주를 한다고 답한 (B)가 정답이 된다. go on a trip(여행하다)이란 표현을 암기하고 전치사 on이 함께 쓰이는 것을 기억해 두자.

round-the-world 세계 일주의

8 Who do you expect to make a hiring decision?
영W (A) We're short of staff.
영M (B) Personnel department.
(C) At the end of the month.

누가 고용 결정을 내릴 것으로 예상하십니까?
(A) 우리는 직원이 부족합니다.
(B) 인사부요.
(C) 월 말에요.

의문사 who 질문으로 사람 이름, 부서명, 회사명 등이 정답으로 연결되는 경우가 많다. (B)는 부서명으로만 답을 주고 있으므로 가장 확실한 정답이 된다.

make a decision 결정을 내리다 be short of ~이 부족하다

9 Do you need any help?
미W (A) No, this one is nice.
영W (B) Please go to the cashier.
(C) Yes, I'm looking for a camera.

도움이 필요하십니까?
(A) 아니요, 이것이 좋습니다.
(B) 계산대로 가십시오.
(C) 네, 카메라를 찾고 있습니다.

직원이 고객에게 질문하는 상황으로 도움이 필요한 상황을 이야기한 (C)가 정답이다. 단순한 해석보다는 대화의 상황을 떠올리면서 해석하는 연습을 해야 한다.

10 What's the new assistant's name?
미W (A) Next to my office.
미M (B) He's starting next Monday.
(C) It is Christopher Lee.

새 비서의 이름이 뭐죠?
(A) 제 사무실 옆에요.
(B) 그는 다음 주 월요일에 시작합니다.
(C) Christopher Lee입니다.

새 비서의 이름을 물었으므로 이름을 말해준 (C)가 정답이다.

11 When can we get together again?
영M (A) It has been sent to you already.
영W (B) How about tomorrow?
(C) Take one.

우리는 언제 또 만날 수 있나요?
(A) 그것은 당신에게 이미 발송되었어요.
(B) 내일은 어때요?
(C) 하나 가지세요.

의문사 when이 핵심으로 만날 시점에 대한 답으로 (B)가 가장 적절하다.

get together 만나다

12 How much is the fare to Atlanta?
미M (A) About thirty dollars.
미W (B) No, I walked there.
(C) To get a discount.

Atlanta에 가는 운임은 얼마죠?
(A) 30달러 정도요.
(B) 아니요, 거기 걸어갔어요.
(C) 할인을 받으려고요.

질문의 핵심은 운임 금액을 묻는 것으로 정답은 30달러라고 답한 (A)가 된다.

fare (버스, 기차 등의) 운임

13 Would you like to lead the seminar?
영W (A) No, Jennifer is better qualified.
미M (B) I'll read the daily paper.
(C) The opening ceremony is at 2 o'clock.

당신이 세미나를 진행하시겠어요?
(A) 아니오, Jennifer가 더 자격이 있습니다.
(B) 전 일간지를 읽겠습니다.
(C) 개회식은 2시입니다.

제안 의문문으로 세미나 진행을 하겠냐고 물었으므로, 거절한 후 다른 사람이 더 자격을 갖췄다고 답한 (A)가 정답이다. (B)는 lead의 유사 발음 함정인 read를 이용한 오답이다.

lead 진행하다, 이끌다 qualified 자질을 갖춘, 자격을 갖춘 daily paper 일간지 opening ceremony 개회식

14 You've been to this café before, haven't you?
미W (A) I'd like some tea.
영M (B) No, it's my first time.
(C) After you.

이 카페에 와 본 적이 있으시죠, 그렇지 않나요?
(A) 차를 좀 주세요.
(B) 아니오, 처음입니다.
(C) 당신 먼저요.

부가 의문문으로 특정 장소에 가 본 경험이 있는지를 묻고 있으므로 처음이라고 답한 (B)가 정답이다.

15 What should we talk about at the managers'
영M meeting?
미W (A) They will join us there.
(B) The advertising budget.
(C) Okay, sounds good.

매니저 회의에서 우리는 무엇에 대한 얘기를 해야 할까요?
(A) 그들은 거기에서 저희와 합류할 겁니다.
(B) 광고 예산이요.
(C) 네, 좋습니다.

의문사 what 질문으로 회의 안건이 '무엇'인지를 물었으므로 광고 예산이라고 답한 (B)가 정답이다. 의문사 의문문에 대한 답으로 Yes/No가 불가능한 것처럼 (C)의 okay 표현도 불가능하다.

managers' meeting 매니저 회의 join 합류하다 budget 예산

16 You should try the salmon sandwich at Molly's.
영W (A) With hot sauce.
영M (B) That'll be after lunch.
(C) I have and it was delicious.

당신은 Molly's에서 연어 샌드위치를 먹어보셔야 해요.
(A) 매운 소스와 함께요.
(B) 점심 후가 될 것입니다.
(C) 먹어봤는데 정말 맛있었어요.

평서문으로 you should라는 어투에서 제안의 의도임을 파악할 수 있다. 특정 레스토랑의 메뉴를 추천하고 있으므로 이미 먹어보았고 맛이 좋았다고 답한 (C)가 정답이다. (A)는 salmon sandwich를 들었을 때 연상되는 hot sauce를 이용한 오답이다.

try 먹어보다, 시도하다

17 Where is a good place to buy souvenirs?
미W (A) Late spring is usually best.
영W (B) Most tourists like Paris Blooms a lot.
(C) You must pay in cash.

기념품을 사기에 좋은 장소가 어디인가요?
(A) 늦봄이 보통 제일 좋습니다.
(B) 대부분의 관광객들은 Paris Blooms를 매우 좋아합니다.
(C) 당신은 현금으로 지불해야 합니다.

의문사 where 질문으로 기념품 살 곳을 물었으므로 상점의 이름을 들어 답한 (B)가 정답이 된다. (A)는 when 질문에 대한 답이고 (C)는 지불 방법에 대한 내용으로 buy souvenirs를 들었을 때 연상되는 pay in cash를 이용한 오답 함정이다.

souvenir 기념품 tourist 관광객 in cash 현금으로

18 You haven't registered yet, have you?
미W (A) I'm doing it now.
미M (B) The seminar was too long.
(C) Not quite enough.

당신은 아직 등록하지 않았어요, 그렇죠?
(A) 지금 하고 있습니다.
(B) 세미나가 너무 길었어요.
(C) 별로 충분치 않았어요.

등록 완료 여부를 묻는 부가 의문문이다. (A)에서 지금 하고 있다고 했으므로 질문에 대해서는 No라고 답하는 것이므로 정답이다. (B)는 register를 들었을 때 연상되는 seminar를 이용한 함정이고, (C)는 충분치 않았다고 말하고 있어 문맥에서 벗어난 답이 된다.

register 등록하다 quite 꽤

19 Which car is yours?
영M (A) The one parked in the corner.
영W (B) Isn't it Sarah's?
(C) The red one or blue one?

어떤 차가 당신의 것인가요?
(A) 코너에 주차되어 있는 차요.
(B) Sarah의 것이 아닌가요?
(C) 빨간 것인가요 아니면 파란 것인가요?

의문사 which 질문으로 which 뒤에 따라 나오는 명사를 반드시 기억해 두자. 어떤 차인지를 물었고 정답의 the one은 대명사로 질문의 car를 받는다. 특정 장소에 주차한 그 차를 가리켜 답하므로 (A)가 정답이 된다. (B)는 연상어 오류이고 it에 해당하는 명사를 파악할 수 없는 대명사 오류이기도 하다.

20 Aren't the package designs due today?
미M (A) The package engineering department.
미W (B) The deadline has been extended.
(C) Usually we do.

포장 디자인 마감이 오늘까지 아닌가요?
(A) 포장 기술 부서요.
(B) 마감은 연장되었어요.
(C) 저희는 보통 그렇게 합니다.

질문의 핵심어는 마감의 의미를 가진 due이다. 오늘 마감인지 묻는 말에 (B)에서 마감이 연장되었다고 했으니 질문에 대해 No라고 답한 것이 된다.

due 마감인 extend 연장시키다

21 Would you like to stay in an executive suite or
영W should I book a smaller room?
미M (A) I'm sure he will be there.
(B) I don't think I need that much space.
(C) It is an interesting book.

특실에 머물고 싶으세요 아니면 좀 더 작은 방을 예약할까요?
(A) 그는 거기에 올 것입니다.
(B) 그렇게 넓은 공간은 필요 없을 것 같아요.
(C) 그것은 재미있는 책입니다.

선택 의문문으로 특실과 작은 방이 선택 사항이 된다. (B)의 넓은 공간이 필요 없다는 것은 a smaller room을 패러프레이징한 표현이므로 정답이 된다.

executive suite (호텔 등의) 특실 book 예약하다

22 In what currency is oil traded?
미W (A) Yes, for personal reasons.
영M (B) It is our current list of prices.
(C) In U.S. dollars.

어떤 화폐로 석유가 거래됩니까?
(A) 네, 개인적인 사유로요.
(B) 이것이 현재 저희 가격 리스트입니다.
(C) 미국 달러로요.

의문사 what 뒤의 명사 currency까지 한 번에 해석하는 것이 중요하다. 어떤 화폐로 거래되는지 물었으므로 정답은 (C)가 맞다. (B)는 currency – current를 이용한 유사 발음 함정이다.

currency 화폐 trade 거래하다 personal reason 개인적인 이유

23 Why has the board of directors decided to
영M reorganize our firm?
미W (A) To make us more efficient.
(B) The director is available now.
(C) At Gate 7.

왜 이사회는 우리 회사를 구조 조정하기로 결정했나요?
(A) 우리를 더 효율적으로 만들려고요.
(B) 이사님은 지금 계십니다.
(C) 7번 게이트에서요.

회사의 조직 개편 이유를 물었으므로 정답으로 가능한 것은 (A)뿐이다. director를 반복 사용한 (B)는 함정이 된다.

reorganize 구조 조정하다 efficient 효율적인

24 Leisel studied Chemistry at university, didn't she?
영W (A) She studied Physics.
영M (B) Yes, I ordered some laboratory equipment.
(C) Just a few days ago.

Leisel이 대학 때 화학을 전공했어요, 그렇지 않나요?
(A) 그녀는 물리를 전공했어요.
(B) 네, 저는 실험 장비를 주문했어요.
(C) 불과 며칠 전에요.

Yes/No 여부를 묻는 질문으로 전공 과목이 Chemistry가 아닌 Physics였다고 답한 (A)가 정답이다.

laboratory equipment 실험 장비

25 Didn't the director sign the agreement?
미W (A) She can't join us.
영W (B) No, it hasn't been finalized.
(C) He's changing the letters on the sign.

부장님이 계약서에 사인하지 않았나요?
(A) 그녀는 저희와 합류할 수 없어요.
(B) 아니오, 그건 아직 마무리되지 않았어요.
(C) 그가 간판의 글자를 바꾸고 있습니다.

Yes/No 여부를 묻는 질문으로 부장님이 계약서에 서명을 했는지 여부를 묻고 있다. (B)에서 it은 the agreement(계약서)를 가리키므로 아직 마무리되지 않았다는 것은 사인을 하지 않았다는 뜻이므로 정답이다. (A)와 (C)는 내용상 문맥에서 벗어나므로 정답이 될 수 없다.

agreement 계약서 letter 글자 sign 간판

26 Is Roger or Jessica organizing the company's annual
미W functions?
미M (A) It is held every year.
(B) He's the chief editor.
(C) Someone else has offered to do the job this time.

Roger 혹은 Jessica 중 누가 회사의 연례 행사들을 준비할 건가요?
(A) 그것은 매년 열립니다.
(B) 그는 수석 편집장이에요.
(C) 이번에는 다른 사람이 그 일을 하겠다고 했어요.

질문의 핵심인 선택 사항은 Roger와 Jessica였으나 둘 다 아닌 someone else라고 답할 수 있으므로 (C)가 가장 자연스러운 정답이 된다.

organize (행사 등을) 조직하다, 준비하다 function 행사

27 Could you make sure the projector in the meeting
영M room works?
영W (A) Sorry I missed the morning meeting.
(B) I just checked it.
(C) She works too much.

회의실의 프로젝터가 작동하는지 확인해 주시겠습니까?
(A) 아침 미팅에 못 가서 죄송합니다.
(B) 제가 방금 확인했어요.
(C) 그녀는 일을 너무 많이 합니다.

확인을 요청한 것이 프로젝터였으므로 방금 확인했다고 답한 (B)가 정답이다.

28 Haven't you turned in your expense report yet?
미M (A) I turned down the volume.
미W (B) Yes, before lunch time.
(C) Sure, if it's not expensive.

비용 보고서를 제출하지 않으셨나요?
(A) 볼륨을 줄였습니다.
(B) 제출했어요, 점심 시간 전에요.
(C) 그럼요, 만약 비싸지 않으면요.

부정 의문문의 not은 해석하지 않는 것이 중요하다. 질문의 핵심은 동사 turn in(제출하다)에 대한 Yes/No 여부이고 (B)의 Yes는 제출했다는 의미가 된다.

turn in 제출하다 turn down (소리나 온도를) 줄이다

29 Won't it take too long to complete the floor plan?
영W (A) Not if we start right now.
미M (B) It was an hour-long lecture.
(C) No, they don't want to do that.

평면도를 완성하는 데 너무 오래 걸리지 않을까요?
(A) 우리가 지금 시작한다면 오래 안 걸려요.
(B) 그것은 한 시간짜리 강의였어요.
(C) 아니요, 그들은 그것을 원치 않아요.

설계도 완성에 너무 오래 걸릴지를 물었으므로 지금 시작을 한다면 괜찮다고 답한 (A)가 정답이다.

take long to ~하는 데 오래 걸리다 floor plan 평면도

30 Let me get you a safety helmet before you enter the construction site.
미W (A) The building looks old.
영M (B) Read the safety manual carefully.
(C) There's one here.

공사 현장에 들어가기 전에 안전모를 가져다 드릴게요.
(A) 그 빌딩은 오래돼 보입니다.
(B) 안전 매뉴얼을 꼼꼼히 읽으세요.
(C) 여기에 하나 있네요.

안전모를 가져다 주겠다고 말한 질문의 도입부가 핵심이다. (C)의 여기 있다는 것은 가져다 줄 필요가 없다는 의미이므로 자연스러운 정답이 된다.

safety helmet 안전모 construction site 공사 현장

31 It is always very crowded in the financial district.
영M (A) Well, it's pretty deserted on weekends.
미W (B) No, she's not that strict.
(C) They offer financial services.

금융가는 항상 매우 붐벼요.
(A) 음, 주말에는 꽤 한산하지요.
(B) 아니요, 그녀는 그렇게 엄격하지 않아요.
(C) 그들은 금융 서비스를 제공합니다.

평서문의 핵심 내용이 금융가가 붐빈다는 것이므로 똑같이 금융가에 대해서 주말에는 한산하다고 말한 (A)가 가장 자연스러운 답변이 된다. (B)는 district - strict 유사 발음을 이용한 함정이다.

PART 3

Questions 32-34 refer to the following conversation. (미M) (미W)

M Here are some dress shoes you might be interested in, Ms. Hanson. They're made of leather. They are stylish yet comfortable to wear.

W Oh, they look nice. But do they come in lighter colors? I already have too many black shoes.

M Of course Ms. Hanson. These shoes are also available in brown and gray. Would you like to try them on?

W Yes, can I try on the brown ones?

M Absolutely, just wait here for a second, and I'll go get them from the stock room.

남 Hanson 씨, 여기 마음에 드실 만한 정장 구두가 있습니다. 가죽으로 만들어졌고 착용하기 편하면서도 스타일이 좋습니다.

여 오, 좋네요. 그런데 좀 더 밝은 색상으로도 나오나요? 이미 검은색 구두가 너무 많거든요.

남 물론입니다 Hanson 씨. 이 구두는 갈색과 회색으로도 있습니다. 한 번 신어보시겠습니까?

여 네, 갈색으로 신어볼 수 있을까요?

남 물론입니다. 잠시만 기다려 주세요. 창고에 가서 가져다 드리겠습니다.

leather 가죽 try on (상품을 사기 전에) 착용해 보다 stock room 창고

32 Where most likely are the speakers?
(A) In a factory
(B) In a store
(C) In a post office
(D) In a restaurant

화자들은 어디에 있을 것 같은가?
(A) 공장
(B) 상점
(C) 우체국
(D) 레스토랑

장소를 유추하는 질문으로 대화의 도입부에 dress shoes에 대한 언급을 했을 때 이미 store에 있음을 알 수 있다.

33 What does the woman ask for?
(A) Directions to a clothing shop
(B) Proof of purchase
(C) An additional discount
(D) Merchandise in another color

여자는 무엇을 요청하는가?
(A) 옷가게에 가는 길 안내
(B) 구매 증명서
(C) 추가 할인
(D) 다른 색상의 상품

여자의 대사에서 정답의 단서를 찾자. 여자가 같은 상품이 lighter colors로 나오는지 물었으므로 정답은 (D)가 된다.

34 What will the man probably do next?
(A) Go to the storage room
(B) Pay for a purchase
(C) Speak to his manager
(D) Send a package

남자는 다음에 무엇을 할 것 같은가?
(A) 창고로 가기
(B) 구매품 값 지불하기
(C) 매니저와 이야기하기
(D) 소포 보내기

향후 행동의 단서는 후반부에 등장한다. 남자가 I'll go get them from the stock room(창고에서 물건을 가져오겠다)이라고 했으므로 정답은 (A)가 된다.

Questions 35-37 refer to the following conversation. (영W) (영M)

W Hey Carlos, you're in charge of ordering office supplies, aren't you?

M Yes. I am actually putting together a list of supplies right now. Do you want to add something to the list?

W Yes. I need a box of envelopes for the invitations I'm sending out on Thursday.

M Okay. If I place an order today, the delivery should arrive on Wednesday. Is that okay with you?

W Yes, that's fine. Please let my assistant know when you get the supplies on Wednesday.

여 이봐요 Carlos, 사무용품의 주문을 담당하고 있죠, 그렇지 않나요?

남 맞습니다. 실은 지금 구매할 물건의 목록을 작성하고 있었어요. 목록에 추가할 것이 있나요?

여 네. 목요일에 발송할 초대장을 위해 봉투 한 박스가 필요합니다.

남 알겠습니다. 오늘 주문을 하면, 수요일에 배송될 거예요. 괜찮으시겠어요?

여 네, 좋습니다. 수요일에 물건을 받으시면 제 비서에게 알려 주세요.

in charge of ~의 책임을 맡다 put together ~을 만들다, 작성하다 invitation 초대장

35 What is the man doing now?
(A) Making a list of supplies
(B) Reading a magazine
(C) Packing his belongings
(D) Designing an invitation

남자는 지금 무엇을 하고 있는가?
(A) 물품 목록 작성
(B) 잡지 읽기
(C) 소지품 싸기
(D) 초대장 디자인

키워드는 now이므로 남자가 현재 하고 있는 일에 집중하자. I am actually putting together a list of supplies right now 부분에서 정답은 (A)임을 알 수 있다. 리스트, 보고서 등을 작성하다라는 의미로 put together가 자주 사용된다.

36 When is the shipment expected to arrive?
(A) On Monday
(B) On Tuesday
(C) On Wednesday
(D) On Thursday
배송은 언제 도착할 것으로 예상되는가?
(A) 월요일
(B) 화요일
(C) 수요일
(D) 목요일

여러 요일이 언급되기 때문에 배송이 도착하는 시점을 정확하게 포착하는 게 중요하다. 오늘 주문하면 the delivery should arrive on Wednesday라고 했으므로 정답은 (C)가 된다.

37 What is the man asked to do when he receives the package?
(A) Contact an assistant
(B) Place an order
(C) Pay a bill
(D) Call a delivery company
남자가 소포를 받으면 무엇을 하기를 요청 받는가?
(A) 비서에게 연락하기
(B) 주문하기
(C) 청구 요금 내기
(D) 배송 업체에 전화하기

여자가 남자에게 요청하는 내용을 찾는 질문으로 물건이 도착하면 비서에게 알려달라고 요청하므로 (A)가 정답이 된다.

Questions 38-40 refer to the following conversation. (미M) (미W)

M Excuse me. How much is the parking fee per hour here?
W I'm sorry, but we don't accept cars from outside. The parking area is only for the residents of the building.
M Oh, I didn't know that. Do you know anywhere nearby that I could go?
W Well, you should try the commercial bank at the corner of Eighth and Davidson. The bank's closed today so you can park there for free.
M Oh, that's good to know. I appreciate your help.

남 실례합니다. 이곳에 주차하는 게 시간당 얼마인가요?
여 죄송하지만 저희는 외부 차량은 받지 않습니다. 이 주차장은 이 빌딩의 거주자들만을 위한 것입니다.
남 아, 그걸 몰랐네요. 근처에 제가 갈 만한 곳이 있을까요?
여 Eighth와 Davidson 가 모퉁이에 있는 은행에 한 번 가보세요. 오늘 은행이 문을 닫아서 무료로 주차할 수 있을 거예요.
남 좋은 정보네요. 도와주셔서 감사합니다.

accept 받다 resident 거주민

38 Who most likely is the woman?
(A) A bank clerk
(B) A parking attendant
(C) A local resident
(D) A real estate agent
여자는 누구일 것 같은가?
(A) 은행 직원
(B) 주차장 직원
(C) 지역 주민
(D) 부동산 중개인

남자가 여자에게 주차 요금을 묻는 맨 앞부분에서 이미 여자의 직업을 주차장 직원으로 유추할 수 있다.

39 What is the problem?
(A) A bank is closed for business.
(B) A man has forgotten his access code.
(C) A parking garage is currently full.
(D) A facility is exclusively for its residents.
무엇이 문제인가?
(A) 은행이 문을 닫았다.
(B) 남자는 출입 코드를 잊어버렸다.
(C) 주차장이 현재 꽉 찼다.
(D) 시설물이 주민들만을 위한 것이다.

문제점으로 언급된 부분은 This parking area is only for the residents of the building(이 빌딩의 거주민들만 주차장을 이용할 수 있다)이라고 했으므로 정답은 (D)가 된다.

40 What does the woman suggest the man do?
(A) Open a bank account
(B) Return the next day
(C) Use public transportation
(D) Go to a different location
여자는 남자에게 무엇을 하라고 제안하는가?
(A) 은행 계좌 열기
(B) 다음 날 다시 오기
(C) 대중교통 이용하기
(D) 다른 장소로 가기

여자 대사에서 정답을 찾아야 하는 질문이다. 특정 주소의 은행을 언급하면서 은행이 문을 닫아 무료로 주차할 수 있을 거라고 했으므로 정답은 (D)가 맞다.

Questions 41-43 refer to the following conversation. (영M) (영W)

M Good morning, Linda. How's the survey report coming along? I'd like to take a look at it before I present it at the board meeting tomorrow.
W It's almost done. I just need another hour to double check the charts and figures. Should I give you a hard copy of the report or would you prefer to read it on the screen?
M You can just e-mail it to me. And could you prepare handouts for tomorrow's meeting?
W Sure. How many people will be attending?
M Well, I'm not sure yet. Could you check with me later this afternoon to see how many copies should be made?

남 안녕하세요, Linda. 설문 보고서는 어떻게 진행되고 있나요? 내일 이사회 회의에서 발표를 하기 전에 살펴보고 싶은데요.
여 거의 끝났습니다. 한 번만 더 차트와 수치를 검토해보면 됩니다. 인쇄를 해서 드릴까요 아니면 컴퓨터 화면을 통해서 읽어보시겠어요?
남 그냥 이메일로 보내 주시면 됩니다. 그리고 내일 미팅 때 쓸 유인물도 준비해 주시겠어요?
여 알겠습니다. 몇 분이나 참석하시죠?
남 음, 아직 확실치가 않네요. 몇 부를 인쇄해야 할지 오후에 다시 저한테 확인해 주시겠어요?

double check 한 번 더 확인하다 hard copy 인쇄본 handout 인쇄물, 유인물

41 What is the woman currently working on?
(A) A feature article
(B) A financial summary
(C) A survey report
(D) A cost estimate

여자는 현재 무엇을 작업 중인가?
(A) 특집 기사
(B) 재무 요약본
(C) 설문 보고서
(D) 비용 견적서

남자가 여자에게 How's the survey report coming along?라면서 설문 보고서가 어떻게 진행되고 있는지 물었으므로 현재 여자가 작업 중인 일은 설문 보고서가 된다.

42 What is the man supposed to do tomorrow?
(A) Calculate some figures
(B) Attend a meeting
(C) Watch a video
(D) Have a conference call

남자는 내일 무엇을 하기로 되어 있는가?
(A) 수치 계산하기
(B) 미팅 참석하기
(C) 비디오 보기
(D) 화상 회의하기

질문의 키워드는 tomorrow이다. I present it at the board meeting tomorrow(내일 이사 회의에서 발표를 할 것이다)라고 했으므로 정답은 (B)가 된다.

43 What information will the man give the woman later?
(A) The number of attendees
(B) The cost of an event
(C) The location of a meeting
(D) The time of a presentation

남자는 여자에게 어떤 정보를 나중에 줄 것인가?
(A) 참석자의 수
(B) 행사의 비용
(C) 미팅의 장소
(D) 발표의 시간

여자가 참석자의 수를 물었을 때 Could you check with me later this afternoon to see how many copies should be made(몇 부를 인쇄해야 할지 오후에 다시 물어보라)라고 했으므로 나중에 알려줄 정보는 참석자의 수가 된다.

Questions 44-46 refer to the following conversation. (영M) (미W)

M Hi, this is Sam Carver calling from Albany Medical Center. A few days ago, I placed an order for some medical equipment and I got the shipment this morning. But the thermometers I ordered were not in the box.
W Hold on a second. Let me check your account. Well, I see that the items you ordered were sent separately from each manufacturer. The thermometers will be delivered in the next few days.
M Okay. Is there a tracking number I can use to check the status of my order?
W Of course. I'll look it up for you.

남 안녕하세요, 저는 Albany Medical Center의 Sam Carver입니다. 며칠 전에 제가 의료 기기를 주문했고 오늘 아침에 배송을 받았습니다. 그런데 박스 안에 주문한 체온계가 없었습니다.
여 잠시만 기다리세요. 고객님의 계정을 확인해 보겠습니다. 음, 주문하신 물건들이 각각의 공급업체에서 따로 보내졌네요. 체온계는 며칠 후에 배달이 될 것입니다.
남 알겠습니다. 주문의 상태를 확인할 수 있는 운송 번호가 있을까요?
여 그럼요. 제가 찾아봐 드리겠습니다.

medical equipment 의료 기기 thermometer 체온계 account (고객의) 계정 tracking number 운송 번호 status 상태 look up 찾아보다

44 What is the man calling about?
(A) An incomplete shipment
(B) A missing document
(C) An incorrect address
(D) A damaged product

남자는 무엇에 관해서 전화하는가?
(A) 불완전한 배송
(B) 없어진 서류
(C) 부정확한 주소
(D) 손상된 상품

도입부의 상황 설명을 정확히 이해해야 정답을 고를 수 있다. 상품을 주문했고 배송을 받았으나 thermometer(체온계)가 보이지 않는다고 했으므로 모든 상품이 다 온 것이 아님을 알 수 있다. 이 내용을 한 마디로 an incomplete shipment라고 표현할 수 있다.

45 What does the woman say caused the problem?
(A) Some items were not available.
(B) A mailing address was not correct.
(C) The order was sent from different places.
(D) A delivery truck broke down.

여자는 무엇이 문제를 야기시켰다고 하는가?
(A) 일부 상품이 재고가 없었다.
(B) 배송 주소가 정확하지 않았다.
(C) 주문이 다른 장소들에서 보내졌다.
(D) 배달 트럭이 고장 났다.

여자는 상품이 다 도착하지 않은 이유에 대해 the items you ordered were sent separately from each manufacturer라고 말하며 각각의 생산업체에서 따로 보내졌다고 했으므로 정답은 (C)가 된다.

46 What does the woman say she will do?
(A) Contact a delivery company
(B) Cancel a bill
(C) Provide a coupon
(D) Find a number

여자는 무엇을 하겠다고 말하는가?
(A) 배송 회사에 연락하기
(B) 청구서 취소하기
(C) 쿠폰 제공하기
(D) 번호 찾아보기

남자가 먼저 tracking number가 있는지 물었고 여자가 이를 찾아보겠다고 했으므로 정답은 (D)가 맞다.

Questions 47-49 refer to the following conversation. 미W 미M

W Adrian, have you seen the folder where we keep all the patient files? I thought I left it on my desk, but I can't find it.
M I'm sorry. I have it right here, Dr. Williams. I took it from your desk this morning to update the contact information of some patients.
W Oh, that's no problem. I just wanted to take a look at Ms. Garcia's medical file before I see her.
M Right. She's supposed to be here in 10 minutes. Let me find the file and bring it over to you.

여 Adrian, 환자 파일을 모아두는 폴더를 본 적 있나요? 책상 위에 두었다고 생각했는데 찾을 수가 없네요.
남 죄송합니다. 여기 제가 가지고 있어요 Williams 박사님. 일부 환자들의 연락 정보를 고치려고 아침에 제가 책상에서 가져갔어요.
여 오, 괜찮습니다. 진료 전에 Garcia 씨의 진료 파일을 보려고 했어요.
남 맞네요. 그분은 10분 후에 오시기로 되어 있죠. 제가 지금 파일을 찾아서 가져다 드릴게요.

patient file 환자 파일 contact information 연락 정보 medical file 의료 파일

47 Where most likely are the speakers?
(A) In a customer service department
(B) In a medical office
(C) In a furniture shop
(D) In a coffee shop

화자들은 어디에 있을 것 같은가?
(A) 고객 서비스부
(B) 병원
(C) 가구점
(D) 커피숍

장소를 유추할 때는 화자들의 업무 내용이 힌트가 된다. 여자가 patient file(환자 파일)을 찾고 있는 부분에서 이미 정답은 병원임을 알 수 있다.

48 What is mentioned about Ms. Garcia?
(A) She has provided new contact information.
(B) She recently started working at a medical clinic.
(C) She has moved into a new house.
(D) She has an appointment with a doctor today.

Garcia 씨에 대해서 무엇이 언급되는가?
(A) 새로 바뀐 연락처를 제공했다.
(B) 최근에 병원에서 일하기 시작했다.
(C) 새 집으로 이사했다.
(D) 오늘 의사와 진료 예약이 있다.

Garcia 씨의 이름이 언급되는 부분을 유심히 듣자. 여자는 Garcia 씨를 진료하기 전에 그녀의 파일을 보고 싶다고 했고 남자 역시 10분 후에 그녀가 오기로 되어 있다고 했으므로 정답은 (D)가 된다.

49 What will the man probably do next?
(A) Find a document
(B) Contact a patient
(C) Repair a computer
(D) Make a reservation

남자는 다음에 무엇을 할 것 같은가?
(A) 서류 찾기
(B) 환자에게 연락하기
(C) 컴퓨터 고치기
(D) 예약하기

대화의 마지막 부분에 남자가 환자의 파일을 찾아서 갖다 주겠다고 했으므로 정답은 (A)이다.

Questions 50-52 refer to the following conversation. 영W 영M

W Welcome back! You're listening to Channel 3 local business news. Today's special guest is Kurt Russell, the owner of DE Motor Suppliers. Mr. Russell, I understand you're planning to open your third manufacturing plant here in Redwood.
M That's right. The new factory will produce auto parts for car engines. But what excites me most is that this facility will create more than a thousand jobs, which will help revive the local economy. And that is my goal as a businessman.
W I'm so glad to hear that, Mr. Russell. And when will this wonderful facility begin operating?
M The construction is almost done. So it will officially open sometime in April.

여 돌아오신 걸 환영합니다! 여러분은 채널3 지역 비즈니스 뉴스를 듣고 계십니다. 오늘의 특별 초대손님은 DE Motor Suppliers의 소유주인 Kurt Russell입니다. Russell 씨, 이곳 Redwood에 세 번째 생산 공장을 열려고 계획 중이라고 알고 있습니다.
남 맞습니다. 새 공장에서는 자동차 엔진에 사용되는 부품을 생산할 것입니다. 그러나 저를 가장 흥분시키는 일은 이 공장이 천 개 이상의 일자리를 창출할 것이며 지역 경제를 되살리는 데 한 몫을 할 것이라는 점입니다. 그리고 그것은 기업가로서 저의 목표이기도 합니다.
여 그 얘기를 들으니 정말 기쁩니다, Russell 씨. 그런데 이 훌륭한 공장은 언제 가동을 시작하게 됩니까?
남 공사는 거의 끝났습니다. 따라서 4월 중에 공식적으로 문을 열 것입니다.

special guest 초대 손님 owner 소유주 manufacturing plant 생산 공장 auto part 자동차 부품 excite 신 나게 만들다, 흥분시키다 revive 되살리다 local economy 지역 경제 officially 공식적으로

50 Who most likely is the man?
(A) A reporter
(B) A factory worker
(C) A local entrepreneur
(D) A mayor

남자는 누구일 것 같은가?
(A) 기자
(B) 공장 인부
(C) 지역 기업가
(D) 시장

남자의 직업을 유추하는 질문으로 도입부에 여자가 남자를 소개하는 내용에서 단서를 찾을 수 있다. 남자를 Kurt Russell로 소개하면서 the owner of DE Motor Suppliers라고 설명했으므로 기업체의 소유주, 즉 기업가임을 알 수 있다. 정답은 (C)이다.

51 What goal does the man mention?
(A) Increasing employment
(B) Restoring old buildings
(C) Creating new car models
(D) Establishing an economic policy

남자는 어떤 목표를 언급하는가?
(A) 고용을 증가시키는 것
(B) 오래된 건물을 복구하는 것
(C) 신차 모델을 만드는 것
(D) 경제 정책을 설립하는 것

남자가 목표와 관련된 얘기를 할 때가 정답 포인트이다. 새 생산 공장이 일자리를 창출해 내는 점이 가장 흥분되는 일이라고 언급한 후 And that is my goal as a businessman이라고 했으므로 남자의 목표는 일자리 창출로 인한 경제 활성화라고 볼 수 있다.

52 What does the woman ask about?
(A) The number of new employees
(B) The opening date
(C) The cost of construction
(D) A building plan

여자는 무엇에 관해 묻는가?
(A) 신입 직원의 수
(B) 개관 날짜
(C) 건설비
(D) 건축 도면

여자가 질문하는 내용이 정답이 되므로 And when will this wonderful facility begin operating?에서 공장이 가동되는 시점, 즉 개관 날짜를 묻고 있음을 확인한다.

Questions 53-55 refer to the following conversation. 미W 미M

W Hey, Pete. Is it true that the power went out at the Preston Factory yesterday? I'm worried because we have to send the customized coffee mugs to Salinas Products by tomorrow.

M Don't worry, Gina. The Preston Factory had a blackout for a couple of hours yesterday, but it was after the order was already sent.

W Oh, I'm relieved to hear that. They're supposed to distribute the mugs with the company logo at the promotional event next week.

M Well, the shipment will arrive at Salinas Products by tomorrow at the latest. So I think everything will be fine.

여 저기요, Pete. 어제 Preston공장에 전기가 나갔었다는 게 사실인가요? 내일까지 Salinas Products로 주문 제작된 머그컵을 보내줘야 해서 걱정이 되네요.

남 걱정 말아요, Gina. 어제 두어 시간 정도 Preston 공장에서 정전이 되었지만, 그건 이미 그 주문품을 보낸 후였어요.

여 아, 그 말을 들으니 안심이 되네요. 그들은 다음 주에 있을 홍보 행사에서 회사의 로고가 박힌 머그컵을 나눠주기로 되어 있거든요.

남 음, 배송은 늦어도 내일까지 Salinas Products에 도착할 거예요. 그러니 다 잘될 것 같네요.

go out (전기 등이) 나가다 customized 주문 제작된 blackout 정전 distribute 나눠주다 promotional event 홍보 행사 shipment 선적

53 What are the speakers mainly discussing?
(A) The location of a promotional event
(B) The opening of a new factory
(C) The shipment of some goods
(D) The cause of a power failure

화자들은 무엇에 대해 주로 논의하는가?
(A) 홍보 행사의 장소
(B) 새 공장의 개장
(C) 일부 상품의 배송
(D) 정전의 원인

대화의 주제를 찾는 질문으로 도입부에 정전이 언급되었으나 원인에 대한 대화는 아니었으므로 (D)는 함정이 된다. 특정 회사에 보내기로 한 mugs의 배송에 대해 이야기하는 대화이므로 정답은 (C)가 맞다.

54 What does the woman imply when she says, "Oh, I'm relieved to hear that"?
(A) She is happy that a delivery will arrive on time.
(B) She is satisfied with the quality of some products.
(C) She feels better after receiving treatment.
(D) She likes to hear other people's opinions.

여자가 "아, 그 말을 들으니 안심이 되네요"라고 말한 의도는 무엇인가?
(A) 여자는 배송이 제때에 도착하리라는 것에 만족한다.
(B) 여자는 일부 상품의 질에 만족한다.
(C) 여자는 치료를 받은 후에 몸이 나아졌다.
(D) 여자는 다른 사람들의 견해를 듣고 싶어한다.

화자의 의도를 파악하는 문제로 해당 표현의 앞뒤 문맥에서 단서를 찾아야 한다. 공장의 정전 때문에 배송이 늦어질까 걱정하는 여자에게 남자가 배송이 보내진 후에 정전이 있었다고 말했고 이에 대해 Oh, I'm relieved to hear that이라고 언급하였으므로 정답은 (A)가 된다.

55 According to the woman, what will happen next week?
(A) A factory tour
(B) A trade show
(C) A demonstration
(D) A promotional event

여자에 따르면, 다음 주에 무슨 일이 있을 것인가?
(A) 공장 견학
(B) 무역 박람회
(C) 시연
(D) 홍보 행사

여자 대사에서 질문의 힌트인 next week을 잘 노려 듣자. 세부 정보를 순발력 있게 잡는 질문이므로 at the promotional event next week가 들렸을 때 바로 정답을 (D)로 선택한다.

Questions 56-58 refer to the following conversation. (영M) (미W)

M Hello, I'm calling about my utility bill. I paid it online two weeks ago, but this morning I received a late payment notice in the mail.
W Oh, I'm sorry to hear that. Could you give me your account number and your name please?
M It's 577011 and my name is Jeremy Kwan.
W Please hold the line while I check your account, Mr. Kwan. Oh, there have been some billing errors since we installed our new software last month. And a late notice was sent out to you by mistake. So, don't worry about the late fee. I'll correct your payment information right away.

남 여보세요, 고지서 때문에 전화드립니다. 2주일 전에 온라인으로 돈을 지불했는데, 오늘 아침에 우편물에서 체납 통지서를 받았습니다.
여 오 죄송합니다. 당신의 계정 번호와 이름을 알려 주시겠어요?
남 577011이고, Jeremy Kwan입니다.
여 Kwan 씨, 계정을 확인하는 동안 전화를 끊지 말고 기다려 주십시오. 오, 저희가 지난달에 소프트웨어를 설치한 이후로 청구상의 실수가 있어 왔는데요. 귀하에게도 실수로 체납 통지가 발송되었네요. 그러니 연체료에 관하여 신경 쓰지 마십시오. 제가 즉시 귀하의 지불 정보를 수정해 놓겠습니다.

utility bill 전기·가스·수도 요금 late payment notice 체납 통지서 hold the line 전화를 끊지 않고 기다리다 billing error 청구상의 실수 by mistake 실수로 late fee 연체료 correct 정정하다

56 Why is the man calling?
(A) To report a billing mistake
(B) To request a copy of a receipt
(C) To provide a correct address
(D) To close a bank account

남자는 왜 전화하고 있는가?
(A) 청구서 실수를 보고하려고
(B) 영수증 사본을 요구하려고
(C) 정확한 주소를 제공하려고
(D) 은행 계좌를 닫으려고

남자의 전화 목적을 묻는 질문으로 도입부 남자 대사에서 I'm calling about my utility bill이 언급된 후 2주 전에 돈을 냈는데 체납 통지서가 왔다는 부분에서 정답을 (A)로 선택할 수 있다.

57 What change was made last month?
(A) Some new employees were hired.
(B) Wages were raised.
(C) A new line of products was added.
(D) Some new software was installed.

지난달에 어떤 변화가 있었는가?
(A) 새로운 직원이 고용되었다.
(B) 임금이 올랐다.
(C) 신상품이 추가되었다.
(D) 새로운 소프트웨어가 설치되었다.

세부 사항 질문으로 키워드는 last month이다. we installed our new software last month라고 언급되는 부분에서 정답이 (D)임을 알 수 있다. 질문의 키워드가 들렸을 때 순발력 있게 정답을 처리하는 것이 오답을 줄이는 방법이다.

58 What does the woman offer to do?
(A) Send a letter of apology
(B) Open a new account
(C) Correct the mistake
(D) Offer a discount

여자는 무엇을 해 주겠다고 하는가?
(A) 사과 편지 보내기
(B) 새로운 계정 열기
(C) 오류 수정하기
(D) 할인 제공하기

여자가 남자를 위해 해주겠다고 하는 내용을 포착한다. I'll correct your payment information right away라고 말하며 정보를 수정해 주겠다고 한 (C)가 정답이다.

Questions 59-61 refer to the following conversation. (영W) (미M)

W Jason, Mr. Kenta just called to talk about his house remodeling project. Mr. and Mrs. Kenta really want to see the floor plan as soon as possible. You have a meeting with them tomorrow morning, right?
M Yes, at 10 a.m. But would you mind taking my place? I'd like to be there, but it's the only time I can see my doctor before he leaves for a conference tomorrow afternoon.
W Hmm... I don't think we should postpone the meeting either. Alright, I'll meet with them for you.
M Oh, thank you very much. All you'll need for the meeting is the floor plan and I can e-mail it to you right away.

여 Jason, Kenta 씨가 방금 주택 리모델링에 관해서 전화를 하셨어요. Kenta 씨 부부는 평면도를 최대한 빨리 보고 싶다고 하시네요. 내일 오전에 그분들과 미팅이 있는 거 맞죠?
남 네 아침 10시예요. 그런데 저 대신 해주실 수 있을까요? 저도 그 자리에 나가고 싶지만 제 담당 의사가 내일 오후 컨퍼런스에 가기 전에 진료를 볼 수 있는 유일한 시간이어서요.
여 흠… 우리는 미팅을 미룰 수도 없긴 해요. 좋습니다, 당신 대신 그 분들을 만나도록 할게요.
남 오, 정말 감사합니다. 미팅에 필요한 건 평면도뿐이고요 제가 지금 바로 이메일로 보내겠습니다.

floor plan 평면도 take one's place ~의 자리를 대신하다

59 What is the purpose of Mr. Kenta's call?
(A) To discuss a remodeling project
(B) To reschedule a meeting
(C) To arrange a trip
(D) To revise a contract

Kenta 씨가 전화를 한 목적은 무엇인가?
(A) 리모델링 프로젝트에 대해서 논의하려고
(B) 미팅의 일정을 다시 잡으려고
(C) 출장 일정을 정하려고
(D) 계약서를 수정하려고

Kenta 씨라는 이름이 키워드이고 전화를 했다는 사실까지 미리 염두에 두고 대화를 듣자. Mr. Kenta just called to talk about his house remodeling project(주택 리모델링 프로젝트에 관해서 Kenta 씨가 전화를 했다)라고 언급했으므로 정답은 (A)가 된다.

60 Why does the man say, "But would you mind taking my place"?
(A) To reschedule the meeting
(B) To ask the woman to finish a building plan
(C) To hold an event in another city
(D) To ask the woman to meet with the clients

왜 남자는 "그런데 저 대신 해주실 수 있을까요"라고 말하는가?
(A) 회의의 일정을 다시 잡으려고
(B) 여자에게 평면도를 완성하라고 부탁하려고
(C) 다른 도시에서 행사를 열려고
(D) 여자에게 고객들과 만나 달라고 부탁하려고

"But would you mind taking my place?"의 의미는 "저 대신 해주시겠어요?"인데 남자가 이 표현을 한 후 회의에 갈 수 없는 이유가 진료 예약과 고객 미팅 시간이 겹쳤기 때문이라고 설명했으므로 정답은 여자에게 대신 미팅에 나가 달라는 (D)가 된다.

61 What does the man say he will send the woman?
(A) A floor plan
(B) A list of suppliers
(C) A cost estimate
(D) A construction schedule

남자는 여자에게 무엇을 보내겠다고 하는가?
(A) 평면도
(B) 공급업체 목록
(C) 가격 견적서
(D) 공사 스케줄

남자가 여자에게 미팅에 필요한 것은 a floor plan이라고 하며 지금 보내겠다고 했으므로 정답은 (A)가 된다.

Questions 62-64 refer to the following conversation with three speakers. (미M) (미W) (영W)

M Ms. Quinn, thank you so much for agreeing to be the guest lecturer in my class. My students are really looking forward to your lecture.
W1 Oh, it's my pleasure. This is my first time in Madison Town, and it's an absolutely gorgeous village. You two are lucky to live here.
W2 I'm glad you like it here, Ms. Quinn. We'd like to show you around the town while you are here. When would be a good time for you?
W1 **Oh, that's very kind of you.** As you know, I have to leave as soon as my lecture ends tomorrow. So how about we go out to dinner tonight?
W2 Sounds great. How about you, Joshua?
M Perfect! There's a great Cuban restaurant on the waterfront. It has a fantastic view of the lake and you can enjoy live music there every night.

남 Quinn 씨, 제 수업에 초청 연사가 되기로 하셔서 정말 감사드립니다. 제 학생들이 당신의 강연을 정말 기대하고 있어요.
여1 오, 저도 기쁘네요. 이번이Madison Town에 처음인데, 정말로 아름다운 마을이네요. 두 분은 여기에 살 수 있어 행운이네요.
여2 이곳을 좋아하시니 기쁩니다, Quinn 씨. 여기 계신 동안에 저희가 동네를 구경시켜 드리고 싶어요. 언제가 시간이 좋으세요?
여1 **오, 정말 친절하시네요.** 아시다시피, 전 내일 강의가 끝나면 바로 떠나야 합니다. 그래서 오늘 저녁 식사를 하는 건 어떨까요?
여2 좋습니다. 어떠세요, Joshua?
남 좋죠! 강가 쪽에 근사한 쿠바 레스토랑이 있어요. 강가 전망도 환상적이고 라이브 공연도 매일 밤 즐길 수 있어요.

gorgeous 아름다운, 예쁜 waterfront 강가, 물가

62 Who most likely is Ms. Quinn?
(A) A student
(B) A restaurant manager
(C) A guest lecturer
(D) A business owner

Quinn 씨는 누구일 것 같은가?
(A) 학생
(B) 레스토랑 매니저
(C) 초청 강사
(D) 사업가

3인 대화로 이름을 잘 파악하는 것이 중요하다. 대화의 도입부에 Quinn 씨의 이름을 부르면서 초청 강사가 되어 주기로 해서 감사하다고 했으므로 정답은 (C)가 맞다.

63 What does Ms. Quinn mean when she says, "Oh, that's very kind of you"?
(A) She is thankful for the invitation.
(B) She wants to use a specific kind of product.
(C) She needs to prepare for her lecture.
(D) She likes the village very much.

Quinn 씨가 "오, 정말 친절하시네요"라고 말한 의미가 무엇인가?
(A) 그녀는 초대에 감사하다.
(B) 그녀는 특정 상품을 이용하기 원한다.
(C) 그녀는 강의를 준비해야 한다.
(D) 그녀는 이 마을을 매우 좋아한다.

의도 파악 질문에서 가장 중요한 것은 해당 표현의 앞, 뒤 문맥이다. 동네를 구경시켜 주고 싶다는 제안을 받고 "오, 정말 친절하시네요"라고 답했으므로 정답은 (A)가 된다.

64 What does the man say about the restaurant?
(A) It serves Indian food.
(B) It has a great view.
(C) It is always crowded.
(D) It has opened recently.

남자는 레스토랑에 대해서 무엇을 말하는가?
(A) 인도 음식을 판매한다.
(B) 경치가 좋다.
(C) 항상 붐빈다.
(D) 최근에 오픈하였다.

남자 대사에서 레스토랑에 대한 정보가 몇 가지 나왔으나 보기와 일치하는 부분은 It has a fantastic view of the lake이므로 정답은 (B)이다.

Questions 65-67 refer to the following conversation and chart. 영M 미W

M Sarah, these are the results of a recent survey conducted at our community center. We gave a questionnaire to 300 of our members asking if they are satisfied with the programs we offer.
W Well, it is interesting to see how differently each age group responded to the services we offer. I see that this age group is the happiest of all.
M Yes, that group consists mostly of parents with young children. They feel that we offer a variety of programs for both adults and children and that is reflected in the survey result. As you can see, the second happiest group is the under-13 age group.
W I see. Is there any particular program they like the best?
M Well, the Sunday morning baseball game is very popular.
W Right. On the other hand, this age group here is the least satisfied with our programs. What is the problem?
M Many of the members in that age group are interested in learning something new, like a foreign language or painting. So they want us to offer more classes.

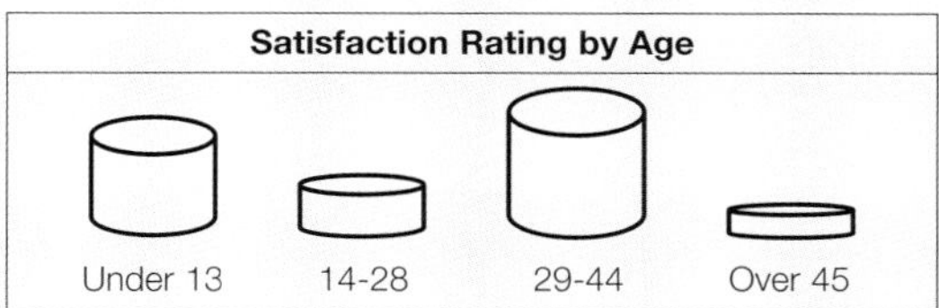

남 Sarah, 여기 우리 커뮤니티 센터에서 설문 조사한 결과입니다. 회원 중에서 300명에게 설문지를 주었고 우리가 제공하는 프로그램에 대해서 만족하는지를 물었습니다.
여 음, 우리가 제공하는 서비스에 대해서 각 연령대가 다르게 응답한 것이 흥미롭네요. 이 연령대가 가장 만족한 그룹이군요.
남 네, 그 그룹은 대부분 어린 아이를 둔 부모들로 구성되어 있어요. 그들은 우리가 성인과 아이들 둘 다를 위한 다양한 프로그램을 제공한다고 느끼고 있고 이 부분이 설문 결과에 반영이 되었습니다. 보시다시피, 두 번째로 만족한 그룹이 13세 미만 연령대입니다.
여 그렇군요. 이들이 가장 좋아하는 특정한 프로그램이 있나요?
남 음, 일요일 야구 경기가 굉장히 인기가 좋아요.
여 그렇군요. 반면에, 여기 이 연령대 그룹은 우리 프로그램에 대해 가장 만족도가 낮네요. 무엇이 문제죠?
남 그 연령대의 많은 회원들은 외국어나 그림 같이 뭔가 새로운 것을 배우는 데 관심이 많습니다. 그래서 저희가 더 많은 수업을 제공하기 원하고 있어요.

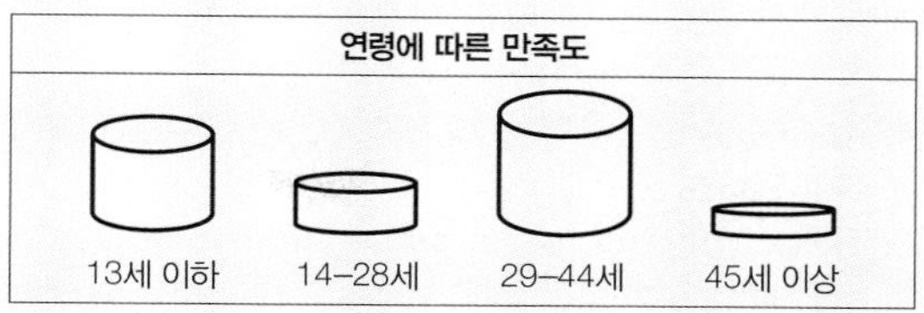

questionnaire 설문지 be satisfied with ~에 만족하다 age group 연령대 consist of ~로 구성되다 a variety of 다양한 particular 특정한

65 Where do the speakers most likely work?
(A) At a research center
(B) At an art gallery
(C) At a fitness club
(D) At a community center

화자들은 어디에서 일할 것 같은가?
(A) 연구 센터
(B) 아트 갤러리
(C) 체육관
(D) 커뮤니티 센터

도입부에 화자들이 주고 받는 내용은 커뮤니티 센터의 프로그램 만족도 설문조사 결과에 대한 것이었으므로 정답은 (D)가 된다.

66 What are the speakers mainly discussing?
(A) A family membership
(B) Promoting a new program
(C) A schedule change
(D) The results of a recent survey

화자들은 주로 무엇에 대해 이야기하는가?
(A) 가족 멤버십
(B) 새 프로그램을 홍보하는 것
(C) 스케줄 변경
(D) 최근 설문 조사의 결과

대화의 도입부에 these are the results of a recent survey conducted at our community center라고 하면서 연령별 특성을 이야기하므로 정답은 (D)이다.

67 Look at the graphic. Which age group wants the center to offer more classes?
(A) Under 13
(B) 14-28
(C) 29-44
(D) Over 45

시각 정보를 보시오. 어떤 연령대가 센터에서 더 많은 수업을 제공하길 원하는가?
(A) 13세 이하
(B) 14–28세
(C) 29–44세
(D) 45세 이상

새로운 것을 배우고 싶어하고 센터가 더 많은 수업을 제공하기 원하는 연령대는 만족도가 가장 낮은 그룹(the least satisfied with our programs)이었으므로 정답은 (D)가 된다.

Questions 68-70 refer to the following conversation and brochure. (영W) (미M)

W Welcome to City Sights of New York. How can I help you?
M Hello. I'm here to get some information about sightseeing tours of the city. Do you offer single-day tours?
W Yes, we have two different types of day trips. Here, there's more information in this brochure. They both begin at 9 a.m., but the half-day tour goes only until lunchtime. The full-day tour includes the Statue of Liberty ferry ride and ends at 8 p.m.
M The full-day tour sounds great because I really want to see the Statue of Liberty. And do you offer a discount for students? That would be even better!
W Yes, if you choose the full-day tour and present your student ID, you can get a 20 percent discount.
M I'll take a full-day ticket. Uh-oh, I didn't bring my ID with me. Can I still get the discounted price?
W I'm sorry but that's not possible.

City Sights of NY		
	Adult	Senior/Student
Half Day City Tour	$60	$50
Full Day City Tour + Ferry	$100	$80

여 City Sights of New York에 오신 것을 환영합니다. 어떻게 도와 드릴까요?
남 안녕하세요. 도시 관광 투어에 대해 알아보려고요. 하루 투어도 제공하나요?
여 네, 두 종류의 하루 투어가 있습니다. 여기 이 안내 책자에 더 많은 정보가 있어요. 둘 다 아침 9시에 시작되지만 반일 투어는 점심 시간까지만 투어가 지속됩니다. 종일 투어는 자유의 여신상 페리 탑승까지 포함하여 저녁 8시에 끝이 납니다.
남 저는 자유의 여신상을 정말 보고 싶기 때문에 종일 투어가 좋을 것 같네요. 그리고 학생은 할인을 해주시네요? 더 좋군요!
여 네, 종일 투어를 선택하시고 학생증을 제시하시면, 20퍼센트 할인을 받을 수 있어요.
남 종일 투어 티켓을 구입하겠습니다. 이런, 제가 신분증을 가져오지 않았네요. 그래도 할인을 받을 수 있을까요?
여 죄송하지만 그건 불가능합니다.

City Sights of NY		
	성인	경로/학생
반일 시티 투어	60달러	50달러
종일 시티 투어+페리	100달러	80달러

sightseeing tour 관광 투어 single-day tour 하루 투어 Statue of Liberty 자유의 여신상

68 What is the man asking about?
(A) A sightseeing tour
(B) A concert schedule
(C) Directions to an attraction
(D) A famous artist

남자는 무엇에 관하여 문의하는가?
(A) 관광 투어
(B) 콘서트 일정
(C) 관광 명소에 가는 길
(D) 유명한 예술가

I'm here to get some information about sightseeing tours of the city에서 관광 투어에 대해 문의하고 있음을 알 수 있다. 정답은 (A)이다.

69 According to the woman, what is included in the full-day city tour?
(A) A museum tour
(B) A Broadway show
(C) A ferry ride
(D) A seafood lunch

여자에 따르면, 종일 시티 투어에는 무엇이 포함되는가?
(A) 박물관 투어
(B) 브로드웨이 쇼
(C) 페리 탑승
(D) 해산물 점심

질문의 키워드인 full-day city tour를 잘 듣자. The full-day tour includes the Statue of Liberty ferry ride and ends at 8 p.m.에서 자유의 여신상을 보는 페리 탑승을 포함한다고 했으므로 정답은 (C)가 맞다.

70 Look at the graphic. How much will the man pay for a tour?
(A) $50
(B) $60
(C) $80
(D) $100

시각 정보를 보시오. 남자는 투어에 얼마를 낼 것인가?
(A) 50달러
(B) 60달러
(C) 80달러
(D) 100달러

가격표에 따르면 일반가와 학생 할인가가 구별되어 있다. 남자는 full-day tour를 선택하고 학생 할인을 받고자 했으나 I didn't bring my ID with me(신분증을 가져오지 않았다)라고 하자 여자가 학생증 없이는 할인이 불가하다고 했으니 최종적으로 낼 금액은 100달러가 된다.

PART 4

Questions 71-73 refer to the following message. (미W)

Hello, this message is for Mr. Duffey. This is Mary Wilson calling from DK Airlines. I'm calling to let you know that we've located your suitcase from Flight 703. We'll send it to the Palace Hotel where you're staying while in London. You will probably receive it by tomorrow morning. If you have any questions, please contact us at 800-555-0118. Once again, we're sorry for the inconvenience and thank you for flying with DK Airlines.

안녕하세요. 이 메시지는 Duffey 씨에게 남기는 것입니다. DK Airlines에서 전화드리는 Mary Wilson입니다. Flight 703에서 당신의 여행 가방을 찾아서 알려 드립니다. 런던에 계시는 동안 머무시는Palace Hotel로 가방을 보내겠습니다. 내일 오전까지는 받아볼 수 있습니다. 질문이 있으시면 800-555-0118로 연락 주십시오. 다시 한 번 불편을 드려 죄송하고 DK Airlines를 이용해 주셔서 감사합니다.

locate 찾다 inconvenience 불편

71 Where does the speaker most likely work?
(A) At an airport lounge
(B) At a travel agency
(C) At an airline
(D) At a car rental agency

화자는 어디서 일할 것 같은가?
(A) 공항 라운지
(B) 여행사
(C) 항공사
(D) 렌터카 업체

메시지의 시작 부분에서 화자 본인을 밝히는 This is Mary Wilson calling from DK Airlines 에서 항공사에서 일하는 직원임을 알 수 있다.

72 What is the woman calling about?
(A) A travel itinerary
(B) A boarding pass
(C) A piece of luggage
(D) A hotel reservation

여자는 무엇에 관해 전화하는가?
(A) 여행 일정표
(B) 탑승권
(C) 짐 가방
(D) 호텔 예약

전화하는 이유로 여행 가방을 찾았기(located your suitcase) 때문이라고 했으므로 정답은 (C)가 된다.

73 When will the shipment arrive at the hotel?
(A) Today
(B) Tomorrow
(C) Next week
(D) In two weeks

배송은 언제 호텔에 도착할 것인가?
(A) 오늘
(B) 내일
(C) 다음 주
(D) 2주일 후

호텔로 짐 가방을 보낼 것이라고 한 후 내일 아침 받게 될 것(You will probably receive it by tomorrow morning)이라고 했으므로 정답은 (B)이다.

Questions 74-76 refer to the following radio broadcast. (영M)

Welcome back everyone. My name is Billy Dyne, your host of *Design Your Home*. On tonight's show, we have a special guest, Earl Davis. As you already know, he is one of the country's leading interior designers. For the next hour Mr. Davis will be sharing interior design tips and ideas from his recent book *Fun Home*. And he will be taking questions from our listeners. So if you have any questions regarding interior design, home decorating or even paint color selection, please give us a call at 555-0100.

환영합니다 여러분. 〈Design Your Home〉의 진행자, Billy Dyne입니다. 오늘 밤의 쇼에는 특별 게스트인 Earl Davis를 모십니다. 아시겠지만, 그는 국내에서 가장 선두적인 인테리어 디자이너 중 한 명입니다. 앞으로 한 시간 동안 Davis 씨는 그의 최신 책인 〈Fun Home〉에 나온 인테리어 조언과 아이디어를 우리에게 알려 줄 것입니다. 그리고 청취자들로부터 질문도 받겠습니다. 그러니 인테리어 디자인, 집 꾸미기, 아니면 페인트 색상 정하기와 관련하여 질문이 있으시다면 저희에게 555-0100로 전화 주십시오.

leading 선두적인 share 나누다, 정보를 주다 regarding ~에 관해

74 Who is Earl Davis?
(A) A show host
(B) An interior designer
(C) A reporter
(D) A publisher

Earl Davis는 누구인가?
(A) 쇼 진행자
(B) 인테리어 디자이너
(C) 기자
(D) 출판인

Earl Davis라는 이름이 초대 손님으로 언급되고 leading interior designer라고 소개되었으므로 정답은 (B)가 된다.

75 What will Mr. Davis discuss on the program?
(A) A critic's review
(B) Some art techniques
(C) Useful investment tips
(D) His recent book

Davis 씨는 프로그램에서 무엇에 대해 이야기할 것인가?
(A) 비평가의 평론
(B) 그림 기술
(C) 유용한 투자 팁
(D) 그의 최근 책

Davis 씨는 그의 최근 책인 〈Fun Home〉에 소개된 인테리어 조언과 아이디어에 대해 이야기한다고 했으므로 정답은 (D)가 맞다.

76 What are the listeners invited to do?
(A) Register for a course
(B) Attend a fashion show
(C) Call in with questions
(D) Choose a color

청취자들은 무엇을 하기를 권고 받는가?
(A) 수업 신청하기
(B) 패션쇼에 참석하기
(C) 질문을 가지고 전화하기
(D) 색상 정하기

게스트가 청취자들의 질문을 받을테니 555-0100번으로 전화 달라고 했으므로 정답은 (C)가 된다.

Questions 77-79 refer to the following excerpt from a meeting.
영W

Good morning everyone. Thank you all for attending today's department meeting. I have some good news. As the head of product development, I'm happy to announce that our new mini sedan, the Zeta 500, has successfully passed the automotive quality control tests and is ready to hit the market. Both our design and engineering teams have worked really hard to develop a luxury mini sedan that provides great mileage and advanced technology. Now, our marketing manager, Grace Lee, will tell us about the plan to unveil the Zeta 500 at the KM International Motor Show next week.

안녕하세요, 여러분. 오늘의 부서 미팅에 참석해 주셔서 감사합니다. 좋은 소식이 있는데요. 상품 개발 부서장으로서 새 미니 세단인 Zeta 500가 성공적으로 품질 검사를 통과하고 시장에 나올 준비가 되었다는 것을 기쁜 마음으로 발표합니다. 우리 디자인팀과 기술팀 모두 높은 연료 효율과 신기술을 제공하는 이 럭셔리 미니 세단을 개발하기 위해서 열심히 일해 주었습니다. 이제 마케팅 매니저인 Grace Lee가 다음 주에 있을 KM International Motor Show에서 Zeta 500를 선보일 계획에 대해 발표하도록 하겠습니다.

production development 상품 개발 quality control test 품질 검사
hit the market 시장에 나오다 provide great mileage 연료 효율이 높다
unveil 선보이다

77 Who most likely is the speaker?
(A) A car dealer
(B) A department director
(C) A factory manager
(D) A company president

화자는 누구일 것 같은가?
(A) 자동차 판매원
(B) 부서장
(C) 공장 매니저
(D) 회사 사장

화자가 본인을 직접 밝힌 부분은 As the head of product development, I'm happy to announce(상품 개발 부서장으로서 발표하게 되어 기쁘다)라고 했으므로 정답은 (B)이다.

78 What does the speaker say about the Zeta 500?
(A) It is faster than the previous model.
(B) It has a powerful engine.
(C) It has won an award.
(D) It is ready to be introduced.

Zeta 500에 대해서 화자는 뭐라고 말하는가?
(A) 이전 모델보다 더 빠르다.
(B) 엔진이 강력하다.
(C) 상을 받았다.
(D) 출시될 준비가 되었다.

신차 모델인 Zeta 500에 대해서 여러 가지가 언급되었으나 보기와 일치하는 부분은 is ready to hit the market(시장에 나갈 준비가 되었다)이다. 신상품 출시와 관련하여 hit the market, be introduced, be released, be launched 등은 모두 뜻이 같은 표현이다.

79 What will Grace Lee discuss?
(A) An upcoming awards ceremony
(B) A manufacturing process
(C) A plan to unveil a new car
(D) A recent motor show

Grace Lee는 무엇에 대해 이야기할 것인가?
(A) 다가오는 시상식
(B) 생산 과정
(C) 신차를 선보일 계획
(D) 최근의 자동차 쇼

Grace Lee가 plan to unveil the Zeta 500에 대해서 발표하겠다고 했으므로 정답은 (C)이다. 자동차 쇼에서 신차를 선보이는 것이므로 (D) A recent motor show는 들리는 단어를 이용한 함정이 된다.

Questions 80-82 refer to the following radio announcement.
미W

Do you have electronic devices at home that you no longer use? Ever wonder how you can get rid of them? Radio CIU and Charles's Electronics Store are collaborating to help you recycle your old home appliances, such as old televisions and mobile phones. You can just bring them to Charles's Electronics Store located on Dundas Street this Sunday from 10 a.m. to 4 p.m. That's not all! As an added bonus, for those of you who participate by bringing in a recyclable item, we will provide a 10% discount coupon that can be used at any of Charles's locations.

집에 더 이상 사용하지 않는 가전제품이 있으신가요? 어떻게 버려야 할지 궁금해하신 적 있으시죠? Radio CIU와 Charles's Electronics Store가 낡은 텔레비전이나 휴대 전화처럼 오래된 가전제품 재활용을 돕기 위해 힘을 합쳤습니다. 여러분은 이번 주 일요일 아침 10시부터 오후 4시까지 Dundas Street에 있는 Charles's Electronics Store로 가져오시기만 하면 됩니다. 그것이 다가 아니죠! 추가 보너스로 재활용이 가능한 물건을 가지고 오셔서 참여하시는 분들께는 Charles's 지점 어디에서든 사용할 수 있는 10퍼센트 할인 쿠폰을 드리도록 하겠습니다.

no longer 더 이상 ~ 않는 get rid of 버리다 home appliances 가전제품 recyclable item 재활용이 가능한 물건 location 지점

80 What is the purpose of the announcement?
(A) To collect old electronics equipment
(B) To promote a charity concert
(C) To thank local residents
(D) To celebrate an anniversary

공지의 목적은 무엇인가?
(A) 오래된 가전 기기들을 수거하려고
(B) 자선 콘서트를 홍보하려고
(C) 지역 주민들에게 감사하려고
(D) 기념일을 축하하려고

공지의 목적은 도입부부터 집중해서 듣자. 더 이상 사용하지 않는 가전제품을 재활용 하도록 돕겠다(help you recycle)고 말했으므로 정답은 (A)가 된다.

81 What does the speaker imply when she says, "That's not all"?
(A) All local residents are invited to an event.
(B) Selected products in the store will be on sale.
(C) Participants will receive an additional bonus.
(D) A radio program will be broadcast on Sunday.

화자가 "그것이 다가 아니죠"라고 말한 의도는 무엇인가?
(A) 모든 지역 주민들이 행사에 초청되었다.
(B) 상점의 일부 상품들만 할인될 것이다.
(C) 참가자들은 추가적인 보너스를 받을 것이다.
(D) 라디오 방송은 일요일에 방송될 것이다.

That's not all은 추가되는 내용을 말하기 앞서 '그것이 다가 아니죠'라는 의미이므로 해당 표현 후에 어떤 내용이 나오는지 파악하면 된다. 참가자들에게 10퍼센트 할인 쿠폰을 주겠다고 했으므로 정답은 (C)가 된다.

82 What will participants receive?
(A) A new television set
(B) Free shipping
(C) A confirmation document
(D) A discount coupon

참가자들은 무엇을 받게 될 것인가?
(A) 새로운 텔레비전
(B) 무료 배송
(C) 확인 증서
(D) 할인 쿠폰

재활용이 가능한 물건을 가지고 오는 참가자들에게 10퍼센트 할인 쿠폰을 주겠다고 했으므로 정답은 (D)가 된다.

Questions 83-85 refer to the following announcement. 영M

Good morning passengers. Welcome aboard the UB Express Line Service to Madison, with stops in Springfield, Greenville and Georgetown. We apologize for the late departure. This was due to a stalled train ahead of us that had to be moved off the tracks. Thankfully, we will be able to make up time along the way so you will arrive at your destination on time. This train is equipped with a dining car where a selection of beverages, snacks and light meals are available. And lastly, please have your tickets ready for inspection. The conductor will be coming through each car shortly. Thank you.

안녕하세요, 승객 여러분. Springfield, Greenville 그리고 Georgetown 역을 거쳐 Madison으로 가는 UB 고속 열차에 탑승하신 것을 환영합니다. 출발이 지연된 것에 대해 사과드립니다. 앞에 멈춰 선 기차를 선로에서 옮기는 것 때문에 지연이 되었습니다. 다행히도 가는 길에 지연된 시간을 따라 잡을 수 있고 여러분의 목적지에는 제때 도착할 것입니다. 이 기차는 여러 종류의 음료와 스낵, 가벼운 식사를 드실 수 있는 식당칸이 마련되어 있습니다. 그리고 마지막으로, 여러분의 표를 검사할 수 있게 준비해 주세요. 차장이 각 칸을 곧 지나가도록 할 것입니다. 감사합니다.

apologize for ~에 대해 사과하다 stalled 멈춘 ahead of ~ 앞에 destination 목적지 be equipped with ~이 장착되어 있다 inspection 검사 conductor (기차의) 차장

83 Where is the announcement most likely taking place?
(A) On a train
(B) At a bus terminal
(C) At an airport
(D) On a boat

공지는 어디서 일어날 것 같은가?
(A) 기차 안
(B) 버스 터미널
(C) 공항
(D) 보트 위

공지의 도입부에 승객들에게 Welcome aboard the UB Express Line Service(UB 고속열차의 탑승을 환영한다)라고 했고 앞에 stalled train이 있어 출발이 지연되었다고 했으므로 정답은 기차가 맞다.

84 What is the cause of the departure delay?
(A) A crew shortage
(B) A disabled train
(C) Foggy weather
(D) Flooded tracks

출발 지연의 원인은 무엇인가?
(A) 인력 부족
(B) 못 움직이는 기차
(C) 안개 낀 날씨
(D) 물에 잠긴 선로

출발 지연에 대해 사과한 후 앞에 멈춰 선 기차(stalled train)가 있어 출발이 지연되었다고 했으므로 정답은 (B)가 된다.

85 What are the listeners asked to do?
(A) Speak to the conductor
(B) View a lunch menu
(C) Conduct an inspection
(D) Take out their tickets

청자들은 무엇을 할 것을 요청 받는가?
(A) 차장과 이야기하기
(B) 점심 메뉴 보기
(C) 검사 실시하기
(D) 티켓 꺼내기

요청 표현인 please가 사용되면서 have your tickets ready for inspection(표 검사를 위해 티켓을 준비해 놓으라)이라고 했으므로 정답은 (D)가 된다.

Questions 86-88 refer to the following excerpt from a meeting. 미M

As you know, Kyson-Vac has launched its new vacuum cleaner, the Filtrex 202, which is expected to compete directly with our new model. In order to successfully increase our market share, we need to carry out an aggressive marketing campaign. So I'd like all of you in marketing to think of a new strategy to highlight the strength of our vacuum cleaner. Now, Rebecca has analyzed this new competing product and created this report. Please take a close look at it and do not share this information with anyone outside the company.

아시는 것처럼, Kyson-Vac는 우리의 신제품과 직접적으로 경쟁할 것으로 예상되는 새 진공 청소기 Filtrex 202를 출시했습니다. 우리가 성공적으로 시장 점유율을 높이기 위하여, 공격적인 마케팅을 실행할 필요가 있습니다. 따라서 마케팅 부서 모두가 우리 진공 청소기의 장점을 강조할 수 있는 새로운 전략을 생각해 주시길 바랍니다. 자, Rebecca가 이 새로운 경쟁 상품을 분석해서 보고서를 만들었습니다. 보고서를 꼼꼼하게 살펴봐 주시고, 회사 외부의 누구와도 이 정보를 공유해서는 안됩니다.

launch 출시하다, 시작하다 vacuum cleaner 진공 청소기 complete 경쟁하다 increase one's market share 시장 점유율을 높이다 highlight 강조하다 analyze 분석하다 take a look at 살펴보다 share 공유하다

86 According to the speaker, what has Kyson-Vac done recently?
(A) They have revised an advertising campaign.
(B) They have merged with another manufacturer.
(C) They have released a new product.
(D) They have started a special promotion.

화자에 따르면, Kyson-Vac는 최근에 무엇을 했는가?
(A) 광고를 수정했다.
(B) 다른 제조사와 합병했다.
(C) 신제품을 출시했다.
(D) 특별 판촉을 시작했다.

세부 사항 질문으로 Kyson-Vac이라는 회사 이름을 미리 파악한 후에 지문을 듣자. 이 회사는 새 진공 청소기를 출시했다(launched its new vacuum cleaner)고 했으므로 정답은 (C)가 된다.

87 What are listeners encouraged to provide?
(A) Marketing strategies
(B) Product designs
(C) Survey results
(D) Work schedules

청자들이 제공하라고 요청받는 것은 무엇인가?
(A) 마케팅 전략
(B) 상품 디자인
(C) 설문 결과
(D) 업무 스케줄

화자가 청자들에게 제공하라고 요청하는 것을 찾아 듣는다. 상대방에게 요청할 때 쓰이는 힌트 표현인 I'd like all of you to에서 정답을 찾는다. 상품의 장점을 강조할 수 있는 새로운 전략을 생각해보라고 했으므로 정답은 (A)가 된다.

88 What are listeners asked to avoid?
(A) Implementing a new marketing campaign
(B) Contacting other suppliers
(C) Missing an important deadline
(D) Sharing confidential information

청자들은 무엇을 피하라고 요청 받는가?
(A) 새로운 마케팅 캠페인을 실행하는 것
(B) 다른 공급업체에게 연락하는 것
(C) 중요한 마감을 놓치는 것
(D) 기밀 정보를 공유하는 것

청자들이 하지 말아야 할 행동을 정답으로 선택하는 것이 질문의 핵심이다. 마지막 부분에 do not share this information with anyone outside the company라고 언급된 부분에서 회사의 외부인과는 이 정보를 공유하지 말라고 했으므로 청자들이 피해야 할 행동은 (D)가 된다.

Questions 89-91 refer to the following talk. 영M

Welcome to Alexandra Falls. My name is Dan and I'll be your tour guide today. I am very excited to show you the majestic Alexandra Falls, which I'm sure you will not forget. Our tour will last about 3 hours and we will walk about 2 kilometers along the scenic Alexandra Pathway. You are welcome to take pictures during the tour, but you must stay with the group at all times. You're not allowed to wander around on your own. Due to the natural moisture from the falls, the surrounding area is very wet and slippery. So, please watch your step. One final note, please leave any food or beverages on the tour bus because we're going to have a lunch buffet at a nearby restaurant at noon. Okay everyone, let's begin our tour!

Alexandra 폭포에 오신 것을 환영합니다. 저는 Dan이고, 오늘 여러분의 투어 가이드입니다. 여러분께 앞으로 절대 잊지 못하실 이 엄청난 Alexandra 폭포를 보여 드릴 생각에 매우 신이 납니다. 투어는 3시간 정도 소요되고 2킬로미터 정도 경치 좋은 Alexandra 산책로를 따라서 걷게 될 것입니다. 투어 중에 얼마든지 사진을 찍어도 좋지만 항상 그룹과 함께 다니셔야만 합니다. 혼자서 다니시는 것은 허용되지 않습니다. 폭포로부터 나오는 자연적인 습기 때문에 주변이 매우 축축하고 미끄럽습니다. 그러니, 발을 조심하십시오. 마지막 공지는, 정오에 근처 레스토랑에서 점심 뷔페를 먹을 예정이므로 음식과 음료는 투어 버스에 놓고 내려 주세요. 자 여러분, 이제 투어를 시작합시다!

falls 폭포 majestic 위대한, 엄청난 pathway 산책로 surrounding area 주변 지역 slippery 미끄러운

89 What is the main purpose of the talk?
(A) To describe a nature tour
(B) To give directions to a tower
(C) To recommend a travel agency
(D) To introduce a speaker

공지의 주 목적은 무엇인가?
(A) 자연 투어에 대해 설명하려고
(B) 타워까지 가는 길 안내를 하려고
(C) 여행사를 추천하려고
(D) 화자를 소개하려고

도입부에 Welcome to Alexandra Falls(폭포에 온 것을 환영한다)라고 하며 본인을 투어 가이드라고 소개했으므로 정답은 (A)가 된다.

90 What are listeners not allowed to do?
(A) Take photographs
(B) Swim in some areas
(C) Explore the site alone
(D) Use cell phones

청자들은 무엇을 하는 것이 허용되지 않는가?
(A) 사진 찍기
(B) 일부 장소에서 수영하기
(C) 혼자 그 장소 다니기
(D) 휴대 전화 사용하기

허용이 되는 것과 안 되는 것을 구별해서 들을 수 있어야 한다. 사진은 찍어도 되지만 but you must stay with the group at all times(항상 그룹과 함께 있어야 한다)라고 하며 혼자 wander around (주변을 걸어 다니는 것)는 허용되지 않는다고 했으므로 정답은 (C)이다.

91 Why does the speaker say, "So, please watch your step"?
(A) To encourage them to enjoy the beautiful view
(B) To ask them to wear a life vest
(C) To tell them to look around the falls
(D) To warn them not to slip

화자는 왜 "그러니, 발을 조심하십시오"라고 말하는가?
(A) 아름다운 경치를 보라고 권하려고
(B) 구명 조끼를 입으라고 요청하려고
(C) 폭포 주변을 살펴보라고 말하려고
(D) 미끄러지지 말라고 경고하려고

해당 표현 전에 폭포 주변이 축축하고 미끄럽다(wet and slippery)고 했으므로 넘어지지 않도록 발 조심을 하라는 의도이다.

Questions 92-94 refer to the following tour information. (영W)

Welcome everybody to the Carriage Chocolate Factory. The Carriage is the oldest chocolate manufacturer in town, and began operating in 1819. The plant has been in operation in the original building since its founding. First, we're going into the production area, where ingredients are mixed and transformed into different types of chocolate. Since it is quite noisy with all the machines running, information will be given through an audio recording. Each of you will receive a set of headphones as you enter the production area and you're asked to return them once you leave. Once you have the headphones on, adjust the volume as you wish. One last thing before we enter the building! You're not allowed to wander around by yourself during the factory tour. So, be sure to stay with the group at all times. Okay, now everybody, this way please!

여러분 모두 Carriage Chocolate Factory에 오신 것을 환영합니다. 이 공장은 1819년에 가동을 시작한 도시에서 가장 오래된 초콜릿 제조업체입니다. 공장은 그 이후로도 계속 본래 건물에서 운영되어 왔습니다. 먼저, 초콜릿 재료들이 섞이고 각각 다른 모양으로 변형되는 생산 공간으로 들어갈 것입니다. 그곳은 많은 기계들로 매우 시끄럽기 때문에, 오디오 리코딩을 통해 정보가 전달될 것입니다. 여러분은 각각 생산 공간으로 들어가면서 헤드폰을 한 세트씩 받게 되며 나올 때 다시 반납하도록 요청 받을 것입니다. 일단 헤드폰을 받으시면, 볼륨을 조절해 주십시오. 건물에 들어가기 전에 마지막 사항이 있습니다! 공장 견학 중에 혼자서 주변을 돌아다니는 것은 허용되지 않습니다. 따라서, 항상 일행과 함께 계십시오. 자, 여러분 이제, 이쪽으로 오십시오!

manufacturer 제조업체 operations 운영 original 원래의, 본래의 ingredient 재료 transform 변형시키다 return 반납하다 adjust 조절하다 wander 돌아다니다, 방황하다

92 According to the speaker, what is distinctive about the factory?
(A) It has the largest production facilities.
(B) It was built a long time ago.
(C) It has recently been renovated.
(D) It has a number of locations.

화자에 따르면, 공장에 관하여 무엇이 특별한가?
(A) 가장 큰 생산 시설이 있다.
(B) 오래전에 건축되었다.
(C) 최근에 수리되었다.
(D) 많은 지점이 있다.

공장에 대한 특이 사항을 묻는 질문으로, 이 도시에서 가장 오래된 공장으로 운영이 1819년도에 시작되었다는 부분에서 정답을 (B)로 선택한다.

93 What will be distributed to the listeners?
(A) Safety gear
(B) Tour schedules
(C) Headphones
(D) Product samples

청자에게 무엇이 배부될 것인가?
(A) 안전 장비
(B) 견학 스케줄
(C) 헤드폰
(D) 제품 견본

세부 사항 질문으로 배부될 것(나눠질 것)에 집중하여 듣는다. 청자 각자가 받게 될 것으로 바꿔 표현되며 a set of headphones가 언급되었으므로 정답은 (C)가 된다.

94 According to the speaker, what should be avoided during the tour?
(A) Exploring the factory alone
(B) Making noise
(C) Eating and drinking food
(D) Touching equipment
화자에 따르면, 견학 도중 무엇을 피해야 하는가?
(A) 혼자서 공장을 다니는 것
(B) 소음을 내는 것
(C) 음식을 먹거나 마시는 것
(D) 장비를 만지는 것

질문의 핵심은 투어 중 하면 안 되는 일을 보기 중에서 고르는 것이다. You're not allowed to wander around by yourself가 정답의 근거로 avoid 대신 you're not allowed로 바꿔 표현되며 혼자서 주변을 돌아다니는 것이 언급되었으므로 정답은 (A)이다.

Questions 95-97 refer to the following message and invoice.
미W

Hello, this is Cindy Kelly calling from Atkinson Industries. I'm calling about an error on the invoice we received today. According to the bill, we've been charged for 200 shipping crates for August. For the last 2 years we have ordered 200 shipping crates every month. However, we had to decrease our production in August. As a result, we only ordered 100 shipping crates this time. I'd like you to send us a corrected bill as soon as possible. If you have any questions, you can call me at 555-0887. Thank you.

INVOICE			
Bill to: Atkinson Industries 1130 Castlefield Ave. (064) 555–0887		Invoice Num: #00981 Due Date: 2016. 08. 31.	
Date	Item	Quantity	Balance
2016. 08. 05.	Shipping crate	200	$80

안녕하세요. Atkinson Industries의 Cindy Kelly입니다. 저희가 오늘 받은 청구서에 실수가 있어서 전화를 드립니다. 청구서에 따르면, 8월은 200개의 포장 박스에 대해 금액이 청구되어 있습니다. 지난 2년 동안 저희가 매달 200개의 포장 박스를 주문한 것이 맞습니다. 그러나 8월에는 저희가 생산을 줄여야만 했기 때문에 결과적으로 이번에는 100개의 포장 박스만을 주문했습니다. 그러니 최대한 빨리 수정된 청구서를 보내 주셨으면 합니다. 질문이 있으시면 555-0887으로 전화 주십시오. 감사합니다.

청구서			
청구 대상: Atkinson Industries 1130 Castlefield Ave. (064) 555–0887		청구 번호: #00981 만기일: 2016. 08. 31.	
날짜	품목	수량	미납 대금
2016년 8월 5일	포장 박스	200개	80달러

be charged for ~에 대해 청구 받다 shipping crate 포장용 박스 decrease 줄이다 a corrected bill 수정된 청구서

95 What is the speaker calling about?
(A) A manufacturing defect
(B) A late shipment
(C) A new contract
(D) A mistake on a bill
화자는 무엇에 관해서 전화하는가?
(A) 제조 결함
(B) 늦은 배송
(C) 새로운 계약
(D) 청구서상의 실수

메시지의 용건을 말할 때에는 I'm calling about과 같은 표현이 자주 쓰이므로 암기가 필요하다. 청구서상의 오류(an error on the invoice)에 관해 전화한다고 했으므로 정답은 (D)가 된다.

96 Look at the graphic. According to the speaker, what information is incorrect?
(A) Date
(B) Item
(C) Quantity
(D) Due date
시각 정보를 보시오. 화자에 따르면, 어떤 정보가 맞지 않는가?
(A) 날짜
(B) 품목
(C) 수량
(D) 만기일

메시지의 내용이 청구서상의 실수이므로 잘못 기재된 내용에 집중한다. 8월에 생산이 줄었다고 언급한 후 As a result, we only ordered 100 shipping crates(결과적으로, 100개의 포장 박스만 주문했다)라고 했으므로 잘못된 정보는 quantity(수량)가 된다.

97 What does the speaker request?
(A) A corrected invoice
(B) A price estimate
(C) An order number
(D) A full refund
화자는 무엇을 요청하는가?
(A) 수정된 청구서
(B) 가격 견적서
(C) 주문 번호
(D) 전액 환불

메시지의 후반부에 I'd like you to send us a corrected bill as soon as possible(수정된 청구서를 최대한 빨리 보내 달라)이라고 했으므로 정답은 (A)가 된다.

Questions 98-100 refer to the following message and program. 미M

Good morning and welcome to the 11th Annual Professional Chefs Conference. Today, we have a lot of interesting workshops prepared for you, professional chefs. And you can find a copy of the program at the registration desk. Before we start, I have an announcement for those of you planning to attend Chef Woodbury's 10 o'clock cooking workshop. Due to a mechanical problem, Mr. Woodbury's flight was delayed in Chicago. He's on his way now but he won't be arriving until noon today. So there will be a change in the schedule. Please note that the last speaker will present first and the first speaker will be the last. We apologize for any inconvenience this may cause you. If you must leave before 2 p.m., you may request a full refund at the registration desk. Thank you for your understanding.

Workshop Program	
Presenter	Time
Mr. Woodbury	10:00 ~ 10:50
Ms. Roth	11:00 ~ 11:50
Lunch	12:00 ~ 12:50
Mr. Best	13:00 ~ 13:50
Ms. Levine	14:00 ~ 14:50

안녕하세요. 11번째 연례 Professional Chefs Conference에 오신 것을 환영합니다. 오늘 우리는 전문 쉐프들을 위해서 여러 가지 흥미로운 워크숍을 준비하였습니다. 등록 데스크 가시면 프로그램지를 보실 수 있습니다. 시작하기에 앞서, Woodbury 쉐프의 10시 워크숍에 참석하려고 하시는 분들께 공지 사항이 있습니다. Woodbury 씨가 탄 비행기가 기계 결함으로 시카고에서 지연되었습니다. 그는 지금 오는 중이지만 오늘 정오가 되어야 도착할 것입니다. 그래서 스케줄에 변경이 있을 예정입니다. 마지막 연사가 처음 발표를 하고 첫 번째 연사가 마지막이 될 것임을 알아두세요. 불편을 끼쳐 사과드립니다. 만약 오후 2시 전에 가셔야만 한다면 등록 데스크에서 전액 환불을 요청하시면 되겠습니다. 이해해 주셔서 감사합니다.

워크숍 프로그램	
발표자	시간
Woodbury 씨	10시 ~ 10시 50분
Roth 씨	11시 ~ 11시 50분
점심	12시 ~ 12시 50분
Best 씨	13시 ~ 13시 50분
Levine 씨	14시 ~ 14시 50분

professional chef 전문 요리사 mechanical problem 기계 결함, 기술적인 문제

98 What kind of event is taking place?
(A) An annual conference
(B) A television show
(C) A cooking competition
(D) An awards ceremony

어떤 종류의 행사가 열리는가?
(A) 연례 컨퍼런스
(B) 텔레비전 쇼
(C) 요리 경연대회
(D) 시상식

도입부에 언급된 행사의 명칭이 11th Annual Professional Chefs Conference 이므로 정답은 (A) 연례 컨퍼런스가 맞다.

99 What is the problem?
(A) A food festival has been canceled.
(B) A venue has been changed.
(C) A presenter will arrive late.
(D) A flight is fully booked.

무엇이 문제인가?
(A) 푸드 페스티벌이 취소되었다.
(B) 장소가 변경되었다.
(C) 발표자가 늦게 도착할 것이다.
(D) 항공편 예약이 꽉 찼다.

10시 워크숍 발표자의 비행기가 지연되었다고 밝힌 후, 정오가 되어야 도착한다고 했으므로 정답은 (C)가 된다.

100 Look at the graphic. According to the revised schedule, who will be the day's first speaker?
(A) Mr. Woodbury
(B) Ms. Roth
(C) Mr. Best
(D) Ms. Levine

시각 정보를 보시오. 바뀐 스케줄에 따르면, 누가 오늘의 첫 번째 연사가 될 것인가?
(A) Woodbury 씨
(B) Roth 씨
(C) Best 씨
(D) Levine 씨

Woodbury 씨가 늦게 도착하게 되어 일정 변경이 있다고 한 후 마지막 연사가 첫 번째로 발표할 것이라고 했으므로 10시에 처음으로 발표할 사람은 Levine 씨가 된다.

Actual Test 12

PART 1

본책 p.144

1 (A)	2 (C)	3 (C)	4 (B)	5 (C)	6 (D)

PART 2

본책 p.148

7 (A)	8 (A)	9 (B)	10 (C)	11 (C)	12 (B)
13 (A)	14 (A)	15 (A)	16 (B)	17 (A)	18 (C)
19 (C)	20 (B)	21 (A)	22 (B)	23 (C)	24 (A)
25 (B)	26 (A)	27 (B)	28 (C)	29 (B)	30 (A)
31 (C)					

PART 3

본책 p.149

32 (A)	33 (D)	34 (C)	35 (B)	36 (B)	37 (A)
38 (A)	39 (B)	40 (C)	41 (C)	42 (D)	43 (A)
44 (B)	45 (C)	46 (A)	47 (D)	48 (B)	49 (A)
50 (D)	51 (B)	52 (C)	53 (B)	54 (D)	55 (A)
56 (B)	57 (C)	58 (A)	59 (B)	60 (C)	61 (B)
62 (D)	63 (B)	64 (D)	65 (C)	66 (C)	67 (C)
68 (D)	69 (A)	70 (C)			

PART 4

본책 p.153

71 (D)	72 (B)	73 (B)	74 (A)	75 (C)	76 (B)
77 (B)	78 (A)	79 (C)	80 (A)	81 (C)	82 (C)
83 (B)	84 (A)	85 (C)	86 (A)	87 (B)	88 (C)
89 (D)	90 (B)	91 (A)	92 (B)	93 (A)	94 (B)
95 (C)	96 (B)	97 (A)	98 (A)	99 (D)	100 (C)

PART 1

1 (A) A worker watches an assembly line.
미W (B) Defective items are placed in a box.
(C) Boxes are positioned on a conveyor belt.
(D) A woman is preparing food in a sanitary facility.

(A) 작업자가 조립 라인을 보고 있다.
(B) 결함이 있는 제품이 상자에 놓여 있다.
(C) 상자들은 컨베이어 벨트에 놓여 있다.
(D) 여자가 위생 시설에서 음식을 준비하고 있다.

위생 복장을 한 작업자가 조립 라인의 제품을 보고 있다. (D)는 작업자의 복장만 보면 sanitary라는 단어가 솔깃하지만 사진의 상황과 일치하지는 않는다.

assembly line 조립 라인　defective 결함이 있는　conveyor belt 컨베이어 벨트　sanitary 위생의　facility 시설

2 (A) A bicyclist is riding on the sidewalk.
미M (B) High-rise buildings surround the plaza.
(C) A line is painted on the ground.
(D) Lines of bicycles are on display for sale.

(A) 누군가 보도 위에서 자전거를 타고 있다.
(B) 높은 건물들이 광장을 둘러싸고 있다.
(C) 선이 바닥에 그려져 있다.
(D) 자전거 제품들이 판매를 위해 진열되어 있다.

자전거가 많이 주차되어 있지만 판매를 위한 것인지 단순한 주차인지 알기 어렵다. 자전거 뒤쪽으로 바닥에 선이 그어져 있으므로 (C)가 가장 옳은 설명이다.

bicyclist 자전거를 타는 사람　sidewalk 보도, 인도　high-rise building 높은 건물　surround 둘러싸다　plaza 광장　line 제품의 종류

3 (A) This gym has a strict uniform policy.
미W (B) Some members are working with trainers.
(C) The room is unoccupied at the moment.
(D) All the weights and bars have been sold.

(A) 이 체육관은 엄격한 유니폼 규정을 두고 있다.
(B) 일부 회원들이 트레이너와 운동하고 있다.
(C) 방에 지금 아무도 없다.
(D) 모든 역기와 봉들이 팔렸다.

헬스클럽으로 보이는 공간에 운동 기구들만 제자리에 있고 사람은 보이지 않는다.

strict 엄격한　uniform 유니폼, 제복　policy 정책, 규정　unoccupied 아무도 없는　at the moment 현재, 지금　weights 역기　be sold 팔리다

4 (A) She is taking some measurements.
영M (B) Finished items are on the shelf.
(C) The bowls are being washed.
(D) She is carving a wooden spoon.

(A) 여자가 치수를 재고 있다.
(B) 작업이 끝난 제품들이 선반에 있다.
(C) 그릇들이 씻겨지고 있다.
(D) 여자가 나무 숟가락을 깎아서 만들고 있다.

여자가 조각칼로 작업하고 있는데 대기 중인 작품과 완료된 작품들이 선반에 있다.

take a measurement 치수를 재다　carve 조각하다, 깎아서 만들다　wooden 나무로 된

5 (A) Equipment is being stored away.
미W (B) The bags are being emptied.
(C) Large items are being driven on a forklift.
(D) A worker is transporting bags into a truck.

(A) 장비가 보관되고 있다.
(B) 가방들이 비어지고 있다.
(C) 지게차 위에 큰 물품들이 실려 이동되고 있다.
(D) 작업자가 가방을 트럭으로 옮기고 있다.

지게차에 물품들이 실려 어디론가 가고 있다.

store away 저장하다, 보관하다　empty 비우다　forklift 들어 올리는 장치, 지게차　transport 수송하다

6 (A) Drinks have been prepared for every seat.
영M (B) There are electrical outlets everywhere.
(C) Some stools are the only seating available.
(D) The room features abstract artworks.

(A) 마실 것이 모든 자리에 준비되었다.
(B) 여러 군데 전기 콘센트가 있다.
(C) 등받이 없는 의자들이 유일하게 앉을 수 있는 자리이다.
(D) 방에 추상화가 있는 것이 특징이다.

탁자와 의자들이 나란히 정렬되어 있고 벽에 그림이 몇 점 보인다. 전기 콘센트가 여러 군데 있음은 확인할 수 없고 의자들은 모두 등받이가 있는 형태이다.

drinks 마실 것 seat 좌석, 자리 electrical outlet 전기 콘센트 stool 등받이가 없는 의자 feature ~을 특징으로 하다 abstract 추상적인

PART 2

7 Who's leading the session next week?
영W (A) It's Ms. Wacha.
미M (B) In two weeks.
(C) That sounds like fun.

누가 다음 주 세션을 진행하나요?
(A) Wacha 씨입니다.
(B) 2주 후에요.
(C) 재미있을 것 같습니다.

의문사 who 질문으로 이름이 언급된 (A)가 정답이다. (B)는 의문사 when에 대한 답이므로 오답이고, (C)는 제안문에 대한 승낙 답변이다.

lead 이끌다, 지도하다

8 When does the bank open?
미W (A) At 9 in the morning.
영M (B) It's on Broadway Street.
(C) No, I've never been there.

은행은 언제 문을 여나요?
(A) 아침 아홉 시에요.
(B) 그것은 Broadway 가에 있어요.
(C) 아니요, 거기 가 본 적이 없어요.

when 의문문으로 은행의 문 여는 시각을 물었으므로 정답은 (A)이다.

9 Where is the nearest subway station?
영M (A) I'll go by bus.
미W (B) Right down the street.
(C) Yes, very close.

가장 가까운 전철역은 어디인가요?
(A) 전 버스로 갈 거예요.
(B) 바로 길 아래쪽에요.
(C) 네, 매우 가까워요.

의문사 where을 이용하여 전철역이 어디인지 물었으므로 정답은 (B)이다.

10 How can I make sure Lisa gets this invitation?
영W (A) In the hotel lobby.
영M (B) She has the receipt.
(C) Put it on her desk.

제가 어떻게 Lisa가 이 초대장을 받도록 할 수 있을까요?
(A) 호텔 로비에요.
(B) 그녀가 영수증을 가지고 있어요.
(C) 책상 위에 두시면 됩니다.

의문사 how는 방법을 묻는다. Lisa가 초대장을 받을 수 있는 방법을 물었으므로 책상 위에 두라고 한 (C)가 정답이다.

invitation 초대장 receipt 영수증

11 Do you want my home or office number?
미W (A) Tell him to call me.
영W (B) Yes, I think so.
(C) Both, actually.

저의 집 번호를 원하세요, 아니면 사무실 번호를 원하세요?
(A) 그한테 저에게 전화하라고 하세요.
(B) 네, 그럴 거예요.
(C) 실은 둘 다요.

선택 사항은 집 번호 혹은 사무실 번호이므로 둘 다라고 답한 (C)가 정답이다.

12 Why don't we take a coffee break before we
미W continue with the project?
미M (A) Okay, I'll go pick her up.
(B) But today is the deadline.
(C) Make some extra copies, please.

프로젝트를 계속하기 전에 휴식 시간을 갖는 게 어때요?
(A) 좋아요, 제가 가서 그녀를 픽업해 올게요.
(B) 그렇지만 오늘이 마감이에요.
(C) 추가 복사를 해 주세요.

Why don't we는 대표적인 제안 표현이다. 휴식 시간을 갖는 게 어떠냐고 제안했고 오늘이 마감이라고 한 (B)가 이 제안에 대한 거절의 의미를 내포하고 있으므로 정답이 된다.

take a coffee break 휴식 시간을 가지다 continue with ~을 계속하다

13 Mr. Kawasaki is the magazine director, isn't he?
영M (A) Actually, I'm not sure.
영W (B) On the front page.
(C) He is on the phone all day.

Kawasaki 씨가 잡지사 이사님이죠, 그렇지 않나요?
(A) 전 잘 몰라요.
(B) 앞면에요.
(C) 그는 하루 종일 통화 중이에요.

Yes/No 여부를 묻는 질문으로 특정 인물이 회사의 중역인지 물었고 '잘 모르겠다'라고 답한 (A)가 정답이다. '잘 모르겠다'는 식의 표현은 어떤 질문에도 정답이 되는 경우가 많기 때문에 잘 암기해 두자.

14 Do you want to go out for a walk after the meal?
미M (A) I'm not feeling well.
미W (B) The cinema on Broadway.
(C) I won't be late again.

식사 후에 산책 가시겠어요?
(A) 몸이 좋질 않네요.
(B) 브로드웨이에 있는 영화관이요.
(C) 다시는 늦지 않겠습니다.

Do you want to는 제안의 의미로 '~하시겠습니까?'라고 해석한다. 정답도 제안에 대한 승낙 혹은 거절이 된다. 몸이 좋지 않다는 (A)는 제안에 대한 거절의 의미로 정답이 된다.

go for a walk 산책을 가다 do not feel well 몸이 아프다

15 Who has been hired for the project?
영W (A) The HB Architects has.
미M (B) It should be done by Thursday.
(C) To discuss a proposal.

그 프로젝트를 하기 위해 누가 고용되었습니까?
(A) HB Architects요.
(B) 그것은 목요일까지 끝날 것입니다.
(C) 제안서에 대해 토론하기 위해서요.

의문사 who 질문으로 고용된 사람이 누구인지가 핵심 포인트이다. who에 대한 정답으로 회사 이름이 자주 나오므로 기억해 두어야 한다. 정답인 (A) The HB Architects has (been hired for the project)에서 생략된 부분도 함께 알아두자.

be done 끝나다 proposal 제안서

16 Didn't you receive Ms. Taylor's fax?
미W (A) It's my new number.
영M (B) When did she send it?
(C) Submit a tax return.

Taylor 씨의 팩스를 받지 않았나요?
(A) 저의 새 번호입니다.
(B) 그녀가 언제 그걸 보냈나요?
(C) 소득 신고서를 제출하세요.

Yes/No 여부를 묻는 질문으로 핵심은 Taylor 씨가 보낸 팩스를 받았는지 여부이다. (B)는 Taylor 씨가 언제 보냈는지를 되묻고 있으니 받지 못했음을 간접적으로 알 수 있고 정답이 된다. (A)와 (C)는 문맥에서 벗어난 답을 주고 있으므로 오답이다.

submit 제출하다 tax return 소득 신고서

17 How about stopping by the bank before the show?
영M (A) Do we have time?
미W (B) Walk around the city.
(C) They already did.

쇼 시작 전에 은행에 들르는 게 어떨까요?
(A) 우리 시간이 있나요?
(B) 도시 주변을 산책하세요.
(C) 그들은 이미 했어요.

제안 의문문으로 how about -ing?는 '~하는 게 어때요?'라는 제안 표현으로 암기해두자. 은행을 들르는 게 어떨지 제안했고 (A)는 그럴 시간이 있는지 되묻고 있으므로 자연스러운 답변이다. (C)의 경우 they로 받을 수 있는 명사가 없으므로 주어 오류 함정이다.

stop by ~에 들르다 walk around 주위를 산책하다

18 That's the restricted area, isn't it?
영W (A) We need a larger space.
미M (B) Turn right at the next corner.
(C) I have access to it.

저기는 제한 구역이에요, 그렇지 않나요?
(A) 우리는 더 큰 공간이 필요해요.
(B) 다음 코너에서 우회전하세요.
(C) 저는 출입할 수 있어요.

Yes/No 여부를 묻는 질문이다. That(저곳)이 the restricted area(제한 구역)가 맞는지 물었으므로 자신은 출입할 수 있다고 답한 (C)가 정답이 된다.

restricted 제한된 have access to ~에 출입할 수 있다

19 Let's have dinner at the Palace Hotel.
미W (A) The food wasn't ready.
영W (B) For how many days?
(C) Does it have a good place to eat?

Palace 호텔에서 저녁을 먹읍시다.
(A) 음식이 준비되지 않았어요.
(B) 며칠 동안이요?
(C) 먹을 만한 좋은 장소가 있나요?

Let's는 제안할 때 쓰는 표현으로 저녁을 호텔에서 먹자는 제안이었으므로 그곳에 먹을 만한 좋은 곳이 있는지를 되묻는 (C)가 가장 자연스러운 답이 된다.

20 Isn't the drug store open 24 hours a day?
미W (A) No, at the electronics store.
미M (B) Yes, but it's closed on national holidays.
(C) He is a pharmacist.

그 약국은 24시간 문을 열지 않나요?
(A) 아니요, 가전제품 상점에서요.
(B) 네, 그렇지만 공휴일에는 문을 닫습니다.
(C) 그는 약사입니다.

Yes/No 여부로 묻는 핵심은 24시간 문을 여는지이므로 정답은 (B)가 된다.

drug store 약국 national holiday 공휴일 pharmacist 약사

21 CI Investments has several restaurants in their
영M building.
영W (A) I've been to one of them.
(B) Long-term investments.
(C) Where did you find my briefcase?

CI Investments는 빌딩 안에 레스토랑이 여러 개 있어요.
(A) 그중 한 곳에 가본 적이 있어요.
(B) 장기 투자요.
(C) 어디서 제 서류 가방을 찾으셨어요?

평서문의 요지는 CI Investments라는 특정 회사의 건물에 레스토랑이 여러 곳 있다는 것이므로, 정답 역시 이 레스토랑들 중 한 곳에 가봤다고 답한 (A)가 가장 자연스럽다.

long-term 장기의 investment 투자 briefcase 서류 가방

22 Have you signed the agreement or do you need
미M more time to review it?
미W (A) Thank you for the offer.
(B) I think I need another day.
(C) Sorry, I didn't see the sign.

계약서에 서명을 하셨나요 아니면 검토할 시간이 더 필요하세요?
(A) 제안에 감사드립니다.
(B) 하루 더 필요할 것 같습니다.
(C) 죄송하지만, 저는 그 표지판을 못 봤어요.

서명을 이미 했는지 아니면 시간이 더 필요한지 묻고 있으므로 하루가 더 필요하다고 답한 (B)가 정답이다.

agreement 계약서 offer 제안 (사항)

23 I'd suggest we conduct the customer survey after
영W the holiday.
미M (A) To attract more customers.
(B) The holiday promotion was a success.
(C) Let's see when the marketing team is available.

우리가 휴일 후에 고객 설문 조사를 할 것을 제안합니다.
(A) 더 많은 고객을 유치하려고요.

(B) 휴일 프로모션이 성공적이었어요.
(C) 마케팅 팀이 언제 시간이 되는지 한 번 봅시다.

평서문으로 제안하는 내용이 휴일이 지난 후 설문 조사를 하는 것이었으므로 마케팅 팀이 언제 가능한지 보자고 답한 (C)가 정답이다. (A)는 의문사 why 질문에 대한 답이고 (B)는 holiday가 반복 사용된 함정이 된다.

conduct a survey 설문 조사를 하다 attract 유치하다, 끌어 모으다 promotion 판촉 행사

24 Where can I find an ink cartridge?
미W (A) Maria would know.
영M (B) The store is very busy.
(C) Every day at 4.

잉크 카트리지를 어디서 찾을 수 있을까요?
(A) Maria가 알 거예요.
(B) 그 상점은 매우 붐벼요.
(C) 매일 4시에요.

where 의문문으로 어디서 찾을 수 있는지 물었을 때 장소를 직접 말해 주는 것 외에도 알고 있는 다른 사람을 말하는 것도 자연스러운 정답이 된다. 따라서 'Maria라는 사람이 알 것이다'라고 말한 (A)가 정답이 된다. 특히 제3자의 이름이나 직위 등이 언급되면서 '그 사람이 알 것이다', '그 사람이 책임자이다' 등은 어떤 질문과 만나도 정답이 되는 경우가 많으므로 잘 암기해 두자.

25 I think we should replace our office chairs with a
영M more comfortable model.
미W (A) A special type of chair.
(B) Why don't we wait until the next quarter?
(C) It was designed by our Chicago office.

우리 사무실 의자를 좀 더 편안한 모델로 교체하는 것이 좋을 것 같아요.
(A) 특별한 종류의 의자요.
(B) 다음 분기까지 기다리는 것이 어떨까요?
(C) 그것은 시카고 사무실이 디자인했어요.

평서문에 조동사 should가 사용되어 제안의 의미를 갖는다. 의자를 더 편안한 모델로 교체하자는 제안이었고 (B)는 다음 분기까지 기다리자고 했으므로 제안에 대해 거절의 의미를 갖는 정답이 된다.

replace 교체하다 quarter 분기

26 Could you find a box to pack the extra brochures in?
영W (A) I'll see if I can find one in the storage room.
영M (B) Where did you hear that?
(C) It is a present for Martha.

남은 안내 책자를 담아 둘 박스 하나만 찾아 주실래요?
(A) 창고에 하나 있는지 가서 볼게요.
(B) 그것을 어디서 들었어요?
(C) Martha에게 줄 선물이에요.

요청 의문문으로 박스를 찾아 달라는 것이 핵심이므로 정답은 창고에 가서 찾아보겠다고 한 (A)가 맞다.

pack 포장하다, 싸다 see if ~인지 보겠다

27 Why is there such a long wait for the bus?
미W (A) It was the wrong address.
영W (B) There's always a lot of traffic at this time of day.
(C) It is now located on Smith Street.

버스를 타기 위해 왜 이렇게 오래 기다려야 하죠?
(A) 그것은 잘못된 주소였어요.
(B) 매일 이 시간에는 항상 교통이 막혀요.
(C) 그건 이제 Smith 가에 있어요.

버스를 왜 이렇게 오래 기다려야 하는지 묻는 질문으로 가장 그럴 듯한 이유는 (B)이다. 차가 막혀서 버스가 늦게 오기 때문이라고 해석된다.

traffic 교통량 at this time of day 하루 중 이 시간에

28 You are designing the new company logo, aren't
미W you?
미M (A) I already signed the forms.
(B) They usually do.
(C) No, the new graphic artist is doing it.

당신이 회사의 새 로고를 디자인하고 있죠, 그렇지 않나요?
(A) 저는 이미 그 양식에 서명했어요.
(B) 그들은 보통 그렇게 해요.
(C) 아니요, 새로 온 그래픽 디자이너가 하고 있어요.

상대방이 회사의 로고 디자인을 하는 중인지 묻는 말에 the new graphic artist(다른 사람)가 하고 있다고 답한 (C)가 정답이 된다.

29 Will this parcel reach Los Angeles by tomorrow?
영M (A) Yes, it is a wonderful city.
영W (B) If you send it by overnight delivery.
(C) Only carry-on luggage is allowed.

이 소포가 내일까지 로스앤젤레스에 도착할까요?
(A) 네, 그곳은 훌륭한 도시에요.
(B) 익일 배송으로 보내신다면요.
(C) 기내용 짐 가방만 허용됩니다.

질문의 핵심은 소포가 내일까지 도착할지 여부이다. overnight delivery(다음 날 도착하는 배송)를 선택하면 가능하다고 했으므로 정답은 (B)가 된다.

parcel 소포 overnight delivery 익일 배송 carry-on 기내용의

30 Do you know who owns the book store on Pine
미M Avenue?
미W (A) Anthony bought it two months ago.
(B) Yes, I have read her books.
(C) Right across from Kings Avenue.

누가 Pine Avenue에 있는 서점을 소유하고 있는지 아세요?
(A) Anthony가 두 달 전에 사 들였어요.
(B) 네, 그녀의 책들을 읽어 봤어요.
(C) Kings Avenue 맞은편에요.

질문의 중간에 의문사가 있는 경우, 의미를 놓치기가 쉽다. 누가 서점을 소유하고 있는지가 핵심이므로 정답은 (A)가 된다.

own 소유하다 across from ~의 맞은편에

31 What kind of experience do you have in finance?
영W (A) It was a great experience.
미M (B) Was that their final offer?
(C) I've been working as an accountant for 5 years.

재무 분야에서 어떤 경력이 있나요?
(A) 그것은 좋은 경험이었어요.
(B) 그것이 그들의 최종 제안 금액인가요?
(C) 저는 회계사로 5년간 일하고 있습니다.

재무 분야의 경력을 물었으므로 회계사로 5년간 일하고 있다고 답한 (C)가 정답이 된다. 또한 experience라는 단어는 토익에서 '경력'이라는 의미로 더 많이 쓰임을 기억해 두자.

offer 제안, 제안된 금액

PART 3

Questions 32-34 refer to the following conversation. (영M) (미W)

M Jenny, are you attending the economics conference in Australia next week?
W Yes, I am leaving on Saturday. It'll be my first time in Australia so I am pretty excited.
M I'm sure you'll enjoy the country. I wish I could be there but I have to finish this financial summary by next Wednesday.
W Oh, that's too bad. This year's conference sounds quite interesting, so I wish I could go with you.

남 Jenny, 다음 주 호주에서 열리는 경제 컨퍼런스에 참석하나요?
여 네, 토요일에 떠나요. 호주가 이번이 처음이라 신 나요.
남 분명히 좋아하실 거예요. 저도 가고 싶지만 이 재무 요약본을 다음 주 수요일까지 끝내야만 하거든요.
여 오, 안타깝네요. 올해의 컨퍼런스는 굉장히 흥미진진할 것 같아서 함께 갈 수 있었으면 했는데요.

economics 경제 financial summary 간략한 재무제표

32 Why is the woman going to Australia?
(A) To attend a conference
(B) To visit her relatives
(C) To open a branch office
(D) To get a new job

여자는 왜 호주에 가는가?
(A) 컨퍼런스에 참석하려고
(B) 친척을 방문하려고
(C) 지점을 열려고
(D) 새 직장을 얻으려고

질문의 키워드인 Australia에 주목하는 것이 포인트이다. 여자에게 경제 컨퍼런스에 참석하는지 묻는 부분에서 정답을 (A)로 선택한다.

33 What is the woman excited about?
(A) Working with the man
(B) Learning a foreign language
(C) Making new friends
(D) Travelling to another country

여자는 무엇에 대해서 신이 났는가?
(A) 남자와 함께 일하는 것
(B) 외국어를 배우는 것
(C) 새로운 친구를 사귀는 것
(D) 다른 나라를 여행하는 것

질문의 키워드인 excited는 It'll be my first time in Australia so I am pretty excited에서 찾을 수 있다. 호주는 처음이라서 신 난다고 했으므로 정답은 (D)가 맞다.

34 What does the man have to do by next Wednesday?
(A) Finalize the terms of an agreement
(B) Participate in a discussion
(C) Complete a financial report
(D) Make a flight reservation

남자는 수요일까지 무엇을 해야 하는가?
(A) 계약서의 조항 마무리하기
(B) 토론 참석하기
(C) 재무 보고서 끝내기
(D) 항공편 예약하기

남자가 다음 주 수요일까지 해야 할 일이 있음을 미리 염두에 두고 듣는 것이 중요하다. I have to finish this financial summary by next Wednesday에서 정답은 (C)임을 알 수 있다.

Questions 35-37 refer to the following conversation. (영M) (영W)

M Excuse me. Is this the Park View Building?
W Yes, it is. How can I help you?
M I'm here for a job interview with Ms. Katie Sullivan at 11 o'clock. Could you tell me where her office is located?
W It is on the eighth floor, suite 803. When you get to the eighth floor, you'll see her office to your right.
M Thank you very much. Could you tell Ms. Sullivan that I am here?

남 실례합니다. 여기가 Park View Building인가요?
여 네, 그렇습니다. 어떻게 도와 드릴까요?
남 전 11시에 Katie Sullivan 씨와 면접 약속이 있어서 왔습니다. 그녀의 사무실이 어디인지 알려 주시겠어요?
여 8층 803호입니다. 8층으로 올라가시면, 오른쪽에 그녀의 사무실이 보일 겁니다.
남 감사합니다. Sullivan 씨께 제가 왔다고 알려 주시겠어요?

35 What does the man ask the woman about?
(A) Business hours
(B) Directions to an office
(C) The name of a job applicant
(D) Information about the company

남자는 여자에게 무엇에 대해 묻는가?
(A) 영업시간
(B) 사무실에 가는 방법
(C) 구직자의 이름
(D) 회사에 대한 정보

남자가 여자에게 질문한 내용은 면접관의 사무실을 묻는 것이었으므로 (B)가 정답이 된다.

36 Where is Ms. Sullivan's office located?
(A) On the third floor
(B) On the eighth floor
(C) On the eleventh floor
(D) On the twentieth floor

Sullivan 씨의 사무실은 어디에 있는가?
(A) 3층
(B) 8층

(C) 11층
(D) 20층

세부 사항 정보를 묻는 질문은 순발력이 가장 중요하다. It is on the eighth floor, suite 803이 들리는 순간 정답을 처리하자.

37 What will the woman probably do next?
(A) Make a telephone call
(B) Prepare for an interview
(C) Go to another building
(D) Reserve a conference room

여자는 다음에 무엇을 할 것 같은가?
(A) 전화하기
(B) 면접 준비하기
(C) 다른 빌딩으로 가기
(D) 컨퍼런스 룸 예약하기

대화의 후반부에 남자가 여자에게 Could you tell Ms. Sullivan that I am here?라고 요청했으므로 여자는 Sullivan 씨에게 전화를 할 것이다. 정답은 (A)이다.

Questions 38-40 refer to the following conversation. (영W) (미M)

W Hi, I bought this dress a couple of days ago, but it's too large for me. Can I exchange it for a smaller size?
M Well, we do have that dress in smaller sizes but not in blue. Would you like to try it in another color?
W No, I really want to have one in blue. When are you getting a new shipment of these dresses?
M I'm sorry but we won't be getting any more of that style. However, I can call our other store on First Avenue to ask if they have a smaller one in blue.

여 안녕하세요. 제가 이 원피스를 이틀 전에 샀는데 저한테 너무 크네요. 더 작은 사이즈로 교환할 수 있을까요?
남 음, 작은 사이즈가 있기는 한데 파란색으로는 없습니다. 다른 색상을 한번 입어보시겠어요?
여 아니요, 전 파란색을 갖고 싶습니다. 이 원피스는 언제 재고가 다시 들어 오나요?
남 죄송하게도 그 스타일은 더 이상 나오지 않습니다. 그러나 First Avenue에 있는 다른 매장에 전화해서 파란색으로 더 작은 사이즈가 있는지 알아보겠습니다.

exchange 교환하다

38 Where most likely are the speakers?
(A) In a clothing store
(B) In a restaurant
(C) In a warehouse
(D) In a paint shop

화자들은 어디에 있을 것 같은가?
(A) 옷 가게
(B) 레스토랑
(C) 창고
(D) 페인트 가게

대화 장소를 유추할 수 있는 힌트는 거의 도입부에 나온다. 여자가 옷을 여기에서 샀다라고 말했을 때 정답을 (A)로 선택할 수 있다.

39 What is the problem with the woman's purchase?
(A) Its color
(B) Its size
(C) Its quality
(D) Its style

여자의 구매 상품은 무엇이 문제인가?
(A) 색상
(B) 사이즈
(C) 품질
(D) 스타일

여자가 구입한 옷에 대해 too large for me(나에게 너무 크다)라고 했고 더 작은 사이즈로 교환하기 원했으므로 정답은 (B)이다.

40 What does the man offer to do?
(A) Expedite a delivery
(B) Recommend another item
(C) Contact another store
(D) Provide a coupon

남자는 무엇을 해주겠다고 하는가?
(A) 배송을 빠르게 하기
(B) 다른 상품 추천하기
(C) 다른 상점에 연락하기
(D) 쿠폰 제공하기

남자의 대사 마지막 부분에서 I can call our other store on First Avenue를 들었을 때 다른 지점에 전화할 것임을 알 수 있다. 정답은 (C)이다.

Questions 41-43 refer to the following conversation. (미M) (미W)

M Paula, I can't find the materials I've prepared for the meeting. I'm sure I put them in my briefcase when I left home this morning.
W Uh-oh, take your time and try looking in your briefcase again. Have you checked the front pocket as well?
M Yes, I looked everywhere but they are not in here. The meeting's scheduled to begin in 10 minutes. Could you go ahead and set up the projector? I'm going back to my office to see if I left the materials there.
W No problem. Let me bring your laptop computer to the meeting room for you.

남 Paula, 제가 미팅에 쓰려고 준비해 둔 자료들을 찾을 수가 없어요. 아침에 출근할 때 분명히 제 서류 가방에 넣어 두었거든요.
여 저런, 다시 한 번 천천히 서류 가방 안을 보세요. 그 앞 주머니도 확인해 보셨나요?
남 네, 다 찾아봤는데 이 안에는 없네요. 미팅이 10분 후면 시작이에요. 먼저 가셔서 프로젝터를 설치해 주시겠어요? 저는 사무실에 돌아가서 거기 놔두고 왔는지 확인해 볼게요.
여 문제없습니다. 제가 대신 노트북 컴퓨터를 회의실로 가져갈게요.

materials 자료 briefcase 서류 가방 go ahead 먼저 가다 set up 설치하다

41 Why is the man worried?
(A) He missed a bus.
(B) He is late for a presentation.
(C) He cannot find meeting materials.
(D) He lost his briefcase.

남자는 왜 걱정하는가?
(A) 버스를 놓쳤다.
(B) 발표에 늦었다.
(C) 미팅 자료를 찾을 수가 없다.
(D) 서류 가방을 잃어 버렸다.

남자 대사에서 정답을 찾는 것이 포인트이다. I can't find the materials I've prepared for the meeting에서 미팅 때 쓰려고 준비한 자료를 못 찾겠다고 했으므로 정답은 (C)가 된다.

42 What does the man ask the woman to do?
(A) Contact his assistant
(B) Reschedule a meeting
(C) Print out documents
(D) Set up some equipment

남자는 여자에게 무엇을 하라고 요청하는가?
(A) 그의 비서에게 연락하기
(B) 미팅 일정 다시 잡기
(C) 서류 출력하기
(D) 장비 설치하기

요청 표현이 정답에 대한 단서이다. 남자가 먼저 가서 프로젝터를 설치하라고 요청했으므로 정답은 (D)가 된다.

43 Where will the man probably go next?
(A) To his office
(B) To his car
(C) To a meeting room
(D) To a clothing store

남자는 다음에 어디로 갈 것 같은가?
(A) 사무실
(B) 차
(C) 회의실
(D) 옷 가게

대화의 후반부에 남자가 I'm going back to my office라고 했으므로 정답은 (A)이다.

Questions 44-46 refer to the following conversation. 영M 영W

M Hi, Melinda. I heard you visited our branch office in Japan last week. How was your trip?
W It was very good. I had a chance to meet with our online marketing expert and learned a lot about how our products are marketed through the Internet in Asia. I've come up with some ideas to expand our customer base here in the United States through online retail stores.
M That's great. I'm really looking forward to hearing your ideas at the marketing meeting tomorrow morning.
W Oh, yeah. The meeting is at 10, right? I'm going to take some time this afternoon to organize my thoughts for the meeting.

남 안녕하세요, Melinda. 지난주에 일본 지점에 방문하셨다고 들었어요. 출장은 어땠나요?
여 굉장히 좋았어요. 온라인 마케팅 전문가를 만날 기회가 있었고 우리 제품들이 아시아에서는 인터넷을 통해 어떻게 마케팅 되고 있는지 많이 배웠습니다. 여기 미국에서 온라인 매장들을 통해 고객층을 확대할 수 있는 아이디어들이 떠올랐어요.
남 잘됐네요. 내일 아침 마케팅 미팅에서 당신의 아이디어를 빨리 듣고 싶습니다.
여 아, 네. 미팅은 10시 맞죠? 전 오늘 오후에 미팅을 위해 생각을 정리하는 시간을 좀 가지려고 해요.

have a chance to ~할 기회를 갖다 organize one's thoughts 생각을 정리하다

44 What did the woman do last week?
(A) Attended a marketing convention
(B) Visited an overseas branch
(C) Conducted a job interview
(D) Moved to another city

여자는 지난주에 무엇을 했는가?
(A) 마케팅 컨벤션에 참석했다.
(B) 해외 지점을 방문했다.
(C) 면접을 진행했다.
(D) 다른 도시로 이사했다.

last week이 질문의 키워드이다. 남자가 여자에게 you visited our branch office in Japan last week(지난주에 일본 지점을 방문했다)라는 얘기를 들었다고 했으므로 정답은 (B)가 된다.

45 Which department do the speakers work in?
(A) Accounting
(B) Shipping
(C) Marketing
(D) Personnel

화자들은 어떤 부서에서 일하는가?
(A) 회계
(B) 배송
(C) 마케팅
(D) 인사

화자들이 나누는 업무의 내용을 통해 부서를 유추하여 풀자. 여자는 일본에서 제품이 어떻게 마케팅 되는지 배우고 미국에서 사용할 수 있는 아이디어가 생겼다고 했으므로 정답은 (C)가 된다.

46 What is the woman going to do this afternoon?
(A) Prepare for a meeting
(B) Attend a seminar
(C) Speak to a colleague
(D) Read some e-mail

여자는 오늘 오후에 무엇을 할 것인가?
(A) 미팅 준비하기
(B) 세미나 참석하기
(C) 동료와 얘기하기
(D) 이메일 읽기

this afternoon이 질문의 키워드이다. 여자가 오늘 오후는 시간을 갖고 미팅을 위한 생각 정리를 하겠다(to organize my thoughts for the meeting)고 했으므로 정답은 (A)가 맞다.

Questions 47-49 refer to the following conversation. 미W 미M

W Thank you for calling First Airlines. How can I help you?
M Hello. I need to fly to Washington D.C. today to attend an emergency meeting. I know this is last-minute, but are there any evening flights available?
W Unfortunately all the flights are booked tonight. I can put you on the 7 o'clock flight tomorrow morning though.
M Well, the meeting doesn't start until 1 p.m. so I should be able to make it on time. I'll take it.

여 First Airlines에 전화 주셔서 감사합니다. 어떻게 도와 드릴까요?
남 안녕하세요. 긴급 회의 때문에 오늘 워싱턴으로 가야 합니다. 늦은 건 알지만 저녁에 가능한 비행편이 있나요?
여 안타깝게도 오늘 밤은 모든 항공기가 만석입니다. 내일 아침 7시 비행기는 잡아 드릴 수 있는데요.
남 음. 미팅이 오후 1시에 시작이니 참석할 수 있겠네요. 그걸로 하겠습니다.

emergency meeting 비상 회의 last-minute 막판, 최후의 순간

47 What does the man want to do?
(A) Purchase a gift
(B) Send a package
(C) Check in some luggage
(D) Book a flight ticket
남자는 무엇을 하고 싶어 하는가?
(A) 선물 구입하기
(B) 소포 보내기
(C) 짐 부치기
(D) 항공편 예약하기

남자가 I need to fly to Washington D.C. today to attend an emergency meeting에서 급하게 워싱턴에 비행기를 타고 가야 한다고 했으므로 정답은 (D)가 된다.

48 What is the problem?
(A) A passport is lost.
(B) A flight ticket is unavailable.
(C) The man is sick.
(D) The weather is bad.
무엇이 문제인가?
(A) 여권을 분실했다.
(B) 항공편이 없다.
(C) 남자가 아프다.
(D) 날씨가 안 좋다.

남자가 항공편을 예약하고 싶다고 했고 여자가 Unfortunately all the flights are booked tonight(오늘 밤은 항공편이 모두 예약됐다)이라고 했으므로 정답은 (B)가 된다.

49 When will the man leave?
(A) At 7:00 a.m.
(B) At 8:00 a.m.
(C) At noon
(D) At 1:00 p.m.
남자는 언제 떠날 것인가?
(A) 오전 7시
(B) 오전 8시
(C) 정오
(D) 오후 1시

여자가 남자에게 내일 아침 7시 항공편을 예약해 줄 수 있다고 했고 남자는 결국 I'll take it(그걸로 하겠습니다)라고 했으므로 정답은 (A)가 된다.

Questions 50-52 refer to the following conversation. 영M 영W

M This apartment is the largest of the three I've shown you so far. It has a separate dining area and the living room is spacious as well.
W Wow, and the view is great. But the best thing about it is that my office building is very close to here. I can even walk to work. How much is the rent?
M It is 1,200 dollars per month.
W Hmm... **That's more than I was hoping to spend.** Could you give me some time to think it over? I'll call you early next week.

남 이 아파트는 지금까지 보여 드린 3개 중에서 가장 큽니다. 식사 공간이 분리되어 있고 거실 역시 매우 넓습니다.
여 와, 게다가 경치도 좋네요. 그렇지만 가장 좋은 점은 제 사무실이 매우 가깝다는 거예요. 걸어갈 수도 있거든요. 임대료는 얼마죠?
남 한 달에 1200달러입니다.
여 흠… **제가 쓰려고 한 것보다 많네요.** 생각할 시간을 좀 주시겠어요? 다음 주 초에 전화를 드릴게요.

so far 현재까지 separate 분리된 spacious 넓은

50 Who most likely is the man?
(A) A tenant
(B) A home builder
(C) A designer
(D) A real estate agent
남자는 누구일 것 같은가?
(A) 세입자
(B) 주택 건축업자
(C) 디자이너
(D) 부동산 중개인

남자의 직업은 This apartment is the largest of the three I've shown you so far에서 집을 보여주는 직업이라고 알 수 있다. 정답은 (D)가 맞다.

51 What does the woman say about the apartment?
(A) It is fully furnished.
(B) It is conveniently located.
(C) The rent is reasonable.

(D) The living room needs repairs.
여자는 아파트에 대해 뭐라고 말하는가?
(A) 가구가 완비되어 있다.
(B) 편리한 위치에 있다.
(C) 임대료가 적절하다.
(D) 거실이 수리가 필요하다.

여자의 대사 중 사무실과 매우 가깝다는 말은 편리한 위치에 있다는 의미로 이해될 수 있으므로 (B)가 정답이다.

52 What does the woman mean when she says, "That's more than I was hoping to spend"?
(A) The apartment is unnecessarily large.
(B) She has spent a lot of money on furniture.
(C) The rent is more expensive than she expected.
(D) She does not have time to think.
여자가, "제가 쓰려고 한 것보다 많네요"라고 말한 의미는 무엇인가?
(A) 아파트가 불필요하게 넓다.
(B) 여자는 가구에 돈을 많이 썼다.
(C) 임대료는 여자의 예상보다 비싸다.
(D) 여자는 생각할 시간이 없다.

해당 표현 전에 임대료에 대해 언급되었고 여자가 "제가 쓰려고 한 것보다 많네요"라고 말했으므로 임대료가 비싸다는 의미이다.

Questions 53-55 refer to the following conversation. 미M 미W

M Have you checked with the supplier about the auto parts we ordered? It has been a week since we ordered them.
W I just spoke with the supplier. It turns out that they sent the parts to the wrong address so the shipment was returned to them.
M Oh no. We can't finish the repairs on the cars without the parts. Did they say when the parts would arrive?
W By Thursday at the latest. They were very apologetic about the delay, so they're giving us a 10 percent discount.
M Well, that's not bad. I think I should call the customers to tell them their cars will be ready by the end of the week.

남 우리가 주문한 부품에 관해서 공급업체에 확인해 보셨나요? 주문한 지 일주일이 됐어요.
여 방금 업체와 통화를 했습니다. 알고 보니 다른 주소로 부품이 보내져서 그들에게 되돌아 갔다고 합니다.
남 큰일이네요. 그 부품이 없이는 이 차들의 수리를 마칠 수가 없어요. 언제 부품이 도착할거라고 하던가요?
여 늦어도 목요일까지는요. 그들은 매우 미안해하면서 10퍼센트 할인을 제공하겠다고 했습니다.
남 음, 나쁘지 않네요. 고객들에게 전화해서 그들의 차가 이번 주말까지는 준비될 거라고 알려야겠어요.

check with ~에게 묻다, 확인하다 It turns out that ~라고 밝혀지다 apologetic 미안해하는

53 Why was the shipment delayed?
(A) A payment was not made.
(B) The delivery address was wrong.
(C) The manufacturer was understaffed.
(D) Some products were not available.
배송은 왜 지연되었는가?
(A) 지불을 하지 않았다.
(B) 배송 주소가 틀렸다.
(C) 제조업체가 직원이 부족했다.
(D) 상품이 재고가 없었다.

배송의 지연에 대해서 여자가 they sent the parts to the wrong address(잘못된 주소로 배송을 했다)라고 언급했으므로 정답은 (B)가 된다.

54 What did the supplier provide?
(A) A complimentary ticket
(B) A similar product
(C) Special delivery
(D) A reduced price
공급업체는 무엇을 제공했는가?
(A) 무료 티켓
(B) 비슷한 상품
(C) 특별 배송
(D) 할인 가격

배송의 지연에 대해 업체가 미안해하며 10 percent discount를 해 준다고 했으므로 정답은 (D)가 맞다.

55 What will the man probably do next?
(A) Contact some customers
(B) Make some repairs
(C) Order some parts
(D) Use different parts
남자는 다음에 무엇을 할 것 같은가?
(A) 고객들에게 연락하기
(B) 수리하기
(C) 부품 주문하기
(D) 다른 부품 사용하기

남자가 마지막에 I should call the customers(고객에게 전화해서) 수리 일정에 대해 알리겠다고 했으므로 정답은 (A)가 된다.

Questions 56-58 refer to the following conversation. 영M 미W

M Hello, my name is Sam Parker. I'm calling about the guitar classes you advertised on the Internet. Can I get some details about the lessons?
W Hi, Sam. I give guitar lessons 3 evenings per week in my private music studio near the community park. There are 2 openings left at the moment – Tuesday and Thursday evening at 6.
M Well, Thursday works for me. Oh, do you know where I can rent a guitar and how much it might cost?
W Well, my friend Henry Woo runs a musical instrument shop close to my studio. He offers rentals as well. But I think the costs vary. Let me give you his phone number so you can ask him yourself.

남 여보세요, 저는 Sam Parker입니다. 인터넷에 광고를 내신 기타 수업과 관련해서 전화를 드립니다. 수업에 관하여 세부 정보를 얻을 수 있을까요?

여 안녕하세요, Sam. 지역 공원 근처에 있는 제 개인 음악 스튜디오에서 일주일에 세 번의 저녁 시간에 기타 수업을 합니다. 지금은 화요일과 목요일 저녁 6시에 두 타임이 비어 있습니다.

남 그렇다면, 매주 목요일이 좋겠네요. 아, 어디에서 기타를 대여할 수 있고 얼마나 비용이 들지 혹시 아시나요?

여 음, 제 스튜디오에 가까이에서 친구 Henry Woo가 악기 상점을 운영합니다. 그가 대여도 제공하고요. 그러나 비용은 천차만별일 거예요. 직접 물어보시도록 그의 전화번호를 드리도록 할게요.

private 개인적인, 개인의 opening 빈자리 work for (시간, 일정 등이) ~에게 맞다 rent 임대하다 musical instrument 악기 close to ~와 가까운 vary 서로 다르다

56 What is the man calling about?
(A) Moving into a new apartment
(B) Taking some lessons
(C) Opening a new business
(D) Buying a musical instrument

남자는 무엇에 관해 전화하는가?
(A) 새로운 아파트로 이사하는 것
(B) 수업을 듣는 것
(C) 새로 개업하는 것
(D) 악기를 사는 것

남자의 전화 목적은 도입부 I'm calling about the guitar classes에서 바로 (B)로 선택한다.

57 What information does the woman give the man?
(A) Directions to the store
(B) Rental fees
(C) A phone number
(D) Business hours

여자는 남자에게 어떤 정보를 제공하는가?
(A) 상점 가는 길 안내
(B) 임대료
(C) 전화번호
(D) 영업시간

여자가 남자에게 주는 정보를 찾는 문제로 Let me give you his phone number 부분이 정답이다. 전화번호를 주겠다고 했으므로 (C)가 정답이고 (D)의 경우 상점이나 회사의 영업시간을 말하는 것으로, 여자가 수업 스케줄을 말해준 것은 class schedule이지 business hours가 아니므로 정확하게 구별하여 암기해 두자. 예를 들어 기차 출발 시간표는 schedule 혹은 time table이라고 하지 business hours라고 하지 않는 것과 같은 원리이다.

58 What will the man probably do next?
(A) Call a shop
(B) Request a product
(C) Provide contact information
(D) Rent a room

남자는 다음에 무엇을 할 것 같은가?
(A) 상점에 전화하기
(B) 제품 요청하기
(C) 연락처 제공하기
(D) 방 임대하기

남자의 향후 행동은 대화의 후반부에 단서가 나온다. Let me give you his phone number so you can ask him yourself에서 남자가 전화를 할 것임을 알 수 있다. 단, 69번과 거의 동시에 정답이 등장했으므로 고난도 문제 유형에 속한다.

Questions 59-61 refer to the following conversation. (미W) (영M)

W Hey, I just read your article on the must-see attractions in Seattle. I really liked it and the photos of the beaches and food were excellent.

M Yeah, weren't they good? I actually worked on the article with a new photographer, who is really talented. Have you met Sean Walker?

W No, but I really want to work with him on my next assignment now. I'm interviewing the new director of the City Museum next week and I'm sure there will be some nice photo opportunities there. How can I get in touch with him?

M I could give you his phone number but I think you should speak to the editor about arranging a meeting.

여 이봐요, 방금 당신이 쓴 시애틀에서 꼭 가봐야 할 명소에 대한 기사를 읽었어요. 기사가 정말 좋았고 해변과 음식 사진들도 훌륭했어요.

남 네, 진짜 좋지 않나요? 실은 정말 실력 있는 새 사진 작가와 이 기사 작업을 했거든요. Sean Walker를 만나 본 적이 있으세요?

여 아니요, 그렇지만 제 다음 작업에 함께 일하고 싶네요. 다음 주에 City 박물관의 새 관장을 인터뷰 하거든요. 멋진 사진을 촬영할 기회가 좀 있을 거예요. 그에게 어떻게 연락을 취하죠?

남 제가 전화번호를 줄 수도 있지만 편집장님에게 미팅을 주선해 달라고 하는 게 좋겠어요.

must-see attraction 꼭 봐야 하는 명소 work on ~에 대한 작업을 하다 talented 실력 있는 photo opportunities 사진 촬영 get in touch with ~와 연락을 취하다 arrange a meeting 미팅을 주선하다

59 Who most likely is the man?
(A) A photographer
(B) A reporter
(C) A sales representative
(D) A tour guide

남자는 누구일 것 같은가?
(A) 사진 작가
(B) 기자
(C) 영업 사원
(D) 관광 가이드

남자의 직업은 여자가 I just read your article(당신의 기사를 읽었다)이라고 했을 때 이미 기사를 쓰는 기자임을 알 수 있다.

60 What does the man imply when he says, "Yeah, weren't they good"?
(A) He would like to visit the attractions with the woman.
(B) Many tourists have a good time in the city.

(C) He is satisfied with the work of the photographer.
(D) Many people like the photographs.

남자가 "네, 진짜 좋지 않나요"라고 말한 의도는 무엇인가?
(A) 그는 여자와 함께 명소들을 방문하고 싶다.
(B) 많은 관광객들이 도시에서 좋은 시간을 보낸다.
(C) 그는 사진 작가의 작품에 만족한다.
(D) 많은 사람들이 사진을 좋아한다.

해당 표현의 앞뒤 문맥이 가장 중요하다. 여자가 사진에 대해 excellent(훌륭하다)라고 했을 때 "네, 진짜 좋지 않나요"라고 되물었고 이어 새 사진 작가가 매우 실력이 좋았다고 했으므로 정답은 (C)가 맞다.

61 Why is the woman going to the City Museum?
(A) To take a tour
(B) To conduct an interview
(C) To participate in an event
(D) To view some artwork

여자는 왜 City Museum에 가는가?
(A) 투어를 하려고
(B) 인터뷰를 하려고
(C) 행사에 참석하려고
(D) 예술품을 보려고

여자가 I'm interviewing the new director of the City Museum이라고 말하면서 박물관 관장을 인터뷰할 것이라고 했으므로 정답은 (B)이다.

Questions 62-64 refer to the following conversation with three speakers. 미W 영M 미M

W Excuse me. Are you the store manager?
M1 Yes, I am. What can I do for you?
W I'm afraid I spilled coffee beans all over the floor of aisle 3. I just picked the package off the shelf and the bottom of it just broke open.
M1 I can't believe it broke again. This is the third time that's happened this week. There must be some manufacturing problem with the packaging. Hey Adam, have you talked to the supplier about the defective coffee bags? The same packaging just broke again.
M2 Oh, I'm sorry Mr. Jackson. I haven't talked to the supplier yet. Should I do that right now?
M1 No, I'll talk to them myself. Could you go clean aisle 3 where the spill is, Adam?

여 실례합니다. 당신이 상점 매니저인가요?
남1 네, 맞습니다. 무엇을 도와 드릴까요?
여 죄송하지만 제가 3번 통로 바닥에 커피 원두를 다 쏟았어요. 선반에서 커피 봉지를 들었는데 밑 부분이 그냥 터져 버렸어요.
남1 또 터졌다니 믿을 수가 없네요. 이번 주에 벌써 세 번째 그런 일이 있었어요. 포장에 뭔가 제조상의 문제가 있는 게 틀림없어요. 이봐요 Adam, 업체에게 결함 있는 커피 포장에 대해서 얘기했나요? 같은 포장이 또 터졌잖아요.
남2 오, 죄송합니다 Jackson 씨. 아직 업체와 이야기를 못 했어요. 지금 당장 할까요?
남1 아니에요, 제가 직접 얘기하겠습니다. 3번 통로에 쏟아진 것을 좀 치워 주실래요, Adam?

spill 쏟다 package (상품의) 포장 manufacturing problem 제조상의 문제 defective 결함 있는

62 What problem does the woman mention?
(A) A manager is unavailable.
(B) An item is not fresh.
(C) A shopping cart is broken.
(D) A product is spilled on the floor.

여자는 어떤 문제점을 언급하는가?
(A) 매니저가 부재중이다.
(B) 상품이 신선하지 않다.
(C) 쇼핑 카트가 고장 났다.
(D) 상품이 바닥에 쏟아졌다.

여자가 I'm afraid I spilled coffee beans all over the floor라고 했으므로 정답은 (D)가 된다. coffee beans는 a product로 패러프레이징되었다.

63 Why does the store manager say, "I can't believe it broke again"?
(A) The store sign has been damaged.
(B) The same problem has occurred again.
(C) Some items were recalled.
(D) An employee was late for work again.

상점 매니저는 왜 "또 터졌다니 믿을 수가 없네요"라고 말하는가?
(A) 상점 간판이 손상되었다.
(B) 같은 문제가 또 발생했다.
(C) 일부 상품이 수거되었다.
(D) 직원이 또 늦게 출근했다.

3인 대화에서는 이름, 직위 등을 잘 파악하는 게 중요하고, 해당 표현의 앞뒤 문맥을 연결할 수 있어야 하는 질문 유형이다. 여자가 상품의 포장이 터지면서 물건을 쏟았다고 했고 이에 I can't believe it broke again이라고 하면서 이번 주에 세 번째 그런 일이 있었다고 했으므로 정답은 (B)가 맞다.

64 What will Adam probably do next?
(A) Call a supplier
(B) Cancel an order
(C) Examine a package
(D) Clean a spill

Adam은 다음에 무엇을 할 것 같은가?
(A) 공급업체에 전화하기
(B) 주문 취소하기
(C) 포장 살펴보기
(D) 쏟아진 것 치우기

3인 대화에서는 이름, 직위 등을 잘 파악하는 게 중요하다. 상점 매니저가 Could you go clean aisle 3 where the spill is, Adam?이라고 했으므로 Adam은 쏟은 물건을 치울 것이다.

Questions 65-67 refer to the following conversation and list.
미M 영W

M Welcome to Planet Fitness Club. Can I help you?
W Hi. I'd like to get some information about the exercise classes you offer.
M Absolutely. We offer private lessons and group exercise classes. Which would you prefer?
W My work schedule is pretty erratic and I lack the motivation to work out on my own. So I think private sessions would work better for me.
M Well, sounds like it is very important for you to choose the right trainer. Do you happen to have a particular instructor in mind?
W Actually yes. A close friend of mine strongly recommended a trainer who works here. But the problem is that I can't remember her name.
M But do you remember what class she teaches? We have two female instructors.
W Oh yes, I think she teaches some kind of dance class.

Planet Fitness Club	
EX Class	Trainer
Cycling	Morgan
Muscle Conditioning	Kyle
Zumba Dance	Amanda
Cardio Kick	Trevor

남 Planet Fitness Club에 오신 걸 환영합니다. 무엇을 도와 드릴까요?
여 안녕하세요. 여기서 제공하는 운동 수업에 대해 정보를 얻고 싶습니다.
남 물론이죠. 저희는 개인 레슨과 그룹 운동 수업을 제공합니다. 어떤 것을 선호하시죠?
여 제 업무 스케줄이 불규칙한 편이고 저 혼자는 운동에 동기 부여가 약한 편이에요. 그래서 제 생각에는 개인 레슨이 더 잘 맞을 것 같아요.
남 음, 잘 맞는 트레이너를 선택하는 것이 중요할 것 같네요. 혹시 생각하고 계신 특정 트레이너가 있으세요?
여 실은 그렇습니다. 저와 친한 친구 한 명이 여기서 일하는 트레이너 한 분을 강력 추천했어요. 그런데 문제는 그녀의 이름이 기억이 안 나네요.
남 그렇지만 그녀가 가르치는 수업을 기억하시나요? 여자 강사는 두 명이 있어요.
여 아, 네. 무슨 댄스 수업을 가르친다고 했던 것 같아요.

Planet Fitness Club	
운동 수업	강사
사이클링	Morgan
근육 운동	Kyle
줌바 댄스	Amanda
유산소 킥	Trevor

erratic 불규칙한, 일정치 않은 motivation 동기 on one's own 스스로 have ~ in mind ~를 염두에 두다 female 여성의

65 Why is the woman at the fitness club?
(A) To cancel a membership
(B) To provide some feedback
(C) To learn about exercise classes
(D) To participate in a competition

여자는 왜 피트니스 클럽에 있는가?
(A) 멤버십을 취소하려고
(B) 피드백을 제공하려고
(C) 운동 수업에 대해 알려고
(D) 경기에 참여하려고

대화가 피트니스 클럽에서 이루어지고 있음을 미리 염두에 두고 듣는 것이 중요하다. 여자가 I'd like to get some information about the exercise classes you offer라고 말했을 때 정답은 (C)로 선택할 수 있다. get some information과 learn about은 같은 의미를 갖는다.

66 Why does the woman prefer private lessons?
(A) She is highly motivated to work out regularly.
(B) There is no wait for exercise machines.
(C) Her work schedule is quite irregular.
(D) She has worked at the gym before.

여자는 왜 개인 레슨을 선호하는가?
(A) 규칙적으로 운동하려는 동기 부여가 잘 되어 있다.
(B) 운동 기기를 기다리지 않아도 된다.
(C) 그녀의 업무 스케줄이 일정하지 않다.
(D) 여자는 전에 체육관에서 일해본 적이 있다.

질문을 통해 여자는 개인 레슨을 선호한다는 것을 미리 파악해 두자. My work schedule is pretty erratic and I lack the motivation to work out on my own이라고 업무 스케줄이 불규칙한 것과 동기가 부족한 것 두 개가 언급되었으므로 정답은 (C)가 된다. (A)는 반대되는 내용이지만 같은 단어가 들리기 때문에 함정에 빠지기 쉽다.

67 Look at the graphic. Which trainer does the woman want to learn from?
(A) Morgan
(B) Kyle
(C) Amanda
(D) Trevor

시각 정보를 보시오. 여자는 어떤 트레이너로부터 배우길 원하는가?
(A) Morgan
(B) Kyle
(C) Amanda
(D) Trevor

친구로부터 추천 받은 강사의 이름이 기억이 안 나지만 I think she teaches some kind of dance class(무슨 댄스 수업을 가르치는 것 같다)가 정답의 근거이다. Zumba Dance 수업을 하는 Amanda가 정답이 된다.

Questions 68-70 refer to the following conversation and advertisement. (미W) (영M)

W Hi, this bracelet is absolutely gorgeous. I saw an advertisement in today's newspaper that said every item in your showroom is fifty percent off.

M Oh, I'm afraid that sale begins on Saturday. You may want to come back in two days to get a bracelet at a discounted price.

W Hmm... That won't work for me. I've been in Rome for a medical conference for the last few days and I fly back to the United States tomorrow afternoon. But I still want to get a nice bracelet to wear for a banquet tonight. Could you show me this one here?

M Oh, that's a great choice! The ruby mounted in it is genuine so it will last a life time.

W It is just beautiful. I'll take it.

Red Tag SALE SAVE 50% OFF EVERYTHING IN THE SHOWROOM!		
	Regular Price	Sale Price
Diamond Bracelet	$500	$250
Genuine Ruby Bracelet	$300	$150

여 안녕하세요. 이 팔찌는 정말 아름답네요. 오늘 신문에서 이 진열장에 있는 전 품목이 50퍼센트 할인된다는 광고를 봤어요.

남 아, 안타깝게도 그 세일은 토요일에 시작됩니다. 팔찌를 할인가에 구매하시려면 이틀 후에 다시 오시는 게 좋겠네요.

여 흠… 그럴 수가 없어요. 저는 지난 며칠 동안 의학 컨퍼런스 때문에 로마에 와 있었는데 내일 오후에 다시 미국으로 돌아갑니다. 그렇지만 여전히 오늘 저녁 연회 때 할 예쁜 팔찌를 사고 싶네요. 여기 이 제품을 보여 주시겠어요?

남 아, 훌륭한 선택이세요. 거기 박혀 있는 루비는 진품이라 평생 갈 겁니다.

여 정말 아름답네요. 이걸로 주세요.

Red Tag SALE 진열장의 전 품목 50퍼센트 할인!		
	정가	할인가
다이아몬드 팔찌	500달러	250달러
진품 루비 팔찌	300달러	150달러

absolutely 완전히 gorgeous 예쁜, 아름다운 showroom 전시장, 진열 공간 bracelet 팔찌 banquet 연회 mount (보석 등을) 박다 genuine 진품, 진짜

68 What was advertised in the newspaper?
(A) A job opening
(B) A fashion show
(C) A musical performance
(D) A half-off sale

신문에 무엇이 광고 되었는가?
(A) 일자리 공석
(B) 패션쇼
(C) 음악 공연
(D) 반액 세일

질문의 키워드인 advertise, newspaper를 놓치지 말자. 신문 광고에서 every item in your showroom is fifty percent off(전시장의 모든 물건이 50퍼센트 할인)라고 했으므로 정답은 (D)가 된다.

69 What is the purpose of the woman's visit to Rome?
(A) To attend a conference
(B) To purchase some jewelry
(C) To open a business
(D) To write an article

여자가 로마에 방문한 목적은 무엇인가?
(A) 컨퍼런스에 참석하려고
(B) 보석을 구입하려고
(C) 개업하려고
(D) 기사를 쓰려고

여자는 로마에 왔다는 것을 미리 파악하고 듣는다. I've been in Rome for a medical conference for the last few days에서 방문 목적은 컨퍼런스 참석임을 알 수 있다.

70 Look at the graphic. How much will the woman pay for a bracelet?
(A) $150
(B) $250
(C) $300
(D) $500

시각 정보를 보시오. 여자는 팔찌에 얼마를 낼 것인가?
(A) 150달러
(B) 250달러
(C) 300달러
(D) 500달러

시각 정보에는 정가와 할인가가 있음을 유의하자. half-off sale은 토요일에 시작이고 여자는 그 전에 미국으로 돌아가야 하는 상황이다. 여자가 여전히 연회 때 착용할 팔찌를 사고 싶다고 했고 최종적으로 진짜 루비가 박힌 팔찌(The ruby mounted in it is genuine)를 골랐으므로 최종 가격은 루비 팔찌의 정가이다. 정답은 (C)가 된다.

PART 4

Questions 71-73 refer to the following talk. (미W)

Hi David, this is Erica Deacon. You called me earlier to see if I could teach a ballroom dancing class at the community center on Fridays. I'd be happy to, but I'm only available after 4 p.m. since I have other classes to teach in the morning. And I was wondering if there's a dance studio available at the community center for us to use. I was hoping for a room equipped with a full length mirror and stereo system. Please call me back at 555-7002. Thank you.

안녕하세요, David. Erica Deacon입니다. 제가 금요일마다 커뮤니티 센터에서 사교 댄스 수업을 가르칠 수 있는지 아까 전화하셨죠. 기꺼이 하고 싶은데요, 제가 아침에는 다른 수업들이 있어서 오후 4시 이후에만 시간이 됩니다. 그리고 커뮤니티 센터에 저희가 쓸 수 있는 댄스 스튜디오가 있는지 궁금합니다. 벽면 전체가 거울로 되어 있고 스테레오 시스템이 갖춰져 있는 방을 썼으면 합니다. 555-7002로 회신 전화 부탁해요. 감사합니다.

ballroom dancing class 사교 댄스 수업　equipped with ~이 갖추어진　full length mirror 벽면 거울

71 Who most likely is the speaker?
(A) An event organizer
(B) A university student
(C) A hotel clerk
(D) A dance teacher

화자는 누구일 것 같은가?
(A) 행사 기획자
(B) 대학생
(C) 호텔 직원
(D) 댄스 강사

화자가 도입부에 자신이 하는 일에 대한 언급을 한 부분은 You called me earlier to see if I could teach a ballroom dancing class에서 찾을 수 있다. 상대방이 사교 댄스 수업을 담당해 달라는 요청을 했으므로 화자는 댄스 강사이다.

72 What does the speaker agree to do?
(A) To make a donation
(B) To teach a class
(C) To lead a workshop
(D) To host an exhibit

화자는 무엇을 하기로 동의하는가?
(A) 기부를 하기로
(B) 수업을 가르치기로
(C) 워크숍을 진행하기로
(D) 전시회를 열기로

동의하는 것은 보통 상대방이 제안/요청을 한 경우에 성립한다. 화자가 댄스 수업을 가르쳐 달라는 요청을 이미 받았고 이에 대한 답으로 I'd be happy to(기꺼이 그렇게 하겠다)라고 했으므로 정답은 (B)가 된다.

73 What does the speaker request?
(A) Directions to a center
(B) Use of a special room
(C) A list of attendees
(D) Additional funding

화자는 무엇을 요청하는가?
(A) 센터까지 가는 길 안내
(B) 특별실의 사용
(C) 참석자 명단
(D) 추가 기금

화자는 dance studio가 있는지 물으면서 I was hoping for a room equipped with a full length mirror and stereo system(전면 거울과 스테레오 시스템이 갖춰진 룸이었으면 좋겠다)이라고 했으므로 a special room을 사용할 것을 요청하고 있다. 정답은 (B)이다.

Questions 74-76 refer to the following announcement. (영M)

Good afternoon, shoppers! Are you a member of Baldwin Farmers Market? Why not sign up today? If you become a member of Baldwin Farmers Market today, you will receive a basket of fresh farm produce as a gift. For our members only, we're offering discount coupons every month which are not available to the general public. To become part of the Baldwin Farmers family, just stop by the customer service desk by the main entrance and fill out a form.

안녕하세요, 쇼핑객 여러분! 여러분은 Baldwin Farmers Market의 회원이신가요? 오늘 신청을 하시는 게 어떠세요? 오늘 Baldwin Farmers Market의 회원이 되시면, 선물로 신선한 농장 농산물 한 바구니를 받을 수 있습니다. 우리 회원들에게만 일반 고객은 사용할 수 없는 할인 쿠폰을 매달 제공합니다. Baldwin Farmers 가족이 되기 위해서는 정문 옆의 고객 서비스 데스크에 가셔서 양식을 작성해 주시면 됩니다.

sign up (for) 신청하다　farm produce 농장 농산물　general public 일반 대중　stop by ~에 들르다

74 What are the listeners encouraged to do?
(A) Sign up for a membership
(B) Take a tour of the farm
(C) Provide excellent service
(D) Order groceries online

청자들은 무엇을 하라는 권고를 받는가?
(A) 멤버십에 가입하기
(B) 농장 투어 하기
(C) 훌륭한 서비스 제공하기
(D) 온라인으로 식료품 주문하기

정답의 단서는 도입부에 Are you a member of Baldwin Farmers Market? Why not sign up today? 부분에서 벌써 찾을 수 있다. 회원인지 물으면서 오늘 신청하면 어떻겠냐고 했으므로 정답은 (A)가 된다.

75 What can listeners receive today?
(A) A shopping bag
(B) Meal vouchers
(C) Farm produce
(D) A membership card

청자들은 오늘 무엇을 받을 수 있는가?
(A) 쇼핑백
(B) 식사 쿠폰
(C) 농장 농산물
(D) 회원 카드

질문의 키워드는 today이므로 오늘의 혜택에 주목하자. 오늘 회원 가입을 하면 선물로 농장 농산물을 준다고 했으므로 정답은 (C)가 된다.

76 Why should listeners go to the service desk?
(A) To request a catalog
(B) To complete a form
(C) To pay for goods
(D) To return items

청자들은 왜 서비스 데스크로 갈 것인가?
(A) 카탈로그를 요청하려고
(B) 양식을 작성하려고
(C) 상품값을 지불하려고
(D) 상품을 반품하려고

질문의 키워드는 service desk이므로 회원이 되려면 서비스 데스크에 가서 양식을 채우면 된다(stop by the customer service desk by the main entrance and fill out a form)라고 언급된 것으로부터 정답을 (B)로 선택할 수 있다.

Questions 77-79 refer to the following radio report. (영W)

Before we end the final day of the marketing conference, I'd like to make an announcement about the location of tonight's banquet. In your schedule, it is listed as Clare Port Place. However, the banquet has been moved to Terrace Banquet Center located at 1800 Peeler Road. For those of you who are not familiar with the city, we have printed directions to the new venue which are available at the reception desk. Please pick up a copy on your way out. I'll see you all at the banquet tonight.

마케팅 컨퍼런스의 마지막 날을 끝내기에 앞서, 오늘 밤 연회 장소에 대해 공지가 있습니다. 스케줄에 보시면 Clare Port Place라고 쓰여 있는데요. 그러나 장소가 Peeler Road 1800번지에 있는 Terrace Banquet Center로 변경되었습니다. 이 도시가 익숙하지 않은 분들을 위해서 안내 데스크에 새 장소에 대한 약도를 프린트해 놓았습니다. 나가는 길에 한 부씩 가져가세요. 여러분 모두 오늘 밤 연회에서 뵙겠습니다.

banquet 연회, 만찬 venue 장소

77 Where most likely is the announcement being made?
(A) At a farewell party
(B) At a conference
(C) At a job fair
(D) At a sales meeting

공지되는 장소는 어디인가?
(A) 송별 파티
(B) 컨퍼런스
(C) 취업 박람회
(D) 영업 미팅

Before we end the final day of the marketing conference를 통해 마케팅 컨퍼런스에서 공지가 나오고 있음을 알 수 있다. 정답은 (B)이다.

78 According to the speaker, what has changed?
(A) The location of a party
(B) The number of participants
(C) The time of an event
(D) The guest lecturer

화자에 따르면, 무엇이 변경되었는가?
(A) 파티의 장소
(B) 참석자의 인원
(C) 행사의 시간
(D) 초청 연사

질문을 통해 바뀐 것이 있다는 것을 미리 염두에 두고 듣자. 연회의 장소가 Clare Port Place에서 Terrace Banquet Center로 변경되었다고 했으므로 장소가 바뀐 것이다.

79 What will be available to listeners at the reception desk?
(A) Light snacks and beverages
(B) A city map
(C) Directions to a banquet center
(D) A revised schedule

안내 데스크에서 청자들이 이용할 수 있는 것은 무엇인가?
(A) 가벼운 스낵과 음료
(B) 도시 지도
(C) 연회 센터까지 가는 길 안내
(D) 수정된 스케줄

질문의 키워드인 reception desk에 집중하여 정보를 찾자. 연회의 장소가 바뀌었다는 공지를 한 후 we have printed directions to the new venue available at the reception desk(새로운 장소로 가는 길 안내를 인쇄해 안내 데스크에 두었다)라고 했으므로 정답은 (C)가 된다.

Questions 80-82 refer to the following excerpt from a meeting. (미M)

I'd like to make a quick announcement about the company's new payroll system. This new system automatically calculates each employee's paycheck based on the number of hours they work. Therefore, beginning tomorrow, you will need to enter the number of hours you work each day into the computer system. Be sure to use the department code that I've sent you in the e-mail. Erica Yamada in accounting has put together instructions on how to use the system. So if you have difficulty entering your work hours, ask her for a copy of the instructions.

회사의 급여 정산 시스템에 대해서 짧게 공지를 하도록 하겠습니다. 이 새 시스템은 각 직원의 급여를 그들이 일한 시간에 근거하여 자동으로 계산합니다. 그러므로, 내일부터 여러분께서는 매일 컴퓨터 시스템에 근무한 시간을 입력해 주셔야 합니다. 반드시 제가 이메일로 보내 드린 부서 코드를 사용해 주세요. 회계부서의 Erica Yamada가 이 시스템을 어떻게 사용하는지 설명서를 만들어 놓았습니다. 그러니 만약 근무 시간을 입력하는 데 어려움이 있으면 그녀에게 설명서를 한 부 요청하도록 하세요.

payroll system 급여 정산 시스템 automatically 자동적으로 calculate 계산하다 paycheck 월급 put together 구성하여 만들다 have difficulty -ing ~하는 데 어려움을 겪다

80 What is the purpose of the talk?
(A) To explain the new payroll system
(B) To introduce a new employee
(C) To describe a change in the work schedule
(D) To welcome a company executive

담화의 목적은 무엇인가?
(A) 새 급여 정산 시스템에 대해 설명하려고
(B) 신입 사원을 소개하려고
(C) 근무 스케줄상의 변경에 대해 설명하려고
(D) 회사 중역을 환영하려고

목적은 보통 도입부에 언급이 된다. 화자가 the company's new payroll system에 대해 공지가 있다고 했으므로 정답은 (A)가 된다.

81 What are employees asked to do starting tomorrow?
(A) Work overtime to meet a deadline
(B) Wear a security badge at all times
(C) Enter some data into the computer
(D) Attend a training session

직원들은 내일부터 무엇을 하라는 요청을 받는가?
(A) 마감을 맞추기 위해 야근하기
(B) 항상 보안 배지 착용하기
(C) 컴퓨터에 데이터 입력하기
(D) 교육 세션에 참석하기

질문의 키워드는 starting tomorrow이다. 내일부터 근무 시간(the number of hours you work)을 컴퓨터 시스템에 입력하라고 했으므로 정답은 (C)가 된다.

82 Why would an employee contact Erica Yamada?
(A) To schedule some repair work
(B) To ask for a department code
(C) To request some instructions
(D) To explain an accounting error

직원이 Erica Yamada에게 연락을 하는 이유는 무엇일까?
(A) 수리 일정을 잡으려고
(B) 부서 코드를 요청하려고
(C) 설명서를 요청하려고
(D) 회계 실수에 대해 설명하려고

질문의 키워드인 Erica Yamada에 집중하여 듣자. Erica Yamada in accounting has put together instructions(회계부서의 Erica Yamada가 설명서를 작성해 놓았다)라고 언급을 한 후 시스템 사용에 어려움이 있으면 ask her for a copy of the instructions(그녀에게 설명서 한 부를 요청하라)라고 했으므로 정답은 (C)가 맞다.

Questions 83-85 refer to the following introduction. (영W)

It is my honor to present this year's award for excellence in teaching to Professor David King. When Professor King joined the faculty of the Department of Journalism two years ago, our journalism program was struggling financially. **But he turned the program around.** In just two years, he got more funding so the department could purchase professional equipment and provide students with a more hands-on experience. He has been a great inspiration to the students as well. They often comment on how he makes learning fun and they feel lucky to have him as a professor. Now Professor King, please come forward to receive your award.

올해의 훌륭한 교육상을 David King 교수님에게 수여하게 되어 매우 영광입니다. 2년 전 King 교수님이 처음 언론학과의 교수진에 합류했을 때, 우리 학과의 프로그램은 재정적으로 어려움을 겪었습니다. **그러나 그가 이 프로그램을 뒤집었죠.** 단 2년 안에, 그는 더 많은 기금을 받아서 우리 학과가 전문적인 장비를 구입하고 학생들에게 보다 직접적인 경험을 제공할 수 있도록 하였습니다. 그는 학생들에게도 큰 영감이 되어왔습니다. 학생들은 종종 그가 배움을 얼마나 재미있게 만들어 주는지 얘기하고 그를 교수님으로 모시게 되어 행운이라고 생각합니다. 이제 King 교수님, 상을 받기 위해 앞으로 나와 주세요.

excellence in teaching 훌륭한 교육 faculty 교수진 department 학과 hands-on 직접 해볼 수 있는 inspiration 영감, 영감을 주는 사람

83 Where does Mr. King work?
(A) At a research lab
(B) At a university
(C) At a hospital
(D) At a government office

King 씨는 어디에서 일할 것 같은가?
(A) 연구실
(B) 대학
(C) 병원
(D) 공공 기관

질문의 키워드인 King에 집중하자. 첫 번째 단서는 훌륭한 교육상(excellence in teaching)을 받는 사람이고 David King 교수님이라고 불리는 사람이므로 정답은 (B)이다.

84 What does the speaker mean when she says, "But he turned the program around"?
(A) Mr. King worked hard to revive the program.
(B) The program was not well organized.
(C) Mr. King used to work at an investment firm.
(D) The school offers a variety of programs.

화자가 "그러나 그가 이 프로그램을 뒤집었죠"라고 말한 의미는 무엇인가?
(A) King 씨는 프로그램을 되살리기 위해 열심히 노력했다.
(B) 프로그램은 체계적으로 짜여 있지 않았다.
(C) King 씨는 예전에 투자 회사에서 일했다.
(D) 학교는 다양한 프로그램을 제공한다.

의도 파악 문제를 잘 풀려면 해당 표현 앞뒤의 문맥을 이해해야 한다. 처음 교수진에 들어왔을 때는 프로그램이 재정적으로 어려움을 겪고 있었다(struggling financially)고 했고 "But he turned the program around"라며 현재는 기금을 더 받아 전문 장비도 구입하고 학생들에게 체험 기회도 제공할 수 있었다고 했으므로 앞뒤 문맥상 (A)가 맞다.

85 What will probably happen next?
(A) Students will ask questions.
(B) Refreshments will be served.
(C) An award will be presented.
(D) Music will be played.

다음에 무슨 일이 있을 것인가?
(A) 학생들이 질문을 할 것이다.
(B) 다과가 제공될 것이다.
(C) 상이 수여될 것이다.
(D) 음악이 연주될 것이다.

후반부에 Now Professor King, please come forward to receive your award에서 King 교수는 단상 앞으로 나와 상을 받게 될 것이다.

Questions 86-88 refer to the following introduction to an interview. 미W

You're listening to Radio 707. I'm your host Julia Paterson. Tonight, we'll be joined by William Tate, the director of the recent blockbuster, *The Lost City*. This adventure story was shot in Chiclayo, Peru. Mr. Tate wrote the film script himself and stayed in Chiclayo for 5 months, searching for the perfect shooting locations. Through his mesmerizing cinematography, you'll be able to experience the stunning archeological sites and museums of Peru while watching the movie. On today's show, you'll have the opportunity to talk to Mr. Tate, so please call in with any questions or comments.

여러분은 Radio 707를 청취하고 있습니다. 진행자 Julia Paterson입니다. 오늘 밤, 우리는 〈The Lost City〉라는 최신 블록버스터 영화의 감독 William Tate를 모십니다. 이 어드벤처 스토리는 페루의 Chiclayo에서 촬영되었습니다. William은 영화 각본을 직접 쓰고 완벽한 촬영 장소를 찾기 위해 5개월 동안 Chiclayo에서 머물렀습니다. 그의 넋을 잃게 만드는 촬영 기법을 통해, 여러분은 영화를 보고 있는 동안 페루의 근사한 고대 유적지와 박물관을 경험할 수 있을 것입니다. 오늘 프로그램에서 여러분은 Tate 씨와 대화할 수 있는 기회가 있으니, 질문과 의견이 있으시면 전화 주십시오.

host 사회자 blockbuster 블록버스터 영화 be shot (영화 등이) 촬영되다 film script 영화 각본 shooting location 촬영 장소 mesmerizing 넋을 잃게 하는 cinematography 영화 촬영 기법 stunning 눈부신, 놀라운 archeological site 고대 유적지 call in (방송국 등으로 참여를 위해) 전화하다

86 Who is William Tate?
(A) A film director
(B) An actor
(C) An archeologist
(D) A movie-goer

William Tate는 누구인가?
(A) 영화 감독
(B) 배우
(C) 고고학자
(D) 영화 팬

파트 4의 빈출 세부 사항 질문으로, 직업은 이름과 함께 소개되기 때문에 해당 이름이 언급되는 부분에서 순발력 있게 정답을 처리하자. William Tate, the director of the recent blockbuster를 듣고 바로 영화 감독으로 정답을 골라낸다.

87 According to the speaker, what did William do in Peru?
(A) He visited relatives.
(B) He selected shooting places.
(C) He attended a history class.
(D) He learned a foreign language.

화자에 따르면, William은 페루에서 무엇을 했는가?
(A) 친척을 방문했다.
(B) 촬영 장소를 선정했다.
(C) 역사 수업을 들었다.
(D) 외국어를 배웠다.

세부 사항을 묻는 질문으로 in Peru가 키워드이다. William이 Chiclayo라는 페루의 한 도시에 5개월간 체류했다고 언급하면서 완벽한 촬영지를 찾았다(searching for the perfect shooting locations)고 했으므로 정답은 (B)이다.

88 What are listeners invited to do?
(A) Watch a movie
(B) Attend a party
(C) Ask questions
(D) Offer fashion advice

청자들은 무엇을 하도록 권유 받는가?
(A) 영화 보기
(B) 파티에 참석하기
(C) 질문하기
(D) 패션 조언하기

화자가 청자들에게 권유하는 내용을 찾는 질문으로 정답의 근거는 so please call in with questions and comments에서 찾을 수 있다. 질문과 코멘트를 가지고 방송국으로 전화 달라고 했으므로 정답은 (C)가 된다.

Questions 89-91 refer to the following talk. 미M

I'd like to remind all of you in sales that today is the final day to turn in vacation requests using paper forms. If you are currently working on a vacation request form, you must submit the completed form to your manager by the end of the day. Changes will be in effect starting tomorrow. As of tomorrow, paper forms will no longer be processed. So you will have to submit all vacation request forms using the new online system. If you haven't attended any training sessions on how to use the new system yet, please sign up for one. They will be held over the next two weeks. You can contact Sylvia at extension 19 for more information about the sessions.

영업부 직원 모두에게 오늘이 종이 양식을 이용해서 휴가 요청서를 제출할 수 있는 마지막 날이라는 것을 상기시켜 드립니다. 현재 휴가 요청서를 쓰고 있다면, 오늘까지는 매니저에게 완성된 양식을 제출해야만 합니다. 내일부터 변경 사항이 적용될 것입니다. 내일 부로, 종이 양식은 더 이상 처리되지 않을 것입니다. 여러분은 새 온라인 시스템을 이용하여 모든 휴가 요청서를 제출해야만 할 것입니다. 이 새 시스템의 사용 방법에 대한 교육에 아직 참석을 못했다면 지금 신청해 주세요. 교육은 다음 2주일에 걸쳐 열릴 것입니다. 교육에 관한 정보는 Sylvia에게 내선번호 19번으로 전화해 주세요.

turn in 제출하다 vacation request 휴가 신청서 in effect 효과를 갖는

89 What is the purpose of the talk?
(A) To explain a reimbursement system
(B) To close a company event
(C) To assign a new task
(D) To remind employees of a change

담화의 목적은 무엇인가?
(A) 환급 시스템에 대해 설명하려고
(B) 회사 행사를 끝내려고
(C) 새로운 업무를 배정하려고
(D) 직원들에게 변경에 대해 상기시키려고

담화의 목적은 보통 도입부에 언급된다. 오늘이 휴가 신청서를 종이 양식으로 제출할 수 있는 마지막 날임을 상기시켜 준다고 했으므로 정답은 (D)이다.

90 What does the speaker mean when he says, "Changes will be in effect starting tomorrow"?
(A) The new measurements will be more effective.
(B) Employees cannot use paper forms any more.
(C) A deadline must be met by tomorrow.
(D) Employees can request extra days off.

화자가 "내일부터 변경 사항이 적용될 것입니다"라고 말한 의미는 무엇인가?
(A) 새로운 조치들이 더 효율적일 것이다.
(B) 직원들은 종이 양식을 더는 사용할 수 없다.
(C) 내일까지 마감이 지켜져야 한다.
(D) 직원들은 추가 휴가를 신청할 수 있다.

해당 표현의 앞뒤 문맥에서 의미를 파악하자. 오늘이 휴가 신청서를 종이 양식으로 제출할 수 있는 마지막 날임을 언급하고 Changes will be in effect starting tomorrow라고 했으며 내일부터는 온라인으로 제출을 해야 한다고 했으므로 정답은 (B)이다.

91 Why should employees contact Sylvia?
(A) To inquire about training
(B) To reschedule a meeting
(C) To request office supplies
(D) To hand in a report

직원들은 왜 Sylvia에게 연락을 할 것인가?
(A) 교육에 대해 문의하려고
(B) 미팅 일정을 다시 잡으려고
(C) 사무 용품을 요청하려고
(D) 보고서를 제출하려고

키워드는 Sylvia이다. 교육이 있을 것임을 언급한 후 You can contact Sylvia at extension 19 for more information about the sessions(교육에 대한 정보는 Sylvia에게 문의)라고 했으므로 정답은 (A)이다.

Questions 92-94 refer to the following talk. 영W

I'd like to begin by congratulating all our coaches and staff on a great rugby season. This year, two teams in our league, the Men's and Women's Ravens, won their regional championships. We really appreciate all the hard work you put into it. Now that the season has ended, we should start preparing for next season. It's never too early to look for sponsors, because we cover our expenses, such as entry fees and field maintenance, mostly from their generous financial support. It's a win-win situation, because they can increase their brand exposure by advertising in our league newsletters and on signs at the fields. Katie, the marketing manager, will form a team to start contacting local entrepreneurs about becoming sponsors.

먼저 모든 코치와 직원들에게 훌륭한 럭비 시즌을 보낸 것에 대해 축하하고 싶습니다. 올해에, 우리 리그에 있는 두 팀, the Men's와 Women's Ravens가 지역 챔피언 전에서 우승을 하였습니다. 여러분이 열심히 일해주신 것에 대해 진심으로 감사합니다. 이제 시즌이 끝났으니, 우리는 다음 시즌에 대한 준비를 시작해야 합니다. 출전비와 경기장 보수 등의 비용을 대부분 후원자의 재정 지원에서 충당하기 때문에 후원자를 찾는 것은 빠를수록 좋습니다. 그들은 우리 리그의 소식지와 경기장 표지판에 광고하는 것을 통해 브랜드 노출을 늘리기 때문에, 이것은 서로에게 득이 되는 상황입니다. 마케팅 부장인 Katie가 팀을 조직하여 지역 사업가들에게 후원자가 되는 것에 관해서 연락을 하기 시작할 것입니다.

win 우승하다 regional championship 지역 챔피언전 sponsor 후원자 cover (비용을) 충당하다 field maintenance 경기장 보수 win-win 서로에게 득이 되는 brand exposure 브랜드 노출 entrepreneur 기업가

92 Who is the speaker addressing?
(A) News reporters
(B) Sports coaches and league staff
(C) Business owners
(D) Sporting goods store employees

화자는 누구에게 이야기하는가?
(A) 뉴스 기자
(B) 스포츠 코치와 리그 직원
(C) 사업체 소유주
(D) 스포츠 용품 상점 직원

청자가 누구인지 유추하는 질문으로 도입부 I'd like to begin by congratulating all our coaches and staff on a great rugby season에서 듣는 사람들은 coaches와 staff임을 알 수 있다.

93 What does the speaker want to do?
(A) Solicit sponsors
(B) Write an article
(C) Revise an advertisement
(D) Donate money

화자는 무엇을 하기를 원하는가?
(A) 후원자 구하기
(B) 기사 쓰기

(C) 광고 수정하기
(D) 돈 기부하기

화자가 원하는 일은 It's never too early to look for sponsors에서 스폰서를 찾는 것임을 알 수 있다. 지문의 look for sponsors는 보기에서 solicit sponsors로 바꿔 표현되었다. 정답은 (A)이다.

94 What can businesses gain from their sponsorship?
(A) They can reduce their operating costs.
(B) They can advertise their brands.
(C) They can be invited to a local event.
(D) They can get a free newspaper subscription.

업체들은 후원으로부터 무엇을 얻을 수 있는가?
(A) 그들의 운영 비용을 줄일 수 있다.
(B) 그들의 상표를 광고할 수 있다.
(C) 지역 행사에 초대받을 수 있다.
(D) 무료 신문 구독을 할 수 있다.

세부 사항 질문으로 후원업체가 얻을 수 있는 점에 집중한다. 후원업체는 스포츠팀을 위해 비용을 충당해 주는 대신, 광고를 통해 브랜드 노출 효과를 얻을 수 있다고 했으므로 정답은 (B)가 된다.

Questions 95-97 refer to the following message and list. 영M

Hello. This is Bobby Randall from Stella Pharmaceutical Company. I'm calling about ordering a business card. I just started working here as a sales representative and my boss, Mr. Harrison, highly recommended your business. I understand that you have basic card stock and premium coated card stock. Although I'd like my business card printed on glossy paper, I can't afford the premium card stock because my budget is only $40. However, I definitely want double-sided printing. I'll be busy attending new employee orientation sessions all next week. So I'd like to get a sample card by the end of the week so that I can check that everything is correct before you print it. Could you please call me back so we can discuss it in further details? My number is 555-7879. Thank you.

Monk Printing Price List (Business Card)		
Basic	Single–sided Double–sided	$20 $35
Premium	Single–sided Double–sided	$40 $55

안녕하세요. 저는 Stella Pharmaceutical Company의 Bobby Randall입니다. 명함 주문과 관련해서 전화를 드립니다. 저는 영업 사원으로 이곳에서 막 일을 시작했고 상사인 Harrison 씨께서 당신의 업체를 강력하게 추천하셨습니다. 제가 알기로는 기본 명함지와 고급 코팅 명함지가 있으시던데요. 광택 있는 용지에 명함을 찍고 싶지만 예산이 40달러밖에 안 되어서 프리미엄 명함지는 감당할 수가 없네요. 그렇지만, 양면 인쇄는 꼭 하고 싶습니다. 제가 다음 주 내내 신입 사원 오리엔테이션에 참석하느라 바쁠 거예요. 그래서 이번 주까지는 명함 샘플을 받고 인쇄 전에 모든 내용이 정확한지 확인하고 싶습니다. 좀 더 자세한 이야기를 나누기 위해서 전화를 해주시겠습니까? 제 번호는 555-7879입니다. 감사합니다.

Monk Printing 가격표 (명함)		
기본	단면 양면	20달러 35달러
고급	단면 양면	40달러 55달러

card stock 명함 용지 coated 코팅이 된 glossy 광택 있는 double-sided 양면의 sample card 명함 샘플 in further details 더 자세하게

95 Why does the speaker mention Mr. Harrison?
(A) He has worked as a sales representative for years.
(B) He is in charge of ordering office supplies.
(C) He recommended the printing company.
(D) He cannot afford a premium service.

화자는 왜 Harrison 씨를 언급하는가?
(A) 수 년 동안 영업 사원으로 일해 오고 있다.
(B) 사무 용품을 주문하는 일을 맡고 있다.
(C) 이 인쇄 업체를 추천하였다.
(D) 고급 서비스를 감당할 수 없다.

질문의 키워드인 Mr. Harrison을 놓치지 말자. 명함 주문 건 때문에 전화를 했다고 말한 후 my boss, Mr. Harrison, highly recommended your business에서 상사인 Harrison 씨가 강력하게 추천해 줬다고 했으므로 정답은 (C)가 된다.

96 Look at the graphic. What type of card stock did the speaker choose?
(A) Basic single-sided
(B) Basic double-sided
(C) Premium single-sided
(D) Premium double-sided

시각 정보를 보시오. 화자는 어떤 종류의 명함지를 선택했는가?
(A) 기본 단면 인쇄
(B) 기본 양면 인쇄
(C) 고급 단면 인쇄
(D) 고급 양면 인쇄

화자가 명함지에 대해 언급한 내용을 종합해 보면, 우선 예산이 40달러라서 프리미엄은 안 된다고 했고 그렇지만 double-sided를 원한다고 했으므로, 예산에 맞으면서 고급 용지가 아닌 Basic double-sided를 주문하고 싶다는 의미가 된다. 정답은 (B)이다.

97 What does the speaker want to do by the end of the week?
(A) Check a sample copy of his business card
(B) Purchase an item at a discounted price
(C) Meet with an international client
(D) Order from a recommended company

화자는 이번 주 말까지 무엇을 하고 싶어 하는가?
(A) 명함 샘플 확인하기
(B) 할인 가격으로 상품 구입하기
(C) 해외 고객과 미팅하기
(D) 추천 받은 회사로부터 주문하기

질문의 키워드는 by the end of the week임을 잊지 말자. 이번 주 말까지 하고 싶어 하는 일은 I'd like to get a sample card by the end of the week에서 볼 수 있듯이, 명함 샘플을 확인하는 일이다.

Questions 98-100 refer to the following message and list. 미W

Okay everyone. Before we end today's meeting, I'd like to update you on the upcoming office relocation to Jefferson Tower. You will be pleased to know that this new location has a great view of the city because our office will be located on the 23rd floor. As you already know, the move will take place on Friday, November 30th, just three days from now. So I'd like you to start sorting out important documents and packing up your personal items. Also we have decided which moving company to hire. It was not an easy decision because the price estimates varied from company to company. Even though the moving company we decided to hire is the second most expensive, they are very skilled at moving office furniture and sensitive equipment. We don't want any of our expensive photography equipment to be damaged during the move.

List of Moving Companies	
Company	Price Quote
1. Best Movers	$5,000
2. GTA Moving Co.	$10,000
3. Smart Movers	$7,000
4. Cargo Professionals	$3,500

좋습니다 여러분. 오늘 미팅을 끝내기 전에, Jefferson Tower로 사무실을 이전하는 것에 관해 보고를 하겠습니다. 사무실이 23층에 위치해서 도시의 멋진 전경을 볼 수가 있다는 사실에 기쁘실 겁니다. 이미 알고 계시는 것처럼, 이사는 단 3일 후인, 11월 30일 금요일에 있을 것입니다. 그래서 여러분이 중요한 파일을 분류하고 개인적인 짐을 싸는 일을 시작해 주셨으면 합니다. 또한 우리는 고용할 이삿짐 업체를 결정했습니다. 가격 견적서가 회사별로 차이가 많아서 결정하는 것이 쉽지는 않았습니다. 우리가 고용하기로 결정한 회사는 두 번째로 비싼 업체임에도 불구하고, 이들은 사무용 가구와 민감한 장비를 옮기는 데 뛰어난 곳입니다. 우리는 이사하는 도중에 비싼 사진 장비가 손상되는 걸 원하지는 않으니까요.

이삿짐 업체 리스트	
회사	가격 견적
1. Best Movers	5,000달러
2. GTA Moving Co.	10,000달러
3. Smart Movers	7,000달러
4. Cargo Professionals	3,500달러

office relocation 사무실 이전 take place 일어나다, 발생하다 sort out 분류하다 personal item 개인적인 물건 be skilled at ~에 뛰어나다 sensitive equipment 민감한 장비

98 What does the speaker mention about the new office?
(A) It has an impressive view.
(B) It is located close to a subway station.
(C) It is more spacious than the old one.
(D) It is opening on the 23rd of May.

화자는 새로운 사무실에 대해서 뭐라고 언급하는가?
(A) 경치가 좋다.
(B) 지하철 역과 가깝다.
(C) 예전 것보다 더 넓다.
(D) 5월 23일에 문을 연다.

Jefferson Tower의 새 사무실에 대해서 23층에 있기 때문에 도시의 전경이 좋다(this new location has a great view of the city)고 했으므로 정답은 (A)이다.

99 What are employees asked to do?
(A) Submit a document
(B) Compare two moving companies
(C) Turn off office equipment
(D) Pack their belongings

직원들은 무엇을 할 것을 요청 받는가?
(A) 서류 제출하기
(B) 두 개의 이삿짐 업체 비교하기
(C) 사무기기의 전원 끄기
(D) 소지품 싸기

요청 표현과 함께 직원들이 요청 받은 내용은 중요 서류를 분류하는 것과 개인 짐을 짐 싸는 것이었으므로 정답은 (D)가 맞다.

100 Look at the graphic. Which moving company has been hired?
(A) Best Movers
(B) GTA Moving Co.
(C) Smart Movers
(D) Cargo Professionals

시각 정보를 보시오. 어떤 이삿짐 업체가 고용되었는가?
(A) Best Movers
(B) GTA Moving Co.
(C) Smart Movers
(D) Cargo Professionals

시각 정보의 견적 금액과 함께 확인하는 것이 포인트이다. 고용하기로 결정한 회사는 두 번째로 비싼(the second most expensive) 업체라고 했으므로 정답은 (C)가 된다.